CW01333667

AWS SERVERLESS IOT

A Hands On Project Based Approach

AWS SERVERLESS IOT

A Hands On Project Based Approach

First Edition

Inexpensive IoT Projects to take you from Zero to AWS IoT Hero

Stephen Borsay

AWS Serverless IoT
Inexpensive IoT Projects to take you from Zero to AWS IoT Hero
First Edition

Paperback Edition.
ISBN 979-8-9867878-1-7
Designed in the United States of America.

Introduction to the Book

This book is a friendly and approachable guide to getting started programming IoT devices to communicate with IoT-centric services on the AWS cloud. The intended goal of the book is for the reader to use either a real IoT device, or a free virtual IoT device, to transmit data to AWS. Once the IoT data is on the AWS cloud, then that data can be stored, transformed, queried, filtered, and visualized with AWS IoT-centric services.

This book covers various AWS services such as IoT Core, Lambda, S3, QuickSight, SageMaker, API Gateway, DynamoDB, Timestream, WebSocket's, IoT Analytics, and other AWS services. The IoT devices used to connect to AWS explained in this book will be the ESP8266, ESP32, or the Raspberry Pi. The book is designed to use any or all of these popular and inexpensive IoT devices. Alternately, the reader can choose to use a free virtual IoT device if the reader doesn't intend to purchase any IoT hardware.

The intent of the book is for it to be a hands-on experience, covering projects and activities using IoT centric services on AWS to make data lakes, fill databases, and use IoT sensor readings for visualizing and dashboarding using static websites hosted on AWS. All of this will be accomplished at little to no cost on AWS using a serverless design flow.

When working with IoT devices which transmit data to AWS, serverless IoT services can save the customer a tremendous amount of money. Instead of setting up an "always on" EC2 instance, the developer can utilize individual serverless AWS services only as needed. All the projects in this book are intended to be no, to ultra-low cost. Fake sensor data can be generated on the IoT device to further save the reader money by not having to purchase ancillary sensors and other additional hardware for the IoT device.

The ultimate goal of this book is to walk the user through a range of hands-on projects that will expose them to most of the essential serverless IoT services AWS offers. These are also the cloud services that most employers would look for when hiring a developer or an IoT engineer. These are also the same serverless cloud services that you can use to make your own IoT designs for your own projects.

Who is this book designed for: I designated this book for the beginning to intermediate software developer who wants to learn more about IoT and serverless cloud services on AWS. The book would also be suitable for the cloud developer new to IoT. Finally, the book is applicable for the IoT and embedded device engineer who is unfamiliar with developing for cloud services on AWS but wishes to learn.

How best to learn IoT on AWS: A final word on this topic is surprisingly important. It is vital that the reader understand that the process of learning is not usually how they think they learn but rather how their subconscious retains information. If this pedagogical approach sounds overly opaque or abstruse let me just relate my experience from teaching on multiple platforms: you will learn best not by reading or studying but by "doing." Therefore, I have designed this book for "doers." That means that I'm asking you to do the steps required to complete the projects in this book and not just read the chapters straight through and expect to understand the process. My main goal is to follow a linear learning path which allows anyone to learn and succeed if they follow the steps in this book. Therefore, do yourself a favor and spend the two to three hours required to 'walk through' all the steps needed to complete each project.

I am very customer focused on my desire to see others find success. Saying that, I will do my best to answer all questions through the contact information provided.

Stephen Borsay

IoT Development Board Recommendations

The recommended embedded IoT devices for the course are the inexpensive ESP32 DevKitC or the ESP8266 12-E. You can also use any WiFi capable Raspberry Pi. I wrote the book, so you don't have to start out breadboarding or connecting additional sensors or components to your development board.

If you use the ESP32 DevKitC, as I recommend as the best choice for the book, then I recommend that your DevKitC has one of the following Espressif chips onboard:

ESP32-WROOM-D

ESP32-WROOM-DA

ESP32-WROOM-32E

ESP32-WROOM-32U

ESP32-WROOM-32UE

ESP32-WROVER-E

ESP32-WROVER-IE

If all you want to do is use the Arduino IDE to program your device with the included scripts from chapter 4, then you are free to use any of the many compatible ESP devices that Arduino supports.

Code Used in the Book

I have created a GitHub page for all the code used in this book, it can be found at:

https://github.com/sborsay/AWS-Serverless-IoT-Book

To access the code, simply go to the relevant chapter and you should see the code there. Also, note that any necessary corrections or clarifications will also be included in the relevant chapter on the GitHub page as well.

It is extremely difficult to keep all the code in the book formatted to be copied correctly and pasted into the readers IDE and programming tools without formatting errors. This formatting problem is especially true of code in Python for obvious reasons. Therefore, if you are getting problems or errors in code copied directly from the eBook or Kindle it is likely a formatting or word-wrapping issue that is causing the problem. GitHub, being designed from the ground up for code, doesn't have these issues. The final code authority should always be the GitHub repository for the book.

This book is here to help you get your job done. If you see anything lacking, make sure to issue a pull request directly on GitHub or contact me directly if that is easier for you. My plan is to correct mistakes and ambiguities as quickly as possible.

In general, if example code is offered with this book, you may use it in your programs and documentation. You do not need to contact me, but you should reference where you are getting the code from and give due accreditation.

About the Author

Stephen Borsay has a bachelor's degree in Computer Engineering and a passion for teaching and training electronic hobbyists, computer programmers, and engineers in IoT and cloud technologies. He has experience designing and developing embedded systems, FPGA's, IoT technologies, and device to cloud integrations.

Stephen has run Meetup groups, hackathons, engineering workshops, spoken at engineering conventions, and has successfully developed online training courses to help developers and engineers learn difficult concepts and advance their careers. Stephen was recognized in 2020 as an AWS IoT Hero, one of only two currently in the Americas

Designing and developing the Cloudboard IoT device has been his latest interest. The Cloudboard is an IoT training tool designed around the ESP32 and can be found at *Cloudboard.cc*. The intent behind the Cloudboard is to provide an IoT training device, with multiple sensors integrated on-board, that comes with hands-on tutorials covering IoT-centric services in the cloud.

How to Contact the Author

Twitter: *@Embedded_IoT_*

Email: *Borsay@gmail.com*

My Resources for IoT

My GitHub: *https://github.com/sborsay*

Cloudboard Homepage: *Cloudboard.cc*

My YouTube Channel: *https://www.youtube.com/channel/UCiwFO9083gofF-OJMZsYIdg*

My Udemy Courses: *https://www.udemy.com/user/stv/*

Chapter Contents

Chapter 1 - AWS Provisioning and CLI Configuration **1**

Set up your AWS free tier account and retrieve your AWS account credentials for administrator privileges. After setting up your account, download and install the free AWS CLI to expediate AWS commands from the command line. Test your AWS CLI configuration to send a basic JSON payload to AWS IoT Core using your SigV4 credentials. After the initial test from the CLI run a Bash script to automate IoT payload transmission to the MQTT server-side broker on AWS IoT Core.

Chapter 2 - Creating, Configuring, and Activating AWS IoT Device Certificates and IoT Policies **16**

Create TLS 1.2 compliant security certificates on AWS IoT Core. After downloading your Root CA, Client/Device certificate, and your Private Key activate them and then design and attach an IoT policy to the security certificates. Place the certificates in a local folder on your computer. You will then test your certificates with the free cURL tool to ensure that they are working correctly.

IoT Device Programming

Chapter 3 - Using a Virtual IoT Device to Publish Data to AWS IoT Core with MQTT **31**

Download and configure the MQTT.fx GUI tool with your security credentials, IoT endpoint, and protocol information to publish and subscribe to IoT data. After configuring the virtual IoT tool and testing that it is capable of publishing and subscribing to IoT payloads from your AWS account you will then use a JavaScript test program to automate transmitting IoT data payloads to AWS IoT Core.

[Chapter 4 - ESP32 and ESP8266 IoT Device Programming with Arduino to AWS IoT Core](#) **49**

Install and configure the Arduino IDE for programming your IoT device. Implement the Arduino scripts found in the chapters GitHub for the ESP32 or ESP8266 device. Upload the Arduino code to your IoT device and then transmit your IoT data using MQTT and the publish and subscribe features to communicate with AWS.

[Chapter 5 - ESP32 and ESP8266 IoT Device Programming with MicroPython to AWS IoT Core](#) **74**

Download, install, and configure the free IDE for MicroPython called "Thonny." Use the Python programming language in the Thonny IDE to program your IoT devices to communicate with AWS IoT Core. You will implement the MicroPython programs found in the chapters GitHub for the ESP32 or the ESP8266 device. Configure and transfer the security certificates to your IoT device then upload the Python code to your IoT device to transmit your IoT data using MQTT publish and subscribe functionality to communicate with AWS.

[Chapter 6 - ESP32 and ESP8266 IoT Device Programming with Mongoose OS to AWS IoT Core](#) **106**

Download, install, and configure the MOS tool for programming your IoT device in JavaScript. Implement the program provided by Mongoose for sending IoT data to AWS IoT Core using MQTT and the Pub/Sub model. Then implement a custom JavaScript program from the chapters GitHub which will make the devices IoT payload more suitable f or the IoT centric services on AWS.

[Chapter 7 - Programming the Raspberry Pi with the AWS IoT Device SDK in Python](#) **116**

Use the AWS IoT Device SDK in Python to program your Raspberry Pi. Install the AWS IoT Device SDK and run the provided Pub/Sub sample application program. View the IoT messages from the sample app in the AWS IoT MQTT test console. After the sample app is run successfully you will then run the modified PubSub program, from the chapters GitHub page, to transmit JSON IoT payloads using MQTT on your Raspberry Pi to AWS.

Chapter 8 - Programming the Raspberry Pi with the AWS IoT Device SDK in Node.js **135**

Use the AWS IoT Device SDK in Node.js/JavaScript to program your Raspberry Pi. Install AWS IoT Device SDK and run the provided index.js sample app. View the IoT payloads from the sample app in the MQTT test client on AWS IoT Core. After the sample app is run successfully you will then run a modified index.js program, from the chapters GitHub page, to transmit JSON IoT payloads using MQTT on your Raspberry Pi to AWS.

Prerequisites for AWS IoT Cloud Development

Chapter 9 - Prerequisite One: Creating an AWS S3 Public Bucket for IoT Data and Static Website Hosting **153**

Create a public S3 bucket from the console with an open bucket policy, configure CORS, and make an accessible ACL. Then configure the S3 bucket to host a static website for future visualizations of IoT data. Repeat the same tasks as before but instead of using the console, use the AWS CLI to create an open and public S3 bucket and upload a bucket policy, CORS, and an index.html file for hosting a static website.

Chapter 10 - Prerequisite Two: AWS IoT Core with Lambda **177**

Design am AWS Lambda function to republish a JSON payload to a MQTT topic using JavaScript or Python. Test the function and subscribe to the MQTT topic with an IoT device or the MQTT test client. Set up a 'Rule" in AWS IoT Core to send a IoT payload to Lambda to test the publishing function.

AWS Services for IoT

Chapter 11 - Developing a Threshold Tester with AWS SNS and Topic Republishing in IoT Core **202**

Using AWS IoT Core, you will develop two Rules. The first Rule will test the incoming temperature threshold of an IoT payload. If the threshold exceeds a given value an alert will be issued by a topic republishing rule. In the second use case a SNS topic notification rule will be developed to alert the user if a threshold condition is exceeded from an incoming stream of IoT payloads.

Chapter 12 - Developing the World's Simplest Synchronous Serverless AWS IoT Dashboard **222**

In this project you will start by designing a Rule in AWS IoT Core to publish IoT data payloads to a public S3 bucket. Then a static website will be developed for the public bucket which will visualize the latest IoT sensor readings by polling the IoT data object in the S3 public bucket. A line chart will visualize all the subsequent IoT sensor readings with continuous synchronous polling of the data in delivered to S3.

Chapter 13 - Designing the World's Simplest IoT Data Lake on AWS **241**

In this chapter you will design rule in AWS IoT Core to send IoT payloads with their own unique 'key' to S3. Using S3 as a IoT data repository for storing each of your sensor readings you will then upload a static website in the same S3 bucket which will read all the sensor readings by key in the S3 bucket. The JavaScript code will then produce a visualization with a free graphing package from the static s3 hosted website.

Chapter 14 - Using Kinesis Data Firehose for IoT **261**

Kinesis Firehose offers a high frequency, memory buffered transmission pipeline for IoT data that is well suited to multi-device, fan-in architectures. For this project you will set up a Kinesis Data Firehose which is can be used for IoT data queuing and handling massive IoT data ingest. First you will design a transformation Lambda function as well as S3 bucket retention for the IoT data. Then you will design the Kinesis Firehose to ingest data from an IoT Core Rule and then transform the IoT data with the Lambda function. Once the transformed IoT data is in the S3 bucket the data will be visualized with AWS QuickSight as well as graphed with a custom coded JavaScript website hosted on S3.

Chapter 15 - Using AWS DynamoDB for IoT **290**

In this chapter you will use DynamoDB as a data repository for IoT data. First, you will create a Rule in IoT Core to send data to DynamoDB Version 2. You will also add a "Time-To-Live" function into the data table. Once the IoT sensor readings are held as items in the database you will design a Lambda function to extract each item with a scan operation of the data table. You will then create an endpoint with API Gateway to access the scanning Lambda function from an external website. Finally, you will upload a static website to S3 with the API Gateway endpoint embedded into the JavaScript Code which will send a GET request to the Lambda function to return all the IoT items in the data table for visualization using the static webpage hosted on S3.

Chapter 16 - Using AWS Timestream for IoT **335**

AWS Timestream is a timeseries database well suited for IoT data. In this chapter you will design a Rule in IoT Core to dispatch IoT data to fill a Timestream database. Then you will explore the unfiltered results with an integrated, third-party visualization service called "Grafana". After this is complete you will explore the Timestream sensor readings in the AWS business intelligence offering: AWS QuickSight. Next you will develop a Lambda function to extract all the IoT items in your Timestream database. Then you will use a Function URL from Lambda as an endpoint in a S3 static website host to extract all the Timestream IoT data for visualization.

Chapter 17 - Putting it All Together with AWS IoT Analytics **381**

AWS IoT Analytics offers a complete processing chain for IoT data. In this chapter you will set up an IoT Analytics Channel, Pipeline, Datastore, and Dataset. Once these services are developed you will designate an S3 public bucket as a repository for your IoT sensor readings after connecting the Channel to IoT Core with a Rule. Then you will send sensor data through the chain to the bucket to verify the architecture. Once the process is verified you will then design a Lambda function to insert into the IoT Analytics Pipeline for ETL. The results of this process will be visualized in both AWS QuickSight and with a custom static website hosted on S3.

Chapter 18 - Building A Real-Time Serverless IoT Dashboard with AWS WebSockets **424**

AWS WebSockets offers a constant connection between the client and the server. Earlier you built the Worlds Simplest IoT dashboard but had to rely on synchronous polling. Using the AWS WebSockets protocol, you can get close to real time performance with bidirectional IoT ingestion and consumption with asynchronous transmissions. First, you will design two Lambda functions. The first 'connection' lambda will extract the unique connection ID from your S3 static webhost and store it in the AWS parameter Store. You will then create a rule to send the IoT data readings to your 'messaging' Lambda function. Your second 'messaging' lambda will use an API Gateway endpoint to dispatch your IoT sensor readings to your static website hosted in S3 with an "always-on" WebSocket connection.

Chapter 1 -

AWS Cloud Side Provisioning and AWS CLI Configuration

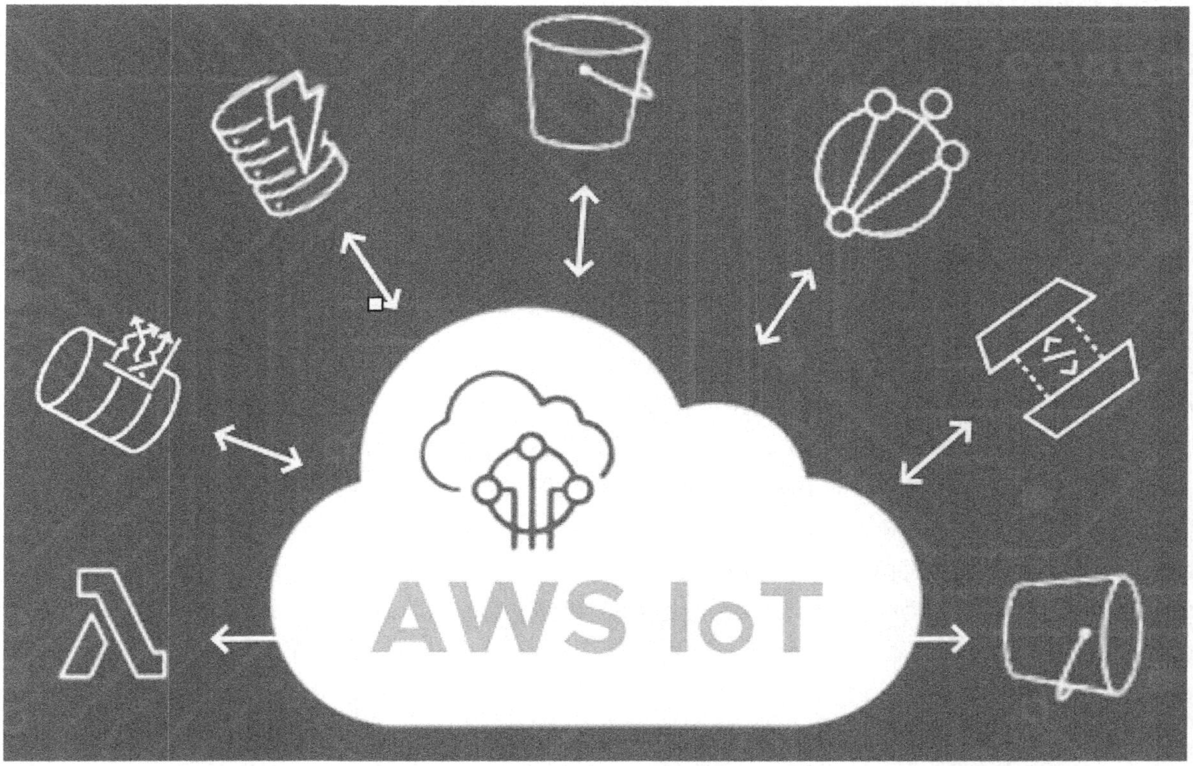
AWS IoT

Step 1 - Create your AWS Account
Step 2 - Create an AWS Account Admin User and get your SigV4 Credentials
Step 3 - Install the AWS CLI
Step 4 - Configure the AWS CLI with your SigV4 Credentials
Step 5 - Use the AWS CLI to send Test IoT Payloads to AWS IoT Core

Step 6 - Run a Bash Script with the AWS CLI to Automate Publishing IoT Data to AWS IoT Core

---

Step 1 - Create your AWS Account

To get started with AWS the first thing you must do is create an AWS cloud account. If you don't have an AWS account, you are in luck. Why is this? Because you are entitled to a year of free services (with certain exceptions) as a long going promotion AWS uses to entice new users.

Sign up here:

https://aws.amazon.com/free/

Step 2 - Create an AWS Account Admin User and get your SigV4 Credentials

All AWS accounts need an "Administrator." This 'Admin' could also be thought of as the "root" or "superuser" who controls the account. An administrator can create sub-users with more limited permissions which curtail access rights on the AWS account to prevent intentional or unintentional problems, caused by unintended users, doing unauthorized actions. Sub-users with lesser privileges are very important for a corporate account, however they are much less important for the purposes of this book. In this book the assumption is that all IoT testing on AWS will be handled by an individual user on their own account as the "root" user.

As a consistent theme throughout this book, you will see that I don't like to repeat publicly available instructional material that is produced by expert, in-house technical writers, being paid large salaries. It is a waste of both your time and mine. There is enough original material in this book that there is no need for 'filler' material. Therefore, please follow AWS documentation on assigning a root administrator (you) for your AWS account and collecting your SigV4 security credentials. Remember to save your SigV4 credentials (access key and secret access key) in a safe place, you will need them to set up the AWS CLI required for the book.

Below is a link to instruct you on setting up your root Admin user:

https://docs.aws.amazon.com/IAM/latest/UserGuide/getting-started_create-admin-group.html

Step 3 - Install the AWS CLI

The AWS CLI (command line interface) is an essential tool for using AWS. Hypothetically everything you do in the console (The AWS GUI) can be accomplished faster by just using the AWS CLI. However, using the AWS CLI for teaching purposes is a bad heuristic for the readers learning. Therefore, I will only use the AWS CLI when necessary or helpful, I won't use it just to expedite the development processes. The AWS CLI can be extremely useful and there are even certain, essential, things when completing AWS IoT centric tasks, that can only be accomplished with the AWS CLI. The following instructions tell you how to configure the AWS CLI for any popular operating system. The installer is very sophisticated, so it installs all the necessary Python dependencies and sets the environmental variables for you automatically.

In this book you will use the AWS CLI version two. As an aside a major difference between the two AWS CLI versions is that version two sends all IoT data as 'base64' encoded by default. Surprisingly the encoding is not for security. Base64 encoding is just a much more efficient method for transmitting data between computers. This is important when sending massive amounts of data and transmitting large data payloads quickly.

Install the AWS CLI using the link below:

https://docs.aws.amazon.com/cli/latest/userguide/getting-started-install.html

Step 4 - Configure the AWS CLI with your SigV4 Credentials

You have already received your AWS SigV4 credentials in Step 2. I recommend using the 'us-east-1' region (North Virginia) as your home region when configuring the AWS CLI. This preference for us-east-1 is because that region has the most AWS services available immediately, and it is consistently one of the least expensive regions for AWS services. The only real benefit of using a geographically closer region to your location is less latency between the user and an AWS data center.

Corporate AWS accounts may have compliance issues related to their AWS region selection.

You can get further info on configuring your AWS CLI here:

https://docs.aws.amazon.com/cli/latest/userguide/cli-configure-quickstart.html

The AWS CLI will prompt you to input four parameters during configuration. The fields should be filled out as shown below, with the corresponding 'access key' and 'secret access key' that was acquired earlier when you created your administrator account in AWS IAM:

```
> aws configure

AWS Access Key ID [None]: <YOUR-ACCESS-KEY-HERE>
AWS Secret Access Key [None]: <YOUR-SECRET-ACCESS-KEY>
Default region name [None]: us-east-1
Default output format [None]: json
```

After configuring the AWS CLI, you can enter the following command at the command prompt:

```
aws iot describe-endpoint --endpoint-type iot:Data-ATS
```

The command should return something like this but on your computer:

```
C:\Users\borsa>aws iot describe-endpoint --endpoint-type iot:Data-ATS
{
    "endpointAddress": "a32qaa131oyees-ats.iot.us-east-1.amazonaws.com"
}
```

This is your AWS IoT endpoint which you will use extensively throughout this book. Remember, if you change AWS regions you must change the region portion of your AWS IoT endpoint.

I also created a video for the procedure if you need further details: https://youtu.be/_K-Jbm61B2s

The AWS CLI can connect to the AWS message broker using 'SigV4' authentication over HTTPS. The AWS proprietary security protocol is called Signature Version 4 (SigV4) and it employs the access key and the secret access key that you received from AWS IAM and used to configure the AWS CLI.

Below is a table describing which protocols and security methods are palatable to the AWS message broker. In this course you will be mostly using MQTT(S) over port 8883 with TLS1.2 using security certificates, however as mentioned previously, for this section you are using the AWS CLI with SigV4 authentication over HTTPS. Although MQTT with TLS1.2 requires a special protocol not available on the AWS CLI, the AWS CLI can still "talk" to the message broker on AWS IoT Core. However, since the AWS CLI uses HTTPS, it can only send IoT payloads and not receive IoT payloads from the AWS cloud.

Protocols, port mappings, and authentication

How a device or client connects to the message broker by using a device endpoint depends on the protocol it uses. The following table lists the protocols that the AWS IoT device endpoints support and the authentication methods and ports they use.

Protocols, authentication, and port mappings

Protocol	Operations supported	Authentication	Port	ALPN protocol name
MQTT over WebSocket	Publish, Subscribe	Signature Version 4	443	N/A
MQTT over WebSocket	Publish, Subscribe	Custom authentication	443	N/A
MQTT	Publish, Subscribe	X.509 client certificate	443†	x-amzn-mqtt-ca
MQTT	Publish, Subscribe	X.509 client certificate	8883	N/A
MQTT	Publish, Subscribe	Custom authentication	443†	mqtt
HTTPS	Publish only	Signature Version 4	443	N/A
HTTPS	Publish only	X.509 client certificate	443†	x-amzn-http-ca
HTTPS	Publish only	X.509 client certificate	8443	N/A
HTTPS	Publish only	Custom authentication	443	N/A

Step 5 - Use the AWS CLI to send Test IoT Payloads to AWS IoT Core

As discussed in the previous step, AWS allows messages to be sent to AWS IoT Core using either device security certificates, which will be discussed in the next chapter, or by using SigV4 security credentials configured on your AWS CLI. Since you will be working directly with the security certificates on your own IoT devices in the next section, and since you have already ensured that your AWS CLI works with your SigV4 credentials by using the 'describe-endpoint' command, the test in this step just serves as additional verification.

Now you can have some fun and test everything out that you have just completed in this chapter in an AWS IoT centric way. First, you will send a basic IoT payload to AWS IoT Core using the AWS CLI directly, then you will run a bash script that works on any computer with any operating system that uses the AWS CLI to send emulated JSON IoT payloads to the AWS IoT Core service.

To begin the test, go to the AWS IoT Core console by navigating there yourself or clicking this link:

https://console.aws.amazon.com/iot

What is 'AWS IoT Core?' AWS IoT Core is a managed cloud service that allows you to connect devices easily, and securely interact with cloud applications and other devices." However, for the purposes of this book you should think of AWS IoT Core as a cloud based, server side, MQTT message broker that routes incoming and outgoing device messages, and can dispatch those messages (JSON IoT payloads), to a variety of IoT centric AWS services.

To send IoT payloads to AWS IoT Core make sure you are currently in your intended AWS region:

Within the AWS console navigate to AWS IoT Core → MQTT test client:

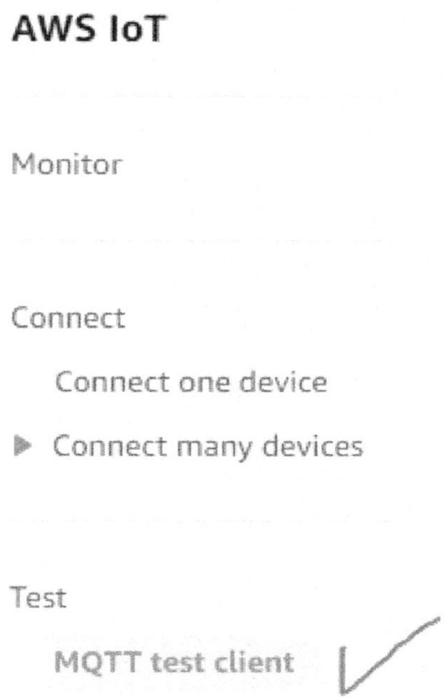
AWS IoT
Monitor
Connect
Connect one device
Connect many devices
Test
MQTT test client

Under the "Subscribe tab" type: “*outTopic*” and then press the “Subscribe” button:

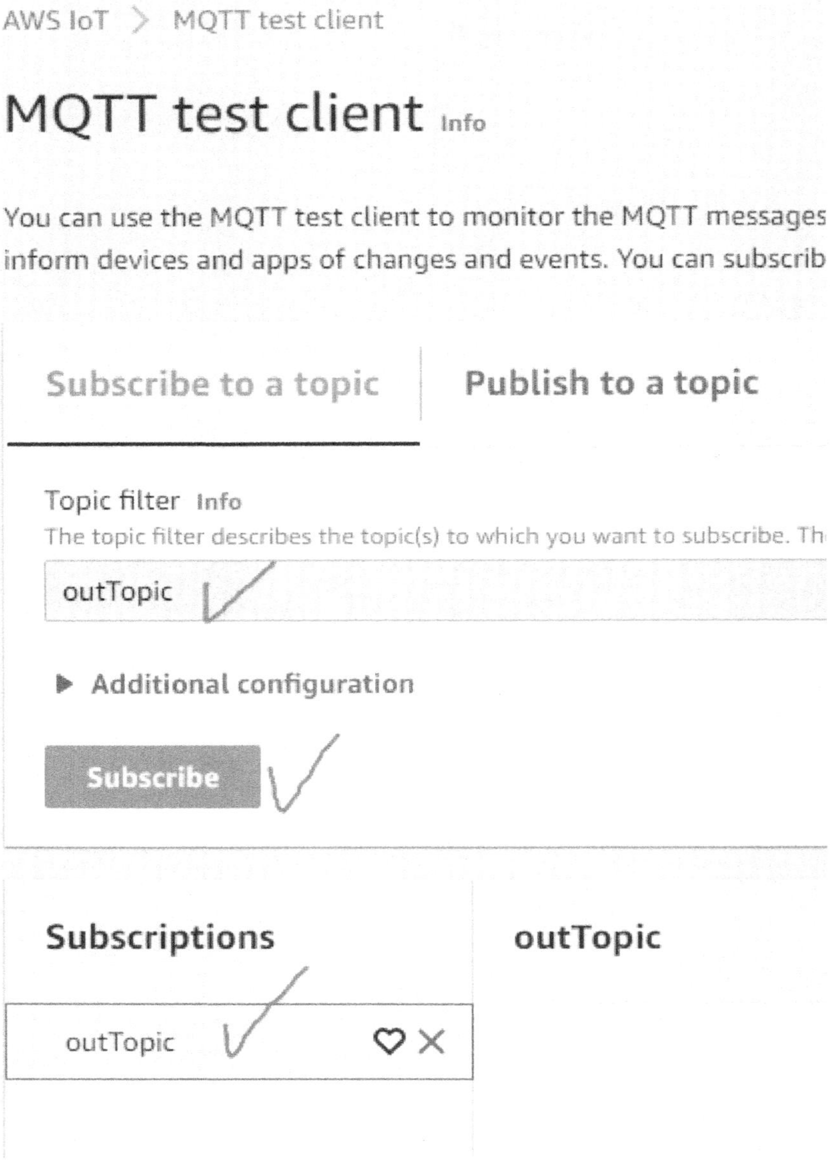
AWS IoT > MQTT test client
MQTT test client Info
You can use the MQTT test client to monitor the MQTT messages
inform devices and apps of changes and events. You can subscrib
Subscribe to a topic
Publish to a topic
Topic filter Info
The topic filter describes the topic(s) to which you want to subscribe. Th
outTopic
Additional configuration
Subscribe
Subscriptions
outTopic
outTopic

At the command prompt on your local computer enter the following test payload into the AWS CLI (if you are not using 'us-east-1' then change the region flag):

```
aws --region us-east-1 iot-data publish --topic "outTopic" --cli-binary-format raw-in-base64-out --payload "{\"uptime\": 123,\"temp\": 55,\"humidity\": 77}"
```

If your CLI is configured correctly you should see the following output in the MQTT test client when you subscribed to "outTopic." Also note you could just subscribe to "#" which is a wildcard/hash to catch all incoming MQTT topics.

- As an aside, you don't need to use the region flag in the AWS CLI command if you are scripting to the same region as your AWS CLI is configured to as its 'home' region.

- If you are interested in how MQTT topics with wildcards work in AWS IoT Core this is a great resource: https://docs.aws.amazon.com/iot/latest/developerguide/topics.html

---

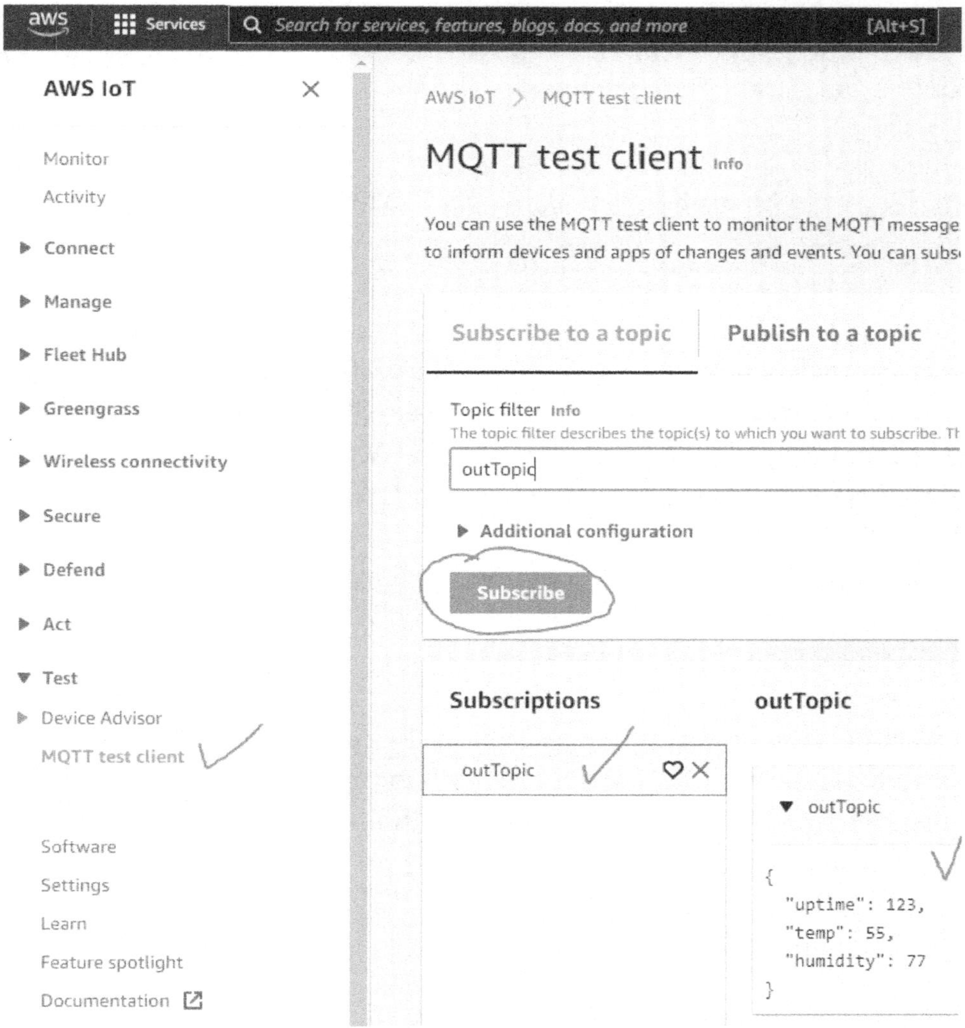
aws
Services
Search for services, features, blogs, docs, and more
[Alt+S]
AWS IoT
Monitor
Activity
Connect
Manage
Fleet Hub
Greengrass
Wireless connectivity
Secure
Defend
Act
Test
Device Advisor
MQTT test client
Software
Settings
Learn
Feature spotlight
Documentation
AWS IoT > MQTT test client
MQTT test client Info
You can use the MQTT test client to monitor the MQTT message
to inform devices and apps of changes and events. You can subs
Subscribe to a topic
Publish to a topic
Topic filter Info
The topic filter describes the topic(s) to which you want to subscribe.
outTopic
Additional configuration
Subscribe
Subscriptions
outTopic
outTopic
outTopic
{
"uptime": 123,
"temp": 55,
"humidity": 77
}

Another useful technique you can try from the AWS CLI for IoT JSON payload testing is to transmit a whole JSON file of fake sensor data to IoT Core in one batch. Why would you want to use this method over an automated test program sending a stream of random IoT readings? Well, if you wanted to test a machine learning model in AWS SageMaker or test out an AWS Kinesis Analytics batching configuration this could be a very useful technique for biasing a sample of IoT sensor readings. I have included a "sample.json" file in the GitHub for this chapter in array JSON formatting. JSON array style formatting is needed when batching data. To send the file of sample IoT sensor readings to IoT Core from the AWS CLI simply enter the command below at the command prompt on your computer. Use the region flag if needed if not using your home region with the "sample.json" file from the same directory in which you issue the AWS CLI command:

```
aws iot-data publish --topic "outTopic" --cli-binary-format raw-in-
base64-out --payload file://sample.json
```

Step 6 - Run a Bash Script with the AWS CLI to Automate Publishing IoT Data to AWS IoT Core

For the final test of the AWS CLI communicating with the AWS IoT message broker, you will use a Bash script to send automated fake JSON IoT data payloads to the MQTT test client on AWS IoT Core. If using the Windows operating system, you may need to install the free 'Git for Windows' to run Bash shell scripts.

Git for Windows can be found and downloaded here:

https://gitforwindows.org/

Depending on how Bash is configured on your PC you may need to navigate to the Git prompt to execute the Bash script provided in this chapter below. Just Google "How to run a Bash script on X", with 'X' being the name of your operating system to determine the appropriate method.

Below is the original Bash script:

https://aws.amazon.com/blogs/iot/integrating-iot-data-with-your-data-lake-with-new-aws-iot-analytics-features

The modified version of the Bash script used in this chapter can be found on the chapters GitHub:

https://github.com/sborsay/AWS-Serverless-IoT-Book/blob/main/Chapter-1-AWS-Configuration/Bash_Script.sh

I have already altered the test script to transmit just temperature and humidity data. Simply insert your AWS region ('us-east-1') and MQTT topic name ('outTopic' or 'iot/bash') into the test script where indicated. The Bash script uses your AWS CLI version two to deliver the payload to IoT Core (using your SigV4 credentials over HTTPS). You can also change the number of payloads published (iterations) and wait time between each publish (interval) to produce as much fake IoT data as you like.

- Be careful of using unnecessary blank spaces with bash scripts - padding matters.

```
#!/bin/bash
mqtttopic='<Insert-Your-IoT-Topic-Here>'
iterations=10
wait=2
region='<Insert-Your-AWS-Test-Region-Here>'
profile='default'

for (( i = 1; i <=$iterations; i++)) {

    #Added these randomizers, Temperature in Fehr
    minT=-20
    maxT=120
    numberT=$(expr $minT + $RANDOM % $maxT)

    #humidity % cannot exceed 100
    minH=0
    maxH=100
    numberH=$(expr $minH + $RANDOM % $maxH)

  temperature=$(($numberT ))
  humidity=$(($numberH ))

  echo "Publishing message $i/$ITERATIONS to IoT topic $mqtttopic:"
  echo "temperature: $temperature"
  echo "humidity: $humidity"
```

```
#use below for AWS CLI V2
 aws iot-data publish --topic "$mqtttopic" --cli-binary-format raw-in-base64-
out --payload "{\"temperature\":$temperature,\"humidity\":$humidity}" --
profile "$profile" --region "$region"

  sleep $wait
}
```

Now save the above code, giving it a name like "iot_tester.sh".

Before running the script locally, go to the AWS console and go to AWS IoT Core:

https://console.aws.amazon.com/iot

Within the AWS console navigate back to AWS IoT Core → MQTT test client. Under the "Subscribe to a topic" tab type “outTopic” or “iot/bash” or whatever publishing topic name you used in the Bash script you saved it locally on your computer. In this example you can use the wildcard ‘#’ hash/pound to catch all the incoming MQTT topics to your AWS account.

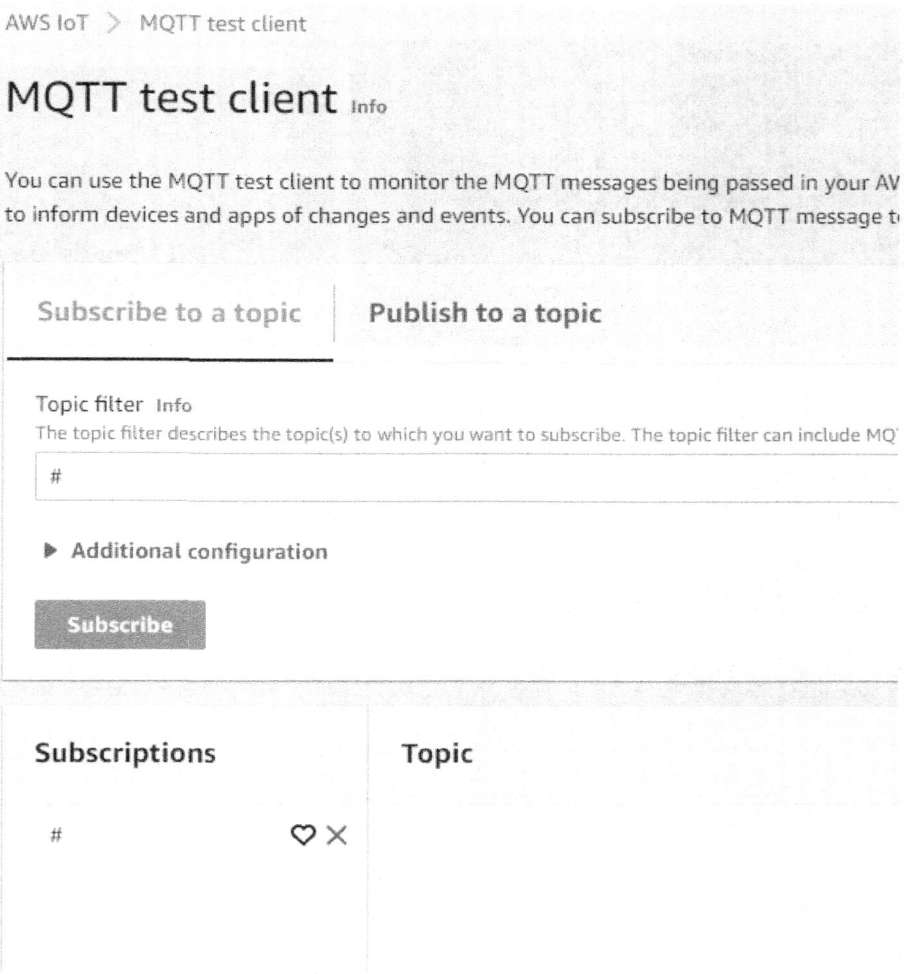
AWS IoT > MQTT test client
MQTT test client Info
You can use the MQTT test client to monitor the MQTT messages being passed in your AV
to inform devices and apps of changes and events. You can subscribe to MQTT message t
Subscribe to a topic
Publish to a topic
Topic filter Info
The topic filter describes the topic(s) to which you want to subscribe. The topic filter can include MQ
#
Additional configuration
Subscribe
Subscriptions
Topic
#

Now go to the directory on your computer where you saved the 'iot_tester.sh' script and execute the IoT data producer Bash shell script. Activating the Bash script at the command prompt looks like this on a Windows PC:

```
$
iot.tester.sh
```

Simply enter the entire file name at the command prompt and press; '*Enter*':

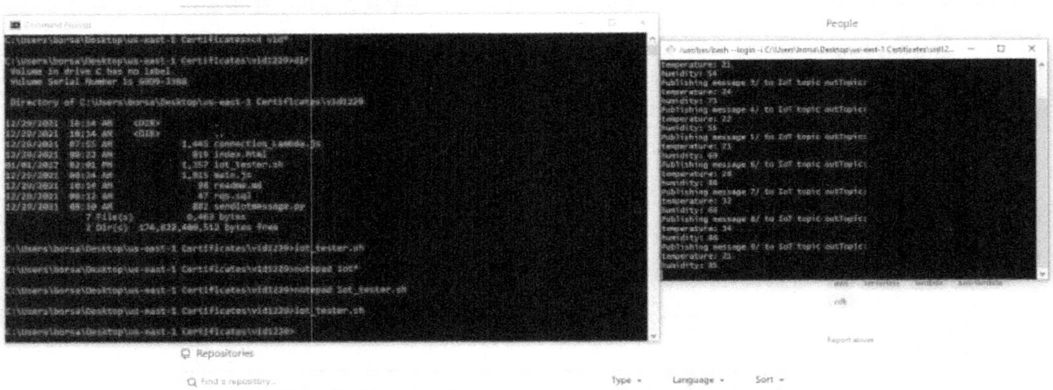

Now return to the MQTT test client in AWS IoT Core. You previously subscribed to the '#' wildcard topic to catch all topics incoming to your account. You should see the incoming JSON IoT fake sensor readings transmitted from the AWS CLI delivered to your MQTT test client that look like those below.

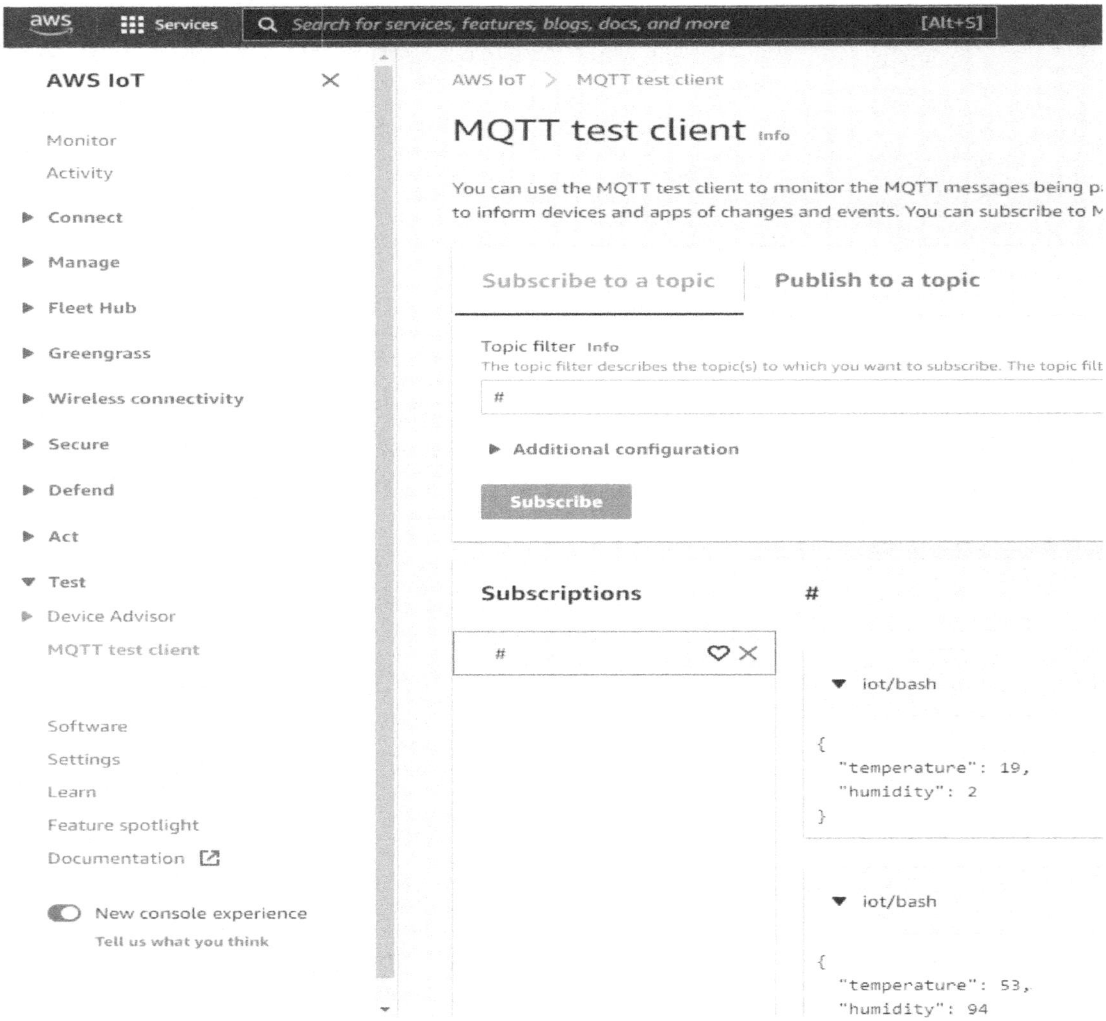

aws
Services
Search for services, features, blogs, docs, and more
[Alt+S]
AWS IoT
Monitor
Activity
Connect
Manage
Fleet Hub
Greengrass
Wireless connectivity
Secure
Defend
Act
Test
Device Advisor
MQTT test client
Software
Settings
Learn
Feature spotlight
Documentation
New console experience
Tell us what you think
AWS IoT > MQTT test client
MQTT test client Info
You can use the MQTT test client to monitor the MQTT messages being p
to inform devices and apps of changes and events. You can subscribe to M
Subscribe to a topic
Publish to a topic
Topic filter Info
The topic filter describes the topic(s) to which you want to subscribe. The topic filt
#
Additional configuration
Subscribe
Subscriptions
#
#
iot/bash
{
"temperature": 19,
"humidity": 2
}
iot/bash
{
"temperature": 53,
"humidity": 94

Congratulations, you have now successfully signed up for an AWS account, created a root admin, collected your SigV4 credentials, configured the AWS CLI, and tested the CLI to communicate with AWS IoT Core using both a publish command, and a Bash script to generate fake IoT data. Soon you will be implementing IoT transmissions with a more sophisticated virtual device as well as using physical IoT devices like the ESP8266, ESP32, and Raspberry Pi to send IoT data to AWS.

Chapter 2 - Creating, Configuring, and Activating AWS IoT Device Certificates and IoT Policies

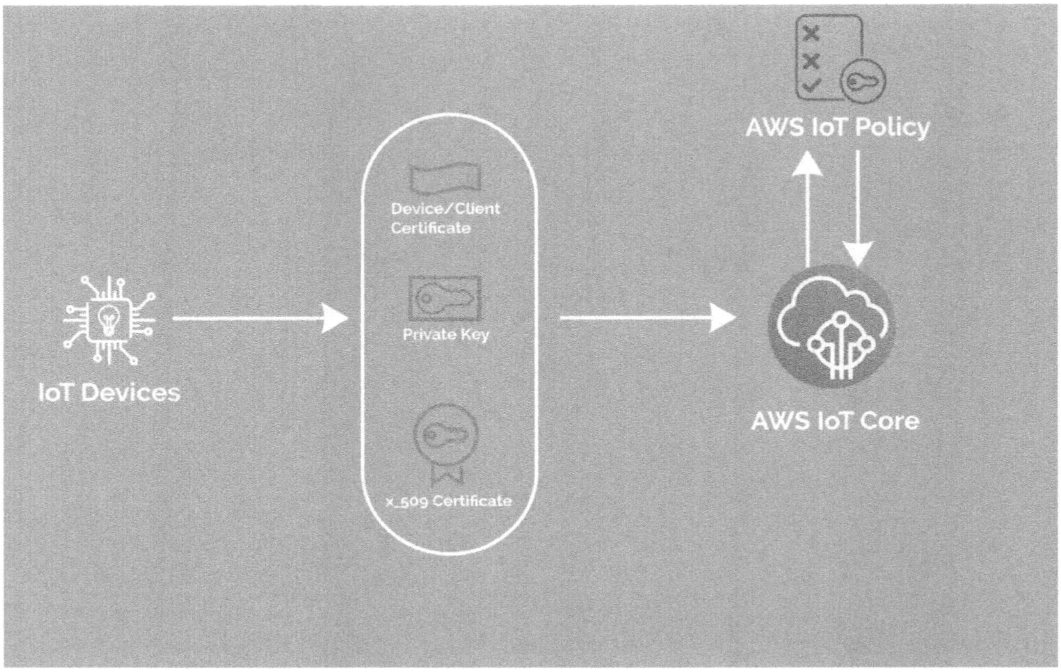
AWS IoT Policy
Device/Client Certificate
Private Key
x_509 Certificate
IoT Devices
AWS IoT Core

In the previous chapter you set up the AWS CLI. You configured the AWS CLI to work with your AWS account with AWS's SigV4 credentials which consist of the access key and the secret access key. However, these credentials are not sufficient to communicate with AWS from an IoT device. SigV4 is an AWS proprietary credential authentication protocol which is not IoT specific, more importantly, industry standards for IoT device security are heavily tilted towards certificate authentication when performing IoT device to cloud integration.

Later in the chapter I will demonstrate how to connect to AWS via HTTPS through the free cUR tool. However, as you saw in the protocol chart from the previous chapter, HTTPS to AWS IoT Core transmission doesn't facilitate bi-directional communication, making it generally an inferior choice compared to MQTT. Finally, you may see WebSockets and wonder what exactly that is. While using MQTT over WebSockets on the device is often redundant, AWS WebSockets can be very useful for "Real-time" IoT applications. In a later chapter in this book, we will have a chance to dive deep into AWS WebSockets and produce some unique and useful results with real-time dashboarding utilizing AWS Lambda and AWS API Gateway. For this chapter we will cover creating device certificates and attaching an IoT policy to them so that your ESP8266, ESP32, or Raspberry Pi can utilize bidirectional communications with AWS.

Having decided the best solution was to use certificate security authentication with the MQTT protocol we can now proceed with the next steps. The first thing we will want to do is get the three needed device security certificates that will link our IoT device to our specific AWS account and region. To do this we will first download the three necessary certificates. Once we have the certificates held on a local folder on our computer, we then need to assign a IoT policy to those certificates. A policy is a list of permissions that grant privileges relating to what the certificate bearing IoT device is allowed to do on AWS. The IoT policy allows service authorization as opposed to the device certificates which provide user authentication. The idea behind this security process is that we only want to give the IoT device enough privileges to accomplish everything we need, but not enough privileges to cause potential damage (see the AWS "least privilege" model). The assigning of permission policies attached to "Roles" can be a full-time job in itself - "AWS IAM Account Administrator". However, we are fortunate as I will assume everyone is using their own personal, non-corporate AWS accounts as a sole user. Thus, we can avoid these potential privileges headaches by giving both our IoT device, and the IoT centric AWS services, broad and powerful privileges. If AWS privileges need to be revoked or curtailed later, this can be done by the user at any time.

Step 1 - Download the AWS Device Security Certificates
Step 2 - Create and Attach an AWS Policy to the Device Security Certificates
Step 3 - Test the IoT Device Security Certificates and IoT Policy with the Free cURL Tool

---

Step 1 - Download the AWS Device Certificates

I have made a video explaining the process of creating certificates and attaching an IoT policy:

https://www.youtube.com/watch?v=sdgXt7Sq2dM&t=178s

The first step to create your security certificates is to navigate in the AWS console to AWS IoT Core.

https://console.aws.amazon.com/iot

Now that you are in AWS IoT Core go to Security → Certificates:

Security
Intro
Certificates
Policies

Then on the upper right, choose to "Add certificate" then drop-down to "Create certificate"

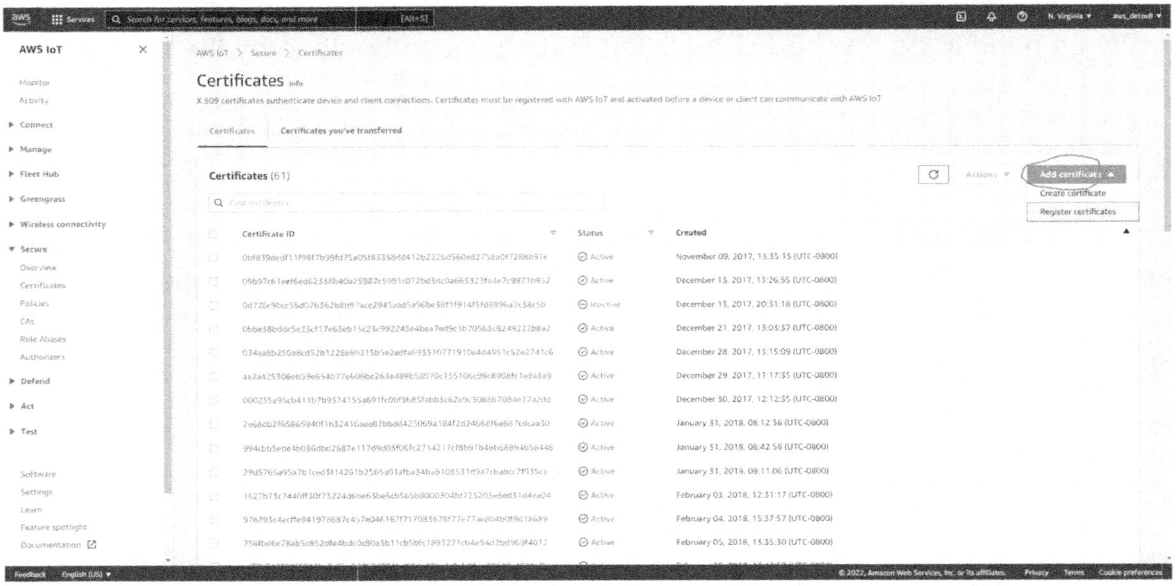
AWS IoT
Certificates
Certificates (61)
Add certificate
Create certificate
Register certificates
Certificate ID
Status
Created

$

$

Now you will choose to auto-generate activated certificates. Also make sure the certificates are "active" on creation. If you forget to activate the certificates, they will not work on your IoT devices until they are activated.

Once these two options are selected press the "Create" button.

$

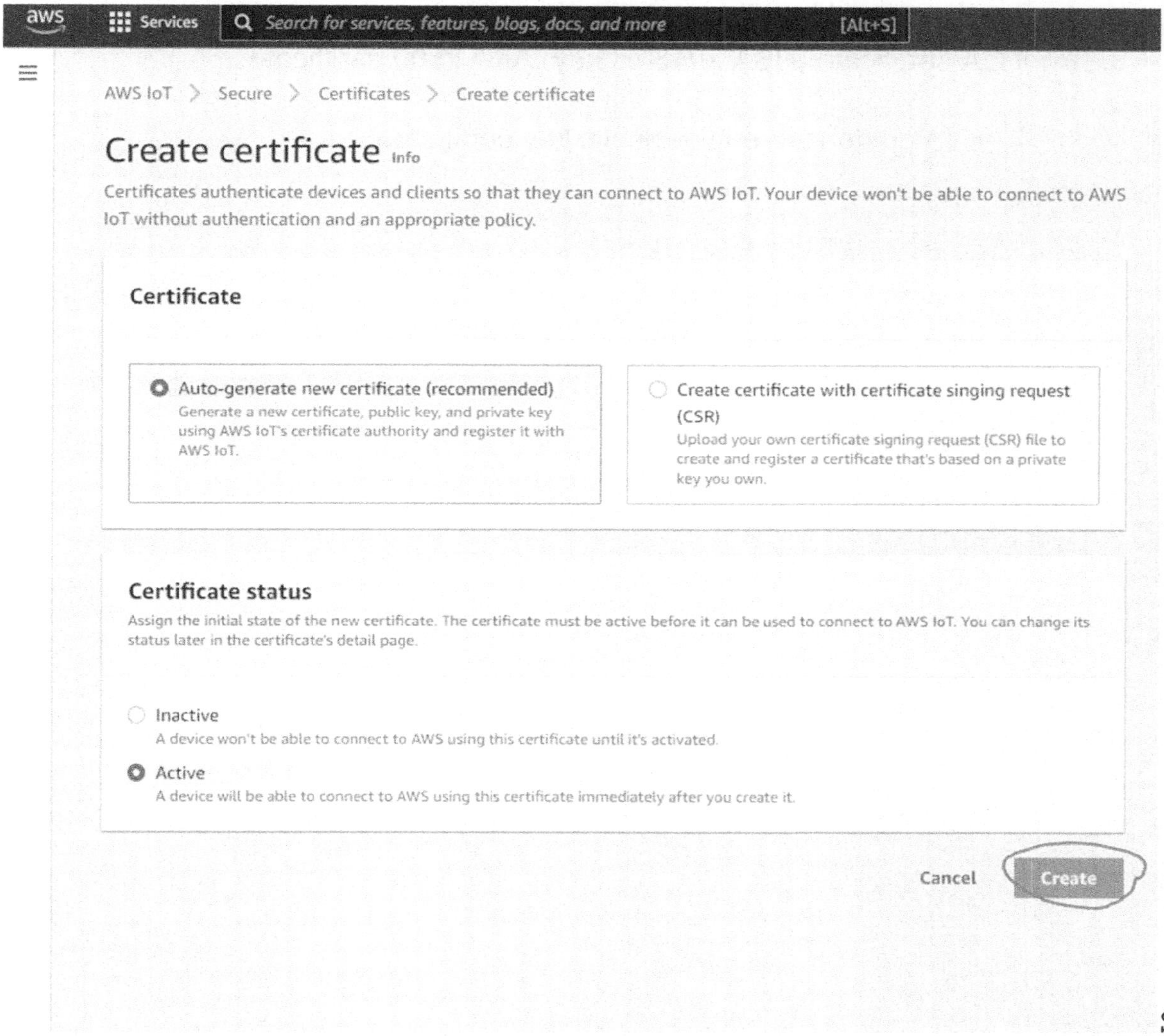
aws
Services
Search for services, features, blogs, docs, and more
[Alt+S]
AWS IoT > Secure > Certificates > Create certificate
Create certificate Info
Certificates authenticate devices and clients so that they can connect to AWS IoT. Your device won't be able to connect to AWS IoT without authentication and an appropriate policy.
Certificate
Auto-generate new certificate (recommended)
Generate a new certificate, public key, and private key using AWS IoT's certificate authority and register it with AWS IoT.
Create certificate with certificate singing request (CSR)
Upload your own certificate signing request (CSR) file to create and register a certificate that's based on a private key you own.
Certificate status
Assign the initial state of the new certificate. The certificate must be active before it can be used to connect to AWS IoT. You can change its status later in the certificate's detail page.
Inactive
A device won't be able to connect to AWS using this certificate until it's activated.
Active
A device will be able to connect to AWS using this certificate immediately after you create it.
Cancel
Create

$

Next, you will download the three certificates you need to connect your IoT devices to AWS IoT Core. You will use these same certificates whether you are using an ESP32, ESP8266, Raspberry Pi, or MQTT.fx as a virtual device. Again, other than

SigV4 credentials, using these security certificates linked to an AWS account is the only way for an IoT device to authenticate and communicate with the message broker on AWS IoT Core. Which IoT device communication protocol you use: MQTT, HTTPS, or MQTT over WebSockets is your choice. Don't confuse security protocols with communication protocols.

Download the following three certificates:

1. Device certificate (AKA Client certificate)
2. Private Key
3. Root CA certificate (RSA 2048 bit key) AKA x509 certificate.

- You don't need the public key certificate

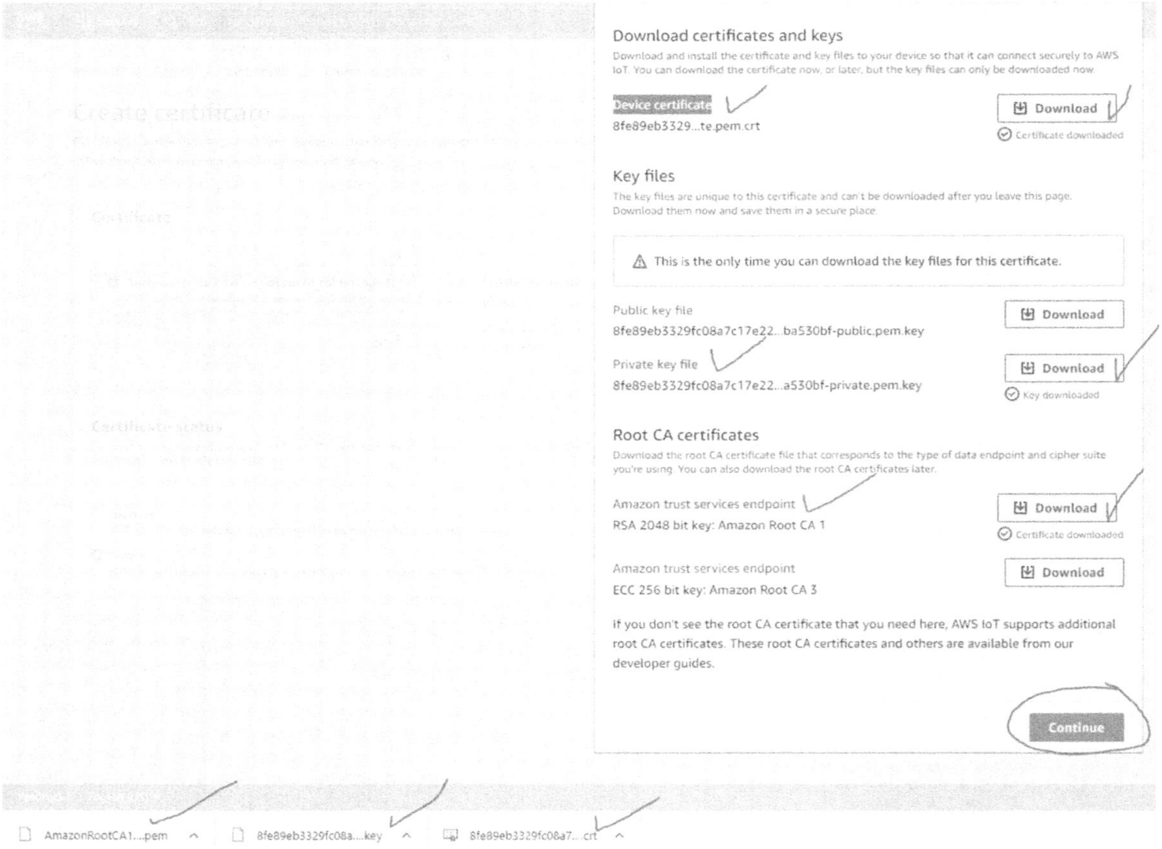

Download certificates and keys
Download and install the certificate and key files to your device so that it can connect securely to AWS IoT. You can download the certificate now, or later, but the key files can only be downloaded now.
Device certificate
8fe89eb3329...te.pem.crt
Download
Certificate downloaded
Key files
The key files are unique to this certificate and can't be downloaded after you leave this page. Download them now and save them in a secure place.
This is the only time you can download the key files for this certificate.
Public key file
8fe89eb3329fc08a7c17e22...ba530bf-public.pem.key
Download
Private key file
8fe89eb3329fc08a7c17e22...a530bf-private.pem.key
Download
Key downloaded
Root CA certificates
Download the root CA certificate file that corresponds to the type of data endpoint and cipher suite you're using. You can also download the root CA certificates later.
Amazon trust services endpoint
RSA 2048 bit key: Amazon Root CA 1
Download
Certificate downloaded
Amazon trust services endpoint
ECC 256 bit key: Amazon Root CA 3
Download
If you don't see the root CA certificate that you need here, AWS IoT supports additional root CA certificates. These root CA certificates and others are available from our developer guides.
Continue

After you downloaded all three certificates, place them in a secure folder in a location on your computer that you will remember. I speak from experience when I tell you it is a very good idea to keep each certificate set in a separate folder where you know how to locate them when needed. It is also a good idea to label the certificate folder with the region the certificates were created in. Other than the X509 Root CA certificate, the security certificates only work in the AWS region of their creation. You will need to use the three security certificates frequently throughout this book. Reusing the same certificates between devices is unadvisable during production IoT development but it makes things easier for the IoT prototyping done in this book.

Here I placed my certificates in their own folder identified by region. Also, I included a command box to show you the full file extension. Knowing the full file extension is important as you will need it several times over the course of this book in multiple projects. On Windows the file extensions are often displayed truncated as they are here with the client/device certificate. Finally, notice I made a second folder in which I renamed the certificates to something more convenient (certificate, private, and root). This is a useful shortcut if you don't want to copy and paste these ridiculously long certificate names every time you need to use them. Do not overwrite the certificates file extensions!

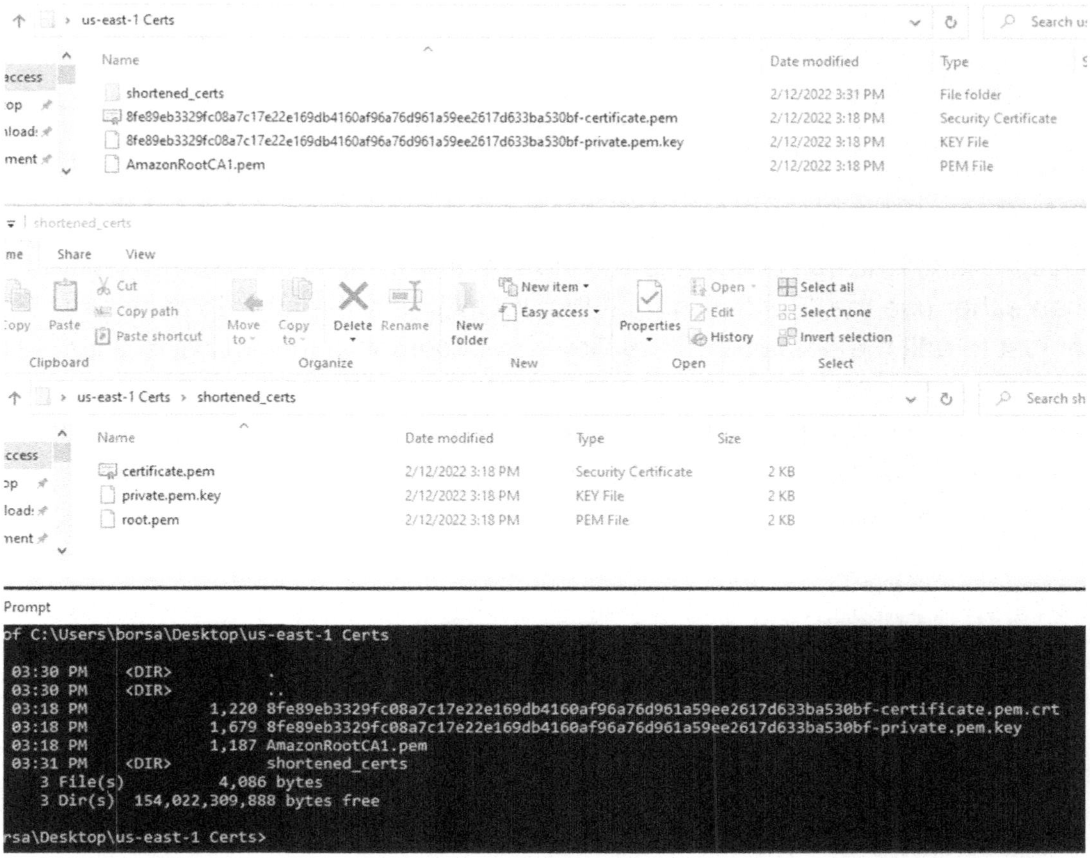
us-east-1 Certs
Name
Date modified
Type
shortened_certs
2/12/2022 3:31 PM
File folder
8fe89eb3329fc08a7c17e22e169db4160af96a76d961a59ee2617d633ba530bf-certificate.pem
2/12/2022 3:18 PM
Security Certificate
8fe89eb3329fc08a7c17e22e169db4160af96a76d961a59ee2617d633ba530bf-private.pem.key
2/12/2022 3:18 PM
KEY File
AmazonRootCA1.pem
2/12/2022 3:18 PM
PEM File
Share
View
Cut
Copy path
Paste shortcut
Paste
Clipboard
Move to
Copy to
Delete
Rename
Organize
New item
Easy access
New folder
New
Properties
Open
Edit
History
Select all
Select none
Invert selection
Select
us-east-1 Certs › shortened_certs
Name
Date modified
Type
Size
certificate.pem
2/12/2022 3:18 PM
Security Certificate
2 KB
private.pem.key
2/12/2022 3:18 PM
KEY File
2 KB
root.pem
2/12/2022 3:18 PM
PEM File
2 KB
Prompt
of C:\Users\borsa\Desktop\us-east-1 Certs
03:30 PM <DIR> .
03:30 PM <DIR> ..
03:18 PM 1,220 8fe89eb3329fc08a7c17e22e169db4160af96a76d961a59ee2617d633ba530bf-certificate.pem.crt
03:18 PM 1,679 8fe89eb3329fc08a7c17e22e169db4160af96a76d961a59ee2617d633ba530bf-private.pem.key
03:18 PM 1,187 AmazonRootCA1.pem
03:31 PM <DIR> shortened_certs
3 File(s) 4,086 bytes
3 Dir(s) 154,022,309,888 bytes free
rsa\Desktop\us-east-1 Certs>

Step 2 - Create and Attach an AWS Policy to the Device Security Certificates

Now that you have downloaded your certificates and activated them you may think that you are done. Surprisingly you are not yet done as you must attach an AWS permissions "policy" to your certificates. The IoT policy that you design will dictate the scope of AWS actions and services that you are allowed to use on the cloud from your IoT device.

Go back to IoT Core, and then to IoT Core → Security→Policies and then select the "Create policy" button:

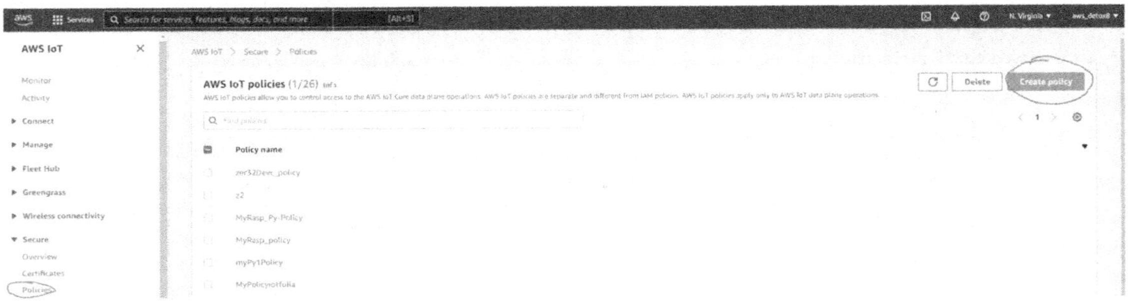
AWS IoT
Connect
Manage
Fleet Hub
Greengrass
Wireless connectivity
Secure
AWS IoT policies (1/26)
Delete
Create policy
Policy name

To design the IoT device policy to attach to your newly created security credentials you can either use the "Builder" or edit the JSON policy directly. In this case it is easier just to edit the default JSON policy. To accomplish this first give your policy a name. Here I named mine "AllIoTAccessPolicy," you can name yours whatever you like as long as you remember your policy name. Then choose "JSON" on the lower right and simply add and edit the default policy by adding an asterisk in two places in the JSON policy:

```
"Action": "*",
"Resource": "*"
```

"*" = all actions and all resources

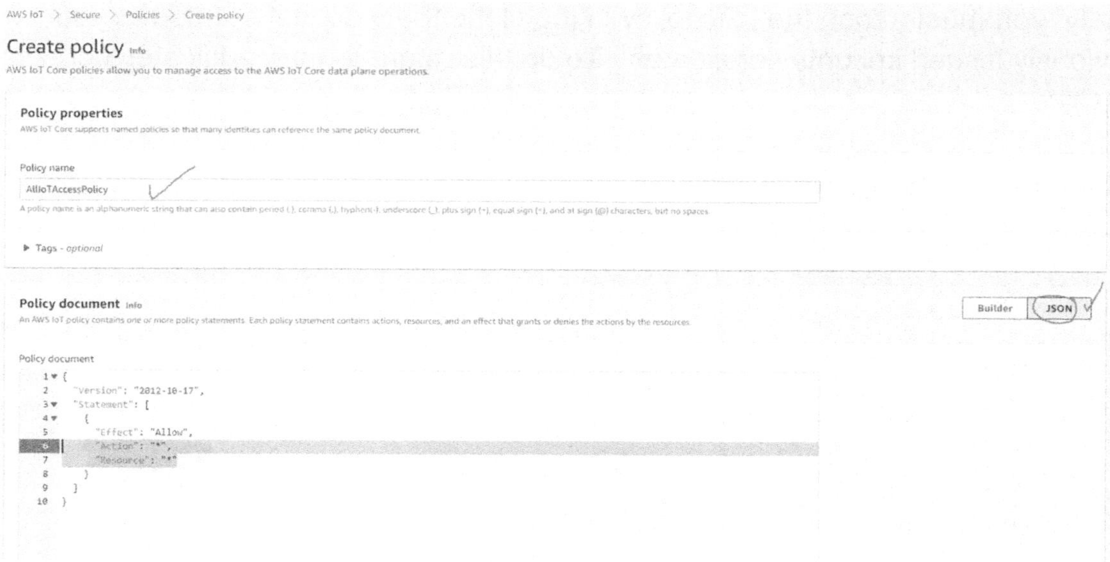
AWS IoT > Secure > Policies > Create policy
Create policy Info
AWS IoT Core policies allow you to manage access to the AWS IoT Core data plane operations.
Policy properties
Policy name
AllIoTAccessPolicy
Tags - optional
Policy document Info
Builder
JSON
Policy document
{
"Version": "2012-10-17",
"Statement": [
{
"Effect": "Allow",
"Action": "*",
"Resource": "*"
}
]
}

By using the asterisk wildcard character, you have given these security certificates the right to use any AWS services and any resource within those services on your AWS account. This is the most powerful policy you could create and certainly violates the "least privilege" AWS axiom, but again, in this case it is acceptable being that you are using it in a private account with one user. If you like you can also alter the policy or make a new one to restrict the certificates privileges.

Remember, this IoT policy is held only on the cloud so even though your certificates are deployed on an IoT device in the wild you can always expand or restrict the attached IoT policy privileges any time you like by editing the policy associated with the security certificates. Also realize that the security certificates are linked to just your AWS account and in just the AWS region in which they were created.

- The x509 root certificate is fungible between all AWS regions and accounts but don't discuss that, it is a secret!

After completing the "Policy document" choose the "Create" button on the lower left of the screen to finalize creating your all access IoT policy.

Create

Finally, you must attach the IoT policy in the cloud that you just created to your previously issued security certificates. To do this return to the certificates console in IoT Core:

Security
Intro
Certificates
Policies

Now choose “Actions” and then “Attach policy”:

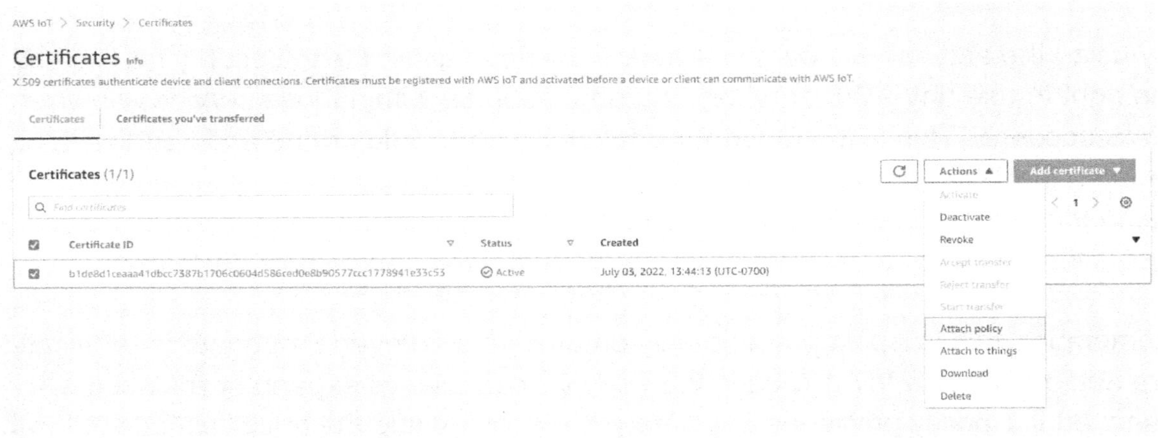
AWS IoT > Security > Certificates
Certificates Info
X.509 certificates authenticate device and client connections. Certificates must be registered with AWS IoT and activated before a device or client can communicate with AWS IoT.
Certificates
Certificates you've transferred
Certificates (1/1)
Actions
Add certificate
Certificate ID
Status
Created
b1de8d1ceaaa41dbcc7387b1706c0604d586ced0e8b90577ccc1778941e33c53
Active
July 03, 2022, 13:44:13 (UTC-0700)
Deactivate
Revoke
Attach policy
Attach to things
Download
Delete

Now choose which policy to attach to your certificates, probably the policy you just created would be the best choice:

Attach policies to the certificate b1de8d1ceaaa41dbcc7387b1706c0604d586ced0e8b90577ccc1778941e33c53.
Policies
Choose policies to attach to this certificate. The certificate can have up to 10 policies attached to it.
Choose AWS IoT policy
AllIoTAccessPolicy
ancel
Attach policies

Step 3 - Test the IoT Device Certificates and IoT Policy with the Free cURL Tool

Now you will test the active security certificates with their attached IoT policy to ensure they work correctly with AWS. If the certificates don't work in this test they will not work on your physical or virtual IoT devices so it is very important to figure out any issue with the certificates now rather than later in which it may not be clear what is failing. Half of the IoT device connection problems my students contact me about are due to issues with their certificates not working properly. To test your security certificates, you are going to use the free cURL tool. This tool comes preinstalled with most operating systems: PC, MacOS, and Linux. However, unlike MacOS and Linux the cURL tool preinstalled for Windows will not work correctly for the intended purposes. For this reason, as well as for the certificate conversion tool you will use later in the book, I highly recommend you download the free "Git for Windows" if you are on a PC. You should have already installed the Git tool in the last chapter if using Windows. Git for windows has a suite of very useful tools for IoT developers.

AWS provides their own documentation for testing device certificates with cURL here:

https://docs.aws.amazon.com/iot/latest/developerguide/http.html

I find their directions pretty good if you are using MacOS or Linux, but I will add my own directions below which I think will be easier to follow and are more relevant to Windows users.

Git for Windows can be found here and downloaded:

https://gitforwindows.org/

After download, open a command prompt and navigate to the default location for the 'curl.exe' installed by Git for Windows. Again, do not use the default curl.exe in the *windows/system32* folder.

The default location for the newly installed cURL tool in Windows should be:

```
C:\Program Files\Git\mingw64\bin>
```

Next, copy your set of three AWS security certificates to the same directory as listed above. Now you may be thinking "why don't I do this correctly and set the environmental variables to execute the cURL tool from anywhere on the computer?" While that may be the correct method, I am choosing to use this lazy technique because it is easier and less prone to error. You are welcome to do it the professional way if you already know how.

After copying your certificates to the "*Program Files\Git\mingw64\bin*" folder return to IoT Core:

https://console.aws.amazon.com/iot

Navigate to the 'MQTT test client' and "Subscribe" to "#" to catch all incoming MQTT topics:

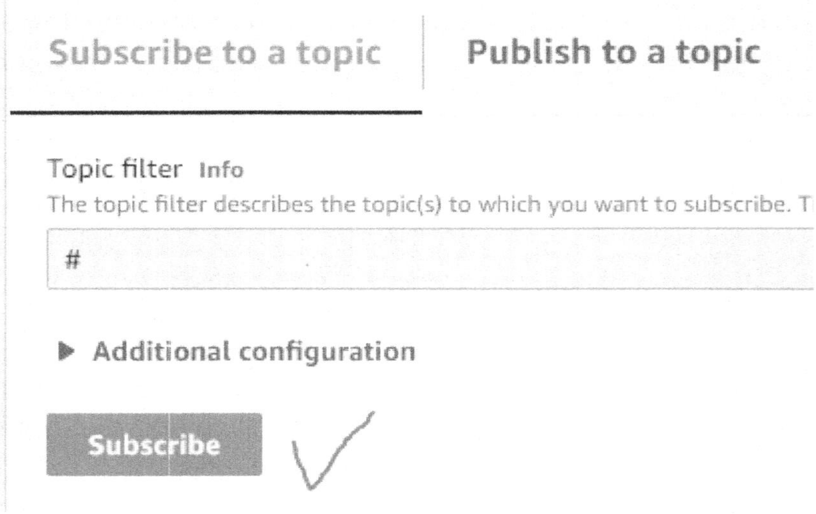
Subscribe to a topic
Publish to a topic
Topic filter Info
The topic filter describes the topic(s) to which you want to subscribe. T
#
Additional configuration
Subscribe

You will now need to retrieve your IoT endpoint which was described in the last chapter by using the AWS CLI. You can also find your IoT endpoint for any AWS region by going to IoT Core→Settings on the left side pane in IoT Core:

▶ Fleet Hub

Device Software

Billing groups

Settings

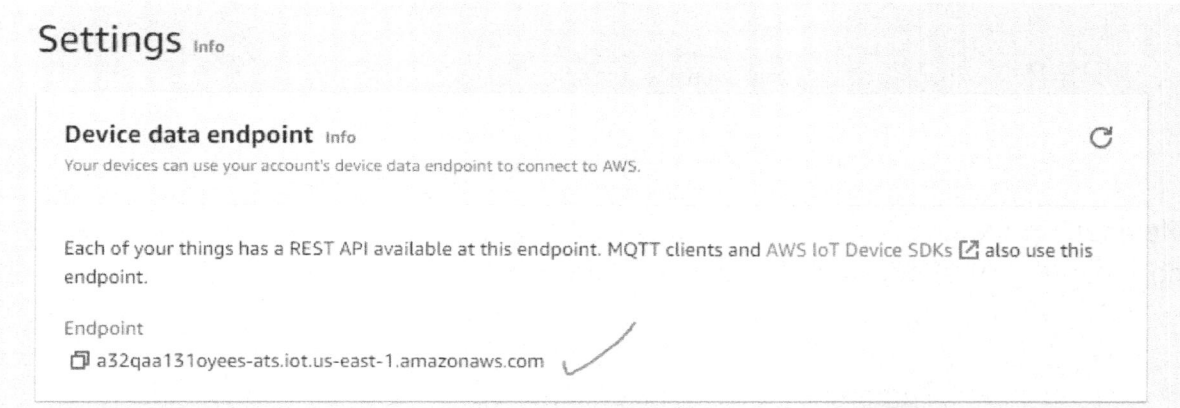

Settings Info

Device data endpoint Info

Your devices can use your account's device data endpoint to connect to AWS.

Each of your things has a REST API available at this endpoint. MQTT clients and AWS IoT Device SDKs also use this endpoint.

Endpoint

a32qaa131oyees-ats.iot.us-east-1.amazonaws.com

Copy your regional IoT endpoint and insert it on this line at the end of the cURL commands:

```
"https://<INSERT-YOUR-IOT-DATA-ENDPOINT-HERE>:8443/topics/outTopic?qos=1"
```

Once your security certificates are copied into the '*Program Files\Git\mingw64\bin* folder' you can now use the following cURL commands at the command prompt from that directory. Make sure your security certificate names match the name you are using in the commands below:

```
  curl --tlsv1.2 ^
  --cacert Amazon-root-CA-1.pem ^
  --cert client.pem.crt ^
  --key private.pem.key ^
  --request POST ^
  --data "{\"Temperature\": 77, \"Humidity\": 88, \"Time\": 12349876}" ^
"https://<INSERT-YOUR-IOT-DATA-ENDPOINT-HERE>:8443/topics/outTopic?qos=1"
```

Now open the command prompt in windows by using the Windows key + R then typing ‘cmd’ into the box and pressing ‘enter’.

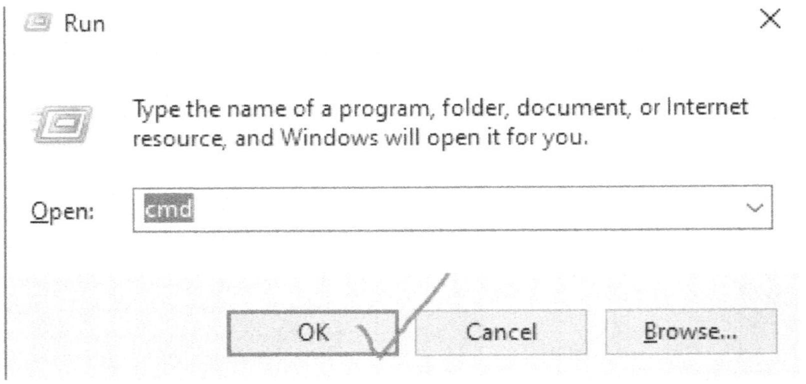
Run
Type the name of a program, folder, document, or Internet resource, and Windows will open it for you.
Open:
cmd
OK
Cancel
Browse...

Navigate to the correct directory and issue the listed cURL commands from the command prompt but with your own IoT endpoint.

- Remember the ‘^’ carrot continuation character is specific to Windows. In Linux based system you would use the "\" as the line continuation command.

Command Prompt

```
C:\Program Files\Git\mingw64\bin>  curl --tlsv1.2 ^
More?    --cacert Amazon-root-CA-1.pem ^
More?    --cert client.pem.crt ^
More?    --key private.pem.key ^
More?    --request POST ^
More?    --data "{\"Temperature\": 77, \"Humidity\": 88, \"Time\": 12349876}" ^
More?    "https://a32qaa131oyees-ats.iot.us-east-1.amazonaws.com:8443/topics/outTopic?qos=1"
```

If the command was successful, and you transmitted your payload correctly, you will receive this notice in the command prompt but with a different ‘*traceId*’:

{"message":"OK","traceId":"f24ad444-c2fc-b42a-c7fa-e1216097c553"} "message":"OK" indicates a successful delivery. If you received a "message":"null" that usually indicates a problem with your certificates or you are in a different region from where your certificates were created.

Going back to the MQTT test client on IoT Core and your payload should have appeared in the "Subscriptions" box:

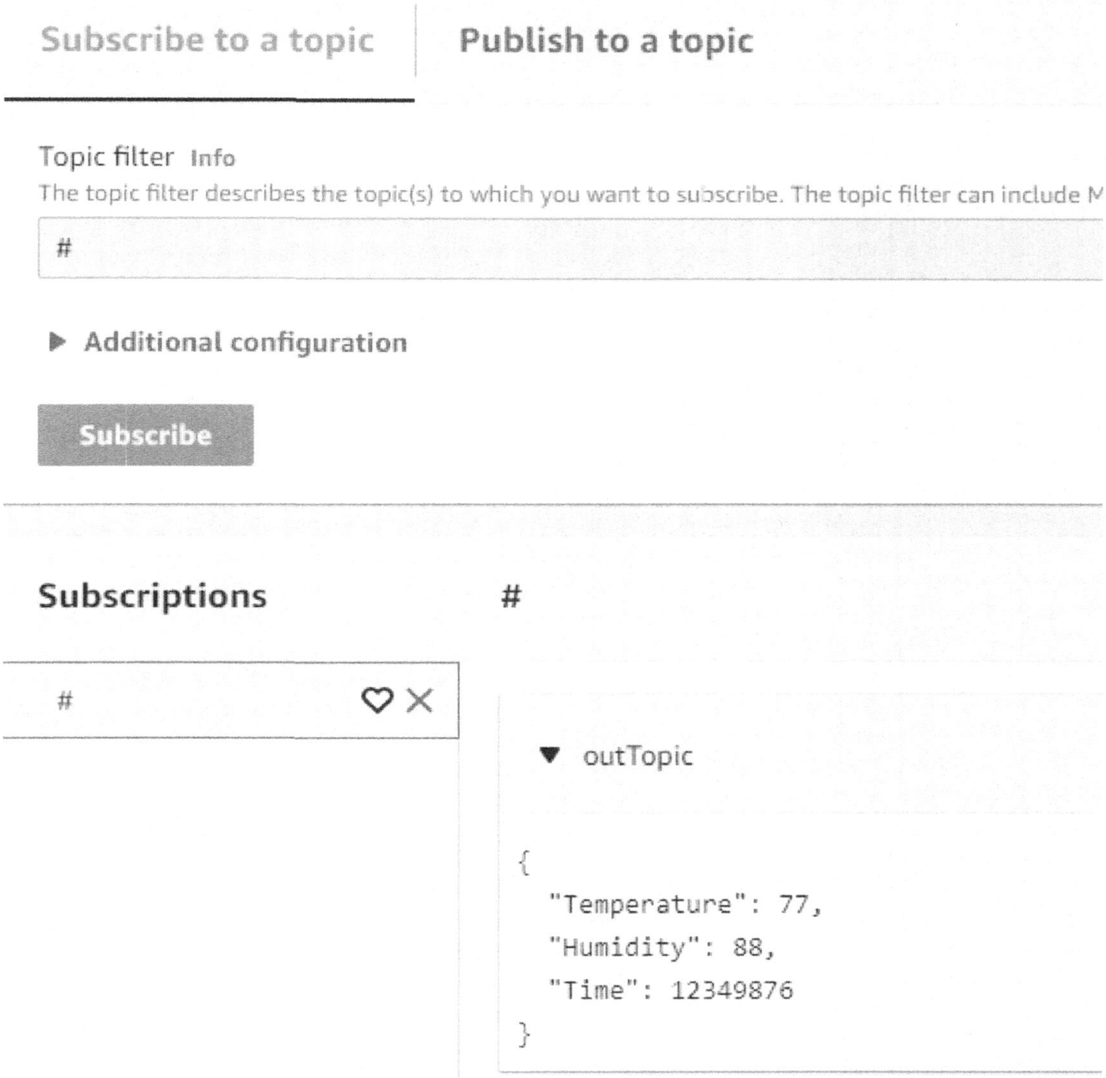
Subscribe to a topic
Publish to a topic
Topic filter Info
The topic filter describes the topic(s) to which you want to subscribe. The topic filter can include
#
Additional configuration
Subscribe
Subscriptions
#
#
outTopic
{
"Temperature": 77,
"Humidity": 88,
"Time": 12349876
}

It should be noted that the cURL tool also uses HTTPS just like the AWS CLI, but instead of SigV4 security you have used certificate security and TLS 1.2. In the next chapter you will use MQTT.fx as a virtual device which uses MQTT(s) over port 8883 with certificate security and the MQTT protocol has the advantage of bidirectional communication which HTTPS does not have when interacting with the message broker on AWS.

Congratulations, now you have working device security certificates with an IoT policy attached. You can reuse these certificates for the rest of the book for both physical and virtual IoT devices.

Chapter 3 -
Using a Virtual IoT Device to Transmit Data to AWS with MQTT

Using a virtual IoT device instead of a physical IoT device to transmit messages to AWS IoT Core could be useful for several reasons, some of these reasons are:

A) The developer does not have a physical IoT device available.
B) It is inconvenient to upload code to the IoT device for every change to the device's firmware.
C) The developer wants custom control over the number of IoT messages sent, duration, and frequency.
D) The IoT vendor is undecided or ambivalent about IoT device component or firmware specifications.

Another important factor to consider when using an IoT device as a teaching heuristic is the advantages of using a virtual IoT device for behavior transparency without getting confused by ancillary hardware considerations. We have already discussed transmission protocols like MQTT, WebSockets, and HTTPS as well as authorization and authentication standards like SigV4 and TLS1.2 certificate secured security. Mixing and matching these protocols can be very confusing to the new IoT engineer or developer.

In this chapter you will utilize a virtual device to transmit and receive IoT data from the server side MQTT broker on AWS IoT Core. You will use a test JavaScript program that will send fake IoT data, as JSON formatted payloads, to AWS IoT Core. Your virtual IoT device will be a free client side MQTT broker called MQTT.fx. MQTT.fx is a MQTT Client written in Java and based on Eclipse Paho. This is an easy-to-use tool with a graphical user interface that provides a simple way to ramp up IoT to cloud testing. There are other free and paid MQTT client brokers available such as HiveMQ, Bevywise, EMQ, and Mosca, however MQTT.fx's easy to use GUI makes it a standout.

MQTT.fx uses the Mosquitto MQTT client broker on your computer but wraps it in a very nice graphical user interface (GUI) which increases its ease of use. Another benefit of using this tool is that the Mosquito MQTT client inside the MQTT.fx tool comes with all the needed dependencies included for the Windows OS. While I found the Eclipse MQTT broker to be relatively easy to use and install on Linux and Mac OS, the Windows configuration is much more involved as you would need to install various dependency packages. Fortunately, MQTT.fx solves this issue for us in one simple package.

It is important to note that once data is received in AWS IoT Core it can be dispatched to any AWS service we like. While we have many IoT centric AWS services that are pre-built with a connector to AWS IoT Core through various "rule actions," we can also access the rest of the AWS services ecosystem through Lambda functions, which also have a pre-configured connector from AWS IoT core.

Step 1 - Download and Install the MQTT.fx Tool
Step 2 - Configure MQTT.fx with your AWS IoT Endpoint and Security Certificates
Step 3 - Connect to AWS IoT Core and Send a Test IoT Payload
Step 4 - Program a MQTT.fx Test Script for Automated Publishing to AWS IoT Core

---

Step 1 - Download and Install the MQTT.fx Tool

The newest version of MQTT.fx has recently become a paid product, however you can download a free three-month trial of the latest version which is suitable for the chapter's requirements here:

https://softblade.de/en/welcome/

You can also find the free forever version 1.7 which I use in this chapter that can be downloaded below (this is one long URL, not two separate addresses):

https://web.archive.org/web/20210514230412/https://www.jensd.de/apps/mqttfx/1.7.1

- A properly formatted link is on the chapters GitHub page.

After installing MQTT.fx for your operating system you need to configure it with your security certificate credentials and AWS IoT endpoint so it can send messages as a virtual IoT device to AWS IoT Core.

Step 2 - Configure MQTT.fx with your AWS IoT Endpoint at Security Certificates

Open MQTT.fx and select the gear icon:

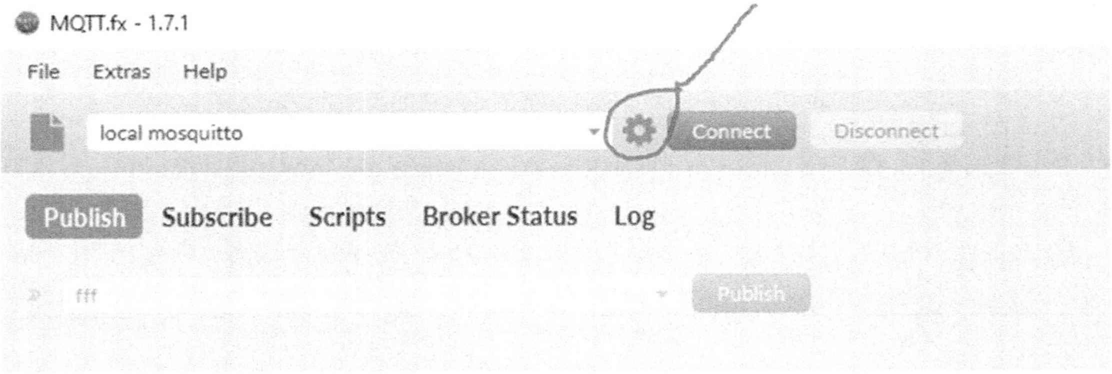

MQTT.fx - 1.7.1
File
Extras
Help
local mosquitto
Connect
Disconnect
Publish
Subscribe
Scripts
Broker Status
Log
fff
Publish

Now you have two fields to fill out in the next screen. You must enter your AWS IoT endpoint, and your MQTT(s) port. For the IoT endpoint you could retrieve it in two different ways if you forgot to save it from the previous chapters. Either enter the following command from the command prompt using the AWS CLI:

```
aws iot describe-endpoint --endpoint-type iot:Data-ATS
```

Or go to:

https://console.aws.amazon.com/iot

Then select "settings" on the lower left of your screen, and then copy your AWS IoT endpoint.

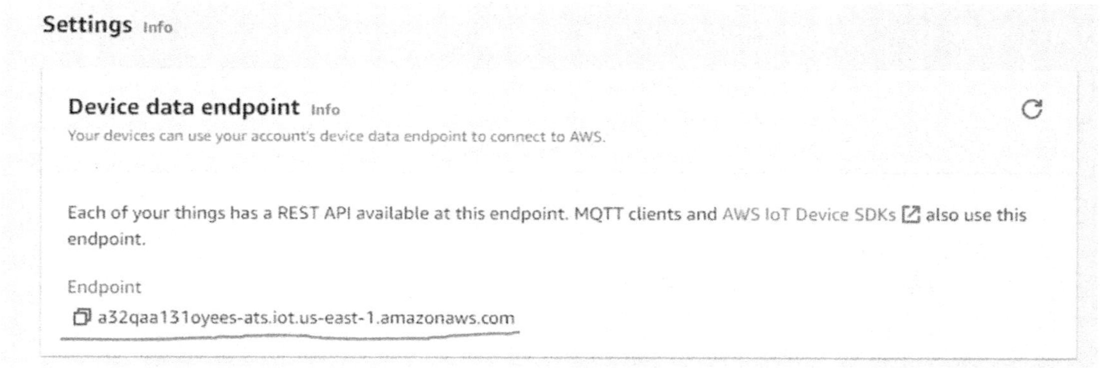
Settings Info
Device data endpoint Info
Your devices can use your account's device data endpoint to connect to AWS.
Each of your things has a REST API available at this endpoint. MQTT clients and AWS IoT Device SDKs also use this endpoint.
Endpoint
a32qaa131oyees-ats.iot.us-east-1.amazonaws.com

A) Fill out the "Broker Port" as 8883. The MQTT protocol specifies two ports by standard convention: 1883, and 8883. Port 1883 is for MQTT unsecured, and port 8883 is for MQTT(s) which is secured. AWS IoT Core only accepts MQTT secured connections on port 8883 and 443.

B) The MQTT protocol standard requires a unique Client ID for each device connecting to the MQTT server-side broker. The name of the Client ID doesn't matter. You can use the name generated by the tool or choose your own. When you have multiple devices, especially when using device shadows, you must remember to set each MQTT Client ID individually, forgetting this often leads to anomalous problems that many new users have a hard time debugging.

Here is what your screen should look like below, but now with your own AWS IoT endpoint and Client ID:

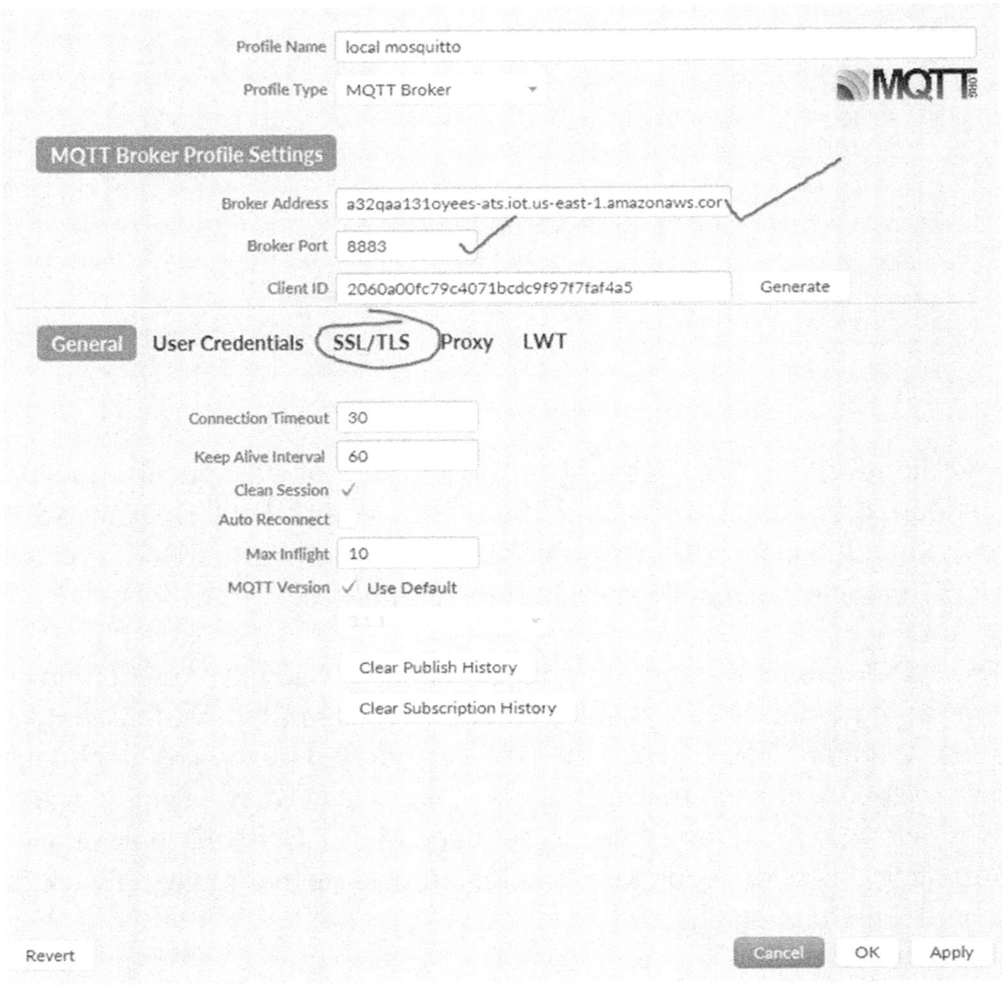
Profile Name
local mosquitto
Profile Type
MQTT Broker
MQTT
MQTT Broker Profile Settings
Broker Address
a32qaa131oyees-ats.iot.us-east-1.amazonaws.com
Broker Port
8883
Client ID
2060a00fc79c4071bcdc9f97f7faf4a5
Generate
General
User Credentials
SSL/TLS
Proxy
LWT
Connection Timeout
30
Keep Alive Interval
60
Clean Session
Auto Reconnect
Max Inflight
10
MQTT Version
Use Default
Clear Publish History
Clear Subscription History
Revert
Cancel
OK
Apply

Now select the "SSL/TLS" tab. SSL stands for 'Secure Sockets Layer' and TLS stands for 'Transport Layer Security'. The terms are often used interchangeably but just know that TLS is an updated version of SSL. AWS IoT requires TLS version 1.2 or above to connect to AWS IoT Core. By using your three security certificates, as well as several other security implementations 'under the hood', you meet the TLS 1.2 criteria for AWS IoT acceptability.

Now you must configure a total of seven things on the SSL/TLS" tab.

1. Check to "Enable SSL/TLS"
2. Set the protocol as TLS 1.2
3. Check "Self-signed certificates"
4. CA File: set the path to where you saved the root certificate, this is also known as the x509, or as AWS calls it, the AmazonRootCA1.

5. Client Certificate File: set the path to the client certificate, this is also known as the device certificate.
6. Private Key File: set the path to the private key.
7. Make sure the "PEM Formatted" box is selected.

Select "Apply" and then "Ok" and go back to the main screen.

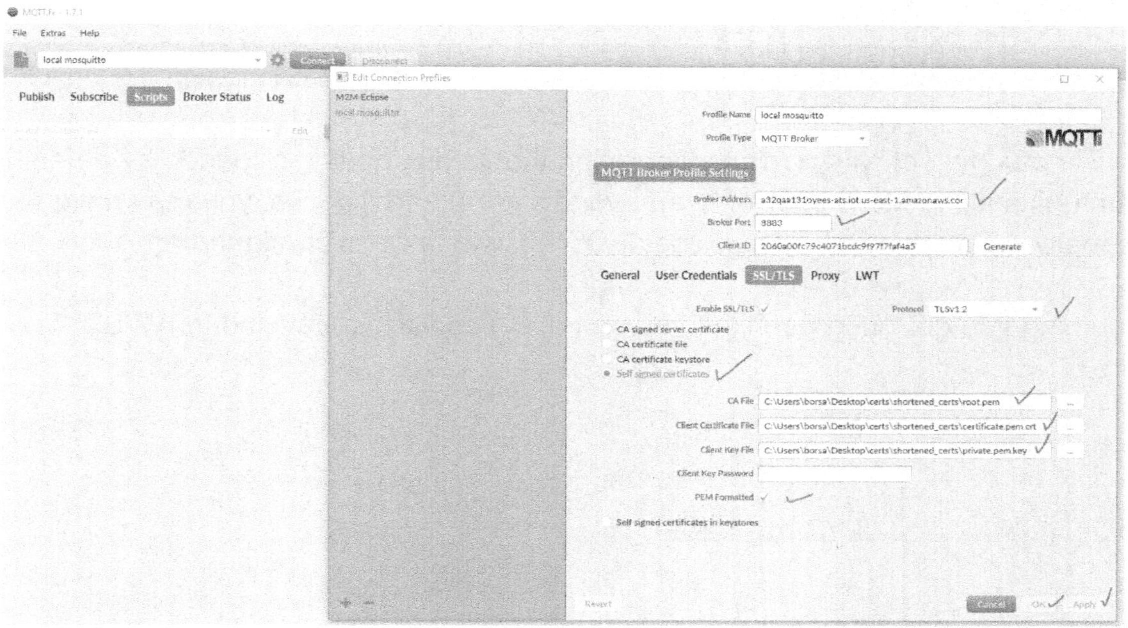

File Extras Help
local mosquitto
Publish Subscribe Scripts Broker Status Log
Edit Connection Profiles
M2M Eclipse
Profile Name local mosquitto
Profile Type MQTT Broker
MQTT
MQTT Broker Profile Settings
Broker Address a32qaa131oyees-ats.iot.us-east-1.amazonaws.com
Broker Port 8883
Client ID
Generate
General User Credentials SSL/TLS Proxy LWT
Enable SSL/TLS
Protocol TLSv1.2
CA signed server certificate
CA certificate file
CA certificate keystore
Self signed certificates
CA File C:\Users\borsa\Desktop\certs\shortened_certs\root.pem
Client Certificate File C:\Users\borsa\Desktop\certs\shortened_certs\certificate.pem.crt
Client Key File C:\Users\borsa\Desktop\certs\shortened_certs\private.pem.key
Client Key Password
PEM Formatted
Self signed certificates in keystores
Revert
Cancel
OK
Apply

Step 3 - Connect to AWS IoT Core and Send a Test IoT payload

You are now ready to connect your virtual device to AWS IoT Core. Here is the moment of truth! Press the "connect" button and if you configured everything properly then you will get the literal green light. Now MQTT.fx is connected to the AWS message broker on AWS IoT Core. Congratulations!

File Extras Help
Disconnect
Publish Subscribe Scripts Broker Status Log

If you get a red light than there is either a problem with your security certificates or some other aspect of your MQTT.fx configuration. If this is the case, then first review your MQTT.fx configuration for errors and then check that your AWS security credentials are activated with a proper IoT policy attached and try again.

Troubleshooting tip:

MQTT.fx has an unfixed problem, the file:

C:\Users\<your-computer>\AppData\Local\MQTT-FX\mqttfx-config.xml

The file can get set with a misconfiguration that keeps getting reloaded by default. Even uninstalling MQTT.fx won't remove this corrupted file. So, you may have to manually delete this file to truly reset MQTT.fx with a good configuration.

Assuming you got the green light you can now send a test payload to AWS IoT Core.

Go back to:

https://console.aws.amazon.com/iot

Next, go to the MQTT test client in AWS IoT Core and select the "Subscribe to a topic" tab. Subscribe to "iot/#", use the pound/hash symbol so the broker will accept all topics starting with 'iot/#''. This is a useful way to accept multiple topics from multiple devices as well as facilitate a "fan in" architecture to assist with large scale data ingest which may include too many messages for IoT core to handle under a single, static topic. For massive IoT data ingest you may have to utilize multiple incoming topic subscriptions, or AWS Kinesis Firehose, or the KCL client in AWS, but this is an expensive service and a more advanced conversation best saved for a discussion of production design.

Your screen should look like the image below after subscribing to the "iot/#" topic on the MQTT test client:

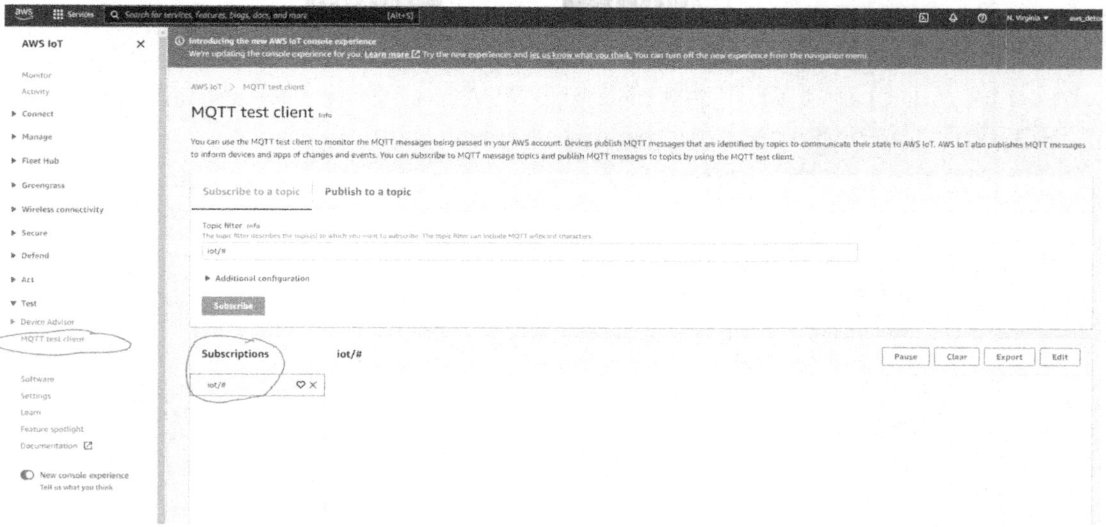

Now let's send a simple IoT payload from MQTT.fx to the message broker on AWS IoT Core. From MQTT.fx paste in the test payload below in JSON format.

```
{
  "temperature": 44,
  "humidity": 66
}
```

Next, when you enter a topic name to publish under, you will want to use a topic that starts with "iot/", here I use "iot/mqttfx". Now press the "Publish" button.

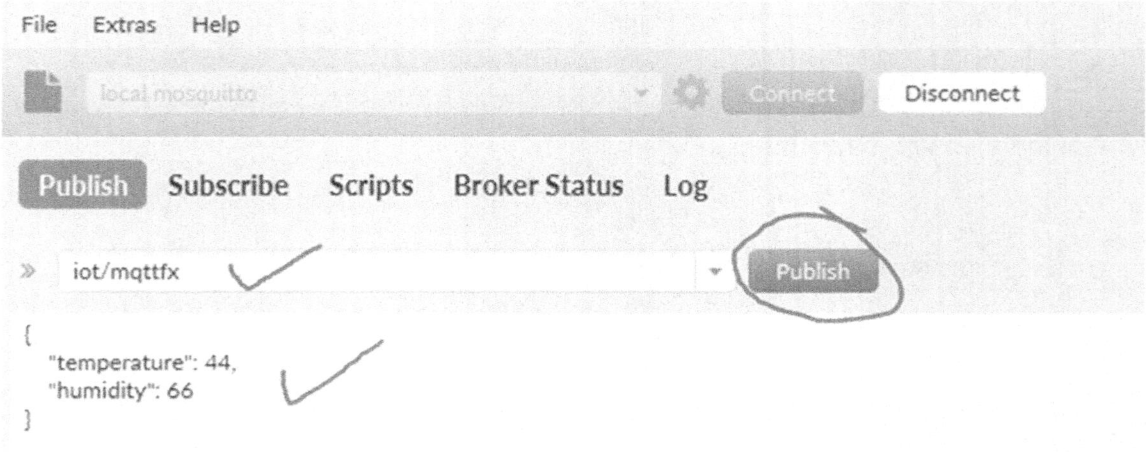

File Extras Help
local mosquitto
Connect
Disconnect
Publish Subscribe Scripts Broker Status Log
iot/mqttfx
Publish
{
"temperature": 44,
"humidity": 66
}

Returning to your open MQTT test client on AWS IoT Core you should have seen your JSON IoT payload appear in the subscription window.

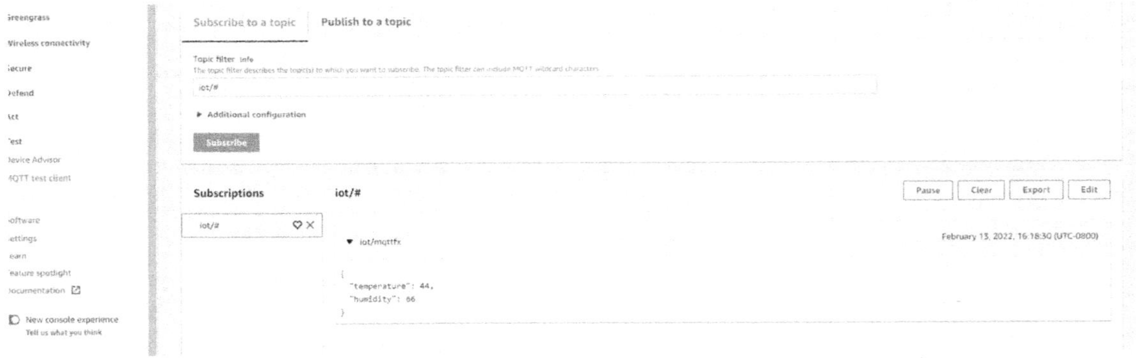

Subscribe to a topic
Publish to a topic
Topic filter
iot/#
Additional configuration
Subscribe
Subscriptions
iot/#
Pause
Clear
Export
Edit
iot/mqttfx
"temperature": 44,
"humidity": 66

Great, now you can reverse the transmission and publish a payload from IoT Core to MQTT.fx.

Within MQTT.fx select the “Subscribe” tab and then enter the same topic as you used as your subscription topic in AWS IoT Core: “iot/#”

Now press the “Subscribe” button.

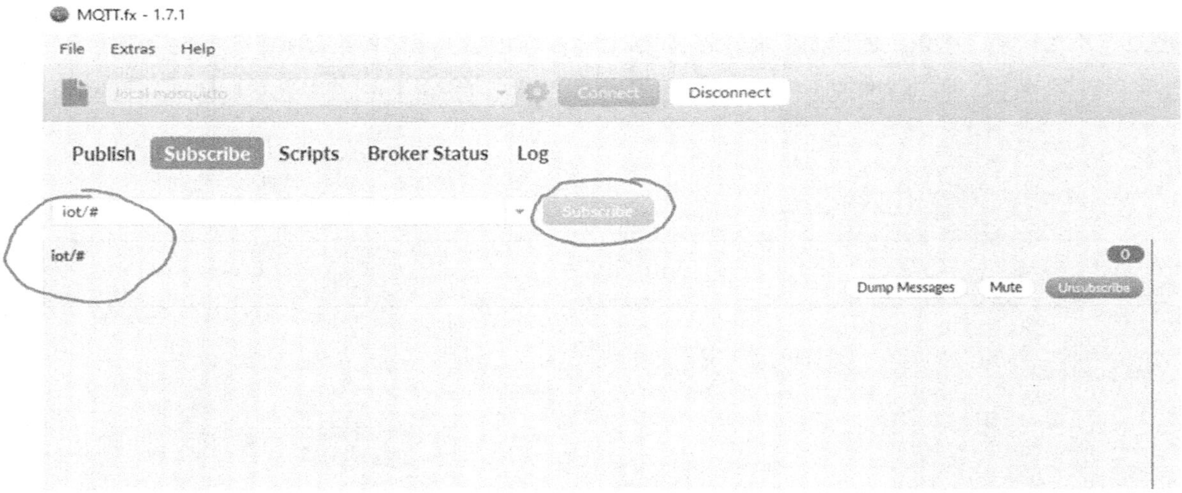

MQTT.fx - 1.7.1
File
Extras
Help
Connect
Disconnect
Publish
Subscribe
Scripts
Broker Status
Log
iot/#
Subscribe
iot/#
Dump Messages
Mute
Unsubscribe

MQTT.fx is now ready to receive any published messages linked to your account credentials in your chosen AWS region that start with “iot/”.

Go back to AWS IoT Core and select the "Publish to a topic". Publish to the topic "iot/mqttfx"." Enter the topic and keep the default "Hello…" message payload or alter it as you like, just ensure it stays in JSON format. Now press the 'Publish' button.

Subscribe to a topic
Publish to a topic
Topic name
iot/mqttfx
Message payload
{
"message": "Hello from AWS IoT console"
}
Additional configuration
Publish
Subscriptions
iot/#
Pause
Clear
Export
Edit
iot/#
iot/mqttfx
February 13, 2022, 16:22:28 (UTC-0800)
{
"message": "Hello from AWS IoT console"
}

As you can now anticipate when returning to the MQTT.fx console, you should have received the message published from AWS IoT Core.

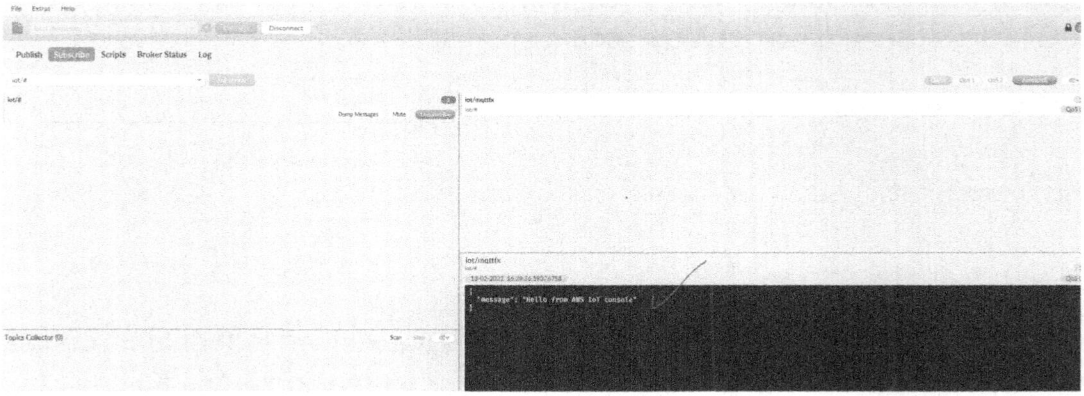
Disconnect
Publish
Subscribe
Scripts
Broker Status
Log
iot/mqttfx
"message": "Hello from AWS IoT console"

Now that you know MQTT.fx and the MQTT test client on AWS IoT Core can talk to each other. Stay tuned for a more meaningful example where you automate the process with a test script developed for MQTT.fx.

Also remember that you don't even need to be logged into your AWS account to transmit messages. You can send IoT messages from the AWS CLI, cURL tool, Bash shell script, or MQTT.fx to AWS IoT Core from wherever you are in the world as your credentials are always active and the AWS message broker is always up. Also, you could use the AWS CLI or the cURL tool like you did in the previous chapter to send messages via a topic to both IoT Core and MQTT.fx. However, also remember, the AWS CLI and the cURL tool use the HTTPS protocol, and HTTPS cannot receive messages from AWS IoT Core. So, while the AWS MQTT test client and MQTT.fx can both publish and subscribe via MQTT topics for a robust bidirectional conversation, the less capable AWS CLI and cURL tool can only publish messages. This is just one reason why MQTT.fx is a better virtual IoT device than the AWS CLI or cURL tool even when compared to the versatile Bash script used in the last chapter to send fake IoT data payloads to IoT Core with the AWS CLI.

One weird trick.

Finally, there is one weird trick that is both useful and easy if you have not already figured it out. If you are lazy and don't want to bother opening an external tool or physical IoT device to send IoT data to AWS IoT Core, you can simply send IoT data by using the MQTT test client within IoT Core to both publish and subscribe to messages. This almost feels like cheating.

To demonstrate, imagine your brother Joe is in Timbuktu whilst you are working on your tan in southern California. You can simply "Publish" a JSON message from the MQTT test client in your AWS account such as:

```
{
    "Message": "hey! How are you"
}
```

Your brother Joe will receive the message if he is subscribed to that topic on the same AWS account in the same region. Here is what that looks like if I open two MQTT test clients. I simply duplicate the MQTT test client tab in my browser and set one client for publishing and the other client for subscribing.

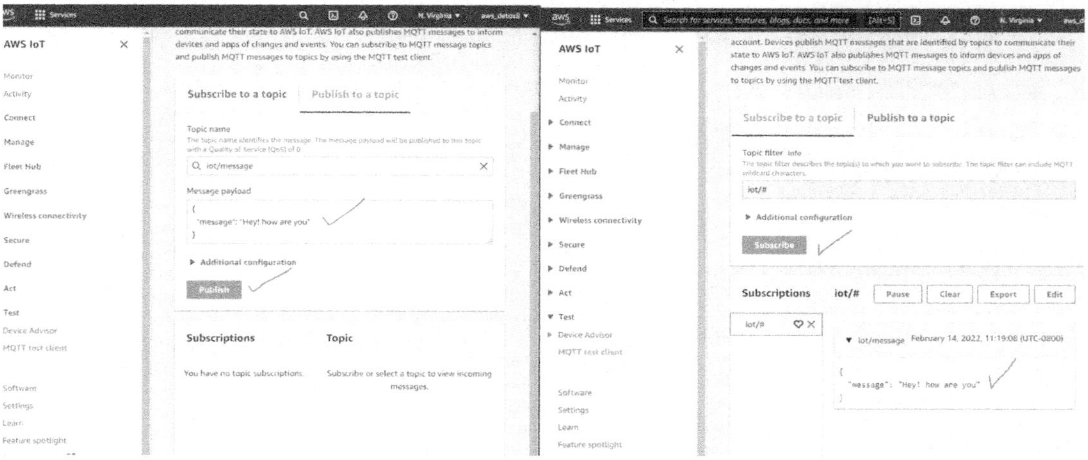

AWS IoT
Subscribe to a topic
Publish to a topic
Topic name
iot/message
Message payload
"message": "Hey! how are you"
Additional configuration
Publish
Subscriptions
Topic
Topic filter
iot/#
Subscribe
Subscriptions
iot/#
Pause
Clear
Export
Edit
iot/message
February 14, 2022, 11:19:08 (UTC-0800)

So, AWS IoT can be your own personal messaging service or chat room assuming you share an account. Of course, a more relevant use of the AWS MQTT test client is to publish fake IoT data payloads if you only want to enter a few dummy payloads to test an AWS design. However, often you will want to send a series of IoT payloads without having to manually type in each payload or use a physical IoT device. In the next step of this chapter, we will discuss exactly that - running a test JavaScript program that produces a series of IoT sensor readings and publishes them to IoT Core for us hands-free.

Another thing to keep in mind is that the partition between the IoT device and cloud allows you to emulate IoT data in such a way that IoT Core is completely agnostic as to the source of the data. Thus, at the end of the day, it may matter less where the IoT data originated from but rather that the data was delivered in the expected quantity, relevant data range, and correct format.

Step 4 - Program a MQTT.fx Test Script for Automated Publishing to AWS IoT Core

Now you will publish data to AWS IoT Core using MQTT.fx to do the repetitive work for you. MQTT.fx uses JavaScript for writing test scripts that can produce IoT data just as your Bash script did earlier. The MQTT.fx tool comes installed with a program called "Switch Fountain Test" but this program isn't suitable for the requirements of this book. I developed a JavaScript program that will produce more relevant IoT data and publish that data to IoT Core.

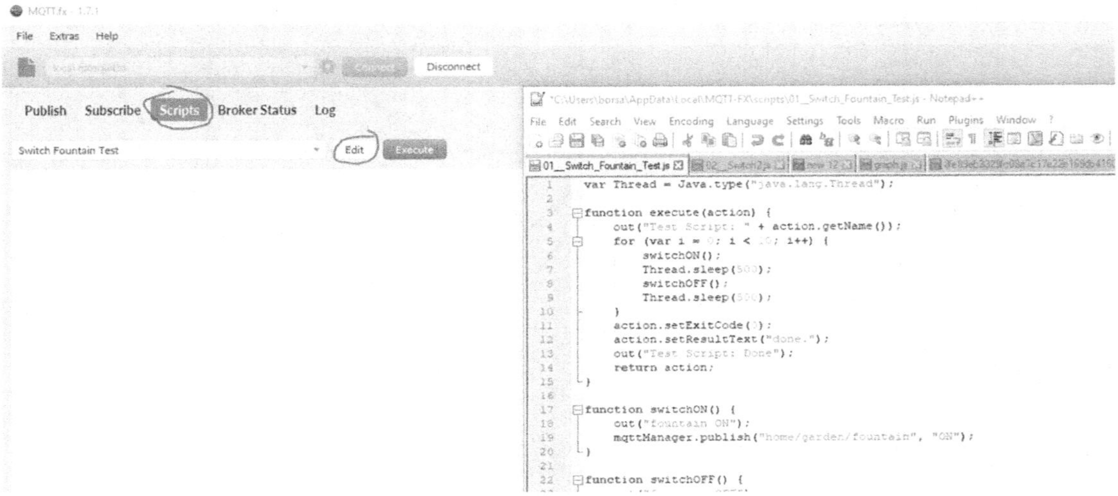

To insert this custom program, open MQTT.fx and go to Scripts→ Edit, and then insert the custom code below into whichever one of your UTF-8 editors opens by default.

```
//MQTT.fx switch fountain, modified by Stephen Borsay

var Thread = Java.type("java.lang.Thread");

var topic = "iot/mqttfx";
var waitTime = 2000;
var iterations = 10;


function execute(action) {
    out("Test Script: " + action.getName());
    for (var i = 0; i < iterations; i++) {
        sendPayload();
        Thread.sleep(waitTime);
    }
    action.setExitCode(0);
    action.setResultText("done.");
    out("Test Script: Done");
    return action;
}

function sendPayload() {

  var temp = Math.round(Math.random()*130);
  var humid = Math.round(Math.random()*100);
  var ts = Date.now();

  var IoT_Payload = {
      "temperature" :  temp,
      "humidity"    :  humid
      "timestamps"  :  ts
    }

var payload = JSON.stringify(IoT_Payload)


  mqttManager.publish(topic, payload);
  out("Topic is:  \n" + topic);
  out("payload sent \n" + payload);
}


function out(message){
```

```
    output.print(message);
}
```

Feel free to change the three variables below in the JavaScript program to suit your preferences:

```
topic = ""; //outgoing topic name
waitTime = ; //in milliseconds
iterations = ; //number of times to send IoT payload
```

The IoT data producer script can also be found on the chapters GitHub. Remember to always refer to the relevant chapters GitHub page for the listed code properly to be properly formatted to work correctly.

After pasting the code into your editor, save the program under a name of your choice but make sure the program name ends in a '.js' extension so that it is recognized as a JavaScript program. If you name the program something other than "Switch Fountain Test" it won't overwrite the default program. You may need to close and then re-open MQTT.fx for the changes to take place and for the new program to appear on the drop-down list of available scripts.

Scripts in MQTT.fx are saved into the following folder by default:

\Users\<NAME>\AppData\Local\MQTT-FX\scripts

On Windows "AppData" is a hidden folder so to access it type "%AppData%" into the Windows search box and hit 'enter,' then navigate to the required folder listed above.

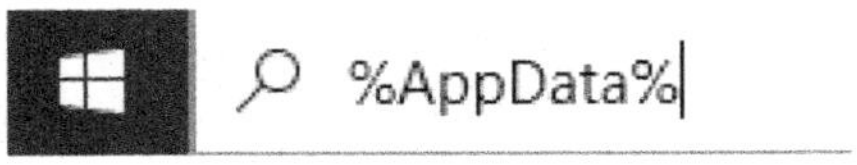
%AppData%

Return to MQTT.fx and select "Connect". After connecting to AWS IoT Core then select the "Scripts" tab and navigate to your newly created JavaScript program and select it. Finally hit the "Execute" button.

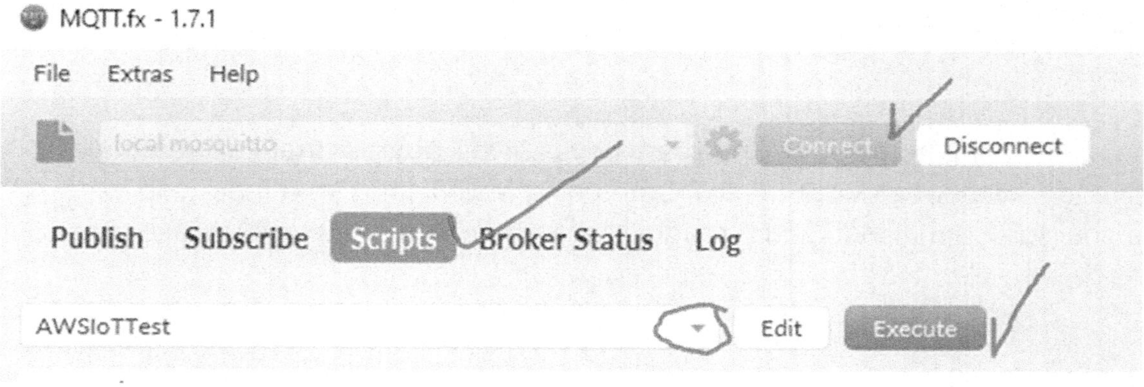

MQTT.fx - 1.7.1
File
Extras
Help
local mosquitto
Connect
Disconnect
Publish
Subscribe
Scripts
Broker Status
Log
AWSIoTTest
Edit
Execute

Just as in the previous example, once you execute the script you should see your IoT data readings stream into IoT Core if you are still subscribed to '#', "iot/#", or "iot/mqttfx" on the MQTT test client.

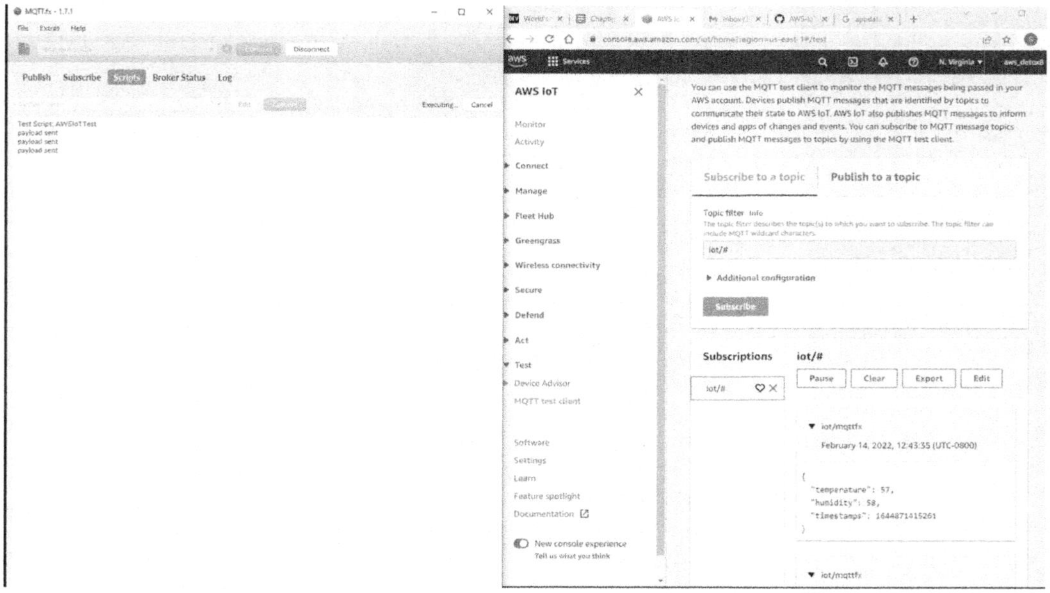

AWS IoT
Subscribe to a topic
Publish to a topic
Subscriptions
iot/#
Pause
Clear
Export
Edit

Congratulations, you have created and used a virtual IoT device utilizing MQTT.fx to publish a single payload manually. Then you used a test script program, written in JavaScript, to stream JSON formatted IoT payloads to AWS IoT Core. You can use MQTT.fx in lieu of a physical IoT device to send and receive IoT payloads to and from AWS IoT Core. Virtual IoT devices are useful when you are feeling lazy, and you don't want to bother setting up a physical device and programming the firmware.

In the coming chapters you will program physical IoT devices that can send and receive IoT sensor data to AWS IoT Core using MQTT, and from there you can have your IoT data dispatched throughout the entire ecosystem of AWS services.

Chapter 4 - ESP32 and ESP8266 IoT Device Programming with Arduino for AWS IoT Core

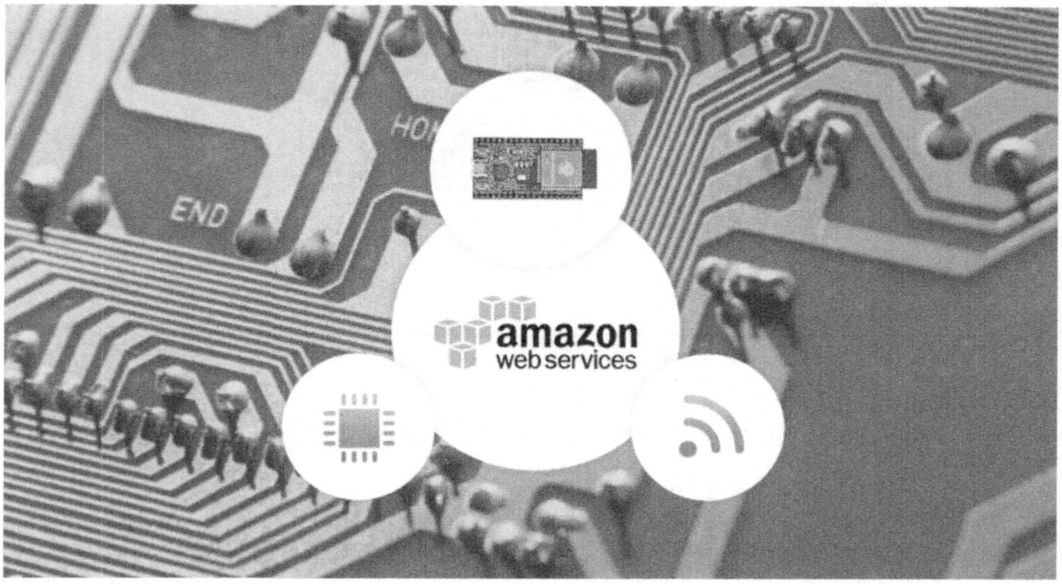
amazon
webservices

In this chapter you will program your ESP physical IoT devices to *'talk'* to AWS IoT Core using the MQTT test client to receive data payloads from the IoT device. Once you confirm that your data payload is being delivered from your device to AWS, then you can start exploring IoT centric AWS services that can consume, store, enrich, transform, and visualize your IoT data.

This chapter will first cover programming the ESP32 and ESP8266 with the Arduino IDE, and then in following chapters, you will explore programming the ESP devices in MicroPython with Thonny, and JavaScript with Mongoose OS. Finally, we will finish out our IoT device section of the book by programming the Raspberry Pi in Python and JavaScript utilizing the AWS-IoT-Device-SDK's.

Arduino has two big advantages over MicroPython and Mongoose OS. First, Arduino has a mature, tested, and proven ecosystem with a large amount of free community resources. Second, Arduino has an extensive range of sensor libraries ready to use for many microcontrollers. This is a huge advantage compared to other programming environments which have a growing, but still limited peripheral library selection for MicroPython and Mongoose OS.

Step 1 - Programming the ESP32 with the Arduino Sketch
Step 2 - Running the Arduino Sketch for the ESP32 and Connecting to AWS IoT Core
Step 3 - Programming the ESP8266 with the Arduino Sketch
Step 4 - Running the Arduino Sketch for the ESP8266 and Connecting to AWS IoT Core

---

Step 1 - Programming the ESP32 with the Arduino Sketch

ARDUINO™

Arduino provides a wonderful and free IDE for programming many common embedded devices. The Arduino "Wiring" language is based on C/C++ but abstracts away many of the low-level embedded device programming details that can be both very tedious and confusing to the beginner.

You can download the newest version of the Arduino IDE here:

https://www.arduino.cc/en/software

I recommend using the ESP32 DevKitC device for this course (see my specific recommendations at the "*IoT Device Recommendations*" preface section of the book). The ESP32 DevKitC is a common board configuration that has been around for several years now and can normally be acquired for under $10 USD. I would not recommend the newest DevKitC's based on Espressif's recent 'C2/C3' or 'S2/S3' series chips quite yet due to IDE compatibility issues. The older DevKitC boards will be compatible not only with Arduino, but with Thonny for MicroPython and Mongoose OS for JavaScript, both of which will be covered in later chapters.

There are many great tutorials for setting up the ESP32 for the Arduino IDE available on the internet, as well as numerous videos on YouTube covering this subject. I don't want to reinvent the wheel and make this book any longer than necessary by adding redundant information, I also don't want to support IDE, board manager, and driver issues which are beyond the purview of this book. Therefore, I will refer you to Rui Santos's excellent free online tutorials which cover these issues extensively (*Random Nerd Tutorials*). I highly recommend any of his paid products as well as they are all first rate. To find his and many other of these resources for setting up the ESP32 or ESP8266 in the Arduino environment simply Google "*setting up the ESP32/ESP8266 in Arduino".*

The following Arduino sketch will be used to program your ESP32 development board within the Arduino IDE. You should now know how to compile and upload basic Arduino sketches to your ESP32, as a prerequisite to the rest of this chapter.

This sketch below is mostly the work of some other talented engineers who are experts in cryptography, networks, and embedded systems. You can see the attributions to these other projects in the comments at the top of the Arduino sketches if you want to explore the original sketches yourself. I have made certain modifications to these sketches to improve them for the purposes of this book. I have also noted in the comments on the sketches where modifications took place.

I have modified the original sketch below so that it can send an entire JSON payload with randomly generated environmental variable values. You will need to know your WiFi network name, password, and region specific AWS IoT endpoint to configure your own Arduino sketch. You will also need to insert the three device security certificates (Client/Device certificate, Private key, and x.509 root certificate) that you created on AWS in an earlier chapter. Place all the configuration data as indicated in the sketch below:

A) WiFI Netwok name (2.4 GHz only)
B) WiFI Password
C) AWS IoT Endpoint (AWS region specific)
D) Publish MQTT topic name
E) Subscribe MQTT topic name
F) Client/Device Certificate
G) Private Key
H) Root (X.509) CA Certificate
I) Client ID (must be unique if using more than one device)

Also, make sure to download the two required libraries below:

WiFiClientSecure.h found at:

https://github.com/espressif/arduino-esp32

PubSubClient.h found at:

https://github.com/knolleary/pubsubclient

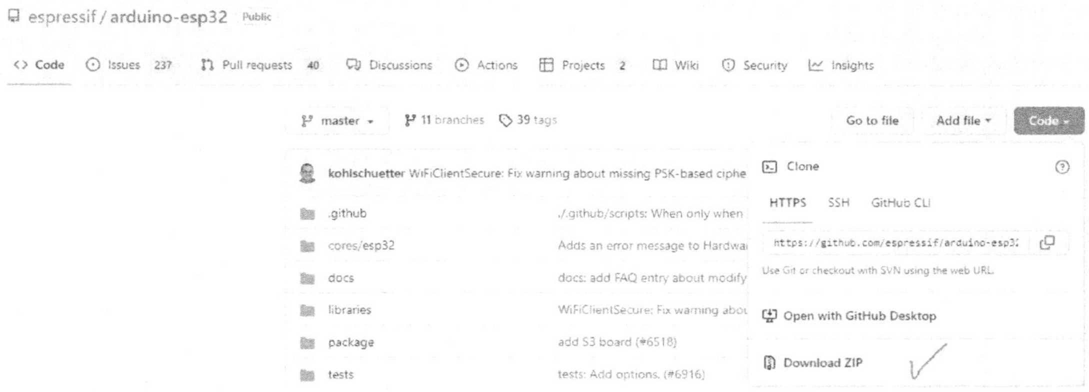

espressif / arduino-esp32
Public
Code
Issues 237
Pull requests 40
Discussions
Actions
Projects 2
Wiki
Security
Insights
master
11 branches
39 tags
Go to file
Add file
Code
Clone
HTTPS
SSH
GitHub CLI
Use Git or checkout with SVN using the web URL.
Open with GitHub Desktop
Download ZIP
.github
cores/esp32
docs
libraries
package
tests

Then when in the Arduino IDE you can use:

Sketch→Include Library→Add .ZIP Library...

To include the required libraries into your Arduino sketch.

You can find all the Arduino code on the chapters GitHub page. Copying code from the relevant chapters GitHub page is more reliable for programming than copying code from eBooks due to character translation and formatting.

The fields to modify in the sketch with variable names:

```
const char* ssid = The name of your WiFi Network
const char* password = Your WiFi Network Password
const char* awsEndpoint = Your AWS IoT endpoint
const char* pubTopic = The name of the topic published from the device
const char* subTopic = The name of the topic subscribed to on the device
```

- Open the AWS security certificates in an UTF-8 editor on your computer and then copy and paste your three security certificates in the appropriate section of the sketch below:

```
/* ESP32 AWS IoT
 *
 * Author: Anthony Elder
 * License: Apache License v2
 * Sketch Modified by Stephen Borsay
 * https://github.com/sborsay
 * Add in Char buffer utilizing sprintf to dispatch JSON data to AWS IoT Core
 * Use and replace your own SID, PW, AWS Account Endpoint, Client cert,
private cert
 *
 * Contributors to AWS IoT Program for Arduino include those below:
 *
 * https://github.com/HarringayMakerSpace/awsiot
 *
https://github.com/Ameba8195/Arduino/blob/master/hardware_v2/libraries/MQTTCl
ient
 * examples/amazon_awsiot_basic/amazon_awsiot_basic.ino
 * https://github.com/igrr
 * https://github.com/copercini/esp32-iot-examples/blob/master/ESP32_aws_iot
```

```
 * https://github.com/256dpi/arduino-mqtt
 */

#include <WiFiClientSecure.h>
#include <PubSubClient.h> // install with Library Manager, I used v2.6.0

const char* ssid = "<YOUR NETWORK NAME>";
const char* password = "<YOUR NETWORK PASSWORD>";

//AWS IoT Core--> Settings (Device data endpoint)
const char* awsEndpoint = "<YOUR-AWS-IOT-ENDPOINT>";

const char* pubTopic = "iot/outTopic";
const char* subTopic = "iot/inTopic";

// xxxxxxxxxx-certificate.pem.crt
static const char certificate_pem_crt[] PROGMEM = R"KEY(
-----BEGIN CERTIFICATE-----
XXXXXXXXXXXXXXXXXXXXXXXXXXXXXXXXXXXXXAoccwSpJEkwDQYJKoZIhvcNAQEL
BQAwTTFLMEkGA1UECwxCQW1hem9uIFdlYiBTZXJ2aWNlcyBPPUFtYXpvbi5jb20g
SW5jLiBMPVNlYXR0bGUgU1Q9V2FzaGluZ3RvbiBDPVVTMB4XDTIxMDYyMzAzNDk1
OFoXDTQ5MTIzMTIzNTk1OVowHjEcMBoGA1UEAwwTQVdTIElvVCBDZXJ0aWZpY2F0
ZTCCASIwDQYJKoZIhvcNAQEBBQADggEPADCCAQoCggEBAMlywFsajU0WY53cA2Dv
BdToiQzjBKG/6FKjIYB6D47nn1pvp03xkCewoF09uaKIHam2raL4XV71eeGFvFHj
cn49cfaYPfIsi2Keoxio+H6W+MJZHNt7XE4NiJydqAv+BjC6/aBPRrcP7X+HmDVV
mRbn8uLBnJKRlh6wK1/91q+2e9bpnoNz6IjyUEssQpB9Qtr99FSNl+PNloJr1Ki4
vs4IBJbXXXXXXXXXXXXXXXXXXXXXXXXXXXXXXXXXXXXXXXXXXX6RR9dYGFHU
cwmodbigKYd2IGcEOEfU0NYFlXJJ/7a8Nq8KKfDorZAQwJRkr8gOZR9TkpymiYxu
2SUCAwEAAaNgMF4wHwYDVR0jBBgwFoAUk5u9teDtHdsYtv8EPE/ZVGiubEYwHQYD
VR0OBBYEFFefBYP1bu1wgutG7/0Q3pSbYIYTMAwGA1UdEwEB/wQCMAAwDgYDVR0P
AQH/BAQDAgeAMA0GCSqGSIb3DQEBCwUAA4IBAQCYFcP1pz4el9vBFO5AmTy4MtzM
wpQRyLC/rZpGkBmMxwyAwuweHYnMD2n3jSBcNNoZ69K3lVTpmlw26421P6qtf+Sf
b9e1vZzTtN2izGGNrR93y/3AxA0fCmkD0JNbfomd77uGnyiOOhrX/2b78Kb59vm4
oSjgR4/NU4dM1dJ8isMOaNQxGC1PvOYjFLJlOAEg5VMJUGgfRrqD5d4LVp9k26ok
ArYEEPnFK6wxXl273g+ZS3dED66/Wny6YYZqdGbyuL59DGNnlpjNVkOAYeh/9MZF
TXi8gPMGeExHgXq5oxbkekl58/pm4dkX8Foo0mY8Vfdq5kMqKhtlKQBtQLUp
-----END CERTIFICATE-----
)KEY";

// xxxxxxxxxx-private.pem.key
static const char private_pem_key[] PROGMEM = R"KEY(
-----BEGIN RSA PRIVATE KEY-----
XXXXXXXXXXXXXXXXXXXXXXXXXXXXXXXXXXXXXXXXXXXXXXXoUqMhgHoPjuefWm+n
TfGQJ7CgXT25oogdqbatovhdXvV54YW8UeNyfj1x9pg98iyLYp6jGKj4fpb4wlkc
23tcTg2InJ2oC/4GMLr9oE9Gtw/tf4eYNVWZFufy4sGckpGWHrArX/3Wr7Z71ume
```

```
g3PoiPJQSyxCkH1C2v30VI2X482WgmvUqLi+zggElvA2/eR1uUdWp3VXsaBh49vH
4upVDN/cgx5w2o/V/xZhExG5DpFH11gYUdRzCah1uKAph3YgZwQ4R9TQ1gWVckn/
trw2rwop8OitkBDAlGSvyA5lH1OSnKaJjG7ZJQIDAQABAoIBAAakewVGBdzB3T0K
US40E3wmwsYjAjcXLeDzshobbEHpD08bGWgvi/JTF6abb3CVjmzXMjiKegG0lHVE
RKZqmo7hFc3szTYcE+iHlJcukysRbVhzOcle8vc76QJJDI6ArNGUiOJtWsaUht9K
qFEx5l9j/JVPjwsiM9IFOxjqNNcMXWAMgVvO1PCNxzI5YzUJADNRjccrFxdzl1b7
sbL3TmUnx/sOCQCg2e8UwNfPj8C4vcE/04IO2ew9zfkNZFy2tru3RXJaB+r5v+Mg
he26f9HuYbcAED4Z6/0zTS0EM7BwN7GTaUUaGezDw0ITGXCvqA8SJul7mCYQOdK1
fKWiJiECgYEA7wIhzfY83hewYHb6DJTIaA3HyxgdiCxXyWZmKtaPT/0flaH2k273
wtTyQfiBthpjKH64XXXXXXXXXXXXXXXXXXXXXXXXXXXXXXXXXXXXXXXXXXXXXXXX
/NHmwJgHU7GJHLNM7yO4GrKuGwZlAQwGh75gtm6P7MjnoCmnzgcynep9sW5t2zey
dW8AudSFcVakIi1Q+kWrc92akglYHeRVQwtlfug+pnbbk3V1cBzzGQ63YgZh9FZr
qCCZhjOhqDG8F7EJY7pY3omKn7WGL4pbhstjAm0CgYAbrwyJVbcxJl9InR9Ta7xW
yRnWPWHWTwSQEGtPFPEem7wX0d3Er/rEt3OkDou/swi/PQZWAmYlqXhZ8TXdBvHB
uUlN22J00kFcI5/kg8m5t6ouZz0j4/iPUCp+V8E0NKDMXL1w7pUVBv4xyK/t3MG8
QEaQWXGeWie/Cs3+f5sNKQKBgQCQ72QUFRLBT92sFFcblj0ZbY7fMCLPOG5kU6WX
TQQ9xuqajSE5boGvXRpdBQRFSP42AKW5SETejqjMRvydkH8SffX7MGIBspEkExpK
nL8ijfJ3cuNvm7i1BF0u+bmo+MyXie1q0+sMQGZYSoAkEeFSwfusEAuz2AU4reFp
G/l3yQKBgEMGm87PrO0rcNlcL99pHxT5QjydL9FWvq5eg4dC3yNJcqvd620eXt83
mYcLcO5Q+SWLNm/NjcQCIMZ/cuS1knTDZV3JIT44tCn4Q+Z6OFvy+KNFZOaQc3Ed
Cmr5ttndjNAEfVOUKPN+8wXx4o8Fbd9dkhwggvBaMQhQjaSzzMJs
-----END RSA PRIVATE KEY-----
)KEY";

/* root CA found at:
  https://www.amazontrust.com/repository/AmazonRootCA1.pem
  fungible between regions.  Open cert, free for public consumption
*/
static const char rootCA[] PROGMEM = R"EOF(
-----BEGIN CERTIFICATE-----
MIIDQTCCAimgAwIBAgITBmyfz5m/jAo54vB4ikPmljZbyjANBgkqhkiG9w0BAQsF
ADA5MQswCQYDVQQGEwJVUzEPMA0GA1UEChMGQW1hem9uMRkwFwYDVQQDExBBbWF6
b24gUm9vdCBDQSAxMB4XDTE1MDUyNjAwMDAwMFoXDTM4MDExNzAwMDAwMFowOTEL
MAkGA1UEBhMCVVMxDzANBgNVBAoTBkFtYXpvbjEZMBcGA1UEAxMQQW1hem9uIFJv
b3QgQ0EgMTCCASIwDQYJKoZIhvcNAQEBBQADggEPADCCAQoCggEBALJ4gHHKeNXj
ca9HgFB0fW7Y14h29Jlo91ghYPl0hAEvrAIthtOgQ3pOsqTQNroBvo3bSMgHFzZM
9O6II8c+6zf1tRn4SWiw3te5djgdYZ6k/oI2peVKVuRF4fn9tBb6dNqcmzU5L/qw
IFAGbHrQgLKm+a/sRxmPUDgH3KKHOVj4utWp+UhnMJbulHheb4mjUcAwhmahRWa6
VOujw5H5SNz/0egwLX0tdHA114gk957EWW67c4cX8jJGKLhD+rcdqsq08p8kDi1L
93FcXmn/6pUCyziKrlA4b9v7LWIbxcceVOF34GfID5yHI9Y/QCB/IIDEgEw+OyQm
jgSubJrIqg0CAwEAAaNCMEAwDwYDVR0TAQH/BAUwAwEB/zAOBgNVHQ8BAf8EBAMC
AYYwHQYDVR0OBBYEFIQYzIU07LwMlJQuCFmcx7IQTgoIMA0GCSqGSIb3DQEBCwUA
A4IBAQCY8jdaQZChGsV2USggNiMOruYou6r4lK5IpDB/G/wkjUu0yKGX9rbxenDI
U5PMCCjjmCXPI6T53iHTfIUJrU6adTrCC2qJeHZERxhlbI1Bjjt/msv0tadQ1wUs
N+gDS63pYaACbvXy8MWy7Vu33PqUXHeeE6V/Uq2V8viTO96LXFvKWlJbYK8U90vv
```

```
o/ufQJVtMVT8QtPHRh8jrdkPSHCa2XV4cdFyQzR1bldZwgJcJmApzyMZFo6IQ6XU
5MsI+yMRQ+hDKXJioaldXgjUkK642M4UwtBV8ob2xJNDd2ZhwLnoQdeXeGADbkpy
rqXRfboQnoZsG4q5WTP468SQvvG5
-----END CERTIFICATE-----
)EOF";


WiFiClientSecure wiFiClient;
void msgReceived(char* topic, byte* payload, unsigned int len);
PubSubClient pubSubClient(awsEndpoint, 8883, msgReceived, wiFiClient);

void setup() {
  Serial.begin(115200); delay(50); Serial.println();
  Serial.println("ESP32 AWS IoT Example");
  Serial.printf("SDK version: %s\n", ESP.getSdkVersion());

  Serial.print("Connecting to "); Serial.print(ssid);
  WiFi.begin(ssid, password);
  WiFi.waitForConnectResult();
  Serial.print(", WiFi connected, IP address: ");
Serial.println(WiFi.localIP());

  wiFiClient.setCACert(rootCA);
  wiFiClient.setCertificate(certificate_pem_crt);
  wiFiClient.setPrivateKey(private_pem_key);
}

unsigned long lastPublish;
int msgCount;

void loop() {

  pubSubCheckConnect();

   //to increase buffer size, change MQTT_MAX_PACKET_SIZE
   char fakeData[128];

  float var1 =  random(0,120); //fake number range
  float var2 =  random(0,100);
  sprintf(fakeData,
 "{\"uptime\":%lu,\"temperature\":%.0f,\"humidity\":%.0f}", millis() / 1000,
var1, var2);


  if (millis() - lastPublish > 10000) {
```

```
  boolean rc = pubSubClient.publish(pubTopic, fakeData);
    Serial.print("Published, rc="); Serial.print( (rc ? "OK: " : "FAILED: ")
);
    Serial.println(fakeData);
    lastPublish = millis();
  }
}

void msgReceived(char* topic, byte* payload, unsigned int length) {
  Serial.print("Message received on "); Serial.print(topic); Serial.print(":
");
  for (int i = 0; i < length; i++) {
    Serial.print((char)payload[i]);
  }
  Serial.println();
}

void pubSubCheckConnect() {
  if ( ! pubSubClient.connected()) {
    Serial.print("PubSubClient connecting to: "); Serial.print(awsEndpoint);
    while ( ! pubSubClient.connected()) {
      Serial.print(".");
      pubSubClient.connect("ESPDeviceUniqueIdentifier"); //this is you
clientID
      delay(1000);
    }
    Serial.println(" connected");
    pubSubClient.subscribe(subTopic);
  }
  pubSubClient.loop();
}
```

You don't need your own rootCA (x.509) certificate as you can just reuse the public one that I provide here. This root x.509 certificate is available on multiple locations on the internet so as you can guess that it doesn't provide much extra security. The root certificate is also the only certificate of the three required that is fungible for every AWS region. For your client/device certificate and your private key you can open them in any UTF-8/ANSI compatible editor and copy all the alphanumeric information directly from the certificate and paste it into the Arduino sketch.

You can find your AWS IoT endpoint by going to AWS IoT Core--> Settings (Device data endpoint) or use the AWS CLI as demonstrated earlier

```
aws iot describe-endpoint --endpoint-type iot:Data-ATS
```

There are a few sections of the code that require further explanation:

```
//If you need to increase buffer size, change MQTT_MAX_PACKET_SIZE in
PubSubClient.h
char fakeData[128];
float var1 = random(0,120);
//fake number range, adjust as you like
float var2 = random(0,100);
sprintf(fakeData, "{"uptime":%lu,"temperature":%.0f,"humidity":%.0f}",
millis() / 1000, var1, var2);
```

This section of the code creates a data buffer of 128 characters (1 character = 1 byte in Arduino). You can increase the buffer size if you want to increase the size of the IoT data payload that you transmit to AWS, however you would have to change the maximum MQTT packet size constant in the "*PubSubClient.h*" library header file. Increasing the buffer size could cause slower cycling of the communication and dispatch loop. In my experience you are safe increasing the size up to 512 bytes/chars as needed for your IoT payload. One way to save space in the char buffer is to use *"%.0f"* instead of *"%f"* as a float data type format specifier. The reason this is a good idea is that you can observe that the random number generated has no trailing decimal point digits. The actual DHT11 sensor imitated here also does not provide decimal point precision. Thus, if you don't have to use extended decimal format then you shouldn't. Using abbreviated numeric data types makes your life easier, not only on the device side but also on the cloud side, as many AWS services don't handle lengthy decimal point numbers without extra complications.

After the data buffer is declared there are two variables declared for temperature and humidity. Using randomly generated environmental sensor readings saves the time and hassle of wiring up a real temperature sensor to the ESP board. Despite the extra time involved, the cost of components, and the wiring required for a BME280 or DHT11/22 environmental sensor the actual additional coding complexity is trivial if you decide to implement the Arduino sketch with an actual sensor in your design.

The final line of code fills the data buffer with the fake environmental readings. After the buffer is filled it is dispatched via the MQTT publish function under the outgoing topic which is named "iot/outTopic" and assigned to the 'pubTopic' variable.

```
pubSubClient.publish(pubTopic, fakeData);
```

The publishing cycle repeats every loop, and you can adjust the loop delay if you want either more or less frequent dispatches of the IoT data payload to the AWS message broker.

Below is the subscription function. Every time the program loops it checks if there is a message waiting with the MQTT topic subscription of "iot/inTopic"

```
void msgReceived(char* topic, byte* payload, unsigned int length) {
Serial.print("Message received on ");
Serial.print(topic); Serial.print(": ");
 for (int i = 0; i < length; i++)
 {
    Serial.print((char)payload[i]);
 }
 Serial.println();
 }
```

This section of the code allows the ESP device to receive messages from the AWS message broker based on the subscription topic. The code "unwinds" a char buffer with the incoming data payload sent from the server. You can publish from the AWS MQTT test client and send a message to your ESP device under your designated subscription name of "iot/inTopic". Based on the message received on the device you can do things like blink a light or actuate a GPIO.

Unlike HTTP, and similar to websockets, MQTT is a constant connection, especially suited for frequent sending and receiving of small messages via the *publish* and *subscribe* functions.

Finally, it is worth remembering that each device requires a unique name, called a "*Client ID*" under the standards of the MQTT protocol. This is easily ignored when dealing with one device. But when working with multiple devices or AWS "device shadows", which are designed to be implemented with multiple IoT devices, problems can arise if you don't remember to give each device a unique Client ID.

```
pubSubClient.connect("ESPthingXXXX");
```

The most confusing part of the program is how the security certificates used to meet TLS1.2 requirements on AWS are handled.

The code below Places the certificates into program flash memory on your device:

```
static const char certificate[] PROGMEM = R"EOF(
-----BEGIN CERTIFICATE-----
<Certificate Cypher>
-----END CERTIFICATE-------
)EOF";
```

This flash memory location is a better alternative than using SRAM or IITVSQ $as those memory spaces are more limited, and these lengthy certificates can overflow the allotted space. This is especially true if the certificates are competing with numerous variables in the same memory space on the device. These certificates are only set once, so they don't get reinitialized every time the program loops.

The macros below set the certificates with a premade 'set' function provided by the WiFi Secure library.

```
  WiFiClient.setCACert(rootCA);
  WiFiClient.setCertificate(certificate_pem_crt);
  WiFiClient.setPrivateKey(private_pem_key);
```

Step 2 - Running the Arduino Sketch for the ESP32 and Connecting to AWS IoT Core

After you install drivers, software, and verify that your ESP32 is powered, and shows a connected COM/Serial port you are ready to run the Arduino sketch. Select the COM port your ESP board is connected to and make sure you are using the correct board manager.

- On the chapters GitHub page, I have included an alternative ESP32 sketch which utilizes a different MQTT library and keeps the device security certificates in a separate header file.

Using the ESP32 DevKitC, the newer boards should handle the upload of the code from the Arduino IDE automatically, without the need to press any buttons on the device as you had to when the ESP32 board was first released. Open a Serial monitor once the code is uploaded to the ESP32 and ensure it connects to your WiFi successfully.

```
COM13

, WiFi connected, IP address: 0.0.0.0
PubSubClient connecting to: a32qaal3loyees-ats.iot.us-east-1.amazonaws.com....... connected
Published, rc=OK: {"uptime":15,"temperature":5,"humidity":8}
Published, rc=OK: {"uptime":20,"temperature":94,"humidity":58}
Published, rc=OK: {"uptime":25,"temperature":90,"humidity":69}
Published, rc=OK: {"uptime":30,"temperature":18,"humidity":67}
Published, rc=OK: {"uptime":35,"temperature":63,"humidity":39}
```

Just as you did in the previous sections testing with the AWS CLI using your SigV4 credentials, and testing with MQTT.fx using your security certificates, you will now confirm that your IoT data payload is being delivered successfully from your ESP32 device to AWS IoT Core via MQTT using security certificates.

Navigate within the AWS Console to IoT Core→MQTT test client

https://console.aws.amazon.com/iot

Once within the “Subscribe” pane of the MQTT test client enter the topic name you published from the device, here you previously call your topic “iot/outTopic”, Also you can just subscribe to “#” to catch all incoming topics as discussed earlier. If everything worked correctly then you should see the following results once you upload and run your sketch.

- If you do not see these results, then see the troubleshooting notes at the end of this chapter or on the GitHub.

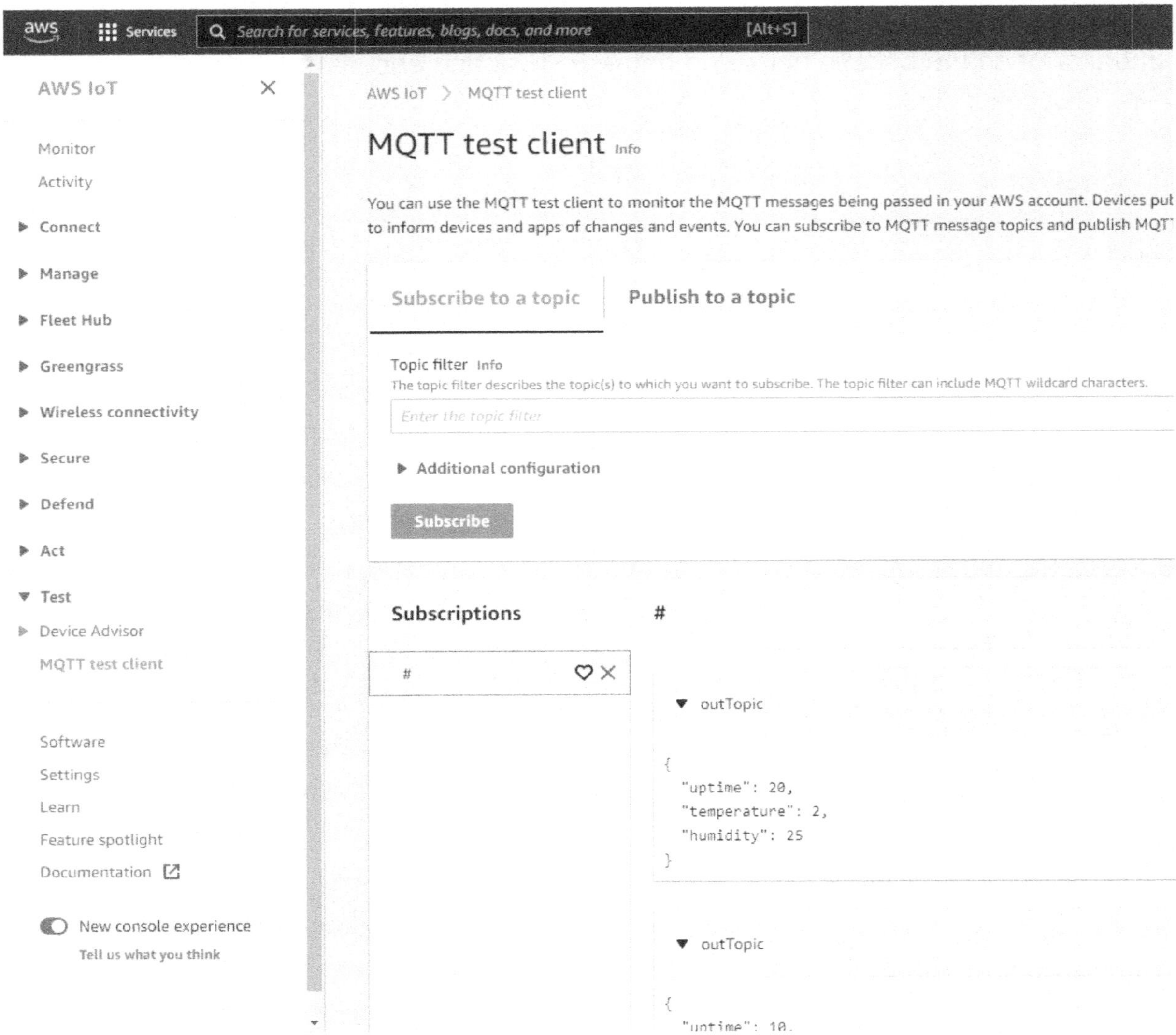
aws
Services
Search for services, features, blogs, docs, and more
[Alt+S]
AWS IoT
Monitor
Activity
Connect
Manage
Fleet Hub
Greengrass
Wireless connectivity
Secure
Defend
Act
Test
Device Advisor
MQTT test client
Software
Settings
Learn
Feature spotlight
Documentation
New console experience
Tell us what you think
AWS IoT > MQTT test client
MQTT test client Info
You can use the MQTT test client to monitor the MQTT messages being passed in your AWS account. Devices pul
to inform devices and apps of changes and events. You can subscribe to MQTT message topics and publish MQT
Subscribe to a topic
Publish to a topic
Topic filter Info
The topic filter describes the topic(s) to which you want to subscribe. The topic filter can include MQTT wildcard characters.
Enter the topic filter
Additional configuration
Subscribe
Subscriptions
#
#
outTopic
{
"uptime": 20,
"temperature": 2,
"humidity": 25
}
outTopic
{

Later in the book you will not want to use "uptime" as a relative time index but rather use the UNIX/Epoch timestamp as an absolute time index. I will show you how to add a timestamp to the payload in a later chapter. In the meantime, if you want to remove the 'uptime' variable from being reported in the IoT payload being transmitted to the MQTT test client simply change the current payload in the Arduino sketch to the one below:

```
sprintf(fakeData,  "{\"temperature\":%.0f,\"humidity\":%.0f}", var1, var2);
```

Step 3 - Programming the ESP8266 with the Arduino Sketch

As mentioned in the IoT device recommendation section of the book there is only one recommend ESP8266 board which is by far the most popular model, The "*ESP8266-12E with NodeMCU1.0*." Within the Arduino sketch there is only one significant change when you compare programming the ESP32 to the ESP8266 within the Arduino IDE for the listed sketch. For the ESP8266 you must have the current time retrieved by the sketch. The reason for this is because an Espressif '*timeout*' related function is disabled by default in the firmware on the ESP8266 but enabled by default on the ESP32. This makes the time update unnecessary for the ESP32 but needed for the ESP8266 device. You can read more of the specifics here:

https://aws.amazon.com/blogs/iot/using-device-time-to-validate-aws-iot-server-certificates/

```
void setCurrentTime() {
  configTime(3 * 3600, 0,"pool.ntp.org", "time.nist.gov");
```

This setCurrentTime() function connects to a time server to receive the current time. If you want to use a time server closer to your location, you can find one at the link below and insert the relevant local URL into your code.

https://www.pool.ntp.org/zone/@

Unlike the ESP32, The ESP8266 sketch included here depends on the board manager installed on the Arduino IDE and whether it is a version above ESP8266 board manager 2.74. The version of the board manager you are using introduces a very minor change which affects how you set and anchor the security certificates. I have included two different ESP8266 sketches, one for board manager 2.0-2.74 and one for board manager 3+. I have included only the code for board manager 3+, however I have provided code for the previous versions of the board manager below 2.74 if you are still using a depreciated package, simply go to this chapters GitHub page to access the code.

You can check your board manager version in the Arduino IDE by going to:

Tools→Board→Boards Manager

Look there for your '*ESP8266 community*' board manager version

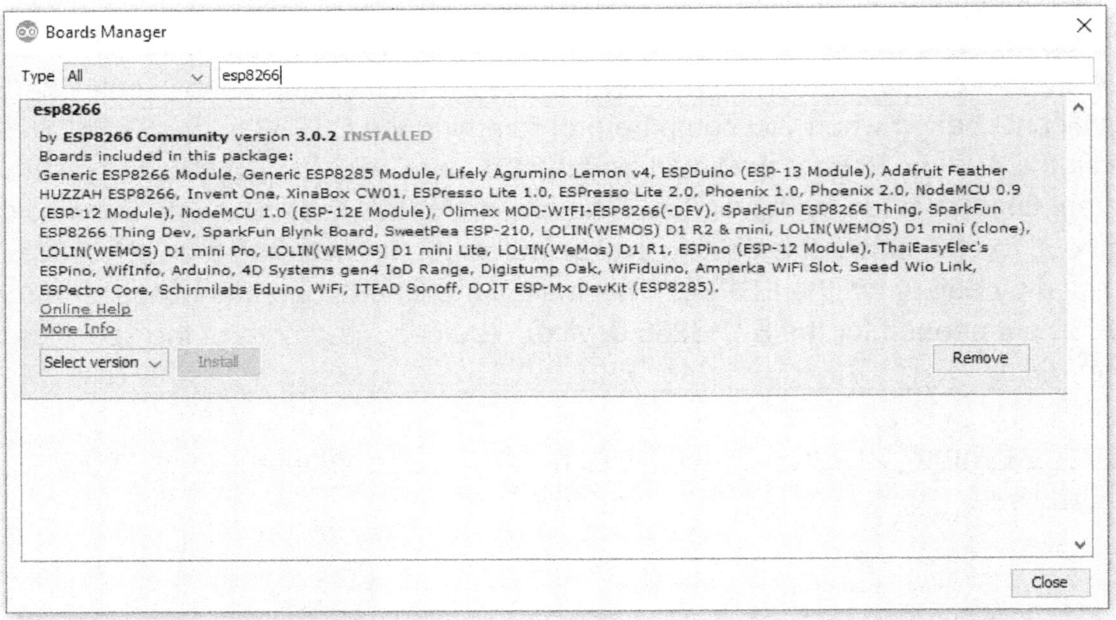
Boards Manager
Type All
esp8266
esp8266
by ESP8266 Community version 3.0.2 INSTALLED
Boards included in this package:
Generic ESP8266 Module, Generic ESP8285 Module, Lifely Agrumino Lemon v4, ESPDuino (ESP-13 Module), Adafruit Feather HUZZAH ESP8266, Invent One, XinaBox CW01, ESPresso Lite 1.0, ESPresso Lite 2.0, Phoenix 1.0, Phoenix 2.0, NodeMCU 0.9 (ESP-12 Module), NodeMCU 1.0 (ESP-12E Module), Olimex MOD-WIFI-ESP8266(-DEV), SparkFun ESP8266 Thing, SparkFun ESP8266 Thing Dev, SparkFun Blynk Board, SweetPea ESP-210, LOLIN(WEMOS) D1 R2 & mini, LOLIN(WEMOS) D1 mini (clone), LOLIN(WEMOS) D1 mini Pro, LOLIN(WEMOS) D1 mini Lite, LOLIN(WeMos) D1 R1, ESPino (ESP-12 Module), ThaiEasyElec's ESPino, WifInfo, Arduino, 4D Systems gen4 IoD Range, Digistump Oak, WiFiduino, Amperka WiFi Slot, Seeed Wio Link, ESPectro Core, Schirmilabs Eduino WiFi, ITEAD Sonoff, DOIT ESP-Mx DevKit (ESP8285).
Online Help
More Info
Select version
Install
Remove
Close

Also, make sure to download the two required libraries for the ESP8266. The first library is different than the required library for the ESP32.

ESP8266WiFi.h found at:

https://github.com/esp8266/Arduino

PubSubClient.h found at:

https://github.com/knolleary/pubsubclient

Then when in the Arduino IDE you can use:

Sketch→Include Library→Add .ZIP Library…

To add the required libraries to your sketch directly from the downloaded zip folder from GitHub.

You will need the following WiFi network and AWS IoT endpoint to configure your sketch. You will also need to insert your three device security certificates (Client/Device certificate, Private key, and x.509 root certificate) that you created in a previous chapter. Place all the configuration data as indicated in the sketch below.

A) WiFI Netwok name (2.4 GHz only)
B) WiFI Password
C) AWS IoT Endpoint (AWS Region Specific)
D) Publishing MQTT topic name
E) Subscribing MQTT topic name
F) Client/Device Certificate
G) Private Key
H) Root (X.509) CA Certificate
I) Client ID (must be unique if using more than one device)

The fields to modify in the sketch with variable names:

```
const char* ssid = The name of your WiFi Network
const char* password = Your WiFi Network Password
const char* awsEndpoint = Your AWS IoT endpoint
const char* pubTopic = The name of the topic published from the device
const char* subTopic = The name of the topic subscribed to on the device
```

- Open the AWS security certificates in an UTF-8 editor on your computer and then copy and paste your three security certificates in the appropriate section of the sketch below.

You can find all the Arduino code on the chapters GitHub page. Copying code from the relevant chapters GitHub page is more reliable for programming than copying code from eBooks due to character translation and formatting.

The code for the ESP8266 is as follows:

```
/* ESP8266 AWS IoT
 *
 *----------------------------
 *
 * Compile this only if using ESP8266 version 3+, not backwards comparable
 *
 *#Tools--> Board--> Board Manager-->ESP8266 version 3+ by ESP8266 Community
 *
 *##Older ESP8266 sketch is not forward compatible
 *
```

```
 * --------------------------------
 *
 *
 * Simplest possible example (that I could come up with) of using an ESP8266
with AWS IoT.
 * No messing with openssl or spiffs just regular pubsub and certificates in
string constants
 *
 * This is working as at 3rd Aug 2019 with the current ESP8266 Arduino core
release:
 * SDK:2.2.1(cfd48f3)/Core:2.5.2-56-g403001e3=20502056/lwIP:STABLE-
2_1_2_RELEASE
 *
 * Author: Anthony Elder
 * License: Apache License v2
 * https://github.com/HarringayMakerSpace/awsiot
 * https://github.com/earlephilhower/bearssl-esp8266
 * https://github.com/igrr
 *
 * Sketch Modified by Stephen Borsay for www.udemy.com/course/exploring-aws-
iot/
 * https://github.com/sborsay
 * Add in EOF certificate delimiter
 * Add in Char buffer utilizing sprintf to dispatch JSON data to AWS IoT Core
 * certs obfuscated, use your own, but you can share root CA / x.509 until
revoked
 */

#include <ESP8266WiFi.h>
#include <PubSubClient.h>

const char* ssid = "<Your-WiFi-Network-Here>";
const char* password = "<Your-Password-Here>";

//AWS IoT Core--> Settings (Device data endpoint)
const char* awsEndpoint = "<YOURACCOUNTID-ats.iot.REGION.amazonaws.com>";

// For the two certificate strings below paste in the text of your AWS
// device certificate and private key:

// xxxxxxxxxx-certificate.pem.crt
static const char certificatePemCrt[] PROGMEM = R"EOF(
-----BEGIN CERTIFICATE-----
XXXXXXXXXXXXXXXXXXXXXXXXXXXXXXXXXXXXXXXXXXXXXXXXXXXXXXXXXXXXXXXX
BQAwTTFLMEkGA1UECwxCQW1hem9uIFdlYiBTZXJ2aWNlcyBPPUFtYXpvbi5jb20g
```

```
SW5jLiBMPVNlYXR0bGUgU1Q9V2FzaGluZ3RvbiBDPVVTMB4XDTIyMDIxMjIzMDQy
NVoXDTQ5MTIzMTIzNTk1OVowHjEcMBoGA1UEAwwTQVdTIElvVCBDZXJ0aWZpY2F0
ZTCCASIwDQYJKoZIhvcNAQEBBQADggEPADCCAQoCggEBAOhy3rpzRWRrnNwoRRSZ
WQu74bD26FDBNTp1K3cejOK7A+HoTixdxYxJ0hv6Cv/9SEbfoBasP59oiTCUhgtX
NYWfi5iYOoGJQbDycKhmWvcBOZqi6m4l+2w5LjOUOqjoo1e3+iEmz+kZb7QFBN2j
zain1RWgNwA+AjcrclsnY7g4zy/Zn9NBEqD8YDkTqDoZF03gPb7y/USPKxZy3rI8
kyU0Gk1rS8acqXXXXXXXXXXXXXXXXXXXXXXXXXXXXXXX6ME0AzrdqhN/pcN3OZ/a
Iy/vxCiRAkVYCQhj/qWPz+qV9KK2teesfeJCiqUzHMfFaWq/919GzfdZeopAzAkL
WS8CAwEAAaNgMF4wHwYDVR0jBBgwFoAUfoVNZfc8zl7iSbOrFGqHVtNfB7UwHQYD
VR0OBBYEFXXXXXXXXXXXXXXXXXXXXXXXXXXXXXXXXXXXXXXXXXXXXXXXXXXXR0P
AQH/BAQDAgeAMA0GCSqGSIb3DQEBCwUAA4IBAQCVspP/8JhHk3Tn7bhT2uojxsmS
idIjCYQwOR2ESYAMyvYnyKDdzJ11G+mRk0htSV75U0fLu1Nz7UYv3znrTXCdbPN7
/YOEK+O1B05ldvWshGI4SUmTBeLEuSOcyKnlW6O5BVZlpeb8IqkF/gWo67Hn0miJ
TKkWaN0sRO83ybMbI3HbVXMIfymn2FOZ806oa010HwRwaFccfz/s7gXfFtd4JCWd
tMhwrYshIylUdFPOZ/T+7rsMpd3jWNWRht5/XbC3Ai6ZdGHBqXMEW3cOUeOHpkBX
VHv+/MIcw7KNf60NQFzWG5wMkCgmvmeQkBjSSOOxFDIxB0MeiLuSL/+8OCgx
-----END CERTIFICATE-----
)EOF";

// xxxxxxxxxx-private.pem.key
static const char privatePemKey[] PROGMEM = R"EOF(
-----BEGIN RSA PRIVATE KEY-----
XXXXXXXXXXXXXXXXXXXXXXXXXXXXXXXXXXXXXXXXXXXXXXXXXXXXXXXXXXXXXXXX
LF3FjEnSG/oK//1IRt+gFqw/n2iJMJSGC1c1hZ+LmJg6gYlBsPJwqGZa9wE5mqLq
biX7bDkuM5Q6qOijV7f6ISbP6RlvtAUE3aPNqKfVFaA3AD4CNytyWydjuDjPL9mf
00ESoPxgOROoOhkXTeA9vvL9RI8rFnLesjyTJTQaTWtLxpyoTdlobS9PtnT6YDBC
JuLNXwTGs/smaZjowTQDOt2qE3+lw3c5n9ojL+/EKJECRVgJCGP+pY/P6pX0ora1
56x94kKKpTMcx8Vpar/3X0bN91l6ikDMCQtZLwIDAQABAoIBACedVAoQlRXtJRl8
H3HIRJ20Ul1XZvZERy8EQvkVEsudNactcQ0smfszpYQxE+jWoJe7isvyZRFkvmSy
GzoZjbyNGTxTTT1ASBrA5qQ8dWo9IjURaMSG4pdqE06lB24734KWjyFRPQOr2xah
+FdRkD4bBDygRl9bMgN2+xE/XXXXXXXXXXXXXXXXXXXXXXXXXXXXXXXXXXXXXXXX
qH3fT9O6I68y3ZYX3piD5tRDFZ7Mjh4Z6NbA3b01Vs8YXfc2zumxJ1GGzCTTc1wa
3iCI5SkCgYEA9+m8M27nmAPfNlU7OQW4SmZvam5I9jjzj4YefWmg2EHSKQX6eNio
jElGybYiFTBKB0hSLEDg/f+MZnVCStrlzBHI4W8Gc/8ltOK6AXqrjN673Gu/y+C6
y9kwRA9JicMohe1a8FlyLHcTx/LCSQ0BQ9noXzbCU64/hS0rOjprr3UCgYEA8Af+
8+Fqf40kGUO8SGNEFti+lVS5b8dpnmyMx4nj+3+iQhy1uggl1zF3L/0derTnrTXk
9O0rgUi8DtI1EgKiSYwWwiN7GTIFeh8P2szrWFbL0Dx454Y0kVzk8WLpVXHYucIf
5431ov3HXXXXXXXXXXXXXXXXXXXXXXXXXXXXXXXXXXXXXXXXXXXXXXdqHsqXhFlS
uUUIfmon/DbmBF8BiLyIlRZmqdDnkG84OA3z0ai72v22pTcnSKDk85p0f18AVOfg
NPc9ilc2MdrumNbDf4SSvAf64eqDfmqYHw4lW6zGHuoCMrNMCg+z/BbXL1/RsW89
2sknUg6oZWQjuRfp5VxJUK0CgYEAlfKYzef67NXSQEo1XA9PIOqkHIvCEFdF3uc3
BwxYNOvmBGEFEcM3SHipWXxJJzfOJ0Gs12k2LVyvxp6A8tBca4+tQ/iAVRwPmdu/
vtMXDqeiSWMNsK0BN/INP9Knq24kkt73qWLgmcLqWblF6s9OAmKgEPfoL3hi0w5C
kbo3pisCgYEA2IG2F6+geLdLPO8IQxnHL1bBs7TGQDru25Hk1o8fG72VSuZzViQ/
x4xwm2x8hI6HUjZ315P39emB5382XWnhsI9LkuJufna0KtxoiBocWDFHxA6GIOz/
```

```
6U0+bpP3rpPJlP07/LTQdEx/tbYBsKsTKhSZPtkuH4mLILuh93GBVvo=
-----END RSA PRIVATE KEY-----
)EOF";

// This is the AWS IoT CA Certificate from:
// https://docs.aws.amazon.com/iot/latest/developerguide/
// This one in here is the 'RSA 2048 bit key: Amazon Root CA 1
// until January 16, 2038 so unless it gets revoked
static const char caPemCrt[] PROGMEM = R"EOF(
-----BEGIN CERTIFICATE-----
MIIDQTCCAimgAwIBAgITBmyfz5m/jAo54vB4ikPmljZbyjANBgkqhkiG9w0BAQsF
ADA5MQswCQYDVQQGEwJVUzEPMA0GA1UEChMGQW1hem9uMRkwFwYDVQQDExBBbWF6
b24gUm9vdCBDQSAxMB4XDTE1MDUyNjAwMDAwMFoXDTM4MDExNzAwMDAwMFowOTEL
MAkGA1UEBhMCVVMxDzANBgNVBAoTBkFtYXpvbjEZMBcGA1UEAxMQQW1hem9uIFJv
b3QgQ0EgMTCCASIwDQYJKoZIhvcNAQEBBQADggEPADCCAQoCggEBALJ4gHHKeNXj
ca9HgFB0fW7Y14h29Jlo91ghYPl0hAEvrAIthtOgQ3pOsqTQNroBvo3bSMgHFzZM
9O6II8c+6zf1tRn4SWiw3te5djgdYZ6k/oI2peVKVuRF4fn9tBb6dNqcmzU5L/qw
IFAGbHrQgLKm+a/sRxmPUDgH3KKHOVj4utWp+UhnMJbulHheb4mjUcAwhmahRWa6
VOujw5H5SNz/0egwLX0tdHA114gk957EWW67c4cX8jJGKLhD+rcdqsq08p8kDi1L
93FcXmn/6pUCyziKrlA4b9v7LWIbxcceVOF34GfID5yHI9Y/QCB/IIDEgEw+OyQm
jgSubJrIqg0CAwEAAaNCMEAwDwYDVR0TAQH/BAUwAwEB/zAOBgNVHQ8BAf8EBAMC
AYYwHQYDVR0OBBYEFIQYzIU07LwMlJQuCFmcx7IQTgoIMA0GCSqGSIb3DQEBCwUA
A4IBAQCY8jdaQZChGsV2USggNiMOruYou6r4lK5IpDB/G/wkjUu0yKGX9rbxenDI
U5PMCCjjmCXPI6T53iHTfIUJrU6adTrCC2qJeHZERxhlbI1Bjjt/msv0tadQ1wUs
N+gDS63pYaACbvXy8MWy7Vu33PqUXHeeE6V/Uq2V8viTO96LXFvKWlJbYK8U90vv
o/ufQJVtMVT8QtPHRh8jrdkPSHCa2XV4cdFyQzR1bldZwgJcJmApzyMZFo6IQ6XU
5MsI+yMRQ+hDKXJioaldXgjUkK642M4UwtBV8ob2xJNDd2ZhwLnoQdeXeGADbkpy
rqXRfboQnoZsG4q5WTP468SQvvG5
-----END CERTIFICATE-----
)EOF";

BearSSL::X509List client_crt(certificatePemCrt);
BearSSL::PrivateKey client_key(privatePemKey);
BearSSL::X509List rootCert(caPemCrt);

WiFiClientSecure wiFiClient;
void msgReceived(char* topic, byte* payload, unsigned int len);
PubSubClient pubSubClient(awsEndpoint, 8883, msgReceived, wiFiClient);

void setup() {
  Serial.begin(115200); Serial.println();
  Serial.println("ESP8266 AWS IoT Example");

  Serial.print("Connecting to "); Serial.print(ssid);
  WiFi.begin(ssid, password);
```

```
  WiFi.waitForConnectResult();
  Serial.print(", WiFi connected, IP address: ");
Serial.println(WiFi.localIP());

  // get current time, otherwise certificates are flagged as expired
  setCurrentTime();

  wiFiClient.setClientRSACert(&client_crt, &client_key);
  wiFiClient.setTrustAnchors(&rootCert);
}

unsigned long lastPublish;
int msgCount;

void loop() {

  pubSubCheckConnect();

  //to increase buffer size, change MQTT_MAX_PACKET_SIZE
   char fakeData[128];

  float var1 =  random(0,120); //fake number range
  float var2 =  random(0,100);
  sprintf(fakeData, "{\"uptime\":%lu,\"temperature\":%f,\"humidity\":%f}",
millis() / 1000, var1, var2);

  if (millis() - lastPublish > 5000) {
  boolean rc = pubSubClient.publish("outTopic", fakeData);
    Serial.print("Published, rc=");
    Serial.print( (rc ? "OK: " : "FAILED: ") );
    Serial.println(fakeData);
    lastPublish = millis();
  }
}

void msgReceived(char* topic, byte* payload, unsigned int length) {
  Serial.print("Message received on "); Serial.print(topic); Serial.print(":
");
  for (int i = 0; i < length; i++) {
    Serial.print((char)payload[i]);
  }
  Serial.println();
}

void pubSubCheckConnect() {
```

```
  if ( ! pubSubClient.connected()) {
    Serial.print("PubSubClient connecting to: "); Serial.print(awsEndpoint);
    while ( ! pubSubClient.connected()) {
      Serial.print(".");
      pubSubClient.connect("ESPthing");
    }
    Serial.println(" connected");
    pubSubClient.subscribe("inTopic");
  }
  pubSubClient.loop();
}

void setCurrentTime() {
  configTime(3 * 3600, 0, "pool.ntp.org", "time.nist.gov");

  Serial.print("Waiting for NTP time sync: ");
  time_t now = time(nullptr);
  while (now < 8 * 3600 * 2) {
    delay(500);
    Serial.print(".");
    now = time(nullptr);
  }
  Serial.println("");
  struct tm timeinfo;
  gmtime_r(&now, &timeinfo);
  Serial.print("Current time: ");
  Serial.print(asctime(&timeinfo));
}
```

Just as you did in the previous sections testing the AWS CLI with your SigV4 credentials, and MQTT.fx testing with security certificates, you will now confirm that your data payload is being delivered successfully from your ESP8266 device to AWS IoT Core via MQTT.

Navigate within the AWS console to IoT Core or use the link below:

https://console.aws.amazon.com/iot

Once within the "Subscribe to a topic" pane of the MQTT test client enter the topic you published from the device, "iot/outTopic". Also, you can just subscribe to "#" or "iot/#" to catch all incoming topics as discussed earlier. If everything worked correctly then you should see the following results once you upload and run your sketch.

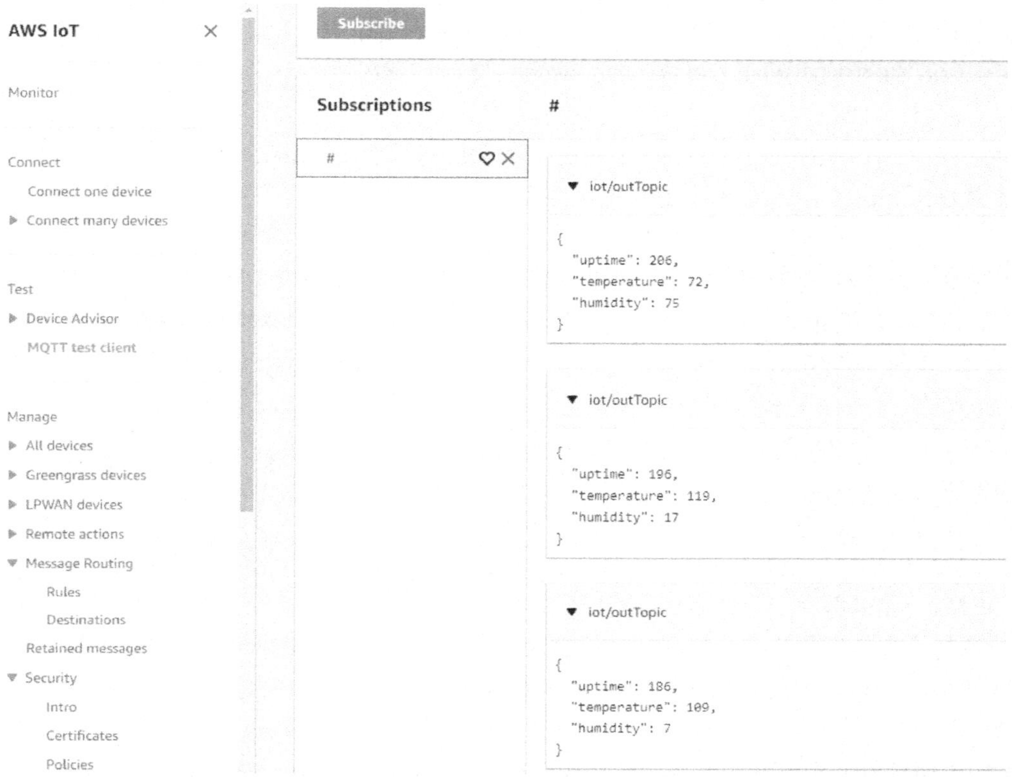
AWS IoT
Monitor
Connect
Connect one device
Connect many devices
Test
Device Advisor
MQTT test client
Manage
All devices
Greengrass devices
LPWAN devices
Remote actions
Message Routing
Rules
Destinations
Retained messages
Security
Intro
Certificates
Policies
Subscribe
Subscriptions
#
#
iot/outTopic
{
"uptime": 206,
"temperature": 72,
"humidity": 75
}
iot/outTopic
{
"uptime": 196,
"temperature": 119,
"humidity": 17
}
iot/outTopic
{
"uptime": 186,
"temperature": 109,
"humidity": 7
}

Congratulations You have successfully programed either your ESP32 or ESP8266 IoT device in the Arduino IDE and successfully transmitted a randomized IoT payload to the MQTT message broker on AWS IoT Core. You will be using Arduino with your ESP board for future projects unless you decide to use MicroPython with the Thonny IDE or JavaScript with Mongoose OS.

Troubleshooting ESP8266 and ESP32 connection issues

For these tips and more see the GitHub page for the chapter

1. Make sure you are on a 2.4GHz network, and not 5GHz, the ESP IoT device only communicates at 2.4GHz.

2. Make sure your IoT device AWS endpoint region matches the current AWS region in your console and on the browser.

3. Make sure port 8883 on your computer isn't being blocked by your network admin, this is the port that MQTT(s) traditionally communicates. AWS IoT Core requires you send MQTT data over secure port 8883 or 443.

4. Make sure your onboard device security certificates match your AWS IoT Core region, the x509 is fungible between regions.

5. Make sure you attached an AWS IoT Policy to your security certificates. If you have not, you will see the connection on the monitor tab, but no data will appear on the MQTT test client.

6. Don't exceed your 'char' buffer in your Arduino sketch. The MQTT protocol requires payloads get sent by time and size over cycles. If you overload the buffer, the device may not transmit or receive the payload. To solve this issue for large payloads in your sketch you can increase the size of your buffer by changing the value of MQTT_MAX_PACKET_SIZE constant in the PubSubClient.h header file from 128 to 256 or 512 bytes to solve this issue. This bigger payload allocation will allow longer buffer payloads to be transmitted.

7. If you aren't receiving your devices payload under your subscription topic in AWS IoT Core in the on the MQTT test client, then go to the "Monitor" tab in AWS IoT Core and see if your device is even connecting. Often a IoT device is connecting but the payload isn't being received, the reason for this is usually a problem with your device security certificates. The IoT device will connect but the payload won't pass through if your device certificates aren't activated correctly and have an attached IoT policy. The problem could also be the issue listed previously as the MQTT max payload buffer is exceeded.

If your device connection isn't even showing up in the monitor, then it is likely a hardware issue not a certificate issue. Confirm you are using the correct virtualization package or board manager for your device.

8. Does your serial monitor look like: *M???
????????%^&???*^$#$^

After running your Arduino sketch? Make sure your serial monitor baud rate matches your sketch baud rate (probably 115200).

9. For the ESP8266 only: Make sure you are using the right version of the sketch for your Arduino Board Manager. If you are not receiving IoT payloads on AWS IoT Core, it could be because you are using the wrong ESP8266 sketch for your current Arduino Board Manager package.

Some older or cheaper ESP32 board issues:

Connecting........_____....._____....._____....._____....._____....._____....._____....._
_____....._____
A fatal error occurred: Failed to connect to ESP32: Timed out waiting for packet header

Solution:
While connecting and holding down the 'Boot' button for one second initiates the firmware downloads mode (BOOT button = FLASH button).

Warning: Do not press the Enable (EN)/RESET(RST) Button

Chapter 5 -
ESP32 and ESP8266 Device Programming with MicroPython to AWS IoT Core

MicroPython

MicroPython is a lean and efficient implementation of the Python 3 programming language that uses a subset of the Python standard library that is optimized to run on microcontrollers within constrained memory. MicroPython is free, and when combined with the free Thonny IDE it becomes an easy and efficient way to program the ESP32 or the ESP8266.

I have chosen MicroPython with the Thonny IDE (version 3.3.13) as one of two alternatives to the Arduino language (Wiring C/C++) and the Arduino IDE for those who prefer the ease of the Python programming language. While both languages and IDEs are viable choices for device programming, I will still use Arduino as the primary programming interface for device connections to AWS IoT for the simple fact that it is the most mature tool, with the biggest community developer support base, and possessing the largest selection of sensor libraries available.

Step 1 – Installing the Thonny IDE then Erasing the Memory and Flashing the Firmware to the ESP32 and ESP8266
Step 2 – Programming the ESP32 to Transmit Data to AWS IoT Core
Step 3 – Programming the ESP8266 to Transmit Data to AWS IoT Core

---

Step 1 – Installing the Thonny IDE then Erasing the Memory and Flashing the Firmware to the ESP32 and ESP8266

There are three steps to be accomplished before you can program the ESP devices to transmit and receive data from AWS. First, you must download and install the free Thonny IDE for your OS. Thonny is an integrated development environment for Python that is designed for beginners. It supports different ways of stepping through the code, step-by-step expression evaluation, and detailed visualization of the call stack. Thonny also inherently supports MicroPython on both the ESP32 and ESP8266 devices.

After installing Thonny you must erase all the memory on your IoT device and then you need to "flash" (upload) the ESP32 or ESP8266 board with the MicroPython environment (virtualization). Both steps – erase and flash, must be accomplished before you can program either device.

At this point you may wonder why you did not need to erase and flash your ESP devices when working with the Arduino IDE. The reason is that Arduino automatically does this for you every time you upload a sketch to the device. The benefit of taking the extra step of virtualizing the device for the MicroPython programming environment is that it is a "write once" requirement that eliminates the extra time it takes to upload the hardware abstraction layer every time a new MicroPython program is uploaded to the device. This means that even though MicroPython is a larger and more abstracted language than Arduino's Wiring language (C/C++), it can be programmed to the board faster in the Thonny IDE than the Wiring language on the Arduino IDE.

Install Thonny for your OS, by downloading it here:

https://thonny.org

The following steps for erasing and flashing your ESP32 or ESP8266 are dependent on if you want to do the process manually or if you want to use the Thonny IDE to do it for you. I recommend you use the Thonny IDE to accomplish these prerequisites as it comes with a built-in application for erasing and flashing your ESP device (esptool). However, both the manual process using the esptool, and the erase and flash process using the Thonny IDE take about the same amount of time.

Method 1: the manual process to erase and flash your ESP device:

Install the ESP tool by downloading it at:

https://github.com/espressif/esptool

Or from the Windows command prompt enter:

```
pip install esptool
```

Download the latest MicroPython binary for your ESP device at:

ESP32:

https://micropython.org/download/esp32

Or if using the ESP8266:

https://micropython.org/download/esp8266

Erase your ESP chips flash memory with the esptool, use "run as administrator" mode" for the command prompt in Windows. To enable the "administrator" role on your Windows machine:

1. Enter for '*cmd*' in the Windows search box.
2. Click on the '*Run as administrator'* option.

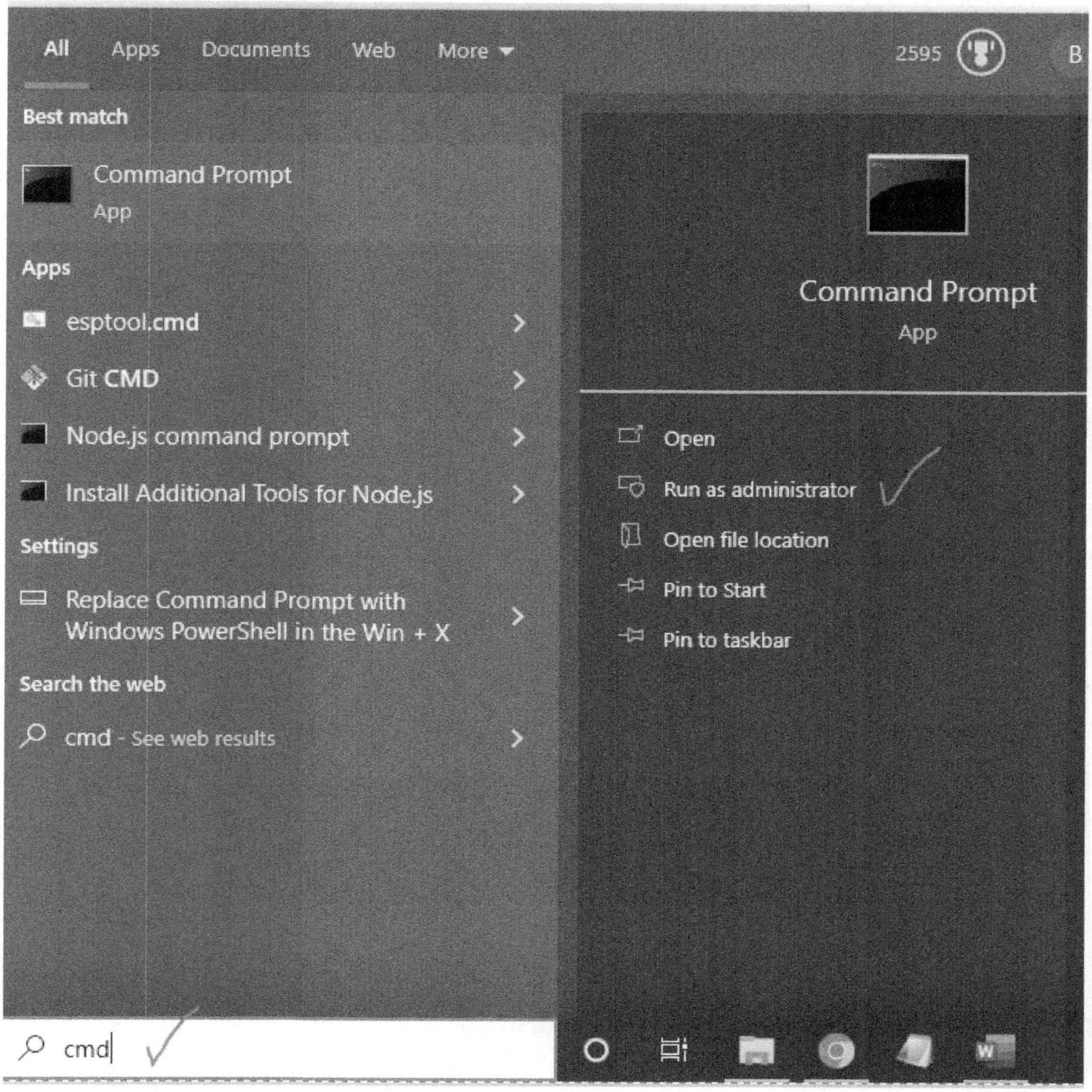
All
Apps
Documents
Web
More
2595
Best match
Command Prompt
App
Apps
esptool.cmd
Git CMD
Node.js command prompt
Install Additional Tools for Node.js
Settings
Replace Command Prompt with Windows PowerShell in the Win + X
Search the web
cmd - See web results
Command Prompt
App
Open
Run as administrator
Open file location
Pin to Start
Pin to taskbar
cmd

Alternately simply right click the command prompt if you have a desktop icon and select "*Run as administrator.*"

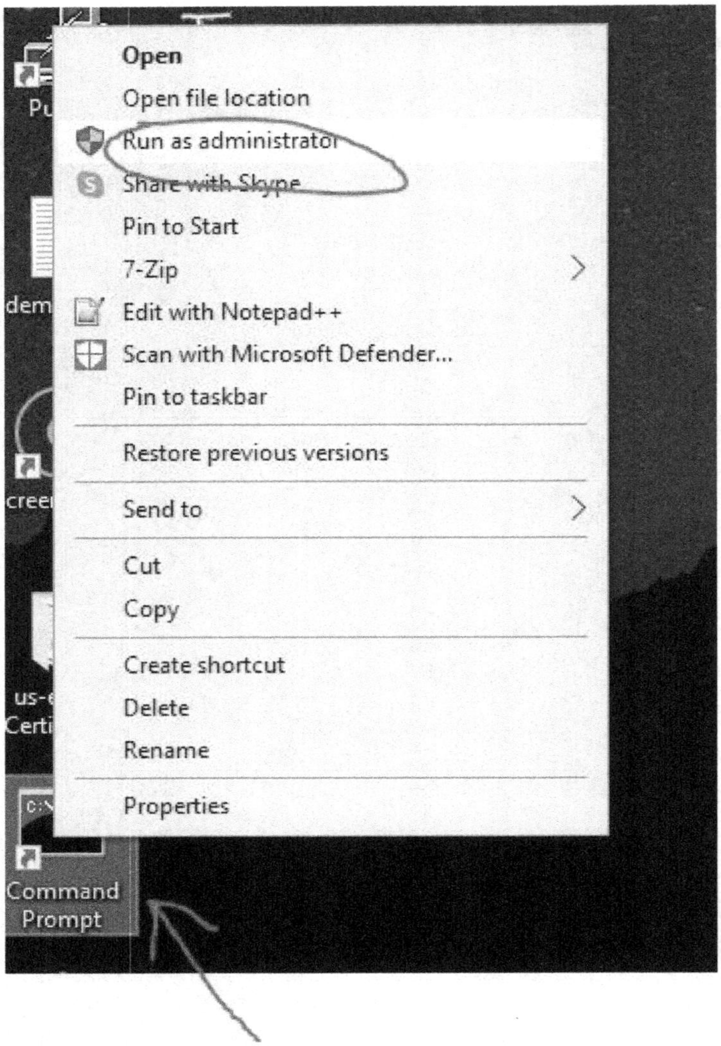
Open
Open file location
Run as administrator
Share with Skype
Pin to Start
7-Zip
Edit with Notepad++
Scan with Microsoft Defender...
Pin to taskbar
Restore previous versions
Send to
Cut
Copy
Create shortcut
Delete
Rename
Properties
Command Prompt

To view this procedure for non-Windows systems, go here:

https://docs.micropython.org/en/latest/esp32/tutorial/intro.html

Connect your ESP device to your computer with a USB cord, then for the ESP32 on Windows type the following commands at the command prompt:

```
python -m esptool --chip esp32 erase_flash
```

or

For the ESP8266 on Windows, type the following commands at the command prompt:

```
python -m esptool -chip esp8266 erase_flash
```

Next, upload the ESP MicroPython binary to your ESP device. For the ESP32 on Windows, type the following commands at the command prompt after filling out the required fields:

```
python -m esptool -chip esp32 -port COM<YOUR-COM-PORT-HERE> write_flash -z
0x1000 esp32-<YOUR-BIN-HERE>.bin
```

Example:

```
python -m esptool -chip esp32 -port COM3 write_flash -z 0x1000 esp32-
20220117-v1.18.bin
```

For the ESP8266 on Windows, type the following commands at the command prompt after filling out the required fields:

```
python -m esptool -chip esp8266 -port COM<YOUR-COM-PORT-HERE> write_flash -
flash_mode dio -flash_size detect 0x0 esp8266-<YOUR-BIN-HERE>.bin
```

Example:

```
python -m esptool -chip esp8266 -port3 write_flash -flash_mode dio -
flash_size detect 0x0 esp8266-20220117-v1.18.bin
```

Method 2: Using the Thonny IDE to erase and flash your ESP device

Even when using Thonny you must download the latest firmware to flash your ESP device, however unlike using the manual process detailed above you may not have to download the esptool manually if you are using Thonny version 3+. The reason you may not need to download the esptool is because it is automatically installed when you downloaded the Thonny IDE depending on which version you are using. To see if the esptool is already installed go to:

Tools→manage plug-ins

Then search for the *esptool.* The image below shows that it is already installed. If it is not installed, go ahead, and install the esptool plug-in as shown previously.

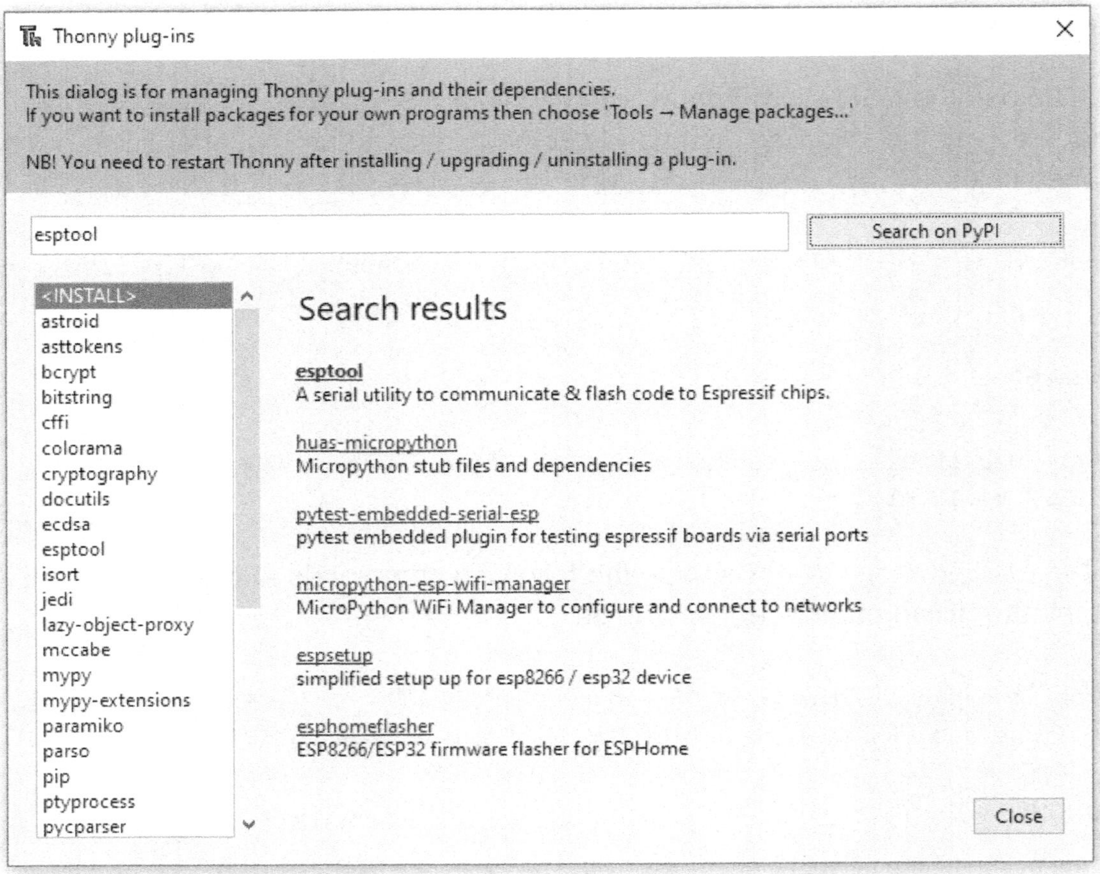
Thonny plug-ins
This dialog is for managing Thonny plug-ins and their dependencies.
If you want to install packages for your own programs then choose 'Tools → Manage packages...'
NB! You need to restart Thonny after installing / upgrading / uninstalling a plug-in.
esptool
Search on PyPI
<INSTALL>
astroid
asttokens
bcrypt
bitstring
cffi
colorama
cryptography
docutils
ecdsa
esptool
isort
jedi
lazy-object-proxy
mccabe
mypy
mypy-extensions
paramiko
parso
pip
ptyprocess
pycparser
Search results
esptool
A serial utility to communicate & flash code to Espressif chips.
huas-micropython
Micropython stub files and dependencies
pytest-embedded-serial-esp
pytest embedded plugin for testing espressif boards via serial ports
micropython-esp-wifi-manager
MicroPython WiFi Manager to configure and connect to networks
espsetup
simplified setup up for esp8266 / esp32 device
esphomeflasher
ESP8266/ESP32 firmware flasher for ESPHome
Close

To download the latest MicroPython binary for your ESP device go to:

ESP32:

https://micropython.org/download/esp32/

Or for the ESP8266:

https://micropython.org/download/esp8266/

Next, connect your ESP device to your computer:

Open the Thonny IDE and go to:

Thonny→ tools→options→Interpreter

Set your ESP device type and Serial/COM port and select to: *"install or update firmware"*

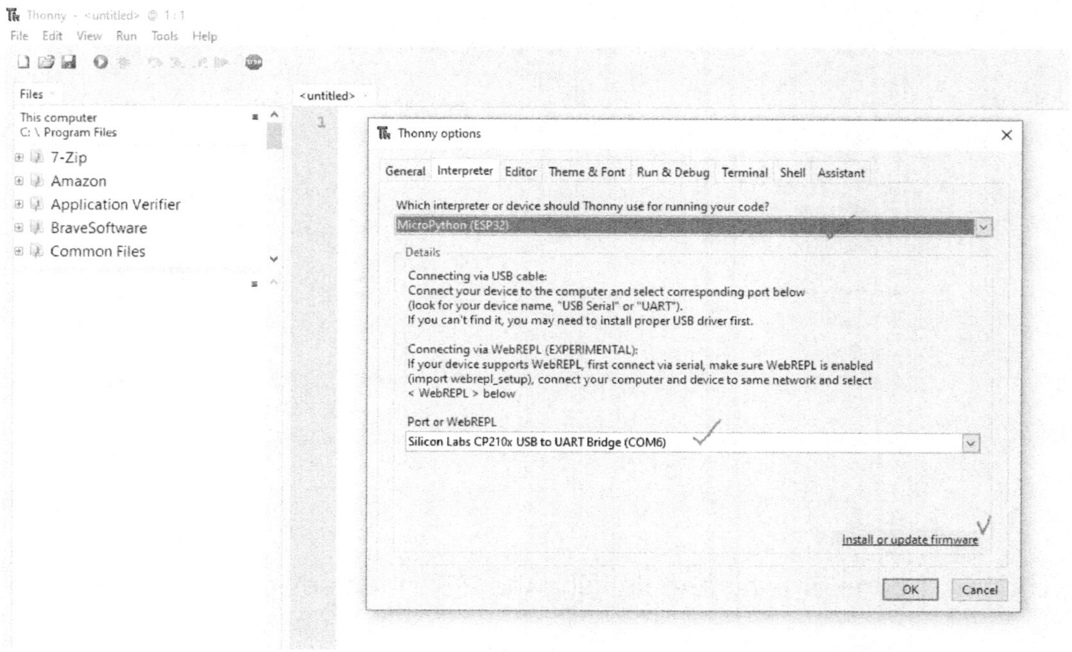

Thonny - <untitled> @ 1 : 1
File Edit View Run Tools Help
Files
This computer
C: \ Program Files
7-Zip
Amazon
Application Verifier
BraveSoftware
Common Files
<untitled>
Thonny options
General Interpreter Editor Theme & Font Run & Debug Terminal Shell Assistant
Which interpreter or device should Thonny use for running your code?
MicroPython (ESP32)
Details
Connecting via USB cable:
Connect your device to the computer and select corresponding port below
(look for your device name, "USB Serial" or "UART").
If you can't find it, you may need to install proper USB driver first.
Connecting via WebREPL (EXPERIMENTAL):
If your device supports WebREPL, first connect via serial, make sure WebREPL is enabled
(import webrepl_setup), connect your computer and device to same network and select
< WebREPL > below
Port or WebREPL
Silicon Labs CP210x USB to UART Bridge (COM6)
Install or update firmware
OK
Cancel

On the next screen select the COM port again and then point the "*Firmware*" to the file location where you downloaded your ESP binary file in the previous step. For the "*Flash Mode*" make sure "*From image file (keep)*" is selected. Make sure the "*Erase flash before installing*" box is checked. Finally, press the "*Install*" button.

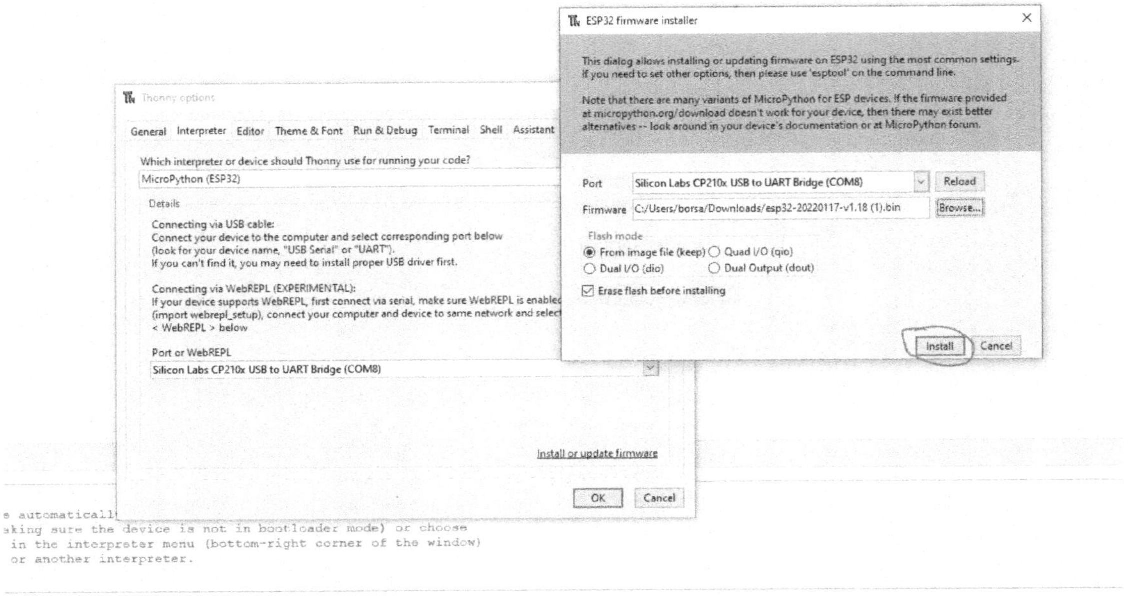
ESP32 firmware installer
This dialog allows installing or updating firmware on ESP32 using the most common settings. If you need to set other options, then please use 'esptool' on the command line.
Note that there are many variants of MicroPython for ESP devices. If the firmware provided at micropython.org/download doesn't work for your device, then there may exist better alternatives -- look around in your device's documentation or at MicroPython forum.
Port
Silicon Labs CP210x USB to UART Bridge (COM8)
Reload
Firmware
C:/Users/borsa/Downloads/esp32-20220117-v1.18 (1).bin
Browse...
Flash mode
From image file (keep)
Quad I/O (qio)
Dual I/O (dio)
Dual Output (dout)
Erase flash before installing
Install
Cancel
Thonny options
General
Interpreter
Editor
Theme & Font
Run & Debug
Terminal
Shell
Assistant
Which interpreter or device should Thonny use for running your code?
MicroPython (ESP32)
Details
Connecting via USB cable:
Connect your device to the computer and select corresponding port below
(look for your device name, "USB Serial" or "UART").
If you can't find it, you may need to install proper USB driver first.
Connecting via WebREPL (EXPERIMENTAL):
Port or WebREPL
Silicon Labs CP210x USB to UART Bridge (COM8)
Install or update firmware
OK
Cancel

After Thonny is done erasing and flashing the ESP then select "*Close*" and then "*OK*."

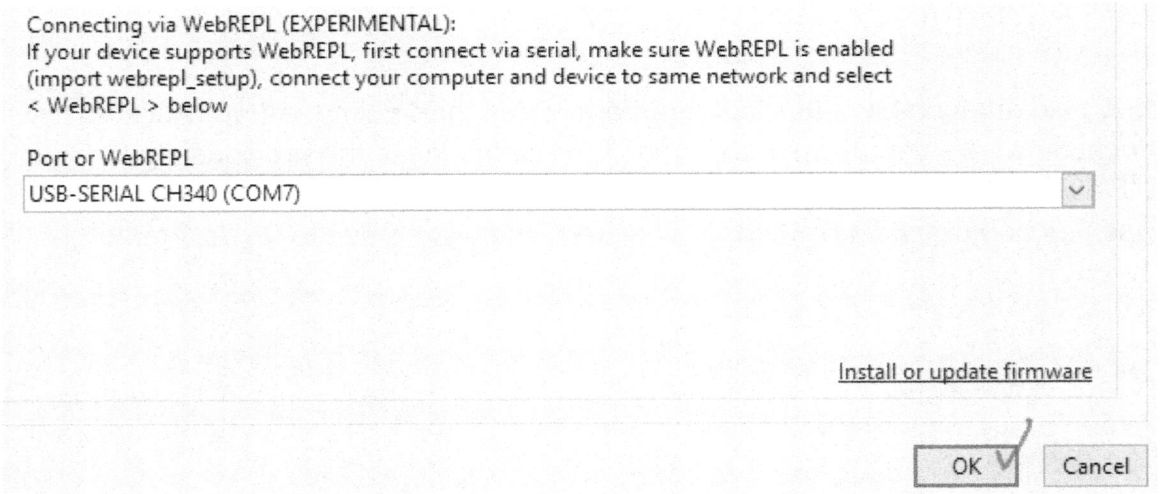
Connecting via WebREPL (EXPERIMENTAL):
If your device supports WebREPL, first connect via serial, make sure WebREPL is enabled (import webrepl_setup), connect your computer and device to same network and select < WebREPL > below
Port or WebREPL
USB-SERIAL CH340 (COM7)
Install or update firmware
OK
Cancel

Great, you have now erased the device memory and flashed the necessary firmware to enable your ESP device to be programmed in MicroPython. This will now allow you to connect and transmit data to AWS IoT.

Step 2 – Programming the ESP32 to Transmit Data to AWS IoT Core

After you have installed Thonny and erased and flashed your ESP device you are now ready to program the device in Thonny to talk to AWS IoT Core using certificate secured MQTT. The code for both the ESP32 and the ESP8266 is very similar, I will point out where they differ when you arrive at that part of the chapter.

I have developed MicroPython code below for the ESP32 to both Publish and Subscribe to AWS IoT Core. Much of the code comes from the MicroPython community. I did have to add some custom code for the subscription function, random number generation, and blinking LED's for indicating the delivery status of the IoT payload. Just as with the previous Arduino sketch there will be fields the developer is expected to fill out and customize for their own MicroPython program.

Open Thonny and go to:

Thonny→ tools→options→Interpreter

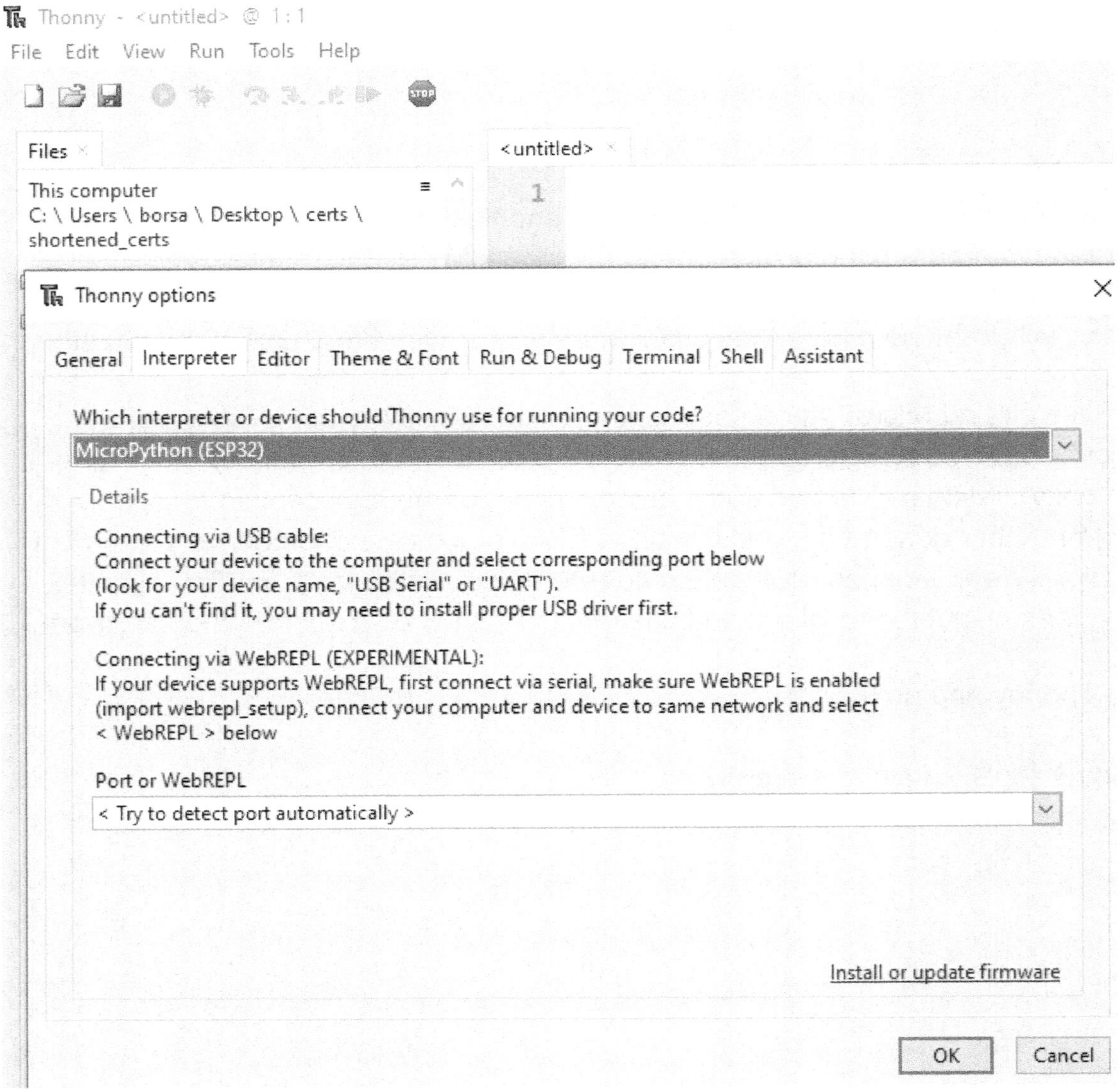
Thonny - <untitled> @ 1 : 1
File Edit View Run Tools Help
Files
<untitled>
This computer
C: \ Users \ borsa \ Desktop \ certs \ shortened_certs
Thonny options
General
Interpreter
Editor
Theme & Font
Run & Debug
Terminal
Shell
Assistant
Which interpreter or device should Thonny use for running your code?
MicroPython (ESP32)
Details
Connecting via USB cable:
Connect your device to the computer and select corresponding port below
(look for your device name, "USB Serial" or "UART").
If you can't find it, you may need to install proper USB driver first.
Connecting via WebREPL (EXPERIMENTAL):
If your device supports WebREPL, first connect via serial, make sure WebREPL is enabled
(import webrepl_setup), connect your computer and device to same network and select
< WebREPL > below
Port or WebREPL
< Try to detect port automatically >
Install or update firmware
OK
Cancel

Make sure you select ESP32, and your com port is set, now open a new file in Thonny by going to:

File→ New

Change the indicated fields to configure the code to your WiFi network and AWS account:

```
MQTT_HOST = "<YOUR-AWS-IOT-ENDPOINT>"
WIFI_SSID = "<Your-WiFi-Network-Name-Here>"
WIFI_PW = "<Your-WiFi-Password>"
```

- *Changing the Client_ID, Publishing topic, and subscription topic is optional.*

Now paste in the code below with your custom modifications detailed above.

The MicroPython code for the ESP32 can be found formatted correctly at the chapters GitHub page. Copying code from the relevant chapters GitHub page is more reliable for programming than copying code from eBooks due to character translation and formatting issues.

```
#AWS MQTT client example for esp32
#https://awsiot.wordpress.com/2019/01/10/connect-8266
#https://forum.micropython.org/viewtopic.php?t=5166
#Original code added by Stephen Borsay for Udemy Course

from umqtt.robust import MQTTClient
import time
import random
import machine
pin = machine.Pin(2)  #blinking is optional, check your LED pin

#Place these Certs at same folder level as your MicroPython program
#No need to alter your AWS Client Cert and Private Key
CERT_FILE = "/certificate.pem.crt"
KEY_FILE = "/private.pem.key"

MQTT_CLIENT_ID = "CurtesyFlush88"
MQTT_PORT = 8883 #MQTT secured

PUB_TOPIC = "iot/outTopic" #coming out of device
SUB_TOPIC = "iot/inTopic"  #coming into device

#Your AWS IoT Endpoint found at IoT Core→Settings
#Change the following three settings
MQTT_HOST = "<YOUR-AWS-IOT-ENDPOINT>" #Your AWS IoT endpoint
WIFI_SSID = "<Your-WiFi-Network-Name-Here>"
WIFI_PW = "<Your-WiFi-Password>"

MQTT_CLIENT = None

print("starting program")

def network_connect():
    print("starting connection method")
```

```
    import network
    sta_if = network.WLAN(network.STA_IF)
    if not sta_if.isconnected():
        print('connecting to network...')
        sta_if.active(True)
        sta_if.connect(WIFI_SSID , WIFI_PW)
        while not sta_if.isconnected():
            pass
    print('network config:', sta_if.ifconfig())

def pub_msg(msg):  #publish is synchronous so we poll and publish
    global MQTT_CLIENT
    try:
        MQTT_CLIENT.publish(PUB_TOPIC, msg)
        print("Sent: " + msg)
    except Exception as e:
        print("Exception publish: " + str€)
        raise

def sub_cb(topic, msg):
    print('Device received a Message: ')
    print((topic, msg))  #print incoming message, waits for loop below
    pin.value(0)         #blink if incoming message by toggle off

def cloud_connect():
    global MQTT_CLIENT

    try:  #Security certs
        with open(KEY_FILE, "r") as f:
            key = f.read()
        print("Got Private Key")

        with open(CERT_FILE, "r") as f:
            cert = f.read()
        print("Got Client/Device Cert")

        MQTT_CLIENT = MQTTClient(client_id=MQTT_CLIENT_ID, server=MQTT_HOST, 
port=MQTT_PORT, keepalive=5000, ssl=True, ssl_params={"cert":cert, "key":key, 
"server_side":False})
        MQTT_CLIENT.connect()
        print('MQTT Connected')
        MQTT_CLIENT.set_callback(sub_cb)
        MQTT_CLIENT.subscribe(SUB_TOPIC)
        print('Subscribed to %s as the incoming topic' % (SUB_TOPIC))
        return MQTT_CLIENT
```

```
    except Exception as e:
        print('Cannot connect MQTT: ' + str€)
        raise

#Start execution
try:
    print("Connecting WiFi 87ayload")
    network_connect()
    print("Connecting to AWS IoT")
    cloud_connect()
    while True: #Loop forever
            pin.value(1)
            pending_message = MQTT_CLIENT.check_msg()  # check for new sub
payload incoming
            if pending_message != 'None':  #check if we have a message
                temp =  random.randint(0, 130)
                humid = random.randint(0, 100)
                deviceTime = time.time()
                print("Publishing")
                pub_msg("{\n  \"temperature\": %d,\n  \"humidity\": %d,\n
\"timestamps\": %d\n}"%(temp,humid,deviceTime))
                print("published payload")
                time.sleep(5)  #A 5 second delay between publishing

except Exception as e:
    print(str€)
```

* The MQTT Client ID is a unique ID, give it any name you like, but choose a different name for every device you program. Unique Client IDs are a requirement of the MQTT protocol.

```
MQTT_CLIENT_ID = "CurtesyFlush88" #Or use your own ID
```

Topic to be published under for outgoing IoT data payloads.

```
PUB_TOPIC = "iot/outTopic" #Payload coming out of the device
```

Topic to subscribe to for incoming IoT data payloads.

```
SUB_TOPIC = "iot/inTopic"  #Payload coming into device
```

Your own AWS IoT endpoint: IoT Core→Settings.

```
MQTT_HOST = "<Your-IoT-Endpoint>"  #Your AWS IoT endpoint
```

At this point, once you have filled out all the required fields and the program is in your Thonny editor you can save it to "MicroPython Device", save it under any name you like.

File→Save as:

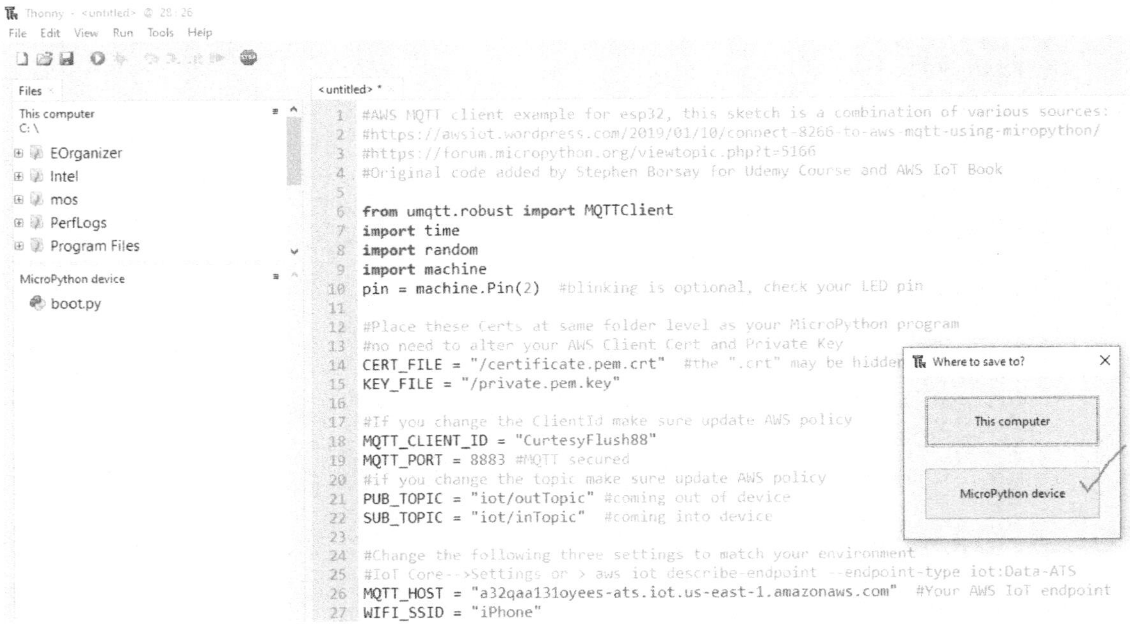

Thonny - <untitled> @ 28 : 26
File Edit View Run Tools Help
Files
This computer
C:\
EOrganizer
Intel
mos
PerfLogs
Program Files
MicroPython device
boot.py
<untitled> *
#AWS MQTT client example for esp32, this sketch is a combination of various sources:
#https://awsiot.wordpress.com/2019/01/10/connect-8266-to-aws-mqtt-using-miropython/
#https://forum.micropython.org/viewtopic.php?t=5166
#Original code added by Stephen Borsay for Udemy Course and AWS IoT Book
from umqtt.robust import MQTTClient
import time
import random
import machine
pin = machine.Pin(2) #blinking is optional, check your LED pin
#Place these Certs at same folder level as your MicroPython program
#no need to alter your AWS Client Cert and Private Key
CERT_FILE = "/certificate.pem.crt" #the ".crt" may be hidden
KEY_FILE = "/private.pem.key"
#If you change the ClientId make sure update AWS policy
MQTT_CLIENT_ID = "CurtesyFlush88"
MQTT_PORT = 8883 #MQTT secured
#if you change the topic make sure update AWS policy
PUB_TOPIC = "iot/outTopic" #coming out of device
SUB_TOPIC = "iot/inTopic" #coming into device
#Change the following three settings to match your environment
#IoT Core-->Settings or > aws iot describe-endpoint --endpoint-type iot:Data-ATS
MQTT_HOST = "a32qaa131oyees-ats.iot.us-east-1.amazonaws.com" #Your AWS IoT endpoint
WIFI_SSID = "iPhone"
Where to save to?
This computer
MicroPython device

If the MicroPython device box doesn't appear you may have to press the "Stop" button first. 

Here I called my program "*AWS_IoT_MicroP.py*"

Make sure you use the .py file extension so the compiler knows that this is a Python file.

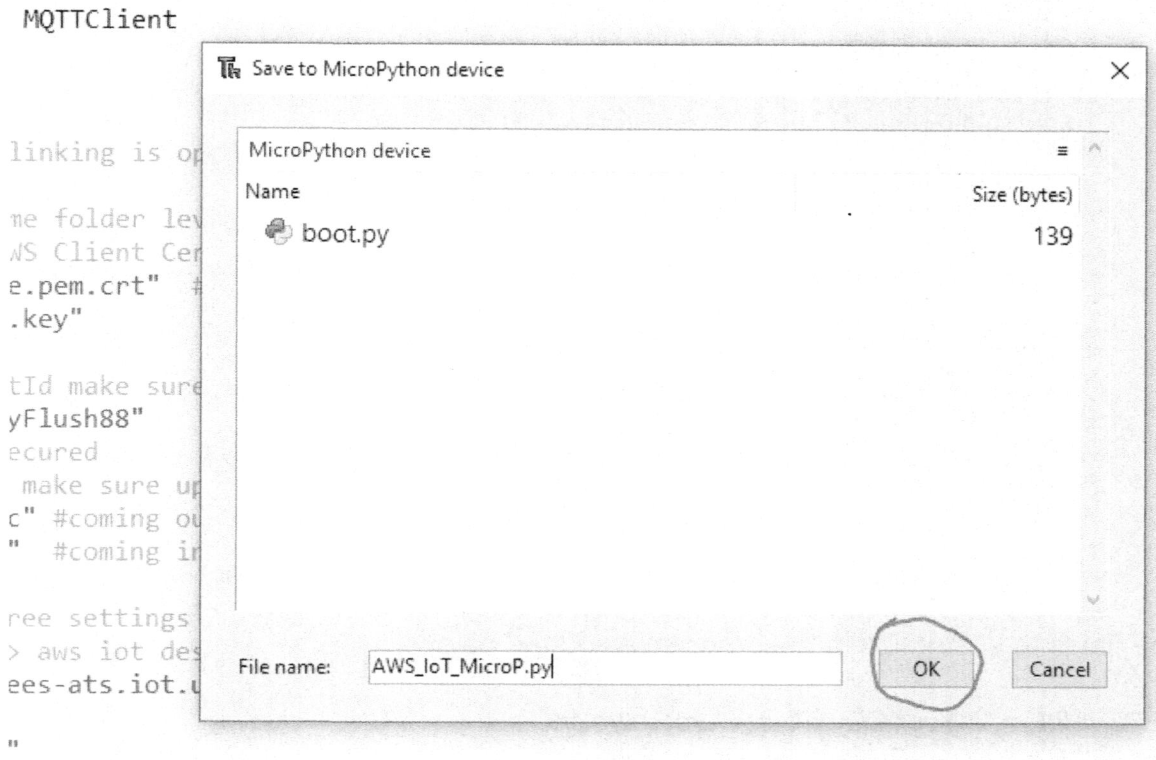
MQTTClient
Save to MicroPython device
MicroPython device
Name
Size (bytes)
boot.py
139
File name:
AWS_IoT_MicroP.py
OK
Cancel

Your Micro Python device pane on the left side of the IDE should now look like the image below:

MicroPython device
AWS_IoT_MicroP.py
boot.py

Transferring your security certificates to the ESP32 device in Thonny

Next, you need to place your client certificate and your private key certificate on the ESP32. If you took my advice, you have a folder on your desktop, organized by AWS region, that has your security certificates inside. Now use the left side pane of Thonny to navigate to where your certificates are held on your local computer. Here I navigated on my desktop to my “shortened certs” folder.

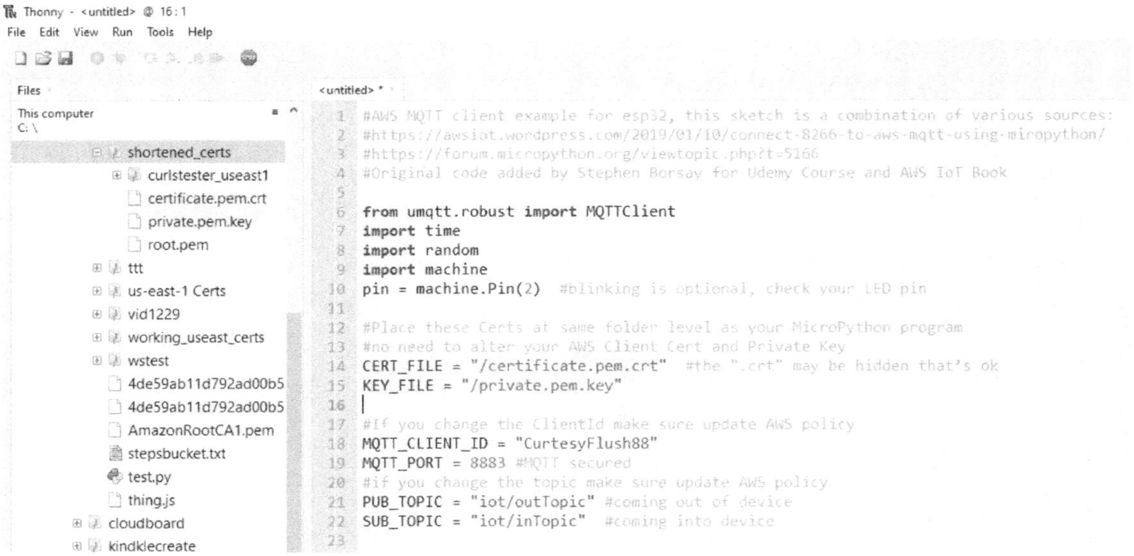
Thonny - <untitled> @ 16 : 1
File Edit View Run Tools Help
Files
This computer
C: \
shortened_certs
curlstester_useast1
certificate.pem.crt
private.pem.key
root.pem
ttt
us-east-1 Certs
vid1229
working_useast_certs
wstest
4de59ab11d792ad00b5
4de59ab11d792ad00b5
AmazonRootCA1.pem
stepsbucket.txt
test.py
thing.js
cloudboard
kindklecreate
<untitled> *
#AWS MQTT client example for esp32, this sketch is a combination of various sources:
#https://awsiot.wordpress.com/2019/01/10/connect-8266-to-aws-mqtt-using-miropython/
#https://forum.micropython.org/viewtopic.php?t=5166
#Original code added by Stephen Borsay for Udemy Course and AWS IoT Book
from umqtt.robust import MQTTClient
import time
import random
import machine
pin = machine.Pin(2) #blinking is optional, check your LED pin
#Place these Certs at same folder level as your MicroPython program
#no need to alter your AWS Client Cert and Private Key
CERT_FILE = "/certificate.pem.crt" #the ".crt" may be hidden that's ok
KEY_FILE = "/private.pem.key"
#If you change the ClientId make sure update AWS policy
MQTT_CLIENT_ID = "CurtesyFlush88"
MQTT_PORT = 8883 #MQTT secured
#if you change the topic make sure update AWS policy
PUB_TOPIC = "iot/outTopic" #coming out of device
SUB_TOPIC = "iot/inTopic" #coming into device

The fields to customize in the program are listed below:

CERT_FILE = "/<Your-Client-Cert-Here>.pem.crt"
KEY_FILE = "/<Your-Private-Key-Here>.pem.key"

And name the client and private key certificates in your MicroPython program to match the names on your local computer:

```
CERT_FILE = "/certificate.pem.crt"
KEY_FILE = "/private.pem.key"
```

I called my client cert (also called device certificate) and private key certificate: "certificate" and "private." You can change the name as you like just to ensure that the file extension remains *pem.crt* and *pem.key* respectively.

To transfer your certificates to your ESP32 right click each certificate on your computer to "*Upload to /*." This will move the certificates into memory on the ESP32. Notice that you don't need the root certificate (x.509), just the client/device certificate and the private key. Make sure the certificate names in your folder on your computer match the names you gave them in your Thonny program.

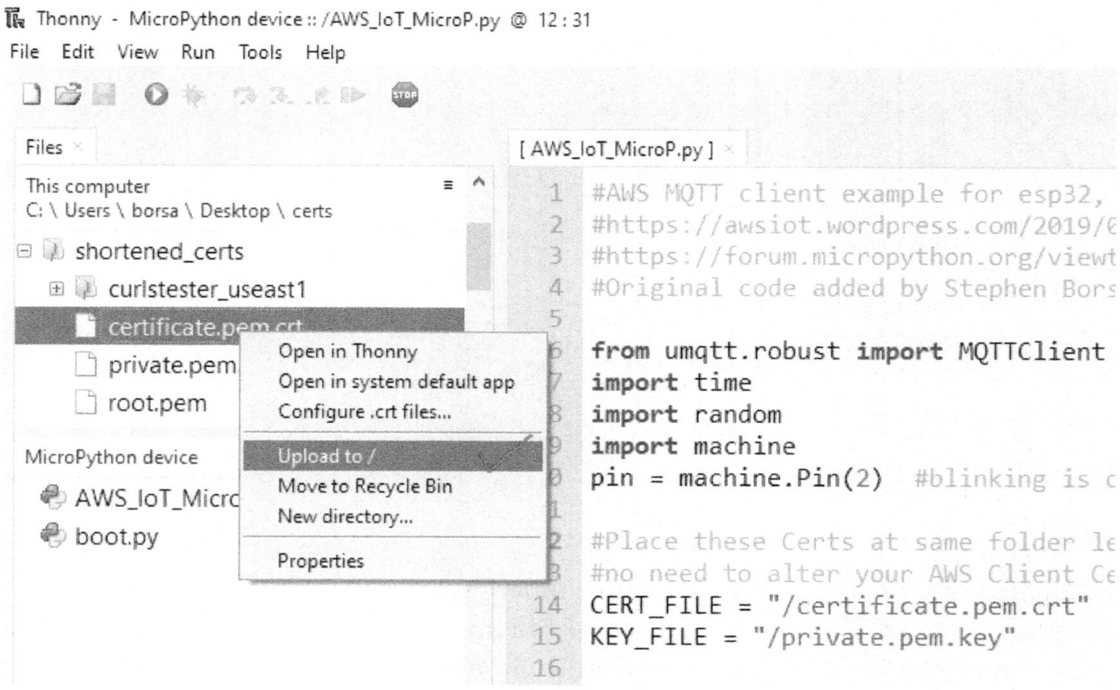
Thonny - MicroPython device :: /AWS_IoT_MicroP.py @ 12 : 31
File Edit View Run Tools Help
Files
This computer
C: \ Users \ borsa \ Desktop \ certs
shortened_certs
curlstester_useast1
certificate.pem.crt
private.pem
root.pem
MicroPython device
AWS_IoT_Micrc
boot.py
Open in Thonny
Open in system default app
Configure .crt files...
Upload to /
Move to Recycle Bin
New directory...
Properties
[AWS_IoT_MicroP.py]
#AWS MQTT client example for esp32,
#https://awsiot.wordpress.com/2019/
#https://forum.micropython.org/viewt
#Original code added by Stephen Bors
from umqtt.robust import MQTTClient
import time
import random
import machine
pin = machine.Pin(2) #blinking is c
#Place these Certs at same folder le
#no need to alter your AWS Client Ce
CERT_FILE = "/certificate.pem.crt"
KEY_FILE = "/private.pem.key"

Upload both your client certificate and private key. After uploading both your certs to your device the ESP32 device pane should look like this:

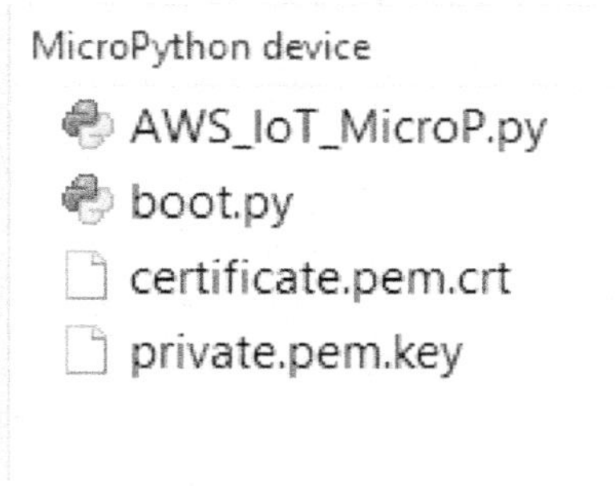
MicroPython device
AWS_IoT_MicroP.py
boot.py
certificate.pem.crt
private.pem.key

Now run the program by going to:

Run→ Run current script

Or simply by pressing the run button  on the menu

The program should connect to WiFi and start publishing sensor readings to AWS IoT Core.

```
Shell
}
published payload
Publishing
Sent: {
  "temperature": 0,
  "humidity": 88,
 "timestamps": 704821277
}
published payload
```

As explained earlier, you may notice how much faster the MicroPython program compiles and uploads to the device than Arduino. Again, this is because you have already virtualized the ESP with the MicroPython framework. As you remember from your compiler design class in college, under normal circumstances a compiled C/C++ binary should be much faster and efficient than a transpired python file. However, that is not the case here due to the "virtualization" you completed earlier.

Just as with Arduino you can make sure the payloads are getting published to AWS by going to the MQTT test client in AWS IoT Core and subscribing to the "#" wildcard topic.

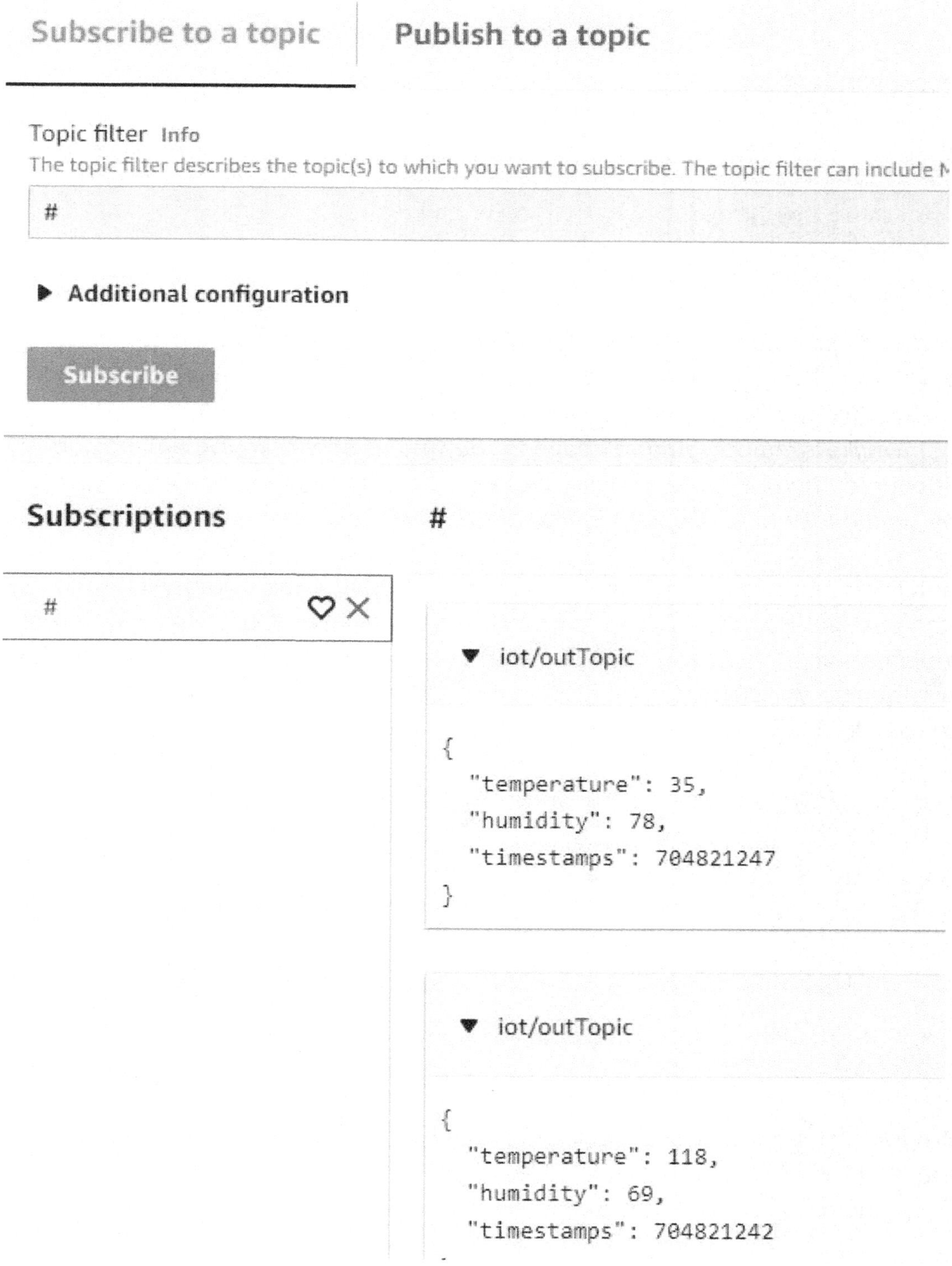
Subscribe to a topic
Publish to a topic
Topic filter Info
The topic filter describes the topic(s) to which you want to subscribe. The topic filter can include
#
Additional configuration
Subscribe
Subscriptions
#
#
iot/outTopic
{
"temperature": 35,
"humidity": 78,
"timestamps": 704821247
}
iot/outTopic
{
"temperature": 118,
"humidity": 69,
"timestamps": 704821242

You can also send messages from AWS IoT Core to your ESP32 by publishing from the MQTT test client and subscribing on the device using a subscription topic:

```
SUB_TOPIC = "iot/inTopic"  #IoT 94ayLoad coming into device
```

The subscription function:

```
def sub_cb(topic, msg):
    print('Device received a Message: ')
    print((topic, msg))  #print incoming message, waits for Loop below
    pin.value(0)         #bLink if incoming message by toggLe off
```

Contrast this subscription method in MicroPython to the subscription function using Arduino with the Wiring programming language based on C/C++. Note how much more intuitive and simpler the MicroPython program is as a highly abstracted language. Unlike Arduino you don't have to "unwind" a char buffer in a conditional loop. Of course, the downside of using more abstracted, higher-level languages on hardware, is the loss of bit flipping control of low-level implementation details.

Congratulations, you were able to configure the ESP32 and the Thonny IDE and upload the custom program to send IoT payloads to AWS IoT Core. Now for a real-world implementation you can check out what external sensor libraries are available in MicroPython so you can start integrating real sensors with your device and send real time data to AWS.

https://docs.micropython.org/en/latest/library/index.html

https://github.com/mcauser/awesome-micropython

Step 3 – Programming the ESP8266 to Transmit Data to AWS IoT Core

When programming the ESP8266 in the Thonny IDE there are just a couple of extra considerations I will discuss below. However, you will find the directions identical to the ESP32 otherwise, so I won't repeat the same directions unless it is relevant.

Follow the same initial setup by erasing the device memory and then flashing the ESP8266 with the MicroPython firmware either manually from the command line or using the Thonny IDE as described in Step 1. For the ESP8266 you will have to perform a security certificate conversion described below before you can upload and run the ESP8266 MicroPython program to transmit data to AWS IoT core.

The first difference from the ESP32 directions is that the 'random' library doesn't work well on the ESP8266. To generate random numbers for the fake environmental variables, you would use the modulo operator ("%") with the time method. While this did not generate as wide a range of truly random numbers as the random library would have, it was sufficient for attaining a functional result.

Now let's discuss the only significant difference between the MicroPython program for the ESP32 and the MicroPython program for the ESP8266. The certificate formatting with the default file extensions, as they were downloaded from AWS, will not work by default for the ESP8266 they did for the ESP32. So, you must convert the two security certificates to the more primitive, computer readable "DER" format for them to work correctly in the MicroPython program. To do this format conversion you will need the openSSL tool. This tool should be available by default on Mac and Linux. However, for Windows you won't find an acceptable version installed by default. To get the openSSL tool just download the free toolset included by default in "**Git for Windows**". If you decided to test your security certificates with cURL to AWS IoT Core, as I demonstrated in an earlier chapter, you already have this tool on your computer. The "Git for Windows" *toolset* includes other useful development tools as well. You can find the free Git for Windows download here:

https://gitforwindows.org/

Once the tool is downloaded you have two options when using 'openSSL' to convert your certificates. The proper way to do the conversion is to create an "environmental variable" so you can access openSSL from anywhere on your computer. The lazy way is to copy and paste your client certificate and private key from your certificate folder into the same folder where openSSL is located.

In Windows, after installing "Git for Windows," the openSSL.exe can be found in:

C:\Program Files\Git\usr\bin>

You likely are going to need "administrator" privileges to paste the certificates and run openSSL on Windows. To use "run as administrator" mode" for the command prompt in Windows:

1. Enter "*cmd*" in the Windows search box.
2. Click on the "*Run as administrator*" option.

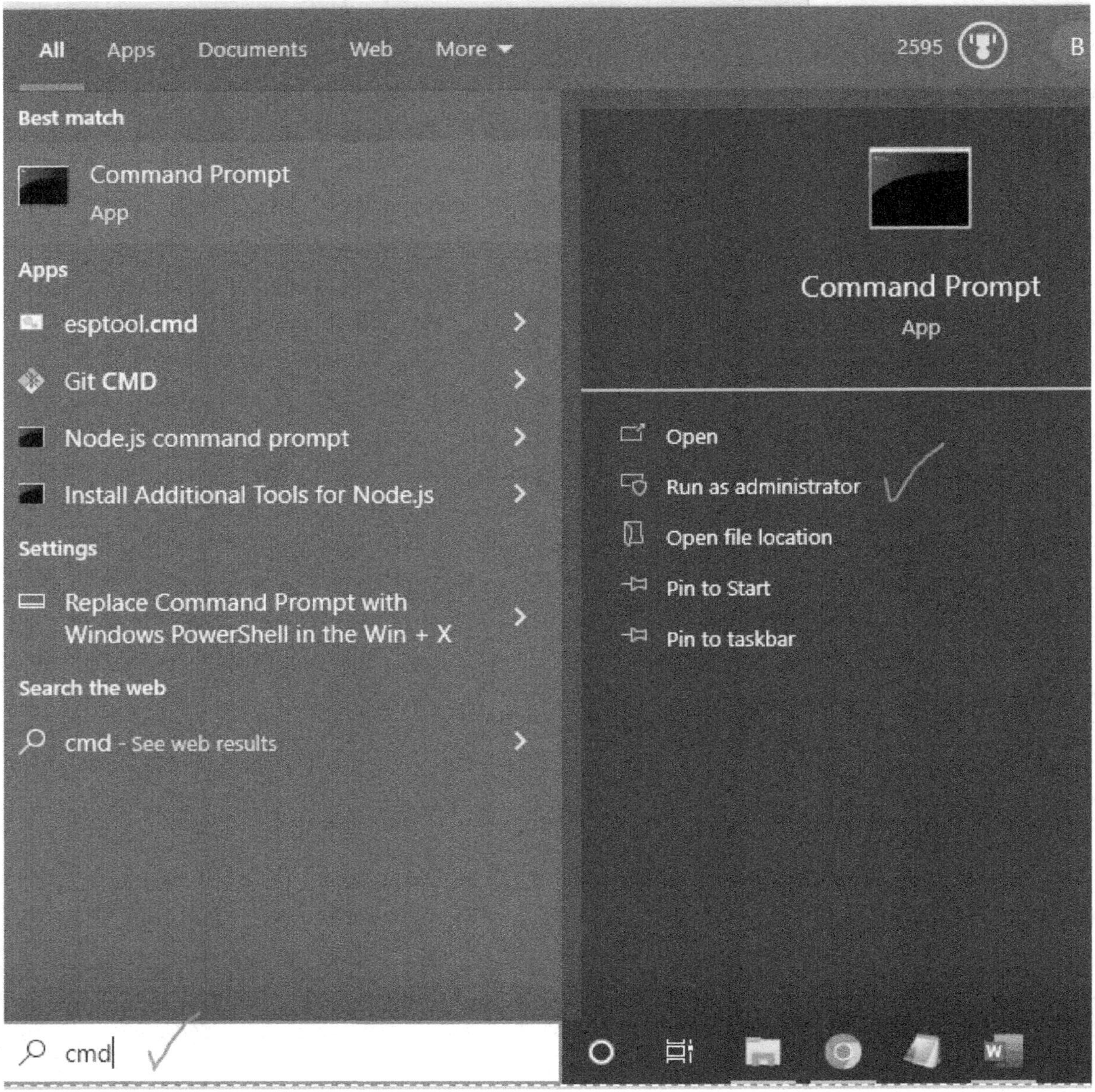

All
Apps
Documents
Web
More
2595
B
Best match
Command Prompt
App
Apps
esptool.cmd
Git CMD
Node.js command prompt
Install Additional Tools for Node.js
Settings
Replace Command Prompt with Windows PowerShell in the Win + X
Search the web
cmd - See web results
Command Prompt
App
Open
Run as administrator
Open file location
Pin to Start
Pin to taskbar
cmd

Alternately simply right click the command prompt if you have a desktop icon and select “Run as administrator.”

$

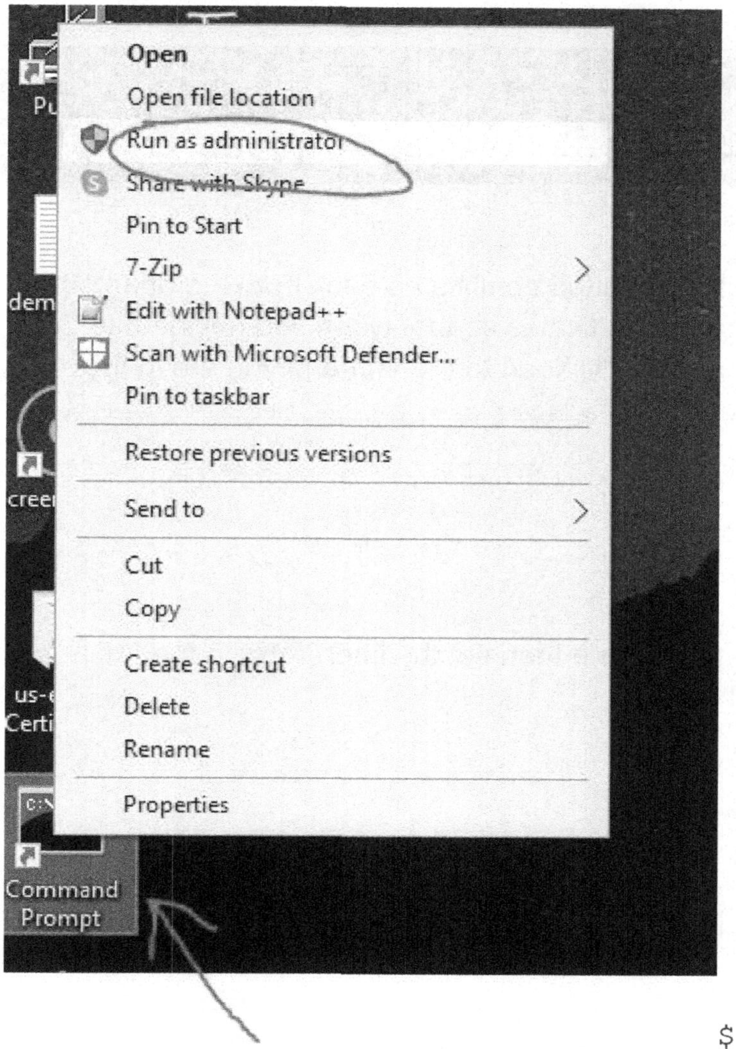
Open
Open file location
Run as administrator
Share with Skype
Pin to Start
7-Zip
Edit with Notepad++
Scan with Microsoft Defender...
Pin to taskbar
Restore previous versions
Send to
Cut
Copy
Create shortcut
Delete
Rename
Properties
Command Prompt

$

After pasting the certificates in the same folder as the openSSL tool use the following commands naming the DER certs whatever name you like.

Example:

```
openssl x509 -in 5d65748f80-certificate.pem.crt
 -out ClientCert.cert.der -outform DER
```

And:

```
openssl rsa -in 5d65748f80-private.pem.key
 -out privateKey.key.der -outform DER
```

- These commands should be all on one line, I am using two lines here due to eBook formatting

Command Prompt
C:\Program Files>cd git
C:\Program Files\Git>cd us*
C:\Program Files\Git\usr>cd bin
C:\Program Files\Git\usr\bin>openssl x509 -in 5d65748f80-certificate.pem.crt -out ClientCert.cert.der -outform DER

That's it. Now move the new "DER" formatted certificates back from the openSSSL folder to where you keep your original certificates so that when you navigate to the local directory within Thonny and use the "Upload to /" command you are in the correct folder on your local computer.

Return to the Thonny IDE and go to:

Tools→Options→ Interpreter

Connect the ESP8266 to your computer and then set the interpreter to the ESP8266 and the occupied COM Port:

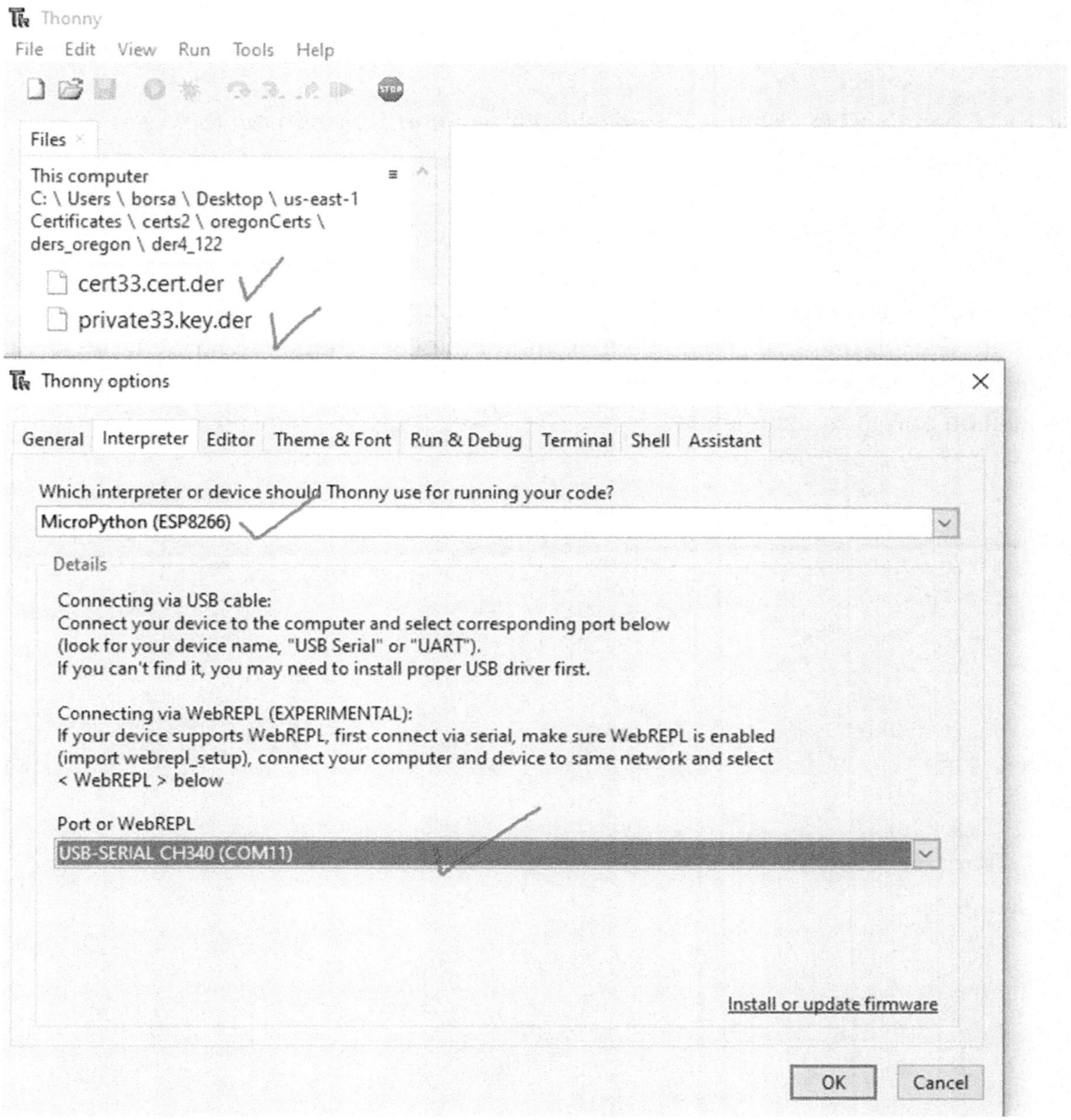
Thonny
File Edit View Run Tools Help
Files
This computer
C: \ Users \ borsa \ Desktop \ us-east-1 Certificates \ certs2 \ oregonCerts \ ders_oregon \ der4_122
cert33.cert.der
private33.key.der
Thonny options
General Interpreter Editor Theme & Font Run & Debug Terminal Shell Assistant
Which interpreter or device should Thonny use for running your code?
MicroPython (ESP8266)
Details
Connecting via USB cable:
Connect your device to the computer and select corresponding port below
(look for your device name, "USB Serial" or "UART").
If you can't find it, you may need to install proper USB driver first.
Connecting via WebREPL (EXPERIMENTAL):
If your device supports WebREPL, first connect via serial, make sure WebREPL is enabled
(import webrepl_setup), connect your computer and device to same network and select
< WebREPL > below
Port or WebREPL
USB-SERIAL CH340 (COM11)
Install or update firmware
OK
Cancel

Now open a new file in Thonny by going to:

File→ New

Change indicated fields to configure the code to your WiFi network and AWS account:

```
MQTT_HOST = “<YOUR-AWS-IOT-ENDPOINT>”     #Your AWS IoT endpoint
```

```
WIFI_SSID = "<Your-WiFi-Network-Name-Here>"
WIFI_PW = "<Your-WiFi-Password>"
```

- *Changing the Client_ID, Publishing topic, and Subscription topic are optional.*

Paste in the ESP8266 code below with the modifications.

The MicroPython code for the ESP8266 can be found formatted correctly at the chapters GitHub page. Copying code from the relevant chapters GitHub page is more reliable for programming than copying code from eBooks due to character translation and formatting issues.

```
#AWS MQTT client cert example for esp8266, this sketch
#https://awsiot.wordpress.com/2019/01/10/connect-8266
#https://forum.micropython.org/viewtopic.php?t=5166
#Originalcode added by Stephen Borsay for Udemy Course
#AWS MQTT Connect Pub/Sub

from umqtt.robust import MQTTClient
import time
import random
import machine
pin = machine.Pin(2)

#Convert your AWS Certs with OpenSSL
#Open.SSL install in→ C:\Program Files\Git\usr\bin>
CERT_FILE = "/<Your-Client-Cert>.cert.der"
KEY_FILE = "/<Your-Private-Key>.key.der"

#ClientId should be unique per device
MQTT_CLIENT_ID = "HeavyPetter33"
MQTT_PORT = 8883 #MQTT Secured

#Pub and Sub topics
PUB_TOPIC = "iot/outTopic" #coming out of device
SUB_TOPIC = "iot/inTopic"  #coming into device

#Change the following three settings
MQTT_HOST = "<Your-AWS-IoT-Endpoint>"
WIFI_SSID = "<Your-WiFi-Network>"
WIFI_PW = "<Your-WiFi-Password>"
```

```
MQTT_CLIENT = None  #empty object

print("Starting program...")

def network_connect():
    print("In network connect method")
    import network
    sta_if = network.WLAN(network.STA_IF)
    if not sta_if.isconnected():
        print('connecting to network...')
        sta_if.active(True)
        sta_if.connect(WIFI_SSID , WIFI_PW)
        while not sta_if.isconnected():
            pass  # I do nothing and like it
    print('network config:', sta_if.ifconfig())

def pub_msg(msg):  #publish is synchronous so we poll and publish
    global MQTT_CLIENT
    try:
        MQTT_CLIENT.publish(PUB_TOPIC, msg)
        print("Sent: " + msg)
    except Exception as e:
        print("Exception publish: " + str€)
        raise

def sub_cb(topic, msg):
    print('Device received a Message: ')
    print((topic, msg))  #print incoming message asynchronously
    pin.value(0) #blink if incoming message by toggle off

def cloud_connect():
    global MQTT_CLIENT

    try:
        with open(KEY_FILE, "r") as f:
            key = f.read()

        print("set private key")

        with open(CERT_FILE, "r") as f:
            cert = f.read()

        print("set client cert")
```

```
        MQTT_CLIENT = MQTTClient(client_id=MQTT_CLIENT_ID, server=MQTT_HOST,
port=MQTT_PORT, keepalive=5000, ssl=True, ssl_params={"cert":cert, "key":key,
"server_side":False})
        MQTT_CLIENT.connect()
        print('Network Connected')
        MQTT_CLIENT.set_callback(sub_cb)
        MQTT_CLIENT.subscribe(SUB_TOPIC)
        print('Subscribed to %s as the incoming topic' % (SUB_TOPIC))
        return MQTT_CLIENT
    except Exception as e:
        print('Cannot connect MQTT: ' + str€)
        raise

#Start Loop
try:
    print("Connecting to WiFi Network")
    network_connect()
    print("Connecting to AWS IoT")
    cloud_connect()
    print("Entering Loop")
    while True: #Loop forever
            pin.value(1)
            pending_message = MQTT_CLIENT.check_msg()
            if pending_message != 'None':  #check for new message
                temp = (time.time())%99   #because randomint doesn't work
                humid = (time.time())%98
                deviceTime = time.time()
                pub_msg("{\n  \"temperature\": %d,\n  \"humidity\": %d,\n
 \"timestamps\": %d\n}"%(temp,humid,deviceTime))
                print("OK Published payload")
                time.sleep(5)  # 5 second delay between publishing

except Exception as e:
    print(str€)
```

Fill in all the indicated fields in the program and then File→Save to the ESP8226 device, making sure to name your program something ending in the "*.py*" (Python) file extension.

Transferring your security certificates to the ESP8266 in Thonny

Next, you need to place your client certificate and your private key certificate on the ESP8266. If you took my advice, you have a folder on your desktop, organized by

AWS region, that has your DER formatted security certificates inside. Now use the left side pane of Thonny to navigate to where your certificates are held on your local computer. Move your DER certificates to the ESP8266 by right clicking the certificates on your computer and then using the "Upload to /" command and transferring the certificates to your ESP8266 device.

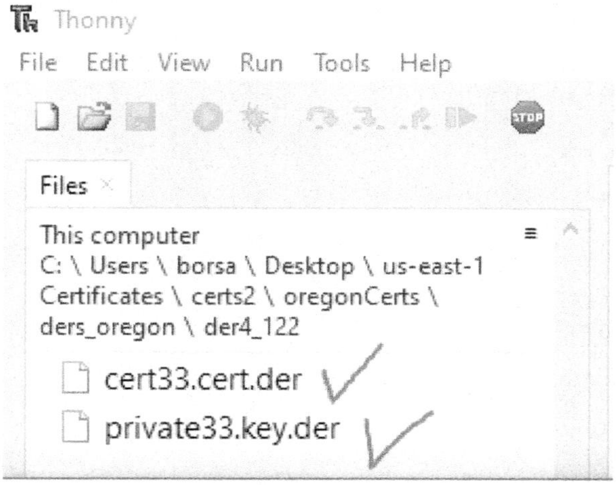

Thonny
File Edit View Run Tools Help
Files
This computer
C: \ Users \ borsa \ Desktop \ us-east-1 Certificates \ certs2 \ oregonCerts \ ders_oregon \ der4_122
cert33.cert.der
private33.key.der

Your certificates should be transferred to your ESP8266 device with the following format extension in your MicroPython program in Thonny:

```
CERT_FILE = "/<Your-Client-Cert>.cert.der"
KEY_FILE = "/<Your-Private-Key>.key.der"
```

In this example I named my client/device certificate "cert33" and my private key as "private33." After I right clicked them to upload them to the ESP8266 the certificates now appear on the MicroPython device pane shown below. Also, note that the certificate names on the device match exactly the names on the MicroPython program.

```
CERT_FILE = "/cert33.cert.der"
KEY_FILE = "/private33.key.der"
```

The certificate names should exactly match those in the MicroPython program and those uploaded to the ESP8266 device.

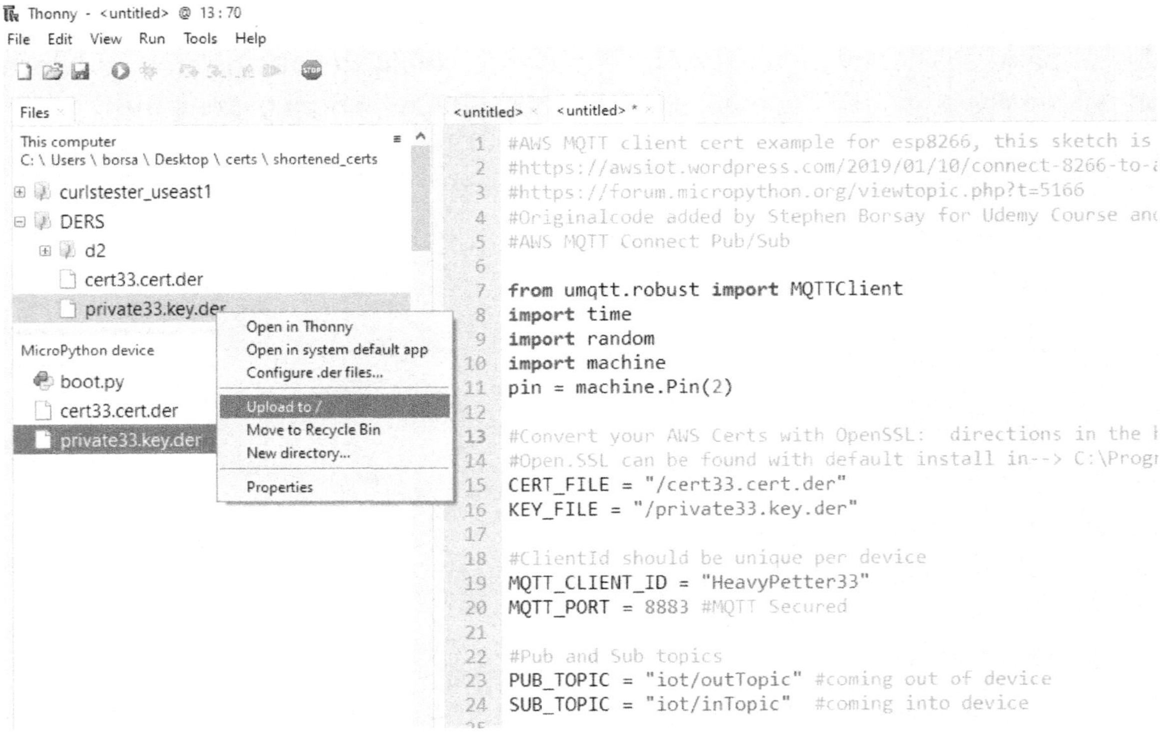

Thonny - <untitled> @ 13 : 70
File Edit View Run Tools Help
Files
This computer
C: \ Users \ borsa \ Desktop \ certs \ shortened_certs
curlstester_useast1
DERS
d2
cert33.cert.der
private33.key.der
MicroPython device
boot.py
cert33.cert.der
private33.key.der
Open in Thonny
Open in system default app
Configure .der files...
Upload to /
Move to Recycle Bin
New directory...
Properties
<untitled>
<untitled> *
#AWS MQTT client cert example for esp8266, this sketch is
#https://awsiot.wordpress.com/2019/01/10/connect-8266-to-
#https://forum.micropython.org/viewtopic.php?t=5166
#Originalcode added by Stephen Borsay for Udemy Course an
#AWS MQTT Connect Pub/Sub
from umqtt.robust import MQTTClient
import time
import random
import machine
pin = machine.Pin(2)
#Convert your AWS Certs with OpenSSL: directions in the
#Open.SSL can be found with default install in--> C:\Progr
CERT_FILE = "/cert33.cert.der"
KEY_FILE = "/private33.key.der"
#ClientId should be unique per device
MQTT_CLIENT_ID = "HeavyPetter33"
MQTT_PORT = 8883 #MQTT Secured
#Pub and Sub topics
PUB_TOPIC = "iot/outTopic" #coming out of device
SUB_TOPIC = "iot/inTopic" #coming into device

Use File→Save in Thonny once you transferred the certificates to your device to save the MicroPython program.

Now run the program by selecting to:

Run→Run current script

Or simply by pressing the run button  on the menu

The program should connect, after some time, start publishing sensor readings to AWS IoT Core. You can see these readings by subscribing to "#" on the MQTT test client in IoT Core.

```
  "humidity": 53,
  "timestamps": 707915989
}
OK Published payload
Sent: {
  "temperature": 60,
  "humidity": 58,
  "timestamps": 707915994
}
```

As a final note a promising new MicroPython IDE for devices has been recently released called "Mu". Mu offers the same functionality as Thonny with both the erase and flash features for the ESP32 and ESP8266. It is designed to be even easier to use than Thonny. It can be downloaded at:

https://codewith.mu/

Congratulations, you have now been able to erase, flash, and program both the ESP32 and the ESP8266 with the Thonny IDE using the MicroPython language. The next steps would be to explore the sensor libraries available for MicroPython and then to modify to the test programs for your own needs.

Troubleshooting: see this chapters GitHub for additional troubleshooting

- "Bytes index out of range" error often cause by incorrect endpoint/wrong AWS region.

Chapter 6 -
Using Mongoose OS and JavaScript with AWS

Mongoose OS is an operating system for your ESP32 and ESP8266 capable of running a constrained subset of the JavaScript language on microcontrollers. This is similar to MicroPython running a subset of Python on microcontrollers. Since JavaScript is the most popular development language for web applications it makes sense that when using device to cloud interfacing JavaScript can be a suitable choice if you would like to keep things consistent.

Mongoose offers other services for microcontrollers, like over the air updates (OTA) and paid services as well. For this chapter we will just focus on the standard functionality of programming microcontrollers with a JavaScript program capable of connecting and sending JSON IoT data payloads to the AWS message broker.

Another nice feature of Mongoose OS is that it handles device security for you without the developer manually having to configure the JavaScript program with security credentials. Mongoose uses your AWS CLI to create device certificates and an IoT policy in your AWS account. Mongoose OS then provisions your AWS security certificates onto the ESP device automatically. Because of this clever automation you never actually see the certificates being created or embedded on your ESP device unless you go to AWS IoT Core and look for the security certificates.

In this chapter you can find the basic setup directions for Mongoose OS. For this section only of the book I am not going to provide you with instructions on how to set up and run Mongoose. The reason for this abeyance is not the authors insouciance, but rather that Mongoose OS has provided an excellent walk through of exactly how to accomplish this complete process that I could not improve upon. What I can provide is a modification of the basic Mongoose OS program to send IoT payloads to AWS IoT Core that are more suitable for the IoT projects we will be working on later in this book.

Mongoose OS provides an instructional for building and uploading a sample JavaScript application to your ESP device. After completing this configuration process there are two AWS specific steps to accomplish in a separate Mongoose tutorial which will allows Mongoose OS to embed AWS security certificates on your device and then upload a custom "metrics.js" JavaScript program to transmit a nested JSON formatted payload from your ESP device to AWS IoT. Finally, I will supply a custom Mongoose program to upload to your device which will provide a more suitable IoT payload.

You can download Mongoose OS here:

https://mongoose-os.com/

Upon starting the MOS application at the top of the MOS tool screen the GUI allows you to select the COM port that your ESP device is connected to as well as choose which ESP board you are developing on:

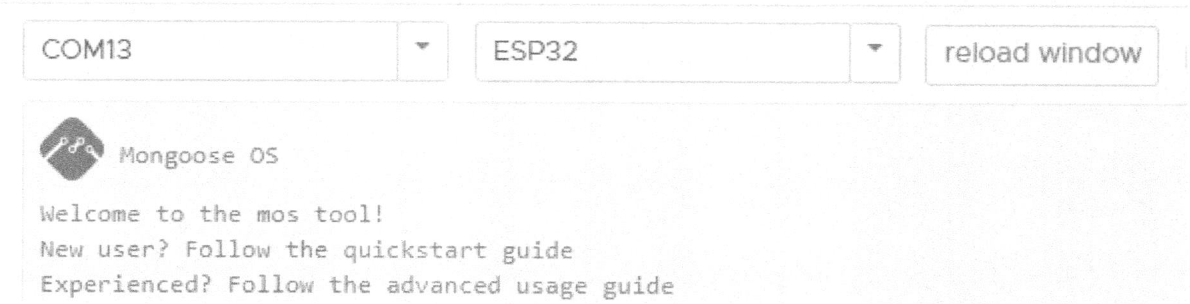
COM13
ESP32
reload window
Mongoose OS
Welcome to the mos tool!
New user? Follow the quickstart guide
Experienced? Follow the advanced usage guide

Unlike Arduino or MicroPython, the JavaScript code is exactly the same with either ESP MCU.

After starting the MOS tool follow steps 1-7 below, (you can do steps 8-10 later, as they are not essential).

https://mongoose-os.com/docs/mongoose-os/quickstart/setup.md

These steps show you how to:

1. Download and install MOS tool (*completed*)
2. Start the MOS tool (*completed*)
3. Install drivers for your ESP dev board (already completed if you used Arduino or MicroPython)
4. Create a new MOS app directory with the necessary files
5. Build the test program
6. Flash(upload) the test program to your device
7. Set up your WiFi credentials on the device

The next part of the walk-through provided by Mongoose is shorter and AWS IoT specific. After you complete the seven steps above in the "*Mongoose Quickstart Guide*", you can proceed below. So far you may have noticed that none of the instructions above were AWS specific, nor did they use the AWS CLI.

The next few steps can be found here:

https://mongoose-os.com/docs/mongoose-os/cloud/aws.md

From the URL tutorial link above the step that uses the AWS CLI to construct your certificates is the following command:

```
mos aws-iot-setup -aws-region YOUR_AWS_REGION
```

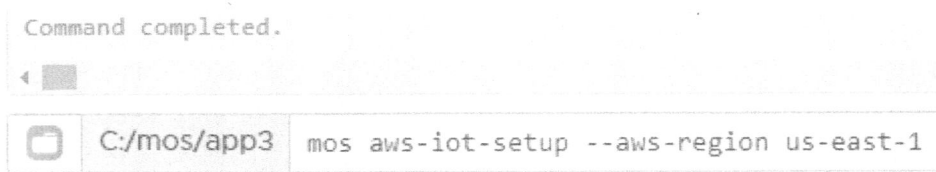

```
Command completed.
```

```
C:/mos/app3   mos aws-iot-setup --aws-region us-east-1
```

After using the AWS IoT setup command, you should see a dialog like this below:

```
AWS region: us-east-1
```

```
Attaching policy "mos-default" to the certificate...
Attaching the certificate to "esp32_E04C38"...
Writing certificate to aws-esp32_E04C38.crt.pem...
Uploading aws-esp32_E04C38.crt.pem (1139 bytes)...
Writing key to aws-esp32_E04C38.key.pem...
Uploading aws-esp32_E04C38.key.pem (227 bytes)...

Updating config:
  aws.thing_name =
  mqtt.enable = true
  mqtt.server = a3456789oyees-ats.iot.us-east-1.amazonaws.com:8883
  mqtt.ssl_ca_cert = ca.pem
  mqtt.ssl_cert = aws-esp32_E04C38.crt.pem
  mqtt.ssl_key = aws-esp32_E04C38.key.pem
```

Now that the certificates are created, and a "mos-default" IoT policy has also been created and attached to the certificates, the demonstration program will start sending IoT payloads to the AWS message broker. Mongoose OS provides this demonstration program called "init.js" that sends nested JSON payloads to the AWS message broker in your AWS account. The published topic is for several device shadows but for you to see the messages, just go to the MQTT test client on AWS IoT Core and 'Subscribe' to *"$aws/things/#"*, *"$aw/things/#/shadow/get/accepted"*, or just "#".

At this point the demonstration program *'init.js'* is running and AWS MQTT test client console looks like the image below whilst receiving messages:

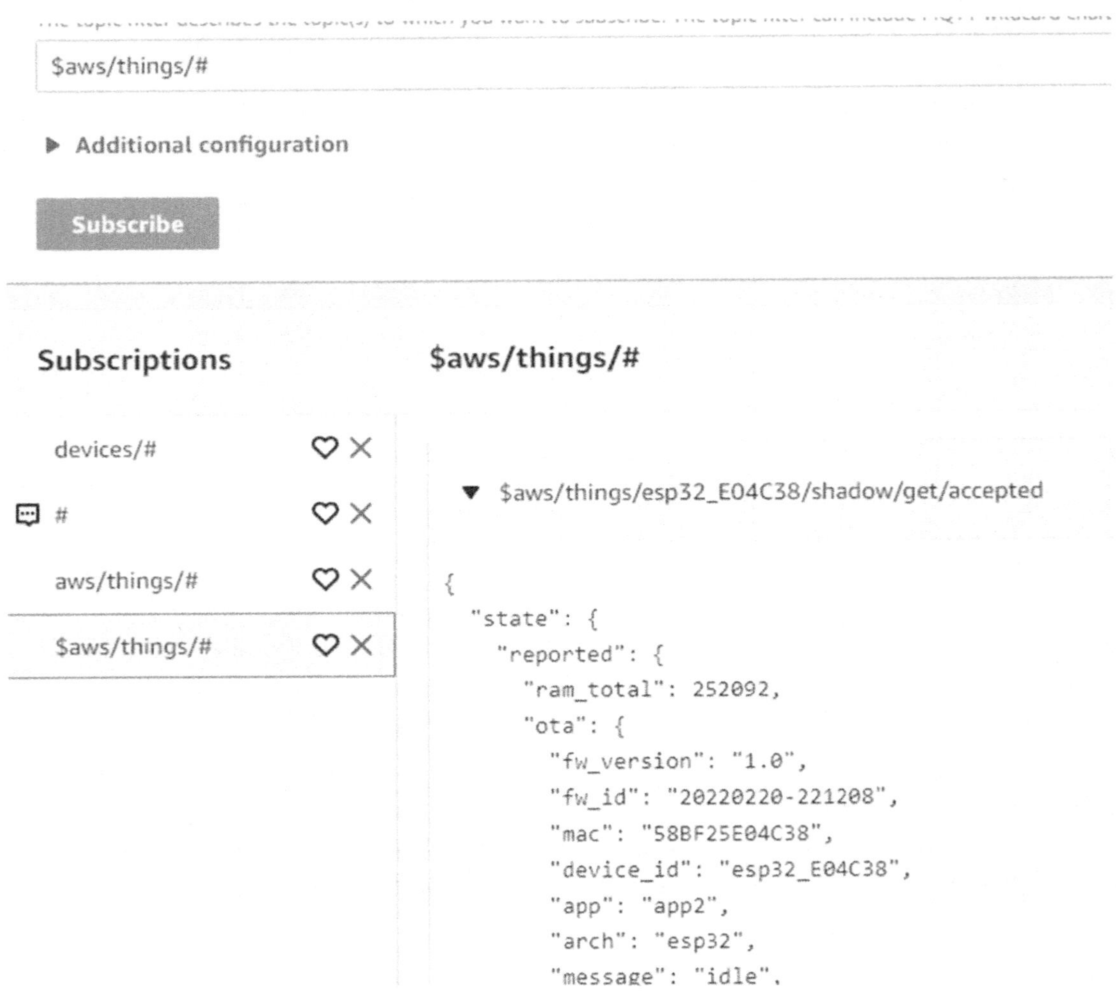
$aws/things/#
Additional configuration
Subscribe
Subscriptions
$aws/things/#
devices/#
#
aws/things/#
$aws/things/#
$aws/things/esp32_E04C38/shadow/get/accepted
{
"state": {
"reported": {
"ram_total": 252092,
"ota": {
"fw_version": "1.0",
"fw_id": "20220220-221208",
"mac": "58BF25E04C38",
"device_id": "esp32_E04C38",
"app": "app2",
"arch": "esp32",
"message": "idle",

As a side note this “state…reported” nested JSON format is required for AWS device shadows.

You can see that the MOS tool sets up the IoT device by configuring the device specifically for your AWS account. You can inspect the new “Thing” group that the MOS tool created by going to:

AWS IoT Core→Manage→All Devices→Things

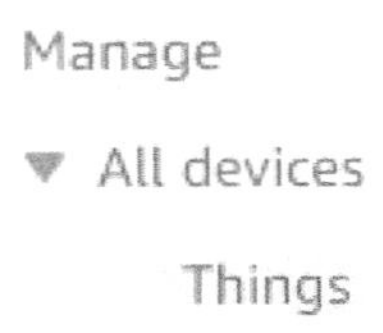
Manage
All devices
Things

This “Thing” group includes all three of your security certificates and enables device shadows.

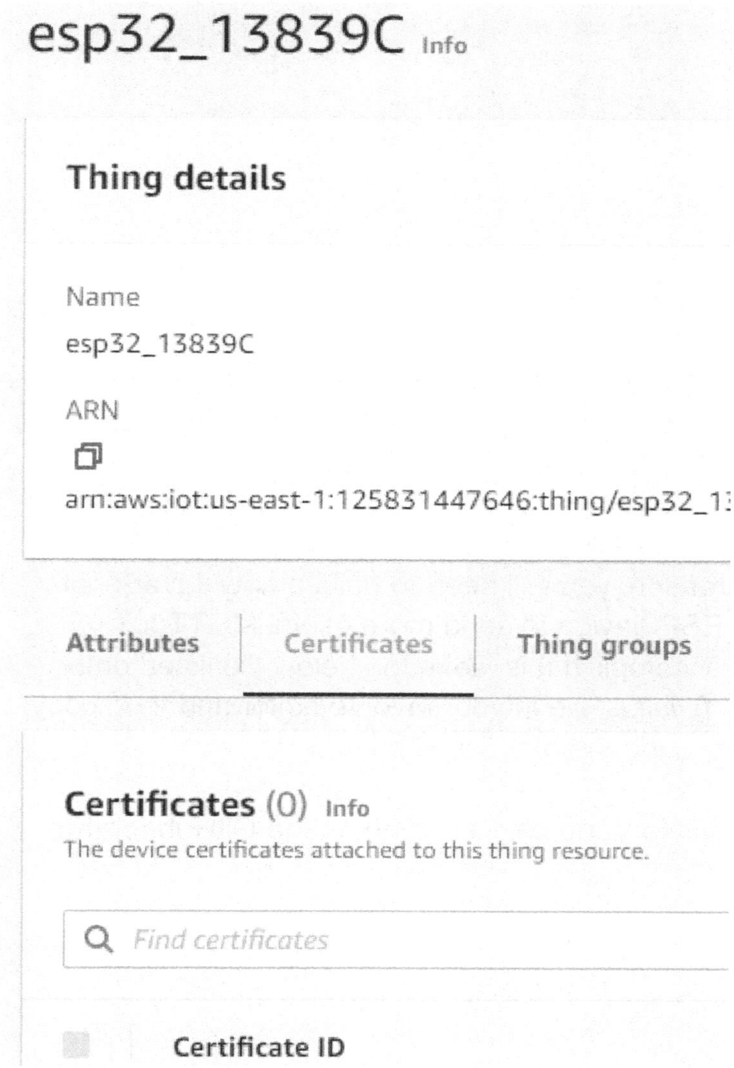
esp32_13839C Info
Thing details
Name
esp32_13839C
ARN
arn:aws:iot:us-east-1:125831447646:thing/esp32_1
Attributes
Certificates
Thing groups
Certificates (0) Info
The device certificates attached to this thing resource.
Find certificates
Certificate ID

You will also notice if you examine the newly created certificates in your account that the MOS tool created and attached an IoT AWS policy to your certificates called “mos-default”, this policy grants full IoT permissions.

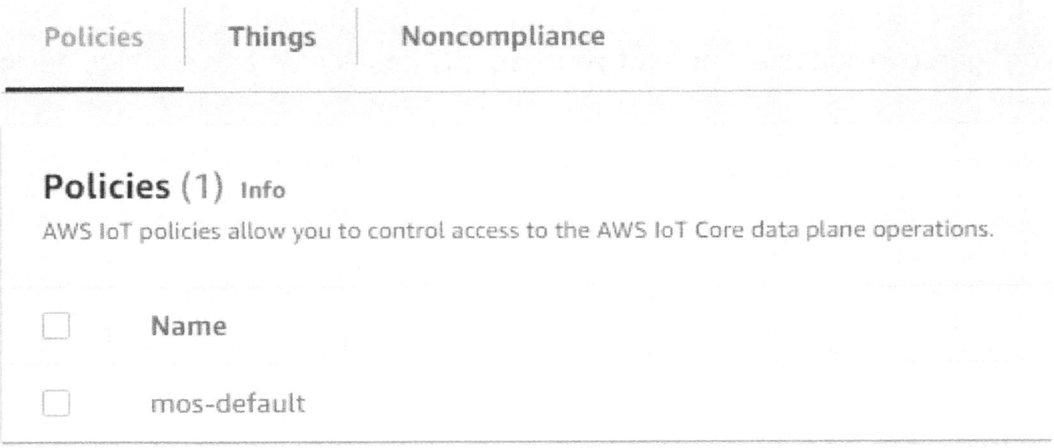
Policies
Things
Noncompliance
Policies (1) Info
AWS IoT policies allow you to control access to the AWS IoT Core data plane operations.
Name
mos-default

Most of the work is already done for you by following these easy to implement steps supplied by Mongoose. However, the demo program that is provided by Mongoose is not a suitable for the projects in this book. For the projects in the following chapters, you will want to publish a non-nested, simplified JSON payload with variable values that can be used by the AWS services that you will be utilizing through AWS IoT Core. For this reason, you will need to build a new JavaScript program and then flash it to your ESP device to send more useful MQTT IoT messages to AWS IoT Core. To accomplish this, save the below file listed onto your device. To do this open the *‘fs/init.js’* file in your favorite editor and then copy and paste the following code overwriting the old *“init.js”* code.

The correctly formatted modified ‘init.js’ code can be found on the GitHub for the chapter as well.

```
load(‘api_config.js’);
load(‘api_gpio.js’);
load(‘api_mqtt.js’);
load(‘api_net.js’);
load(‘api_sys.js’);
load(‘api_timer.js’);
load(‘api_math.js’); //for Math.random

let pubTopic = ‘iot/outTopic’;
let subTopic = ‘iot/inTopic’;


Timer.set(2000 /* milliseconds */, Timer.REPEAT, function() {
  let message = JSON.stringify({ ‘temperature’: Math.random() * 130,
```

```
                                  'humidity':      Math.random() * 100,
                                  'timestamps':   Timer.fmt('%H:%M:%S',
Timer.now()),
                                  'device_ID' :   Cfg.get('device.id')
                                  });
  let ok = MQTT.pub(pubTopic, message, 1);
  print('Published:', ok);

  print('The Time is:', Timer.fmt('%H:%M:%S', Timer.now()));
}, null);


MQTT.sub(subTopic, function(conn,subTopic, message2) {
   print('Got message:', message2);
}, null);
```

- Make sure to keep the file name as "*init.js*"

Copy the new code above and save it as '*init.js*' in the 'fs' folder. Now you only need to complete two more steps, as the previous eight steps are already configured by setting up and executing the previous '*init.js*' file. After you overwrite the old '*init.js*' file with the new code above execute these two commands below in the MOS console:

```
mos put fs/init.js
```

C:/mos/app1
mos put fs/init.js

```
mos call Sys.Reboot
```

C:/mos/app1
mos call Sys.Reboot

These two commands should be sufficient to upload and then reinitialize the code on your ESP device. After these two steps are executed, the device should automatically start sending the customized IoT payloads from the modified JavaScript program.

In the AWS IoT Core console go back to the MQTT test client and on the "Subscription topic" field, enter "iot/outTopic" or simply "#" and then click "Subscribe to topic".

Now observe the new messages coming into the MQTT test client susbscription pane:

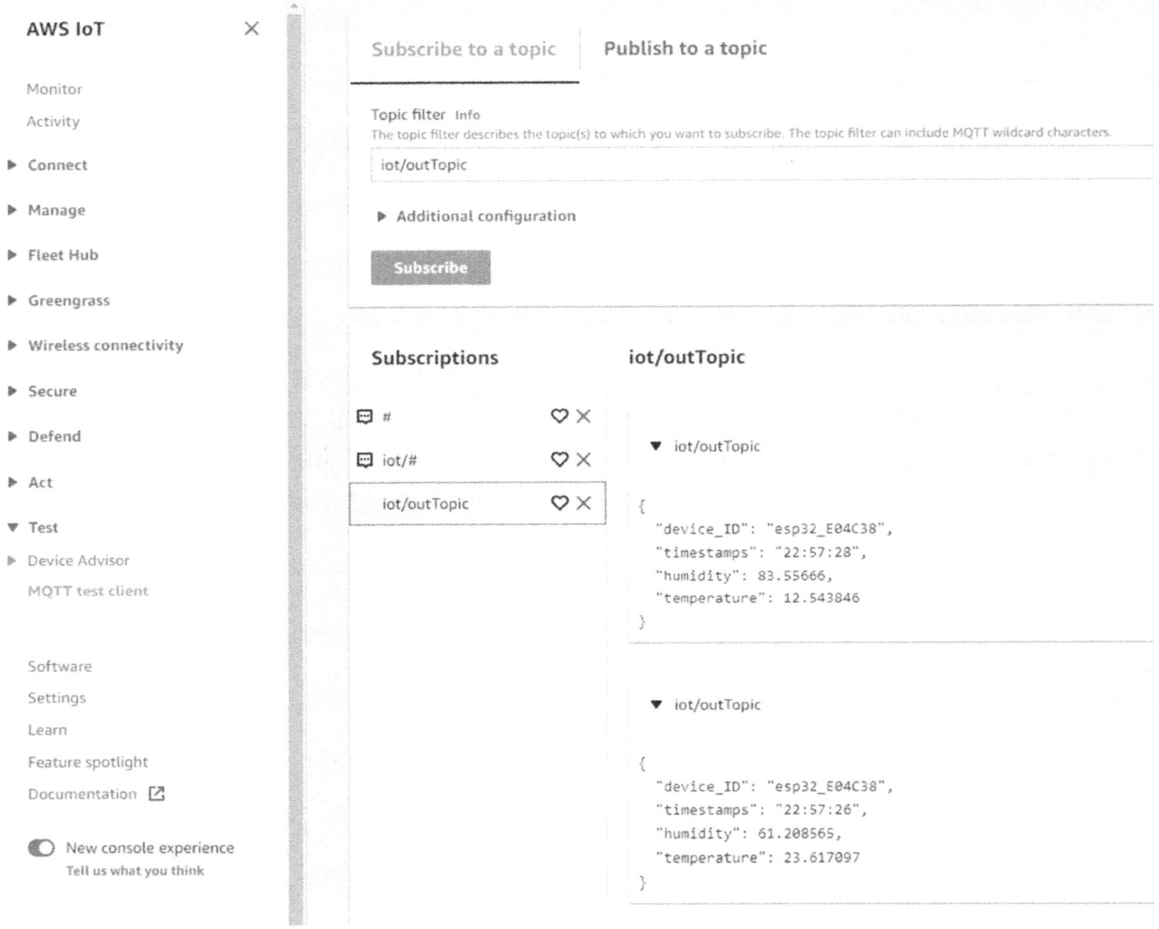

AWS IoT
Monitor
Activity
Connect
Manage
Fleet Hub
Greengrass
Wireless connectivity
Secure
Defend
Act
Test
Device Advisor
MQTT test client
Software
Settings
Learn
Feature spotlight
Documentation
New console experience
Tell us what you think
Subscribe to a topic
Publish to a topic
Topic filter Info
The topic filter describes the topic(s) to which you want to subscribe. The topic filter can include MQTT wildcard characters.
iot/outTopic
Additional configuration
Subscribe
Subscriptions
#
iot/#
iot/outTopic
iot/outTopic
iot/outTopic
{
"device_ID": "esp32_E04C38",
"timestamps": "22:57:28",
"humidity": 83.55666,
"temperature": 12.543846
}
iot/outTopic
{
"device_ID": "esp32_E04C38",
"timestamps": "22:57:26",
"humidity": 61.208565,
"temperature": 23.617097
}

Congratulations, you have successfully used the MOS tool to upload your JavaScript code to your ESP32 or ESP8266 device, configure AWS security certificates with an IoT policy, and send IoT payloads from your ESP device to AWS IoT Core with a modified "*init.js*" program.

Don't forget to explore the Mongoose OS GitHub for more IoT examples and projects you can use with your ESP device and AWS. You can check out the

Mongoose GitHub for sensor libraries and additional code examples from the links of this chapters GitHub page.

Chapter 7 -
Programming the Raspberry Pi with the AWS IoT Device SDK in Python

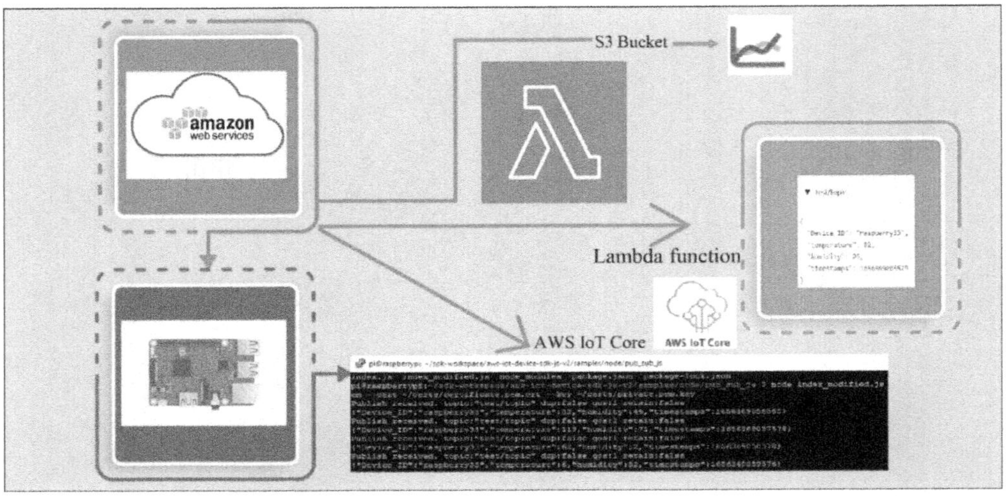

S3 Bucket
amazon web services
Lambda function
AWS IoT Core
AWS IoT Core

The AWS IoT Device SDKs helps you quickly and easily connect your Raspberry Pi to AWS. The SDKs include open-source libraries, developer guides with samples, and porting guides so that you can build innovative IoT products or solutions on your choice of hardware platforms. The SDKs currently come in five flavors: Java, JavaScript, Python, C++, and Embedded C. The most popular and easy to work with IoT Device SDKs are the ones using the higher-level languages of Python and JavaScript.

When comparing the Raspberry Pi to the ESP32 or ESP8266 the biggest distinction is that the Rpi is a powerful single board computer (SBC), with an application processor, and a full operating system. This contrasts with the ESP32 and ESP8266 which both have a less powerful Microcontroller (MCU), with a limited OS, and thus are unable to run the AWS SDK's. There are pros and cons to each system related to capability, cost, power consumption, programmability, and the ability to interface with larger systems. Understanding how to integrate both types of devices, embedded and SBCs, with AWS provides maximum flexibility when solving IoT device to cloud integration challenges.

$

Requirements to run the AWS IoT Device SDKs:$

$

- Raspberry Pi 3 Model B or more recent model. This might work on earlier versions of the Raspberry Pi, but they have not been tested.
- Raspberry Pi OS (32-bit) or later installed. AWS recommends using the latest version of the Raspberry Pi OS. Earlier versions of the OS might work, but they have not been tested.

  $

Much of the instructions in this chapter are taken from AWS documentation for the Raspberry Pi. I have modified the AWS instructions as needed for our use case.

Further AWS reference for using the AWS IoT SDK for Python version 2 on the Raspberry Pi can be found here:

https://github.com/aws/aws-iot-device-sdk-python-v2/blob/main/documents/PREREQUISITES.md

$

https://github.com/aws/aws-iot-device-sdk-python-v2

Raspberry Pi
AWS IoT Core

$

$

Step 1 – Install the AWS IoT SDK for Python Version 2
Step 2 – Configure the Security Certificates on the Raspberry Pi
Step 3 – Run the Python MQTT pubsub.py Program to Publish Messages to AWS IoT Core
Step 4 – Modify and Run the pubsub.py Program to Deliver Custom IoT Payloads to AWS IoT Core

---

Step 1 – Install the AWS IoT SDK for Python Version 2

AWS provides instructions on how to install all the prerequisite tools on the Raspberry Pi before you get started with a basic test program. The best method for learning is to get the simple string message test program from the SDK working ("pubsub.py") and then move on to using a customized Python program that will better meet the requirements for the projects in this book. Also note the documentation and the setup is slightly different between the official AWS online documentation and the AWS GitHub documentation for the SDKs. Always follow the GitHub documentation when sufficient, as it contains the latest changes.

Before you install the AWS IoT Device SDK and sample code, make sure your system is up-to-date and has the required tools and libraries to install the SDKs. Also make sure your Rpi device can connect to Wfi by editing the "wpa_supplicant.conf" file on the device so it knows the WiFi network name and password to automatically connect. Again, follow the following steps at:

```
lxxtw>33kmxlyf2gsq 3e{ w3e{ w1hsx1hizmgi1who1t}xlsr1z6'Mrwxepexmsr$
$
$
```

AWS dynamically updates this document, so it is the best source for current information. From your home directory on the Raspberry Pi create a workspace directory:

```
mkdir sdk-workspace
cd sdk-workspace
```

Clone the Python IoT Device SDK repository into that folder:

```
git clone https://github.com/aws/aws-iot-device-sdk-python-v2.git
```

Install the SDK using '*pip*':

```
python3 -m pip install ./aws-iot-device-sdk-python-v2
```

The '*sdk-workspace*' directory should now contain the Python SDK:

```
pi@raspberrypi: ~/sdk-workspace
pi@raspberrypi:~/sdk-workspace $ dir
aws-iot-device-sdk-js-v2  aws-iot-device-sdk-python-v2
```

The steps outlined on the GitHub installation are:

A) Set up your device (complete)
B) Install the required tools and libraries for the AWS IoT Device SDK (complete)
C) Install AWS IoT Device SDK (complete)
D) Upload Security certificates (covered in Step 2)
E) Install and run the sample app (covered in Step 3)
F) View messages from the sample app in the AWS IoT console (covered in Step 3)
G) Modify and upload the sample app (covered in Step 4)
H) View messages from the modified sample app in the AWS IoT console (covered in Step 4)

Step 2 – Configure the Security Certificates on the Raspberry Pi

The sample app requires the AWS security certificate files to be installed onto the Rpi. I will cover this section separately from the AWS provided documentation because it is important that it is done correctly, and the provided screenshots should be helpful. To install the security certificate files, create a 'certs' subdirectory from your Rpi home directory by running these commands:

```
cd ~
mkdir certs
```

In the newly created ~/certs directory, copy the private key, client/device certificate, and root CA certificate that have been kept on your PC. If you have changed the name of the AWS security certificates that is fine, just make sure you modify the names below to your own names for the relevant certificates.

You may have to use the 'sudo' command from the command line if you don't have the required permissions to write files to your Raspberry Pi:

https://raspberry-projects.com/pi/command-line/sudo

```
pi@raspberrypi:~ $ dir
                          Desktop    node_modules        sdk-workspace
                          Documents  package-lock.json   Templates
Bookshelf                 Downloads  Pictures            Videos
certs                     Music      Public
pi@raspberrypi:~ $
```

$

Which method you use to copy the security certificate files to your device depends on your PC and your operating system. In my case I just work through an ethernet connection to the Rpi using a command prompt from the free "Putty" SSH tool. I am also using the free "FileZilla" FTP program. I use the built-in editor 'Nano' on the Rpi to edit files as needed for small modifications.

Below is an image of using my Raspberry Pi's IP address to connect to FileZilla. I attained my Rpi Ipv4 address by just typing in "ifconing" on my Rpi after I logged in to the device on Putty.

$

$

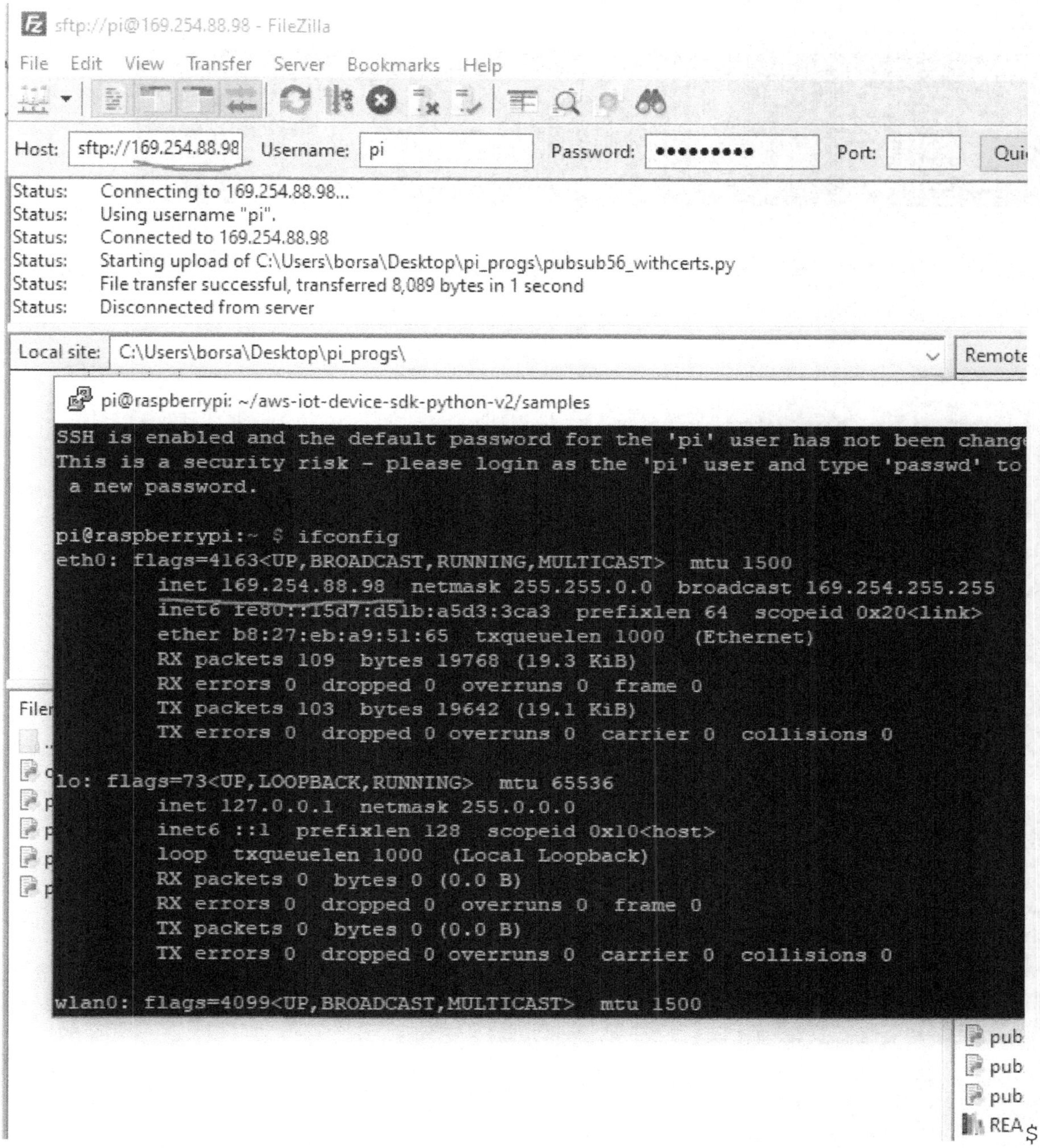
sftp://pi@169.254.88.98 - FileZilla
File Edit View Transfer Server Bookmarks Help
Host: sftp://169.254.88.98 Username: pi Password: •••••••••• Port:
Status: Connecting to 169.254.88.98...
Status: Using username "pi".
Status: Connected to 169.254.88.98
Status: Starting upload of C:\Users\borsa\Desktop\pi_progs\pubsub56_withcerts.py
Status: File transfer successful, transferred 8,089 bytes in 1 second
Status: Disconnected from server
Local site: C:\Users\borsa\Desktop\pi_progs\
pi@raspberrypi: ~/aws-iot-device-sdk-python-v2/samples
SSH is enabled and the default password for the 'pi' user has not been chang
This is a security risk - please login as the 'pi' user and type 'passwd' to
a new password.
pi@raspberrypi:~ $ ifconfig
eth0: flags=4163<UP,BROADCAST,RUNNING,MULTICAST> mtu 1500
inet 169.254.88.98 netmask 255.255.0.0 broadcast 169.254.255.255
ether b8:27:eb:a9:51:65 txqueuelen 1000 (Ethernet)
RX packets 109 bytes 19768 (19.3 KiB)
RX errors 0 dropped 0 overruns 0 frame 0
TX packets 103 bytes 19642 (19.1 KiB)
TX errors 0 dropped 0 overruns 0 carrier 0 collisions 0
lo: flags=73<UP,LOOPBACK,RUNNING> mtu 65536
inet 127.0.0.1 netmask 255.0.0.0
inet6 ::1 prefixlen 128 scopeid 0x10<host>
loop txqueuelen 1000 (Local Loopback)
RX packets 0 bytes 0 (0.0 B)
RX errors 0 dropped 0 overruns 0 frame 0
TX packets 0 bytes 0 (0.0 B)
TX errors 0 dropped 0 overruns 0 carrier 0 collisions 0
wlan0: flags=4099<UP,BROADCAST,MULTICAST> mtu 1500

$

$

$

I save my certificates to my Rpi by opening the built-in “nano” editor and then copy/paste in each of the three certificates alphanumeric values.

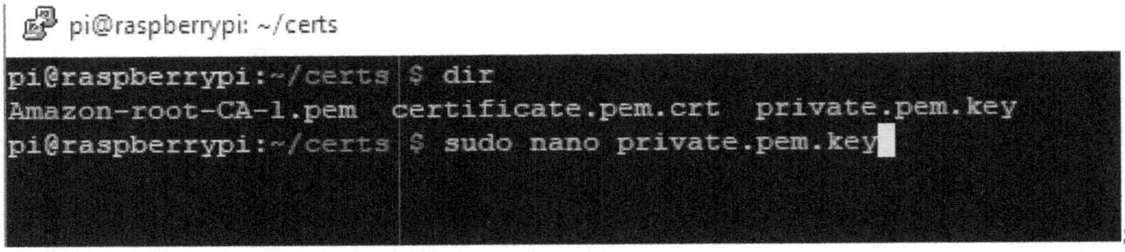
pi@raspberrypi: ~/certs
pi@raspberrypi:~/certs $ dir
Amazon-root-CA-1.pem certificate.pem.crt private.pem.key
pi@raspberrypi:~/certs $ sudo nano private.pem.key

$

Here is a semi-obfuscated image of my private key being pasted in:

$

pi@raspberrypi: ~/certs
GNU nano 3.2
private.pem.key
-----BEGIN RSA PRIVATE KEY-----
J1ZC7vhsPboUME1OnUrdx6M4rsD4ehO
LF3FjEnSG
+LmJg6gY1BsPJwqGZa9wE5mqLq
biX7bDkuM5Q6qOijV7f6ISb
NqKfVFaA3AD4CNytyWydjuDjPL9mf
00ESoPxgOROoOhkXTeA9vvL9RI8rFnLesjyTJTQaTWtLxpyoTdlobS9PtnT6YDBC
JuLNXwTGs/smaZjowTQDOt2qE3+lw3c5n9ojL+/EKJECRVgJCGP+pY/P6pX0oral
56x94kKKpTMcx8Vpar/3X0bN9116ikDMCQtZLwIDAQABAoIBACedVAoQ1RXtJR18
H3HIRJ20U11XZvZERy8EQvkVEsudNactcQ0smfszpYQxE+jWoJe7isvyZRFkvmSy
GzoZjbyNGTxTTT1ASBrA5qQ8dWo9IjURaMSG4pdqE061B24734KWjyFRPQOr2xah
+FdRkD4bBDygR19bMgN2+xE/4EXHzZcPmFgwJEdvmf6/bXob24cbp2aldRIhNtP/
MluGcy6rv02X/0FC6wXTWgaELnuabHF7hLwDweEsDPBicVnWkDUoLv1BYYbNAEQ3
qH3fT9O6I68y3ZYX3piD5tRDFZ7Mjh4Z6NbA3b01Vs8YXfc2zumxJ1GGzCTTclwa
3iCI5SkCgYEA9+m8M27nmAPfN1U7OQW4SmZvam5I9jjzj4YefWmg2EHSKQX6eNio
jE1GybYiFTBKB0hSLEDg/f+MZnVCStrlzBHI4W8Gc/81tOK6AXqrjN673Gu/y+C6
y9kwRA9JicMohela8FlyLHcTx/LCSQ0BQ9noXzbCU64/hS0rOjprr3UCgYEA8Af+
8+Fqf40kGUO8SGNEFti+1VS5b8dpnmyMx4nj+3+iQhylugg11zF3L/0derTnrTXk
9O0rgUi8DtI1EgKiSYwWwiN7GTIFeh8P2szrWFbL0Dx454Y0kVzk8WLpVXHYucIf
543lov3H61zUDINw61AopC0NmJ483LvyhMdtFZMCgYEAnnrt05dXN4dqHsqXhF1S
uUUIfmon/DbmBF8BiLyI1RZmqdDnkG84OA3z0ai72v22pTcnSKDk85p0f18AVOfg
[Read 27 lines]
^G Get Help
^O Write Out
^W Where Is
^K Cut Text
^J Justify
^C Cur Pos
^X Exit
^R Read File
^\ Replace
^U Uncut Text
^T To Spell
^_ Go To Line

$

After each certificate is pasted into the editor then use CNTR+X to exit nano, then use ‘y’ to confirm to save each certificate.

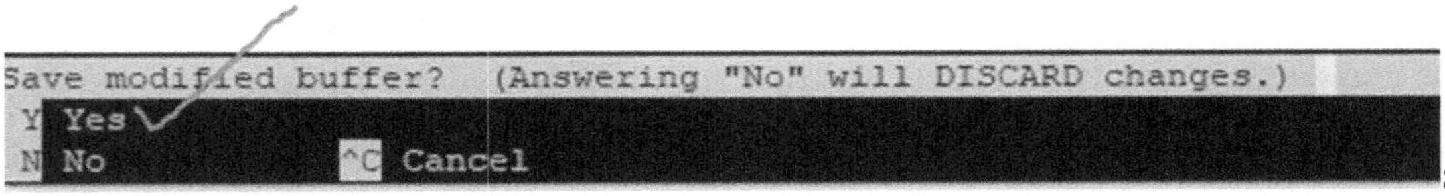
Save modified buffer? (Answering "No" will DISCARD changes.)
Y Yes
N No
^C Cancel

The commands in the next section assume that your security certificate files are stored on the Rpi device to the location and name shown on this table:

Certificate file names

File	File path
Root CA certificate	~/certs/Amazon-root-CA-1.pem
Device certificate	~/certs/certificate.pem.crt
Private key	~/certs/private.pem.key

$

It doesn't matter what you call your certificates, just keep the names consistent when you issue commands from your Rpi command prompt.

```
pi@raspberrypi:~/certs $ dir
Amazon-root-CA-1.pem  certificate.pem.crt  private.pem.key
pi@raspberrypi:~/certs $
```

$

Instead of using the built-in "nano" editor on the device, you can use a UTF-8 editor of your choice on your computer and then use Filezilla to transfer the security certificates to your Rpi. I find using FileZilla with an editor on my PC to be an easier method when editing files while using the RPI "heedlessly" rather than in a desktop configuration.

Step 3 – Run the Python MQTT pubsub.py Program to Publish to AWS IoT Core

$

$

To install and run the sample pubsub.py app, navigate to the sample's directory on your Rpi:

pi@raspberrypi:~/sdk-workspace/aws-iot-device-sdk-python-v2/samples

To run the sample "pubsub.py" program, you will need your AWS IoT endpoint. To find your IoT endpoint go to:

AWS IoT Core→ Settings:

AWS IoT
Settings

Or using the AWS CLI Command:

```
aws iot describe-endpoint -endpoint-type iot:Data-ATS
```

$

The argument parser from the command line will take in your account specifics and include them in the 'pubsub.py' program AWS provides in the Python IoT Device SDK. To run the sample program with your security certificates and endpoint simply enter the following command at the Rpi's command prompt from the samples folder after you insert your own AWS IoT endpoint and certificate names:

```
python3 pubsub.py -endpoint <Your-AWS-IoT-Endpoint> --ca_file ~/certs/Amazon-root-CA-1.pem -cert ~/certs/certificate.pem.crt -key ~/certs/private.pem.key
```

After entering the command above on your Rpi's command prompt, you should observe the following results:

$

Connected!
Subscribing to topic 'test/topic'...
Subscribed with QoS.AT_LEAST_ONCE
Sending 10 message(s)
Publishing message to topic 'test/topic': Hello World! [1]
Received message from topic 'test/topic': b'"Hello World! [1]"'
Publishing message to topic 'test/topic': Hello World! [2]
Received message from topic 'test/topic': b'"Hello World! [2]"'
Publishing message to topic 'test/topic': Hello World! [3]
Received message from topic 'test/topic': b'"Hello World! [3]"'
Publishing message to topic 'test/topic': Hello World! [4]

$

$

$

Ensure that the sample '*pubsub.py'* program:

A) Connects to the AWS IoT message broker for your account.
B) Publishes 10 messages to the topic: test/topic.
C) Displays output like the following if you subscribe to "#" on the MQTT test client.

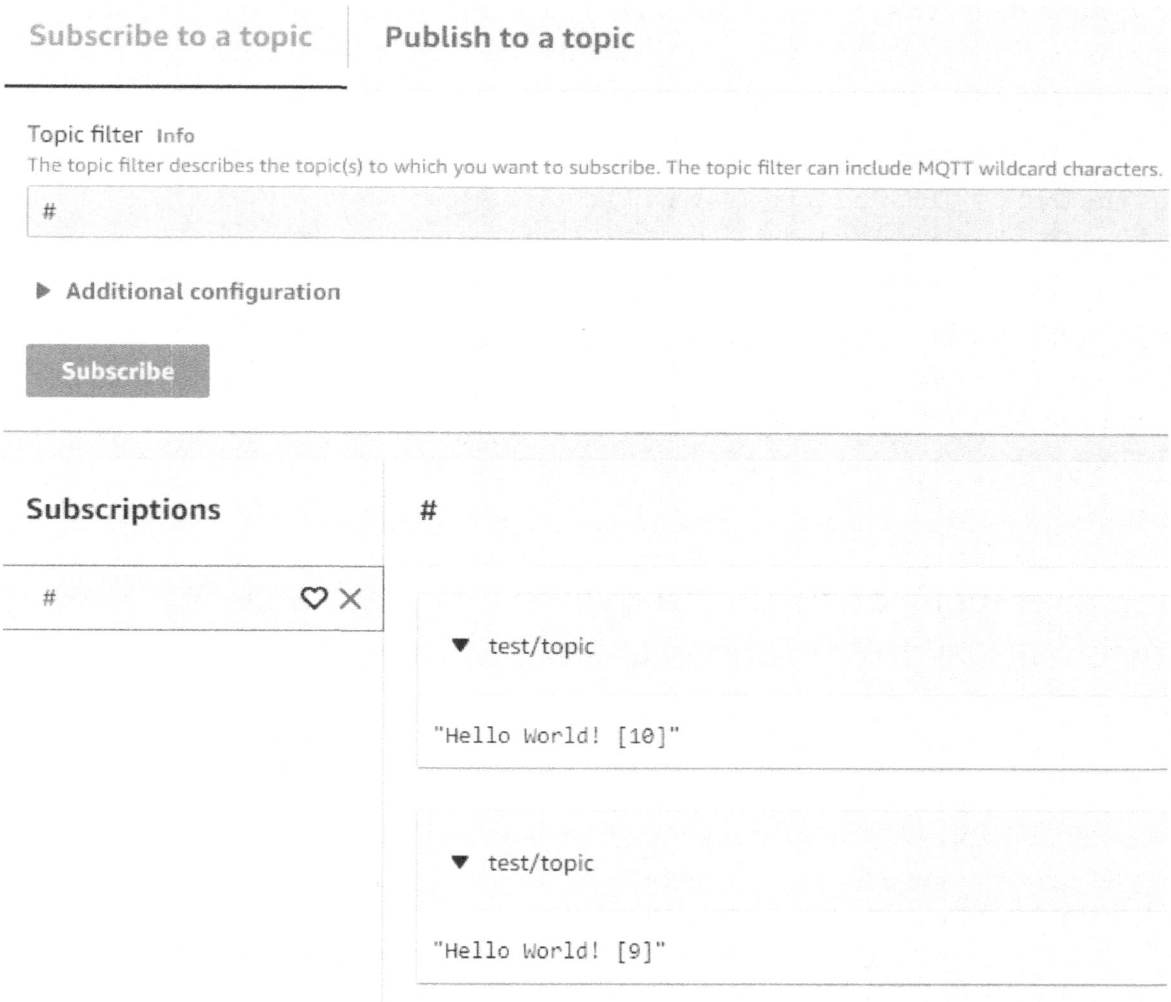
Subscribe to a topic
Publish to a topic
Topic filter Info
The topic filter describes the topic(s) to which you want to subscribe. The topic filter can include MQTT wildcard characters.
#
Additional configuration
Subscribe
Subscriptions
#
#
test/topic
"Hello World! [10]"
test/topic
"Hello World! [9]"

Now you should examine the “pubsub.py” program and see if you can figure out exactly how it works. The first thing to understand is that if you look closely at the ‘pubsub.py’ program, the IoT payload transmission message is nowhere in the actual program. So where is the MQTT topic – ‘test/topic’ declared? Where is the “Hello World” string that gets published to AWS IoT Core originating from? The answer is that these parameters are coming from another file called “command_line_utils.py” which is located in the same directory as the “pubsub.py” program:

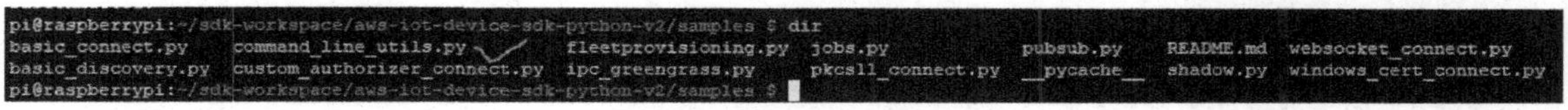
pi@raspberrypi:~/sdk-workspace/aws-iot-device-sdk-python-v2/samples $ dir
basic_connect.py command_line_utils.py fleetprovisioning.py jobs.py pubsub.py README.md websocket_connect.py
basic_discovery.py custom_authorizer_connect.py ipc_greengrass.py pkcs11_connect.py __pycache__ shadow.py windows_cert_connect.py
pi@raspberrypi:~/sdk-workspace/aws-iot-device-sdk-python-v2/samples $

If you want to see where the arguments are inherited in the "pubsub.py" program from the external program "command_line_utils.py" look on lines 82 and 83 of the code:

```
message_topic = cmdUtils.get_command(cmdUtils.m_cmd_topic)
message_string = cmdUtils.get_command(cmdUtils.m_cmd_message)
```

Good work, now that you have the basic messaging program working on your Rpi, you can now modify the 'pubsub.py' program to better reflect the requirements going forward with a more suitable IoT payload to send MQTT messages to AWS IoT Core.

$

$

Step 4 – Modify and Run the Python Program to Deliver Custom JSON IoT Payloads to AWS IoT Core

$

$

To modify the 'pubsub.py' program to best fit the projects in this book you must add in the needed variables to the outgoing IoT payload and then generate some random sensor values for those variables. You have two options as to where to make this JSON IoT payload modification. You can either modify the "command_line_utils.py" to deliver the modified JSON payload in lieu of the current simply string message of Hello World!," or you can modify the "pubsub.py" program by creating a variable containing the JSON payload, and simply overwrite the inherited external message. I choose to do the later as I believe it is better programming practice to leave constants and settings in the header file, "command_line_utils.py", and change the dynamic variables in the implementation file, which is this case is "pubsub.py".

You can do this payload modification in the loop section of the Python code by adding the variables in JSON format into the Python "pubsub.py" program as shown below:

$

```
    while (publish_count <= message_count) or (message_count == 0):
        data = {
            "temperature": random.randint(0, 130),
            "humidity": random.randint(0, 100),
            "timestamps": int(time.time())
```

```
}
```

After you generate the JSON IoT payload it is formatted for the MQTT publish function and then included in the dispatch payload to publish to AWS IoT Core:

```
message_json = json.dumps(data)
mqtt_connection.publish(
    topic= "iot/rpi",
    payload=message_json,
    qos=mqtt.QoS.AT_LEAST_ONCE)
```

As you may have noticed I overwrote the inherited topic from "test/topic" to "iot/rpi".

You can also set the message count designator to 0 so that the loop runs forever, or until you manually stop the program (use CTRL+Z). You can also set the iterations to whatever number you like (line 28 of the program).

```
$
cmdUtils.register_command("count", "<int>", "The number of messages to send
(optional, default='10').", default=0, type=int)
$
```

Finally, you may wish to slow down the loop cycle so that the device sends fewer sensor readings than one per second by default. To change the message publishing frequency on the Rpi adjust the delay setting in the program:

```
$
time.sleep(1)
```

The code below adds in random values for the environmental sensor IoT payload in the while loop. To do this the "random" Python package has been imported into the program. The modified program is configured so that instead of 10 loops before it disconnects it loops forever. The time interval dictating the loop delay is also modified from one to three seconds. The code below has all the modifications mentioned above edited into the Python code. Copy the modified code below:

```
$
# Copyright Amazon.com, Inc. or its affiliates. All Rights Reserved.
# SPDX-License-Identifier: Apache-2.0.

from awscrt import mqtt
import sys
```

```
import threading
import time
from uuid import uuid4
import json
import random  # added to generate random numbers

# This sample uses the Message Broker for AWS IoT
# through an MQTT connection. On startup
# subscribes to a topic, and begins publishing messages
# The device should receive those same messages
# since it is subscribed to that same topic.

# Parse arguments
import command_line_utils;
cmdUtils = command_line_utils.CommandLineUtils("PubSub - Send and receive
messages through an MQTT connection.")
cmdUtils.add_common_mqtt_commands()
cmdUtils.add_common_topic_message_commands()
cmdUtils.add_common_proxy_commands()
cmdUtils.add_common_logging_commands()
cmdUtils.register_command("key", "<path>", "Path to your key in PEM format.",
True, str)
cmdUtils.register_command("cert", "<path>", "Path to your client certificate
in PEM format.", True, str)
cmdUtils.register_command("port", "<int>", "Connection port. AWS IoT supports
443 and 8883 (optional, default=auto).", type=int)
cmdUtils.register_command("client_id", "<str>", "Client ID to use for MQTT
connection (optional, default='test-*').", default="test-" + str(uuid4()))
#Set payload IoT publish to run indefinitely by using "default=0"
cmdUtils.register_command("count", "<int>", "The number of messages to send
(optional, default='10').", default=0, type=int)
# Needs to be called so the command utils parse the commands
cmdUtils.get_args()

received_count = 0
received_all_event = threading.Event()

# Callback when connection is accidentally lost.
Def on_connection_interrupted(connection, error, **kwargs):
    print("Connection interrupted. Error: {}".format(error))


# Callback when an interrupted connection is re-established.
Def on_connection_resumed(connection, return_code, session_present,
**kwargs):
```

```
    print("Connection resumed. Return_code: {} session_present:
{}".format(return_code, session_present))

    if return_code == mqtt.ConnectReturnCode.ACCEPTED and not
session_present:
        print("Session did not persist. Resubscribing to existing topics...")
        resubscribe_future, _ = connection.resubscribe_existing_topics()

        # Cannot synchronously wait for resubscribe result
        # Evaluate result with a callback instead.
        Resubscribe_future.add_done_callback(on_resubscribe_complete)


def on_resubscribe_complete(resubscribe_future):
        resubscribe_results = resubscribe_future.result()
        print("Resubscribe results: {}".format(resubscribe_results))

        for topic, qos in resubscribe_results['topics']:
            if qos is None:
                sys.exit("Server rejected resubscribe to topic:
{}".format(topic))


# Callback when the subscribed topic receives a message
def on_message_received(topic, payload, dup, qos, retain, **kwargs):
    print("Received message from topic '{}': {}".format(topic, payload))
    global received_count
    received_count += 1
    if received_count == cmdUtils.get_command("count"):
        received_all_event.set()

if __name__ == '__main__':
    mqtt_connection =
cmdUtils.build_mqtt_connection(on_connection_interrupted,
on_connection_resumed)

    print("Connecting to {} with client ID '{}'...".format(
        cmdUtils.get_command(cmdUtils.m_cmd_endpoint),
cmdUtils.get_command("client_id")))
    connect_future = mqtt_connection.connect()

    # Future.result() waits until a result is available
    connect_future.result()
    print("Connected!")
```

```
    message_count = cmdUtils.get_command("count")
    message_topic = cmdUtils.get_command(cmdUtils.m_cmd_topic)
    message_string = cmdUtils.get_command(cmdUtils.m_cmd_message)

    # Subscribe
    print("Subscribing to topic '{}'...".format(message_topic))
    subscribe_future, packet_id = mqtt_connection.subscribe(
        topic=message_topic,
        qos=mqtt.QoS.AT_LEAST_ONCE,
        callback=on_message_received)

    subscribe_result = subscribe_future.result()
    print("Subscribed with {}".format(str(subscribe_result['qos'])))

    # Publish message to server desired number of times.
    # This step is skipped if message is blank.
    # This step loops forever if count was set to 0.
    If message_string:
        if message_count == 0:
            print ("Sending messages until program killed")
        else:
            print ("Sending {} message(s)".format(message_count))

        publish_count = 1
        while (publish_count <= message_count) or (message_count == 0):
            data = {
                "temperature": random.randint(0, 130),
                "humidity": random.randint(0, 100),
                "timestamps": int(time.time())
                }

            message = "{} [{}]".format(message_string, publish_count)
            print("Publishing message to topic '{}': {}".format("iot/rpi",
data))
            message_json = json.dumps(data)
            mqtt_connection.publish(
                topic="iot/rpi",
                payload=message_json,
                qos=mqtt.QoS.AT_LEAST_ONCE)
            time.sleep(3)
            publish_count += 1

    # Wait for all messages to be received.
    # This waits forever if count was set to 0.
    If message_count != 0 and not received_all_event.is_set():
```

```
    print("Waiting for all messages to be received...")

received_all_event.wait()
print("{} message(s) received.".format(received_count))

# Disconnect
print("Disconnecting...")
disconnect_future = mqtt_connection.disconnect()
disconnect_future.result()
print("Disconnected!")
```

Save your new pubsub.py program as something like "myPubSub.py" on your Raspberry Pi to the same level in the filesystem hierarchy as the basic "pubsub.py" program in the samples folder. Again, you can either paste the code in manually using an editor like nano on your Rpi or edit the file locally on your computer and then transfer the new "myPubSub.py" program over to the samples folder on your Rpi by using FileZilla.

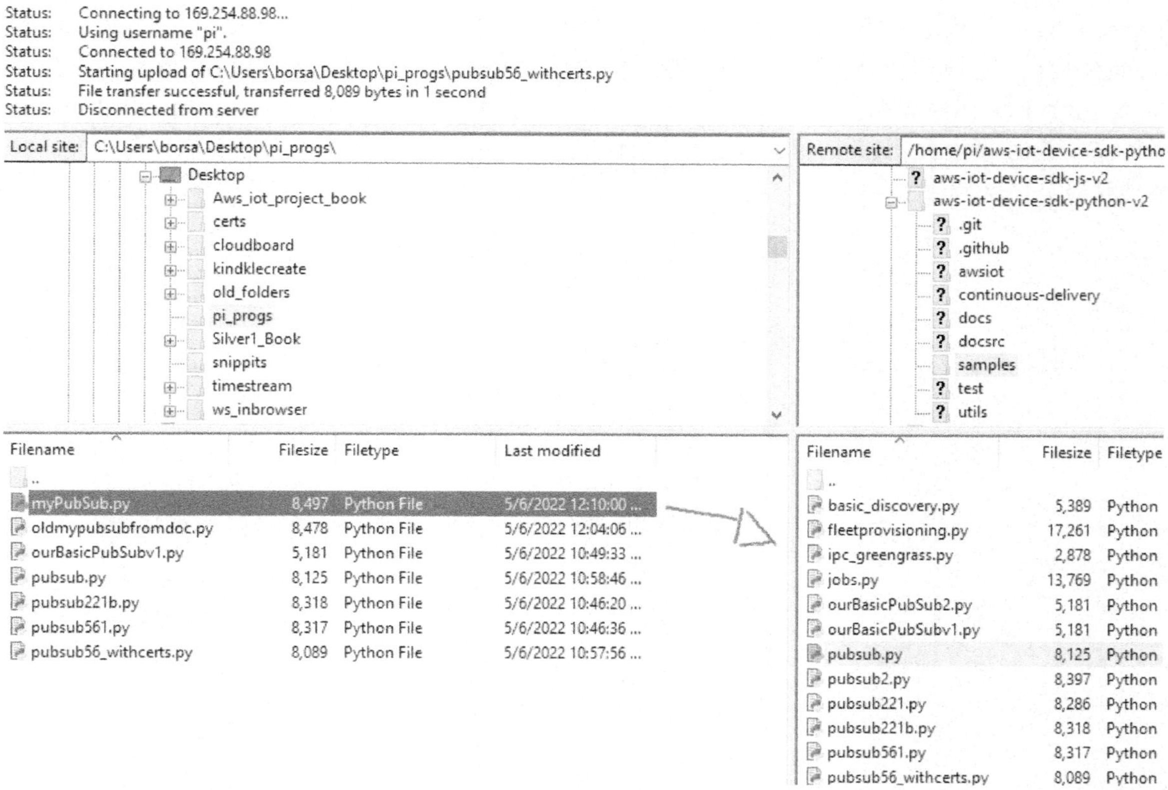

Status: Connecting to 169.254.88.98...
Status: Using username "pi".
Status: Connected to 169.254.88.98
Status: Starting upload of C:\Users\borsa\Desktop\pi_progs\pubsub56_withcerts.py
Status: File transfer successful, transferred 8,089 bytes in 1 second
Status: Disconnected from server
Local site: C:\Users\borsa\Desktop\pi_progs\
Desktop
Aws_iot_project_book
certs
cloudboard
kindklecreate
old_folders
pi_progs
Silver1_Book
snippits
timestream
ws_inbrowser
Filename Filesize Filetype Last modified
myPubSub.py 8,497 Python File 5/6/2022 12:10:00 ...
oldmypubsubfromdoc.py 8,478 Python File 5/6/2022 12:04:06 ...
ourBasicPubSubv1.py 5,181 Python File 5/6/2022 10:49:33 ...
pubsub.py 8,125 Python File 5/6/2022 10:58:46 ...
pubsub221b.py 8,318 Python File 5/6/2022 10:46:20 ...
pubsub561.py 8,317 Python File 5/6/2022 10:46:36 ...
pubsub56_withcerts.py 8,089 Python File 5/6/2022 10:57:56 ...
Remote site: /home/pi/aws-iot-device-sdk-pytho
aws-iot-device-sdk-js-v2
aws-iot-device-sdk-python-v2
.git
.github
awsiot
continuous-delivery
docs
docsrc
samples
test
utils
Filename Filesize Filetype
basic_discovery.py 5,389 Python
fleetprovisioning.py 17,261 Python
ipc_greengrass.py 2,878 Python
jobs.py 13,769 Python
ourBasicPubSub2.py 5,181 Python
ourBasicPubSubv1.py 5,181 Python
pubsub.py 8,125 Python
pubsub2.py 8,397 Python
pubsub221.py 8,286 Python
pubsub221b.py 8,318 Python
pubsub561.py 8,317 Python
pubsub56_withcerts.py 8,089 Python

Simply right click the file to upload it to your Rpi using FileZilla. Your new custom program is now on your Rpi in your samples folder. Navigate back to the 'samples' directory:

~/sdk-workspace/aws-iot-device-sdk-python-v2/samples

Then to run the new "myPubSub.py" program, insert your IoT endpoint, and use the following command at the command prompt from within the samples directory to execute the program:

```
python3 myPubSub.py -endpoint <Your-AWS-IoT-Endpoint> --ca_file
~/certs/Amazon-root-CA-1.pem -cert ~/certs/certificate.pem.crt -key
~/certs/private.pem.key
```

Executing the command will result in similar output as the Rpi runs indefinitely:

You can view the incoming payload result by using MQTT.fx if the tool is logged into your account with the proper security certificates and matching AWS region. You could also use the MQTT test client on IoT Core at the same time and it would work as well. The image below shows the program when monitored in AWS IoT Core on the MQTT test client:

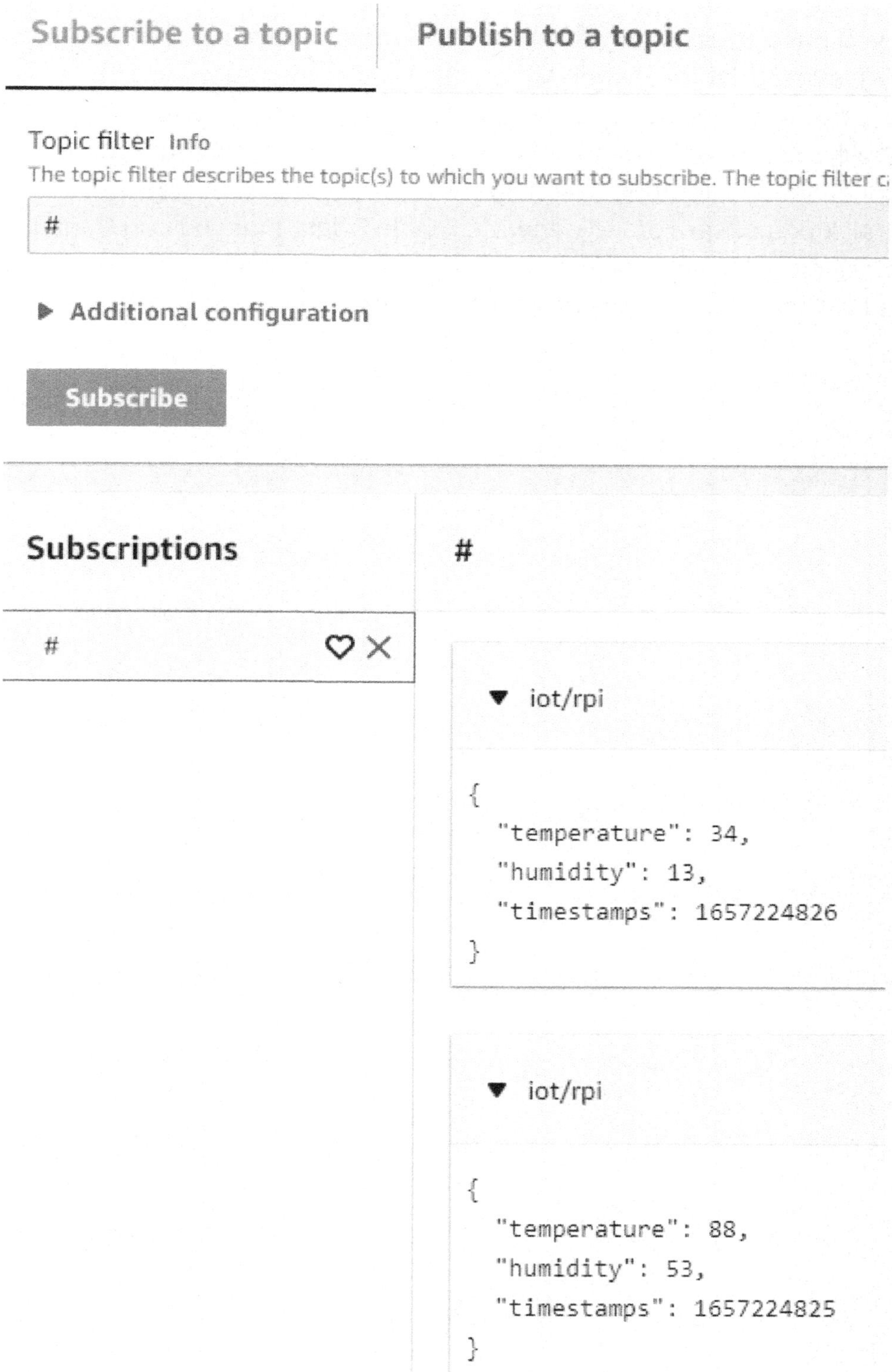
Subscribe to a topic
Publish to a topic
Topic filter Info
The topic filter describes the topic(s) to which you want to subscribe. The topic filter c
#
Additional configuration
Subscribe
Subscriptions
#
#
iot/rpi
{
"temperature": 34,
"humidity": 13,
"timestamps": 1657224826
}
iot/rpi
{
"temperature": 88,
"humidity": 53,
"timestamps": 1657224825
}

$

Congratulations, you have successfully run the Python test program 'pubsub.py' from the AWS IoT Device SDK for Python V2. After running the basic MQTT "pubsub.py" program you were able to modify the program to send a JSON IoT payload with multiple sensor variables to AWS IoT Core. For a more realistic experience the Rpi has many libraries available for importing into the AWS IoT SDK that are made for all kinds of sensors to generate real IoT data that you can transmit to AWS IoT Core. Simply look for any Python sensor libraries designed for the Raspberry Pi and then import them into your Python code.

$ $

Chapter 8 -
Programming the Raspberry Pi with the AWS IoT Device SDK in JavaScript

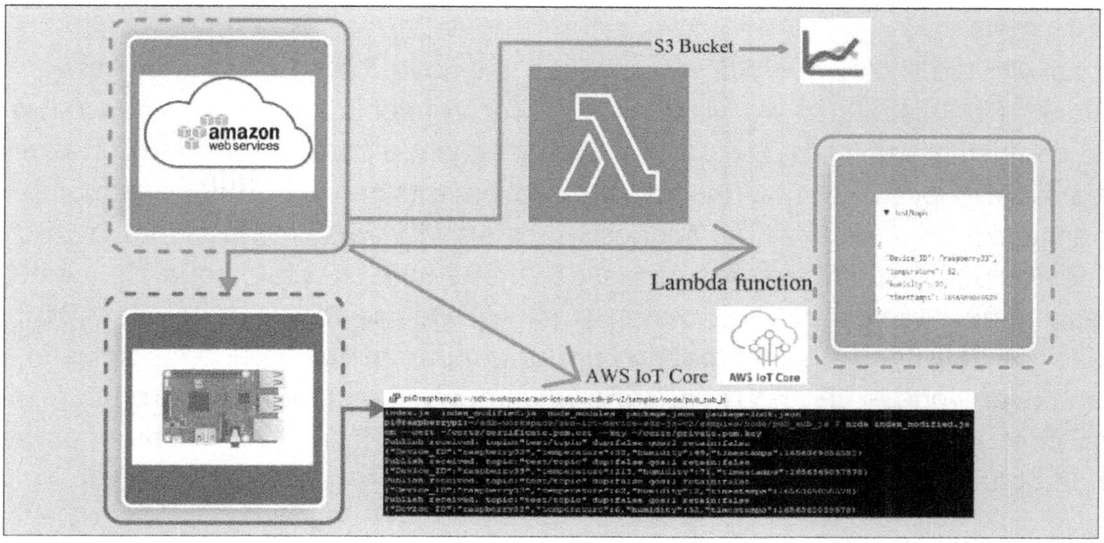
S3 Bucket
amazon
web services
Lambda function
AWS IoT Core
AWS IoT Core

The AWS IoT Device SDKs helps you quickly and easily connect your Raspberry Pi to AWS. The SDKs include open-source libraries, developer guides with samples, and porting guides so that you can build innovative IoT products or solutions on your choice of hardware platforms. The SDKs currently come in five flavors: Java, JavaScript, Python, C++, and Embedded C. The most popular and easy to work with IoT Device SDKs are the ones using the higher-level languages of Python and JavaScript.

When comparing the Raspberry Pi to the ESP32 or ESP8266 the biggest distinction is that the Rpi is a powerful single board computer (SBC), with an application processor, and a full operating system. This contrasts with the ESP32 and ESP8266 which both have a less powerful Microcontroller (MCU), with a limited OS, and thus are unable to run the AWS IoT Device SDK's. There are pros and cons to each system related to capability, cost, power consumption, programmability, and the ability to interface with larger systems. Understanding how to integrate both types of devices, embedded and SBCs, with AWS provides flexibility when solving IoT device to cloud integration challenges.

$

- Raspberry Pi 3 Model B or more recent model. This might work on earlier versions of the Raspberry Pi, but they have not been tested.
- Raspberry Pi OS (32-bit) or later. We recommend using the latest version of the Raspberry Pi OS. Earlier versions of the OS might work, but they have not been tested.

Just as with the Python IoT SDK for devices, the JavaScript SDK comes in two versions. For this tutorial we will use the newer Version 2. In my experience it is more confusing and a little too cleverly designed when compared to the first version of the JavaScript SDK, but it has some improvements as well. You're welcome to use either version you like but I suggest you start with version two of the JavaScript IoT device SDK and if that gives you issues then return to version one. In most cases I would simply recommend the Python IoT Device SDK over the JavaScript IoT Device SDK for the same reason I prefer programming Lambda functions in Python over Node.js. Python is generally a superior language, compared to JavaScript, for handling applications that don't need to facilitate asynchronous web related behaviors.

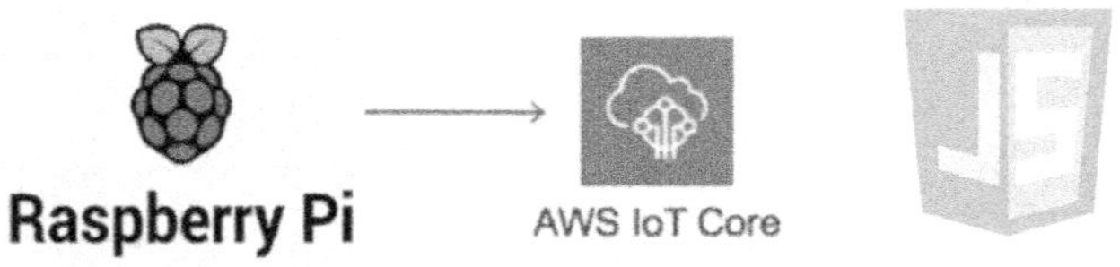
Raspberry Pi
AWS IoT Core

Step 1 – Install the AWS IoT Device SDK for JavaScript Version 2
Step 2 – Configure the AWS Security Certificates on the Raspberry Pi
Step 3 – Run the JavaScript index.js Program to Publish to AWS IoT Core
Step 4 – Modify and Run the New index.js Program to Deliver IoT Payloads to AWS IoT Core

---

Step 1 – Install the AWS IoT Device SDK for JavaScript Version2

AWS provides the following Installation directions at:

https://github.com/aws/aws-iot-device-sdk-js-v2#Installation

I will provide a few of the relevant parts of the installation here with the needed modifications for your own project. The first consideration is:

DO NOT INSTALL THE SDK WITH NPM

There is a known problem with the file structures with NPM installation that I personally experienced. Use the instructions on the GitHub to "Build the V2 SDK from source".

Just like with the previous Python SDK example you will run a basic JavaScript MQTT Publish/Subscribe example program and then you will develop a custom modified JavaScript program more suitable for your needs.

Install Node:

```
sudo apt-get install -y nodejs
```

You can check your node version by

```
node -v
```

Build the JavaScript V2 SDK from source

Create a workspace directory to hold the SDK files:

```
mkdir sdk-workspace
cd sdk-workspace
```

Clone the repository to access the samples:

```
git clone -recursive https://github.com/aws/aws-iot-device-sdk-js-v2.git
```

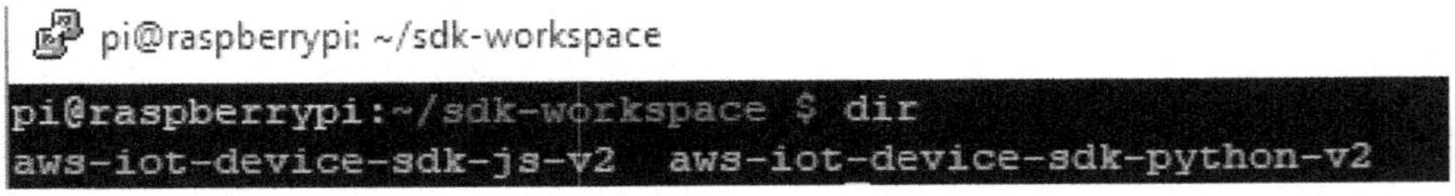
pi@raspberrypi: ~/sdk-workspace
pi@raspberrypi:~/sdk-workspace $ dir
aws-iot-device-sdk-js-v2 aws-iot-device-sdk-python-v2

Go to the new JavaScript SDK directory and then ensure all submodules are properly updated:

```
cd aws-iot-device-sdk-js-v2
```

```
git submodule update -init -recursive
```

Install the SDK:

```
npm install
```

Step 2 – Configure the AWS Security Certificates on the Raspberry Pi

The JavaScript programs require the AWS security certificate files to be installed on the device. I will cover this section separately from the AWS provided documentation because it is important it is done correctly, and the provided screenshots should be helpful.

To install the security certificate files, create a certs directory in your home directory by running these commands at the command line of your Raspberry Pi:

```
cd ~
mkdir certs
```

In the ~/certs directory, copy the private key, client/device certificate, and root CA certificate that have been kept on your PC. If you have changed the name of the AWS security certificates that is fine, just make sure you modify the names below to your own names for the relevant certificates.

You may have to use the 'sudo' command from the command line if you don't have inherent permission to write files to your Raspberry Pi:

https://raspberry-projects.com/pi/command-line/sudo

How you copy the certificate files to your device depends on your PC and your operating system. In my case I just work through an ethernet connection to the RPi using a command prompt from the free "Putty" SSH tool. I am also using the free "FileZilla" FTP program. I also use the built-in editor 'nano' on the RPi to edit files as needed

Below is an image of using my Raspberry Pi's IP address to connect to FileZilla. I attained my RPi IPv4 address by just typing in "ifconing" on my RPi after I logged into the device on Putty.
$

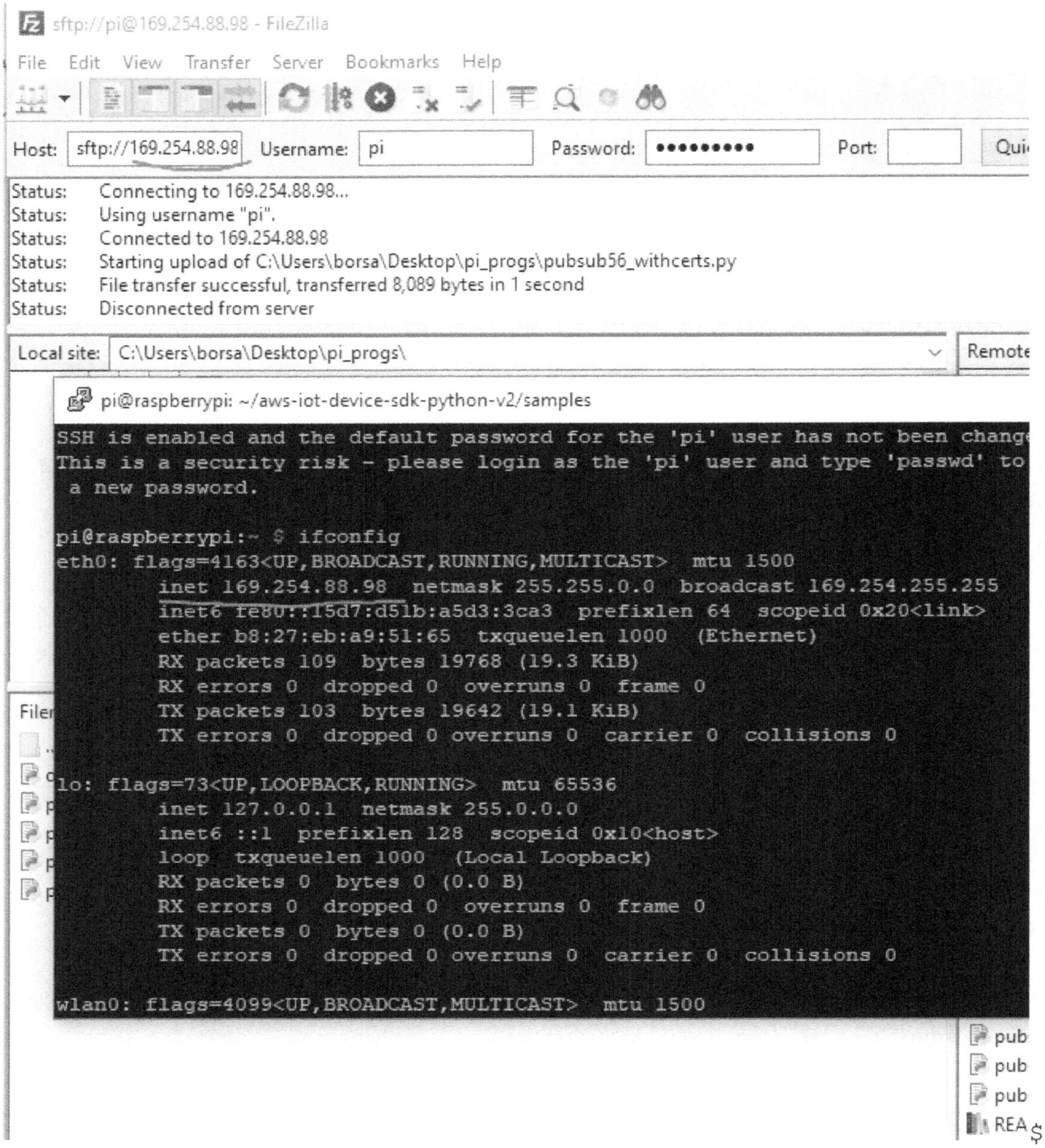
sftp://pi@169.254.88.98 - FileZilla
File Edit View Transfer Server Bookmarks Help
Host: sftp://169.254.88.98 Username: pi Password: ••••••••• Port:
Status: Connecting to 169.254.88.98...
Status: Using username "pi".
Status: Connected to 169.254.88.98
Status: Starting upload of C:\Users\borsa\Desktop\pi_progs\pubsub56_withcerts.py
Status: File transfer successful, transferred 8,089 bytes in 1 second
Status: Disconnected from server
Local site: C:\Users\borsa\Desktop\pi_progs\
pi@raspberrypi: ~/aws-iot-device-sdk-python-v2/samples
SSH is enabled and the default password for the 'pi' user has not been chang
This is a security risk - please login as the 'pi' user and type 'passwd' to
a new password.
pi@raspberrypi:~ $ ifconfig
eth0: flags=4163<UP,BROADCAST,RUNNING,MULTICAST> mtu 1500
inet 169.254.88.98 netmask 255.255.0.0 broadcast 169.254.255.255
inet6 fe80::15d7:d51b:a5d3:3ca3 prefixlen 64 scopeid 0x20<link>
ether b8:27:eb:a9:51:65 txqueuelen 1000 (Ethernet)
RX packets 109 bytes 19768 (19.3 KiB)
RX errors 0 dropped 0 overruns 0 frame 0
TX packets 103 bytes 19642 (19.1 KiB)
TX errors 0 dropped 0 overruns 0 carrier 0 collisions 0
lo: flags=73<UP,LOOPBACK,RUNNING> mtu 65536
inet 127.0.0.1 netmask 255.0.0.0
inet6 ::1 prefixlen 128 scopeid 0x10<host>
loop txqueuelen 1000 (Local Loopback)
RX packets 0 bytes 0 (0.0 B)
RX errors 0 dropped 0 overruns 0 frame 0
TX packets 0 bytes 0 (0.0 B)
TX errors 0 dropped 0 overruns 0 carrier 0 collisions 0
wlan0: flags=4099<UP,BROADCAST,MULTICAST> mtu 1500

$

I save my certs to my RPi by opening the built-in "nano" editor on my RPi and pasting in each of the three certificates alphanumeric codes.

$

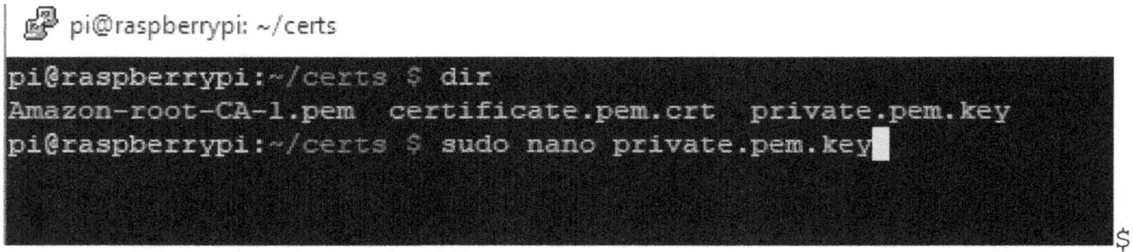
pi@raspberrypi: ~/certs
pi@raspberrypi:~/certs $ dir
Amazon-root-CA-1.pem certificate.pem.crt private.pem.key
pi@raspberrypi:~/certs $ sudo nano private.pem.key

Here is a semi-obfuscated image of my private key being pasted in:

$

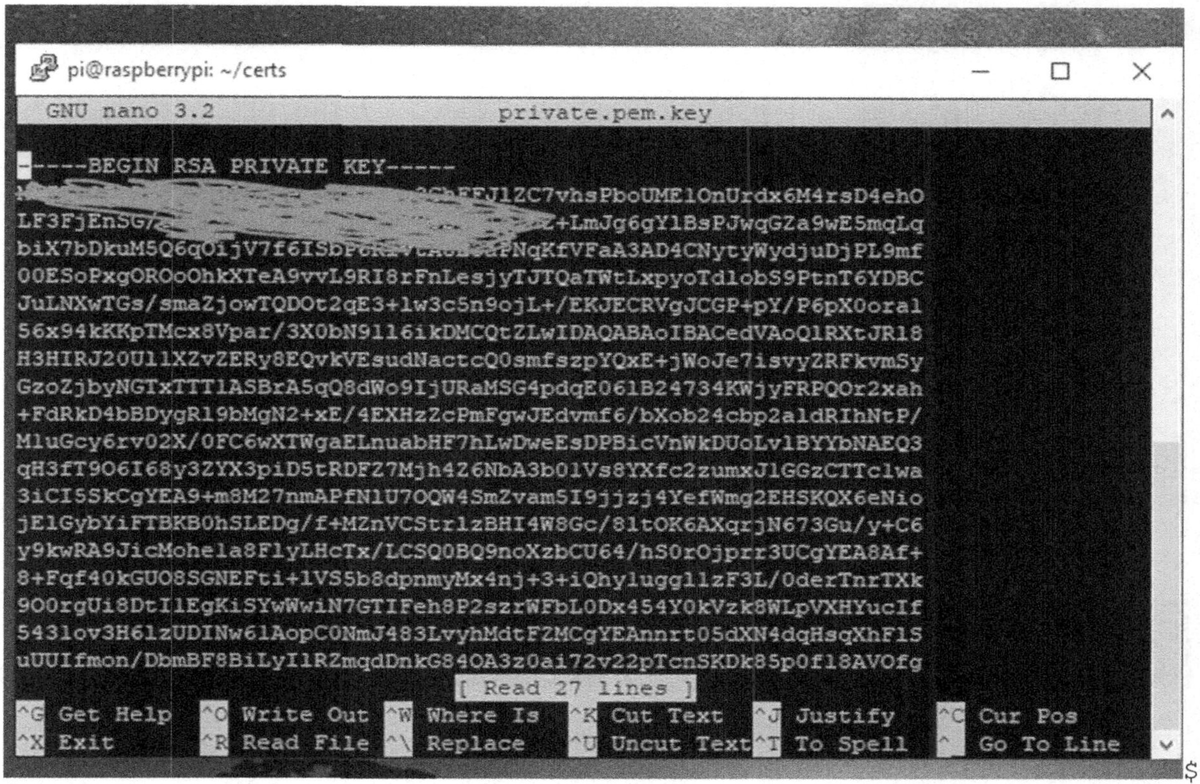
pi@raspberrypi: ~/certs
GNU nano 3.2
private.pem.key
-----BEGIN RSA PRIVATE KEY-----
J1ZC7vhsPboUME1OnUrdx6M4rsD4ehO
LF3FjEnSG/
+LmJg6gY1BsPJwqGZa9wE5mqLq
biX7bDkuM5Q6qOijV7f6ISb
NqKfVFaA3AD4CNytyWydjuDjPL9mf
00ESoPxgOROoOhkXTeA9vvL9RI8rFnLesjyTJTQaTWtLxpyoTdlobS9PtnT6YDBC
JuLNXwTGs/smaZjowTQDOt2qE3+lw3c5n9ojL+/EKJECRVgJCGP+pY/P6pX0oral
56x94kKKpTMcx8Vpar/3X0bN9116ikDMCQtZLwIDAQABAoIBACedVAoQ1RXtJR18
H3HIRJ20U11XZvZERy8EQvkVEsudNactcQ0smfszpYQxE+jWoJe7isvyZRFkvmSy
GzoZjbyNGTxTTT1ASBrA5qQ8dWo9IjURaMSG4pdqE061B24734KWjyFRPQOr2xah
+FdRkD4bBDygR19bMgN2+xE/4EXHzZcPmFgwJEdvmf6/bXob24cbp2aldRIhNtP/
MluGcy6rv02X/0FC6wXTWgaELnuabHF7hLwDweEsDPBicVnWkDUoLv1BYYbNAEQ3
qH3fT9O6I68y3ZYX3piD5tRDFZ7Mjh4Z6NbA3b01Vs8YXfc2zumxJ1GGzCTTc1wa
3iCI5SkCgYEA9+m8M27nmAPfN1U7OQW4SmZvam5I9jjzj4YefWmg2EHSKQX6eNio
jE1GybYiFTBKB0hSLEDg/f+MZnVCStr1zBHI4W8Gc/81tOK6AXqrjN673Gu/y+C6
y9kwRA9JicMohela8FlyLHcTx/LCSQ0BQ9noXzbCU64/hS0rOjprr3UCgYEA8Af+
8+Fqf40kGUO8SGNEFti+1VS5b8dpnmyMx4nj+3+iQhylugg11zF3L/0derTnrTXk
9O0rgUi8DtI1EgKiSYwWwiN7GTIFeh8P2szrWFbL0Dx454Y0kVzk8WLpVXHYucIf
543lov3H61zUDINw61AopC0NmJ483LvyhMdtFZMCgYEAnnrt05dXN4dqHsqXhF1S
uUUIfmon/DbmBF8BiLyI1RZmqdDnkG84OA3z0ai72v22pTcnSKDk85p0f18AVOfg
[Read 27 lines]
^G Get Help
^O Write Out
^W Where Is
^K Cut Text
^J Justify
^C Cur Pos
^X Exit
^R Read File
^\ Replace
^U Uncut Text
^T To Spell
^_ Go To Line

$

$

After each certificate is pasted into the editor then use CNTR+X to exit Nano, then use ‘y’ to confirm to save each certificate.

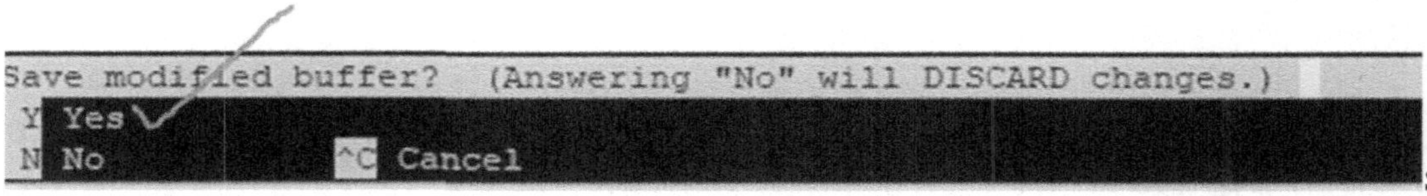
Save modified buffer? (Answering "No" will DISCARD changes.)
Y Yes
N No
^C Cancel

$

The commands in the next section assume that your security certificate files are stored on the device as shown in this table:

Certificate file names

File	File path
Root CA certificate	~/certs/Amazon-root-CA-1.pem
Device certificate	~/certs/certificate.pem.crt
Private key	~/certs/private.pem.key

$

It doesn't matter what you call your certificates, just keep the names consistent when you issue commands from your RPi command prompt.

```
pi@raspberrypi:~/certs $ dir
Amazon-root-CA-1.pem  certificate.pem.crt  private.pem.key
pi@raspberrypi:~/certs $
```

$

Instead of using the built-in “nano” editor on the device, you can use a UTF-8 editor of your choice on your computer and then use Filezilla to transfer the security certificates to your RPi. I find using FileZilla with an editor on my PC to be an easier method when editing files then using the RPI “heedlessly”.

Step 3 - Run the JavaScript MQTT index.js Program to Publish to AWS IoT Core

To install and run the example program

Navigate to the example directory on your RPi as shown below:

```
pi@raspberrypi:~/sdk-workspace/aws-iot-device-sdk-js-
v2/samples/node/pub_sub_js
```

You should now be in the *pub_sub_js* folder (not the *pub_sub* folder)

The location is shown below:

$

```
pi@raspberrypi: ~/sdk-workspace/aws-iot-device-sdk-js-v2/samples/node/pub_sub_js
pi@raspberrypi:~/sdk-workspace/aws-iot-device-sdk-js-v2/samples/node/pub_sub_js $ dir
index.js  node_modules  package.json  package-lock.json
pi@raspberrypi:~/sdk-workspace/aws-iot-device-sdk-js-v2/samples/node/pub_sub_js $
```

$

Now you will need to build the program with its dependencies by using the following command at the RPi command prompt from within the pub_sub_js folder:

```
npm install
```

$

```
pi@raspberrypi:~/sdk-workspace/aws-iot-device-sdk-js-v2/samples/node/pub_sub_js $ npm install
```

The program may take quite a while to build while forming its external dependencies. You can find the complete index.js program here:

https://github.com/aws/aws-iot-device-sdk-js-v2/blob/main/samples/node/pub_sub_js/index.js

After the build process is complete you will need your AWS IoT endpoint for the following commands. To retrieve your AWS IoT endpoint, go to:

AWS IoT Core→ Settings:

AWS IoT > Settings

Or using the AWS CLI command on your PC:

```
aws iot describe-endpoint --endpoint-type iot:Data-ATS
```

The argument parser will take in your specifics from the command line and add them to the 'index.js' program AWS provides in the JavaScript IoT Device SDK. To run the 'index.js' program with your security certificates and endpoint simply enter the following command at the RPi's command prompt:

```
node index.js --endpoint <Your-AWS-IoT-Endpoint> --ca_file ~/certs/Amazon-
root-CA-1.pem --cert ~/certs/certificate.pem.crt --key
~/certs/private.pem.key
```

- Change the name of your security certificates above as needed.

pi@raspberrypi: ~/sdk-workspace/aws-iot-device-sdk-js-v2/samples/node/pub_sub_js
pi@raspberrypi:~/sdk-workspace/aws-iot-device-sdk-js-v2/samples/node/pub_sub_js $ node index.js --endpoint a32qaa13loyees-ats.iot.us-east-1.amazonaws.com --ca_file ~/certs/Amazon-root-CA-1.pem --cert
~/certs/certificate.pem.crt --key ~/certs/private.pem.key

Now the default index.js program will issue exactly ten "Hello World!" messages as shown below:

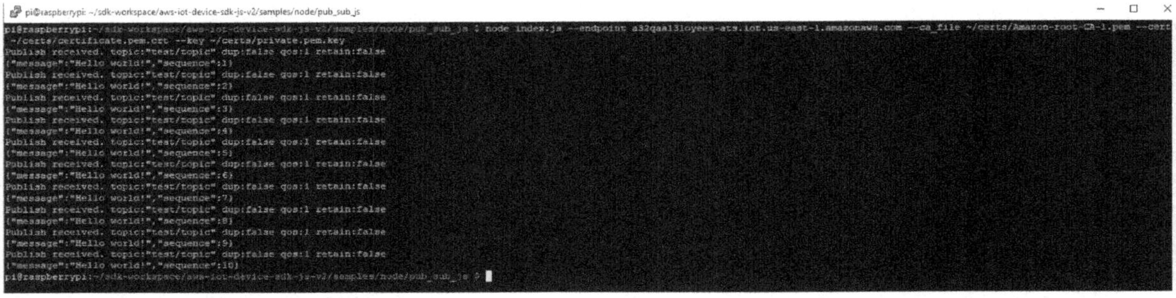
pi@raspberrypi: ~/sdk-workspace/aws-iot-device-sdk-js-v2/samples/node/pub_sub_js
pi@raspberrypi:~/sdk-workspace/aws-iot-device-sdk-js-v2/samples/node/pub_sub_js $ node index.js --endpoint a32qaa13loyees-ats.iot.us-east-1.amazonaws.com --ca_file ~/certs/Amazon-root-CA-1.pem --cert
~/certs/certificate.pem.crt --key ~/certs/private.pem.key
Publish received. topic:"test/topic" dup:false qos:1 retain:false
{"message":"Hello world!","sequence":1}
Publish received. topic:"test/topic" dup:false qos:1 retain:false
{"message":"Hello world!","sequence":2}
Publish received. topic:"test/topic" dup:false qos:1 retain:false
{"message":"Hello world!","sequence":3}
Publish received. topic:"test/topic" dup:false qos:1 retain:false
{"message":"Hello world!","sequence":4}
Publish received. topic:"test/topic" dup:false qos:1 retain:false
{"message":"Hello world!","sequence":5}
Publish received. topic:"test/topic" dup:false qos:1 retain:false
{"message":"Hello world!","sequence":6}
Publish received. topic:"test/topic" dup:false qos:1 retain:false
{"message":"Hello world!","sequence":7}
Publish received. topic:"test/topic" dup:false qos:1 retain:false
{"message":"Hello world!","sequence":8}
Publish received. topic:"test/topic" dup:false qos:1 retain:false
{"message":"Hello world!","sequence":9}
Publish received. topic:"test/topic" dup:false qos:1 retain:false
{"message":"Hello world!","sequence":10}
pi@raspberrypi:~/sdk-workspace/aws-iot-device-sdk-js-v2/samples/node/pub_sub_js $

1

If you subscribe to the default topic or simply '#' on the MQTT test client on AWS IoT Core you will see the output below:

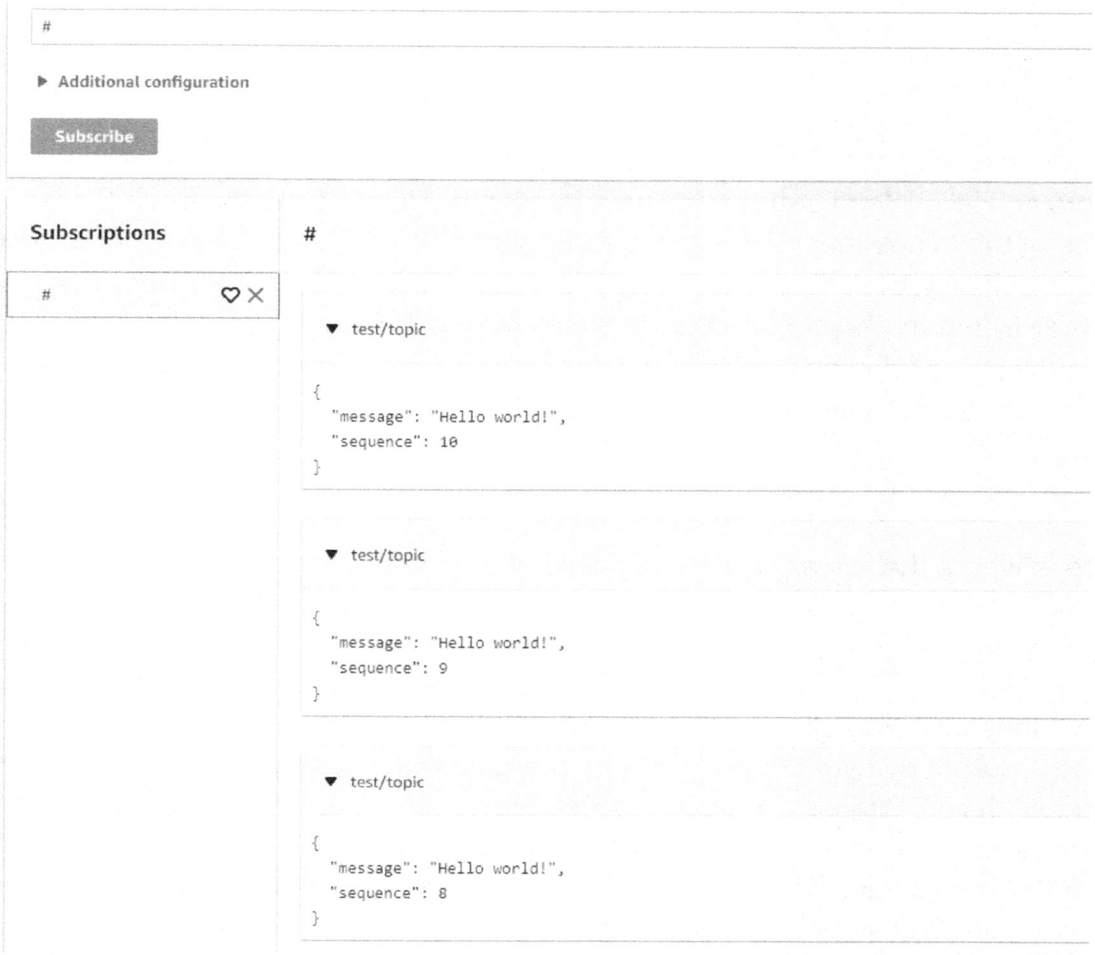
#
▶ Additional configuration
Subscribe
Subscriptions
#
#
▼ test/topic
{
"message": "Hello world!",
"sequence": 10
}
▼ test/topic
{
"message": "Hello world!",
"sequence": 9
}
▼ test/topic
{
"message": "Hello world!",
"sequence": 8
}

You have successfully installed the AWS IoT Device SDK for JavaScript V2 and run the test 'index.js' program. In the next step you will customize the index program to publish a more useful IoT message to the AWS MQTT message broker.

Step 4 - Modify and Run the New index.js Program to Deliver JSON IoT Payloads to AWS IoT Core

Before you modify the 'index.js' program to suit your needs it is important to discuss exactly what is going on in the JavaScript code as it can be confusing. You can also examine the code directly at the AWS GitHub here:

https://github.com/aws/aws-iot-device-sdk-js-v2/blob/main/samples/node/pub_sub_js/index.js

The first thing to understand is, that if you look closely at the 'index.js' program, the IoT payload transmission data is handled similar to the "pubsub.py" program from the previous chapter. So where is the MQTT topic - 'test/topic' declared? Also, where is "Hello World!" string that gets transmitted to IoT Core located? These are some of the things that makes this second version of the JavaScript SDK somewhat more confusing than the first version of the JavaScript IoT Device SDK. The answer is that these parser arguments are coming from another file called "cli_args.js" and this helper file is located in your file structure on your RPi in the util (utility) directory as shown below:

```
aws-iot-device-sdk-js-v2/samples/util/cli_args.js
```

Here is where the *'cli_args.js'* file is called at the top of the *'index.js'* program:

```
const common_args = require('../../util/cli_args');
```

Given these external dependencies you can choose to insert your own IoT payload in the program by overriding the inherited arguments. Alternately, your other option is to edit the 'cli_args.js' file to use a customized IoT payload. I will demonstrate the former technique here. As discussed in the last chapter it is also better practice to modify dynamic variables in an implementation file rather than in a header or "helper" file which is normally meant to handle constant variables and parameters. You are welcome to explore editing the 'cli_args.js' file and determine if that works better for your needs.

If you do decide to alter the 'cli _args.js" file to customize the MQTT IoT payload the code would be located here:

```
.option('message', {
  alias: 'M',
  description: 'Message to publish (optional).',
  type: 'string',
  default: 'Hello world!'
})
```

To customize the IoT payload from the "index.js" file as recommended, you would simply replace the default 'Hello World!" string parameter with your custom JSON payload.

You can also see the developers at AWS have used the loop iterator "op_idx" with a delay thus giving it dual utility. If you studied compiler design and optimization algorithms, you may know to avoid this kind of thing. As I mentioned before there are several ostensibly 'clever' implementation details that make the second version of this SDK somewhat problematic. My final summary is that the original JavaScript SDK V1 was written by very skilled embedded developers at AWS and this latest version was written by very skilled web developers at AWS. Due to my own background, I am likely opinionated towards the former, which may not be fair for being an unbiased observer.

Moving on, you will edit the 'index.js' program by inserting the following IoT JOSN payload to replace the inherited "Hello World!" message:

```
var myPayload = JSON.stringify({
  "Device_ID":    "raspberry33",
  "temperature": Math.floor(Math.random() * 120) + 1,
  "humidity": Math.floor(Math.random() * 100) + 1,
  "timestamps": Date.now()
})
```

Now after inserting the JSON payload above in the 'index.js' file you will simply insert the 'myPayload' variable to the MQTT publishing function by modifying the publish parameter list as shown on the line below:

```
connection.publish(argv.topic, myPayload, mqtt.QoS.AtLeastOnce); //MQTT
publish occurs here
```

You can leave the inherited MQTT topic name and publishing loop counter defaulted to ten iterations. Both the MQTT topic and the publish payload loop counter can either be overwritten locally or modified in the "cli_args.js' file as stated before.

You can find all the programming code on the chapters GitHub page. Copying code from the relevant chapters GitHub page is more reliable for programming than copying code from eBooks due to character translation and formatting.

Below is the entire code for 'index.js' but with the edits discussed for the custom IoT payload:

```
/**
 * Copyright Amazon.com, Inc. or its affiliates. All Rights Reserved.
```

```
* SPDX-License-Identifier: Apache-2.0.
*/

const iotsdk = require('aws-iot-device-sdk-v2');
const mqtt = iotsdk.mqtt;
const TextDecoder = require('util').TextDecoder;
const yargs = require('yargs');
const common_args = require('../../util/cli_args');

yargs.command('*', false, (yargs) => {
    common_args.add_direct_connection_establishment_arguments(yargs);
    common_args.add_topic_message_arguments(yargs);
}, main).parse();

async function execute_session(connection, argv) {
    return new Promise(async (resolve, reject) => {
        try {
            const decoder = new TextDecoder('utf8');
            const on_publish = async (topic, payload, dup, qos, retain) => {
                const json = decoder.decode(payload);
                console.log(`Publish received. topic:"${topic}" dup:${dup}
qos:${qos} retain:${retain}`);
                console.log(json);
                const message = JSON.parse(json);
                if (message.sequence == argv.count) {
                    resolve();
                }
            }

            await connection.subscribe(argv.topic, mqtt.QoS.AtLeastOnce,
on_publish);

            for (let op_idx = 0; op_idx < argv.count; ++op_idx) {
                const publish = async () => {
                    const msg = {
                        message: argv.message,
                        sequence: op_idx + 1,
                    };

                    //add the custom code
                      var myPayload = JSON.stringify({
                        "Device_ID":   "raspberry33",
                        "temperature": Math.floor(Math.random() * 120) + 1,
                        "humidity": Math.floor(Math.random() * 100) + 1,
                        "timestamps": Date.now()
```

```
        })

                        const json = JSON.stringify(msg);
                        //MQTT publish occurs here
                        connection.publish(argv.topic, myPayload,
mqtt.QoS.AtLeastOnce);

                    }
                    setTimeout(publish, op_idx * 1000); //change to 3 seconds
                }
            }
            catch (error) {
                reject(error);
            }
        });
}

async function main(argv) {
    common_args.apply_sample_arguments(argv);

    const connection = common_args.build_connection_from_cli_args(argv);

    // force node to wait 60 seconds before killing itself
    // To get rid of this but it requires a refactor of the connection
    // pinning the libuv event loop while the connection is active
    const timer = setInterval(() => { }, 60 * 1000);

    await connection.connect();
    await execute_session(connection, argv);
    await connection.disconnect();

    // Allow node to die if the promise above resolved
    clearTimeout(timer);
}
```

Save the code to a new file, you can name it “index_modified.js”. You can edit the file locally on your RPi by using nano or edit the JavaScript file on your computer in a UTF-8 editor and then move the file over to your RPi by using FileZilla as shown below. Move the modified program file to the same directory as the original ‘index.js’ file:

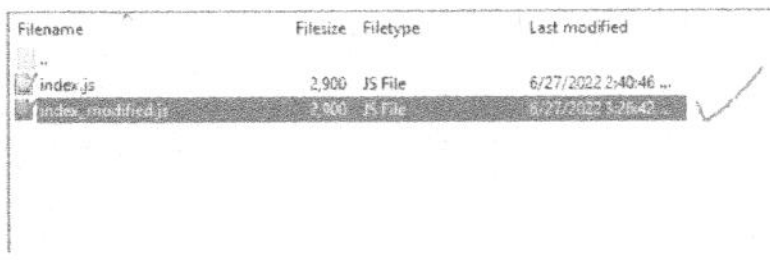
Filename
Filesize
Filetype
Last modified
index.js
index_modified.js

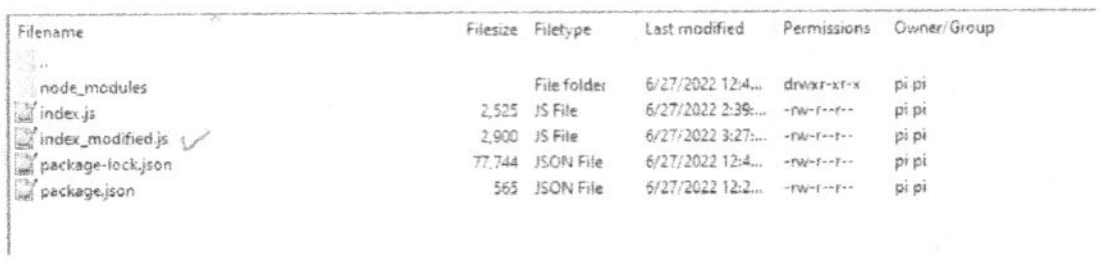
Filename
Filesize
Filetype
Last modified
Permissions
Owner/Group
node_modules
index.js
index_modified.js
package-lock.json
package.json

To run the program, issue the following command from the RPi command prompt in the same directory as before but now with the new customized index file name:

```
node index_modified.js --endpoint <Your-AWS-IoT-Endpoint> --ca_file
~/certs/Amazon-root-CA-1.pem --cert ~/certs/certificate.pem.crt --key
~/certs/private.pem.key
```

You should observe the following result at the command prompt on the Raspberry Pi:

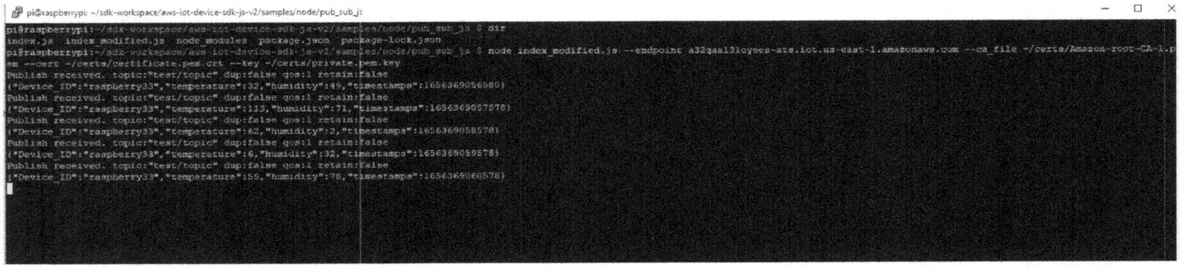
pi@raspberrypi: ~/sdk-workspace/aws-iot-device-sdk-js-v2/samples/node/pub_sub_js
index.js index_modified.js node_modules package.json package-lock.json
Publish received. topic:"test/topic" dup:false qos:1 retain:false
{"Device_ID":"raspberry33","temperature":32,"humidity":49,"timestamps":1656369056580}
Publish received. topic:"test/topic" dup:false qos:1 retain:false
{"Device_ID":"raspberry33","temperature":113,"humidity":71,"timestamps":1656369057578}
Publish received. topic:"test/topic" dup:false qos:1 retain:false
{"Device_ID":"raspberry33","temperature":62,"humidity":2,"timestamps":1656369058578}
Publish received. topic:"test/topic" dup:false qos:1 retain:false
{"Device_ID":"raspberry33","temperature":6,"humidity":32,"timestamps":1656369059578}
Publish received. topic:"test/topic" dup:false qos:1 retain:false
{"Device_ID":"raspberry33","temperature":55,"humidity":78,"timestamps":1656369060578}

And then observing the program execution in the MQTT test client on AWS IoT Core:

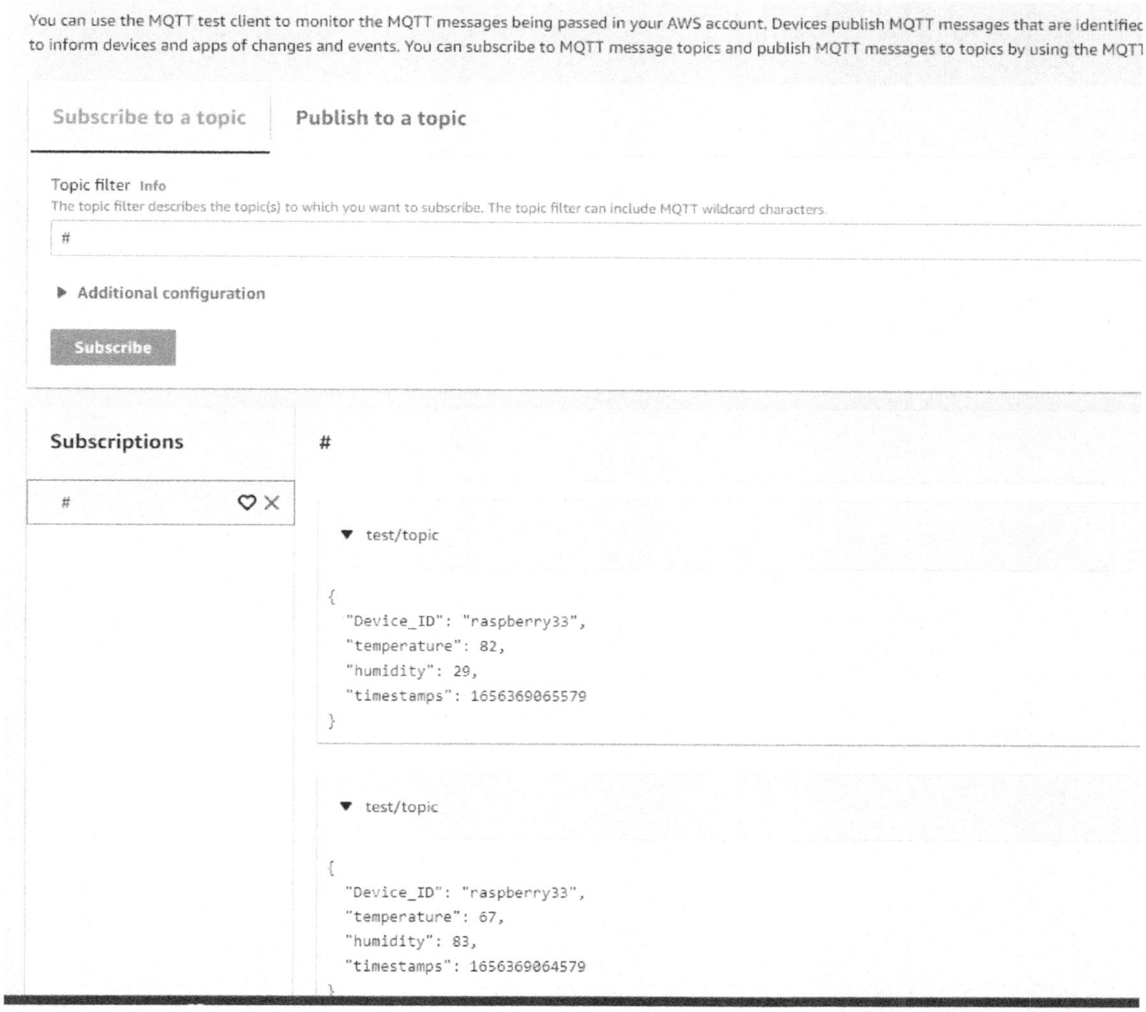
You can use the MQTT test client to monitor the MQTT messages being passed in your AWS account. Devices publish MQTT messages that are identifiec
to inform devices and apps of changes and events. You can subscribe to MQTT message topics and publish MQTT messages to topics by using the MQTT
Subscribe to a topic
Publish to a topic
Topic filter Info
The topic filter describes the topic(s) to which you want to subscribe. The topic filter can include MQTT wildcard characters.
#
Additional configuration
Subscribe
Subscriptions
#
#
test/topic
{
"Device_ID": "raspberry33",
"temperature": 82,
"humidity": 29,
"timestamps": 1656369065579
}
test/topic
{
"Device_ID": "raspberry33",
"temperature": 67,
"humidity": 83,
"timestamps": 1656369064579

Congratulations you were able to use the AWS-IoT-Device-SDK-JS-V2 to send messages with the default 'index.js' program and then send a customized JSON IoT payload with a modified JavaScript MQTT publishing program. To explore further enhancements, you will find that the Raspberry Pi has many sensor libraries that you can implement with the programs included in the JavaScript SDK on your own RPi. Also, the SDK itself has many sample programs to explore.

https://github.com/aws/aws-iot-device-sdk-js-v2

If you find the AWS JavaScript IoT device SDK V2 too confusing, then you may want to use the earlier version of the SDK for JavaScript V1 found below as it is easier to get started with:

https://github.com/aws/aws-iot-device-sdk-js

Chapter 9 -
Prerequisite 1 Creating a S3 Public Bucket for IoT Data Storage and Static Website Hosting

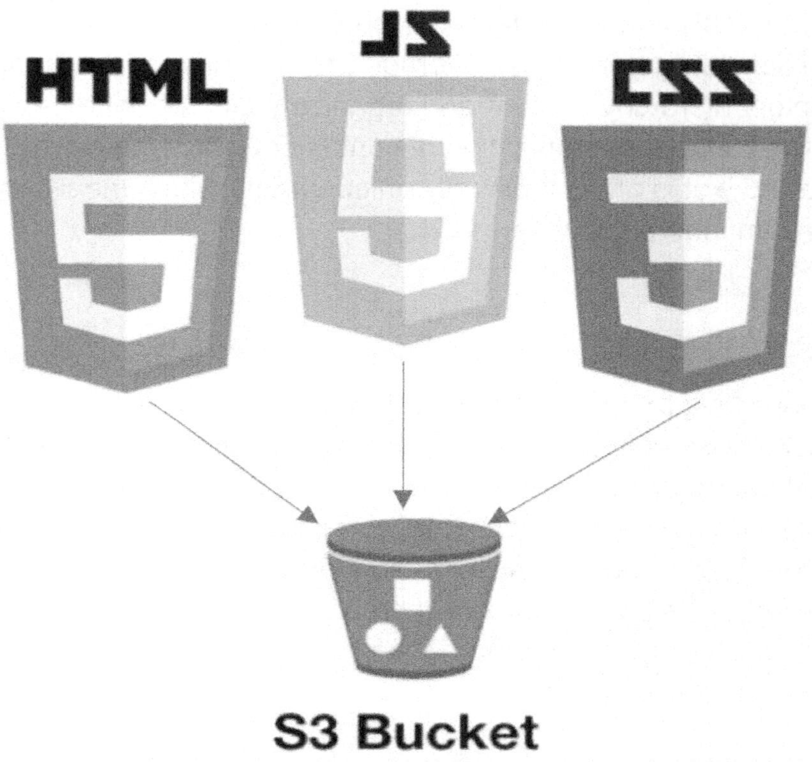

HTML
JS
CSS
S3 Bucket

AWS Simple Storage Service, AKA S3, is the oldest cloud service on AWS and arguably the most important. For IoT it would certainly be in the top three along with IoT Core and Lambda. In a nutshell S3 provides cloud storage for both data and static websites at amazingly low prices. With S3 you can use a S3 bucket for both static web site hosting and IoT data storage for pennies per year.

Throughout this book we will need to create public S3 buckets to both store IoT data and host static websites for visualization of our IoT data. Rather than repeat this same S3 creation process in almost every chapter, it is best to explain the process once here in detail, and then the IoT developer can repeat the process for themselves as needed.

The S3 Storage Structure

S3 provides object storage. It is very important to understand that S3 is not normal file storage. The main implication for this is that when we save data to S3 it is stored as an object blob and not a file. This means we cannot concatenate or append these data objects; the objects must be completely re-written to S3 if we change them. This is a tradeoff that is made to keep the cost of S3 ridiculously low. Traditional file storage and object storage are very different. With file storage you use a directory hierarchy to store and organize your files, whereas in object storage files are stored in a flat organization of containers which we call 'Buckets' and 'keys' in S3. Each bucket is given a globally unique name which means every static website has an inherently unique URL.

Costs

S3's popularity is largely a result of its incredibly low price. This is true for both static website hosting and data store. However, it should be noted that S3 is not capable of hosting dynamic websites so that we must rely on HTTP requests for Lambda functions to serve up dynamic components. So S3 could not use a dynamic language like PHP or host a backend language like Node.js or Python (that is what Lambda is for). AWS has another venerable service called EC2 which is for dynamic website hosting and storage, however its average costs are much higher as a 'live' server instance.

A final relevant fact is that the cost to write objects to S3 is the same, whether it is a huge object or a simple, small JSON sensor payload. Therefore, for production level IoT, you generally would want to "batch" data into large writes (PUTs) to S3. For our purposes the cost differences are so nominal (less than a cent for writing small IoT data sets), that it would not be worth complicating the IoT projects by using batching operations which add extra overhead in exchange for a minor cost reduction.

S3 pricing info can be found here:

https://aws.amazon.com/pm/serv-s3

Data Privacy and Security

In this book we will make public websites for our IoT data. Wouldn't it be better to make everything in our S3 buckets private? All things being equal - yes, the problem is that true privacy adds extra cost as you would need to employ extra AWS services like AWS CloudFront, ACM, and Route 53. Also remember, the IoT data we produce is not normally something we need to keep private; it is mostly just simple environmental readings and IoT visualization code.

We can achieve pretty good privacy ("PGP"), through a simply S3 bucket policy that limits IP access. I will explain that later in this chapter. The best form of privacy is always just not to release your buckets URL to the world.

The second related privacy consideration is potential endpoint exploitation from S3. To explain this imagine I have an S3 bucket with a static website that has a URL created with API Gateway that calls a Lambda function that scans an entire DynamoDB database. This can be a costly operation with large data tables, so I clearly do not want anyone to get my API Gateway endpoint which is embedded in the S3 web code. If the endpoint gets out into the wild the hackers can maliciously keep scanning my database by using my exposed endpoint and running up my AWS bill. There are also other specific means on AWS designed to protect endpoints like API keys, Lambda authorizers, Cognito, and joint web tokens. However, these specific options add overhead for both the developer and the user.

In this prerequisite project we will first create a public S3 bucket with the AWS console and then repeat the process using an express method utilizing the AWS CLI. At the end of the chapter, I will demonstrate a single CLI command to delete your S3 bucket with all the included files.

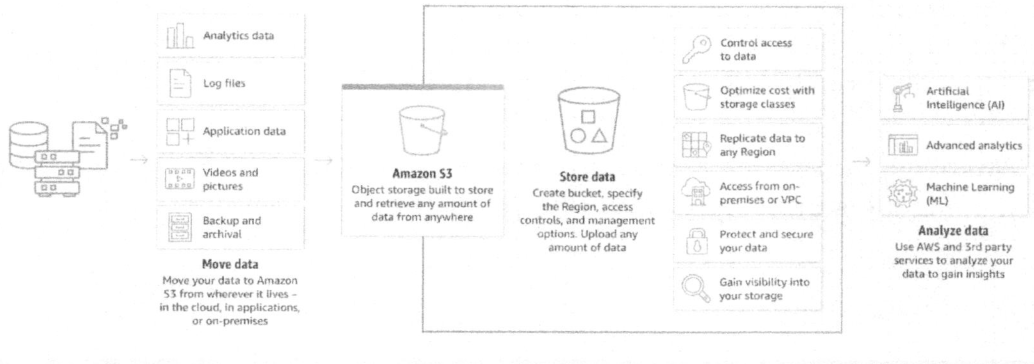

Analytics data
Log files
Application data
Videos and pictures
Backup and archival
Move data
Move your data to Amazon S3 from wherever it lives – in the cloud, in applications, or on-premises
Amazon S3
Object storage built to store and retrieve any amount of data from anywhere
Store data
Create bucket, specify the Region, access controls, and management options. Upload any amount of data
Control access to data
Optimize cost with storage classes
Replicate data to any Region
Access from on-premises or VPC
Protect and secure your data
Gain visibility into your storage
Artificial Intelligence (AI)
Advanced analytics
Machine Learning (ML)
Analyze data
Use AWS and 3rd party services to analyze your data to gain insights

Step 1 - Creating a S3 Bucket from the AWS Console
Step 2 - Enabling a Static Web Host in the S3 Bucket
Step 3 - Creating a S3 Bucket with the AWS CLI
Step 4 - Enabling a Static Web Host in the S3 Bucket from the AWS CLI
Step 5 - Deleting the S3 Bucket and all Files with a Single AWS CLI Command

---

Step 1 - Creating a S3 Bucket from the AWS Console

- Warning: Do not store private information in public buckets, it is publicly readable.

Navigate to S3 from your account or just use this link:

https://s3.console.aws.amazon.com/s3

On the upper right hand of the screen select “Create bucket”

Copy ARN
Empty
Delete
Create bucket

Name your S3 bucket with a globally unique name. The name must be globally unique because you will be granted a unique URL to access it by. Next, choose a bucket region. The best region to start with is the ‘home’ region that your AWS CLI is configured to, probably ‘us-east-1’ (N. Virginia).

- Whenever you create new AWS services, make sure to keep all the services in the in the same region, even the S3 bucket.

Next select “ACLs enabled.”

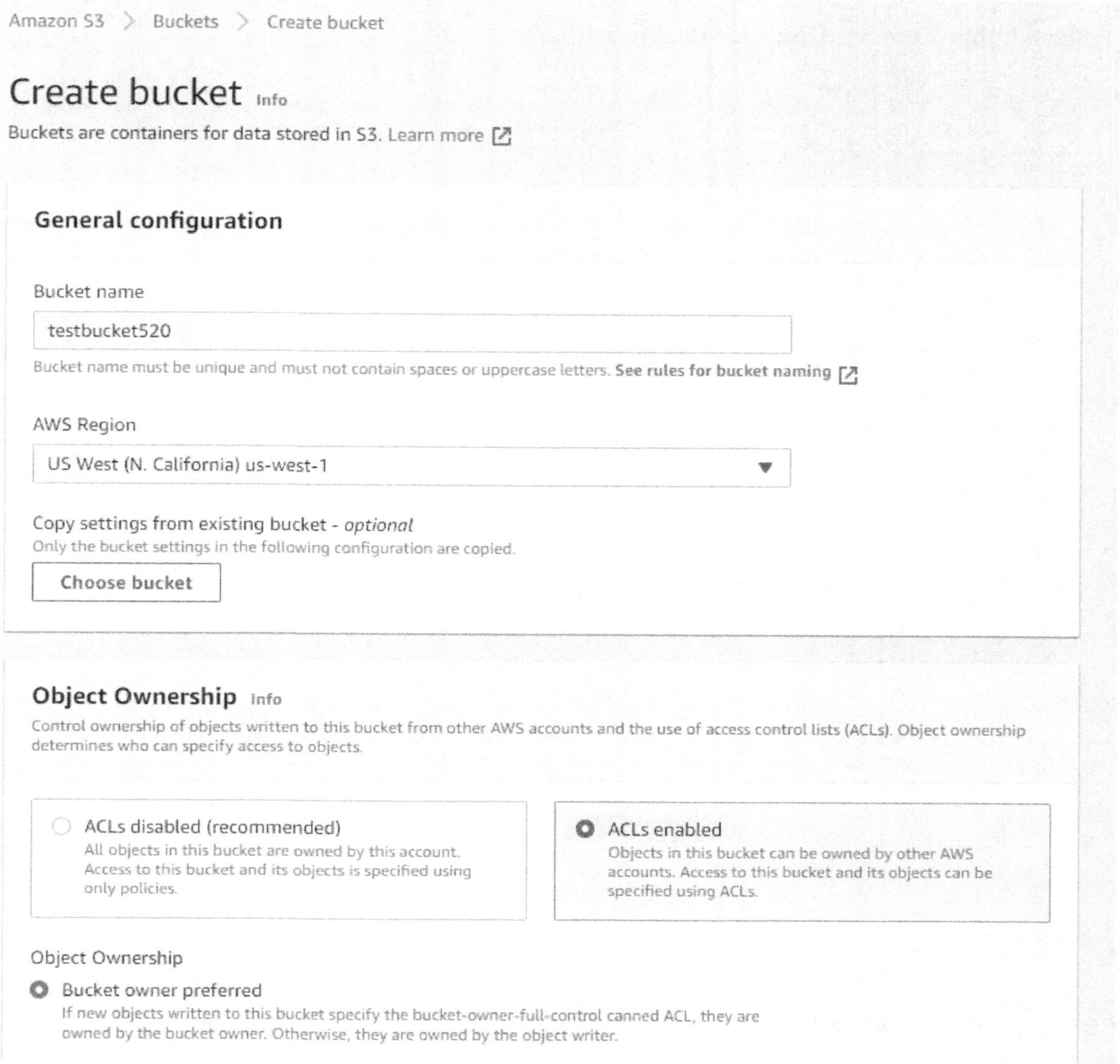
Amazon S3 > Buckets > Create bucket
Create bucket Info
Buckets are containers for data stored in S3. Learn more
General configuration
Bucket name
testbucket520
Bucket name must be unique and must not contain spaces or uppercase letters. See rules for bucket naming
AWS Region
US West (N. California) us-west-1
Copy settings from existing bucket - optional
Only the bucket settings in the following configuration are copied.
Choose bucket
Object Ownership Info
Control ownership of objects written to this bucket from other AWS accounts and the use of access control lists (ACLs). Object ownership determines who can specify access to objects.
ACLs disabled (recommended)
All objects in this bucket are owned by this account. Access to this bucket and its objects is specified using only policies.
ACLs enabled
Objects in this bucket can be owned by other AWS accounts. Access to this bucket and its objects can be specified using ACLs.
Object Ownership
Bucket owner preferred
If new objects written to this bucket specify the bucket-owner-full-control canned ACL, they are owned by the bucket owner. Otherwise, they are owned by the object writer.

Next, unblock your S3 bucket and acknowledge you really want to make it publicly accessible.

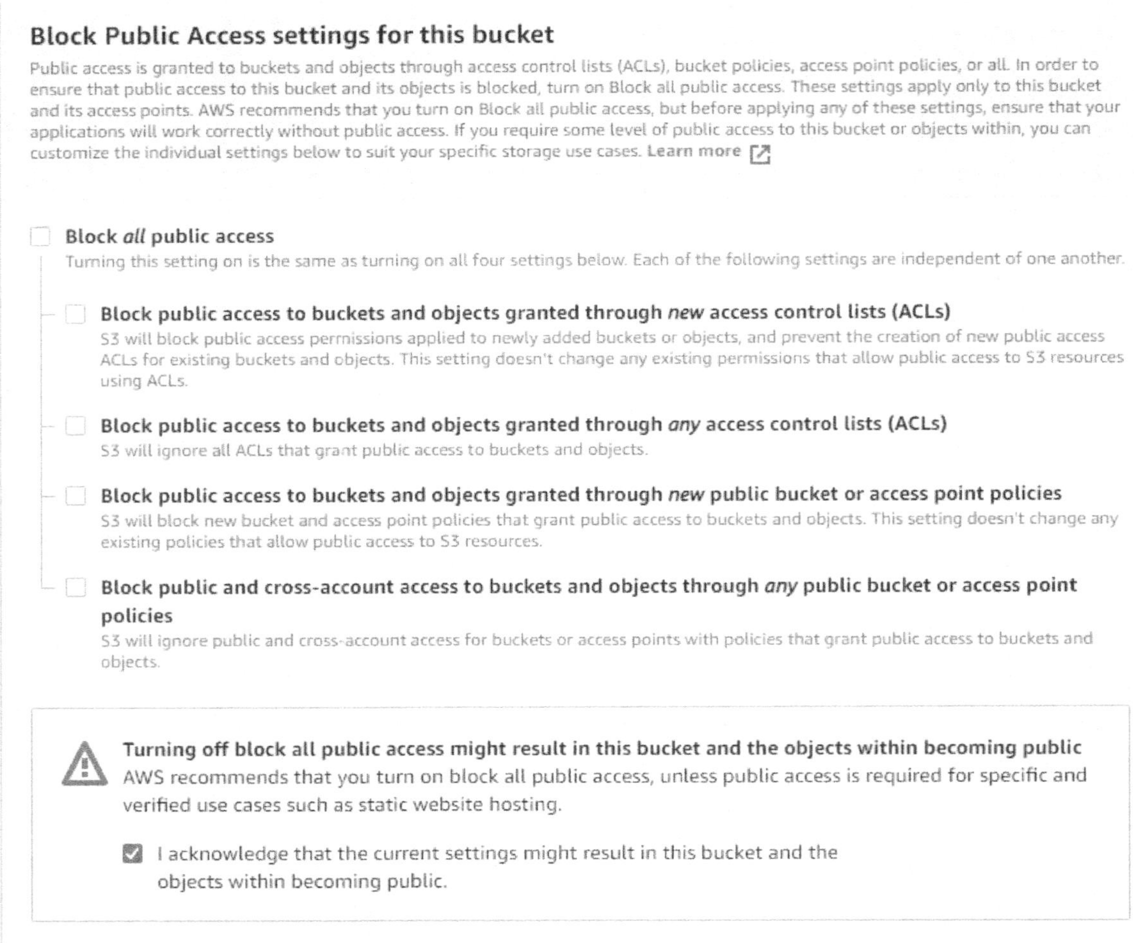
Block Public Access settings for this bucket
Public access is granted to buckets and objects through access control lists (ACLs), bucket policies, access point policies, or all. In order to ensure that public access to this bucket and its objects is blocked, turn on Block all public access. These settings apply only to this bucket and its access points. AWS recommends that you turn on Block all public access, but before applying any of these settings, ensure that your applications will work correctly without public access. If you require some level of public access to this bucket or objects within, you can customize the individual settings below to suit your specific storage use cases. Learn more
Block all public access
Turning this setting on is the same as turning on all four settings below. Each of the following settings are independent of one another.
Block public access to buckets and objects granted through new access control lists (ACLs)
S3 will block public access permissions applied to newly added buckets or objects, and prevent the creation of new public access ACLs for existing buckets and objects. This setting doesn't change any existing permissions that allow public access to S3 resources using ACLs.
Block public access to buckets and objects granted through any access control lists (ACLs)
S3 will ignore all ACLs that grant public access to buckets and objects.
Block public access to buckets and objects granted through new public bucket or access point policies
S3 will block new bucket and access point policies that grant public access to buckets and objects. This setting doesn't change any existing policies that allow public access to S3 resources.
Block public and cross-account access to buckets and objects through any public bucket or access point policies
S3 will ignore public and cross-account access for buckets or access points with policies that grant public access to buckets and objects.
Turning off block all public access might result in this bucket and the objects within becoming public
AWS recommends that you turn on block all public access, unless public access is required for specific and verified use cases such as static website hosting.
I acknowledge that the current settings might result in this bucket and the objects within becoming public.

Keep the rest of the defaults on the page and then select “Create bucket”

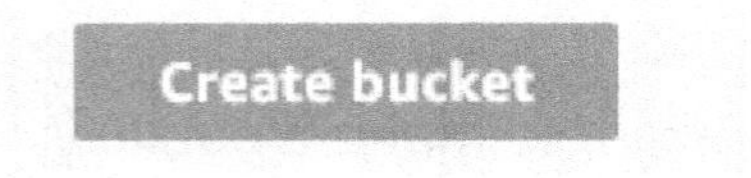
Create bucket

Going back to the buckets list screen you can sort the buckets by creation date to easily find your newly created bucket rather then look for it alphabetically.

Name
AWS Region
Access
Creation date
testbucket520
US West (N. California) us-west-1
Objects can be public
May 20, 2022, 12:14:43 (UTC-07:00)

Open the bucket you just created and go to the permissions tab.

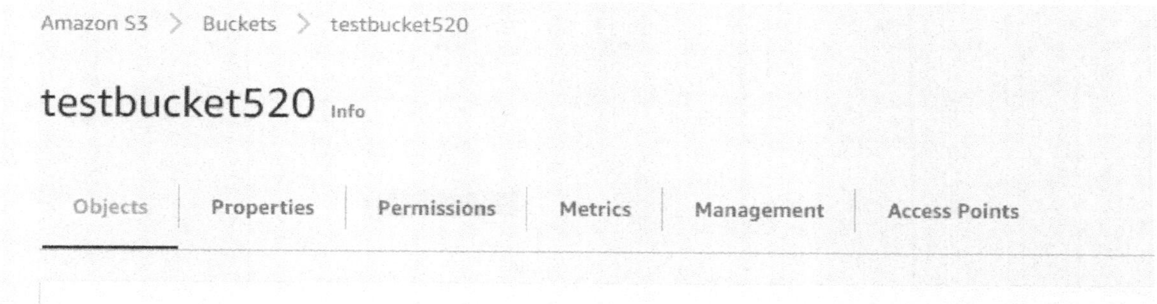

Amazon S3 > Buckets > testbucket520
testbucket520 Info
Objects
Properties
Permissions
Metrics
Management
Access Points

You need to configure the permissions further by first inserting a ‘Bucket policy’. Select the “Edit” button.

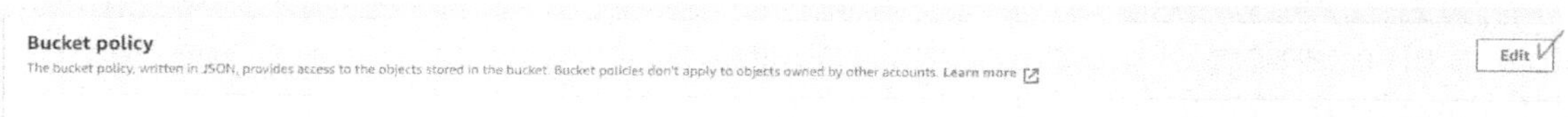

Bucket policy
The bucket policy, written in JSON, provides access to the objects stored in the bucket. Bucket policies don't apply to objects owned by other accounts. Learn more
Edit

Now you have two options with your Bucket policy. You can make a generic *read only policy*, or a *read only by IP policy*. The IP bucket policy will limit anyone who doesn’t have your IP address from seeing the data in your bucket, including any website code you are hosting. IP address restriction is a useful and free way to limit bucket access, however it is not foolproof as IP addresses can be spoofed. Also, you likely have a dynamic IP address that can change regularly unless you pay extra money to your ISP for a static IP address. So remember to check to see if your IP address has changed if you can no longer access objects in your S3 bucket after using an IP restricted bucket policy. If you switch to your phones hotspot or Starbucks WiFi that is also going to provide a new IP address so you would have to adjust your bucket policy accordingly for that new IP address.

Read-only S3 bucket policy

Below is the first example of an open “read-only bucket policy” you can use. You only need to copy/paste your S3 bucket ‘ARN” and place it in the appropriate ‘bucket expression’ location in the policy document. The bucket ARN can be found at the top of the bucket configuration page:

```
"Resource": "<YOUR-BUCKET-ARN-EXPRESSION>/*"
```

After editing the above line for your specific bucket ARN save the policy.

```
{
    "Version": "2012-10-17",
    "Statement": [
        {
            "Sid": "PublicRead",
            "Effect": "Allow",
            "Principal": "*",
            "Action": "s3:GetObject",
            "Resource": "<YOUR-BUCKET-ARN-EXPRESSION>/*"
        }
    ]
}
```

Below is an example of the public read bucket policy with the name of the bucket ARN embedded into the ‘bucket expression.’

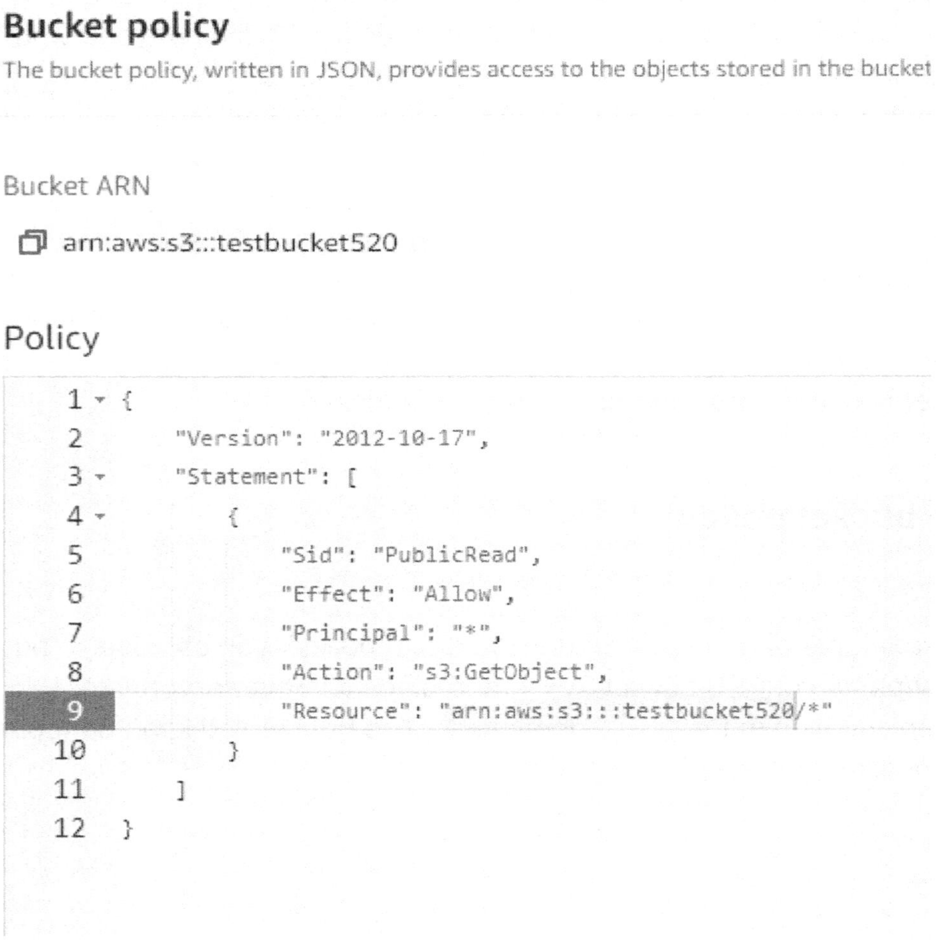
Bucket policy
The bucket policy, written in JSON, provides access to the objects stored in the bucket
Bucket ARN
arn:aws:s3:::testbucket520
Policy
{
"Version": "2012-10-17",
"Statement": [
{
"Sid": "PublicRead",
"Effect": "Allow",
"Principal": "*",
"Action": "s3:GetObject",
"Resource": "arn:aws:s3:::testbucket520/*"
}
]
}

Also make sure to leave the training '/*' after the ARN expression. This allows all the keys and objects within the bucket to also share the same policy.

IP address restricted S3 bucket policy

The following JSON document is a policy example you can use for an *IP address restricted S3 bucket policy*. In the policy example below, you have two lines to modify. The first modification is your bucket ARN:

```
“Resource”: “arn:aws:s3:::<YOUR-BUCKER-NAME-HERE>/*”,
```

The second line to modify is your IP address. To find your Ipv4 address simply go to a website like:

https://whatismyipaddress.com/

```
“aws:SourceIp”: “<YOUR-IP-ADDRESS-HERE>/24”
```

The new *IP limited bucket access policy* is below:

```
{
    “Version”: “2012-10-17”,
    “Id”: “somethingunique”,
    “Statement”: [
        {
            “Sid”: “IPAllow”,
            “Effect”: “Allow”,
            “Principal”: “*”,
            “Action”: “s3:GetObject”,
            “Resource”: “arn:aws:s3:::<YOUR-BUCKER-NAME-HERE>/*”,
            “Condition”: {
                “IpAddress”: {
                    “aws:SourceIp”: “<YOUR-IP-ADDRESS-HERE>/24”
                }
            }
        }
    ]
}
```

Next, you will edit the ACL list you enabled earlier, select “Edit”.

Access control list (ACL)
Grant basic read/write permissions to other AWS accounts. Learn more
Edit

Now check the box for the "List" and "Read" for "Everyone" and finally click the box acknowledging these changes. AWS really wants to make sure you are OK with everyone readings your S3 info if your URL is discovered. However, since we only allowed "GET" access no one can write to (PUT) or delete data from your bucket.

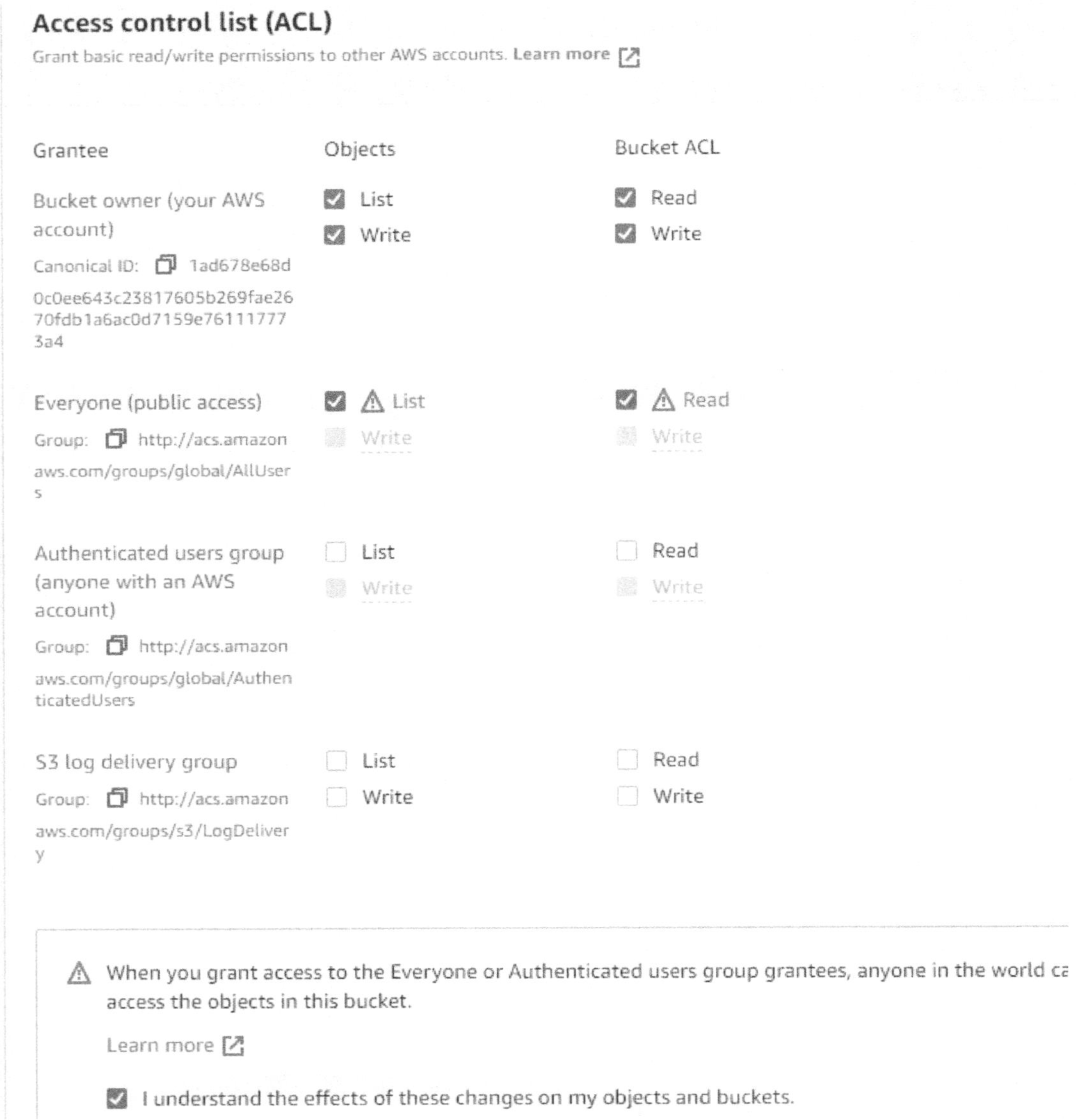
Access control list (ACL)
Grant basic read/write permissions to other AWS accounts. Learn more
Grantee
Objects
Bucket ACL
Bucket owner (your AWS account)
Canonical ID: 1ad678e68d0c0ee643c23817605b269fae2670fdb1a6ac0d7159e761117773a4
List
Write
Read
Write
Everyone (public access)
Group: http://acs.amazonaws.com/groups/global/AllUsers
List
Write
Read
Write
Authenticated users group (anyone with an AWS account)
Group: http://acs.amazonaws.com/groups/global/AuthenticatedUsers
List
Write
Read
Write
S3 log delivery group
Group: http://acs.amazonaws.com/groups/s3/LogDelivery
List
Write
Read
Write
When you grant access to the Everyone or Authenticated users group grantees, anyone in the world ca
access the objects in this bucket.
Learn more
I understand the effects of these changes on my objects and buckets.

Now save your changes to the ACL:

Save changes

CORS configuration (optional):

The last part of configuring S3 permissions is writing the CORS policy but this is optional in most cases. CORS allows bucket access across domains which you might want to restrict but you can also keep open for ease of accessing one bucket in your account from another bucket in your same account.

Select the “Edit” button in the CORS pane:

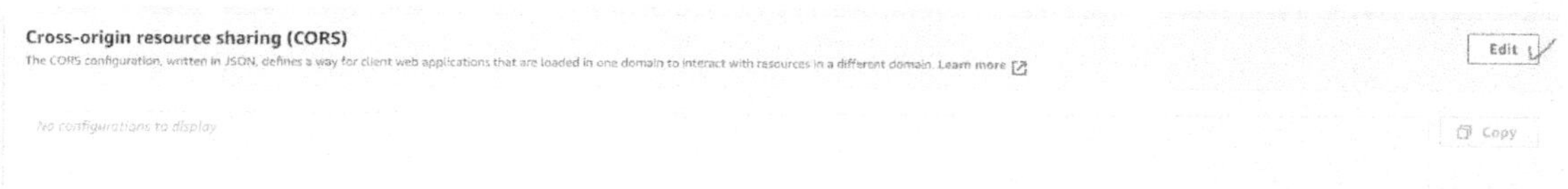
Cross-origin resource sharing (CORS)
The CORS configuration, written in JSON, defines a way for client web applications that are loaded in one domain to interact with resources in a different domain. Learn more
Edit
No configurations to display
Copy

Below is a generic CORS policy you can copy and paste into the CORS editor:

```
[
    {
        “AllowedHeaders”: [
            “Authorization”
        ],
        “AllowedMethods”: [
            “GET”
        ],
        “AllowedOrigins”: [
            “*”
        ],
        “ExposeHeaders”: [],
        “MaxAgeSeconds”: 4000
    }
]
```

This part of configuring your S3 bucket is especially easy because this CORS document does not require any customization.

Now select to “Save changes” to CORS:

Cross-origin resource sharing (CORS)
The CORS configuration, written in JSON, defines a way for client web applications that are loaded in one domain to interact with resources in a different domain. Learn more
[
{
"AllowedHeaders": [
"Authorization"
],
"AllowedMethods": [
"GET"
],
"AllowedOrigins": [
"*"
],
"ExposeHeaders": [],
"MaxAgeSeconds": 4000
}
]
Cancel
Save changes

You have now finished making you bucket public and accessible from anywhere in the world. Just make sure you do not put anything in your bucket you do not want anyone seeing in case your public facing S3 bucket URL is discovered.

Step 2 – Enabling a Static Web Host in the S3 Bucket

It is now time to add a static web host to your S3 bucket. The good news is that you can use the same bucket to both store IoT data and host a static website. You can do one without the other as well, as they are not mutually exclusive. Now return to the buckets base level and select the 'Properties' tab.

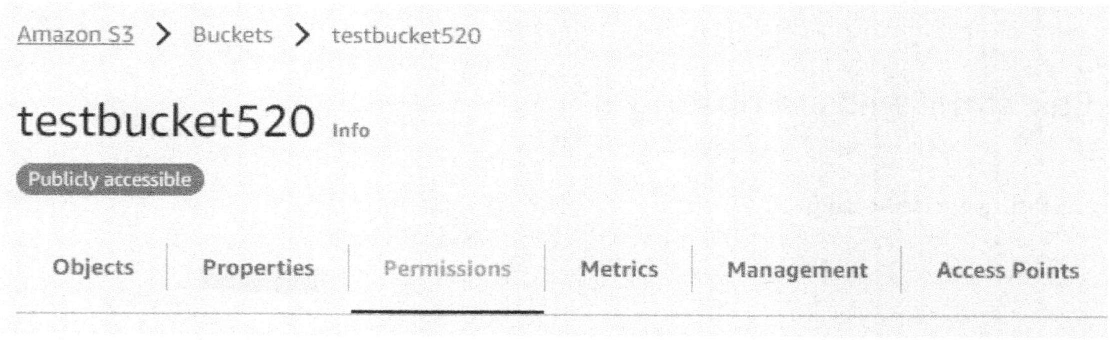
Amazon S3 > Buckets > testbucket520
testbucket520 Info
Publicly accessible
Objects
Properties
Permissions
Metrics
Management
Access Points

Scroll down all the way in the properties page to the “Static website hosting” area and select “Edit”:

Static website hosting
Use this bucket to host a website or redirect requests. Learn more
Edit
Static website hosting
Disabled

To keep things simple, just “Enable” static website hosting, and then name your landing page “index.html”. Do not worry about an error action or redirects.

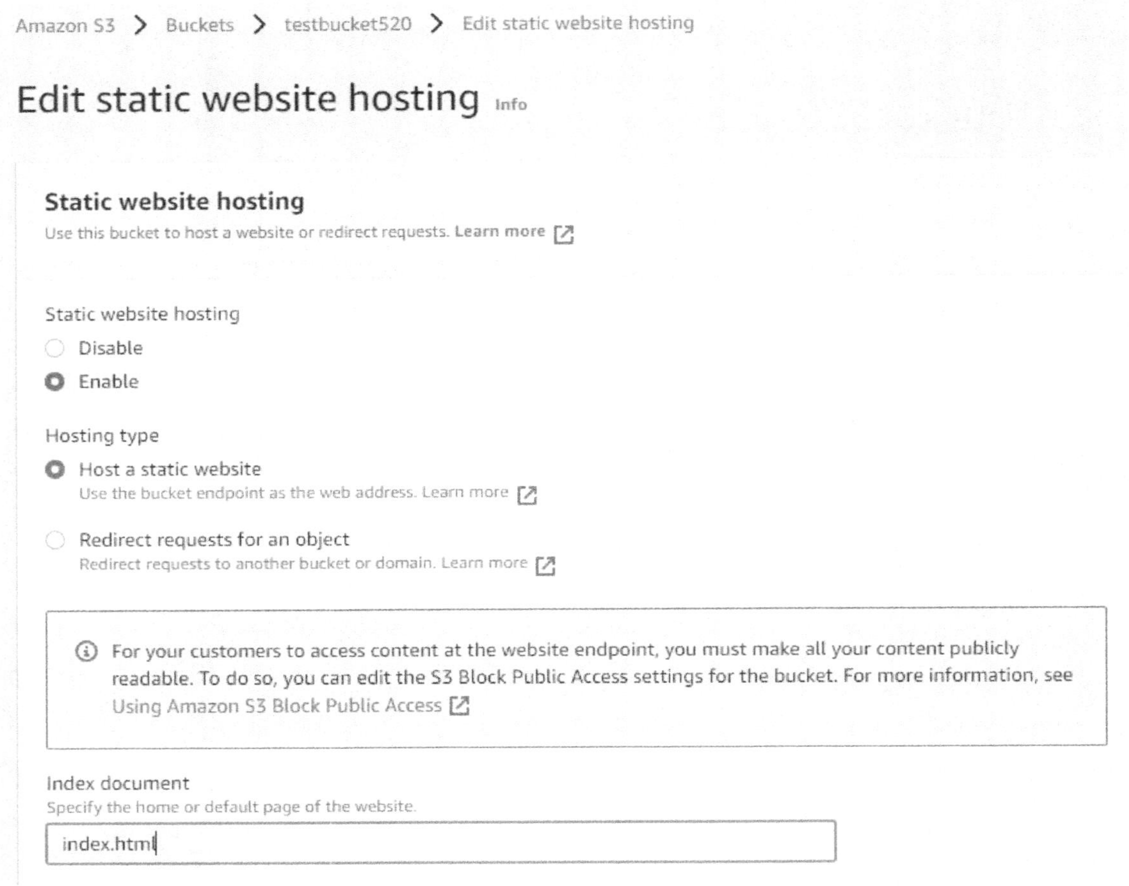

Amazon S3 > Buckets > testbucket520 > Edit static website hosting
Edit static website hosting Info
Static website hosting
Use this bucket to host a website or redirect requests. Learn more
Static website hosting
Disable
Enable
Hosting type
Host a static website
Use the bucket endpoint as the web address. Learn more
Redirect requests for an object
Redirect requests to another bucket or domain. Learn more
For your customers to access content at the website endpoint, you must make all your content publicly readable. To do so, you can edit the S3 Block Public Access settings for the bucket. For more information, see Using Amazon S3 Block Public Access
Index document
Specify the home or default page of the website.
index.html

Now press “Save changes”

Save changes

Now it is time to upload a simple “Hello World” program to test that the index.html works in the wild as a functional website. Return to the buckets base level and select the “Objects” tab. For the *index.html* you can use the following code and then save it as “**index.html**” on your computer.

```
<!DOCTYPE html>
<html lang=”en”>
<head>
  <meta charset=”utf-8”>
  <meta name=”viewport”
     content=”width=device-width, initial-scale=1, user-scalable=yes”>
   <title>Hello World in title</title>
```

```
</head>
<body>
Hello World in body!
</body>
</html>
```

The S3 upload options are either to drag and drop the index.html file, or just browse to the index.html file on your computer to select the file - either method is fine.

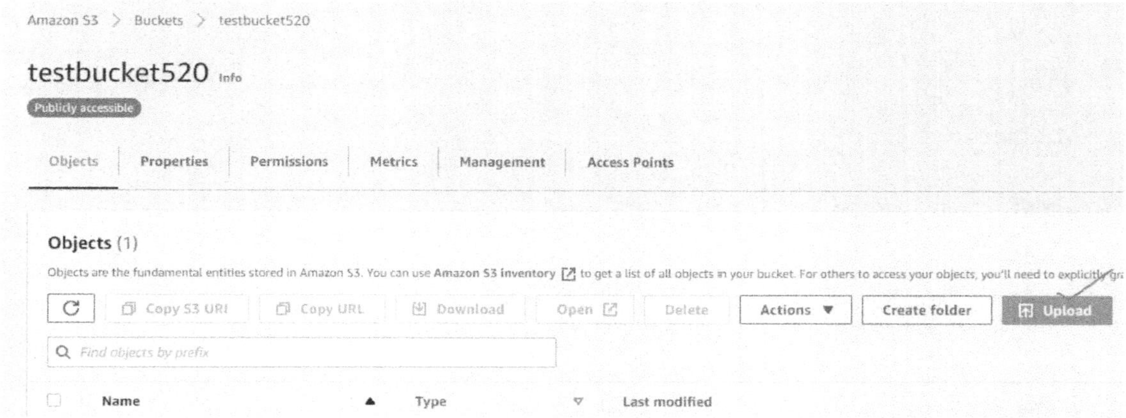

Amazon S3 > Buckets > testbucket520
testbucket520 Info
Publicly accessible
Objects
Properties
Permissions
Metrics
Management
Access Points
Objects (1)
Copy S3 URI
Copy URL
Download
Open
Delete
Actions
Create folder
Upload
Find objects by prefix
Name
Type
Last modified

Now select to "Upload" the index.html file:

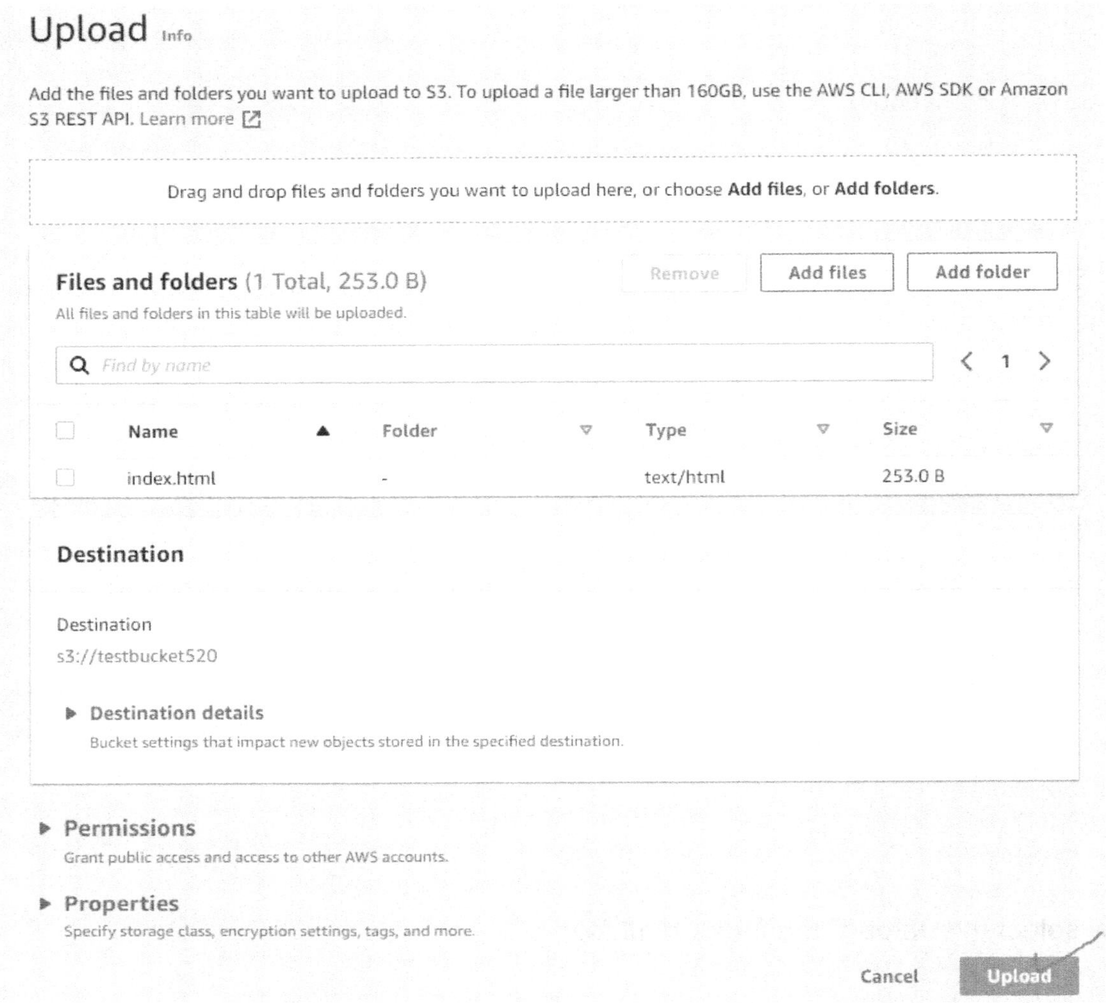
Upload Info
Add the files and folders you want to upload to S3. To upload a file larger than 160GB, use the AWS CLI, AWS SDK or Amazon S3 REST API. Learn more
Drag and drop files and folders you want to upload here, or choose Add files, or Add folders.
Files and folders (1 Total, 253.0 B)
All files and folders in this table will be uploaded.
Remove
Add files
Add folder
Find by name
Name
Folder
Type
Size
index.html
text/html
253.0 B
Destination
Destination
s3://testbucket520
Destination details
Bucket settings that impact new objects stored in the specified destination.
Permissions
Grant public access and access to other AWS accounts.
Properties
Specify storage class, encryption settings, tags, and more.
Cancel
Upload

After clicking the newly uploaded index file, you will see the "Object URL" which is the URL of the index page. You can now right click the URL and open the index.html in a new browser window.

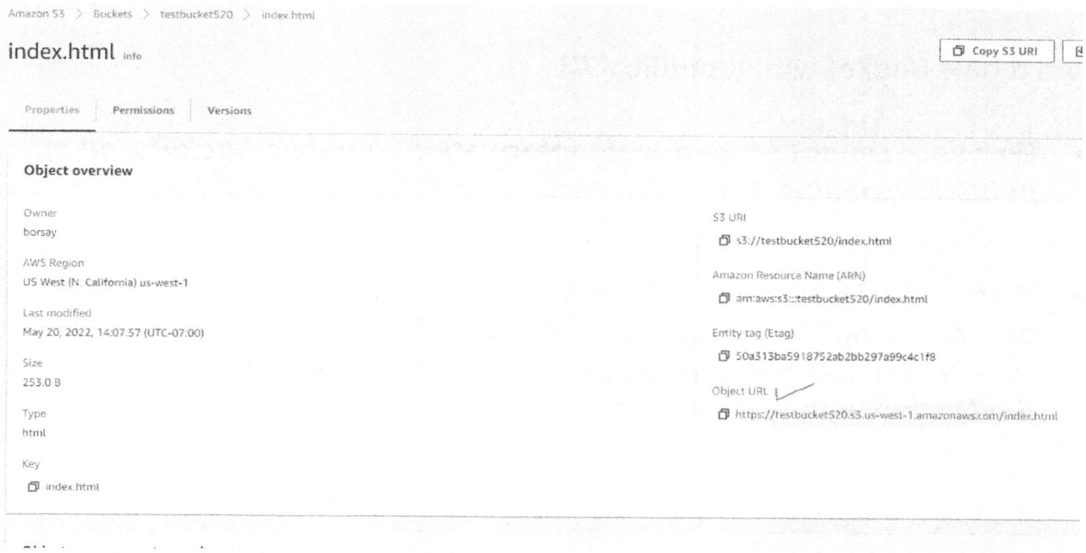
Amazon S3 > Buckets > testbucket520 > index.html
index.html Info
Copy S3 URI
Properties
Permissions
Versions
Object overview
Owner
borsay
AWS Region
US West (N. California) us-west-1
Last modified
May 20, 2022, 14:07:57 (UTC-07:00)
Size
253.0 B
Type
html
Key
index.html
S3 URI
s3://testbucket520/index.html
Amazon Resource Name (ARN)
arn:aws:s3:::testbucket520/index.html
Entity tag (Etag)
50a313ba5918752ab2bb297a99c4c1f8
Object URL
https://testbucket520.s3.us-west-1.amazonaws.com/index.html

The result should now look like the browser image below if you used the same HTML code as I provided.

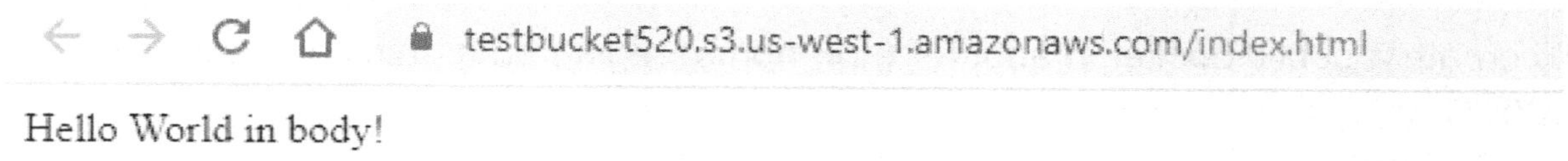
testbucket520.s3.us-west-1.amazonaws.com/index.html
Hello World in body!

Wow, super boring result but don't worry, adding your own CSS and JavaScript to your static website hosted in S3 will make the visualizations much better. Congratulations on your static website in a public S3 bucket. Except for this specific HTML code, you will be following this process throughout this book for designing new and exciting visualizations with IoT data.

Next, you will move on to accomplishing all the same tasks but with just using the AWS CLI without the need to log into your AWS account or use the console.

Step 3 - Creating a S3 Bucket with the AWS CLI

When using the AWS CLI, the S3 bucket commands will default to your "home" region in which your AWS CLI is configured to. If you make a bucket outside your home region, then you will have to use different commands with the 's3API' as I demonstrate below for creating another bucket in 'us-west-2' region.

Create a new bucket with a public ACL

- ***Warning: Do not store private information in public buckets, all info is publicly readable***

- ***Warning: Copying code from the chapters GitHub is more reliable for programming than copying code from eBooks due to UTF-8 character translation and formatting. The CLI Commands below can be found on the GitHub with verified formatting.***

Create a public bucket in your home region with this command in the AWS CLI:

```
aws s3api create-bucket –bucket <Your-Bucket-Name>
--acl public-read
```

To create a public bucket in another (non-home) region enter this command into the AWS CLI:

```
aws s3api create-bucket –bucket <Your-Bucket-Name> --region <AWS-Region>
--create-bucket-configuration LocationConstraint=<AWS-Region> --acl public-
read
```

Here I create a bucket called “testbucket520cli” in us-west-2

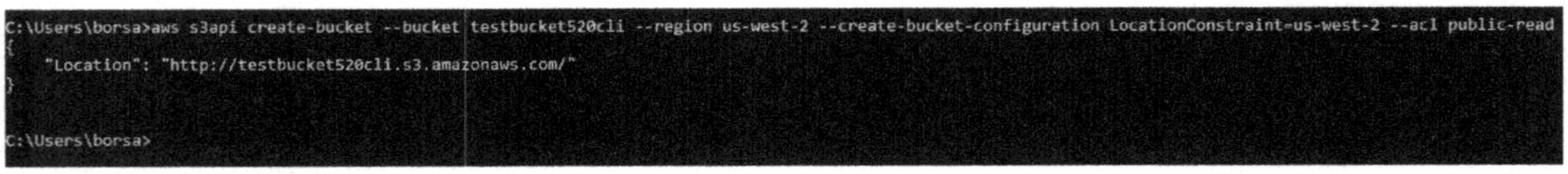
C:\Users\borsa>aws s3api create-bucket --bucket testbucket520cli --region us-west-2 --create-bucket-configuration LocationConstraint=us-west-2 --acl public-read
{
"Location": "http://testbucket520cli.s3.amazonaws.com/"
}
C:\Users\borsa>

Check the result in S3 for the newly created public bucket:

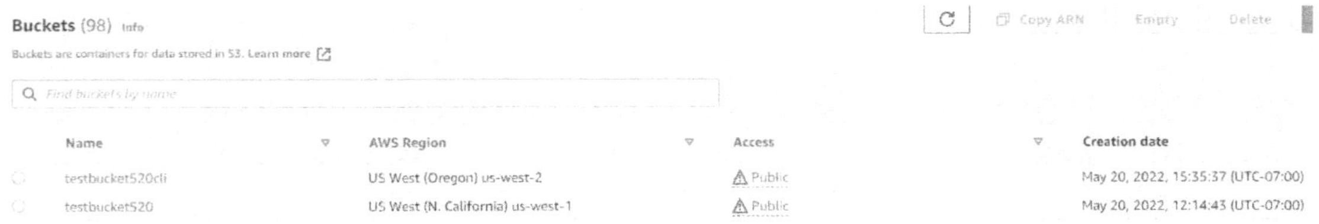
Buckets (98) Info
Buckets are containers for data stored in S3. Learn more
Copy ARN
Empty
Delete
Name
AWS Region
Access
Creation date
testbucket520cli
US West (Oregon) us-west-2
Public
May 20, 2022, 15:35:37 (UTC-07:00)
testbucket520
US West (N. California) us-west-1
Public
May 20, 2022, 12:14:43 (UTC-07:00)

Next you need to create and save the following file in the same folder on your computer that you are currently using with the AWS CLI. So, in my case I will navigate to the folder on my desktop which contains my bucket policy's.

We discussed two different bucket policy's; you can choose to use either one. One is a public read bucket policy and the other is an IP address limited read bucket policy:

File 1 – save as: "*public_policy.json*" after filling out the ARN expression for your bucket name:

```
{
    "Version": "2012-10-17",
    "Statement": [
        {
            "Sid": "PublicRead",
            "Effect": "Allow",
            "Principal": "*",
            "Action": "s3:GetObject",
            "Resource": "<YOUR-BUCKET-ARN-EXPRESSION>/*"
        }
    ]
}
```

If you want to use the IP address limited bucket policy for extra free security then **save as: "*ip_limited_policy.json*"** after filling out the ARN expression for your bucket name:

```
{
    "Version": "2012-10-17",
    "Id": "somethingunique",
    "Statement": [
        {
            "Sid": "IPAllow",
            "Effect": "Allow",
            "Principal": "*",
            "Action": "s3:GetObject",
            "Resource": "arn:aws:s3:::<YOUR-BUCKER-NAME-HERE>/*",
            "Condition": {
                "IpAddress": {
                    "aws:SourceIp": "<YOUR-IP-HERE>/24"
                }
```

```
            }
        }
    ]
}
```

To upload the file to your S3 bucket fill out your bucket name and AWS region and then enter the following command into the AWS CLI:

```
aws s3api put-bucket-policy -region <Your-Region> --policy file://<Your-Policy-Name>.json -bucket <Your-Bucket-Name>
```

Directory of C:\Users\borsa\Desktop\snippits\prereq_s3\policys
05/20/2022 04:06 PM <DIR> .
05/20/2022 04:06 PM <DIR> ..
05/20/2022 04:06 PM 456 ip_limited_policy.json
1 File(s) 456 bytes
2 Dir(s) 138,870,231,040 bytes free
C:\Users\borsa\Desktop\snippits\prereq_s3\policys>aws s3api put-bucket-policy --region us-west-2 --policy file://ip_limited_policy.json --bucket testbucket520cli
C:\Users\borsa\Desktop\snippits\prereq_s3\policys>

The proper response from the AW CLI is no response. Go to the AWS console and check that the S3 bucket→Permissions→Bucket Policy was configured correctly.

Optional: Now it is time to upload your CORS policy if you decide you want cross origin access. However, unlike the bucket policy, the CORS policy must be in a different JSON format than what we used in the AWS console earlier. Create and save the following file in the same location on your PC that you are using the AWS CLI in.

File 2 – save as: ***'cors.json'***

```
{
    "CORSRules": [
      {
        "AllowedOrigins": ["*"],
        "AllowedHeaders": ["Authorization"],
        "AllowedMethods": ["GET"],
        "MaxAgeSeconds": 4000
      }
    ]
  }
```

Fill out the command below with your bucket name and your bucket region and then upload the CORS file to your S3 bucket with the following command from the AWS CLI:

```
aws s3api put-bucket-cors -cors-configuration file://cors.json
--bucket <Your-Bucket-Name> --region <Your-Region>
```

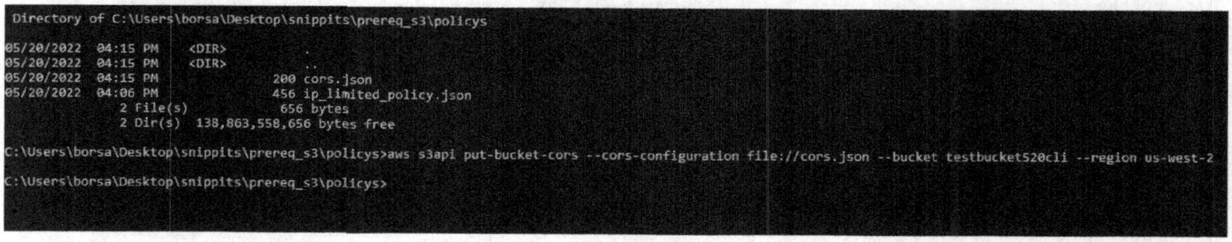

Directory of C:\Users\borsa\Desktop\snippits\prereq_s3\policys
05/20/2022 04:15 PM <DIR> .
05/20/2022 04:15 PM <DIR> ..
05/20/2022 04:15 PM 200 cors.json
05/20/2022 04:06 PM 456 ip_limited_policy.json
2 File(s) 656 bytes
2 Dir(s) 138,863,558,656 bytes free
C:\Users\borsa\Desktop\snippits\prereq_s3\policys>aws s3api put-bucket-cors --cors-configuration file://cors.json --bucket testbucket520cli --region us-west-2
C:\Users\borsa\Desktop\snippits\prereq_s3\policys>

Step 4 - Enabling a Static Web Host in the S3 Bucket from the AWS CLI

To enable static web hosting in your public bucket with a landing page of "index.html", fill out your bucket name and bucket region and enter the following command into the AWS CLI:

```
aws s3 website s3://<Your-Bucket-Name> --region <Your-Bucket-Region> --index-
document index.html
```

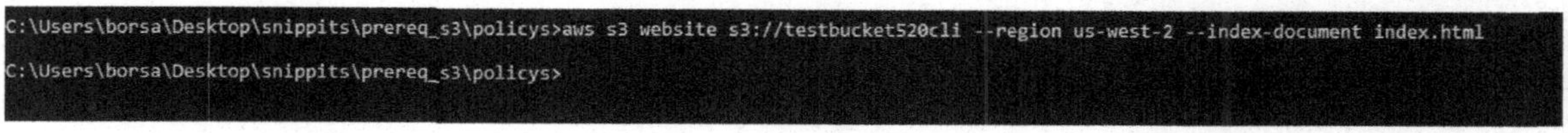

C:\Users\borsa\Desktop\snippits\prereq_s3\policys>aws s3 website s3://testbucket520cli --region us-west-2 --index-document index.html
C:\Users\borsa\Desktop\snippits\prereq_s3\policys>

Create and save the following file in the same local folder on your computer that you are using the AWS CLI from:

File 3 – save as: "*index.html*"

```
<!DOCTYPE html>
<html>
   <body>
      <h1>Hello World</h1>
      <p>My S3 static webhost, add HTML and JavaScript files as needed</p>
   </body>
</html>
```

To upload the index.html file to your S3 bucket fill out your bucket name and AWS bucket region and enter the following command into the AWS CLI:

```
aws s3 cp index.html s3://<Your_Globally_Unique_Bucket_Name_Here> --region <Your-AWS-Region>
```

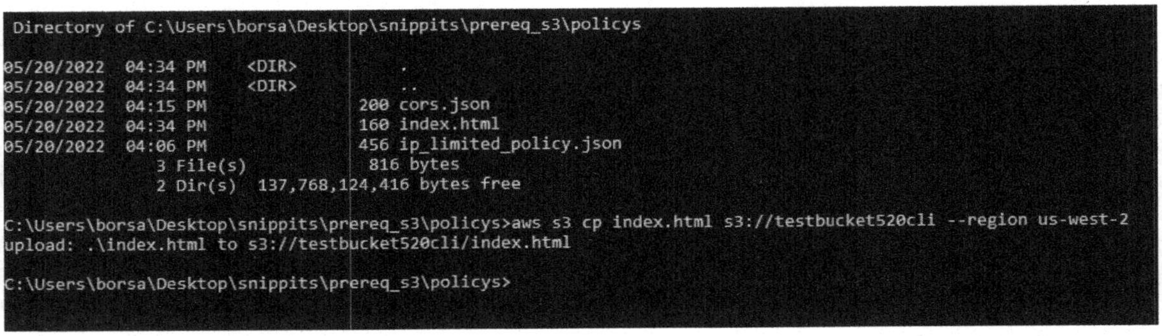

Directory of C:\Users\borsa\Desktop\snippits\prereq_s3\policys
05/20/2022 04:34 PM <DIR> .
05/20/2022 04:34 PM <DIR> ..
05/20/2022 04:15 PM 200 cors.json
05/20/2022 04:34 PM 160 index.html
05/20/2022 04:06 PM 456 ip_limited_policy.json
3 File(s) 816 bytes
2 Dir(s) 137,768,124,416 bytes free
C:\Users\borsa\Desktop\snippits\prereq_s3\policys>aws s3 cp index.html s3://testbucket520cli --region us-west-2
upload: .\index.html to s3://testbucket520cli/index.html
C:\Users\borsa\Desktop\snippits\prereq_s3\policys>

**There is no multifile upload other than recursive file uploads within a specified folder; this would upload all the folder contents to the S3 destination.*

To view the new website in your S3 bucket, navigate to your index pages 'Object URL' and left click the URL to open the page in your web browser:

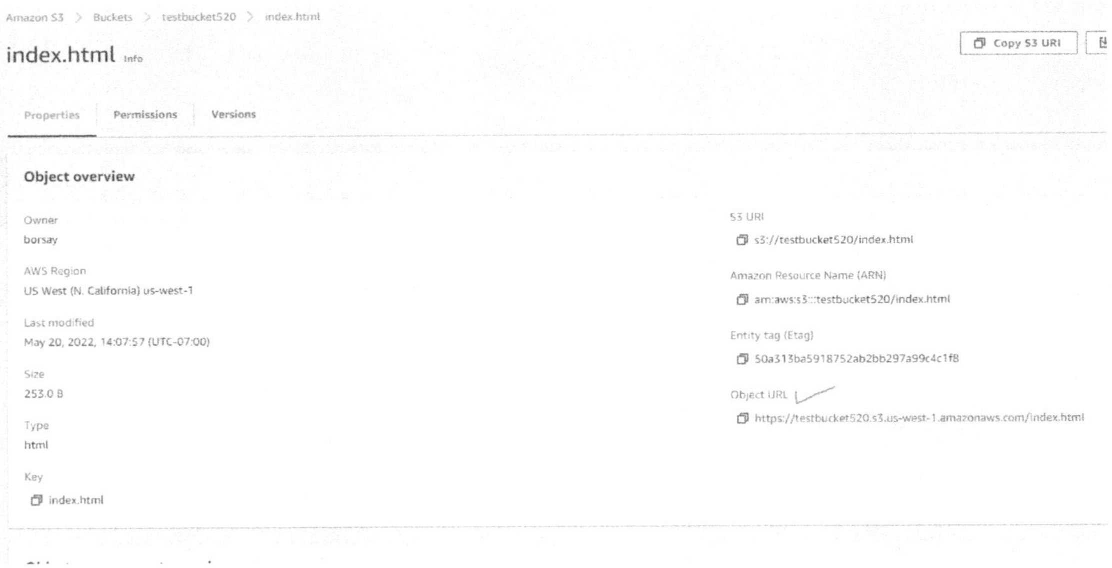

Amazon S3 > Buckets > testbucket520 > index.html
index.html Info
Copy S3 URI
Properties
Permissions
Versions
Object overview
Owner
borsay
AWS Region
US West (N. California) us-west-1
Last modified
May 20, 2022, 14:07:57 (UTC-07:00)
Size
253.0 B
Type
html
Key
index.html
S3 URI
s3://testbucket520/index.html
Amazon Resource Name (ARN)
arn:aws:s3:::testbucket520/index.html
Entity tag (Etag)
50a313ba5918752ab2bb297a99c4c1f8
Object URL
https://testbucket520.s3.us-west-1.amazonaws.com/index.html

And now your website should appear:

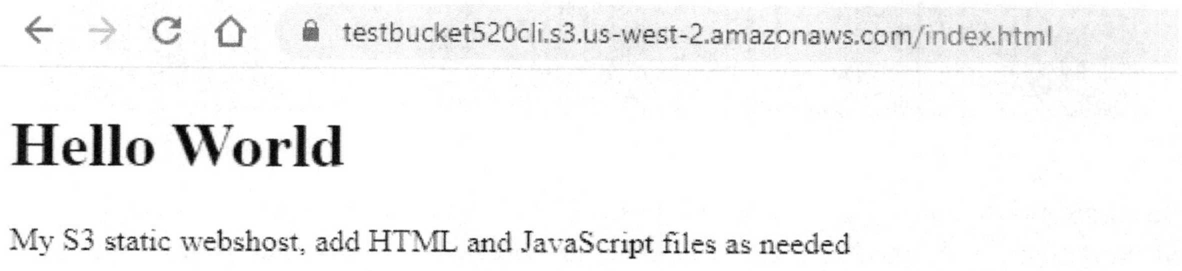
testbucket520cli.s3.us-west-2.amazonaws.com/index.html
Hello World
My S3 static webshost, add HTML and JavaScript files as needed

For another way to navigate to your static webpage go to the 'Object URL' and right click it to open your website in a new tab on your web browser:

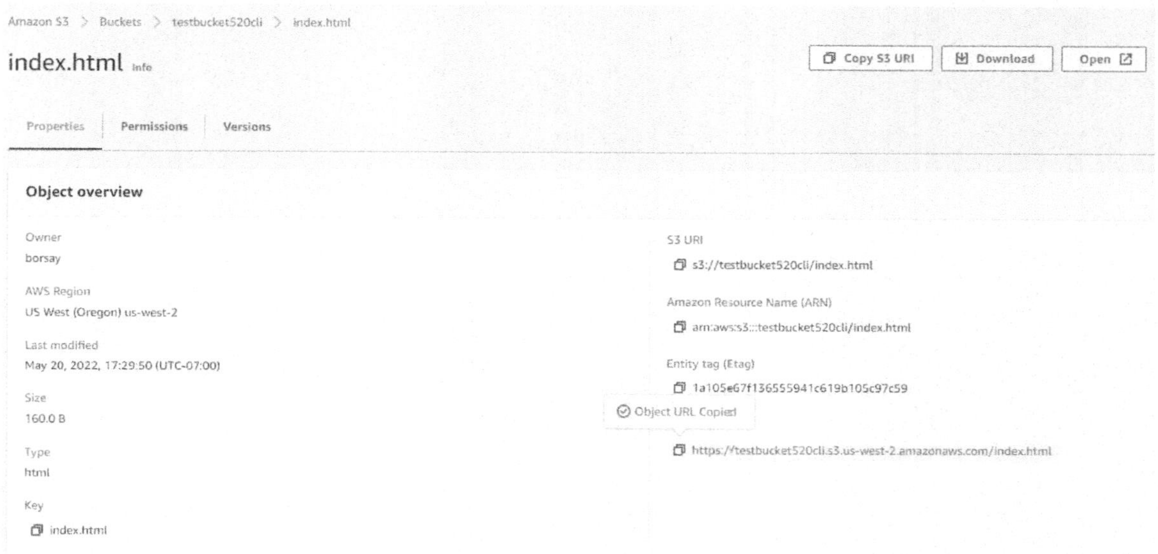
Amazon S3 > Buckets > testbucket520cli > index.html
index.html Info
Copy S3 URI
Download
Open
Properties
Permissions
Versions
Object overview
Owner
borsay
AWS Region
US West (Oregon) us-west-2
Last modified
May 20, 2022, 17:29:50 (UTC-07:00)
Size
160.0 B
Type
html
Key
index.html
S3 URI
s3://testbucket520cli/index.html
Amazon Resource Name (ARN)
arn:aws:s3:::testbucket520cli/index.html
Entity tag (Etag)
1a105e67f136555941c619b105c97c59
Object URL Copied
https://testbucket520cli.s3.us-west-2.amazonaws.com/index.html

Step 5 - Deleting the S3 Bucket and all Files with a Single AWS CLI Command

To remove your S3 bucket and all files in the bucket fill out the bucket name and AWS region and enter the following command into the AWS CLI:

```
aws s3 rb s3://<Your-Bucket-Name> --region <Your-AWS-Region> --force
```

This recursively removes all files and then deletes the S3 bucket.

```
C:\Users\borsa\Desktop\snippits\prereq_s3\policys>aws s3 rb s3://testbucket520cli --region us-west-2 --force
delete: s3://testbucket520cli/index.html
remove_bucket: testbucket520cli

C:\Users\borsa\Desktop\snippits\prereq_s3\policys>
```

Congratulations, you have created a public S3 bucket and then added a static webhost with both the AWS console and the AWS CLI. This process will be useful throughout the rest of the book so you can refer to this prerequisite tutorial as often as needed.

Chapter 10 -
Prerequisite 2 AWS IoT Core with Lambda

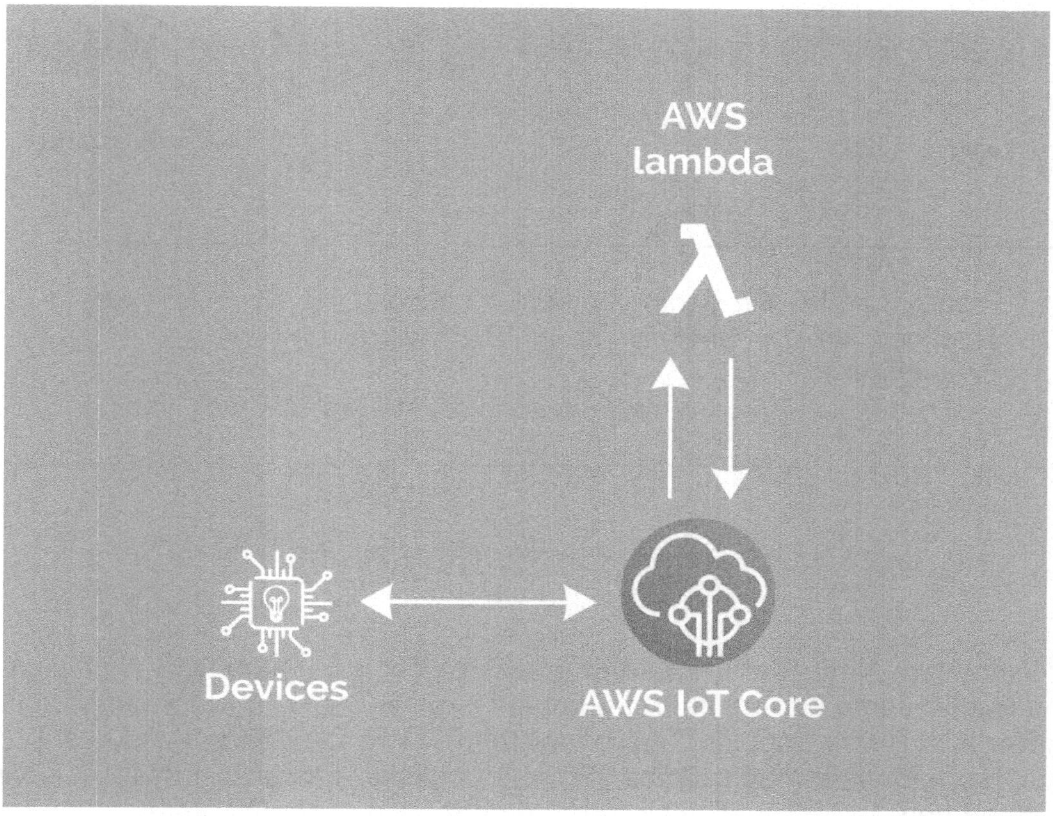
AWS
lambda
Devices
AWS IoT Core

This prerequisite chapter covers two of the three most important AWS services for IoT: IoT Core and Lambda functions. I have already discussed one of the other vital AWS IoT services – S3, in the previous chapter. For this second prerequisite chapter you will create a MQTT publishing Lambda function, test the function, and then integrate the Lambda function into AWS IoT Core. Once the integration is complete, you can then test the configuration with IoT payloads ingested from IoT Core. The purpose of this chapter is to get the reader familiar with an easy design process for essential AWS services that the reader will use throughout the rest of the book.

Lambda is an essential service when dispatching IoT data throughout the AWS ecosystem of services. How does a Lambda function allow you to manipulate IoT data with a vast array of AWS services? Lambda has an invokable SDK with associated APIs. If you use Node.js in Lambda you simply import the AWS-SDK. If you use Python to program your Lambda function, you then import the Boto3 package. Both libraries have thousands of lines of code covering AWS specific APIs for service integration.

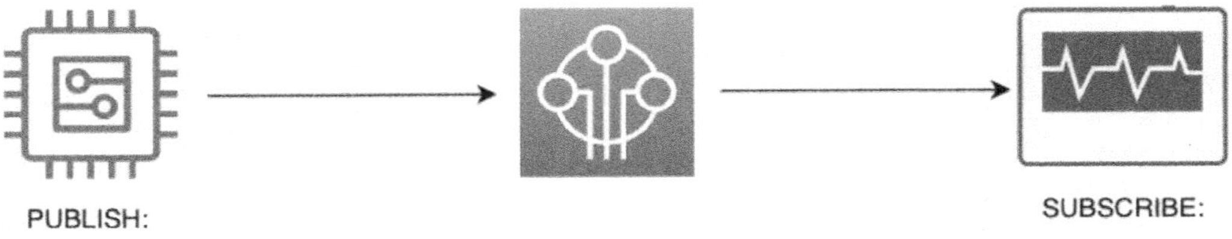
PUBLISH:
SUBSCRIBE:

$

Step 1 - Program an IoT Publishing Lambda Function
Step 2 - Test the Lambda Function with an IoT Payload
Step 3 - Develop an IoT Rule
Step 4 - Test the Rule and Lambda Function with the MQTT Test Client in IoT Core

---

Step 1 - Program an IoT Publishing Lambda Function

It is vital that you understand what the "event" object is in Lambda, and how it works as you will be using it in most of the projects in this book. It is also important that you know how to use Lambda functions with IoT Core to perform various actions on IoT JSON payloads throughout the IoT centric design process. Finally, it is vital to understand how MQTT publishing from Lambda works, as you can use this feature to pass MQTT messages from the Lambda publishing function to the MQTT subscribing function on the IoT device.

Once you are logged into your AWS account Go to AWS Lambda at:

https://console.aws.amazon.com/Lambda

Now "Create" a new Lambda function by pressing the "Create" button on the upper right of the screen:

Last fetched 1 minute ago
Actions
Create function

Name your Lambda function whatever you like and then choose Node.js (version 16.x) or Python (Version 3.8), I will provide Lambda examples of both languages. Use whichever code you are more comfortable with, but due to asynchronous behaviors and how promise "stubbing" is handled in the AWS-SDK for Node.js, I think the Python code will be clearer.

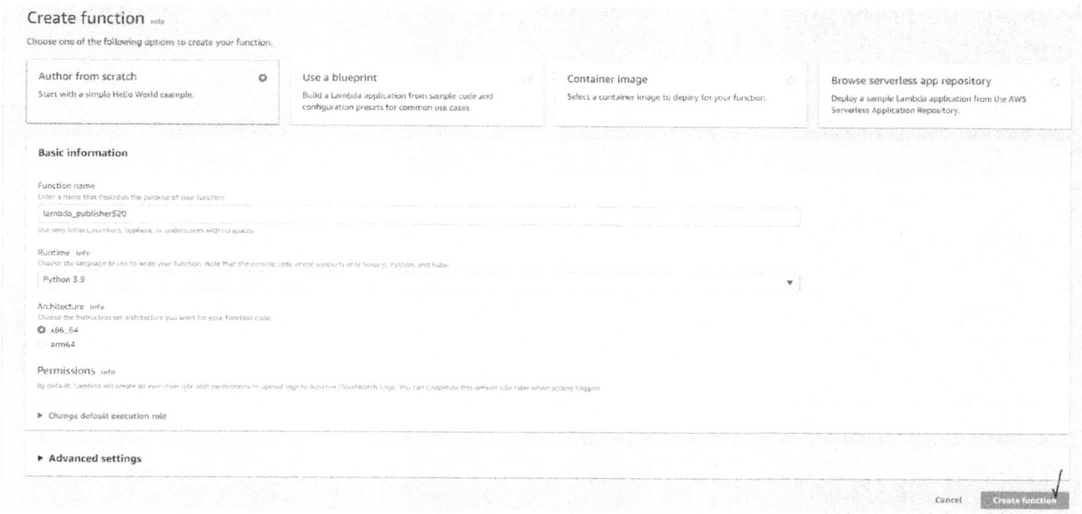

Create function
Choose one of the following options to create your function.
Author from scratch
Start with a simple Hello World example.
Use a blueprint
Build a Lambda application from sample code and configuration presets for common use cases.
Container image
Select a container image to deploy for your function.
Browse serverless app repository
Deploy a sample Lambda application from the AWS Serverless Application Repository.
Basic information
Function name
lambda_publisher520
Runtime
Python 3.9
Architecture
x86_64
arm64
Permissions
Change default execution role
Advanced settings
Cancel
Create function

If using Python fill out the following field in the code below with your own AWS region, I recommended 'us-east-1':

```
region_name='<Your-AWS-Region-Here>'
```

Then paste the following Python code into your Lambda function:

```
import json
import boto3

client = boto3.client('iot-data', region_name='<Your-AWS-Region-Here>')

def lambda_handler(event, context):
    #event['temperature'] = round(((event['temperature'] - 32) / 1.8))
    print(event)
    response = client.publish(
```

```
        topic='fromLambda',
        qos=0,
        payload=json.dumps(event)
    )
    print(response)

    return {
        'statusCode': 200,
        'body': json.dumps('Published to topic')
    }
```

Alternately, if you prefer to use Node.js (version 16.x) instead of Python, create a Lambda function and give it a name of your choice, then fill out the following field in the code:

```
endpoint: '<YOUR-AWS-IOT-ENDPOINT-HERE>'
```

Now copy/paste the Node.js code below into your Lambda function:

```
var AWS = require('aws-sdk');
var iotdata = new AWS.IotData({endpoint: '<YOUR-AWS-IOT-ENDPOINT-HERE>' });

exports.handler = (event) => {
    //event['temperature'] = round(((event['temperature'] - 32) / 1.8))
    console.log("The event object is: " + JSON.stringify(event));
    var params = {
        topic: "fromLambda",
        payload: JSON.stringify(event), //event.Temperature
        qos: 0
    };

    return iotdata.publish(params, function(err, data) {
        if (err) {
            console.log("If error: " + JSON.stringify(err));
        }
        else {
            console.log("Success");
        }
    })
};
```

Both the Python and the JavaScript functions do the same thing, they take an incoming payload as the "event" object into the function. The "event" object can come from the test panel, which you will use soon, or from AWS IoT Core, which you will explore later. Some very simple Lambda functions don't use the "event" object at all, but most non-trivial Lambda functions will use an incoming "event" object and preform various actions on the event object like ETL (extract, transform, load). It is worth noting that the 'event' object is a positional argument, this means you can call it whatever you like as long as it is the first parameter in your Lambda function.

For the use case explained here you are simply taking in a IoT "event" object and publishing it to a topic named "fromLambda". Any MQTT subscribers (using a virtual or physical IoT device) with AWS security certificates and an IoT policy linked to your account can receive the published event payload if they are subscribed to the 'fromLambda" MQTT topic.

Finally, the Node.js Lambda function uses the AWS-SDK whereas the Python Lambda function uses Boto3. These are language specific SDK's which provide hundreds of API's for almost all AWS services. Both the Python and JavaScript Lambda functions provide MQTT publishing ability but not a subscription function from Lambda. AWS wants you to use the MQTT message broker for any MQTT subscription functions required for incoming IoT payloads from external IoT devices.

Here is what the Python code looks like in the Lambda code pane:

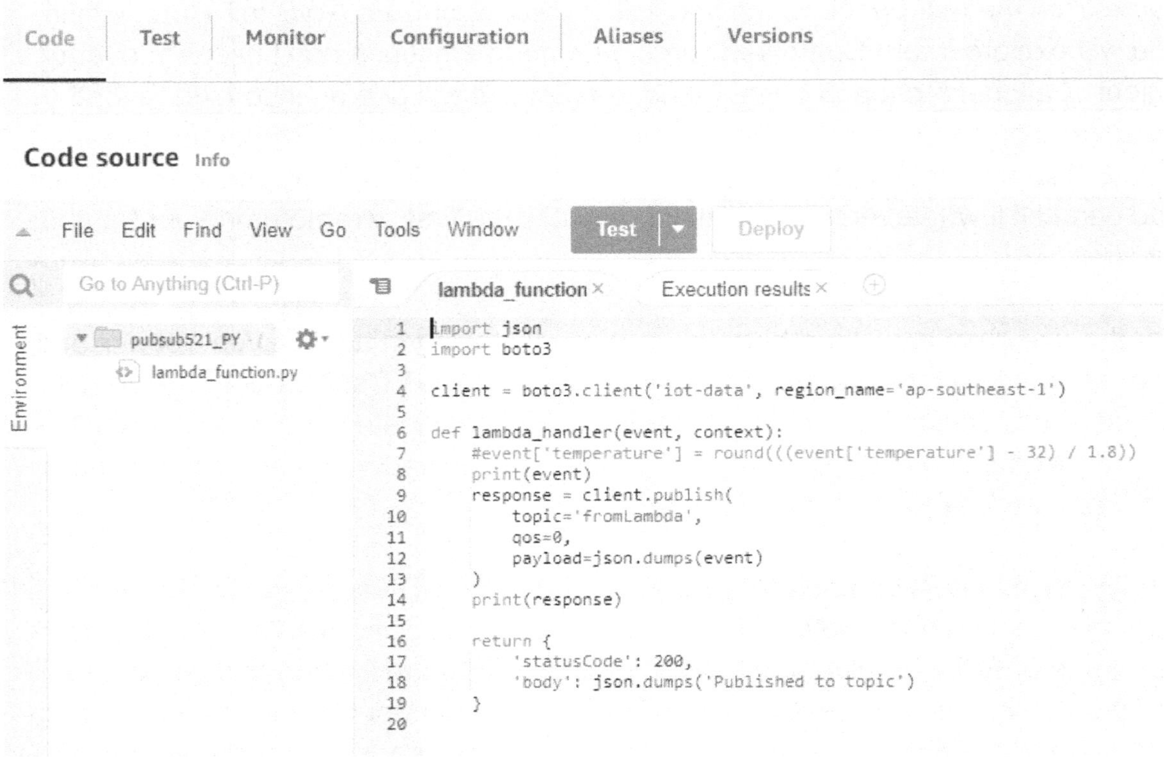
Code
Test
Monitor
Configuration
Aliases
Versions
Code source Info
File Edit Find View Go Tools Window
Test
Deploy
Go to Anything (Ctrl-P)
lambda_function
Execution results
Environment
pubsub521_PY
lambda_function.py
import json
import boto3

client = boto3.client('iot-data', region_name='ap-southeast-1')

def lambda_handler(event, context):
    #event['temperature'] = round(((event['temperature'] - 32) / 1.8))
    print(event)
    response = client.publish(
        topic='fromLambda',
        qos=0,
        payload=json.dumps(event)
)
    print(response)

    return {
        'statusCode': 200,
        'body': json.dumps('Published to topic')
    }

The temperature transform is commented out for now, that will be covered later.

There is one last thing to do before you are ready to move on to testing your Lambda function for IoT payload publishing to your IoT device. You need to give your Lambda permission to access AWS IoT related services. Granting Lambda permissions is a process you will need to do every time you use Lambda with other AWS services. It is boring and tedious but necessary for both security and for enforcing the “least privilege principle” on AWS. For a non-shared private account, limiting permissions are not overly important, but you still must configure them.

To give the required permission to your Lambda function select the “Configuration” tab in your Lambda console.

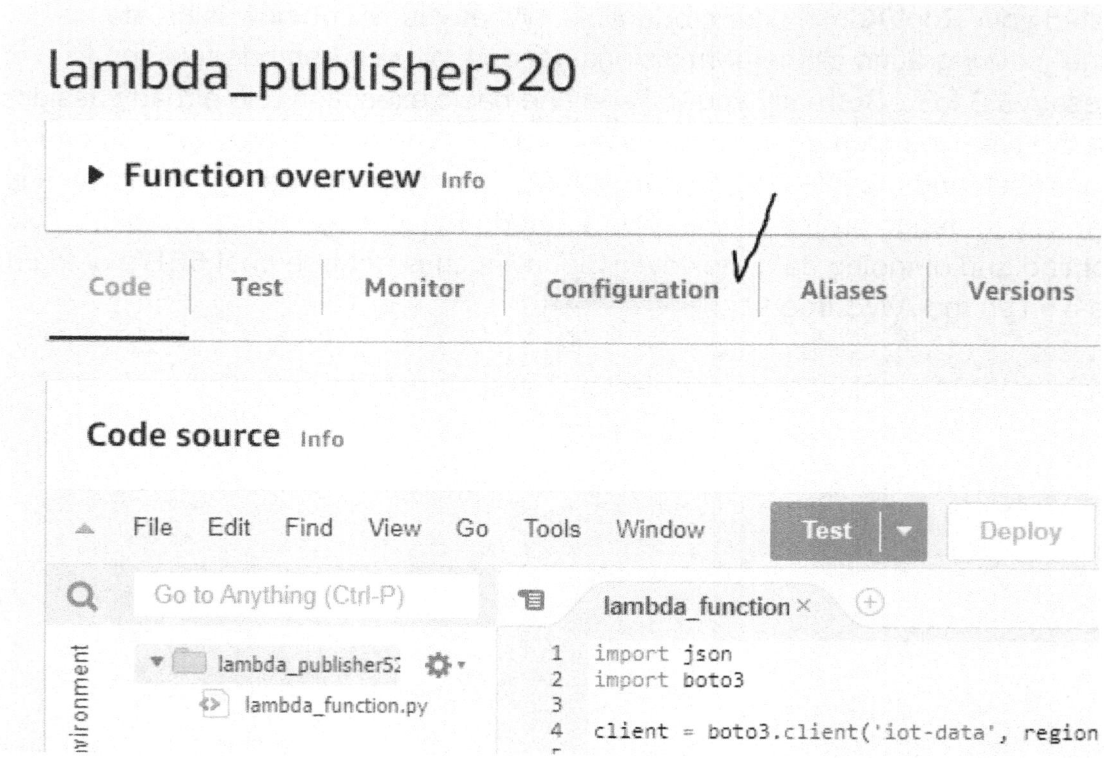
lambda_publisher520
Function overview Info
Code
Test
Monitor
Configuration
Aliases
Versions
Code source Info
File Edit Find View Go Tools Window
Test
Deploy
Go to Anything (Ctrl-P)
lambda_function
lambda_publisher52
lambda_function.py
import json
import boto3
client = boto3.client('iot-data', region

Then go to the ‘Permissions’ tab and click on your ‘Role’ name:

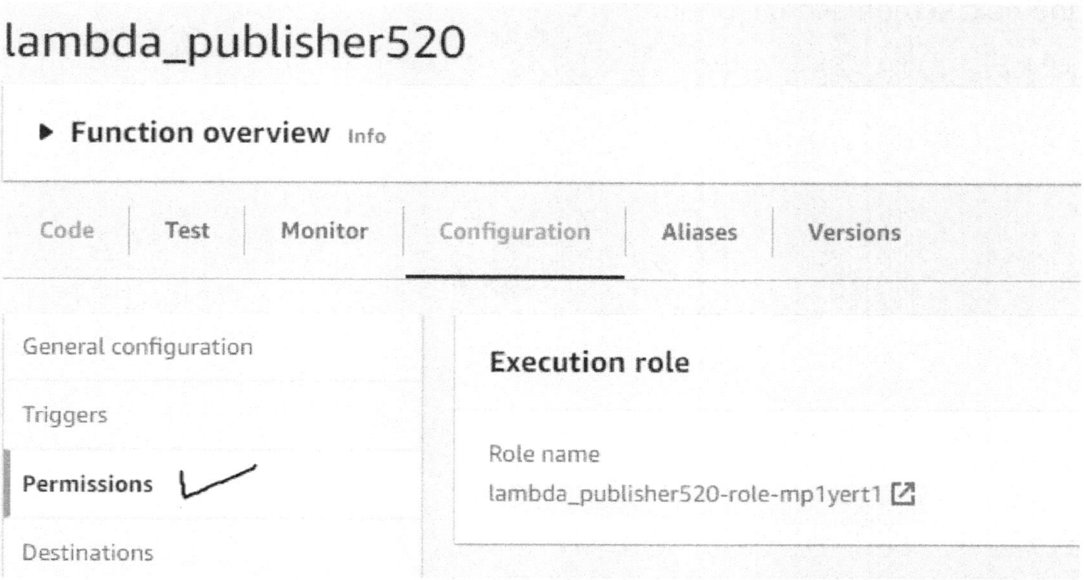
lambda_publisher520
Function overview Info
Code
Test
Monitor
Configuration
Aliases
Versions
General configuration
Triggers
Permissions
Destinations
Execution role
Role name
lambda_publisher520-role-mp1yert1

Clicking the default role will open a window in another AWS service called IAM. You are already familiar with IAM from when you set up your AWS account and created your Root/Admin user credentials. What you will do now is create an "Inline" policy grating all the permissions needed for your Lambda function to access AWS IoT. Currently you will see one basic execution role already assigned from the time you created your Lambda function. The default role lets Lambda access itself and provides log tracing in AWS CloudWatch. Using CloudWatch is a great way to debug problems with your Lambda function as well as monitor incoming and outgoing data, however CloudWatch is not free past 5GB's of log data ingestion on the AWS free tier.

Now in AWS IAM select "Add permissions" and "Create inline policy":

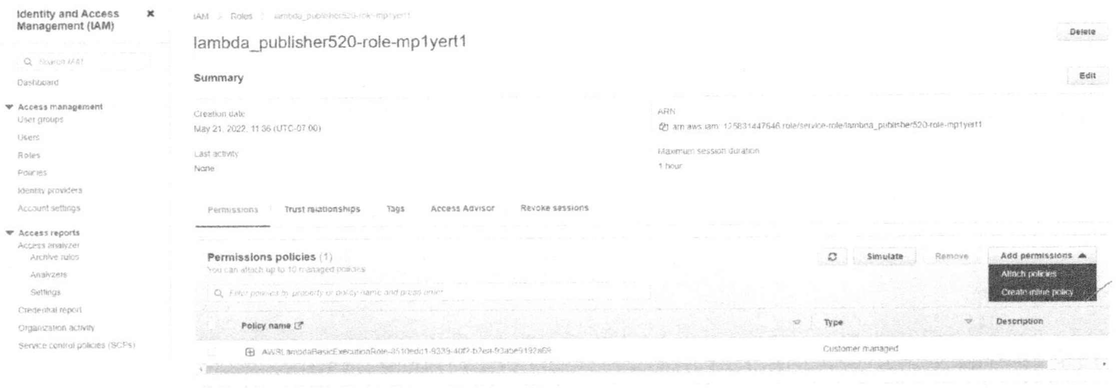
Identity and Access Management (IAM)
lambda_publisher520-role-mp1yert1
Delete
Summary
Edit
Dashboard
Access management
User groups
Users
Roles
Policies
Identity providers
Account settings
Access reports
Access analyzer
Archive rules
Analyzers
Settings
Credential report
Organization activity
Service control policies (SCPs)
Permissions
Trust relationships
Tags
Access Advisor
Revoke sessions
Permissions policies (1)
Simulate
Remove
Add permissions
Attach policies
Create inline policy
Policy name
Type
Description
Customer managed

On the next screen search for "iot":

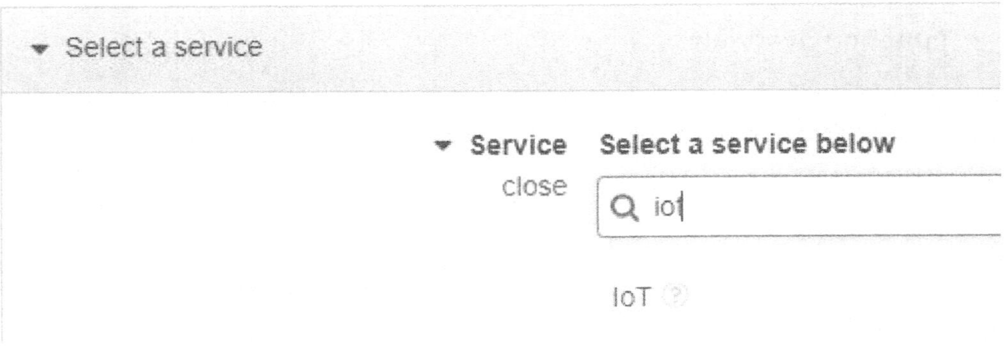
Select a service
Service
close
Select a service below
iot
IoT

Next, select "All IoT Actions"

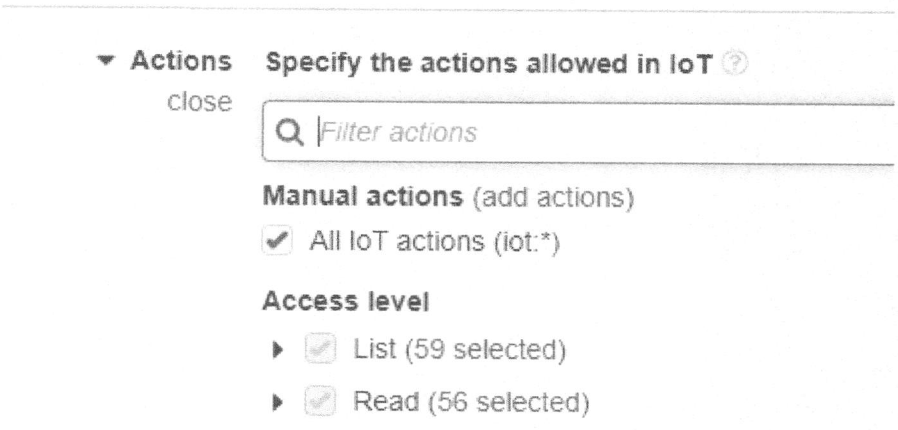
Actions
close
Specify the actions allowed in IoT
Filter actions
Manual actions (add actions)
All IoT actions (iot:*)
Access level
List (59 selected)
Read (56 selected)

And then select "All resources" and then "Review policy".

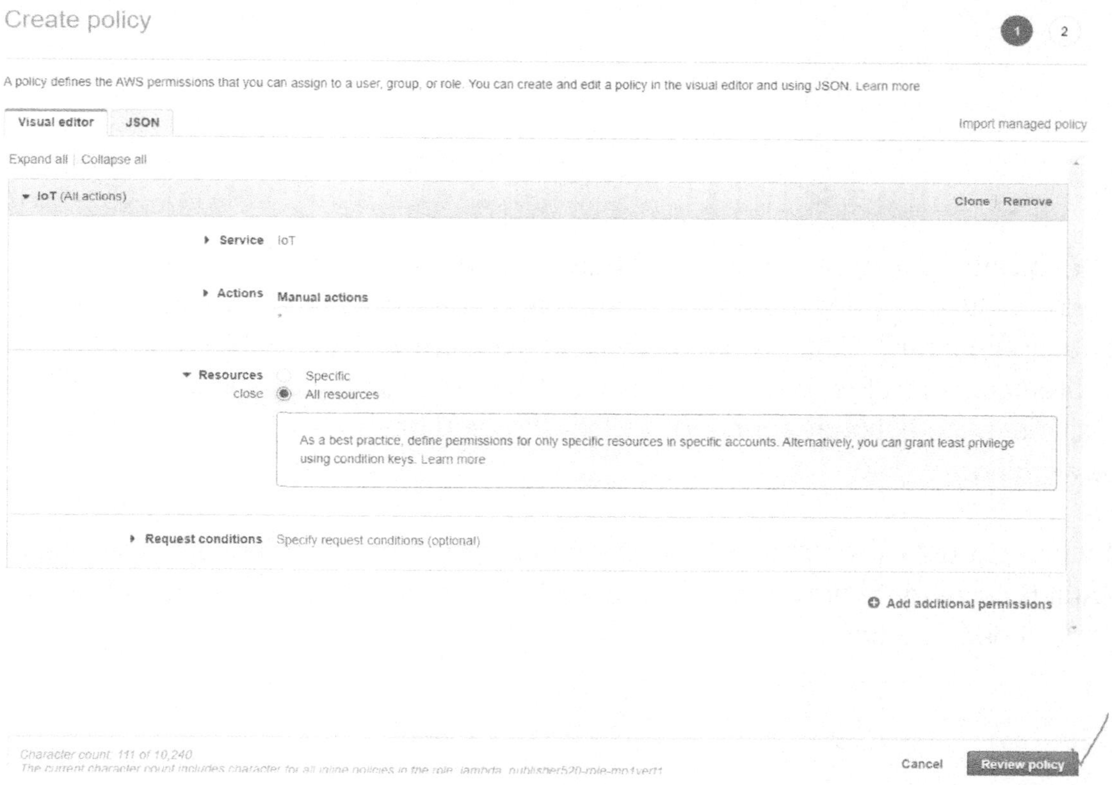
Create policy
A policy defines the AWS permissions that you can assign to a user, group, or role. You can create and edit a policy in the visual editor and using JSON. Learn more
Visual editor
JSON
Import managed policy
Expand all | Collapse all
IoT (All actions)
Clone | Remove
Service IoT
Actions Manual actions
Resources
close
Specific
All resources
As a best practice, define permissions for only specific resources in specific accounts. Alternatively, you can grant least privilege using condition keys. Learn more
Request conditions Specify request conditions (optional)
Add additional permissions
Cancel
Review policy

Give your policy a name and ensure you have 'Full access' to IoT and then press "Create policy."

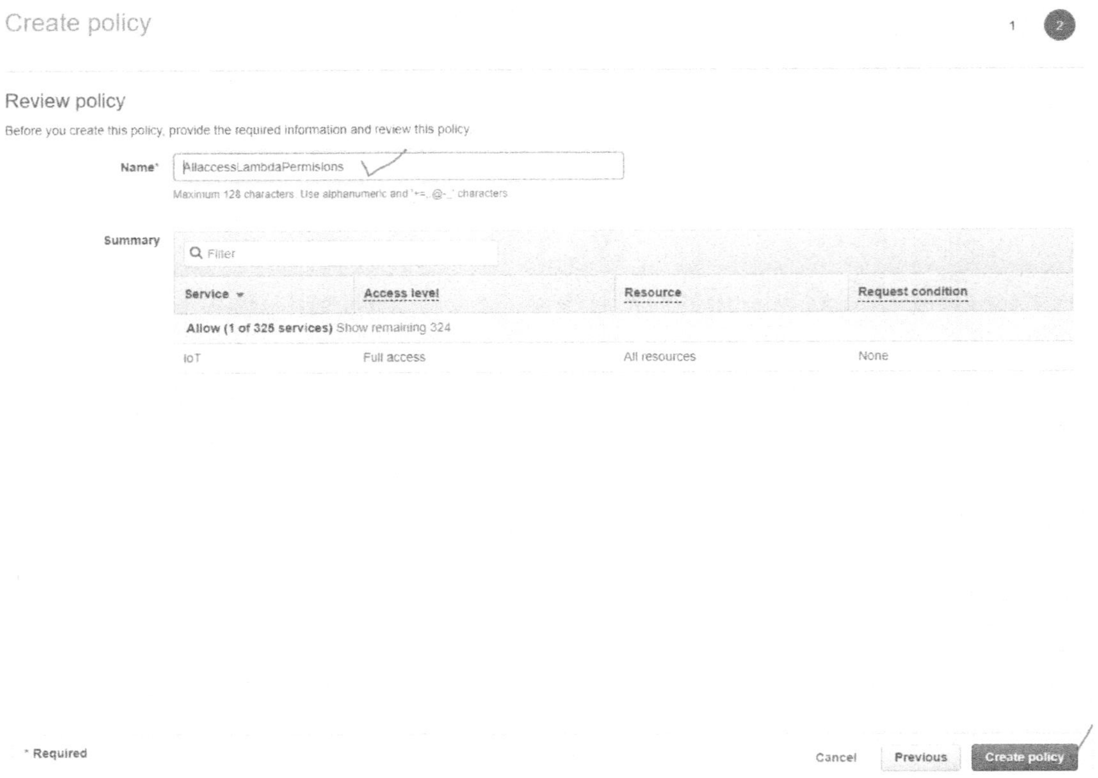
Create policy
1
2
Review policy
Before you create this policy, provide the required information and review this policy.
Name*
AllaccessLambdaPermisions
Maximum 128 characters. Use alphanumeric and '+=,.@-_' characters.
Summary
Filter
Service
Access level
Resource
Request condition
Allow (1 of 325 services) Show remaining 324
IoT
Full access
All resources
None
* Required
Cancel
Previous
Create policy

Again, granting all access and all resources to IoT, or any other AWS service, is not a best practice for privilege administration and you would never do this on a production account. But this is the most convenient way to do things for this small test project. If you like you can always go back and restrict permissions to a specific service action/resource or 'ARN" after you have your IoT design flow tested and working.

Now you should have two policies attached to your Lambda function. The original default policy, and a new policy to access all IoT services and resources from within your Lambda function.

Permissions policies (2)
You can attach up to 10 managed policies
Simulate
Filter policies by property or policy name and press enter
Policy name
Type
AWSLambdaBasicExecutionRole-8510edd1-9339-40f2-b2ea-93abe9192a69
Customer managed
AllaccessLambdaPermisions
Customer inline

Close your IAM panel as you won't need it again in this chapter. You will need another role created in IAM for IoT Core in a bit, but that role will be automatically created for you when you make your 'Rule' in IoT Core. AWS will create a "trigger" role allowing you to send IoT data from IoT Core to your Lambda function.

Step 2 – Test the Lambda Function with an IoT Payload

You are now ready to test your Lambda function and ensure that it can publish incoming IoT event objects to any MQTT topic you choose. To test the Lambda function, go to the test tab in the Lambda function. Give your test event a name and then fill out the JSON event payload with some key-values in JSON format.

```
{
    "temperature": 44,
    "humidity": 77,
    "timestamps": 123456789
}
```

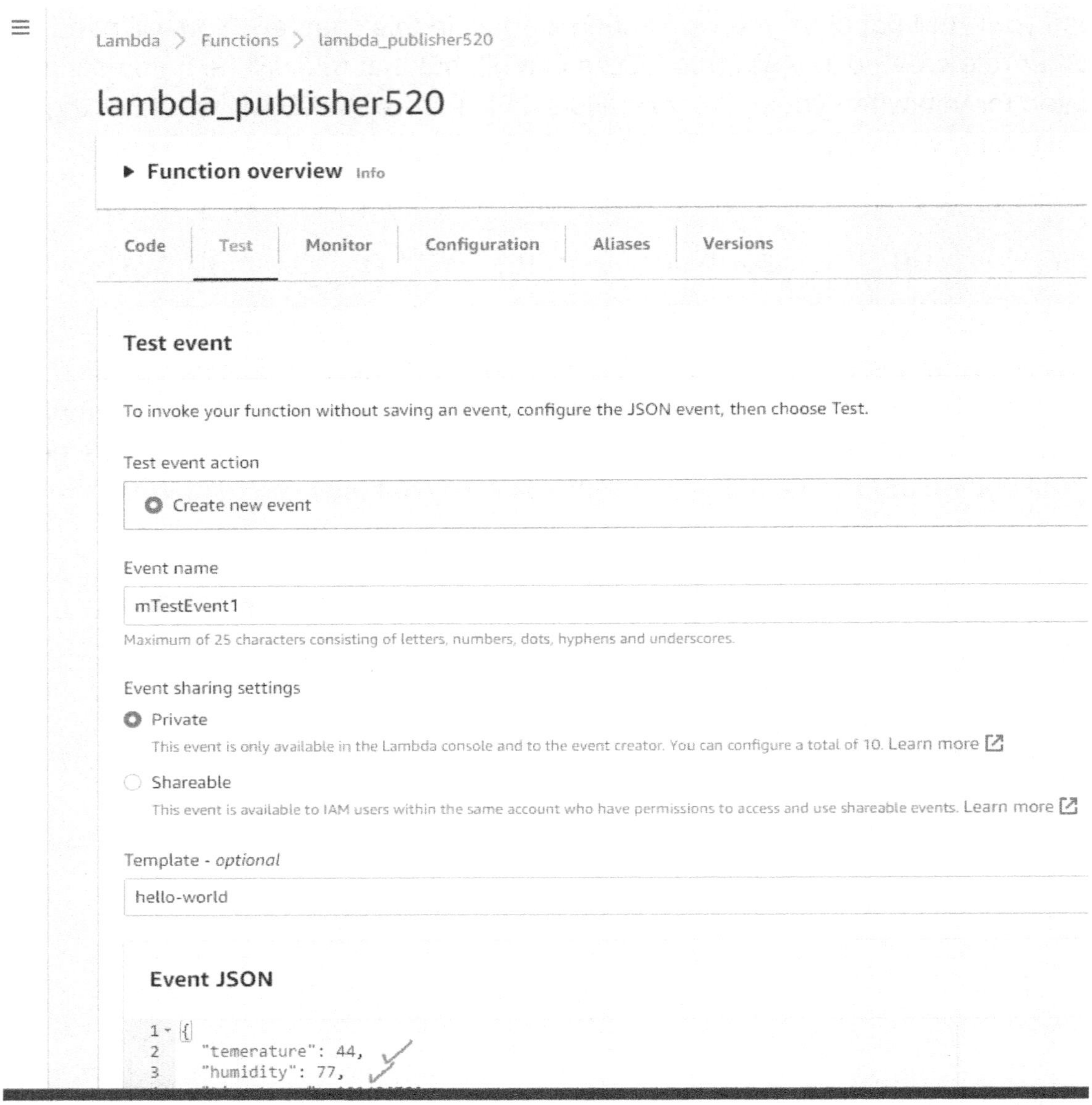
Lambda > Functions > lambda_publisher520
lambda_publisher520
▶ Function overview Info
Code
Test
Monitor
Configuration
Aliases
Versions
Test event
To invoke your function without saving an event, configure the JSON event, then choose Test.
Test event action
Create new event
Event name
mTestEvent1
Maximum of 25 characters consisting of letters, numbers, dots, hyphens and underscores.
Event sharing settings
Private
This event is only available in the Lambda console and to the event creator. You can configure a total of 10. Learn more
Shareable
This event is available to IAM users within the same account who have permissions to access and use shareable events. Learn more
Template - optional
hello-world
Event JSON
1 {
2 "temerature": 44,
3 "humidity": 77,

Press the “Save” button and then press the “Test” button on the upper right of the same screen.

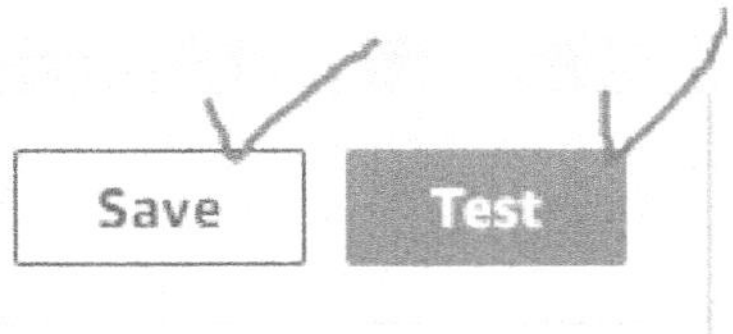
Save
Test

If you have done everything correctly you should see the green execution success message:

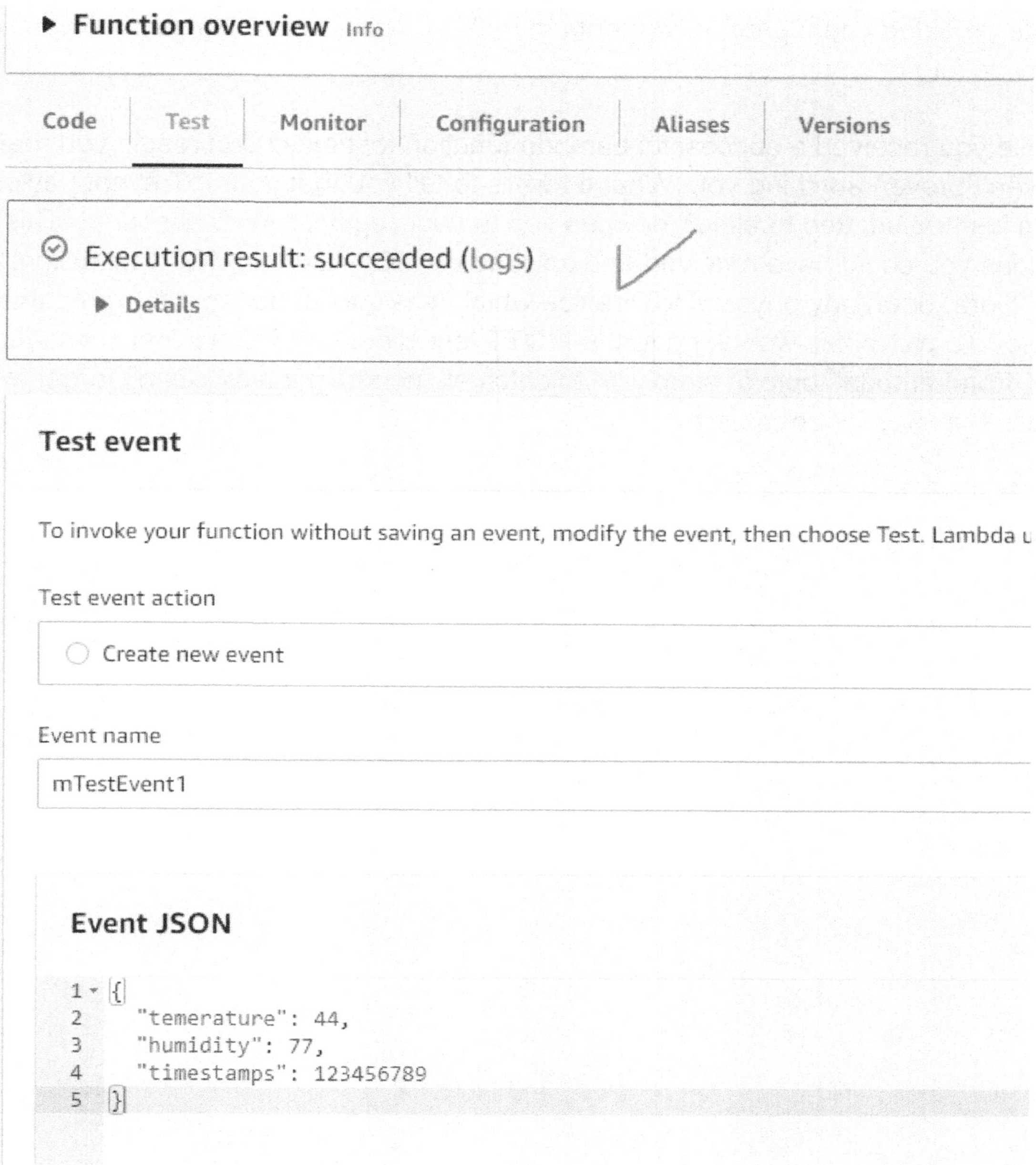
Function overview Info
Code
Test
Monitor
Configuration
Aliases
Versions
Execution result: succeeded (logs)
Details
Test event
To invoke your function without saving an event, modify the event, then choose Test. Lambda u
Test event action
Create new event
Event name
mTestEvent1
Event JSON
{
"temerature": 44,
"humidity": 77,
"timestamps": 123456789
}

It is worthwhile to see the details of the Lambda function test execution by checking the "Execution results" of the test event.

Optional: You can get more details on the test result in AWS CloudWatch by going to:
CloudWatch→Log Groups

And then searching for you latest Lambda execution. The details on the "Execution results" pane will provide a lot of information as well because the Lambda function code provided uses "print" statements in Python, and console logging in Node.js, to provide info on your test results.

While you received a successful Lambda function test execution result, you really haven't proven anything yet. What if I were to tell you that your IoT event payload was just transmitted to all IoT devices tied to your regional AWS account? This means you could have received this payload on MQTT.fx, the MQTT test client on IoT Core, or on any physical IoT device which was subscribed to the "fromLambda" topic. To prove this works, go to the MQTT test client in IoT Core and subscribe to the 'fromLambda' topic or simply '#' to catch all incoming topics. Don't forget to press the "Subscribe" button.

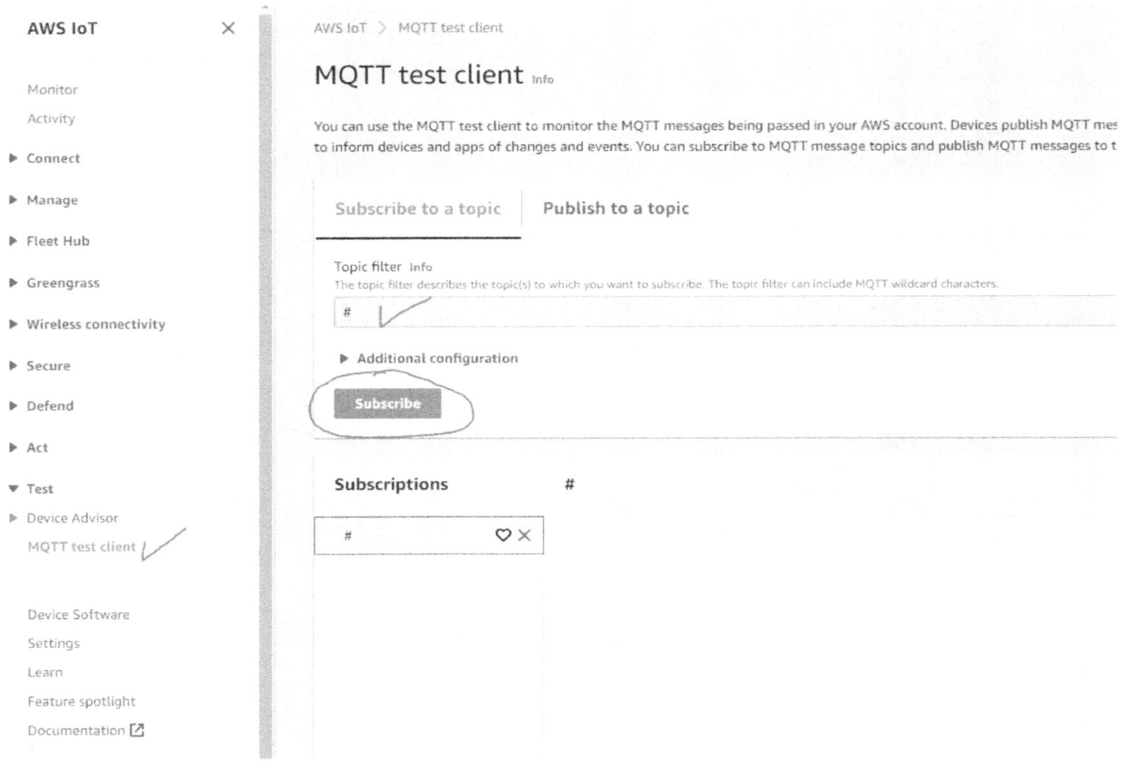
AWS IoT
Monitor
Activity
Connect
Manage
Fleet Hub
Greengrass
Wireless connectivity
Secure
Defend
Act
Test
Device Advisor
MQTT test client
Device Software
Settings
Learn
Feature spotlight
Documentation
AWS IoT > MQTT test client
MQTT test client Info
Subscribe to a topic
Publish to a topic
Topic filter Info
#
Additional configuration
Subscribe
Subscriptions
#
#

Now re-run the same test event on Lambda a few times by pressing the "Test" button. Return to the MQTT test client tab and you should see all the incoming IoT JSON payloads published by your Lambda function under the incoming MQTT topic.

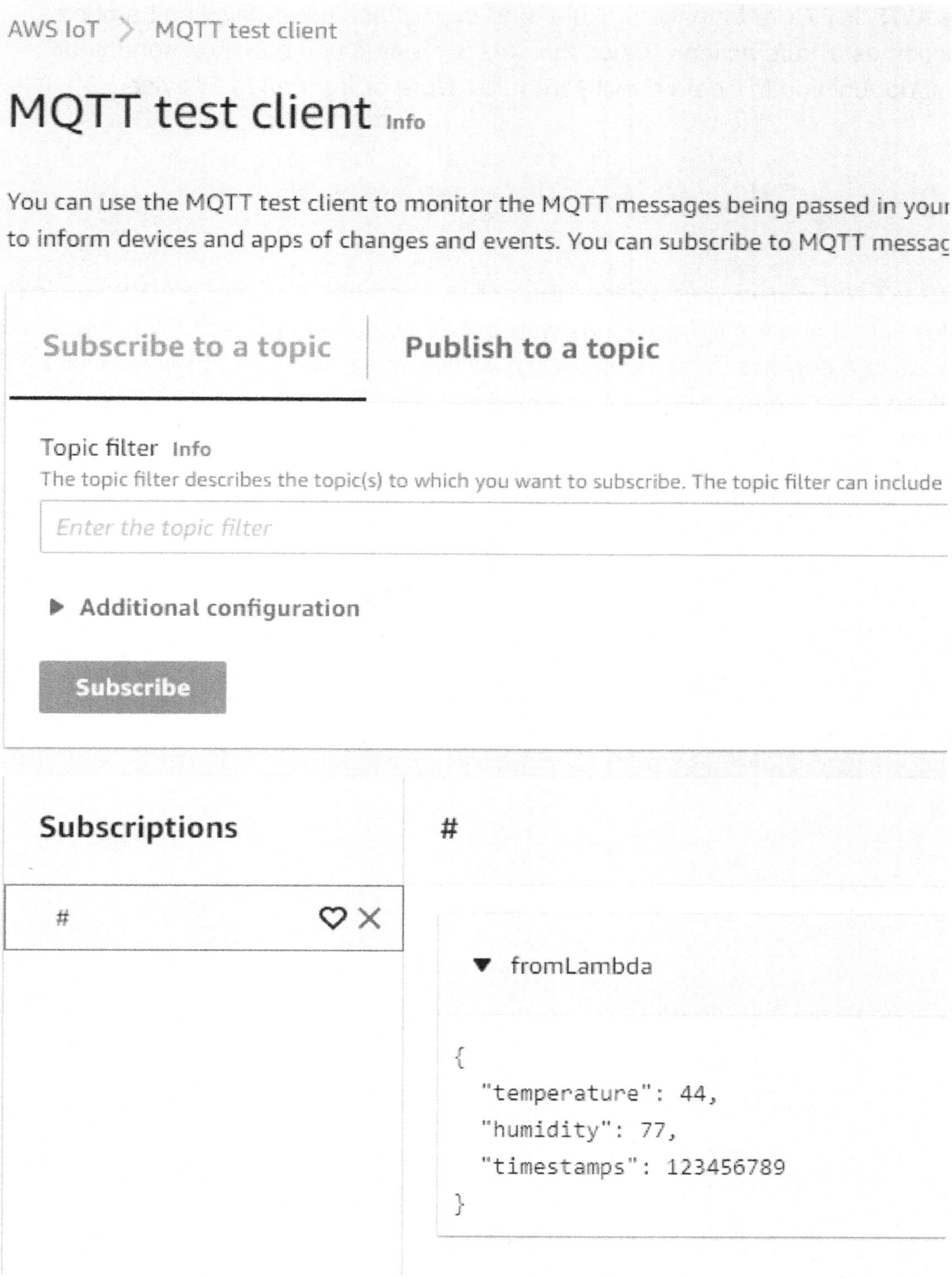
AWS IoT > MQTT test client
MQTT test client Info
You can use the MQTT test client to monitor the MQTT messages being passed in your
to inform devices and apps of changes and events. You can subscribe to MQTT messag
Subscribe to a topic
Publish to a topic
Topic filter Info
The topic filter describes the topic(s) to which you want to subscribe. The topic filter can include
Enter the topic filter
Additional configuration
Subscribe
Subscriptions
#
#
fromLambda
{
"temperature": 44,
"humidity": 77,
"timestamps": 123456789
}

Great, assuming you received the payload demonstrated above you are now you are ready to move on to the second half of this prerequisite chapter in which you will use AWS IoT Core to make a "Rule" and then attach the publishing Lambda function as a "rule action." Once this rule is created you can then send your Lambda function IoT data directly from IoT Core or from an IoT device.

Step 3 - Develop an IoT Rule

AWS IoT Rules give your devices the ability to interact with many AWS services. Rules filter incoming IoT payloads with a Rules Query Statement (RQS) and 'rule actions' are performed based on which AWS service you need to deliver your IoT payload to. You can use rules to support various tasks with many IoT centric AWS services.

Return to IoT Core but now go to Message Routing→Rules

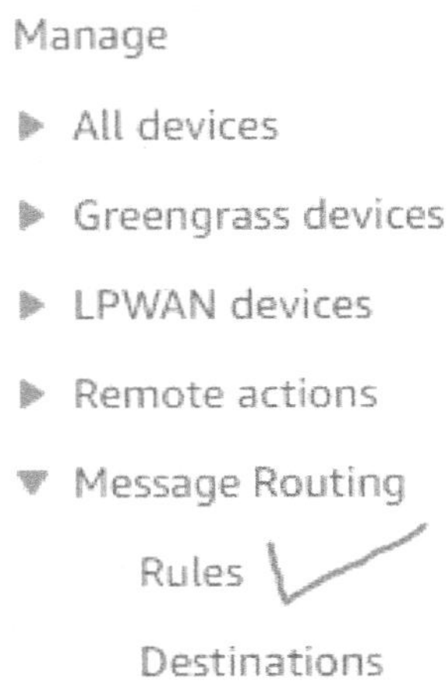
Manage
All devices
Greengrass devices
LPWAN devices
Remote actions
Message Routing
Rules
Destinations

And then press "Create rule":

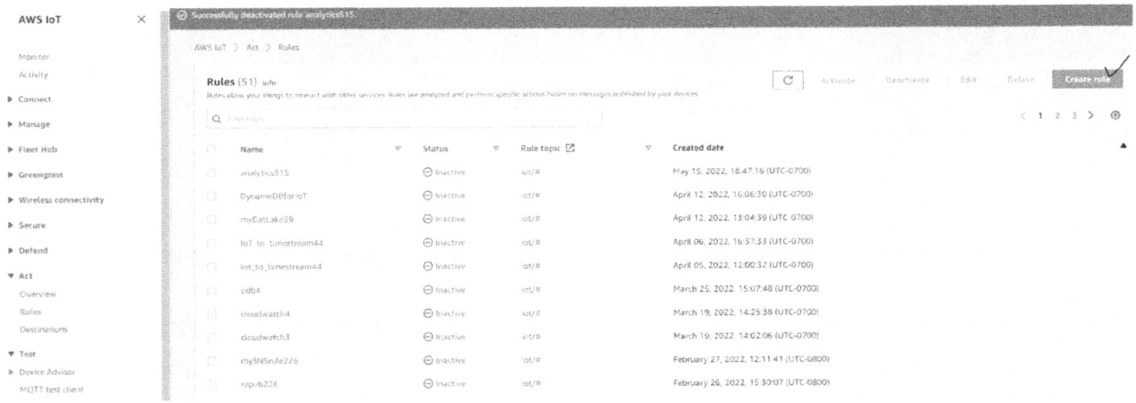
AWS IoT
Rules (51)
Name
Status
Rule topic
Created date
Create rule

- Make sure to create your rule in the same region as the Lambda function and the other AWS services you will be creating in this chapter.

Now give your IoT Core 'Rule' a name. A rule description is optional. Press "Next":

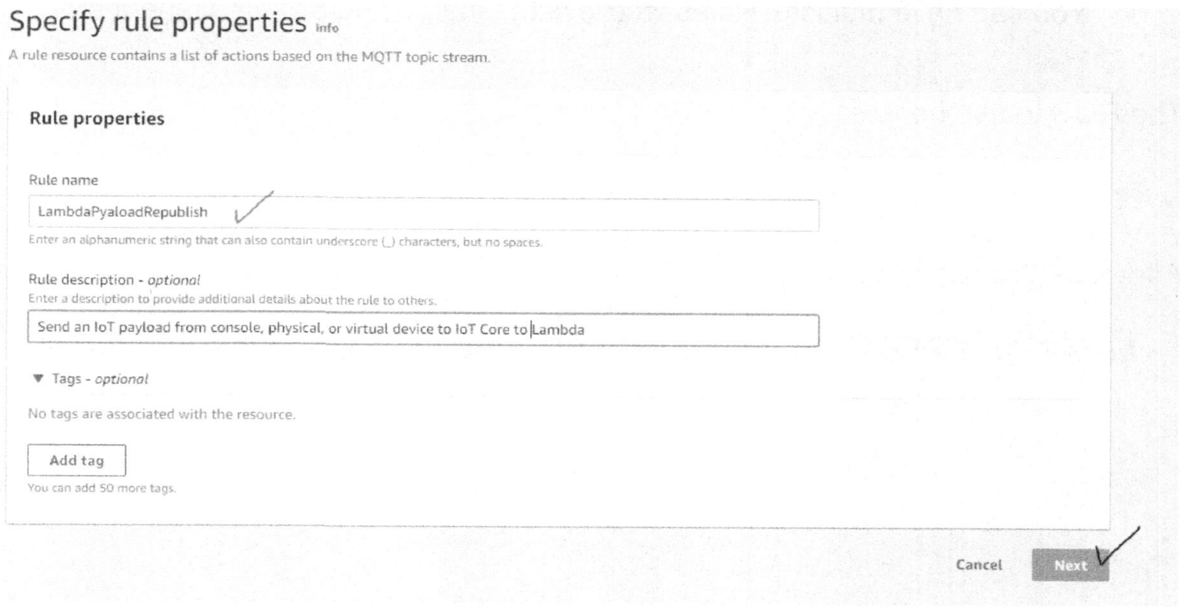

Specify rule properties Info
A rule resource contains a list of actions based on the MQTT topic stream.
Rule properties
Rule name
LambdaPyaloadRepublish
Enter an alphanumeric string that can also contain underscore (_) characters, but no spaces.
Rule description - optional
Enter a description to provide additional details about the rule to others.
Send an IoT payload from console, physical, or virtual device to IoT Core to Lambda
Tags - optional
No tags are associated with the resource.
Add tag
You can add 50 more tags.
Cancel
Next

Now you are going to enter a "Rules Query Statement." The RQS is an SQL statement that allows you to filter, transform, and enhance the incoming IoT payload. You can read more about all the functions built into the RQS in IoT Core rules here:

https://docs.aws.amazon.com/iot/latest/developerguide/iot-sql-functions.html

For this chapter you will keep the RQS simple, you are going to take the entire IoT payload '*', unaltered if the payload is published to "iot/#'. The '#' hash character is predefined to take every payload topic as a wildcard. Thus, if you publish to a topic like 'iot/test' then 'iot/#' will accept it because it starts with the prefix "iot/". If you publish to a topic like 'fromLambda' the RQS will ignore the topic and your IoT Core 'Rule,' and subsequent 'rule action,' will not be triggered. You **do not want** your IoT Rule triggered by the republished topic from your Lambda function.

*Note: Be careful **NOT** to use the same topic name in your Rules Query Statement as in your republishing Lambda function. If you use the same topic, you can create an infinite publish/subscribe loop when you publish an IoT payload. The republished topic will get intercepted by the RQS and sent to the republishing Lambda function again and then accepted by the RQS again, many times per second running up your AWS bill quickly.*

- You can have multiple 'Rules' active with different RQS's simultaneously.

The RQS to use here is:

```
SELECT * FROM 'iot/#'
```

After inserting the RQS above as the "SQL statement" press "Next".

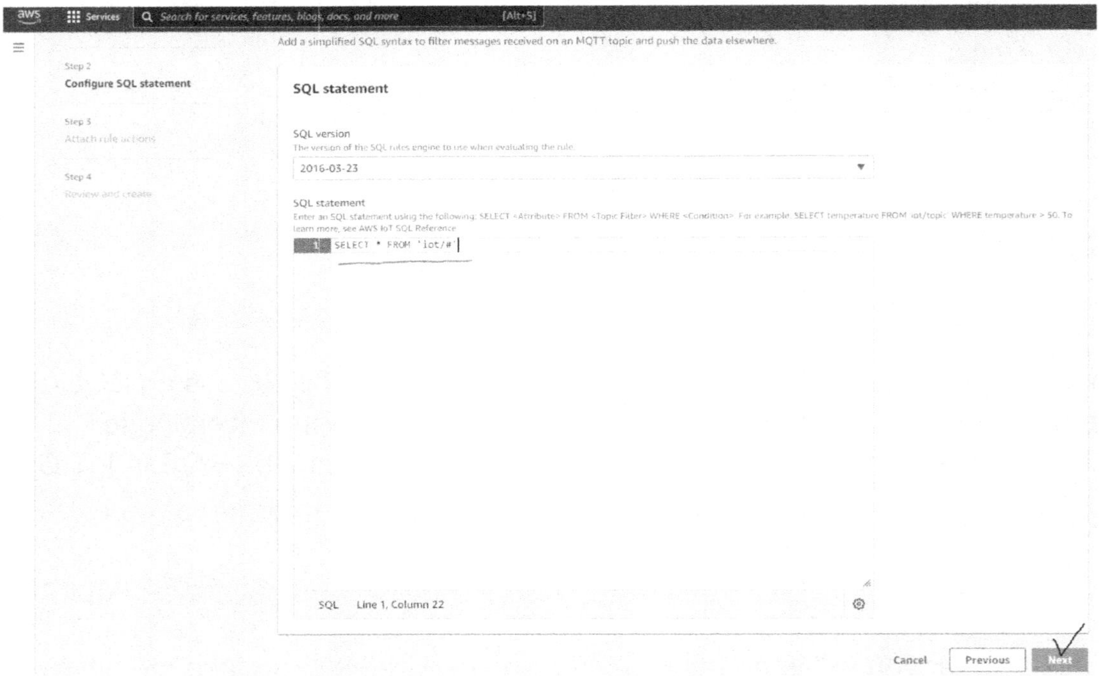
aws
Services
Search for services, features, blogs, docs, and more
[Alt+S]
Add a simplified SQL syntax to filter messages received on an MQTT topic and push the data elsewhere.
Step 2
Configure SQL statement
Step 3
Attach rule actions
Step 4
Review and create
SQL statement
SQL version
The version of the SQL rules engine to use when evaluating the rule.
2016-03-23
SQL statement
Enter an SQL statement using the following: SELECT <Attribute> FROM <Topic Filter> WHERE <Condition>. For example: SELECT temperature FROM 'iot/topic' WHERE temperature > 50. To learn more, see AWS IoT SQL Reference
1 SELECT * FROM 'iot/#'
SQL Line 1, Column 22
Cancel
Previous
Next

Now you will select a "rule action" to attach to your IoT Core "Rule." Rule actions specify what AWS services to link to incoming IoT payloads when a rule is triggered by a matching MQTT topic in the RQS. You can define rule actions to send IoT data to a DynamoDB database, stream IoT data to a Kinesis data Firehose, dispatch IoT data to a S3 bucket, and so on.

You have two fields left to configure in your rule, first select "Lambda" as the 'rule action" and then use the drop-down box to find either the Node.js or Python Lambda function you created in the previous step. Then press "Next":

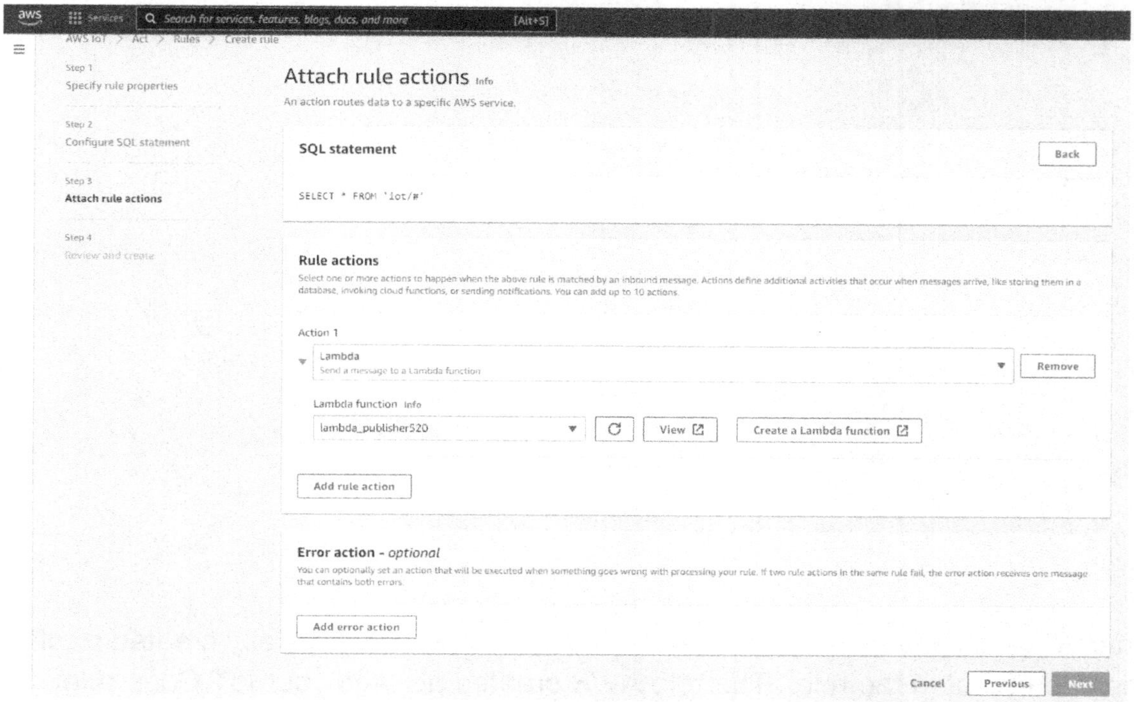

aws
Services
Search for services, features, blogs, docs, and more
[Alt+S]
AWS IoT > Act > Rules > Create rule
Step 1
Specify rule properties
Step 2
Configure SQL statement
Step 3
Attach rule actions
Step 4
Review and create
Attach rule actions Info
An action routes data to a specific AWS service.
SQL statement
Back
SELECT * FROM 'iot/#'
Rule actions
Action 1
Lambda
Send a message to a Lambda function
Remove
Lambda function Info
lambda_publisher520
View
Create a Lambda function
Add rule action
Error action - optional
Add error action
Cancel
Previous
Next

Next you will select to finalize this process by reviewing your rule configuration, and then selecting "Create."

Step 2: SQL statement
Edit
SQL statement
SQL version
2016-03-23
SQL query
SELECT * FROM 'iot/#'
Step 3: Rule actions
Edit
Actions
Lambda
Send a message to a Lambda function
Lambda function
arn:aws:lambda:us-east-1:125831447646:function:lambda_publisher520
Lambda function version
$LATEST
Error action
No error action
Cancel
Previous
Create

What you did not see in this process is that IoT Core automatically created a role when you created the rule. The role AWS created allowed your IoT Core 'rule action' to have access to the MQTT publishing Lambda function you designed earlier.

Now you can see your new 'Rule' at the top of the IoT Core rules menu. Two nice features of the new IoT Core console are that rules are automatically enabled, and they are now searchable by creation date.

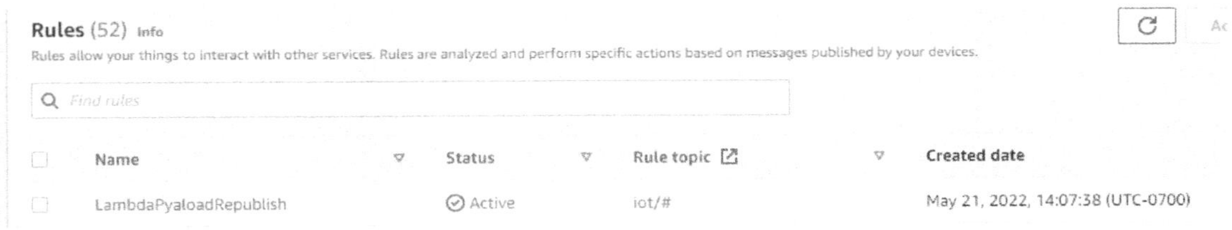
Rules (52) Info
Rules allow your things to interact with other services. Rules are analyzed and perform specific actions based on messages published by your devices.
Find rules
Name
Status
Rule topic
Created date
LambdaPyaloadRepublish
Active
iot/#
May 21, 2022, 14:07:38 (UTC-0700)

If you go back to your Lambda function and refresh the page, you will now see AWS IoT Core as an incoming 'trigger' event.

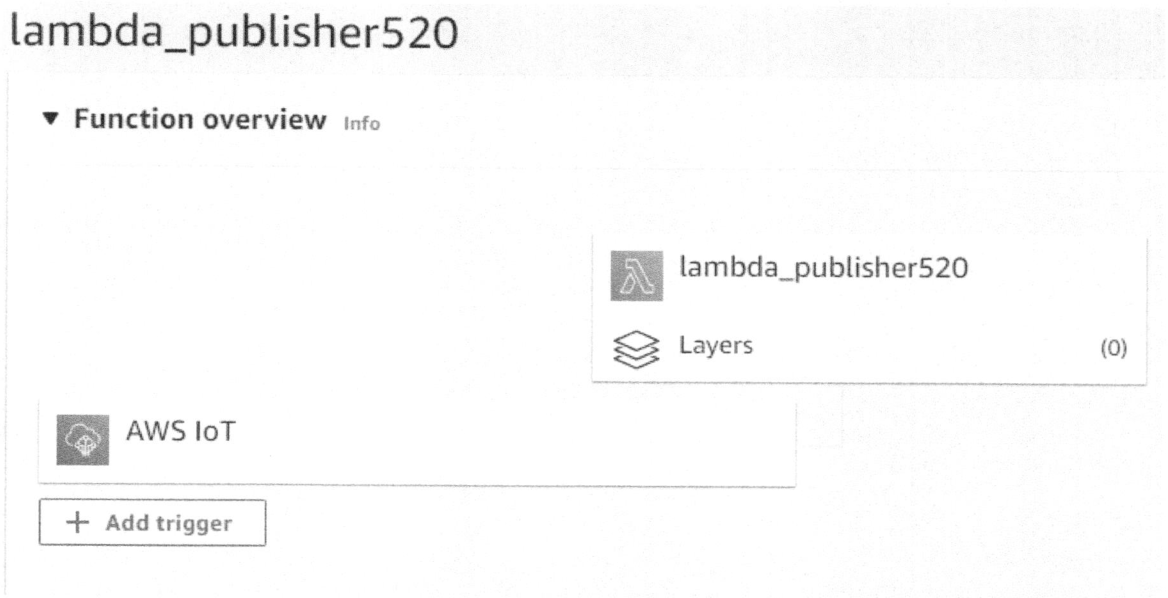
lambda_publisher520
Function overview Info
lambda_publisher520
Layers
(0)
AWS IoT
+ Add trigger

Step 4 – Test the Rule and Lambda Function with the MQTT Test Client in IoT Core

Now your rule is active, and your Lambda function is linked to your IoT Core rule. You can now test a simple publishing action from IoT Core to Lambda. Open two MQTT test clients by duplicating the test client tabs in two browser windows. Open one tab to "Subscribe' to the "fromLambda" topic (or whatever topic name you used in your Lambda function). Open the other tab to 'Publish' to "iot/test".

On the MQTT test client: Select the "Subscribe" tab the enter either "fromLambda" or "#" as the subscription topic.

Then:

On the MQTT test client: Select the "Publish" tab and enter "iot/test" as the publishing topic.

Press the "Publish" button a couple of times.

Publish

The results should look like those below:

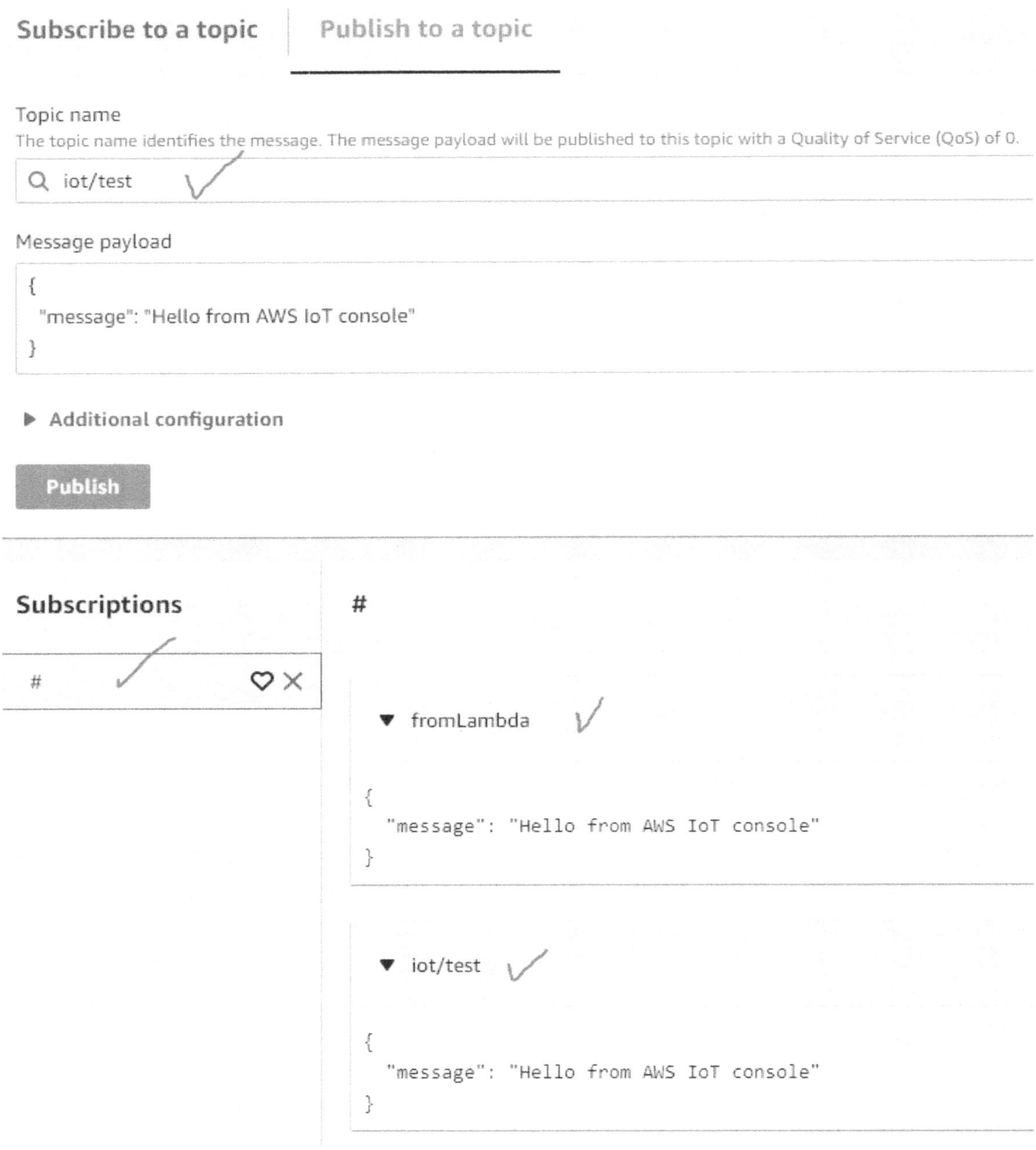
Subscribe to a topic
Publish to a topic
Topic name
The topic name identifies the message. The message payload will be published to this topic with a Quality of Service (QoS) of 0.
iot/test
Message payload
{
"message": "Hello from AWS IoT console"
}
Additional configuration
Publish
Subscriptions
#
#
fromLambda
{
"message": "Hello from AWS IoT console"
}
iot/test
{
"message": "Hello from AWS IoT console"
}

Examine the incoming message and topic in the MQTT test console. If everything is successful, you will see the new incoming message sent from Lambda as "fromLambda" on the subscription tab. This is the result you should expect as Lambda has just republished the "iot/test" message it just received from the MQTT test client with the republished topic name of 'fromLambda' with the same payload the Lambda function just received.

To continue further you can try to transform the outgoing IoT payload from Lambda. Try converting the temperature from Fahrenheit to Celsius in your Lambda function and publish the result to the MQTT test client. I have added the payload temperature conversion code to the Lambdas as comments, simply uncomment the relevant code to enhance the Lambda function and convert the payload temperature.

In the Python Lambda function uncomment this line:

```
event[‘temperature’] = round(((event[‘temperature’] - 32) / 1.8))
```

In the Node.js Lambda function uncomment this line:

```
event.temperature = Math.round(((event.temperature - 32)/1.8));
```

Running the same tests as before, open two MQTT test clients by duplicating the test client tabs in two browser windows. Open one tab to “Subscribe’ to the “fromLambda” topic (or whatever topic name you used in your Lambda function). Open the other tab to ‘Publish’ to “iot/test”.

On the MQTT test client: Select the “Subscribe” tab the enter either “fromLambda” or “#” as the subscription topic

Then:

On the MQTT test client: Select the “Publish” tab and enter “iot/test” as the publishing topic.

Press the “Publish” button.

Publish

From the MQTT test client below are the results:

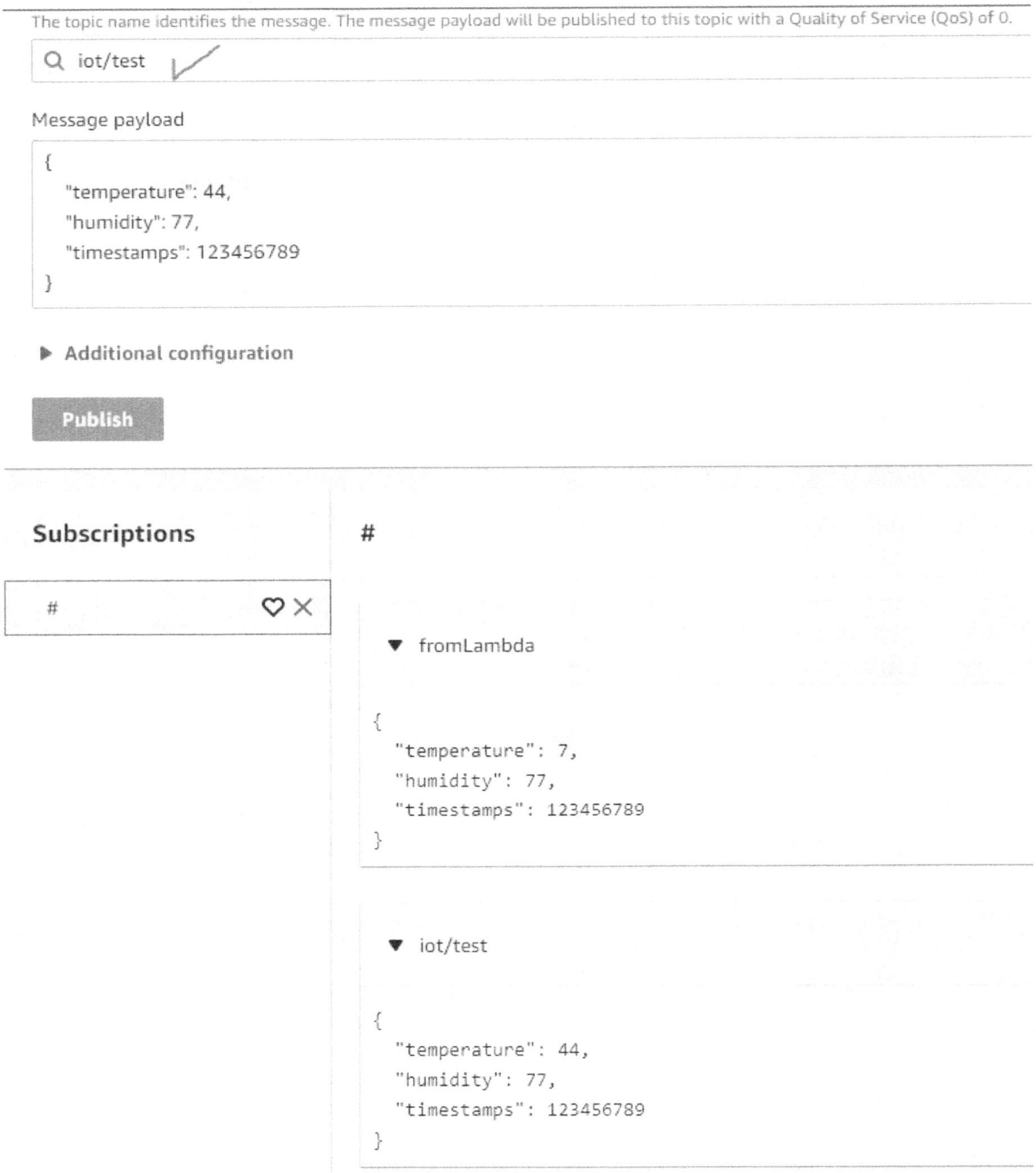
The topic name identifies the message. The message payload will be published to this topic with a Quality of Service (QoS) of 0.
iot/test
Message payload
{
"temperature": 44,
"humidity": 77,
"timestamps": 123456789
}
Additional configuration
Publish
Subscriptions
#
#
fromLambda
{
"temperature": 7,
"humidity": 77,
"timestamps": 123456789
}
iot/test
{
"temperature": 44,
"humidity": 77,
"timestamps": 123456789
}

Notice the temperature converted from Fahrenheit to Celsius when the payload is republished from Lambda. You can now see how it is possible to perform any type of ETL or object transformation you like on IoT payloads in Lambda and then dispatch those converted, enhanced, or transformed payloads directly from Lambda to an IoT device using MQTT, or dispatch the modified payload using the RQS, to another AWS service through an IoT Core 'Rule.' This demonstrates a few reasons how essential and powerful Lambda functions truly are, especially for IoT.

Congratulations, you have now designed a Lambda function and integrated it with IoT Core through a rule. You have also learned how to convert, transform, and enhance IoT payloads in Lambda and republish these enhanced IoT payloads to be utilized by IoT devices or other AWS services.

Chapter 11 - Developing a Threshold Tester with SNS and Topic Republishing in IoT Core

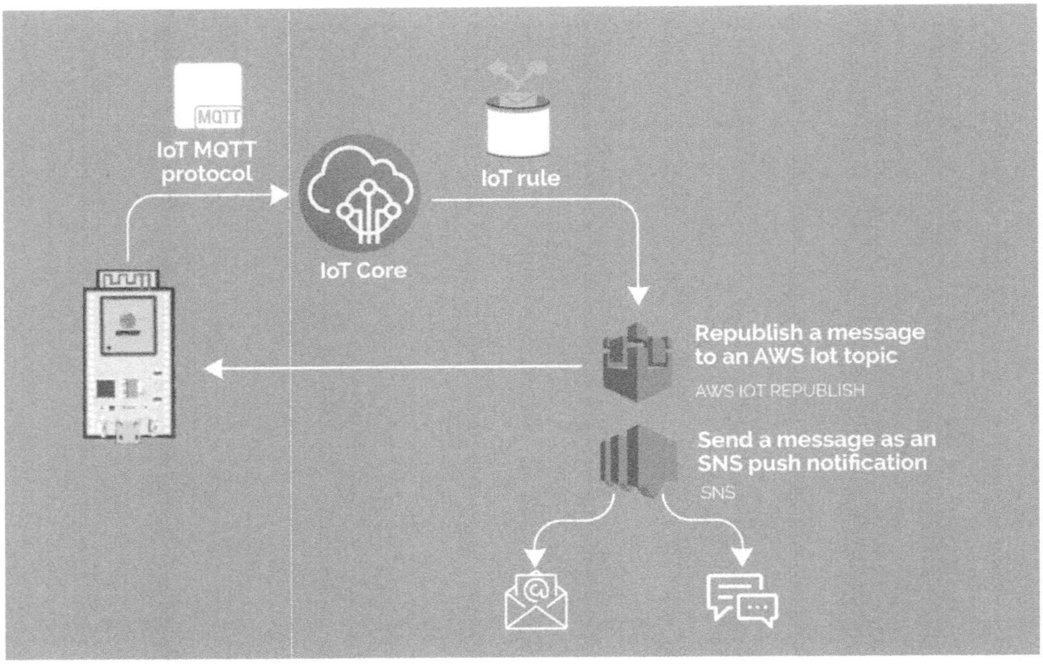
MQTT
IoT MQTT protocol
IoT Core
IoT rule
Republish a message to an AWS Iot topic
AWS IOT REPUBLISH
Send a message as an SNS push notification
SNS

For this first project you will take a standard introductory topic for AWS IoT and then walk through it with two different methods to complete the same objective. For threshold testing you will simply use temperature as the monitored, threshold variable. In the first part of this project, you will use AWS IoT Core and create a rule which republishes the temperature through a "republish" action contingent on if the temperature exceeds a designated threshold value. Along with this first rule in IoT Core you will then create a second rule that utilizes AWS SNS to send an email or text topic. In the first case, with the republishing action to a MQTT subscription topic, it will be considered the "warning" case, while the second rule which uses a text or email alert of high temperature will be considered the "emergency" alert condition.

The practical purpose is to set up an alert temperature so that if we want to create a greenhouse environmental monitor, or some other device in which monitoring a sensor variable is important, we can keep track and send an alert if the variable we are monitoring reaches a certain specified threshold value that would be important to the client or owner.

AWS Services used:

IoT Core

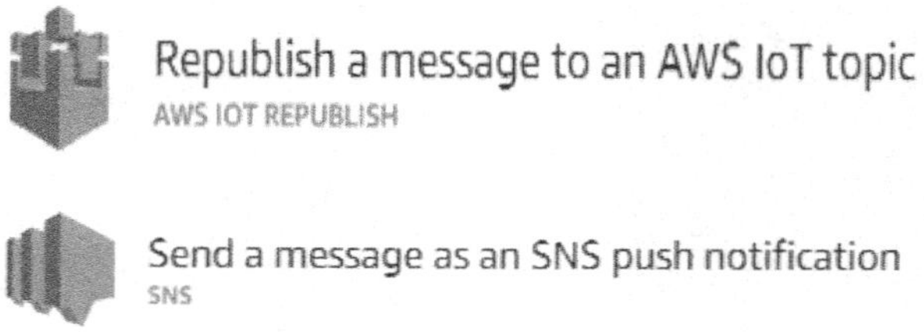
Republish a message to an AWS IoT topic
AWS IOT REPUBLISH
Send a message as an SNS push notification
SNS

Step 1 – Create a Rule to Configure a Republishing Action in IoT Core
Step 2 – Create a Rule and Develop a SNS Action in IoT Core
Step 3 – Test the Republishing and SNS Rules

Step 1 – Create a Rule to Configure a Republishing Action in IoT Core

First, create a “Rule” in AWS IoT Core:

Go to: https://console.aws.amazon.com/iot

Or from the console in IoT Core choose: Message Routing→Rules:

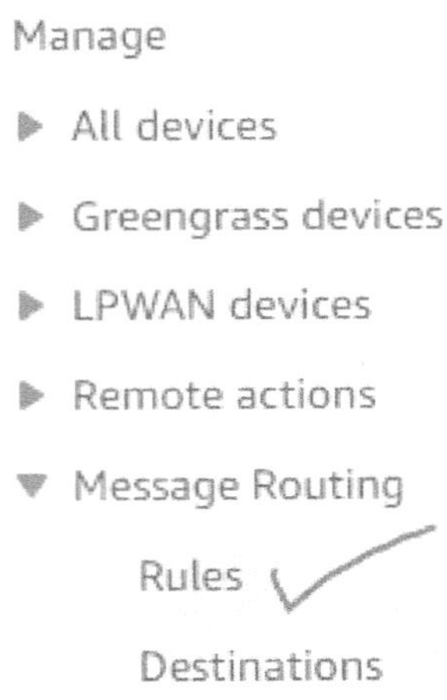
Manage
All devices
Greengrass devices
LPWAN devices
Remote actions
Message Routing
Rules
Destinations

Now Create your Rule:

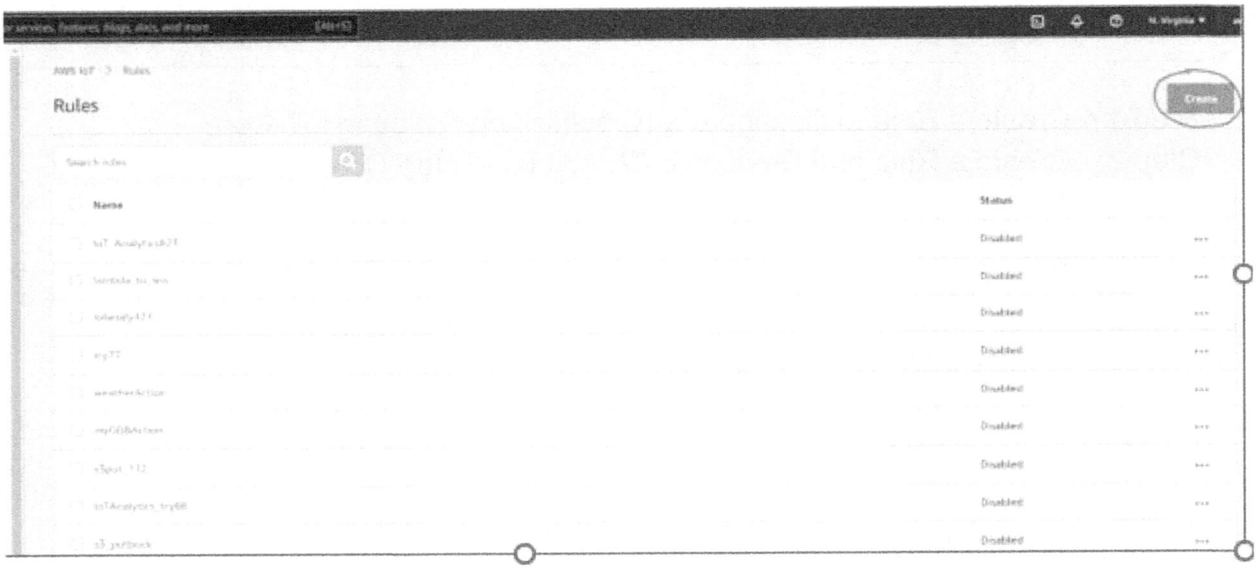
Rules

Here I created a Rule called "Repub226," you can call your rule whatever you like. The first thing to do is to enter the "Rules Query Statement." In this case you want to republish all IoT payloads under a different topic name that exceed 80 degrees. Below is that RQS statement:

```
SELECT temperature as Alert FROM 'iot/#' WHERE temperature > 80
```

As shown in the console in IoT Core:

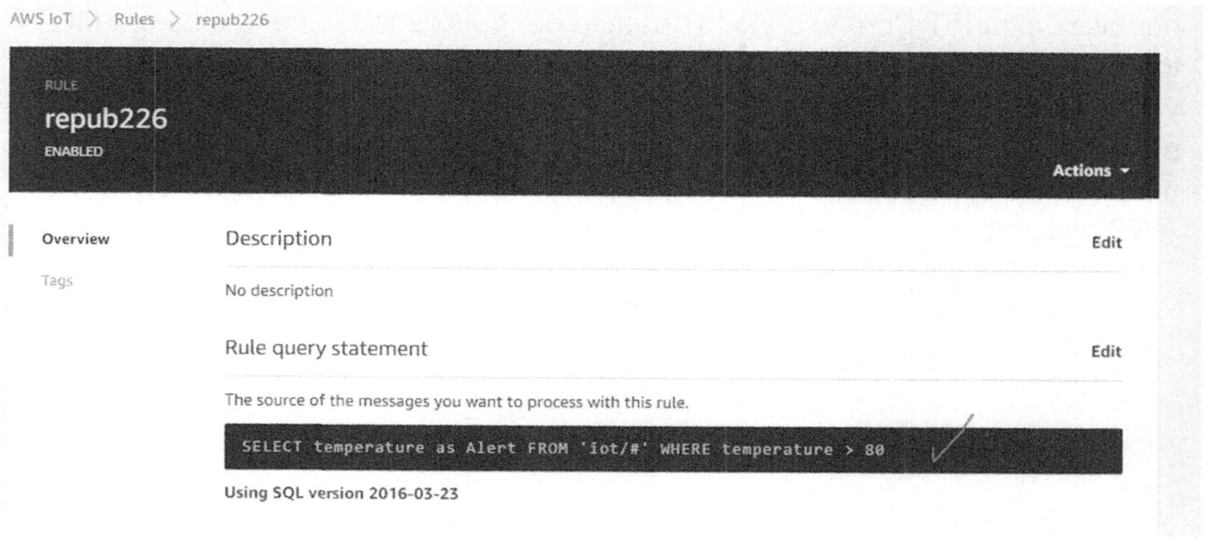
AWS IoT > Rules > repub226
RULE
repub226
ENABLED
Actions
Overview
Tags
Description
Edit
No description
Rule query statement
Edit
The source of the messages you want to process with this rule.
SELECT temperature as Alert FROM 'iot/#' WHERE temperature > 80
Using SQL version 2016-03-23

Now add your republishing 'Action' to your 'Rule'. To do this use the "Next" below the Rules Query Statement.

Next

Now you can configure the topic republishing 'rule action.' Remember this action is only triggered if the temperature coming in from the virtual or real IoT device exceeds the threshold temperature you specified in the Rules Query Statement (RQS).

There are two things to do to configure your rule correctly. First, give the republishing MQTT topic a name, here you use "alert/temp" as the republishing topic. This is a good convention because later, if you want to set up other alerts, you could use various "alert/xyz" topics and then subscribe to "alert/#" to pick up all these different alert topics with subscriptions on your IoT device. Keep the QoS as 0 by default.

Remember the incoming MQTT topic is 'iot/#' as designated by the RQS. However, when the temperature variable exceeds 80 degrees then a new MQTT topic is republished under 'Alert/temp. Only temperatures over 80 degrees get republished under the 'Alert/temp' topic.

The second thing to do is to create a role. This role can be named anything you like but it should be descriptive of the action it is tied to. The 'create role' function gives permission for IoT Core to send IoT data to be republished under a different MQTT topic. Usually, it is easiest to just create a new role than try to reuse an old role. If you want to see the permissions granted in the role that you just created, those permissions can be found in "IAM," which is the AWS service which stores all roles, policies, users, and permissions as you have already seen when you created your AWS account.

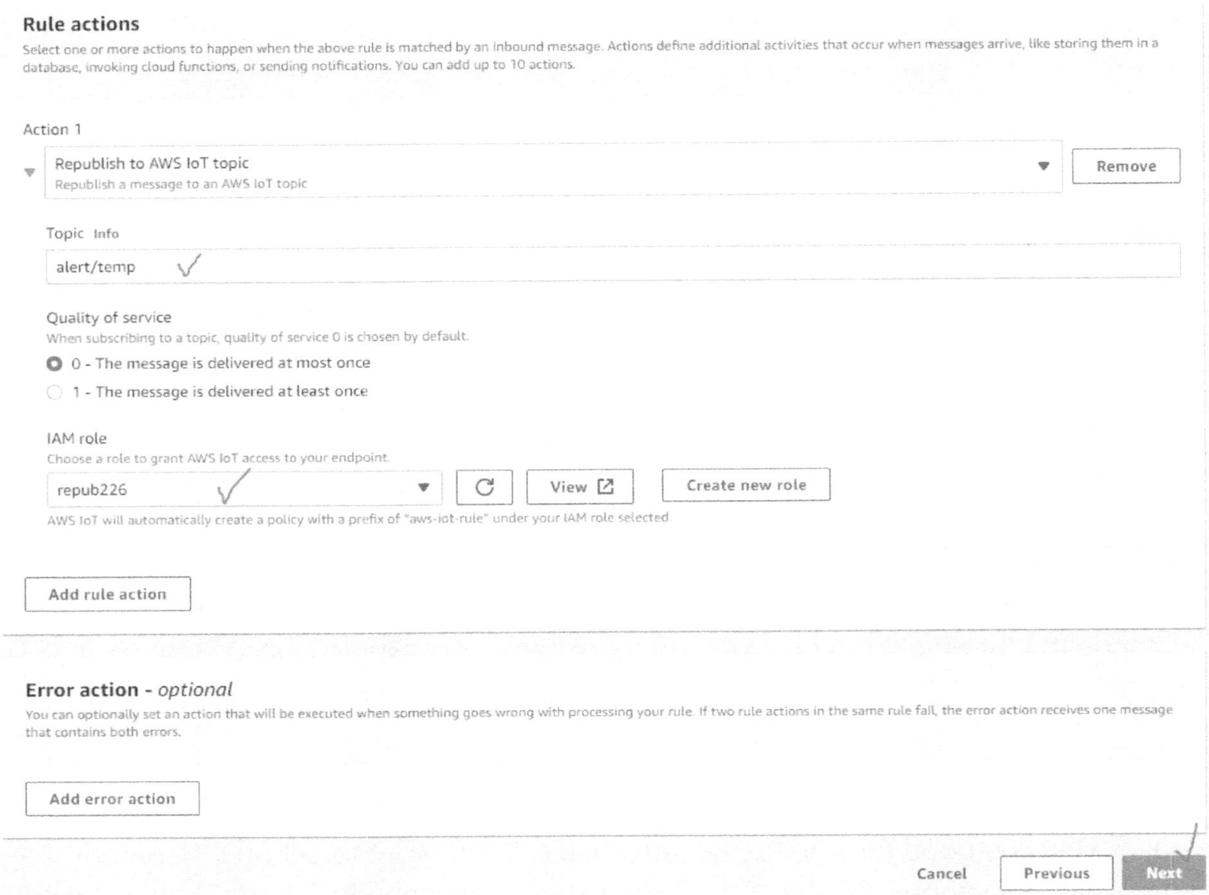

Rule actions
Select one or more actions to happen when the above rule is matched by an inbound message. Actions define additional activities that occur when messages arrive, like storing them in a database, invoking cloud functions, or sending notifications. You can add up to 10 actions.
Action 1
Republish to AWS IoT topic
Republish a message to an AWS IoT topic
Remove
Topic Info
alert/temp
Quality of service
When subscribing to a topic, quality of service 0 is chosen by default.
0 - The message is delivered at most once
1 - The message is delivered at least once
IAM role
Choose a role to grant AWS IoT access to your endpoint.
repub226
View
Create new role
AWS IoT will automatically create a policy with a prefix of "aws-iot-rule" under your IAM role selected
Add rule action
Error action - optional
You can optionally set an action that will be executed when something goes wrong with processing your rule. If two rule actions in the same rule fail, the error action receives one message that contains both errors.
Add error action
Cancel
Previous
Next

After creating your topic name and press the "Next" button:

Next

Finally on the next screen scroll down to the bottom and press "Create":

Create

Now that you have created our republishing rule. This rule will now republish any IoT payload incoming where the temperature is over 80 to a new topic called "alert/temp"

Finally, make sure your Rule is enabled.

Step 2 – Create a Rule and Develop a SNS Action in IoT Core

Now you are ready to add your second rule which will send you an email and/or text when the temperature exceeds another given threshold. Again, you are welcome to base this rule on any variable value you like, so you can use humidity or add your own variable.

First, you must go to AWS SNS and create a topic, then after you have created your topic, you can choose the type of subscription to assign to that topic. Finally, you will return to AWS IoT Core and create a rule using the newly created SNS service.

To get to AWS SNS type "SNS" in the search box of your AWS console or simply use this direct link:

https://console.aws.amazon.com/sns/v3

Now create a topic by choosing the 'Standard' SNS delivery plan, give your topic a name, and then give it a display name of your choice:

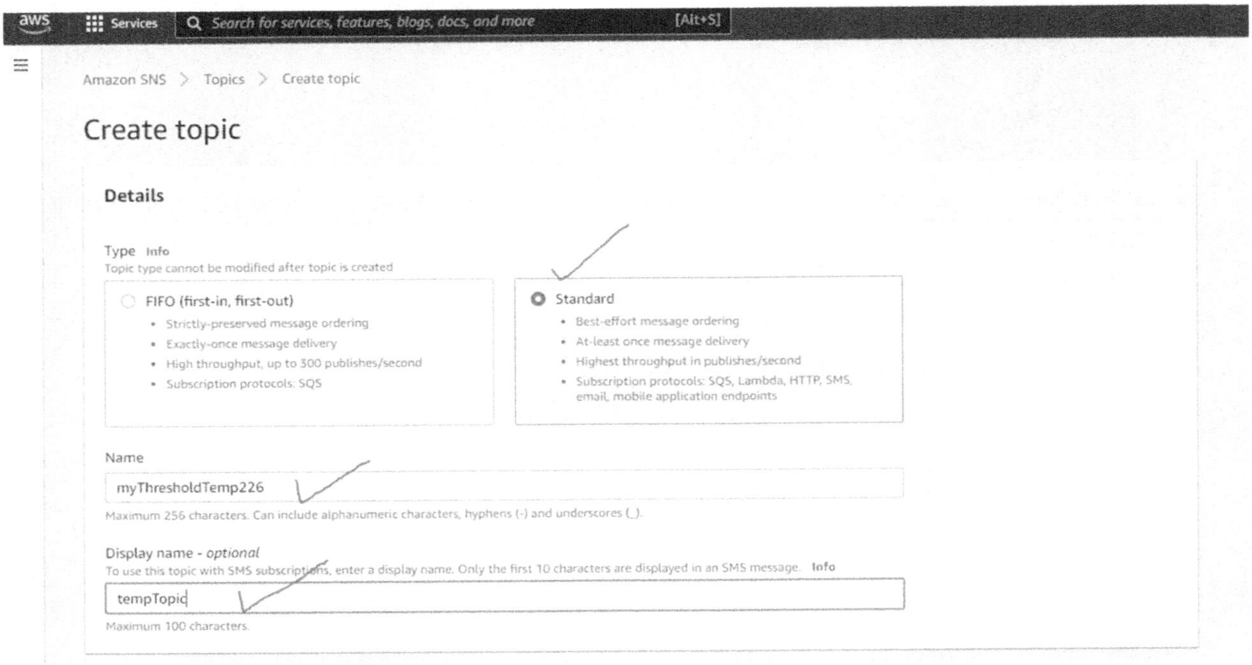
aws
Services
Search for services, features, blogs, docs, and more
[Alt+S]
Amazon SNS > Topics > Create topic
Create topic
Details
Type Info
Topic type cannot be modified after topic is created
FIFO (first-in, first-out)
Strictly-preserved message ordering
Exactly-once message delivery
High throughput, up to 300 publishes/second
Subscription protocols: SQS
Standard
Best-effort message ordering
At-least once message delivery
Highest throughput in publishes/second
Subscription protocols: SQS, Lambda, HTTP, SMS, email, mobile application endpoints
Name
myThresholdTemp226
Maximum 256 characters. Can include alphanumeric characters, hyphens (-) and underscores (_).
Display name - optional
To use this topic with SMS subscriptions, enter a display name. Only the first 10 characters are displayed in an SMS message. Info
tempTopic
Maximum 100 characters.

After you complete the configuration leave all the options as they are by default and press the “Create topic” button.

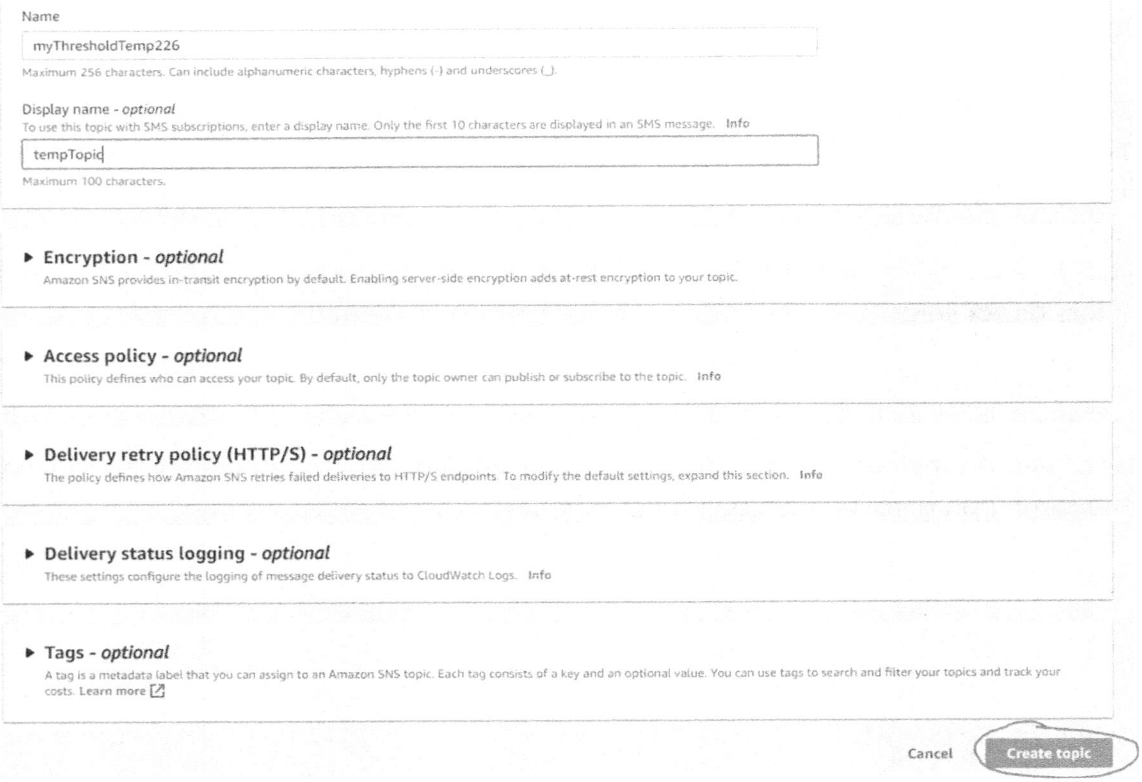
Name
myThresholdTemp226
Maximum 256 characters. Can include alphanumeric characters, hyphens (-) and underscores (_).
Display name - optional
To use this topic with SMS subscriptions, enter a display name. Only the first 10 characters are displayed in an SMS message. Info
tempTopic
Maximum 100 characters.
Encryption - optional
Amazon SNS provides in-transit encryption by default. Enabling server-side encryption adds at-rest encryption to your topic.
Access policy - optional
This policy defines who can access your topic. By default, only the topic owner can publish or subscribe to the topic. Info
Delivery retry policy (HTTP/S) - optional
The policy defines how Amazon SNS retries failed deliveries to HTTP/S endpoints. To modify the default settings, expand this section. Info
Delivery status logging - optional
These settings configure the logging of message delivery status to CloudWatch Logs. Info
Tags - optional
A tag is a metadata label that you can assign to an Amazon SNS topic. Each tag consists of a key and an optional value. You can use tags to search and filter your topics and track your costs. Learn more
Cancel
Create topic

Next, you will create a subscription for your topic. By making these two separate steps you can easily mix and match topics and subscriptions which gives us extra flexibility. At this point press the “Create subscription” button.

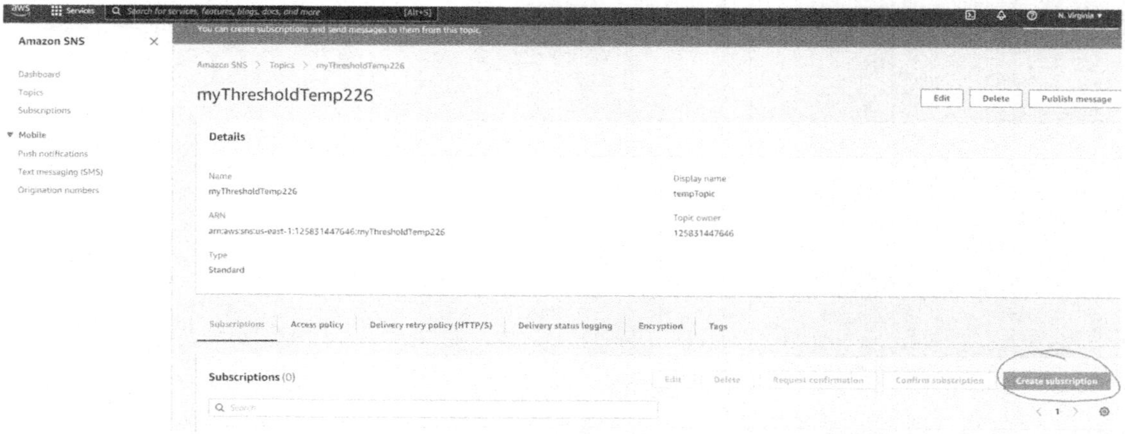
Amazon SNS
Dashboard
Topics
Subscriptions
Mobile
Push notifications
Text messaging (SMS)
Origination numbers
myThresholdTemp226
Edit
Delete
Publish message
Details
Name
myThresholdTemp226
Display name
tempTopic
Type
Standard
Subscriptions
Access policy
Delivery retry policy (HTTP/S)
Delivery status logging
Encryption
Tags
Subscriptions (0)
Create subscription

Now you need to choose a subscription protocol for your topic. The two most common are SMS for text messages and email. Choose email so you don’t get excessive or intrusive texts on your phone number for this test case, however you can choose SMS if you like. Also remember you can add multiple subscriptions to your single topic, so you can get both an email and a text if the temperature exceeds a certain threshold value. You could also make a second subscription for text only so that email would be triggered at one threshold value and text could be triggered at another threshold value. Of course, you would have to make a second IoT Core rule if you did this, because if you add two separate actions under the same rule, they would both get triggered by the same ‘Rules Query Statement’ when filtering by the threshold value.

In this example chose to receive an email notification

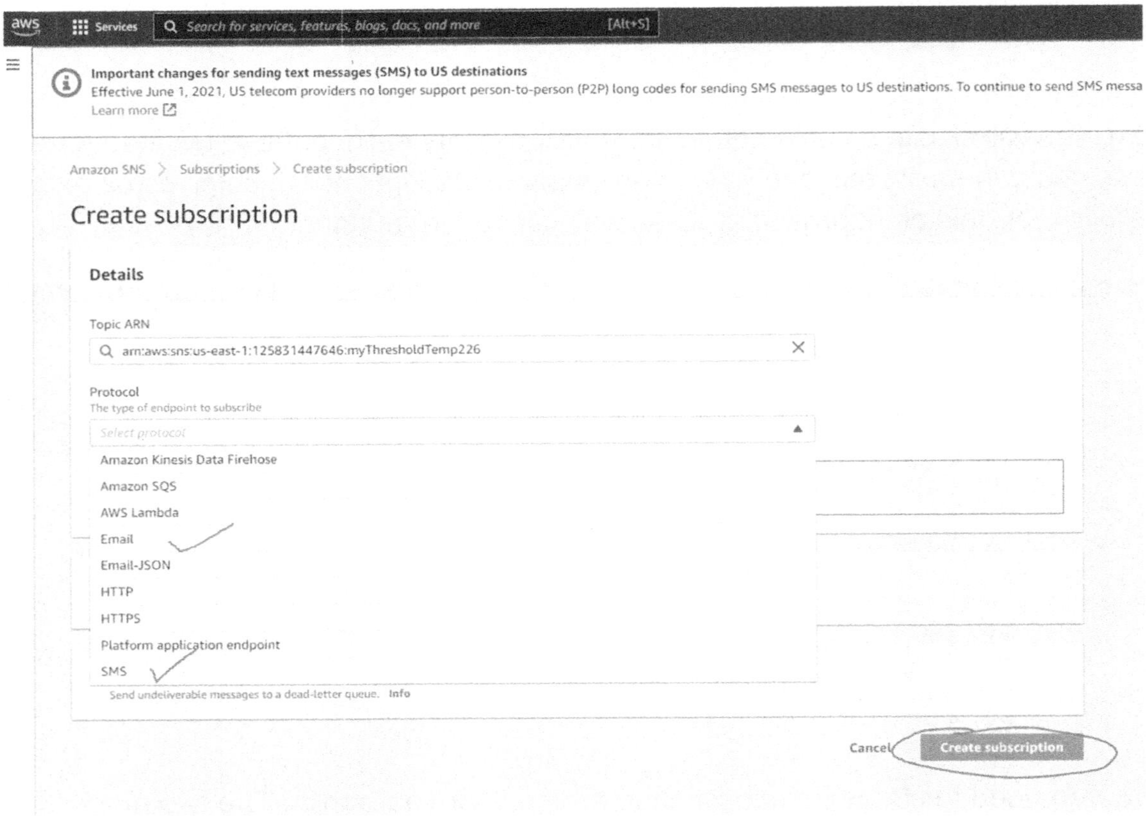
Services
Search for services, features, blogs, docs, and more
[Alt+S]
Important changes for sending text messages (SMS) to US destinations
Effective June 1, 2021, US telecom providers no longer support person-to-person (P2P) long codes for sending SMS messages to US destinations. To continue to send SMS messa
Learn more
Amazon SNS > Subscriptions > Create subscription
Create subscription
Details
Topic ARN
arn:aws:sns:us-east-1:125831447646:myThresholdTemp226
Protocol
The type of endpoint to subscribe
Select protocol
Amazon Kinesis Data Firehose
Amazon SQS
AWS Lambda
Email
Email-JSON
HTTP
HTTPS
Platform application endpoint
SMS
Send undeliverable messages to a dead-letter queue. Info
Cancel
Create subscription

After you select “Create subscription” it shows your email as “Pending confirmation.” At this point you must confirm the protocol for your endpoint (where it will be delivered to) subscription. The reason for this confirmation email or SMS process is obvious; AWS doesn’t want you sending unsolicited messages to spurious endpoints you don’t own containing unwanted alerts, allowing this would turn SNS into a great spamming tool.

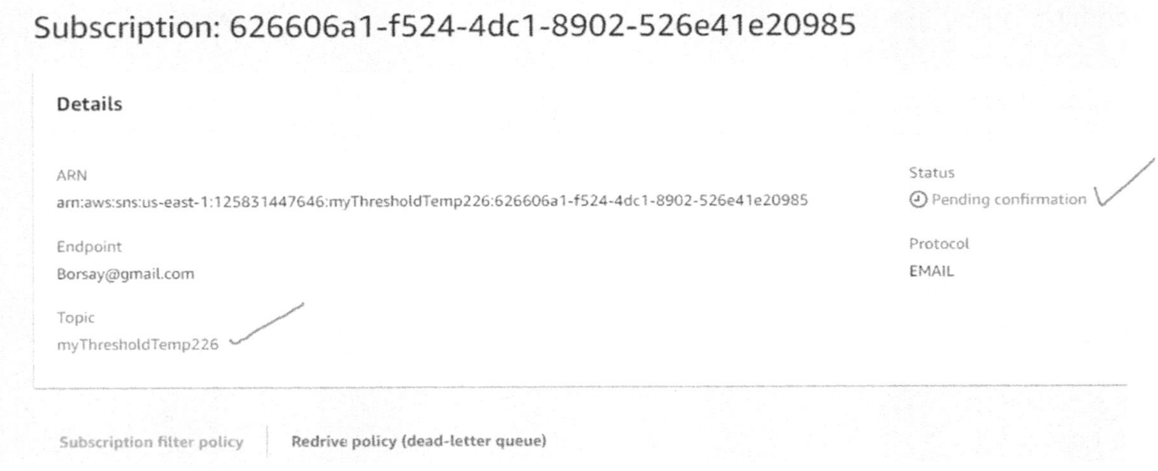
Subscription: 626606a1-f524-4dc1-8902-526e41e20985
Details
ARN
arn:aws:sns:us-east-1:125831447646:myThresholdTemp226:626606a1-f524-4dc1-8902-526e41e20985
Status
Pending confirmation
Endpoint
Borsay@gmail.com
Protocol
EMAIL
Topic
myThresholdTemp226
Subscription filter policy
Redrive policy (dead-letter queue)

Go ahead and confirm you own the email or phone number you assigned in the previous step.

Now that you have created a SNS topic with an attached email or SMS text subscription you can design a new rule with an SNS action to add in the topic with the subscription. To do this return to AWS IoT Core:

https://console.aws.amazon.com/iot

Now create a new rule just as you did previously from IoT Core.

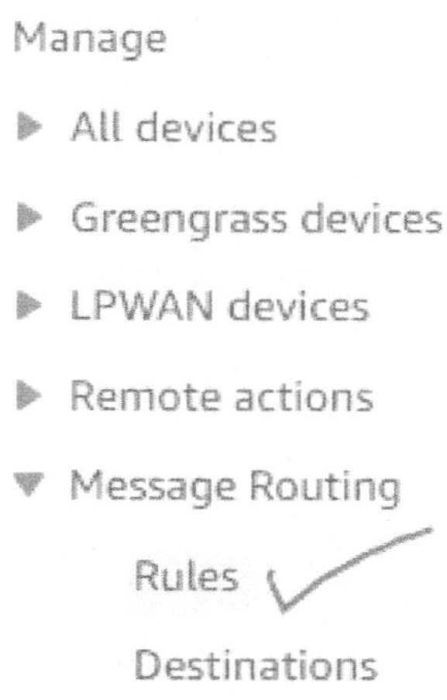
Manage
All devices
Greengrass devices
LPWAN devices
Remote actions
Message Routing
Rules
Destinations

Here I name my new Rule “mySNSrule226.” You can name your rule whatever you like. Note how I changed my RQS to a different threshold value. You can use any value you want, including the one you used for the republishing action, which was 80. Here I choose 90 degrees so you can consider this higher temperature a more exigent situation in which you would want a SMS text or email rather than just a republished MQTT subscription topic.

Use the following SQL line for your RQS:

```
SELECT temperature as Alert FROM ‘iot/#’ WHERE temperature > 90
```

The RQS as shown from the console in IoT Core:

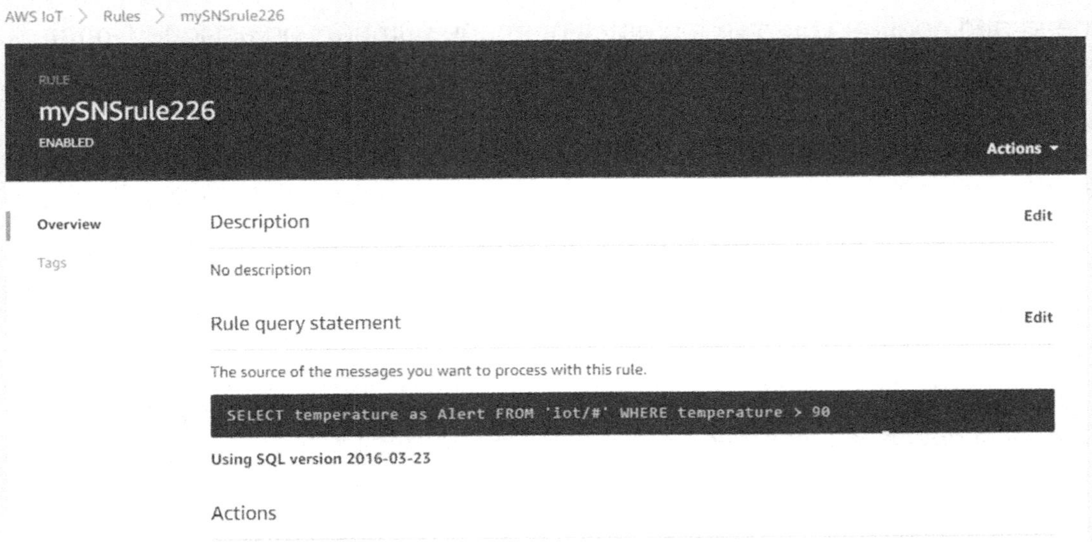

AWS IoT > Rules > mySNSrule226
RULE
mySNSrule226
ENABLED
Actions
Overview
Tags
Description
Edit
No description
Rule query statement
Edit
The source of the messages you want to process with this rule.
SELECT temperature as Alert FROM 'iot/#' WHERE temperature > 90
Using SQL version 2016-03-23
Actions

Next press the "Next" button so you can add the SNS topic you just created.

Next

Now select "Simple Notification Service (SNS)", This allows your IoT Payload to get forwarded to the AWS SNS service and then "pushed" through SNS to your email and/or text subscription.

Next assign the SNS topic you created earlier as the "SNS topic" attached to the 'rule action.'

Choose RAW message format for the alert instead of JSON. The reason to use RAW format for the email SNS is that JSON formatted SNS massages are often rejected by many email services, thus choosing JSON may often result in no email being delivered by major email services.

Finally, create a new IAM role to give permissions to transmit data between IoT Core and your SNS action.

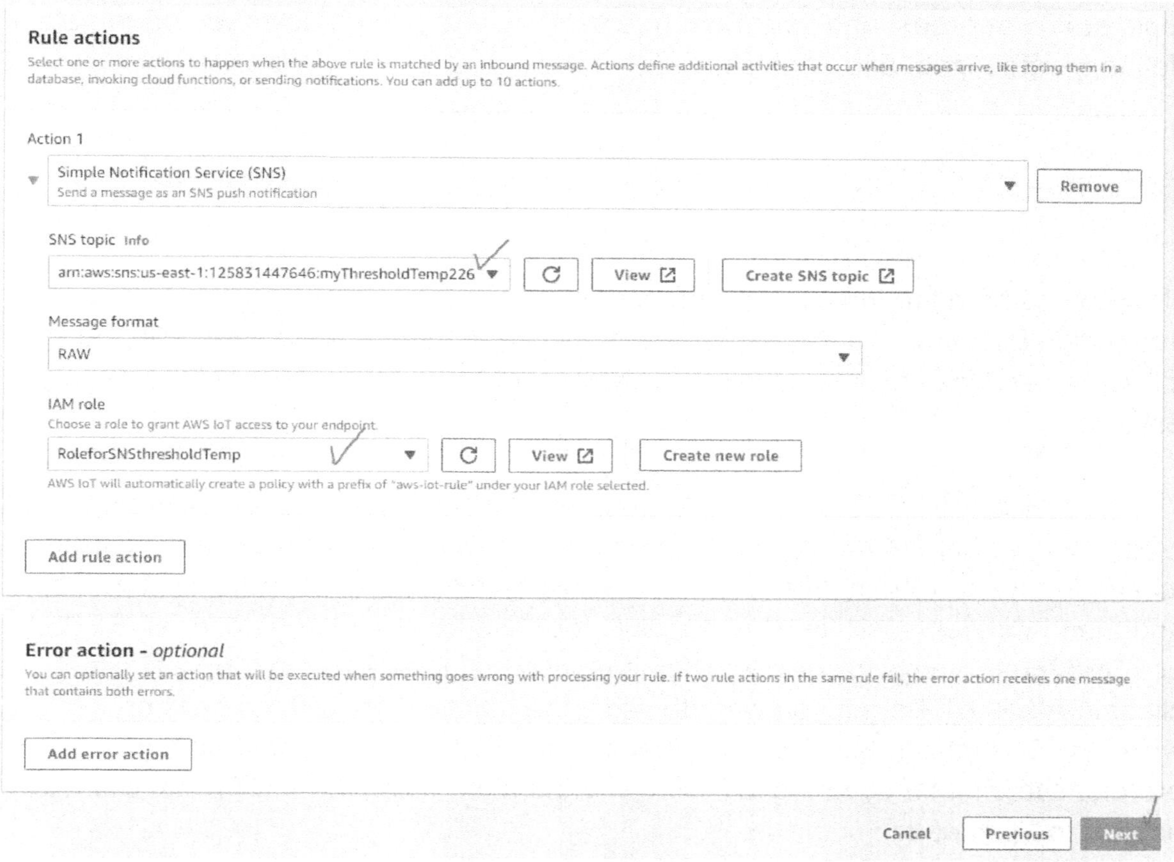
Rule actions
Select one or more actions to happen when the above rule is matched by an inbound message. Actions define additional activities that occur when messages arrive, like storing them in a database, invoking cloud functions, or sending notifications. You can add up to 10 actions.
Action 1
Simple Notification Service (SNS)
Send a message as an SNS push notification
Remove
SNS topic Info
arn:aws:sns:us-east-1:125831447646:myThresholdTemp226
View
Create SNS topic
Message format
RAW
IAM role
Choose a role to grant AWS IoT access to your endpoint.
RoleforSNSthresholdTemp
View
Create new role
AWS IoT will automatically create a policy with a prefix of "aws-iot-rule" under your IAM role selected.
Add rule action
Error action - optional
You can optionally set an action that will be executed when something goes wrong with processing your rule. If two rule actions in the same rule fail, the error action receives one message that contains both errors.
Add error action
Cancel
Previous
Next

After entering all the information above press "Next"

Next

Finally on the next screen scroll down to the bottom and press "Create"

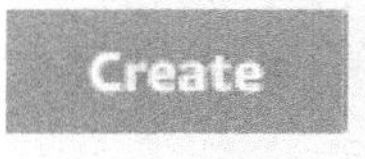
Create

Now your rule should be enabled and showing in the rule's list.

mySNSrule226
Enabled
Disable
Enable
Delete

Now both the republishing rule that publishes your IoT payload to a new MQTT topic at 80+ degrees, and your SNS rule sending a text or email at 90+ degrees are defined, authorized, and enabled.

Step 3 – Test the Republishing Rule and the SNS Rule

Now comes both the fun part and the moment of truth in which you can test your threshold alert system and see if you are notified of high temperatures with the two IoT Core services you just developed and configured using topic republishing and SNS.

You can send IoT JSON payloads through any of the physical or virtual devices that I demonstrated in the IoT section of the book. For this chapter I will demonstrate testing the rules with the attached AWS services with the virtual device, MQTT.fx and then I will demonstrate what it should look like by using Arduino for an ESP32 or ESP8266 IoT physical device. You can also test the design in the MQTT test client in AWS IoT Core if you want to verify the functionality with no bells or whistles. To test it in IoT Core simply follow the testing directions from the prerequisite chapter covering IoT Core with Lambda using the MQTT test client to publish IoT payloads.

Testing with MQTT.fx as a virtual device

Open the MQTT.fx tool and select the gear wheel in the upper right to “connect.” You know you are connected when the green light appears on the right of the screen.

Next, go to the “Subscribe” tab in MQTT.fx and subscribe to the topic “alert/#” This allows you to receive the IoT republished MQTT messages when the temperature exceeds 80 degrees. Remember, you could also just subscribe to the “#” wildcard topic and receive messages from all topics published from your account.

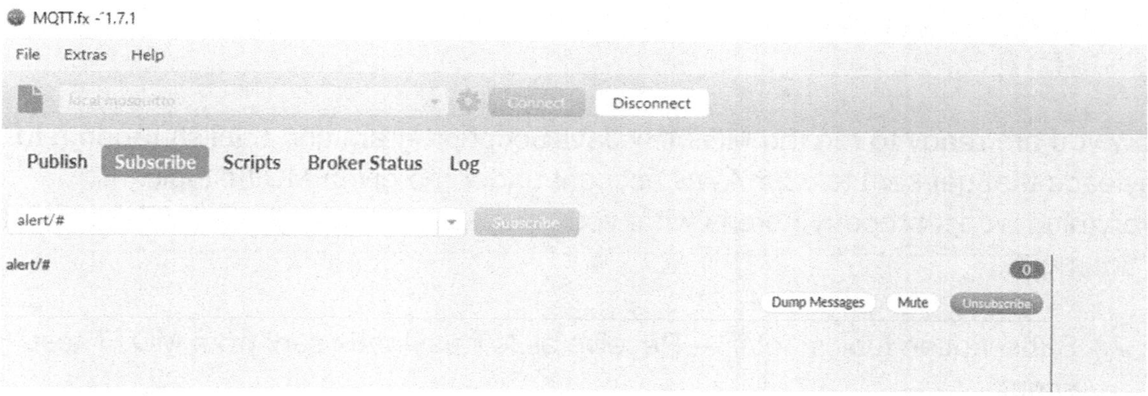
MQTT.fx - 1.7.1
File Extras Help
Disconnect
Publish Subscribe Scripts Broker Status Log
alert/#
alert/#
Dump Messages Mute Unsubscribe

Next go back the MQTT test client in IoT Core and subscribe to both "iot/#" and "alert/#":

https://console.aws.amazon.com/iot

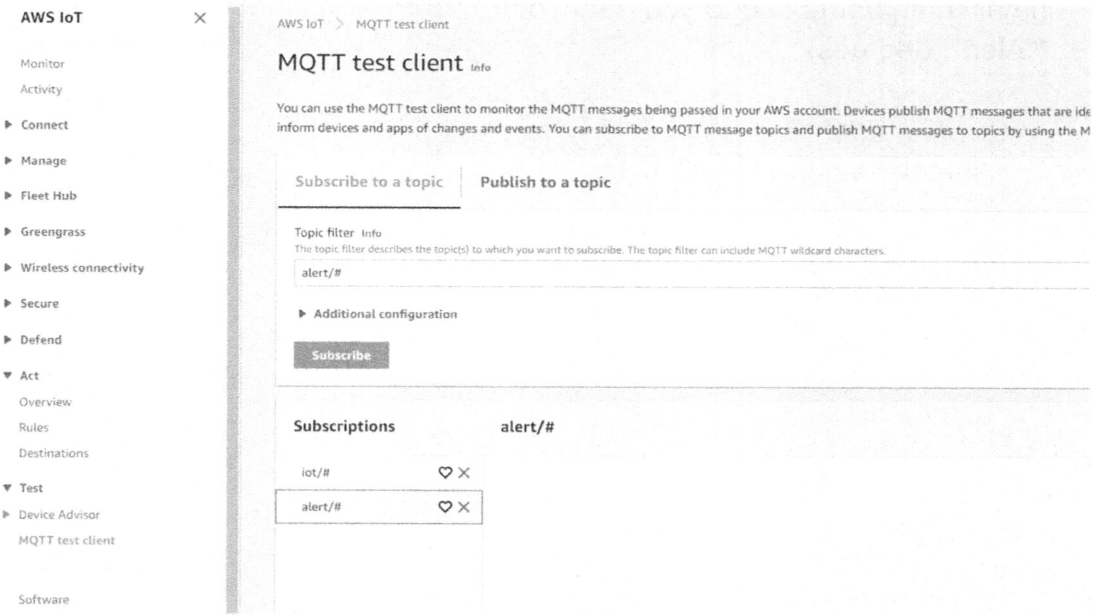
AWS IoT
Monitor
Activity
Connect
Manage
Fleet Hub
Greengrass
Wireless connectivity
Secure
Defend
Act
Overview
Rules
Destinations
Test
Device Advisor
MQTT test client
Software
AWS IoT > MQTT test client
MQTT test client Info
Subscribe to a topic
Publish to a topic
Topic filter Info
alert/#
Additional configuration
Subscribe
Subscriptions
alert/#
iot/#
alert/#

Now go to the "Scripts" tab in MQTT.fx and select your AWS test script. This is the script you programmed in Chapter three, but you can also find it in this chapters GitHub page.

Here I am publishing to the topic of "iot/mqttfx"

```
var topic = "iot/mqttfx";
```

Now you are ready to run the MQTT.fx JavaScript program and publish random IoT payloads that get sent to your AWS account under the given MQTT topic. If everything works properly here is what you can expect to see with a publishing topic of "iot/mqttfx"

A) Subscription topics "iot/#" – Receive all IoT payloads sent from MQTT test script

B) Subscription topic "alert/temp" or "alert/#" – receive {"Alert": degrees} IoT payloads in which the temperature **exceeds 80 degrees**. This is generated from our republishing Rule and received via MQTT topic.

C) When temperatures in IoT payload **exceeds 90 degrees** then an alert is emailed and/or texted to you from your SNS Rule with the IoT payload of {"Alert": degrees}

Below is a sample test run in MQTT.fx:

MQTT.fx - 1.7.1
File Extras Help
local mosquitto
Connect
Disconnect
Publish
Subscribe
Scripts
Broker Status
Log
AWSIoTTest
Edit
Execute
Test Script: AWSIoTTest
Topic is:
iot/mqttfx
payload sent
{"temperature":33,"humidity":8,"timestamps":1646086703162}
Topic is:
iot/mqttfx
payload sent
{"temperature":122,"humidity":12,"timestamps":1646086705168}
Topic is:
iot/mqttfx
payload sent
{"temperature":91,"humidity":77,"timestamps":1646086707171}
Topic is:
iot/mqttfx
payload sent
{"temperature":85,"humidity":19,"timestamps":1646086709177}
Topic is:
iot/mqttfx
payload sent
{"temperature":91,"humidity":44,"timestamps":1646086711180}
Topic is:
iot/mqttfx
payload sent
{"temperature":85,"humidity":41,"timestamps":1646086713182}
Topic is:
iot/mqttfx
payload sent
{"temperature":77,"humidity":85,"timestamps":1646086715183}
Topic is:
iot/mqttfx
payload sent
{"temperature":4,"humidity":10,"timestamps":1646086717186}
Topic is:
iot/mqttfx
payload sent
{"temperature":72,"humidity":56,"timestamps":1646086719193}
Topic is:
iot/mqttfx
payload sent
{"temperature":114,"humidity":37,"timestamps":1646086721194}
Test Script: Done

In this case I show six MQTT IoT payloads that exceed 80 degrees so you would expect six republished alert messages published to “alert/temp.” Four of the six recorded temperatures also exceed 90 degrees so you should also have four emails and/or SMS text messages with the “alert” message if you ran an identical test eventuating in similar results.

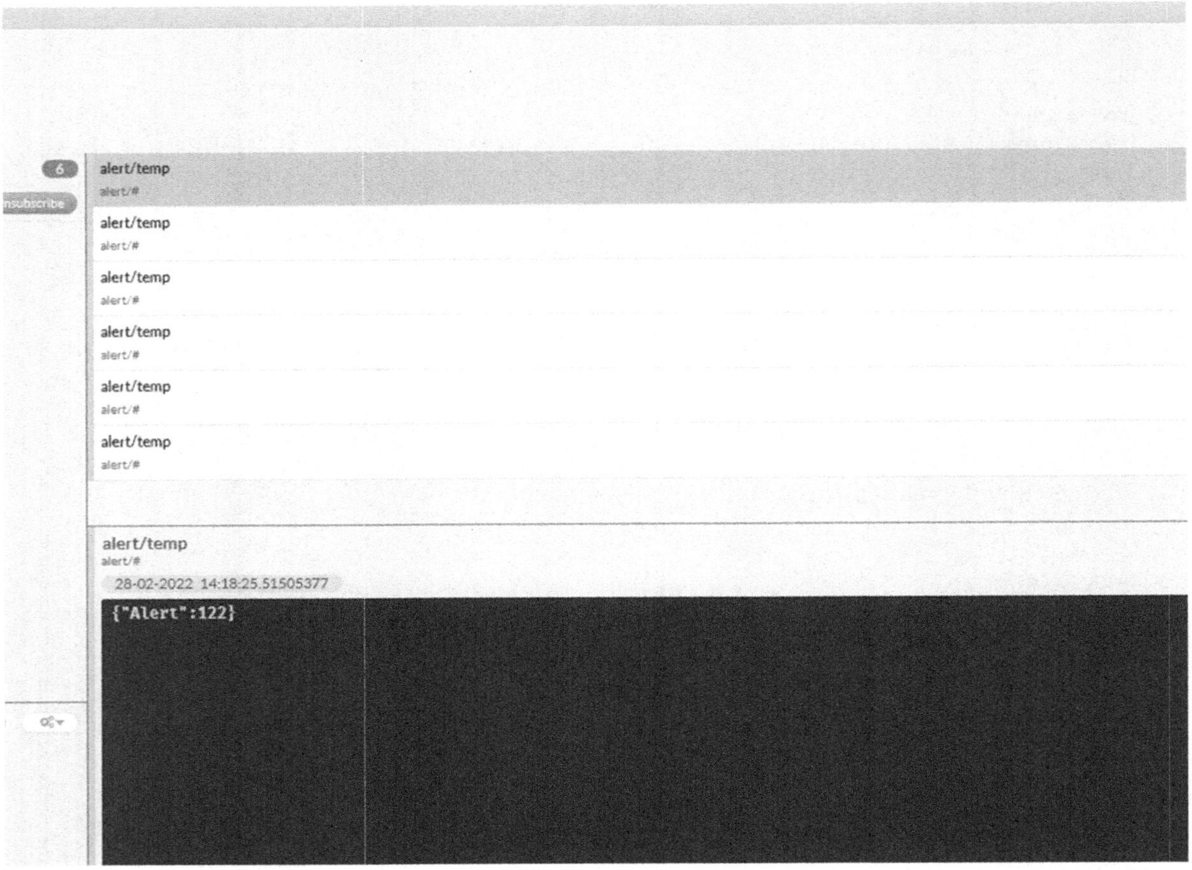
6
alert/temp
alert/#
alert/temp
alert/#
alert/temp
alert/#
alert/temp
alert/#
alert/temp
alert/#
alert/temp
alert/#
alert/temp
alert/#
28-02-2022 14:18:25.51505377
{"Alert":122}

Examining the MQTT test client on IoT Core you can see all the payloads captured under “iot/#” and six of the republished payloads captured under “alert/#”. Both virtual devices capture the same published payloads.

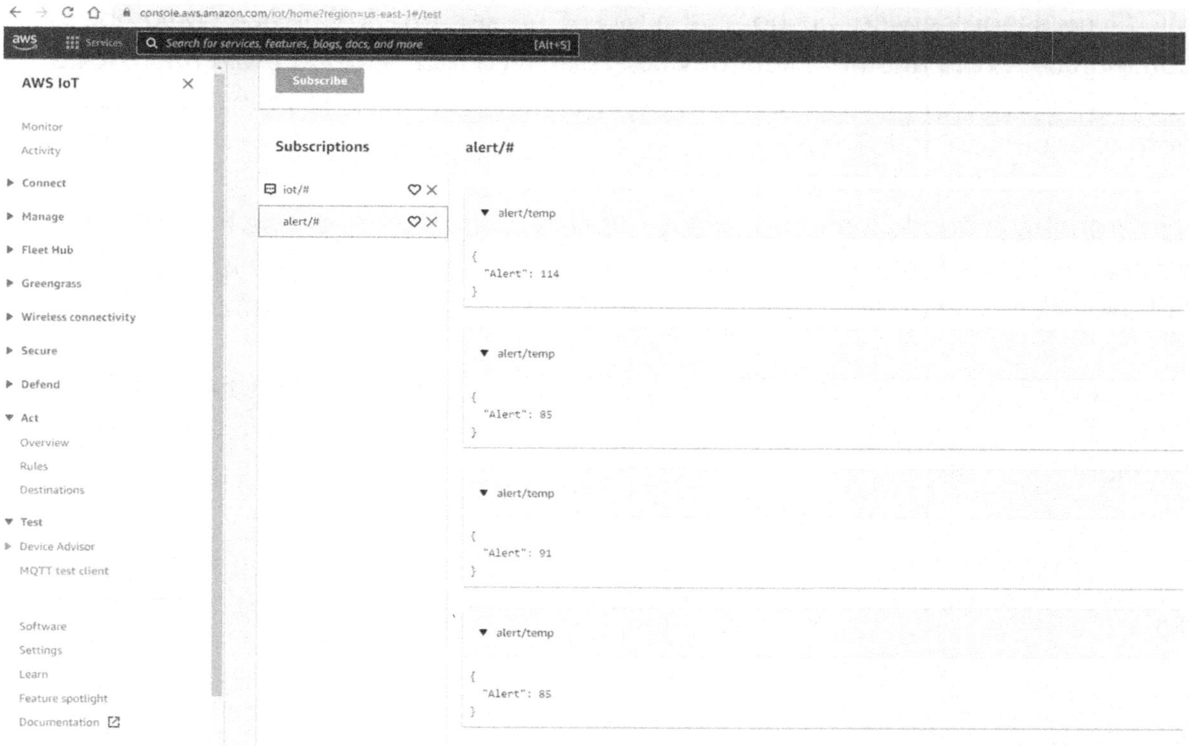
console.aws.amazon.com/iot/home?region=us-east-1#/test
AWS IoT
Monitor
Activity
Connect
Manage
Fleet Hub
Greengrass
Wireless connectivity
Secure
Defend
Act
Overview
Rules
Destinations
Test
Device Advisor
MQTT test client
Software
Settings
Learn
Feature spotlight
Documentation
Subscribe
Subscriptions
iot/#
alert/#
alert/#
alert/temp
{
"Alert": 114
}
alert/temp
{
"Alert": 85
}
alert/temp
{
"Alert": 91
}
alert/temp
{
"Alert": 85
}

Congratulations you have successfully completed this section using MQTT.fx and the MQTT test client along with IoT Core as a virtual device, now if you are interested in trying it in Arduino on your ESP device, you can attempt that next.

Testing with the ESP32 or ESP8266 as a physical device

When using the ESP32 or ESP8266 you will want to make one change to the Arduino sketch so you can capture the republished messages under the "alert/temp" topic. Obviously, it doesn't make much sense for the same device to both publish under a topic and then subscribe to that same message topic. The best option when testing physical devices is to have one device as a MQTT topic publisher and another device as a topic subscriber. For the publishing device you can use MQTT.fx again or use the MQTT test client in IoT Core by selecting the "Publish" tab. If you have two ESP device, feel free to use those as a MQTT publisher and a MQTT subscriber.

Now use the modifications to the previous Arduino script (below) on your ESP device to subscribe to alerts for high temperature sent from MQTT.fx, or IoT Core, the Bash shell script using the AWS CLI, or another ESP device publisher. AWS IoT Core will be the "cloud intermediary" working as the server side MQTT message broker arbitrating the MQTT transmissions, authorizing your account, and passing messages between all devices. Remember without AWS or another server side

MQTT message service, acting as the MQTT broker, one IoT device could not communicate with another client device. This AWS MQTT cloud brokering allows your IoT subscribing device to be anywhere in the world and still receive messages from your publishing IoT device.

It is probably a good idea to optionally "disable" your SNS rule (use the ellipses), otherwise if your Arduino sketch is set to loop, and publish as mine is, then you can get a lot more unwanted emails and/or SMS texts than you may want.

Here is what you should change on your Arduino sketch to use this functionality:

Change:

```
pubSubClient.subscribe("inTopic");
```

To:

```
pubSubClient.subscribe("alert/#");
```

This is the subscription topic, so that when you send messages from MQTT.fx or another virtual or physical IoT device you will receive the "alert" republishing topic if the temperature exceeds 80 degrees.

This is great article on understanding how to utilize subscription topics on the ESP in Arduino:

https://www.baldengineer.com/multiple-mqtt-topics-pubsubclient.html

Finally, be aware that the MQTT 'Client ID' should be unique for each IoT device. If you are only using one device, you can leave the incoming subscription topic as:

```
pubSubClient.connect("ESPthingXXX");//unique identifier
```

Now you can compile, upload, and run the Arduino cript and then open a serial monitor to observe the output. If everything was done correctly you should see the high temperature alert being subscribed to by your ESP device and then being displayed on the serial monitor.

Looking at MQTT.fx and the serial monitor for the ESP sketch you should see something like this:

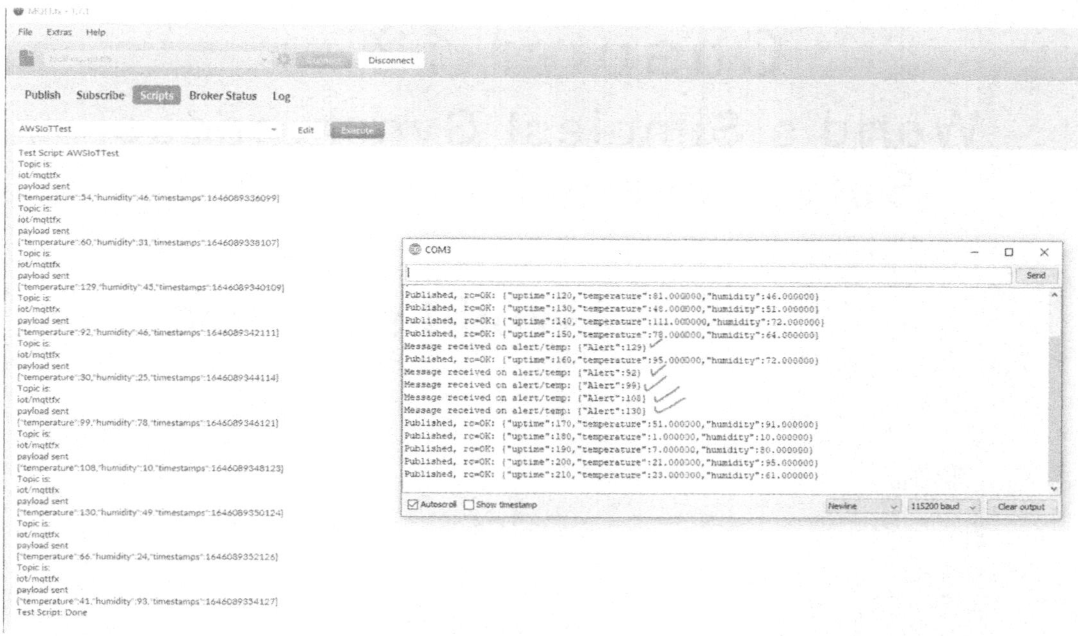

File
Extras
Help
Disconnect
Publish
Subscribe
Scripts
Broker Status
Log
AWSIoTTest
Edit
Execute
COM3
Send
Autoscroll
Show timestamp
Newline
115200 baud
Clear output

You can see that the temperatures over 80 degrees are matching up with the republishing rule output from AWS and the subscription input on your ESP IoT device.

Congratulations, you have finished this chapter's project. You may be wondering is there a better, more flexible way to develop threshold testing on AWS and still have access to SNS and republishing actions rather than just using the Rules Query Statement as a filter in IoT Core. The answer to that is yes! The professional way to accomplish these actions and further ETL is with AWS Lambda. Rather than having added a rule for republishing with an action attached and then adding another rule with an SNS action attached you can just use AWS Lambda with the AWS-SDK or Boto3 to both republish and send a SNS messages based on temperature readings and so much more. You will have plenty of opportunity to implement Lambda functions throughout this book.

Chapter 12 -
World's Simplest Synchronous Serverless IoT Dashboard

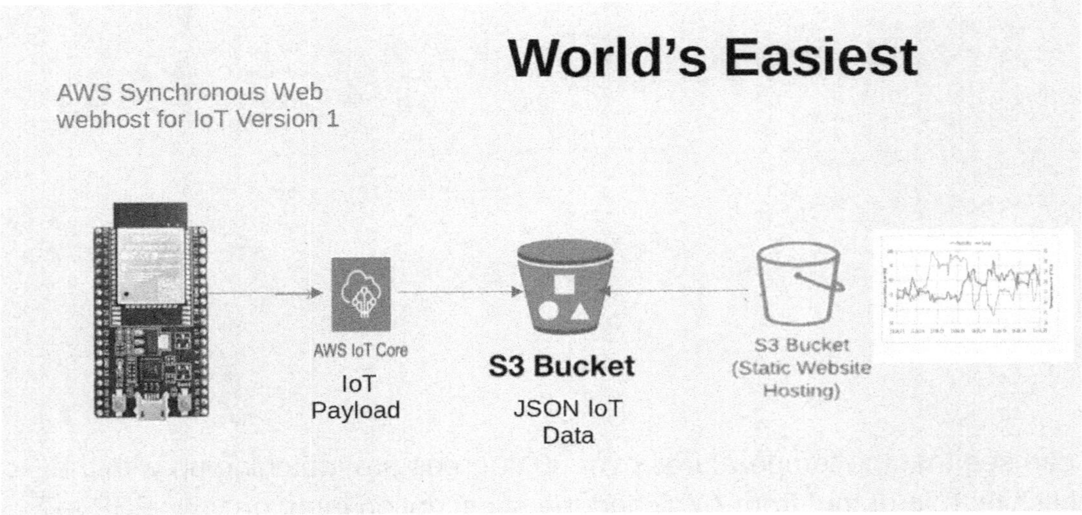

World's Easiest
AWS Synchronous Web
webhost for IoT Version 1
AWS IoT Core
IoT
Payload
S3 Bucket
JSON IoT
Data
S3 Bucket
(Static Website
Hosting)

In this chapter you will create the world's simplest IoT dashboard on AWS. Of course, Worlds' simplest is relevant term as there are easier IoT dashboards that can be created on IoT specific websites that are focused on just a few IoT services. We already know that AWS covers a huge ecosystem of software services in the cloud. The overhead for this professional development environment inherently adds complexity to AWS IoT that more limited IoT websites like, Losant, ThingsSpeak, and Ubidots don't have to contend with.

This chapter covers synchronous polling of IoT data from a S3 bucket. The S3 bucket is used as an IoT data repository with IoT data delivered from AWS IoT Core. For reasons which will soon be obvious, this isn't an optimal IoT design. However, there is an undeniable, inverse correlation between complexity and functionality in this use case. Therefore, this project is a good place to start with AWS IoT. If you are ok with "near real-time" IoT, and some potentially lost IoT data payloads are acceptable, then the simplified design demonstrated here will be useful. I will provide all the code necessary to complete this lab and visualize your own IoT data on your AWS account in this chapters GitHub. Completing this chapter and creating the near real-time custom IoT dashboard is sure to impress your friends, as long as we keep them in the dark about some initial shortcomings to be remedied later.

An assumption of this beginning AWS IoT serverless chapter is that you have a device programmed to send IoT data payloads to AWS IoT Core. You can reference my code in the hardware section of this book, or the GitHub, explaining how to program the device of your choice to publish the relevant IoT payload to AWS IoT Core. You could also use the provided Bash script, the MQTT test client, or the MQTT.fx tool as a virtual device to send data to IoT Core. These virtual IoT devices are a functional substitute for real embedded devices producing and transmitting IoT data.

From a cost standpoint when dealing with S3 writes (PUTs) it is always best to "batch" data as a best practice for production level applications. Also, writing large data files to S3 is the same cost as small writes (PUT's), so keep that in mind when creating a data lake in S3.

- Request pricing for standard storage, the cost for PUT, COPY, POST, or LIST requests ranges from $0.005 per 1000 requests in US regions to $0.007 in other regions.
- Cost to write a JSON payload are as follows, and the cost of running this process for 24 hours at one payload per second would be:
- ((60 x 60 x 24)/1000) x .005 = 43 cents
- Budget accordingly

Sychronous Weather Data on Interval

Line Chart

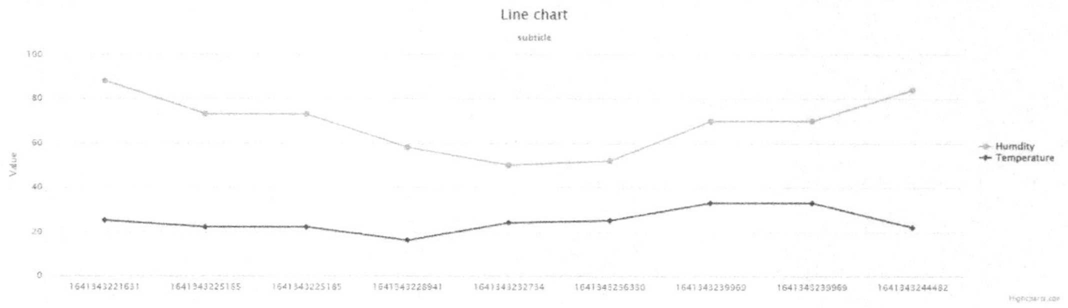
Line chart
subtitle
Value
100
80
60
40
20
0
Humdity
Temperature

Step 1 – Create a Public Bucket in S3 for IoT Data
Step 2 – Design a Rule in AWS IoT Core
Step 3 – Test the Serverless IoT Design Flow
Step 4 – Convert the S3 Bucket into a Static Webhost
Step 5 – Upload the Web Code to Create a Visualization for the IoT Data
Step 6 – Populate the Visualization Using an Automated IoT Data Producer

---

Step 1 – Create a Public Bucket in S3 for IoT Data

As explained in the prerequisite one chapter for S3 you will create a public bucket with either an open bucket policy, or a bucket policy limited by IP address. Again, this public exposure saves you the cost and hassle of obfuscating your bucket contents. Make sure to create your public bucket in the same S3 region as the other services you will be creating in this chapter.

Step 2 – Design a Rule in AWS IoT Core

AWS IoT Core is a wonderful service with a built-in server side MQTT broker that has the ability to dispatch your IoT data payloads to a variety of other AWS IoT centric services. For this chapter you will simply be sending your IoT device data to the S3 bucket you just created in Step 1. To do this you need to create an ''Rule" in IoT Core. You will then use this rule to send your IoT data to the S3 public bucket that you just created.

The first step is to create a new rule in IoT Core. Log into your AWS account and then go to:

https://console.aws.amazon.com/iot

Once at IoT Core select Message Routing→Rule→Create and then select "Create rule"

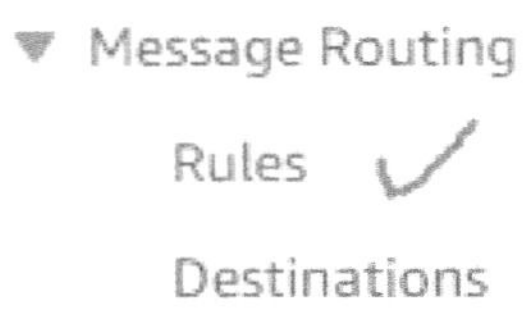
Message Routing
Rules
Destinations

AWS IoT
Rules
Name
Status

Now give your rule a name of your choice. Next, you need to edit the Rules Query Statement (RQS) to select which information you will add to your incoming JSON IoT payload. To make things easier you will use one of the built-in functions AWS provides for the RQS to enrich your IoT data payload.

Enter the SQL statement below into the RQS of your new Rule:

```
SELECT *, timestamp() as timestamps FROM ‘outTopic’
```

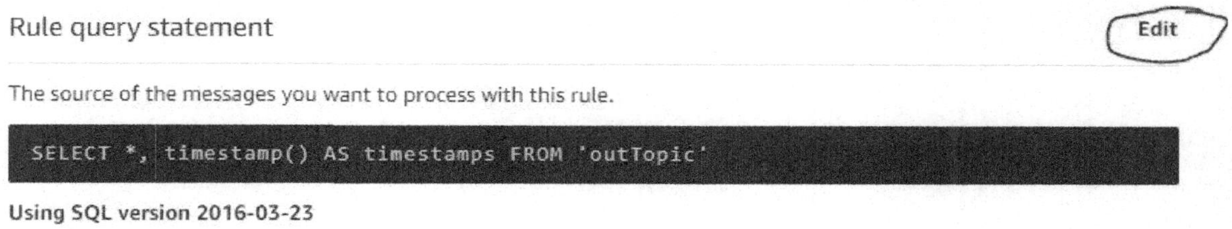
Rule query statement
Edit
The source of the messages you want to process with this rule.
SELECT *, timestamp() AS timestamps FROM 'outTopic'
Using SQL version 2016-03-23

For this rule the RQS is adding a Unix/Epoch timestamp to your incoming IoT JSON payload from a built-in function called ‘*timestamp()*’. The Unix/Epoch ‘timestamp’ is formatted as an absolute measurement, in the form of milliseconds, from the actual date of 1 January 1970. To explore what other built-in functions AWS offers in the Rules Query Statement you can read about them here:

https://docs.aws.amazon.com/iot/latest/developerguide/iot-sql-functions.html

In the RQS you will rename the timestamp as 'timestamps'. The reason for this specific name is that you want the variable name to be a literal match for how you will designate the variable in the JavaScript Code on the upcoming visualization website in S3. The MQTT topic name itself is unimportant for this first tutorial, you can call your MQTT topic whatever name you like, here I call mine 'outTopic' (as it is coming 'out' from my IoT device). In the upcoming chapters the format of specific topic names will be more important in the RQS.

Now press the "Next" button at the bottom of the screen:

Next

Next, you must add an AWS service 'Action' to your 'Rule,' now called a 'rule action.' You will need to send IoT messages to the S3 bucket you created in Step 1 so select that action. You must select the bucket you just created and name the 'Key' (partition) in which to store your IoT data. You also must create a IAM "Role" which will give your "rule action" permission to send data from IoT Core to your S3 bucket.

The tasks to be completed:

1. Select the S3 public open bucket you just created in the "S3 URL" field.
2. Give your "Key" (partition) a name.
3. Select the correct "Canned ACL" of: "bucket-owner-full-control."
4. Create a Role to give your IoT action the correct permission to PUT objects to S3.
5. Press the "Next" button.

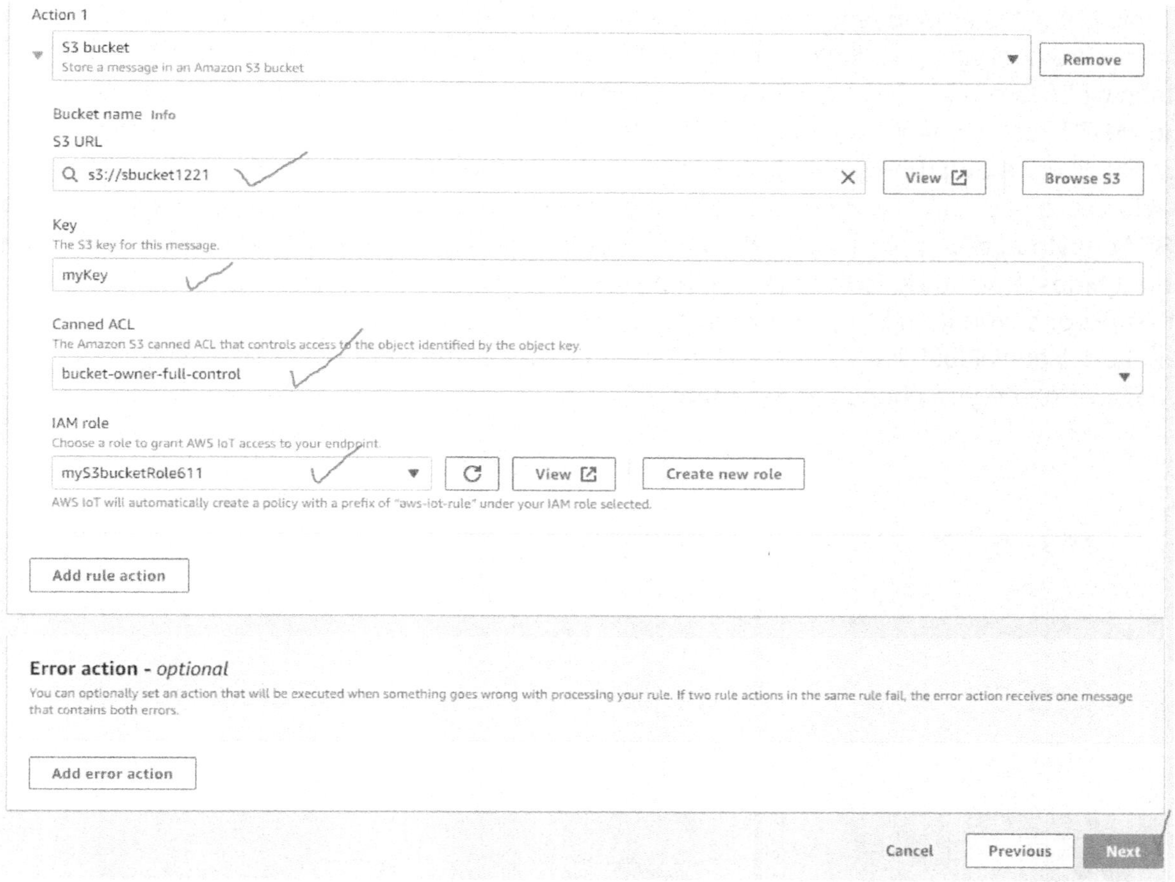
Action 1
S3 bucket
Store a message in an Amazon S3 bucket
Remove
Bucket name Info
S3 URL
s3://sbucket1221
View
Browse S3
Key
The S3 key for this message.
myKey
Canned ACL
The Amazon S3 canned ACL that controls access to the object identified by the object key.
bucket-owner-full-control
IAM role
Choose a role to grant AWS IoT access to your endpoint.
myS3bucketRole611
View
Create new role
AWS IoT will automatically create a policy with a prefix of "aws-iot-rule" under your IAM role selected.
Add rule action
Error action - optional
You can optionally set an action that will be executed when something goes wrong with processing your rule. If two rule actions in the same rule fail, the error action receives one message that contains both errors.
Add error action
Cancel
Previous
Next

After selecting "Next" and reviewing the rule action configuration finalize your rule creation by pressing "Create."

Error action
No error action
Cancel
Previous
Create

Step 3 – Test the Serverless IoT Design Flow

At this point it is time to test the serverless IoT design flow that you developed thus far to make sure everything is working before you move on to uploading the web code to your static website on S3. To test your design flow, you will send some fake IoT data to S3 from the MQTT test client. To do this go to the "MQTT test client" tab on the left side pane on AWS IoT Core and then select the "Publish" tab. This will allow you to send IoT JSON payloads to your public S3 bucket using the rule you just created. Now enter a sample IoT JSON payload of temperature and humidity as shown below. Remember, you don't need to add a timestamp value to the key-value pair of the IoT payload because your RQS adds a UNIX/Epoch timestamp to your incoming IoT payload automatically with the *timestamp()* function. You will publish your JSON IoT payload under the topic name of 'outTopic' or whatever name you choose in the RQS.

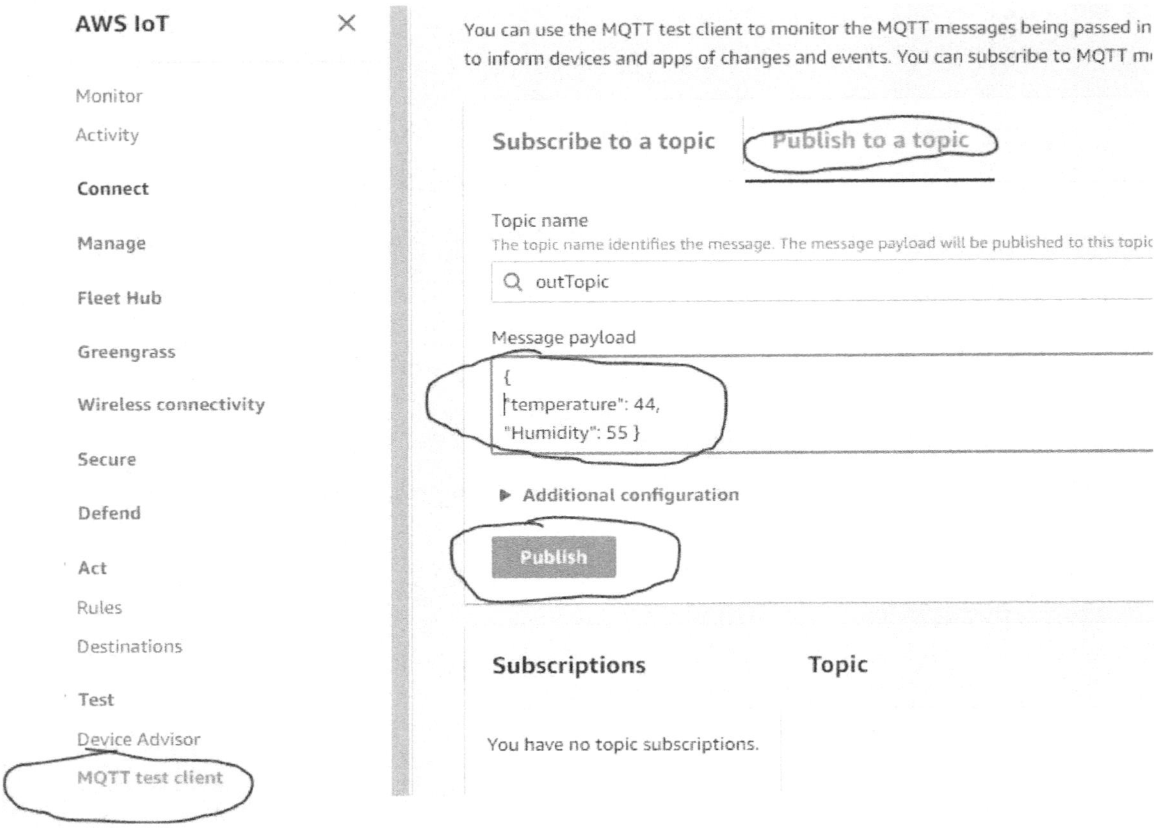

AWS IoT
Monitor
Activity
Connect
Manage
Fleet Hub
Greengrass
Wireless connectivity
Secure
Defend
Act
Rules
Destinations
Test
Device Advisor
MQTT test client
You can use the MQTT test client to monitor the MQTT messages being passed in
to inform devices and apps of changes and events. You can subscribe to MQTT m
Subscribe to a topic
Publish to a topic
Topic name
The topic name identifies the message. The message payload will be published to this topic
outTopic
Message payload
{
"temperature": 44,
"Humidity": 55 }
Additional configuration
Publish
Subscriptions
Topic
You have no topic subscriptions.

Things to do here:

1. Select MQTT test client.
2. Select the Publish tab.
3. Type a test payload in proper JSON format as shown before:

```
{
```

```
    "temperature": 44,
    "humidity": 55
}
```

4. Press the "Publish" button.

Now go to the public bucket you just created in S3. Look under the key that you designated in your rule action in IoT Core. It should be something like the object named "myKey" in this example. Go ahead and download the blob object named "myKey" and open it in the editor of your choice:

Amazon S3
myKey
Download
Open
Object overview

If everything was done correctly you should see the JSON payload you just sent from IoT Core. If you sent multiple payloads, you would only see the last payload sent as the JSON sensor reading object is overwritten in S3 with each successive payload.

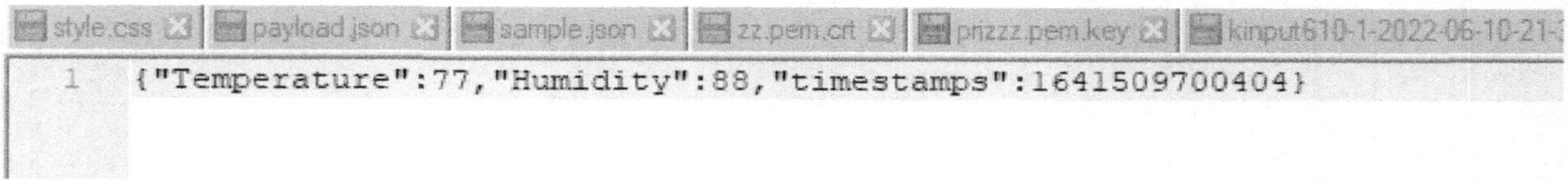

style.css
payload.json
sample.json
zz.pem.crt
prizzz.pem.key
{"Temperature":77,"Humidity":88,"timestamps":1641509700404}

As discussed previously you can't concatenate or edit blob objects in S3. However, there is an easy way to create a data lake with multiple objects with the S3 rule you just created but I will cover that in the next chapter. For this chapter you are only going to fetch the last JSON payload held within S3 on interval (polling).

Step 4 – Convert the S3 Bucket into a Static Webhost

AWS makes it so that the same S3 bucket can be enabled to both hold IoT data and host a static website with a static IP address for pennies a month.

You are now ready to convert your public bucket so that it can facilitate hosting a static website. You could easily have done this in Step 1 and still use the same bucket as a blob object store, as well as a static website, but converting it to a static website now makes more procedural sense for this chapter. The conversion to static web hosting is quite simple as demonstrated in the prerequisite chapter on S3.

Go to your S3 public bucket, select the "Properties" tab, then scroll down to the bottom of the screen where you can edit "Static website hosting" and select "Edit."

Static website hosting

Now 'Enable' static website hosting and name your index file "index.html", this will be your landing page for your visualization website. Click "Save changes" at the bottom of the page and you are good to go.

Buckets
Access Points
Object Lambda Access Points
Multi-Region Access Points
Batch Operations
Access analyzer for S3
Block Public Access settings for this account
Storage Lens
Dashboards
AWS Organizations settings
Feature spotlight
AWS Marketplace for S3
Edit static website hosting Info
Static website hosting
Use this bucket to host a website or redirect requests. Learn more
Static website hosting
Disable
Enable
Hosting type
Host a static website
Use the bucket endpoint as the web address. Learn more
Redirect requests for an object
Redirect requests to another bucket or domain. Learn more
For your customers to access content at the website endpoint, you must make all your content publicly readable. To do so, you can edit the S3 Block Public Access settings for the bucket. For more information, see Using Amazon S3 Block Public Access
Index document
Specify the home or default page of the website
index.html

That's it! Now your public bucket is configured as a webhost with a unique static address that is available worldwide. You have just changed your uber cheap and accessible public bucket into an uber cheap and accessible public bucket that can also host a website with a static IP address.

Step 5 – Upload the Web Code to Create a Visualization for the IoT Data

There are two files to upload to your public bucket and your newly created webhost. The files are called *'index.html'* and *'main.js'*.

The index.html is your launch page. Copy the following code and save it locally as "index.html":

```
<!DOCTYPE html>
<html lang="en">

<head>
    <meta charset="UTF-8">
    <meta name="viewport" content="width=device-width, initial-scale=1.0">
    <meta http-equiv="X-UA-Compatible" content="ie=edge">
    <title>Dashboard</title>
</head>

<body>
    <div class="container">
        <h1>Synchronous Weather Data on Interval</h1>

        <div class="panel panel-info">
            <div class="panel-heading">
                <h3 class="panel-title"><strong>Line Chart</strong></h3>
            </div>
            <div class="panel-body">
                <div id="container1"></div>
            </div>
        </div>
    </div>

    <script src="https://code.jquery.com/jquery-3.1.1.min.js"></script>
    <script src="https://code.highcharts.com/highcharts.js"></script>
    <script src="./main.js"></script>
</body>

</html>
```

The ‘main.js’ is your JavaScript page which visualizes the IoT data. The only change you need to make to the code below is on line 62 of the main.js file. You need to insert the URL of your ‘key’ which is the “Object URL” listed in your S3 bucket. This key is the location of your latest sensor reading in S3. You can find your key’s data object address (URL) by copying it from your S3 bucket as shown by the image below:

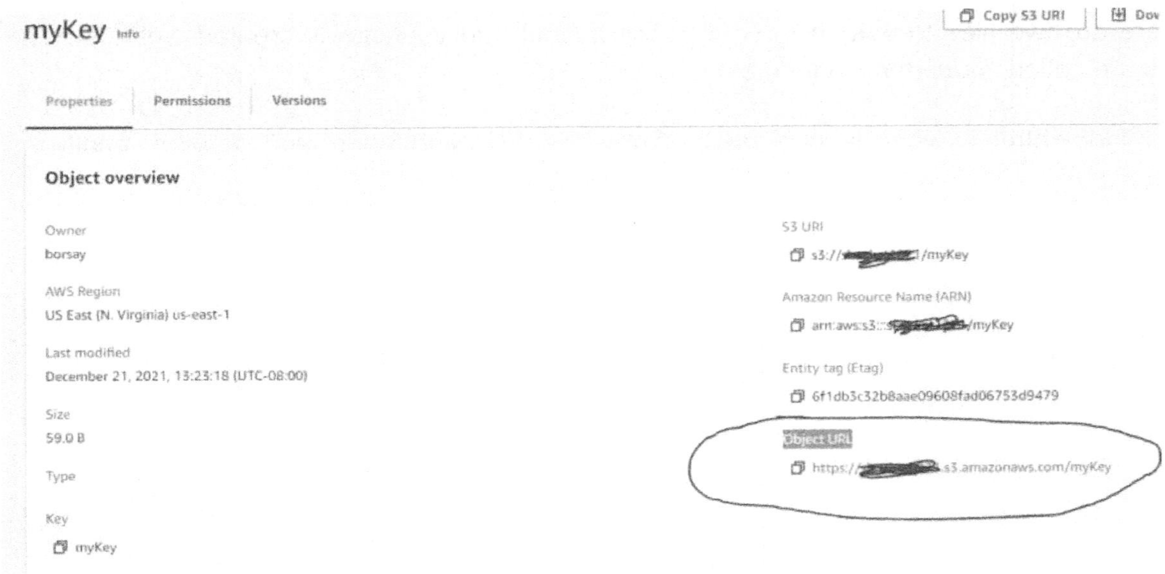
myKey Info
Copy S3 URI
Properties
Permissions
Versions
Object overview
Owner
borsay
AWS Region
US East (N. Virginia) us-east-1
Last modified
December 21, 2021, 13:23:18 (UTC-08:00)
Size
59.0 B
Type
Key
myKey
S3 URI
s3://[redacted]/myKey
Amazon Resource Name (ARN)
arn:aws:s3:::[redacted]/myKey
Entity tag (Etag)
6f1db3c32b8aae09608fad06753d9479
Object URL
https://[redacted].s3.amazonaws.com/myKey

Insert the Object URL of your bucket/key in this line:

```
url: “<https://Insert-Your-IoT-Data-Bucket-With-Key-Here>”
```

Example: *“https://mydatabucket.s3.amazonaws.com/myKey”*

After inserting the Object URL into the code below, save the code below as “*main.js*”:

```
let humArr = [], tempArr = [], upArr = [];
let myChart = Highcharts.chart(‘container1’, {

    title: {
        text: ‘Line chart’
    },

    subtitle: {
        text: ‘subtitle’
    },
```

```
yAxis: {
    title: {
        text: 'Value'
    }
},

xAxis: {
    categories: upArr
},

legend: {
    layout: 'vertical',
    align: 'right',
    verticalAlign: 'middle'
},

plotOptions: {
    series: {
        label: {
            connectorAllowed: false
        }
    }
},
series: [{
    name: 'Humdity',
    data: []
}, {
    name: 'Temperature',
    data: []
}],

responsive: {
    rules: [{
        condition: {
            maxWidth: 500
        },
        chartOptions: {
            legend: {
                layout: 'horizontal',
                align: 'center',
                verticalAlign: 'bottom'
            }
        }
    }]
}
```

```
});

let getWheatherData = function () {
    $.ajax({
        type: "GET",
        url: "<https://Insert-Your-IoT-Data-Bucket-With-Key-Here>",
        dataType: "json",
        async: false,
        success: function (data) {
            console.log('data', data);
            drawChart(data);
        },
        error: function (xhr, status, error) {
            console.error("JSON error: " + status);
        }
    });
}

let drawChart = function (data) {

    let { humidity, temperature, timestamps } = data;

    humArr.push(Number(humidity));
    tempArr.push(Number(temperature));
    upArr.push(Number(timestamps));

    myChart.series[0].setData(humArr , true)
    myChart.series[1].setData(tempArr , true)
}

let intervalTime = 3 * 1000; // 3 second interval polling, change as you like
setInterval(() => {
    getWheatherData();
}, intervalTime);
```

You are now ready to upload the files you just saved locally into your S3 bucket. To do this simply select the 'Objects' tab in your S3 bucket and drag both files to the base level of your bucket. Both files, and your IoT data object ('myKey'), should be on the same level of the partition hierarchy.

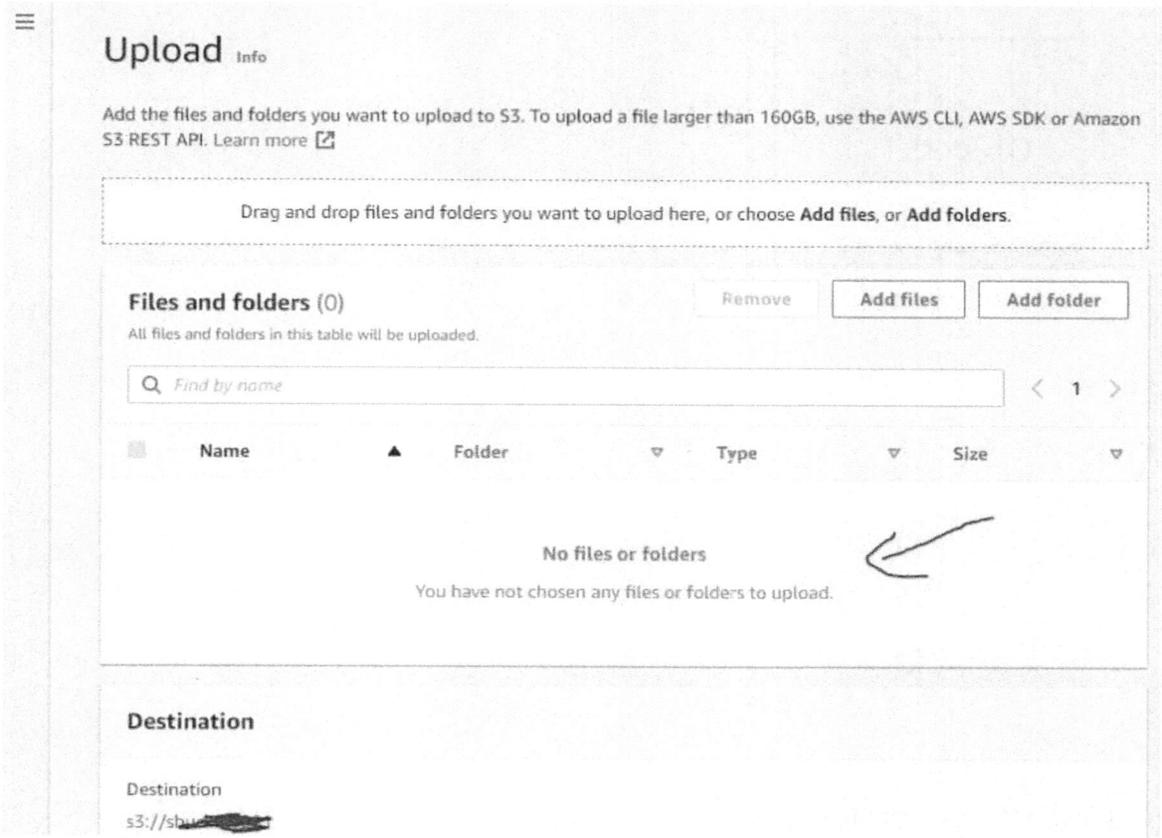
Upload Info
Add the files and folders you want to upload to S3. To upload a file larger than 160GB, use the AWS CLI, AWS SDK or Amazon S3 REST API. Learn more
Drag and drop files and folders you want to upload here, or choose Add files, or Add folders.
Files and folders (0)
All files and folders in this table will be uploaded.
Remove
Add files
Add folder
Find by name
1
Name
Folder
Type
Size
No files or folders
You have not chosen any files or folders to upload.
Destination
Destination
s3://[redacted]

Press the 'upload' button on the bottom right of your screen, and then after both files have been uploaded select the 'Close' button. You should now have three objects in you bucket: your IoT data object with your JSON readings (myKey), as well as your two files ('index.html' and 'main.js').

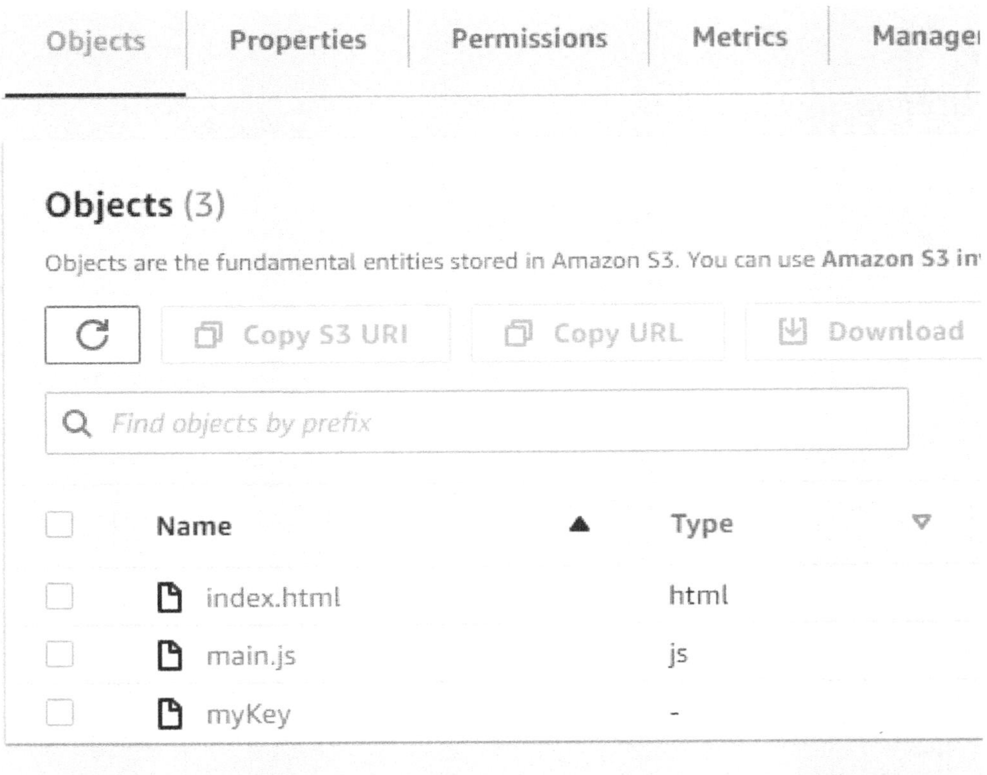
Objects
Properties
Permissions
Metrics
Manage
Objects (3)
Objects are the fundamental entities stored in Amazon S3. You can use Amazon S3 in
Copy S3 URI
Copy URL
Download
Find objects by prefix
Name
Type
index.html
html
main.js
js
myKey
-

The JavaScript code in '*main.js'* works by fetching data from the S3 bucket by a configurable number of seconds (polling). Obviously, it can over and under fetch data on the set interval, but it will provide a nice visualization given a certain amount of delay and possible missed payloads. You will remedy most of these less-than-optimal issues in a later chapter where you will use AWS WebSockets for real-time IoT dashboarding with AWS Lambda for asynchronous messaging. That is an advanced project, employing more AWS services, so we are starting with this simplified project first.

Now is a good time to initiate your static webhost by opening a new web browser tab with your static website URL. The address of your website can be found by going back to the "*index.html*" object in your S3 bucket and then opening the 'Object URL.' Clicking this URL will bring up your website.

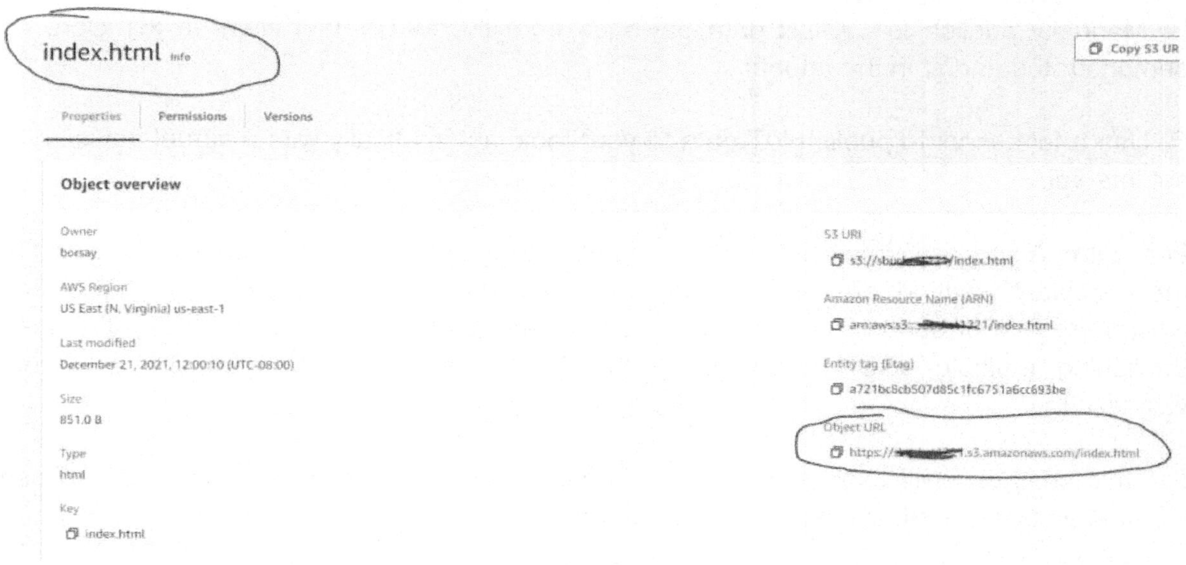
index.html Info
Copy S3 UR
Properties
Permissions
Versions
Object overview
Owner
borsay
AWS Region
US East (N. Virginia) us-east-1
Last modified
December 21, 2021, 12:00:10 (UTC-08:00)
Size
851.0 B
Type
html
Key
index.html
S3 URI
s3://[redacted]/index.html
Amazon Resource Name (ARN)
arn:aws:s3:::[redacted]1321/index.html
Entity tag (Etag)
a721bc8cb507d85c1fc6751a6cc693be
Object URL
https://[redacted].s3.amazonaws.com/index.html

Don't worry if you see a couple of straight lines for temperature and humidity on your website. The visualization is simply extending the last IoT data point that you published from the MQTT test client due to the polling function in the JavaScript code. You will know the data point is stale as the timestamp is duplicated across the X-axis of the chart.

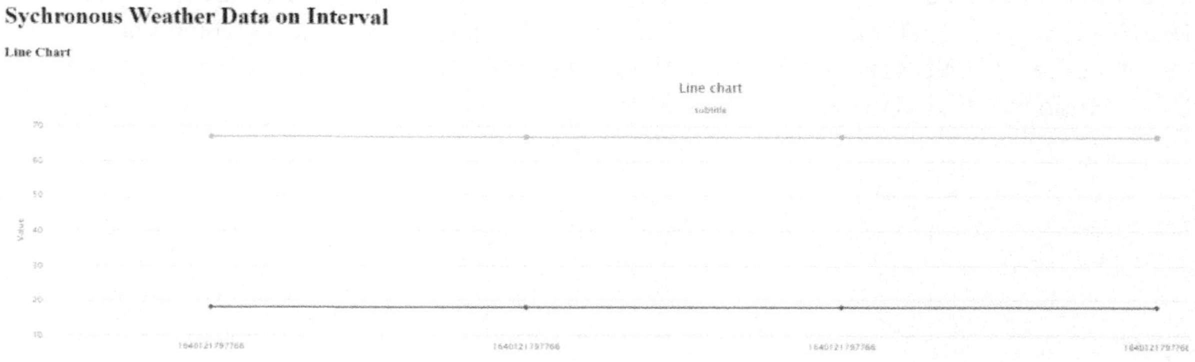
Sychronous Weather Data on Interval
Line Chart
Line chart
subtitle
Values

Step 6 – Populate the Visualization Using an Automated IoT Data Producer

For this last step you have three options to populate the visualization from IoT Core to your webhost in S3.

A) Use a physical IoT device to publish IoT JSON payloads under our topic name.

B) Manually publish IoT JSON data payloads from the MQTT test client in IoT Core as demonstrated earlier in the tutorial.

C) Use a test script to publish IoT data to your topic automatically with a virtual device at a set interval.

For option A you can simply program your device to publish data to IoT core as I instruct in the hardware section of the book in which you programed the ESP devices or the Raspberry Pi. For option B you would have to spend some time manually editing and then publishing multiple JSON payloads in the MQTT test client to generate a decent visualization.

For this chapter I will explain 'option C.' I have already demonstrated this using a Bash script in an earlier chapter of the book, but I will repeat it once again here.

The Bash script has been altered to send just temperature and humidity data. You must change fields at the top of the page of the Bash script to customize it with your MQTT topic name and AWS region in which you developed your AWS 'Rule' for this chapter. The Bash script uses your AWS CLI to deliver the payloads to IoT Core (using your SigV4 credentials). You can also change the number of payloads published (iterations) and wait time between each publish interval to produce as much fake IoT data as you like.

You must change fields at the top of the page in the bash script to customize it for your MQTT topic name (outTopic) and the AWS region ('us-east-1 or other) in which you developed your AWS services for this tutorial. The other two fields, 'iterations' and 'wait time' are optional to edit.

```
#  Adjusted for AWS CLI Version 2, Stephen Borsay
#  Changed 1000 iterations to 5

#!/bin/bash

mqtttopic='<Insert-Your-MQTT-Topic-Here>'
iterations=10
wait=5
region='<Insert-Your-AWS-Region-Here>'
profile='default'

for (( I = 1; I <= $iterations; i++)) {

  #CURRENT_TS=`date +%s`
  #DEVICE="P0"$((1 + $RANDOM % 5))
  #FLOW=$(( 60 + $RANDOM % 40 ))
```

```
  #TEMP=$(( 15 + $RANDOM % 20 ))
  #HUMIDITY=$(( 50 + $RANDOM % 40 ))
  #VIBRATION=$(( 100 + $RANDOM % 40 ))
  temperature=$(( 15 + $RANDOM % 20 ))
  humidity=$(( 50 + $RANDOM % 40 ))

  # 3% chance of throwing an anomalous temperature reading
  if [ $(($RANDOM % 100)) -gt 97 ]
  then
    echo "Temperature out of range"
    TEMP=$(($TEMP*6))
  fi

  echo "Publishing message $i/$ITERATIONS to IoT topic $mqtttopic:"
  echo "temperature: $temperature"
  echo "humidity: $humidity"

 #use below for AWS CLI V2
 aws iot-data publish -topic "$mqtttopic" -cli-binary-format raw-in-base64-
out -payload "{\"temperature\":$temperature,\"humidity\":$humidity}" -profile
"$profile" -region "$region"

  sleep $wait
}
```

Now save the above code, giving it a name like "*iot_tester.sh*". You can run the script by simply installing the program locally on your computer and then from the command prompt typing the name of the script. Bash scripts should work on any operating system. Activating the script in MS Windows from the command prompt looks like the image below:

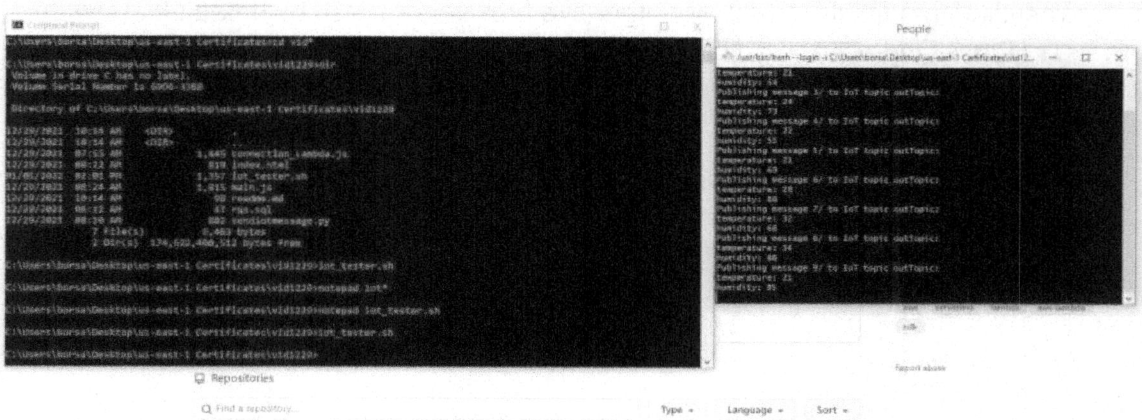

You can now return to your websites index page and see you visualization getting populated by new data points on the delay of your *setInterval()* function in '*main.js*.'

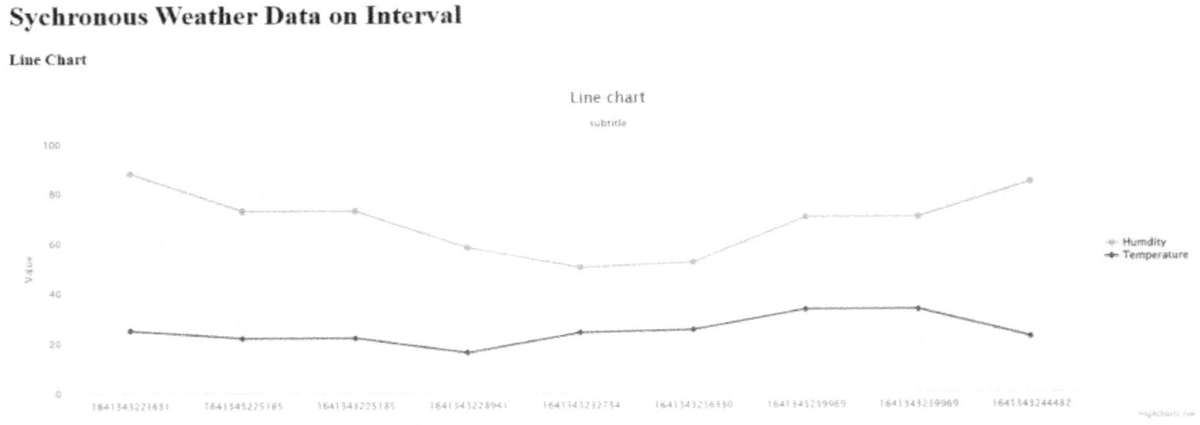
Sychronous Weather Data on Interval
Line Chart
Line chart
subtitle
Value
100
80
60
40
20
0
1641343221631
1641343225185
1641343225185
1641343228941
1641343232734
1641343236330
1641343239969
1641343239969
1641343244482
Humdity
Temperature

Congratulations! You finished the chapter and created the World's Simplest Synchronous Serverless IoT Dashboard. Make sure to keep reading to compare and contrast this chapter to the later chapter covering a more advanced IoT architecture involving AWS WebSockets. This advanced architecture will improve on the basic design here, and offer a superior, "Real-Time" IoT dashboard experience.

A couple of troubleshooting tips for most common issues are offered below:

1. Did you keep your S3 bucket and other AWS services all in the same region?

2. Does your web browsers cache refresh automatically? On my computer Chrome doesn't inherently refresh upon new data, thus I often get stale data from S3 resulting in a flat line chart. My other five browsers refresh by default for new data. Try the S3 index page on other browsers if you are not getting data point updates for the visualization in your current browser. You can also set Chrome to hard refresh the browser and clear the cache.

Chapter 13 - World's Simplest IoT Data Lake on AWS

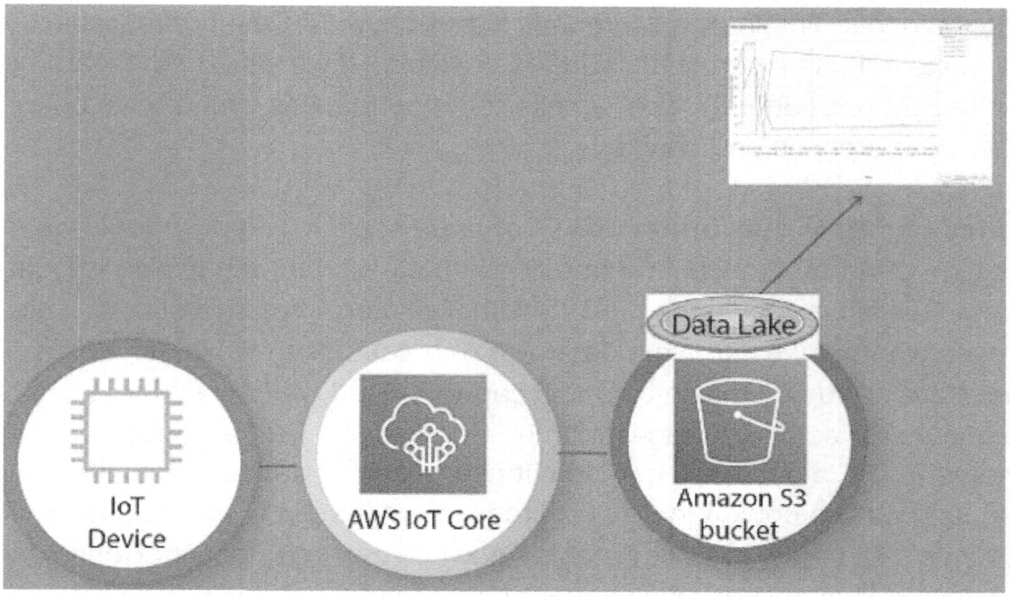
Data Lake
IoT
Device
AWS IoT Core
Amazon S3
bucket

We will spend the next couple of chapters working with data lakes and then databases. Using these two data repository methods is necessary anytime we intend to retain IoT data over time.

Creating an IoT data lakes on AWS can be extremely cheap and easy. A data lake is useful for storing raw data for future modeling and analysis, and for IoT data this is usually what we are looking to do. Often, we don't want to store raw data into a database. Sometimes we must use ETL (extract, transform, load) on IoT data and that can get expensive. However, both the cost and complexity of retrieving data stored on an S3 data lake is contingent on many factors. While I don't want to get into a prolonged discussion on the classical Data Lake vs Database debate for storing IoT data, there are some factors which are relevant when making that decision. Data lakes are generally cheaper for saving IoT data than databases but that depends on many things, including the following factors.

Considerations for IoT data storage: Database vs Data Lake

Size: the size of the data object written to S3. AWS charges the same amount for small writes vs large batch PUTs up to a certain size. Thus, when using S3 for data lakes a fundamental corollary is to always "batch" your data. For professional IoT deployments this is fundamental to consider. Batching data is something we did not do for the "World's Simplest Synchronous Serverless IoT Dashboard" project in an effort to make things as straightforward as possible. If we would have had these small writes, more frequently, over an extended period, this would have been an extremely poor architectural choice.

Frequency of data writes and reads: For large scale IoT deployments we often must design a "fan-in" architecture and queuing pipeline for a massive IoT data ingestion. This is typically done in AWS with Kafka or Kinesis Firehose. This can be the case whether we choose a data lake or a database. However, some databases are billed by time utilized and capacity used, while data lakes are billed by size of puts/writes and storage volume. For massive IoT data ingest, along with small writes/PUTs, a database can be cheaper than a data lake. Usually this is not the case, and, in this book, I try to avoid massive ingestion of IoT data as the cost of adding Kinesis Data Firehose or Kinesis Analytics can add up fast. Considering these factors, it is almost always cheaper for us to use a data lake over a database but in the use cases demonstrated in this book, using either database or a data lake will be inexpensive, especially if you are still on the free tier of AWS.

ELT on IoT Data: We must consider if we need to perform ETL on our IoT data before or after it is written. This is a consideration when using AWS Lambda whether we are using a data lake or a database to store our IoT data. A data lake can remove the need for the complex and expensive ETL processes to condition data before being stored in a database.

Adaptability and Governance: We don't want to turn our data lake into a data swamp so we will want to keep our storage formats consistent. Performing ETL on data retrieval can be painful if not anticipated ahead of time. When we design a database table this problem is largely addressed beforehand if we employ ETL on the frontend. Also, databases often provide better and multiple redundancies for data storage so for very important or private data, a database is often a better solution. IoT data tends to be more fungible than most non-IoT related data.

Storing, Retrieving, and Analyzing IoT Data: Especially considering data analysis and recent advances in artificial intelligence and machine learning, can vary drastically if that IoT data is stored on a data lake versus a database. Scanning and querying for specific data on databases is usually faster but also usually more expensive than data retrieval on a data lake.

Finally, a common practice is combining the best of both data lakes and databases by first storing raw incoming IoT data in a database and then using AWS Data Pipeline or Lambda to move the raw IoT data into a data lake. Once ETL is performed on the data lake, often with using AWS Athena and AWS Glue, we can form tiered data lakes like "bronze, silver, and gold." Within these tiered data lakes, the higher-level data lakes would hold the more refined the data and the lowest level data lakes would contain the original IoT data, consisting mostly of raw, untransformed, or unfiltered data. After the migration of data from the database to the data lake, the database can then be completely deleted if cost savings is important. We will explore using time-to-live (TTL) on our DynamoDB data table in an upcoming chapter to keep data base costs to a minimum.

For our first data lake project we will be using AWS IoT core to send sensor readings to storage on S3 and then visualize the data on a S3 web host. This may sound familiar from the previous project designing the "World's Simplest IoT dashboard." However, this project uses a data lake in S3. This means we don't simply overwrite our IoT sensor readings on a timed interval, rather we save each reading to a S3 bucket as a separate object based on the timestamp of the sensor reading. Then, our website hosted in S3 can use a HTTP request to search for the object key of each sensor reading, retrieve all of the readings from the keys, and then graph those readings using the Chart.js JavaScript framework.

Your first Data Lake

IoT Core
S3 Data Lake
S3 Web Host
Amazon S3 output bucket
Chart.js

Step 1 – Create a S3 Public Bucket with a Static Website
Step 2 – Add a Rule in IoT Core to add each IoT Sensor Reading into S3
Step 3 – Send IoT Data from a Virtual or Physical IoT Device to IoT Core
Step 4 – Add the JavaScript and HTML Code to the S3 Website to Visualize the IoT Data

---

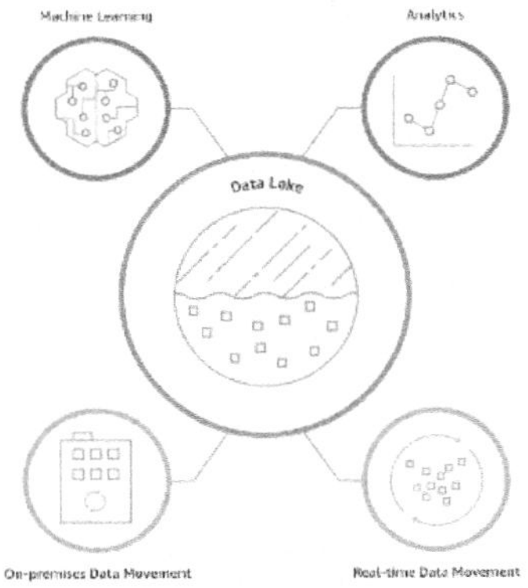
Machine Learning
Analytics
Data Lake
On-premises Data Movement
Real-time Data Movement

Step 1 – Create a S3 Public Bucket with a Static Web Host

Follow the books first prerequisites for S3 public bucket configuration, and then follow the same steps in creating static web host within the public S3 bucket. For this project, configure your bucket for S3 static web hosting for your IoT data visualization with an “index.html” web page.

In this chapter I call my new public bucket: “Datalake39”

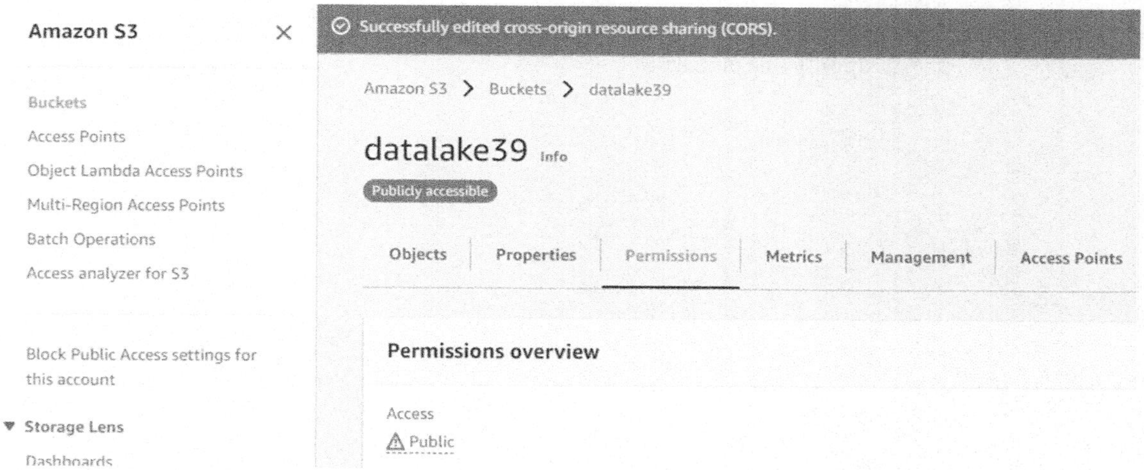
Amazon S3
Buckets
Access Points
Object Lambda Access Points
Multi-Region Access Points
Batch Operations
Access analyzer for S3
Block Public Access settings for this account
Storage Lens
Dashboards
Successfully edited cross-origin resource sharing (CORS).
Amazon S3 > Buckets > datalake39
datalake39 Info
Publicly accessible
Objects
Properties
Permissions
Metrics
Management
Access Points
Permissions overview
Access
Public

Step 2 – Add a Rule in IoT Core to add each IoT Sensor Reading to S3

Go to:

https://console.aws.amazon.com/iot

Create a new rule by going to Message Routing ->Rule

Message Routing
Rules
Destinations

and then "Create" a Rule. Give your new Rule a name like, "myDataLake39"

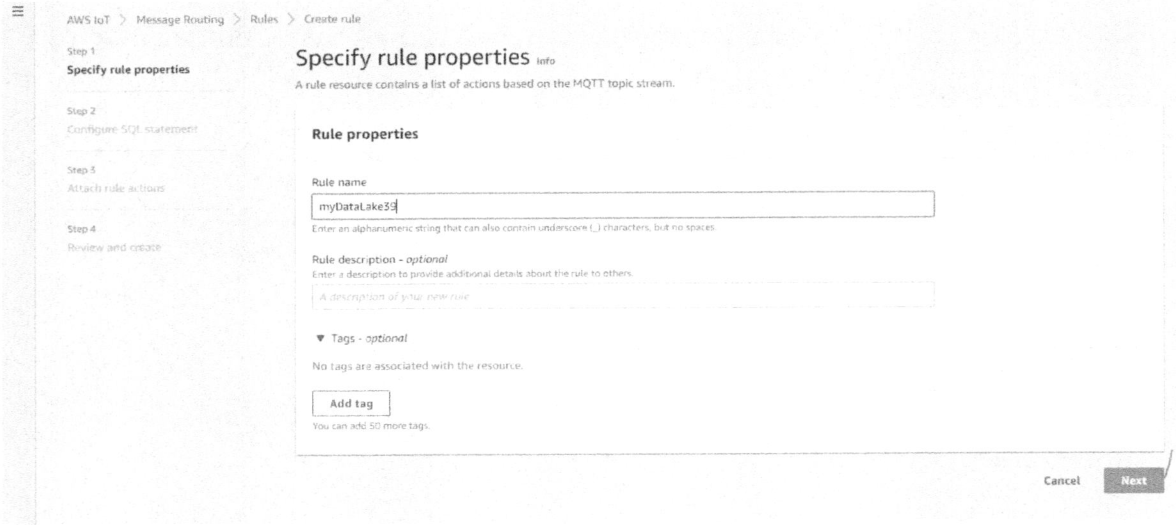
AWS IoT > Message Routing > Rules > Create rule
Step 1
Specify rule properties
Step 2
Step 3
Step 4
Specify rule properties Info
A rule resource contains a list of actions based on the MQTT topic stream.
Rule properties
Rule name
myDataLake33
Rule description - optional
Tags - optional
No tags are associated with the resource.
Add tag
Cancel
Next

Then press "Next"

For the rules query statement (RQS) you will use:

```
SELECT *, timestamp() AS timestamps FROM 'iot/#'
```

This will extract the whole JSON IoT payload and then add a UNIX/Epoch timestamp to the incoming payload by using the built-in timestamp function. Then the RQS will name the new timestamp as "timestamps." The RQS will then accept all topics starting with the topic "iot/".

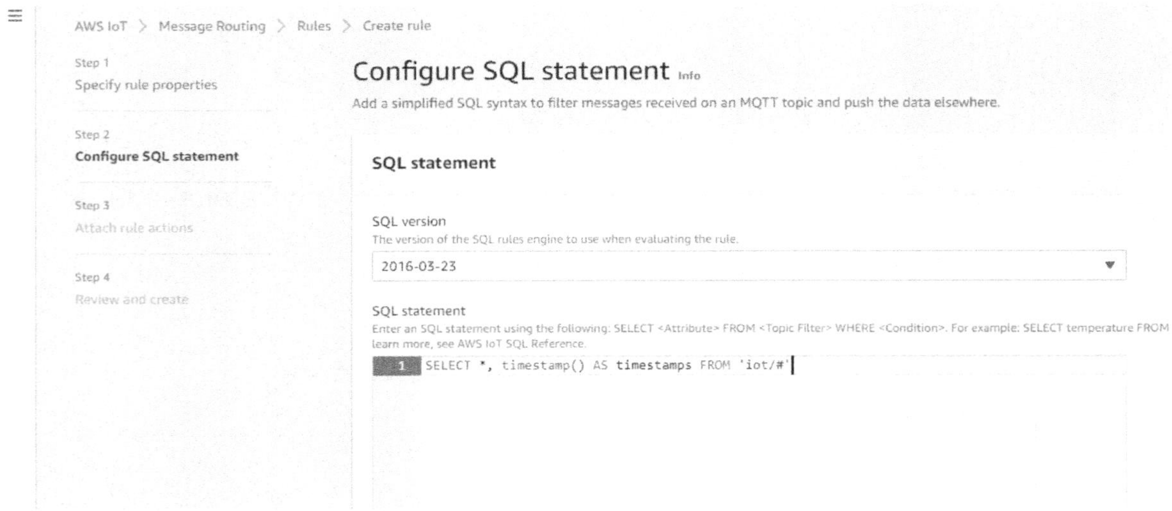
AWS IoT > Message Routing > Rules > Create rule
Step 1
Specify rule properties
Step 2
Configure SQL statement
Step 3
Attach rule actions
Step 4
Review and create
Configure SQL statement Info
Add a simplified SQL syntax to filter messages received on an MQTT topic and push the data elsewhere.
SQL statement
SQL version
The version of the SQL rules engine to use when evaluating the rule.
2016-03-23
SQL statement
Enter an SQL statement using the following: SELECT <Attribute> FROM <Topic Filter> WHERE <Condition>. For example: SELECT temperature FROM
learn more, see AWS IoT SQL Reference.
1 SELECT *, timestamp() AS timestamps FROM 'iot/#'

After the RQS is configured, you are now ready to add your S3 action to your rule by pressing the "Next" button.

Next

For your 'rule action' you will choose to "Store a message in an S3 bucket."

You will now select the S3 bucket that you just created in Step 1, as well as a "key." A "key" in this case is just another name for a partition or folder within the S3 bucket. By using prebuilt functions to create unique "keys" within your S3 bucket you can add some interesting functionality as you will soon observe.

In this example you will use the key:

```
${topic()}/${timestamp()}
```

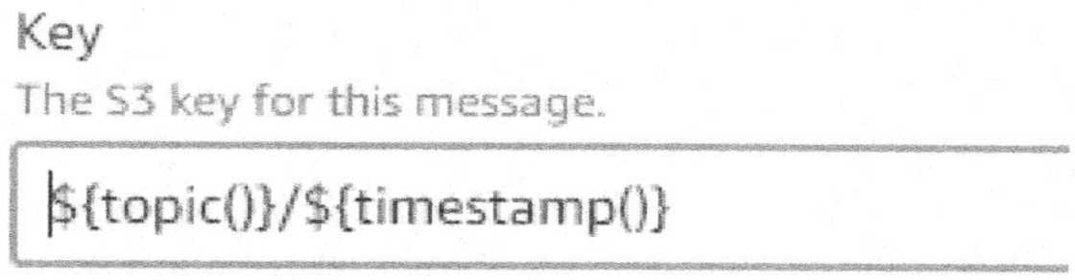
Key
The S3 key for this message.
${topic()}/${timestamp()}

The functionality would be such that the rule receives a message where the incoming MQTT topic is "iot/<Your-Topic>" If the current timestamp is 1649790740526, then this action writes the data to a key called iot/<Your-Topic>/1652119232 in your S3 bucket.

If you use a static key, such as *${topic()}* then obviously you would only get one key in your S3 bucket showing only the latest IoT sensor reading, by adding the timestamp to differentiate the key you get a unique key for each IoT payload.

For "Canned ACL" choose "bucket-owner-full-control" so you can have full privileges to the S3 bucket objects.

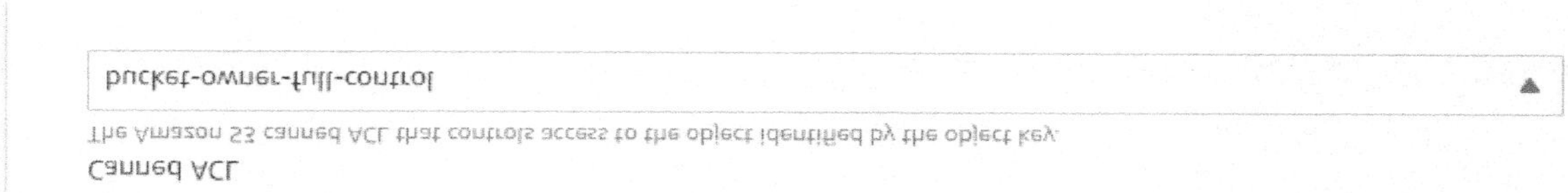
Canned ACL
The Amazon S3 canned ACL that controls access to the object identified by the object key.
bucket-owner-full-control

Next, create a "Role" for your new IoT Action that gives the permission to allow IoT Core to send data to your S3 bucket. Here I call my Role "Datalake39Role."

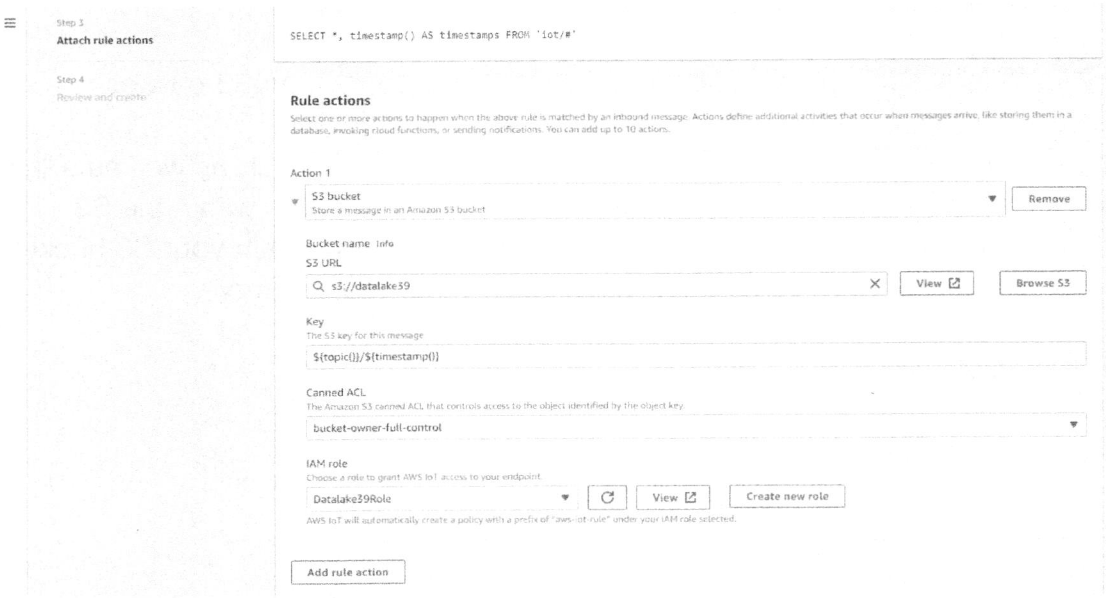

Step 3
Attach rule actions
Step 4
Review and create
SELECT *, timestamp() AS timestamps FROM 'iot/#'
Rule actions
Select one or more actions to happen when the above rule is matched by an inbound message. Actions define additional activities that occur when messages arrive, like storing them in a database, invoking cloud functions, or sending notifications. You can add up to 10 actions.
Action 1
S3 bucket
Store a message in an Amazon S3 bucket
Remove
Bucket name Info
S3 URL
s3://datalake39
View
Browse S3
Key
The S3 key for this message
${topic()}/${timestamp()}
Canned ACL
The Amazon S3 canned ACL that controls access to the object identified by the object key.
bucket-owner-full-control
IAM role
Choose a role to grant AWS IoT access to your endpoint.
Datalake39Role
View
Create new role
AWS IoT will automatically create a policy with a prefix of "aws-iot-rule" under your IAM role selected.
Add rule action

Now select the "Next" button as you don't need to add another rule action.

Next

You can now review your IoT Core rule configuration and finish by pressing the "Create" button.

Create

Your rule should now appear up top, and it will also be searchable by "Created date"

myDatLake39
...

Step 3 – Send IoT Data from a Virtual or Physical IoT Device to IoT Core

At this point you are now ready to start sending IoT data with your AWS IoT Core rule enabled. To publish the IoT messages you can use the MQTT test client, the provided Bash shell script, MQTT.fx, or a physical IoT device. The contents of the IoT payloads for publishing consist of temperature and humidity that looks like the JSON IoT payload below.

```
{
    “temperature”: 55,
    “humidity”: 66
}
```

Remember that spelling and capitalization are important as your variable names must literally match those named in the JavaScript code on the upcoming static website in S3. Also pay attention to how your JSON IoT payload is constructed.

As mentioned before, a helpful tool is https://jsonlint.com/ which will validate that you are constructing proper JSON. Improperly formed JSON will not be able to be ingested by IoT Core

Below I publish ten IoT payloads to the topic “iot/test” and observe them coming into the MQTT test client subscription panel on the IoT Core. To observe the messages, you must subscribe to either “iot/test”, or the superset of “iot/#”, or just “#”.

For the IoT Core Rule to work you don’t actually need to use the MQTT test client console. The console is just for publishing MQTT messages and observing incoming messages. So even if you are not logged into the MQTT test client console, or AWS at all, the IoT Rule you made is still active and any MQTT messages sent to your account under the designated MQTT topic will be received by the AWS IoT message broker and passed to the associated IoT Core rule given a matching MQTT topic.

The IoT messages appear below. Again, don't worry that the "timestamps" variable is not being displayed in the incoming message on the MQTT test client. The timestamp variable gets added to your IoT payload by the RQS before it is dispatched to the selected AWS service by your rule from Step 2.

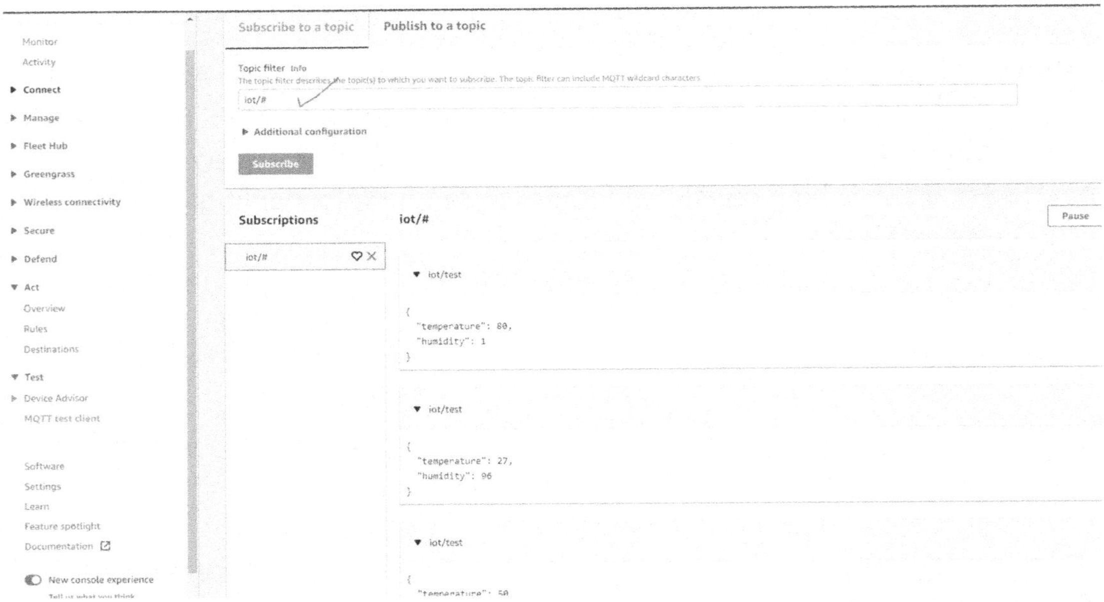
Subscribe to a topic
Publish to a topic
Monitor
Activity
Connect
Manage
Fleet Hub
Greengrass
Wireless connectivity
Secure
Defend
Act
Overview
Rules
Destinations
Test
Device Advisor
MQTT test client
Software
Settings
Learn
Feature spotlight
Documentation
New console experience
Topic filter Info
iot/#
Additional configuration
Subscribe
Subscriptions
iot/#
Pause
iot/test
"temperature": 80,
"humidity": 1
iot/test
"temperature": 27,
"humidity": 96
iot/test

The next step after you created your IoT "Rule," added your S3 "Action," and then transmitted your IoT data to AWS, is to open the S3 bucket that you choose as the destination for your IoT payloads.

Navigate back to S3 and check your bucket.

https://s3.console.aws.amazon.com/s3/buckets

To see your IoT sensor readings look under the topic name and the incoming timestamp keys.

Drilling down into the topic you should see your timestamped readings appear as shown below:

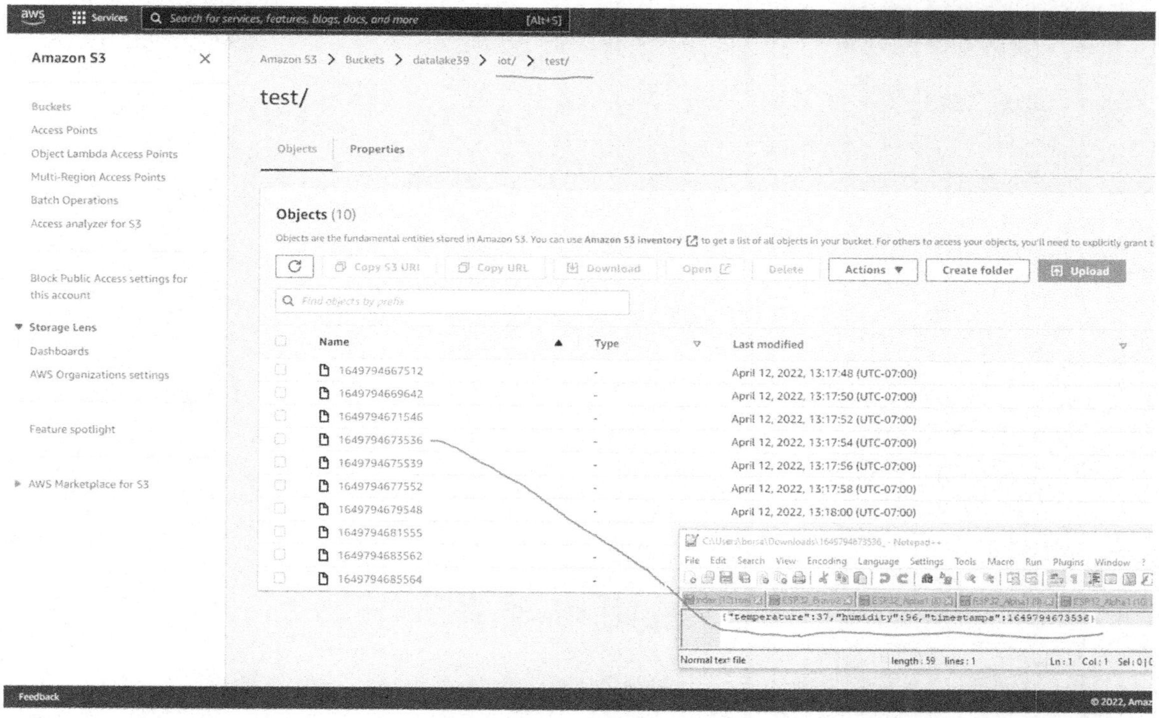
Amazon S3
Buckets
Access Points
Object Lambda Access Points
Multi-Region Access Points
Batch Operations
Access analyzer for S3
Block Public Access settings for this account
Storage Lens
Dashboards
AWS Organizations settings
Feature spotlight
AWS Marketplace for S3
Amazon S3 > Buckets > datalake39 > iot/ > test/
test/
Objects
Properties
Objects (10)
Actions
Create folder
Upload
Name
Type
Last modified
1649794667512
1649794669642
1649794671546
1649794673536
1649794675539
1649794677552
1649794679548
1649794681555
1649794683562
1649794685564
April 12, 2022, 13:17:48 (UTC-07:00)
April 12, 2022, 13:17:50 (UTC-07:00)
April 12, 2022, 13:17:52 (UTC-07:00)
April 12, 2022, 13:17:54 (UTC-07:00)
April 12, 2022, 13:17:56 (UTC-07:00)
April 12, 2022, 13:17:58 (UTC-07:00)
April 12, 2022, 13:18:00 (UTC-07:00)
{"temperature":37,"humidity":96,"timestamps":1649794673536}
Normal text file
Feedback

In this picture I opened a random sensor reading key so that you could see what it should look like once it is downloaded and observed. Despite what Heisenberg may say, observing the data will not change it.

Step 4 – Add the JavaScript and HTML Code to the S3 Website to Visualize the IoT Data

There are three web files to produce the visualization for this chapter. All three web files can be found on the GitHub page for this chapter as well as being listed below.

Now you are ready to upload the web code that will consume the IoT sensor readings and produce a line chart. First step is to create an "*index.html*" page in your S3 bucket after enabling static website hosting in the bucket with the IoT sensor readings sent from IoT Core. Hopefully you have already enabled static webhosting in Step 1, but if not do so now. The file below is the landing page designated by the typical convention of "*index.html*". Upload the file to the base level of your S3 bucket as "*index.html*".

```
<!doctype html>
```

```
<html lang="en">
   <head>
      <title>Title</title>
      <!-Required meta tags →
      <meta charset="utf-8">
      <meta name="viewport" content="width=device-width, initial-scale=1,
shrink-to-fit=no">

      <!-Bootstrap CSS →
      <link rel="stylesheet"
href="https://stackpath.bootstrapcdn.com/bootstrap/4.3.1/css/bootstrap.min.cs
s" integrity="sha384-
ggOyR0iXCbMQv3Xipma34MD+dH/1fQ784/j6cY/iJTQUOhcWr7x9JvoRxT2MZw1T"
crossorigin="anonymous">
      <link rel="stylesheet"
href="https://cdnjs.cloudflare.com/ajax/libs/Chart.js/2.9.3/Chart.css"
integrity="sha256-IvM9nJf/b5l2RoebiFno92E5OnttVyaEEsdemDC6iQA="
crossorigin="anonymous" />
   </head>
   <body>
      <div class="row">
         <div class="col-lg-6">
            <canvas id="myChart" width="200" height="200"
responsive="true"></canvas>
         </div>
      </div>

      <!-Optional JavaScript →
      <!-jQuery first, then Popper.js, then Bootstrap JS →
      <script src="https://code.jquery.com/jquery-3.4.1.min.js"
integrity="sha256-CSXorXvZcTkaix6Yvo6HppcZGetbYMGWSFlBw8HfCJo="
crossorigin="anonymous"></script>
      <script
src="https://cdnjs.cloudflare.com/ajax/libs/popper.js/1.14.7/umd/popper.min.j
s" integrity="sha384-
UO2eT0CpHqdSJQ6hJty5KVphtPhzWj9WO1clHTMGa3JDZwrnQq4sF86dIHNDz0W1"
crossorigin="anonymous"></script>
      <script
src="https://cdnjs.cloudflare.com/ajax/libs/Chart.js/2.9.3/Chart.bundle.min.j
s" integrity="sha256-TQq84xX6vkwR0Qs1qH5AdkP+MvH0W+9E7TdHJsoIQiM="
crossorigin="anonymous"></script>
      <script
src="https://stackpath.bootstrapcdn.com/bootstrap/4.3.1/js/bootstrap.min.js"
integrity="sha384-
```

```
JjSmVgyd0p3pXB1rRibZUAYoIIy6OrQ6VrjIEaFf/nJGzIxFDsf4x0xIM+B07jRM"
crossorigin="anonymous"></script>
      <script src="visualizer.js"></script>
      <script src="main.js"></script>
    </body>
  </html>
```

For the next file you must modify the "*main.js*" file in the four lines listed below so that it will work with your IoT data. Two of the lines for modification require your base bucket URL so that the '*main.js*' file can locate your IoT data partition in the S3 bucket. The other two lines to modify are required so that the main.js program can find your S3 partition 'keys'. Remember because all S3 buckets have globally unique names they also have a globally unique static URL's which makes things easy.

Your base bucket name will take the format of:

```
"https://<YOUR-S3-Bucket>>.s3.<Your-AWS-Region>>.amazonaws.com/",
```

And

```
"https://<YOUR-S3-Bucket>>.s3.<Your-AWS-Region>>.amazonaws.com/" + url,"
```

So, for instance my S3 bucket "datalake39" web address in my home region of *us-east-1* will be:

https://datalake39.s3.us-east-1.amazonaws.com/

Fill in the two places below in the JavaScript code as indicated for your bucket name and bucket region. Do not worry about the "+ url" extension as that is handled automatically by the JavaScript code.

Also, the program will need to know in your file hierarchy as to where the readings are located. So, in this case given the IoT topic that you sent your IoT payloads under and viewed in IoT Core:

```
pos = url.search("<Your-Topic>/"); //We used: "iot/test/"
```

And:

```
if(url.replace("<Your-Topic>/", "+") != "")
```

The "*main.js*" code to place in your S3 bucket, make sure to fill out the necessary four fields in the code below as described above:

```
var timestamps = new Array();
var humidity = new Array();
var temperature = new Array();

// Start by extracting folder/ url from s3 bucket
$.ajax({
    type       : "GET",
    url        : "https://<YOUR-S3-Bucket>>.s3.<Your-AWS-
Region>>.amazonaws.com/",
    254sar254ype : "xml",
    success    : function(xmlData){
        var url = "";
        keys = xmlData.getElementsByTagName("Key");
        for(i=0; I < keys.length; i++) {
            url = keys[i].childNodes[0].nodeValue
            url = url.trim()+"+"

            // Find your locate folder string
            pos = url.search("<Your-Topic>/");  //topic = "iot/test/"
            if(pos > -1) {
                // Detect folder/partition with json file
                if(url.replace("<Your-Topic>/", "+") != "")
                    parseJson(url)
            }
        }

        loadChart(temperature, humidity, timestamps)
    },
    error      : function(){
         alert("Could not retrieve XML file.");
    }
});

var parseJson = function(url) {
    $.ajax({

        type : "GET",
        url : "https://<YOUR-S3-Bucket>>.s3.<Your-AWS-
Region>>.amazonaws.com/" + url,
        254sar254ype : "json",
```

```
        success : function(jsonFile) {
            timestamps.push(jsonFile.timestamps);
            temperature.push(jsonFile.temperature)
            humidity.push(jsonFile.humidity)
        },
        error : function(xhr, status, error) {
            console.error("JSON error: " + status);
        }
    })
}
```

One of my goals in this book is to stay away from explaining web code, however the "*main.js*" is the most challenging of the three files considering code complexity. The first section of code searches through the bucket to find the keys in your file. The second part of the code that concatenates each key to the base URL to ingest the data points for each reading with the subsequent timestamp.

As discussed in the prerequisite chapter on creating an S3 bucket, exposing the base bucket URL is not a huge cost risk, as reading data from S3 is extremely cheap, in fact it is ten times cheaper to read data from S3 than writing data to S3. Later in the book, when you start scanning databases for IoT data, hiding the embedded endpoints to AWS services will become extremely important if not for security reasons than for cost reasons. This simple method of privacy is easily achieved with a free IP limiting policy as discussed in an earlier chapter. You do not want a malicious user discovering your AWS service endpoint and executing it repeatedly.

The final file below for you to upload to your S3 bucket does not require any additional modifications. Copy the file below and upload it to the base level of your S3 bucket, at the same level as the main.js file.

The last file is called "*visualizer.js*", and it implements the Chart.js package.

```
Var loadChart = function( temperature, humidity, timestamps) {
  var ctx = $('#myChart');

  var myChart = new Chart(ctx, {
      type: 'line',
      data: {
          labels: timestamps,
          datasets: [
```

```
            {
                label: "Temperature",
                data: temperature,
                fill: false,
                borderColor: "rgb(255, 0, 0)",
                lineTension: 0.1
            },
            {
                label: "Humidity",
                data: humidity,
                fill: false,
                borderColor: "rgb(0, 0, 255)",
                lineTension: 0.1
            }
        ]
    },
    options: {
        title: {
            display: true,
            text: 'Timestamps',
            position: 'bottom'
        }
    }
});
```

After modifying the main.js file, all three files should be uploaded to the base level of your bucket which holds your sensor readings as it appears below.

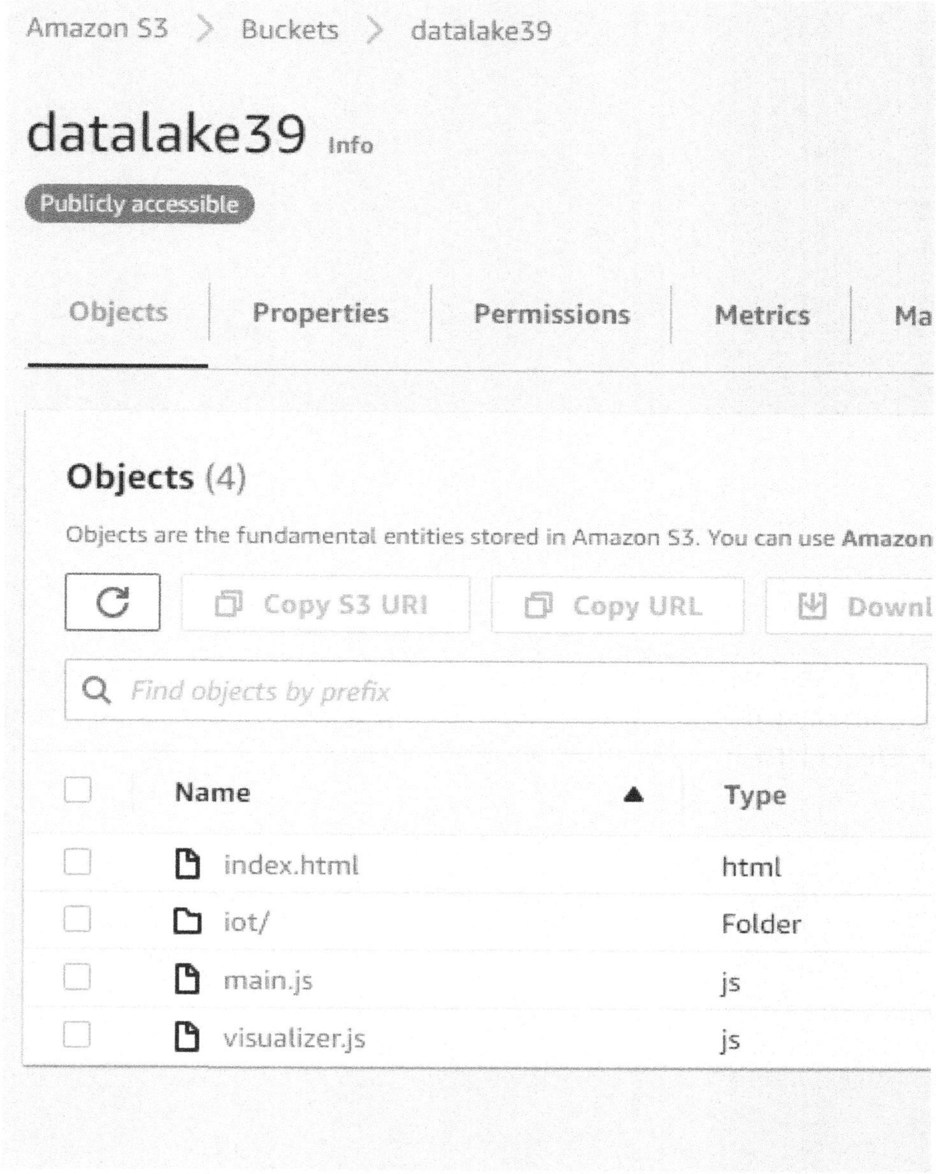
Amazon S3 > Buckets > datalake39
datalake39 Info
Publicly accessible
Objects
Properties
Permissions
Metrics
Ma
Objects (4)
Objects are the fundamental entities stored in Amazon S3. You can use Amazon
Copy S3 URI
Copy URL
Downl
Find objects by prefix
Name
Type
index.html
html
iot/
Folder
main.js
js
visualizer.js
js

After hosting the web files in your bucket, you can now bring up the line chart visualization. The URL for launching the web page can be found in the S3 bucket by going to the 'Objects' tab and then selecting the 'Object URL' of the index.html object.

Bring up the website by either clicking the URL itself, or right clicking the link and bringing up the result in a new tab on your browser.

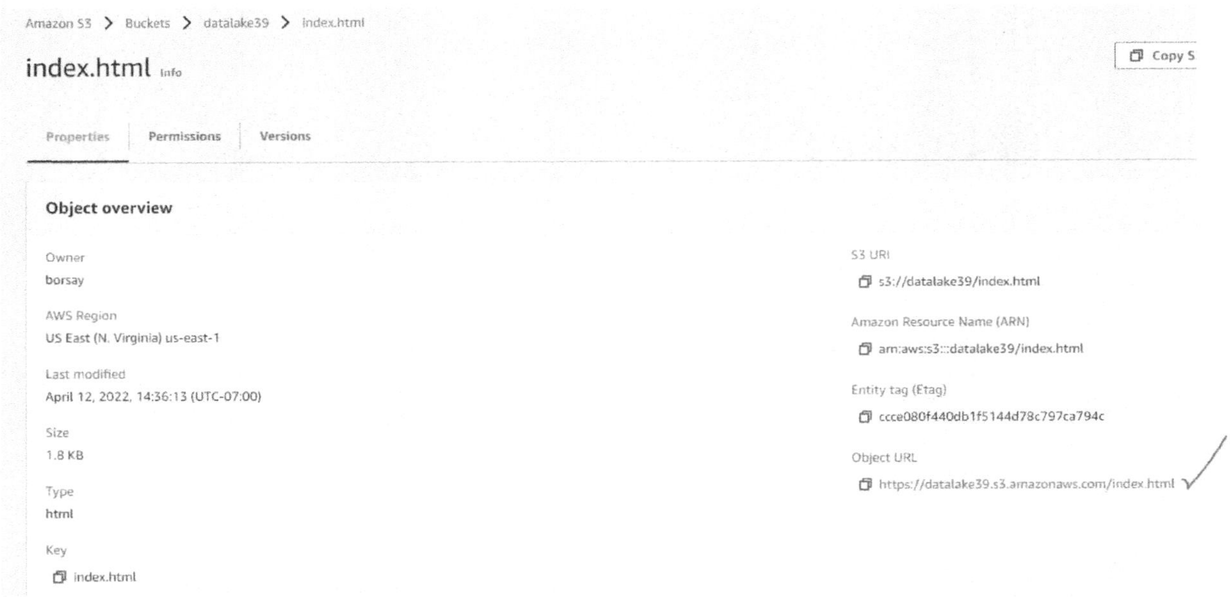
Amazon S3 > Buckets > datalake39 > index.html
index.html Info
Copy S
Properties
Permissions
Versions
Object overview
Owner
borsay
AWS Region
US East (N. Virginia) us-east-1
Last modified
April 12, 2022, 14:36:13 (UTC-07:00)
Size
1.8 KB
Type
html
Key
index.html
S3 URI
s3://datalake39/index.html
Amazon Resource Name (ARN)
arn:aws:s3:::datalake39/index.html
Entity tag (Etag)
ccce080f440db1f5144d78c797ca794c
Object URL
https://datalake39.s3.amazonaws.com/index.html

You should now see the result in a visualization of your sensor readings on your website as demonstrated below. The chart below should appear after opening the index.html Object URL.

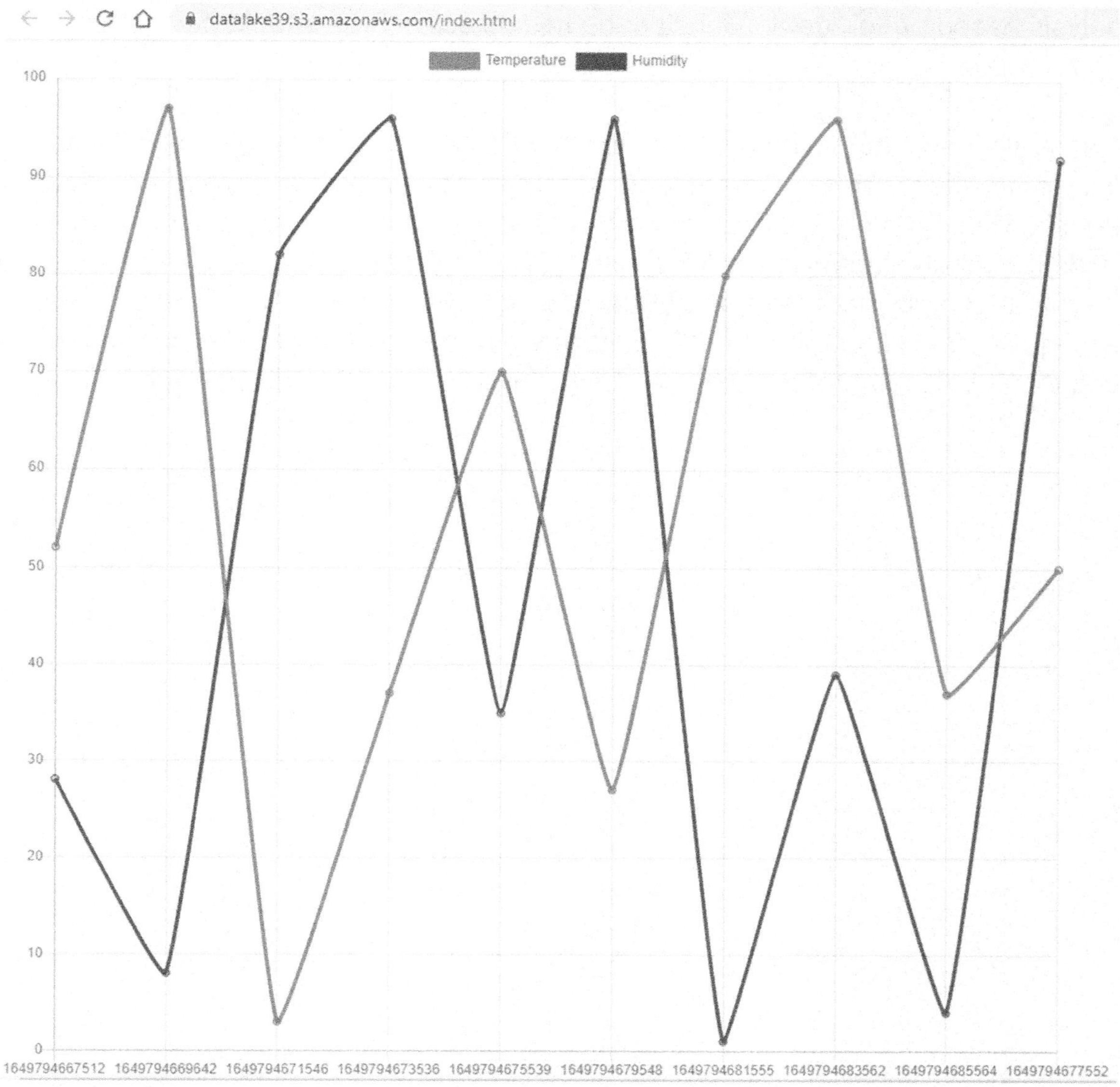
datalake39.s3.amazonaws.com/index.html
Temperature
Humidity
100
90
80
70
60
50
40
30
20
10
0
1649794667512 1649794669642 1649794671546 1649794673536 1649794675539 1649794679548 1649794681555 1649794683562 1649794685564 1649794677552

Clicking on each data point on the line chart should display the sensor value as a tooltip. If your visualization does not load you can click Shift + CTRL+ I in the Chrome browser, or Shift + CTRL + J in most other browsers to check for error messages in the dev tools console to find the problem. Also if you get an empty graph you can try a “hard refresh” to load your visualization by using CTRL + F5.

This is a primitive visualization however the chapter’s objective is not to demonstrate sophisticated modern reactive web code, but rather provide a starting point in which you can implement your own static web page visualizations and analysis based on IoT data. Considering this objective, you should have made a good progress in that direction.

Congratulations, you have now finished this chapter on creating a data lake with multiple sensor readings from IoT data sent from your virtual or physical IoT device. The following chapters should provide the opportunity to explore more sophisticated IoT data methods that utilize AWS Lambda as an intermediatory consumption agent rather than directly accessing a S3 bucket by its URL as this is a rather crude technique. Using Lambda with API Gateway generated endpoints, even without the need for ETL, is the professional way to do things in a production serverless environment.

Chapter 14 –
Kinesis Data Firehose for IoT

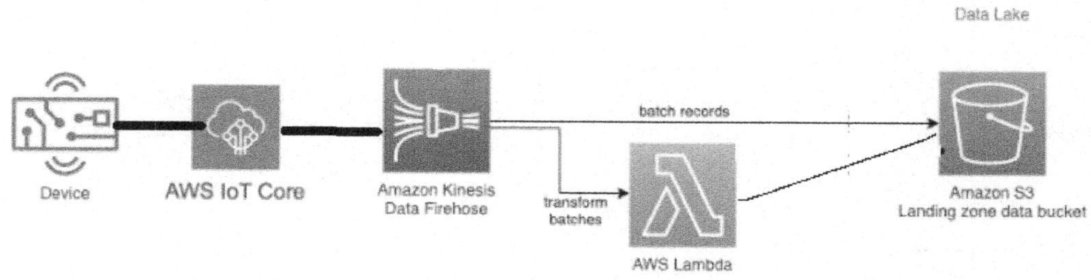
Data Lake
batch records
Device
AWS IoT Core
Amazon Kinesis
Data Firehose
transform
batches
AWS Lambda
Amazon S3
Landing zone data bucket

In this chapter we will be using Kinesis Data Firehose to send IoT data published to AWS IoT Core to S3. We will develop a Lambda function that will serve to enhance the IoT payload, adding in a UUID identifier to the payload, as an example of functional ETL. Finally, we will visualize our IoT data in both QuickSight and a custom coded visualization website hosted on S3.

Just like AWS SQS, Kinesis Data Firehose can act as both a memory buffer and queuing mechanism between IoT Core, Lambda, and our final storage destination in S3. Like Kafka for massive IoT data ingestion, Kinesis Data Firehose provides a queuing service so that we don't suffer from lost IoT data due to cold starts in Lambda or data lose from overlapping transmissions.
To accomplish massive, ingest capabilities Kinesis Data Firehose automatically converts our incoming JSON IoT Payload to a *base64* encoded data stream, just as the AWS CLI does. This encoding becomes important when we decode the IoT data back to human readable JSON before placing it in the S3 bucket.

An excellent article on IoT message buffering and queuing AWS architecture can be found here:

https://www.trek10.com/blog/three-cost-effective-design-patterns-for-aws-iot-data-ingestion

▾ **Amazon Kinesis Data Firehose: How it works**

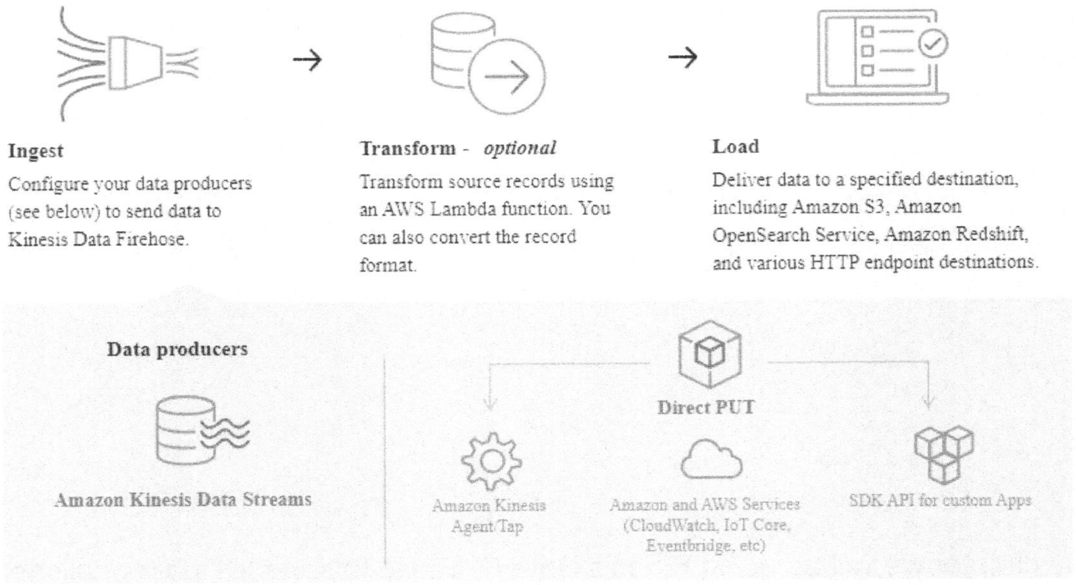
Ingest
Configure your data producers (see below) to send data to Kinesis Data Firehose.
Transform - optional
Transform source records using an AWS Lambda function. You can also convert the record format.
Load
Deliver data to a specified destination, including Amazon S3, Amazon OpenSearch Service, Amazon Redshift, and various HTTP endpoint destinations.
Data producers
Amazon Kinesis Data Streams
Direct PUT
Amazon Kinesis Agent/Tap
Amazon and AWS Services (CloudWatch, IoT Core, Eventbridge, etc)
SDK API for custom Apps

Step 1 – Create a S3 Bucket with a Static Web Host
Step 2 – Develop a Lambda to Transform the IoT Payload
Step 3 – Design a Kinesis Data Firehose Delivery Stream
Step 4 – Create an IoT Rule to Integrate Kinesis Data Firehose
Step 5 – Publish IoT Data to the IoT Rule
Step 6 – Develop a Custom JavaScript Visualization for the Enhanced IoT Data in S3
Step 7 – Create an AWS QuickSight Visualization with the Enhanced IoT Data in S3

Step 1 – Create a S3 Public Bucket with a Static Web Host

Follow the S3 prerequisite chapter of the book to create a public S3 bucket. For this project configure your bucket to enable S3 static web hosting with an '*index.html*' file.

Step 2 – Develop a Lambda to Transform the IoT Payload

You are now going to create a Lambda function to insert into the Kinesis Data Firehose between IoT Core and S3. The purpose of the Lambda function is to transform and enhance your IoT payload coming from IoT Core. There are all types of ETL you can do to the IoT payload with the transformation Lambda, but for this simple example you will just add a unique identifier called a "UUID" into every payload incoming into the Lambda function.

A UUID guarantees a unique identifier for each IoT payload as there are trillions of alphanumeric combinations available from the UUID API. Obviously once you have your Lambda integrated into the design flow you can then develop your own, more complex ETL in Lambda.

Open the Lambda console:

https://console.aws.amazon.com/lambda/

Make sure you are in the same AWS region as your other services

Configure the following settings:

Name – "Choose-A-Lambda-Function-Name".

Runtime – Node.js 16.x.

Choose to "Create function."

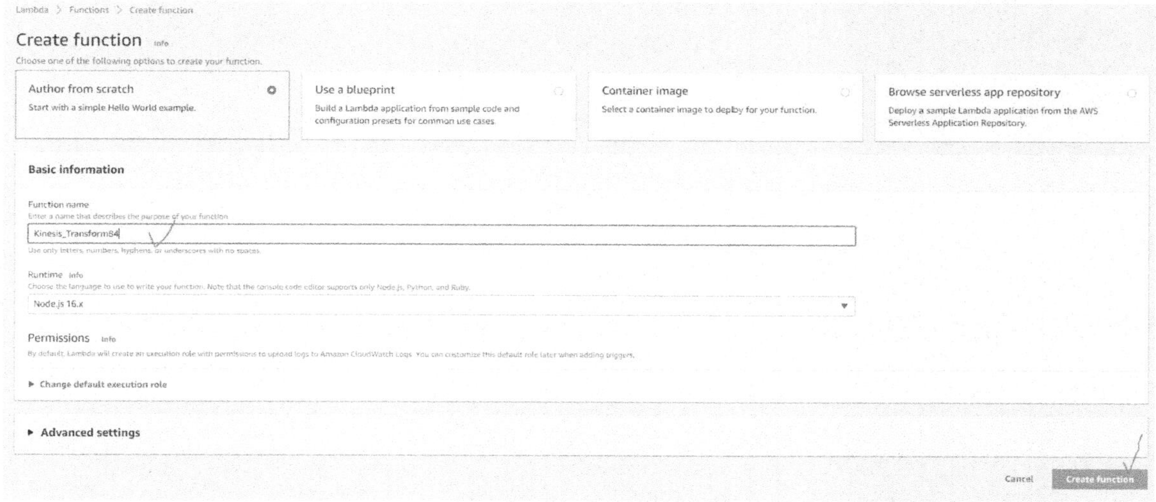
Lambda > Functions > Create function
Create function Info
Choose one of the following options to create your function.
Author from scratch
Start with a simple Hello World example.
Use a blueprint
Build a Lambda application from sample code and configuration presets for common use cases.
Container image
Select a container image to deploy for your function.
Browse serverless app repository
Deploy a sample Lambda application from the AWS Serverless Application Repository.
Basic information
Function name
Kinesis_Transform84
Runtime Info
Node.js 16.x
Permissions Info
Change default execution role
Advanced settings
Cancel
Create function

Insert the following code into your new Lambda function:

```
const AWS = require('aws-sdk');

exports.handler = async (event, context, callback) => {
    const output = event.records.map((record) => {

        let data = Buffer.from(record.data, 'base64').toString('utf8');
        console.log('data :', data);

        if (data) {
            try {
                data = JSON.parse(data);
                data.UUID = AWS.util.uuid.v4();
                data = JSON.stringify(data);
                data = data.replace(/\\n/g, '');
                data = data.replace('}', "},");    //add back trailing comma
                console.log('formation done!', data);
            } catch I {
                console.log('e :', e);

            }
        }

        return {
            recordId: record.recordId,
            result: 'Ok',
           // data: new Buffer(data).toString('base64'),  //depreciated
           data: Buffer.alloc(Object.keys(data).length,
data).toString('base64'),  //create a buffer of dynamic size
        };
    });

    callback(null, { records: output });
};
```

The new Lambda function should now appear in the Lambda code window below:

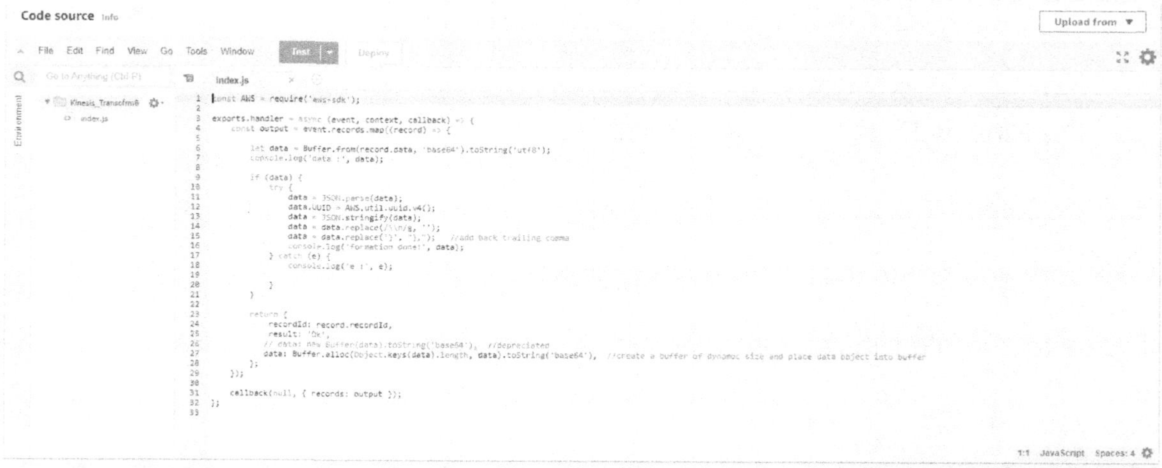
Code source
Upload from
index.js
1:1 JavaScript Spaces: 4

Admittedly this code could look somewhat abstruse, however there are a couple of complications which add complexity to the code due to the way in which IoT payloads are delivered from the Kinesis Data Firehose to the Lambda function.

First, remember the incoming payload is 'base 64 encoded' which means you must convert it out of base64, perform the ETL, and then re-encode the payload. Secondly the IoT data arrives in configurable time windows as you will see when you set up Kinesis Firehose next. This windowed delivery acts as a 'batching' mechanism although you will explicitly state you do not want to batch your IoT data when you configure a IoT Core Rule later in this chapter. Finally, you will not test your Lambda function because it is using base64 encoded streaming data from Kinesis which can only be tested by inserting an unwieldly data blob into the Lambda test window.

The main thing to keep note of is that the Lambda function code is decoding the Incoming IoT data as a stream of payloads. Then the Lambda function is adding a UUID to each payload with the line:

```
data.UUID = AWS.util.uuid.v4();
```

- The AWS 'uuid' is part of the utility library in the AWS-SDK.

After the UUID is added, the payload is returned to the Kinesis Data Firehose and delivered into the S3 bucket. Make sure to "deploy" the Lambda function code.

Step 3 – Design a Kinesis Data Firehose Delivery Stream

Open the Kinesis Data Firehose console at:

https://console.aws.amazon.com/firehose/

Make sure you are in the same AWS region as your other services

Choose to "Create Kinesis Firehose Delivery Stream".

Create delivery stream

Choose source and destination:

- Source: Direct Put
- Destination: Amazon S3
- Delivery stream name: Type a name, or use default name, for the Kinesis delivery stream

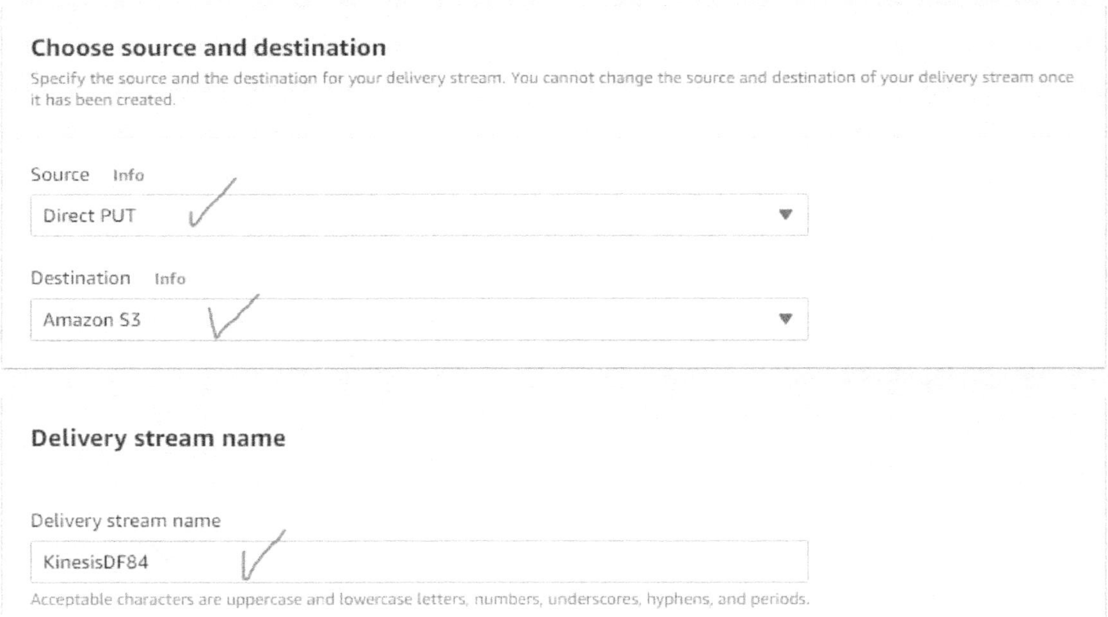
Choose source and destination
Specify the source and the destination for your delivery stream. You cannot change the source and destination of your delivery stream once it has been created.
Source Info
Direct PUT
Destination Info
Amazon S3
Delivery stream name
Delivery stream name
KinesisDF84
Acceptable characters are uppercase and lowercase letters, numbers, underscores, hyphens, and periods.

Data transformation: "

- Transform source records with AWS Lambda" – Choose Enabled

- Choose the Lambda function that you just created
- Leave the other configuration defaults as they are
- Record Format Conversion – leave default "Disabled"

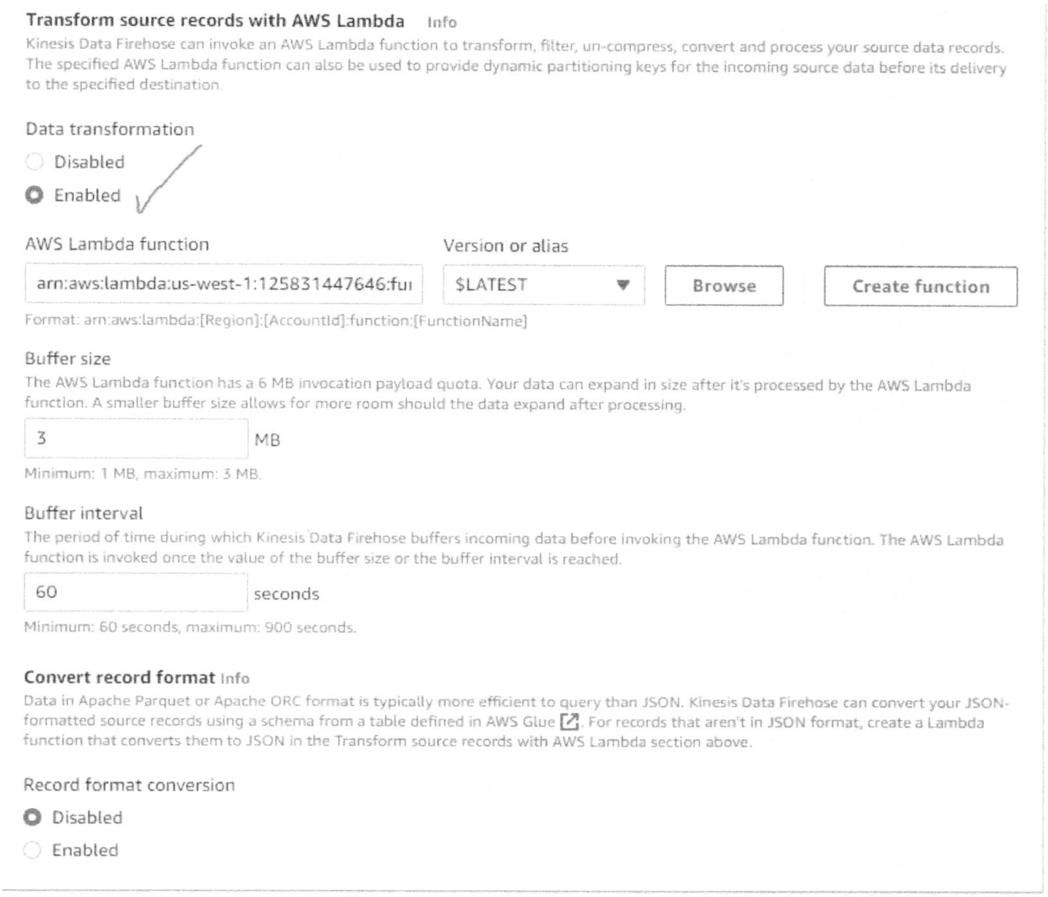
Transform source records with AWS Lambda Info
Kinesis Data Firehose can invoke an AWS Lambda function to transform, filter, un-compress, convert and process your source data records. The specified AWS Lambda function can also be used to provide dynamic partitioning keys for the incoming source data before its delivery to the specified destination.
Data transformation
Disabled
Enabled
AWS Lambda function
Version or alias
arn:aws:lambda:us-west-1:125831447646:fu
$LATEST
Browse
Create function
Format: arn:aws:lambda:[Region]:[AccountId]:function:[FunctionName]
Buffer size
The AWS Lambda function has a 6 MB invocation payload quota. Your data can expand in size after it's processed by the AWS Lambda function. A smaller buffer size allows for more room should the data expand after processing.
3
MB
Minimum: 1 MB, maximum: 3 MB.
Buffer interval
The period of time during which Kinesis Data Firehose buffers incoming data before invoking the AWS Lambda function. The AWS Lambda function is invoked once the value of the buffer size or the buffer interval is reached.
60
seconds
Minimum: 60 seconds, maximum: 900 seconds.
Convert record format Info
Data in Apache Parquet or Apache ORC format is typically more efficient to query than JSON. Kinesis Data Firehose can convert your JSON-formatted source records using a schema from a table defined in AWS Glue. For records that aren't in JSON format, create a Lambda function that converts them to JSON in the Transform source records with AWS Lambda section above.
Record format conversion
Disabled
Enabled

<u>Destination settings:</u>

- S3 bucket – Browse to the S3 bucket you just created in Step 1, make sure it is in the same region your console is currently using
- S3 prefix – Leave this field empty.
- S3 bucket error output prefix – Leave this field empty.
- Buffer hints – Leave defaults

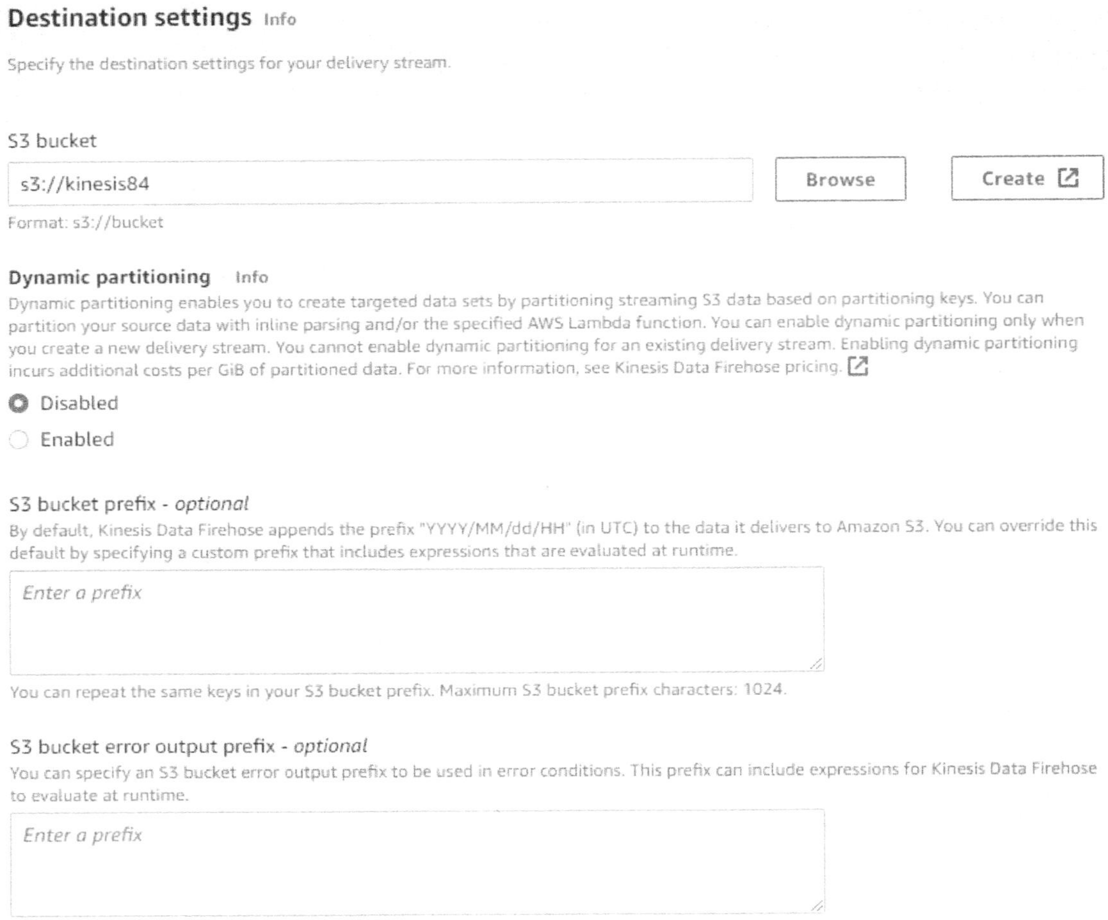
Destination settings Info
Specify the destination settings for your delivery stream.
S3 bucket
s3://kinesis84
Browse
Create
Format: s3://bucket
Dynamic partitioning Info
Dynamic partitioning enables you to create targeted data sets by partitioning streaming S3 data based on partitioning keys. You can partition your source data with inline parsing and/or the specified AWS Lambda function. You can enable dynamic partitioning only when you create a new delivery stream. You cannot enable dynamic partitioning for an existing delivery stream. Enabling dynamic partitioning incurs additional costs per GiB of partitioned data. For more information, see Kinesis Data Firehose pricing.
Disabled
Enabled
S3 bucket prefix - optional
By default, Kinesis Data Firehose appends the prefix "YYYY/MM/dd/HH" (in UTC) to the data it delivers to Amazon S3. You can override this default by specifying a custom prefix that includes expressions that are evaluated at runtime.
Enter a prefix
You can repeat the same keys in your S3 bucket prefix. Maximum S3 bucket prefix characters: 1024.
S3 bucket error output prefix - optional
You can specify an S3 bucket error output prefix to be used in error conditions. This prefix can include expressions for Kinesis Data Firehose to evaluate at runtime.
Enter a prefix

Backup settings – Leave defaults
Advanced settings – Leave defaults

Then choose “Create Delivery Stream”.

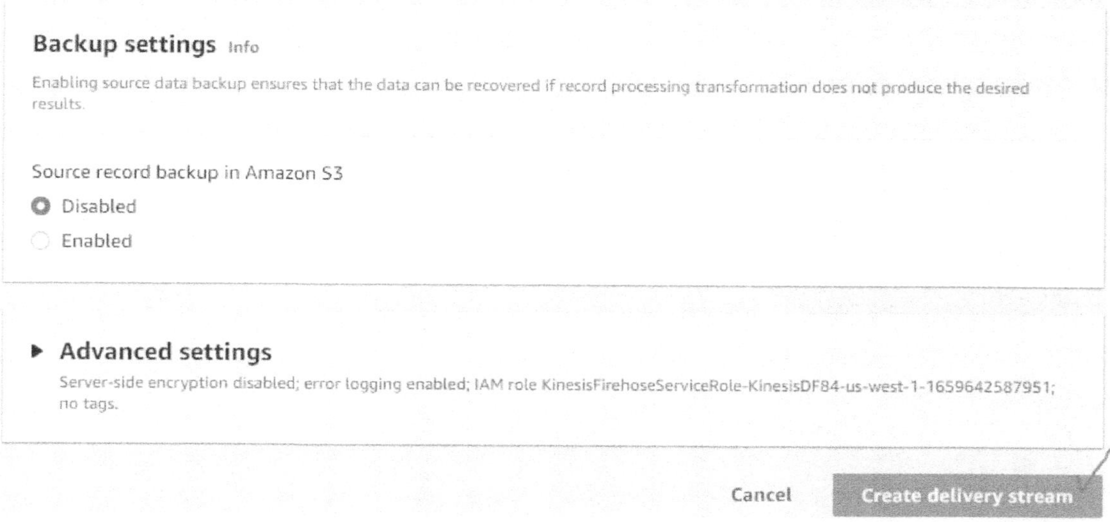
Backup settings Info
Enabling source data backup ensures that the data can be recovered if record processing transformation does not produce the desired results.
Source record backup in Amazon S3
Disabled
Enabled
Advanced settings
Server-side encryption disabled; error logging enabled; IAM role KinesisFirehoseServiceRole-KinesisDF84-us-west-1-1659642587951; no tags.
Cancel
Create delivery stream

The console may suggest you increase the timeout for the Lambda function. This is a good idea for processing high frequency IoT payload delivery. For our use case the default 3 second Lambda timeout is fine. If you decide to increase your Lambda timeout, simply return to your Lambda function, go to the "Configuration" tab, and select to "Edit" the general configuration.

Configuration
Aliases
Versions
General configuration Info
Edit
Description
Memory
128 MB
Ephemeral storage
512 MB

As you can see Kinesis Data Firehose has a lot of configuration options you can explore. For the example in this chapter the main concerns are making sure to include your transformation Lambda function into the Kinesis Data Firehose pipeline, as well as to ensure that the transformed IoT payload reached the S3 bucket that you designated as a data repository and a static web host.

Step 4 – Create an IoT Rule to Integrate Kinesis Data Firehose

Now it is time to create an IoT Rule to transmit the incoming IoT data to the Kinesis Data Firehose for transformation and storage in S3. To do this go to IoT Core:

https://console.aws.amazon.com/iot

Then make a new rule:

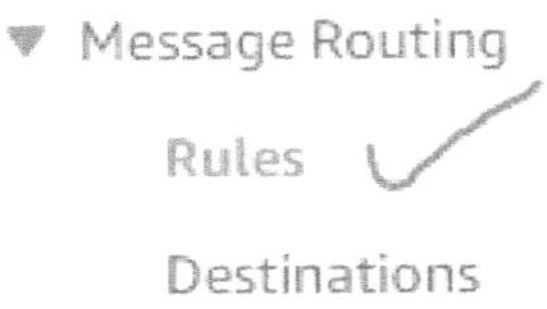
Message Routing
Rules
Destinations

Give your new rule a name and an optional description then select “Next”:

Next

The “Rules Query Statement” for your new rule should be:

```
SELECT *, timestamp() as timestamps FROM 'iot/#'
```

This will add a timestamp to each JSON IoT payload received by the MQTT message broker on IoT Core.

Now press “Next”:

Next

On this console page screen, you have a few things to configure.

1. Choose “Kinesis Firehose Stream” as your action (do not choose “Kinesis Streams”).
2. Choose the Kinesis Firehose you just designed in the previous Step 3.
3. Leave the default “Separator” of “No separator”. This indicates not to add in a character between JSON IoT payloads. The Lambda function adds in a trailing comma after each payload in the transformation.
4. Do not use Batch Mode. Kinesis will deliver streaming data in “time windows” in any case. Batch Mode just adds additional efficiencies if you have large scale ingestion and want to save money. In this use case the difference is nominal.
5. Create a IAM role allowing your IoT Rule to access Kinesis Firehose.

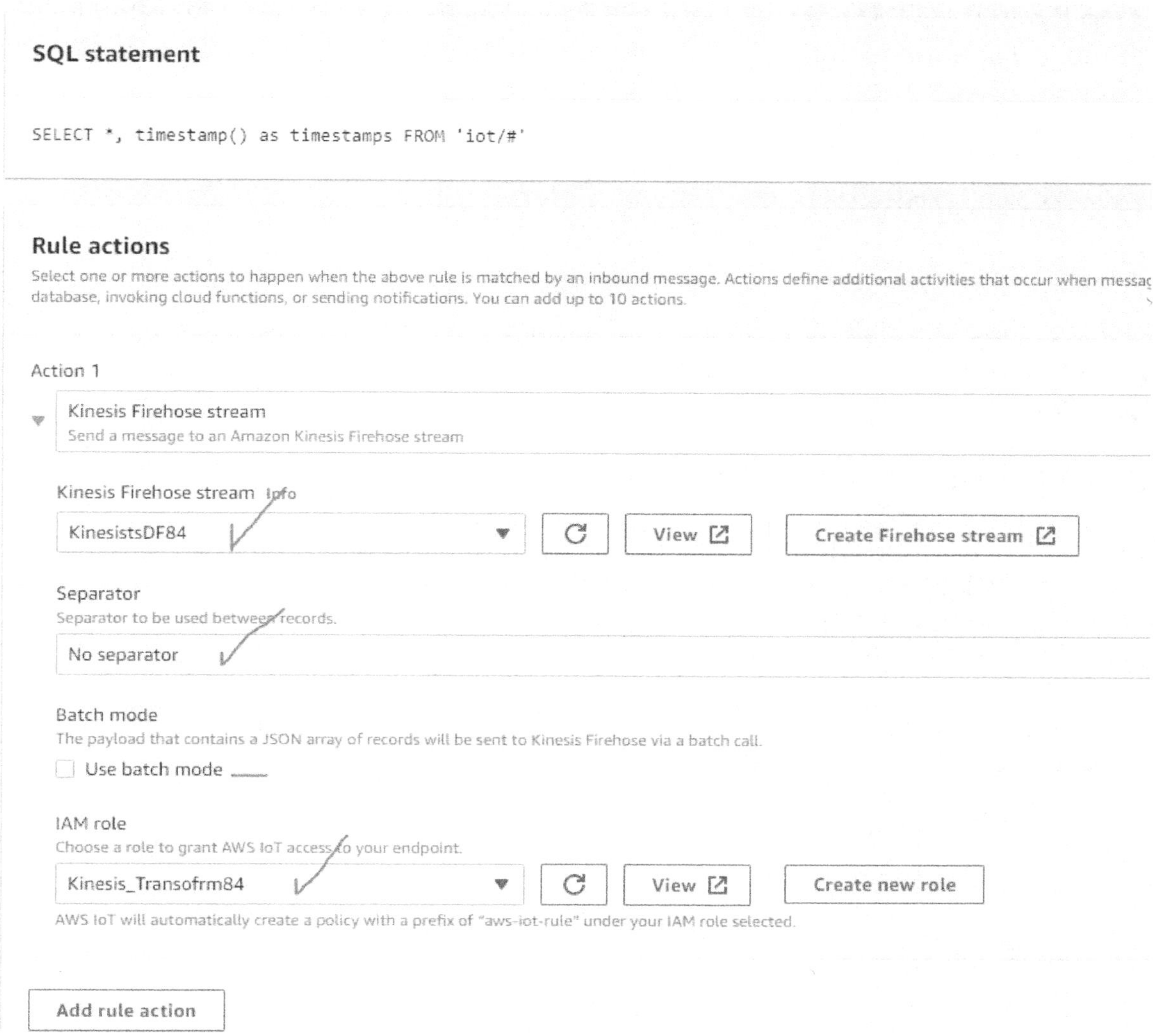
SQL statement
SELECT *, timestamp() as timestamps FROM 'iot/#'
Rule actions
Select one or more actions to happen when the above rule is matched by an inbound message. Actions define additional activities that occur when messag
database, invoking cloud functions, or sending notifications. You can add up to 10 actions.
Action 1
Kinesis Firehose stream
Send a message to an Amazon Kinesis Firehose stream
Kinesis Firehose stream Info
KinesistsDF84
View
Create Firehose stream
Separator
Separator to be used between records.
No separator
Batch mode
The payload that contains a JSON array of records will be sent to Kinesis Firehose via a batch call.
Use batch mode
IAM role
Choose a role to grant AWS IoT access to your endpoint.
Kinesis_Transofrm84
View
Create new role
AWS IoT will automatically create a policy with a prefix of "aws-iot-rule" under your IAM role selected.
Add rule action

Now press “Next”:

Next

Review the new IoT Rule and then select “Create” to finalize the rule:

Create

Good so far, now it is time to test the complete design chain to make sure IoT sensor readings are being accepted by the IoT message broker in IoT Core that are sent to the Kinesis Firehose via your IoT rule, transformed with the Lambda function with the UUID enhancement, and finally appearing as an object in your new S3 bucket.

Step 5 – Publish IoT Data to the IoT Rule

For this section you can use your virtual or physical IoT device to send data or manually enter IoT data into the AWS MQTT test client. You can publish data to the topic "iot/test"

Go back to AWS IoT and then go to the MQTT test client.

Enter the IoT payloads in the "Publish to a topic" tab in the MQTT test client. Publish the following payload or you can choose your own values. Enter a number of JSON payloads (4-12), changing the temperature and humidity values for each payload.

```
{
    "temperature": 92,
    "humidity": 29
}
```

Press the "Publish" button.

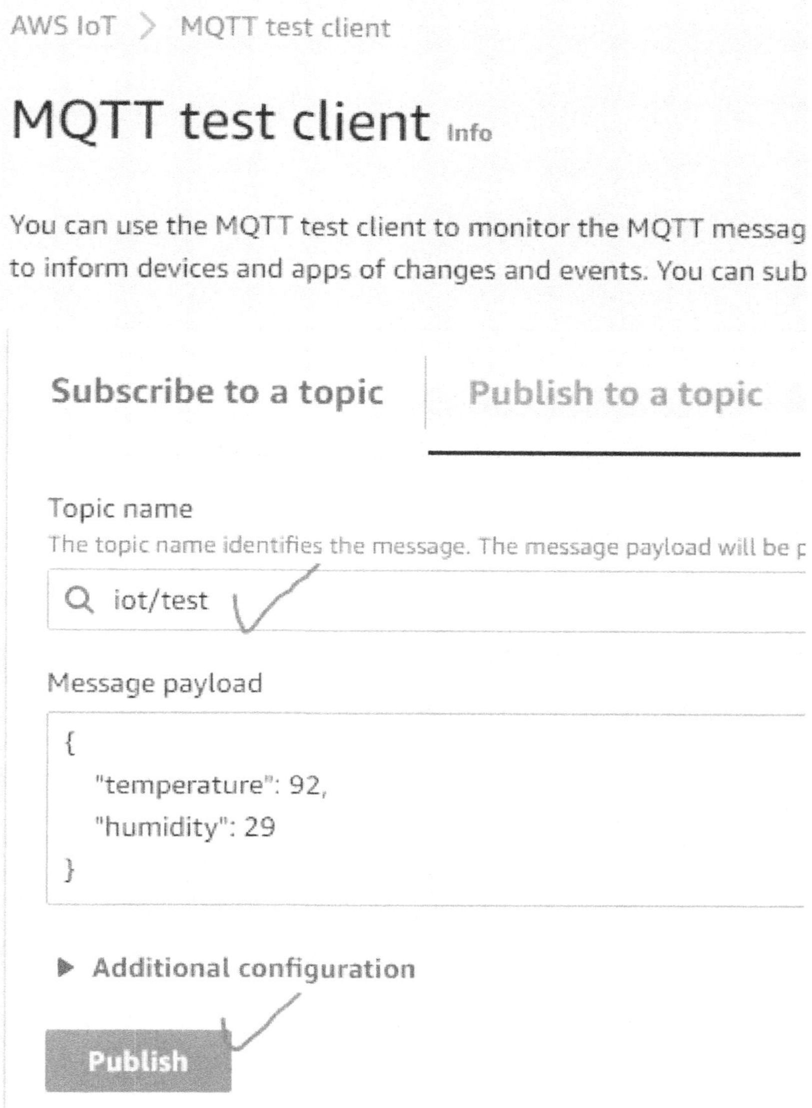
AWS IoT > MQTT test client
MQTT test client Info
You can use the MQTT test client to monitor the MQTT messag
to inform devices and apps of changes and events. You can sub
Subscribe to a topic
Publish to a topic
Topic name
The topic name identifies the message. The message payload will be p
iot/test
Message payload
{
"temperature": 92,
"humidity": 29
}
Additional configuration
Publish

After sending some IoT payloads through this method or any other method you like it is now time to check the S3 bucket to see if the IoT readings reached their final destination.

Go to your S3 bucket created in Step 1 and then drill down into the default key/partition structure automatically that was constructed by Kinesis Firehose. Download the new data object and examine the sensor readings to make sure everything is correct and your IoT rule enhanced your IoT payload with the "timestamps" key-value pair, while your Lambda function transformed your IoT payload and added a "UUID" to each IoT payload.

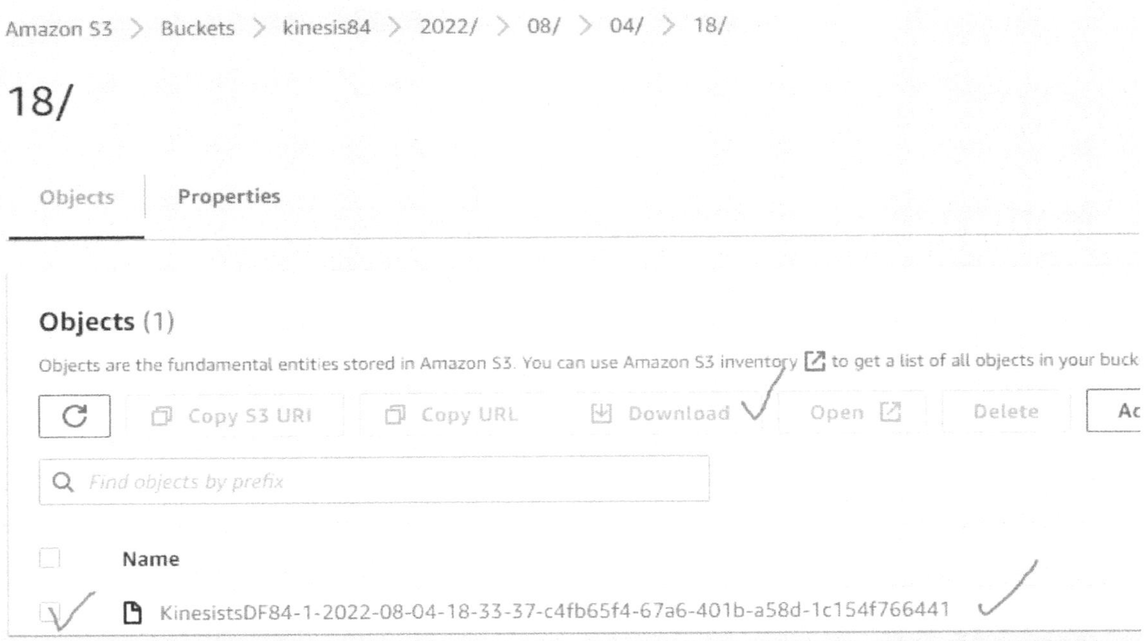
Amazon S3 > Buckets > kinesis84 > 2022/ > 08/ > 04/ > 18/
18/
Objects
Properties
Objects (1)
Objects are the fundamental entities stored in Amazon S3. You can use Amazon S3 inventory to get a list of all objects in your buck
Copy S3 URI
Copy URL
Download
Open
Delete
Find objects by prefix
Name
KinesistsDF84-1-2022-08-04-18-33-37-c4fb65f4-67a6-401b-a58d-1c154f766441

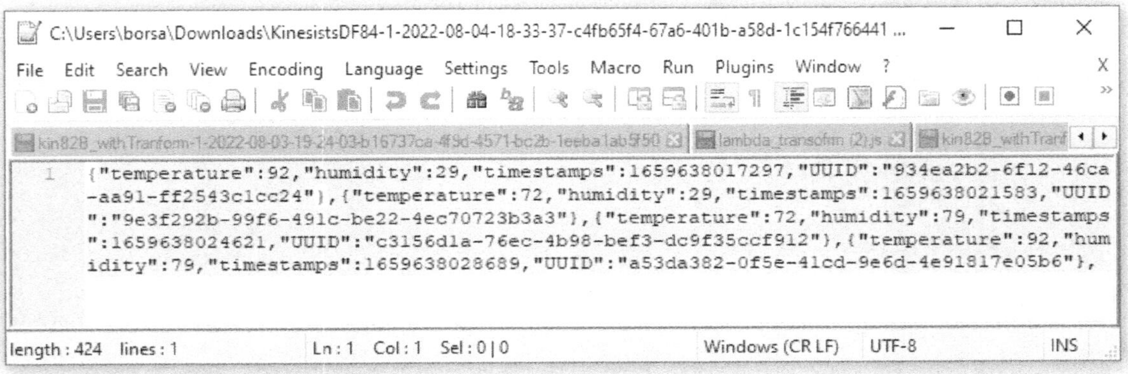
C:\Users\borsa\Downloads\KinesistsDF84-1-2022-08-04-18-33-37-c4fb65f4-67a6-401b-a58d-1c154f766441 ...
File Edit Search View Encoding Language Settings Tools Macro Run Plugins Window ?
lambda_transofrm (2).js
{"temperature":92,"humidity":29,"timestamps":1659638017297,"UUID":"934ea2b2-6f12-46ca-aa91-ff2543c1cc24"},{"temperature":72,"humidity":29,"timestamps":1659638021583,"UUID":"9e3f292b-99f6-491c-be22-4ec70723b3a3"},{"temperature":72,"humidity":79,"timestamps":1659638024621,"UUID":"c3156d1a-76ec-4b98-bef3-dc9f35ccf912"},{"temperature":92,"humidity":79,"timestamps":1659638028689,"UUID":"a53da382-0f5e-41cd-9e6d-4e91817e05b6"},
length : 424 lines : 1
Ln : 1 Col : 1 Sel : 0 | 0
Windows (CR LF) UTF-8 INS

If everything looks good, you are now you are ready to explore the IoT data with your own web visualization on S3.

Step 6 – Develop a Custom JavaScript Visualization for the Enhanced IoT Data in S3

To create the visualization there are three files to upload to the S3 bucket. This is the same S3 bucket that holds your IoT data. You only need to modify the "*main.js*" files JavaScript code for it to work correctly with your IoT data in the S3 bucket.

Enter your S3 bucket URL in both places indicated in the *'main.js'* file. You can retrieve your bucket URL simply by going to the "Objects" tab of your S3 bucket and selecting to "Copy URL".

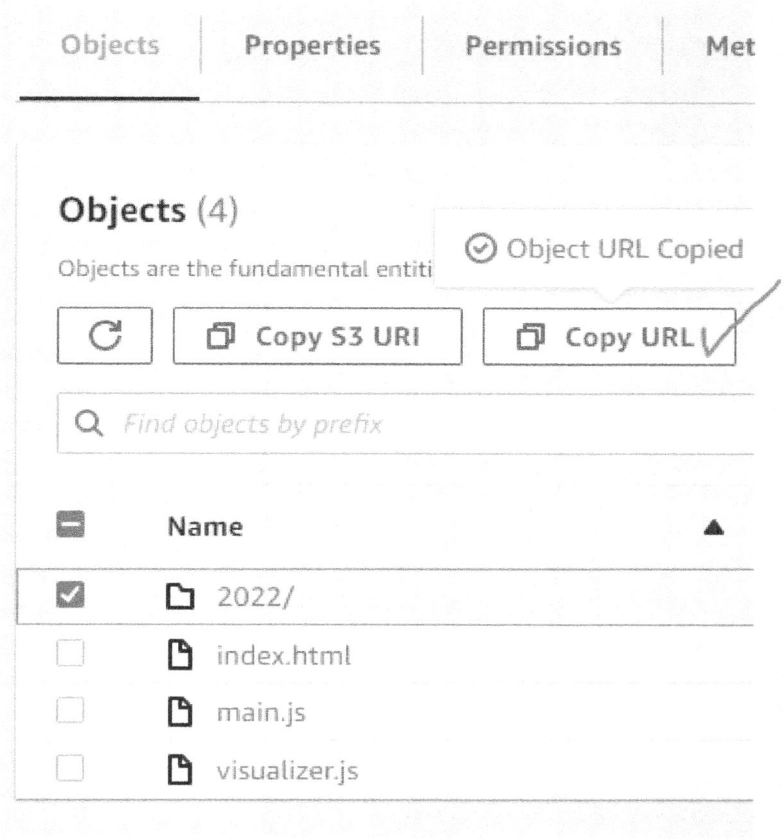

Objects
Properties
Permissions
Met
Objects (4)
Objects are the fundamental entiti
Object URL Copied
Copy S3 URI
Copy URL
Find objects by prefix
Name
2022/
index.html
main.js
visualizer.js

Make sure to remove your key partition from your bucket URL so you are at the base level of your bucket. The copied URL should look like the example link below:

https://<Your-Bucket-Name>t.s3.<Your-AWS-Region>.amazonaws.com

Paste the URL in the line which occurs twice in the "*main.js*" file.

```
"https://<Your-S3-Bucket-Name-Here>/",
```

As always, all the code can be found in more reliable formatting on the books GitHub page.

```
Var timestamps = [];
var humidity = [];
var temperature = [];

// Start by extracting folder2/ url from s3 bucket
$.ajax({
    type      : "GET",
    url       : "https://<Your-S3-Bucket-Name-Here>/",
    276isualiz : "xml",
    success   : function(xmlData, values){
        var url = "";
        var values = {};
        keys = xmlData.getElementsByTagName("Key");
        for(i=0; I < keys.length; i++) {
            url = keys[i].childNodes[0].nodeValue;
            parseText(url, function(getValues) {
                loadLineChart(timestamps,temperature,humidity);
                loadBarChart(timestamps,temperature,humidity);
            })
        }

    },
    error     : function(){
         alert("Could not retrieve XML file.");
    }
})

// Parse file as text
var parseText = function(url, getValues) {
    var values ={ "timestamps":"", "temperature":"", "humidity":"" };
    $.ajax({
        type      : "GET",
        url       : "https://<Your-S3-Bucket-Name-Here>/"" + url,
        276isualiz : "text",
        success   : function(txtFile){
            var jsonArray;
            // Convert text file to JSON Array
            jsonArray = parseToJSONArray(txtFile)
            // Get Values from JSONArray
            jsonArray.forEach(getValuesFromJSON)

            values.timestamps = timestamps
            values.temperature = temperature
            values.humidity = humidity
```

```
                getValues(values)
            },
            error       : function(xhr, status, error){
                alert(status + ' ' + error);
            }
        });
}

// Get timestamps, temperature and humidity from json
var getValuesFromJSON = function(json, index, JSONArray) {
    json = JSON.parse(json)
    timestamps.push(json.timestamps);
    temperature.push(json.temperature)
    humidity.push(json.humidity)
}

// This function converts the text file from server to a JSON Array
var parseToJSONArray = function(txtFile) {
    var json = [];
    var temp = "";
    var I = 0
    while(I < txtFile.length) {
        // console.log(txtFile[i])
        if(txtFile[i] != " ") {
            temp += txtFile[i]
            if(txtFile[i] == "}") {
                I = i+1
                json.push(temp)
                temp = ""
            }
        }
        i+=1
    }
    return json;
}
```

Save the code copied as "*main.js*" and then upload it to the base level of your S3 bucket.

The next file is the "*visualizer.js*". Save this file to your local computer and then upload it to the base level of your S3 bucket as well.

```
Var loadLineChart = function(timestamps, temperature, humidity) {
```

```
    var lineChart = $('#lineChart');

    var myChart1 = new Chart(lineChart, {
        type: 'line',
        data: {
            labels: timestamps,
            datasets: [
                {
                    label: "Temperature",
                    data: temperature,
                    fill: false,
                    borderColor: "rgb(255, 0, 0)",
                    lineTension: 0.1
                },
                {
                    label: "Humidity",
                    data: humidity,
                    fill: false,
                    borderColor: "rgb(0, 0, 255)",
                    lineTension: 0.1
                }
            ]
        },
        options: {
            responsive: true,
            title: {
                display: true,
                text: 'Timestamps',
                position: 'bottom'
            }
        }
    });
}

var loadBarChart = function(timestamps, temperature, humidity) {
    var barChart = $('#barChart');

    var myChart2 = new Chart(barChart, {
        type: 'bar',
        data: {
            labels: timestamps,
            datasets: [
                {
                    label: "Temperature",
                    data: temperature,
```

```
                    backgroundColor: "rgb(255, 0, 0)"
                },
                {
                    label: "Humidity",
                    data: humidity,
                    backgroundColor: "rgb(0, 0, 255)"
                }
            ]
        },
        options: {
            responsive: true,
            barValueSpacing: 20,
            title: {
                display: true,
                text: 'Timestamps',
                position: 'bottom'
            }
        }
    });
}
```

The last file to upload to your bucket is the landing page of "*index.html*". Save this file to your local computer and then upload it to the base level of your S3 bucket.

```
<!doctype html>
<html lang="en">
  <head>
    <title>Title</title>
    <!-Required meta tags →
    <meta charset="utf-8">
    <meta name="viewport" content="width=device-width, initial-scale=1,
shrink-to-fit=no">

    <!-Bootstrap CSS →
    <link rel="stylesheet"
href="https://stackpath.bootstrapcdn.com/bootstrap/4.3.1/css/bootstrap.min.cs
s" integrity="sha384-
ggOyR0iXCbMQv3Xipma34MD+dH/1fQ784/j6cY/iJTQUOhcWr7x9JvoRxT2MZw1T"
crossorigin="anonymous">
    <link rel="stylesheet"
href="https://cdnjs.cloudflare.com/ajax/libs/Chart.js/2.9.3/Chart.css"
integrity="sha256-IvM9nJf/b5l2RoebiFno92E5OnttVyaEEsdemDC6iQA="
crossorigin="anonymous" />
  </head>
```

```
  <body>
    <div class="row">
      <div class="col-lg-6">
        <canvas id="barChart" width="200" height="200"></canvas>
      </div>
      <div class="col-lg-6">
        <canvas id="lineChart" width="200" height="200"></canvas>
      </div>
    </div>


    <!-Optional JavaScript ->
    <!-jQuery first, then Popper.js, then Bootstrap JS ->
    <script src="https://code.jquery.com/jquery-3.4.1.min.js"
integrity="sha256-CSXorXvZcTkaix6Yvo6HppcZGetbYMGWSFlBw8HfCJo="
crossorigin="anonymous"></script>
    <script
src="https://cdnjs.cloudflare.com/ajax/libs/popper.js/1.14.7/umd/popper.min.j
s" integrity="sha384-
UO2eT0CpHqdSJQ6hJty5KVphtPhzWj9WO1clHTMGa3JDZwrnQq4sF86dIHNDz0W1"
crossorigin="anonymous"></script>
    <script
src="https://cdnjs.cloudflare.com/ajax/libs/Chart.js/2.9.3/Chart.bundle.min.j
s" integrity="sha256-TQq84xX6vkwR0Qs1qH5AdkP+MvH0W+9E7TdHJsoIQiM="
crossorigin="anonymous"></script>
    <script
src="https://stackpath.bootstrapcdn.com/bootstrap/4.3.1/js/bootstrap.min.js"
integrity="sha384-
JjSmVgyd0p3pXB1rRibZUAYoIIy6OrQ6VrjIEaFf/nJGzIxFDsf4x0xIM+B07jRM"
crossorigin="anonymous"></script>
    <script src="visualizer.js"></script>
    <script src="main.js"></script>
  </body>
</html>
```

Once all the files are uploaded the base level of your S3 bucket the object hierarchy should appear similar to the image below. The bucket contents show both the hosting of your web code and your IoT data sensor readings.

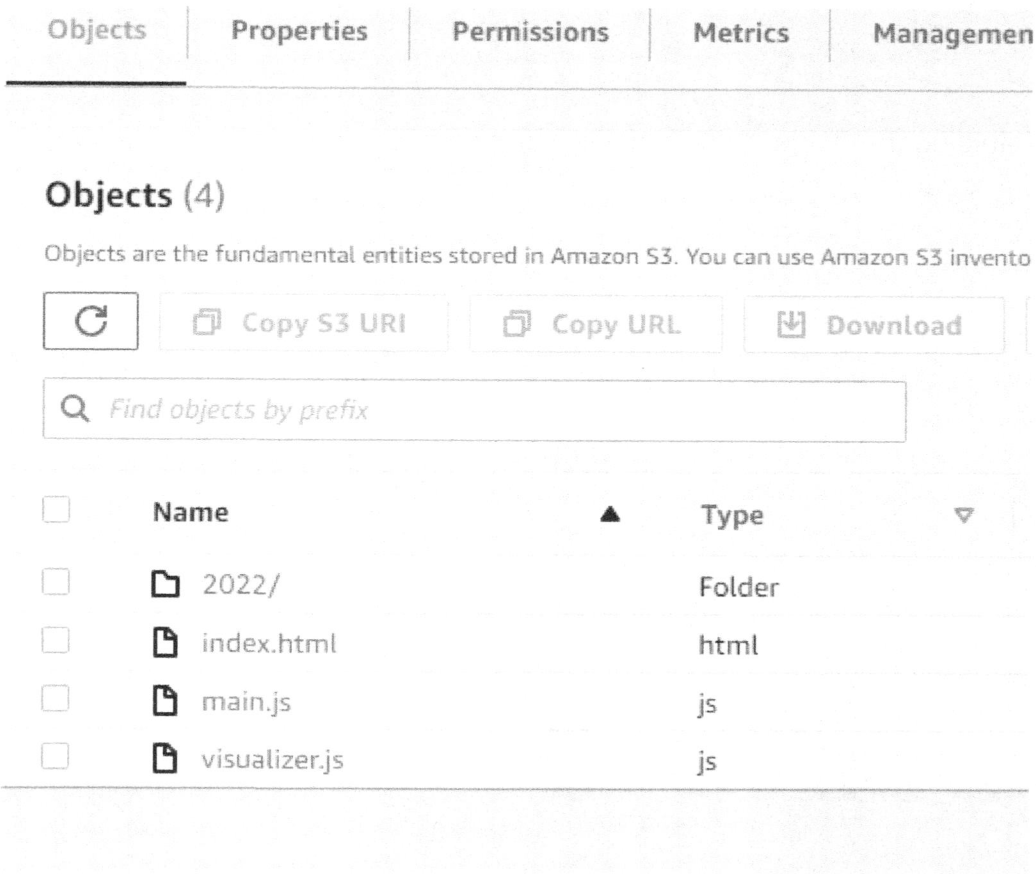
Objects
Properties
Permissions
Metrics
Managemen
Objects (4)
Objects are the fundamental entities stored in Amazon S3. You can use Amazon S3 invento
Copy S3 URI
Copy URL
Download
Find objects by prefix
Name
Type
2022/
Folder
index.html
html
main.js
js
visualizer.js
js

To initiate the visualization of your IoT data navigate to the index.html object in your S3 bucket then either click it to bring up the webpage, or right-click the "Object URL" to open your website in a new tab as demonstrated below:

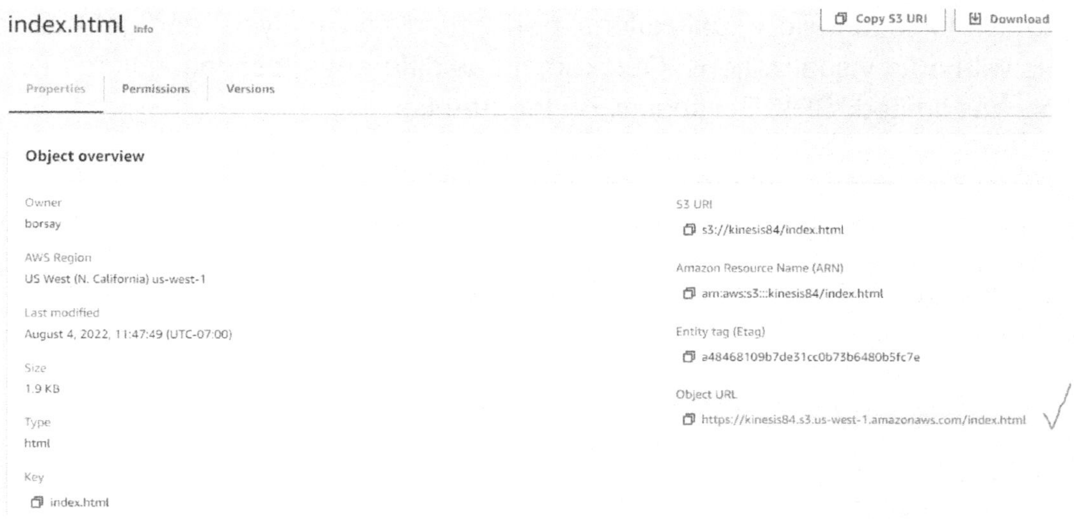
index.html Info
Copy S3 URI
Download
Properties
Permissions
Versions
Object overview
Owner
borsay
AWS Region
US West (N. California) us-west-1
Last modified
August 4, 2022, 11:47:49 (UTC-07:00)
Size
1.9 KB
Type
html
Key
index.html
S3 URI
s3://kinesis84/index.html
Amazon Resource Name (ARN)
arn:aws:s3:::kinesis84/index.html
Entity tag (Etag)
a48468109b7de31cc0b73b6480b5fc7e
Object URL
https://kinesis84.s3.us-west-1.amazonaws.com/index.html

After selecting the "Object URL" of the index.html landing page your visualization should appear.

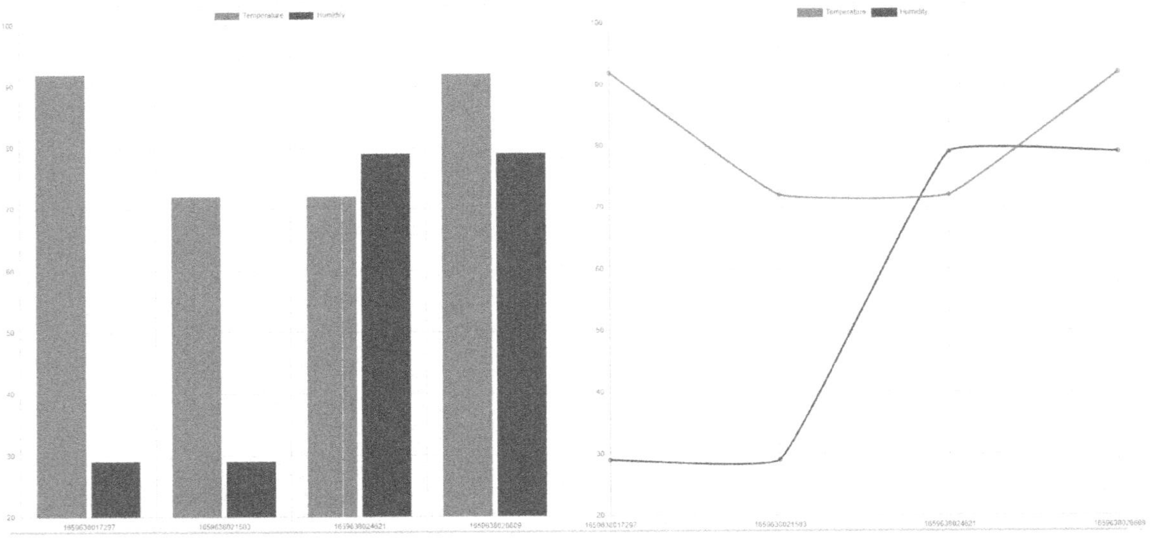

Step 7 – Create an AWS QuickSight Visualization with the Enhanced IoT Data in S3

Amazon QuickSight is a business analytics service, also known as Business Intelligence (BI), that is part of the AWS cloud ecosystem. QuickSight provides easy to use tools to build visualizations, perform ad-hoc analysis, and get business insights with data visualizations. QuickSight has different subscription tiers of use but only has limited "SPICE' capacity on the free tier.

QuickSight has many built-in connectors for AWS services to make integration easy. Unfortunately, QuickSight is not designed to handle Kinesis Firehose output. Fortunately, you only need a simple modification to make your IoT data consumable with QuickSight. This section assumes you have already set up permissions in QuickSight in your home region.

https://docs.aws.amazon.com/QuickSight/latest/user/welcome.html

You will need to change your Kinesis Data Firehose IoT data to proper JSON for QuickSight to be able to consume the IoT data, this process will be explained now.

Download your Kinesis Firehose IoT data object from your s3 bucket:

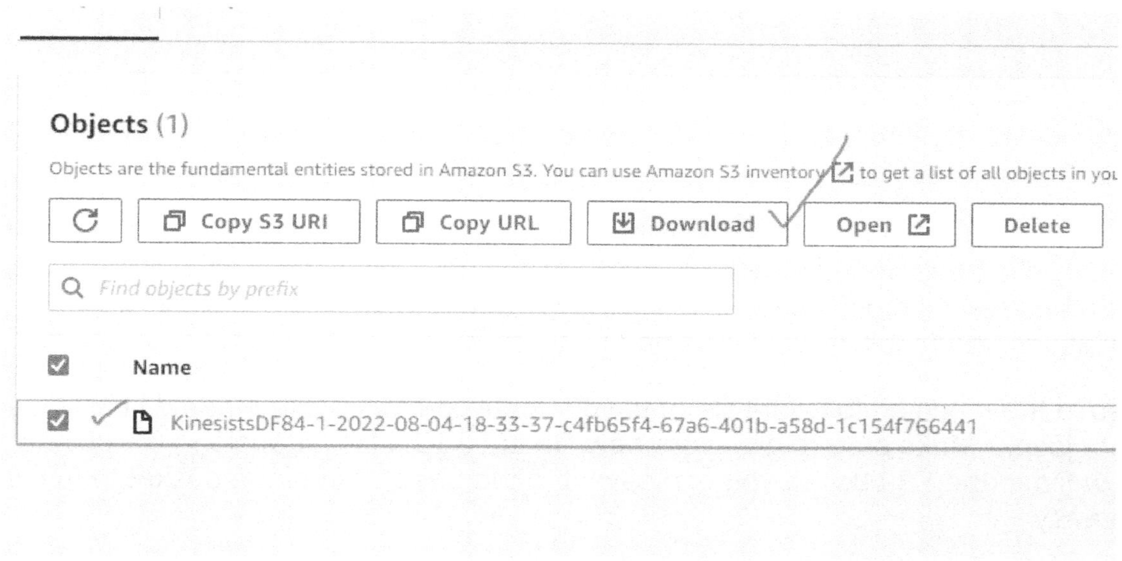
Objects (1)
Objects are the fundamental entities stored in Amazon S3. You can use Amazon S3 inventory to get a list of all objects in you
Copy S3 URI
Copy URL
Download
Open
Delete
Find objects by prefix
Name
KinesistsDF84-1-2022-08-04-18-33-37-c4fb65f4-67a6-401b-a58d-1c154f766441

a. Open the IoT data object in a UTF-8 editor of your choice. Make sure not to add invisible special characters to the object by using a regular word processor.
b. Edit your IoT data to add an open and closing bracket "[<Your-Data>]" as the first and last character in the file.
c. Remove the trailing comma from the last IoT data payload in the data object. You need to have the JSON data in 'array' format.

Your data should now look similar to the data formatted below:

```
[

{"temperature":92,"humidity":29,"timestamps":1659638017297,"UUID":"934ea2b2-6f12-46ca-aa91-ff2543c1cc24"},

{"temperature":72,"humidity":29,"timestamps":1659638021583,"UUID":"9e3f292b-99f6-491c-be22-4ec70723b3a3"},

{"temperature":72,"humidity":79,"timestamps":1659638024621,"UUID":"c3156d1a-76ec-4b98-bef3-dc9f35ccf912"},
```

{"temperature":92,"humidity":79,"timestamps":1659638028689,"UUID":"a53da382-0f5e-41cd-9e6d-4e91817e05b6"}
]

It would now be a good idea to use an online JSON format checker:

https://jsonlint.com/

To ensure you have done everything correctly and have constructed a proper JSON file with these small modifications. If you have not made the correct JSON modifications, then QuickSight won't be able to read and process your data object.

Now save the modified IoT data file onto your local computer with a name like "kindata.json." Make sure to give your new file the JSON file extension. Re-upload the new file to the S3 bucket, you can save it to the base level of the bucket to make things easy.

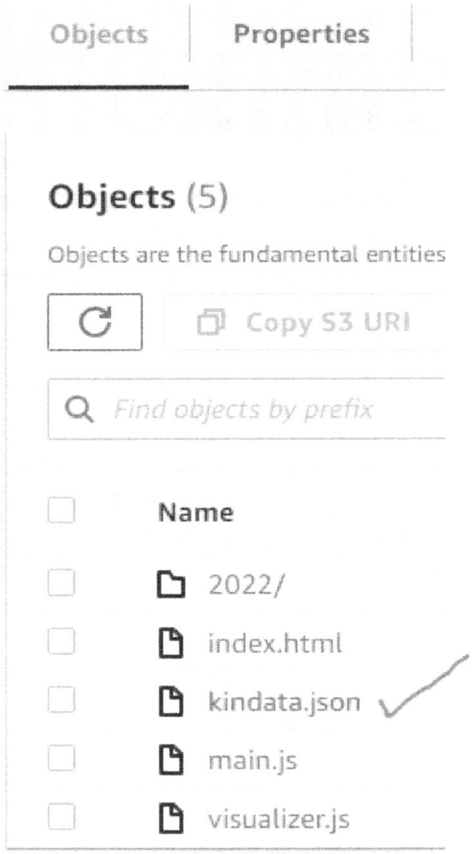
Objects
Properties
Objects (5)
Objects are the fundamental entities
Copy S3 URI
Find objects by prefix
Name
2022/
index.html
kindata.json
main.js
visualizer.js

AWS requires a “manifest” document to utilize custom data in S3. Amazon QuickSight uses the manifest document to identify the files that you want to use and to the upload the settings needed to import the IoT data file, (“kindata.json”) successfully.

To create the manifest, you will need both the bucket S3 URI and the IoT data file S3 URI. The are easy to find by looking at your URL or using the “Copy S3 URI” button directly from S3. Remember to only use the base level S3 URI address for the first location in the manifest, and the S3 URI of the IoT data object path for the second spot within the manifest document.

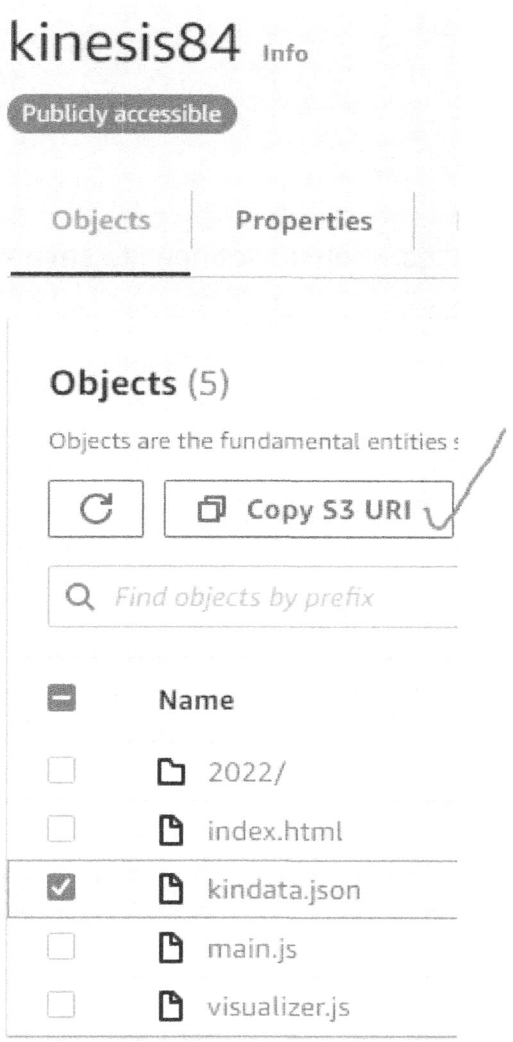

kinesis84 Info
Publicly accessible
Objects
Properties
Objects (5)
Objects are the fundamental entities
Copy S3 URI
Find objects by prefix
Name
2022/
index.html
kindata.json
main.js
visualizer.js

Here is what my completed “manifest.json” file looks like:

```
{
    "fileLocations": [
        {
            "URIs": [
                "s3://kinesis84" //bucket S3 URL
            ]
        },
        {
            "URIPrefixes": [
            "s3://kinesis84/kindata.json" //IoT data object S3 URI
            ]
        }
    ],"globalUploadSettings": {"format":"JSON",
    "delimiter": ","
    }
}
```

Save the file as "*manifest.json*" to your local machine. You do not need to save the manifest file to your S3 bucket.

Now you are ready to upload your IoT data to QuickSight for visualization.

Go to AWS QuickSight:

https://QuickSight.aws.amazon.com

Select the "New Analysis" button on the upper right of the screen:

New analysis

Now select the "New dataset" button on the upper left of the screen:

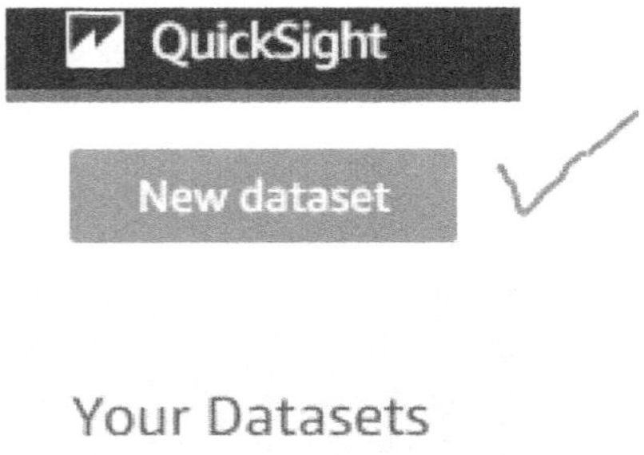
QuickSight
New dataset
Your Datasets

Now select S3 as the dataset location:

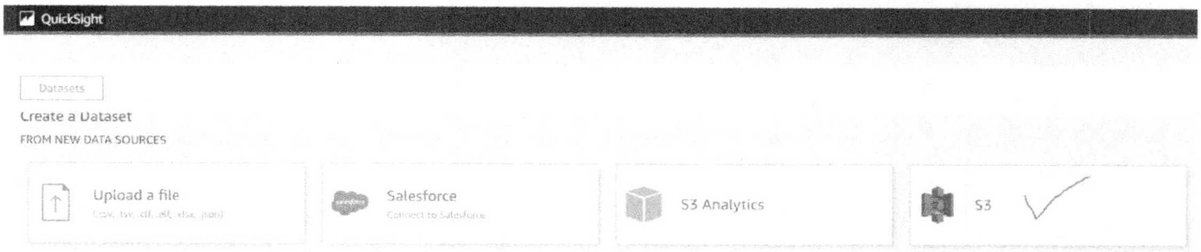

QuickSight
Datasets
Create a Dataset
FROM NEW DATA SOURCES
Upload a file
Salesforce
S3 Analytics
S3

Press the "S3" button and now you must enter the S3 URI of your IoT data object and upload your "*mainfest.json*" file by browsing to its location on your computer.

- The S3 URI of your data object is the same URI you used in the second entry filed of the "*manifest.json*" document.

Make sure you have the "upload" option selected and then press the "Connect" button:

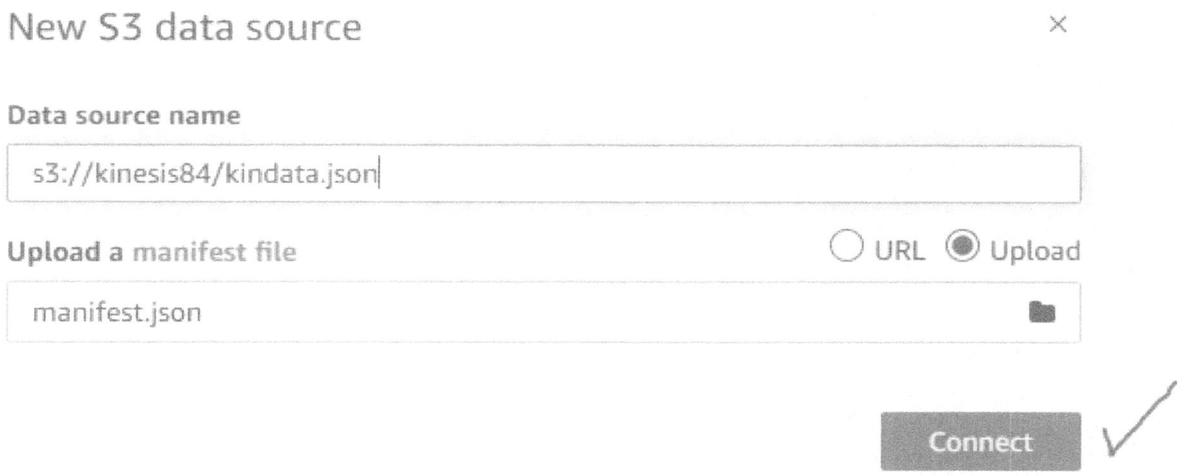

New S3 data source
Data source name
s3://kinesis84/kindata.json
Upload a manifest file
URL
Upload
manifest.json
Connect

If you formatted everything you can now proceed to "Visualize" your data:

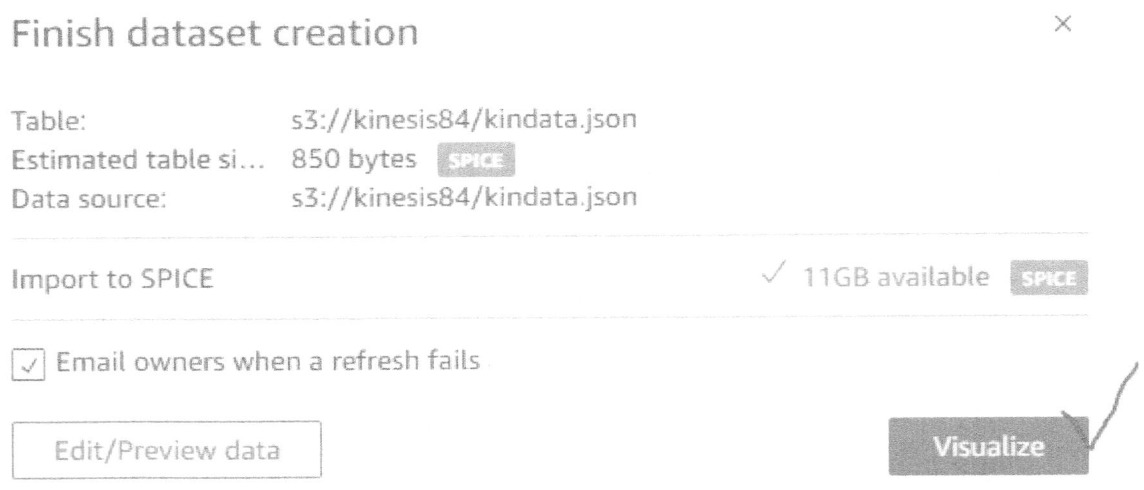
Finish dataset creation
Table: s3://kinesis84/kindata.json
Estimated table si... 850 bytes SPICE
Data source: s3://kinesis84/kindata.json
Import to SPICE
11GB available SPICE
Email owners when a refresh fails
Edit/Preview data
Visualize

Here I select a simple line chart and dragged my IoT variables over to the "Field wells" on the top of the screen to construct a simple visualization.

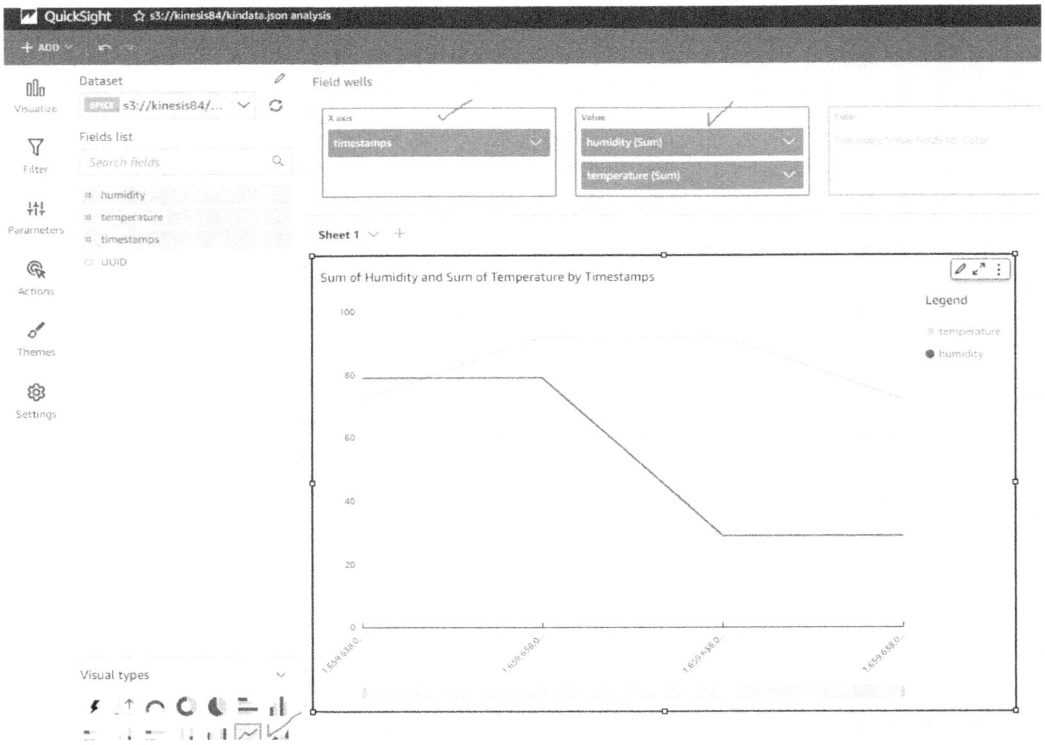
QuickSight
s3://kinesis84/kindata.json analysis
Dataset
s3://kinesis84/...
Fields list
Field wells
timestamps
humidity (Sum)
temperature (Sum)
Sheet 1
Sum of Humidity and Sum of Temperature by Timestamps
Legend
Visual types

With only four readings it is not super exciting but at least it keeps QuickSights SPICE capacity and usage low.

Congratulations, you have designed a transformation Lambda function for enhancing your IoT payload with a UUID and then sending your data to a bucket in S3. After configuring the Kinesis Firehose, you created a rule in IoT Core to add a timestamp and then dispatch your IoT data through Kinesis to be transformed by the Lambda function with a UUID and then finally to reside in your S3 bucket. Once the IoT data was in S3 you were able to visualize the IoT data with both the custom JavaScript code hosted on the static website in S3, as well as use QuickSight with a manifest document for the easy drag and drop creation of a basic visualization.

Chapter 15 - DynamoDB for IoT

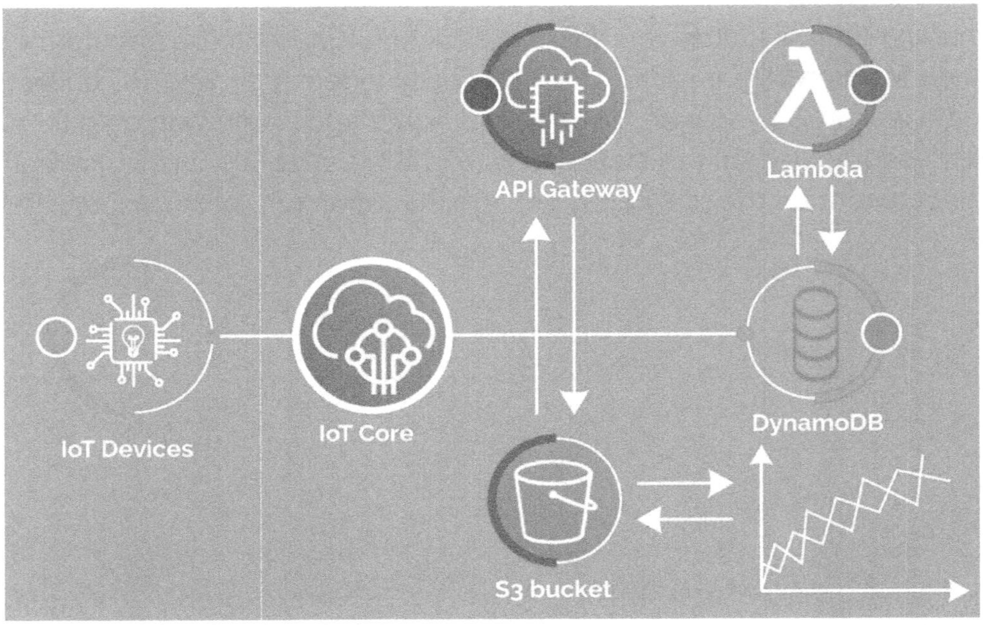
API Gateway
Lambda
IoT Devices
IoT Core
DynamoDB
S3 bucket

AWS offers several databases which are suitable for IoT depending on your needs, performance, and cost considerations. In this chapter we will focus on AWS's flagship database called DynamoDB. DynamoDB is a good database to get started with for IoT for a few reasons. First it is virtually free for allocated services on the free tier, secondly it provides the most documentation and applicable examples for getting started for the new AWS user. Good documentation and demonstrative use cases are essential when learning something as important as a data base.

I have already covered the Database vs. Data Lake arguments briefly in the last chapter so now it is time to create your first database using DynamoDB from IoT Core. After exploring this example there remains an extensive variety of other useful things you can do with your IoT data on DynamoDB.

Step 1 – Create an IoT Core Rule with DynamoDB
Step 2 – Design the Dynamo Database and Table
Step 3 – Enable Time to Live on the Dynamo Table

Step 4 – Produce and Ingest IoT Data Payloads into DynamoDB
Step 5 – Scan DynamoDB for the IoT Items
Step 6 – Visualize the DDB Data with AWS QuickSight (Optional)
Step 7 – Design a Lambda Function to Consume the DynamoDB IoT Data
Step 8 – Test the Lambda Function to Scan the Database
Step 9 – Observe the Return Values in AWS CloudWatch
Step 10 – Create a Rest API for your Lambda Function with API Gateway
Step 11 – Create a Static Website in S3 for Visualization of the DynamoDB IoT Sensor Readings

---

Step 1 – Create an IoT Core Rule with DynamoDB

You will start off with a typical design flow for using DynamoDB for IoT.

First go to AWS IoT Core:

https://console.aws.amazon.com/iot

Now select to create a Rule:

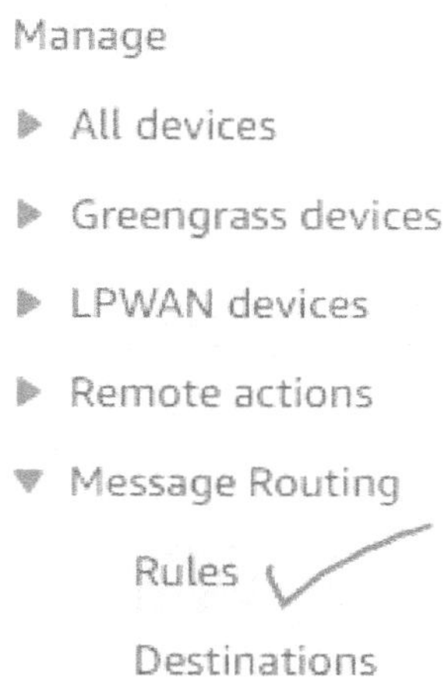
Manage
All devices
Greengrass devices
LPWAN devices
Remote actions
Message Routing
Rules
Destinations

Create a "Rule" and then name your new rule whatever you like, and then use the Rules Query statement (RQS) below:

```
SELECT *, timestamp() as timestamps, floor(timestamp()/1E3 + 1E5) as
ttlExpireOn FROM 'iot/#'
```

```
SELECT *, timestamp() as timestamps, floor(timestamp()/1E3 + 1E5)
    as ttlExpireOn  FROM 'iot/#'
```

This Rules Query Statement (RQS) may seem complicated, but it allows you to utilize some extra functionality when using DynamoDB for IoT. You will set up the Time-to-Live (TTL) in the database soon, but for now you need to design a RQS that will allow you to utilize the TTL.

For the RQS, you select the entire incoming payload by using: *Select **

Then you add the built-in timestamp function*: timestamp()* and call it “timestamps” to be added into the incoming JSON IoT payload as a new variable which reflects current Epoch/UNIX time in milliseconds.

Then divide the *timestamp()* by 1000 (1E3), to get seconds, rather than the milliseconds, which is necessary if you are going to use the Time-To-Live (TTL) function in DynamoDB. TTL is required to be in seconds and Epoch/UNIX timestamps are inherently in milliseconds, thus the need for the conversion from milliseconds to seconds. The TTL is the future time value to automatically expire the database items. This is a great feature to prevent accumulating database items over time that you don’t need. These database items can get very expensive as they use a lot of billable database capacity.

Then the RQS adds 100,000 seconds (1E5), to the TTL as an offset from the current time. This is the time the data will remain in your database after the IoT payload is initially written to your data table before it expires and is removed automatically. 100,000 seconds is a little over one day (27.8 hours). You can adjust this TTL to whatever chronological offset you feel comfortable with. The less frequently you send IoT payloads the longer you can let the items remain in your database and still keep your expenses down. To calculate your own TTL go to this webpage:

https://www.epochconverter.com

The name of the new TTL variable that is added to the JSON payload is: "*ttlExpireOn*"

Another good reason to add a TTL to an IoT database is that IoT data tends to be ephemeral, and unless you need long term storage it is a good idea to delete the data after all viable use. These DDB considerations are due the cost of the "scan" operations that are metered by data size reads in capacity units.

For DynamoDB, the free tier provides 25 GB of storage, 25 provisioned write capacity units (WCU), and 25 provisioned read capacity units (RCU). On the paid tier the first 25 GB consumed per month is still free, and prices start at $0.25 per GB-month thereafter. As the size of your database grows these scans can become more and more costly. It should be noted that when using an IoT data lake with flat cost for reads and writes this consideration is much less important. As a comparison, an S3 data lake costs $0.023 per GB per month for data sitting in S3 standard storage, making DDB storage about ten times more expensive than static data storage.

At this point it is time to design your Dynamo Database version 2 to hold IoT data. You could do this either from AWS IoT Core itself when prompted or create the data table before hand and just link it into your IoT rule.

Step 2 – Design the Dynamo Database and Table

To design the database, duplicate the current tab in your browser, or open a new tab in your browser, and navigate to DynamoDBv2 by going here:

https://console.aws.amazon.com/dynamodbv2

You will be using the 'DynamoDBv2" option, as the older DynamoDB version will not auto-populate non-key fields, instead storing the full message in the table as a single, user-designated field. DDBv2 offers a more timeseries-like database which is better suited for IoT. Another nice feature of DDBv2 is that you don't have to specify attribute fields other than the partition key. The "sort key" would be useful if you needed to sub-sort within the same partition key, but since you are using a timestamp as your partition key that is accurate up to 1/1000 of a second, you wouldn't need to sort within that same partition key. Using this convention may not be the best use case for multiple devices at high frequency, using a fan-in architecture for massive production level IoT data ingestion. Your other attributes fields, “temperature” and “humidity,” will automatically populate in your database table.

Select “Create table” to create your database schema in which to structure your IoT data in DynamoDB.

DynamoDB
Dashboard
Alarms (0)
Manage in CloudWatch
Alarm name
Status
No custom alarms
Create resources
Create table
DAX
DAX clusters (0)
Cluster name
No clusters
Create cluster
Create DAX cluster
What's new

Here I named my database table “DDBv2_forIoT.”

Now you will create a partition key in your own IoT database. A partition key is one of the key attributes in which you can hash data as needed. The incoming field of “timestamps” is a good hash key for IoT, think of “time-series” IoT databases. Choose to use timestamps as a “Number” and not a string from the drop-down box. Remember from your rules query statement when you created your IoT rule, that “timestamps” is simply the timestamp in milliseconds generated by AWS IoT Core when it receives your payload, and the field is automatically added to the IoT payload.

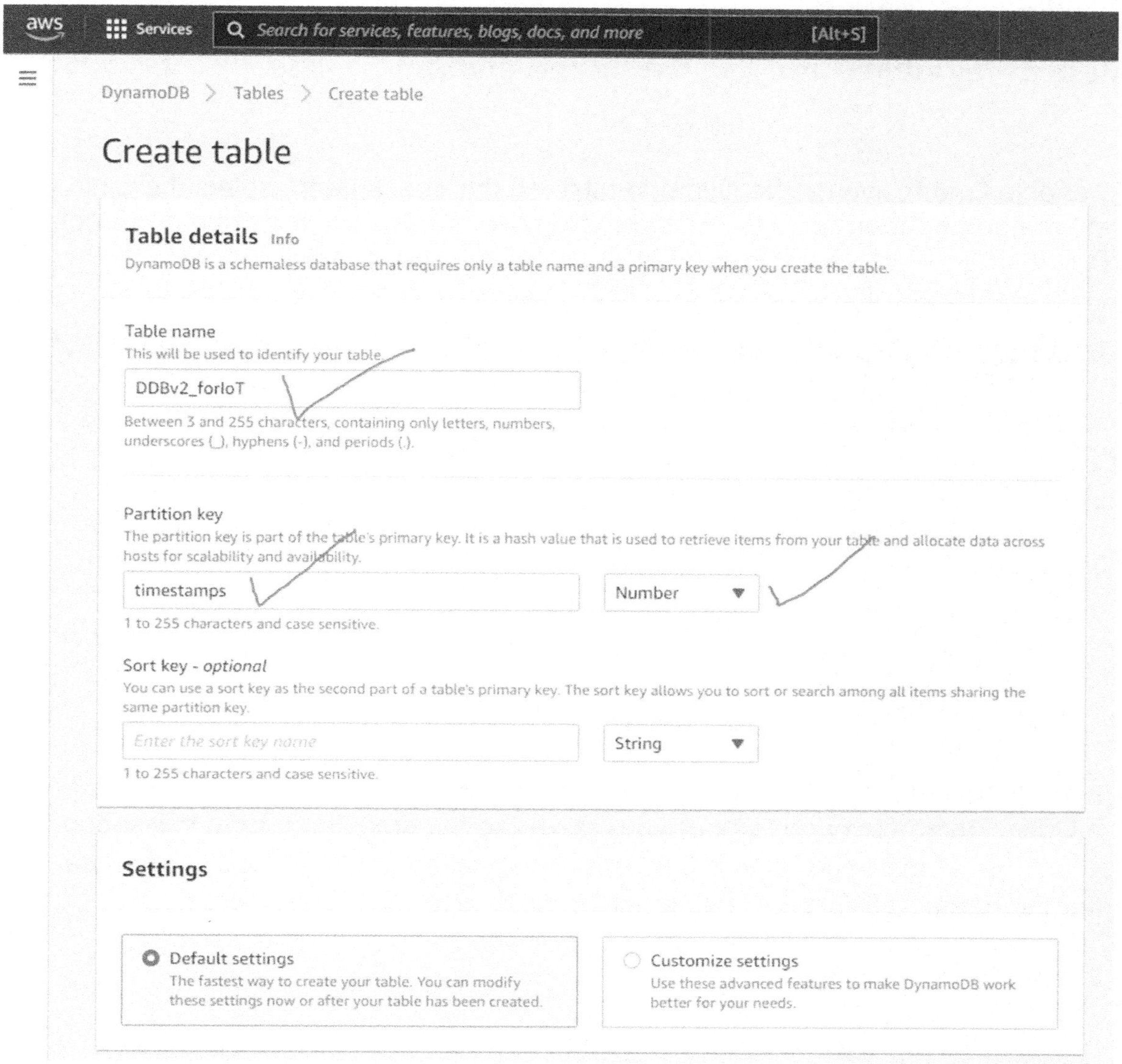
aws
Services
Search for services, features, blogs, docs, and more
[Alt+S]
DynamoDB > Tables > Create table
Create table
Table details Info
DynamoDB is a schemaless database that requires only a table name and a primary key when you create the table.
Table name
This will be used to identify your table.
DDBv2_forIoT
Between 3 and 255 characters, containing only letters, numbers, underscores (_), hyphens (-), and periods (.).
Partition key
The partition key is part of the table's primary key. It is a hash value that is used to retrieve items from your table and allocate data across hosts for scalability and availability.
timestamps
Number
1 to 255 characters and case sensitive.
Sort key - optional
You can use a sort key as the second part of a table's primary key. The sort key allows you to sort or search among all items sharing the same partition key.
Enter the sort key name
String
1 to 255 characters and case sensitive.
Settings
Default settings
The fastest way to create your table. You can modify these settings now or after your table has been created.
Customize settings
Use these advanced features to make DynamoDB work better for your needs.

Leave all the other default settings as they are and choose to "Create table":

Create table

Now you have one more option to configure in the DynamoDB before you can complete your rule in IoT Core. You must set the 'time-to-live' field for your data in the data table.

Step 3 – Enable Time to Live on the Dynamo Table

To enable time to live on the Dynamo table on the next screen, select the table you just created and then go to the "Action" drop down selection and choose "Enable TTL."

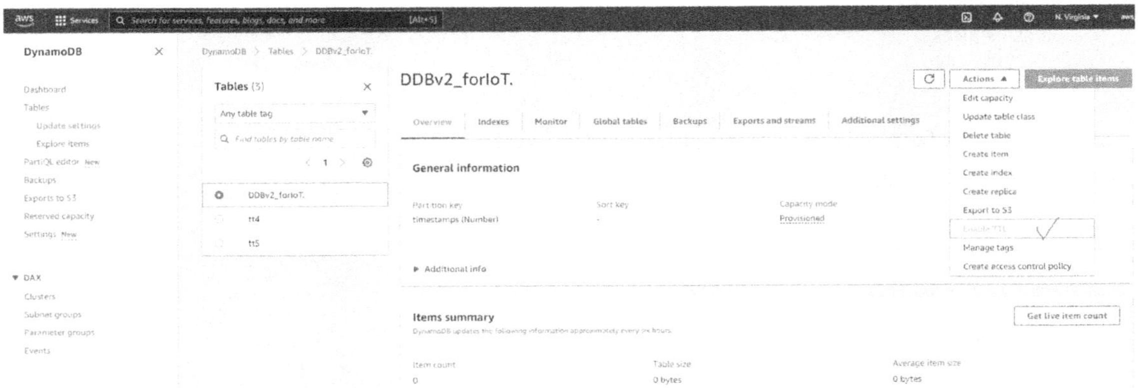

DynamoDB
Tables (3)
DDBv2_forIoT.
Actions
Explore table items
Edit capacity
Update table class
Delete table
Create item
Create index
Create replica
Export to S3
Manage tags
Create access control policy
General information
Items summary
Get live item count

The name of your TTL must match exactly the name you used in the RQS in AWS IoT Core. As you may remember you converted the timestamp from millisecond to second format then added on a time offset and called it "ttlExpireOn." After you enter the name "ttlExpireOn" you must "Enable TTL."

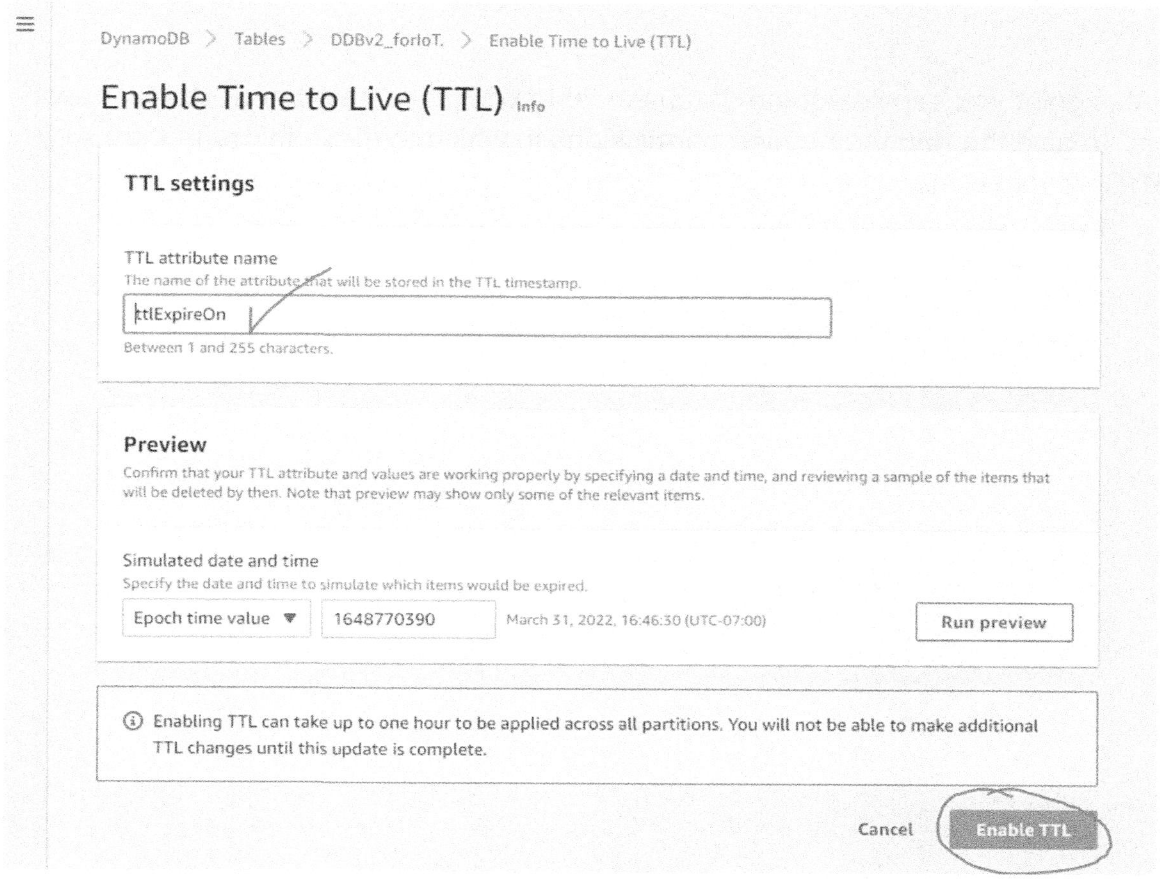
DynamoDB > Tables > DDBv2_forIoT. > Enable Time to Live (TTL)
Enable Time to Live (TTL) Info
TTL settings
TTL attribute name
The name of the attribute that will be stored in the TTL timestamp.
ttlExpireOn
Between 1 and 255 characters.
Preview
Confirm that your TTL attribute and values are working properly by specifying a date and time, and reviewing a sample of the items that will be deleted by then. Note that preview may show only some of the relevant items.
Simulated date and time
Specify the date and time to simulate which items would be expired.
Epoch time value
1648770390
March 31, 2022, 16:46:30 (UTC-07:00)
Run preview
Enabling TTL can take up to one hour to be applied across all partitions. You will not be able to make additional TTL changes until this update is complete.
Cancel
Enable TTL

You don't need to run a preview and see your database IoT objects expire, it is not very exciting. Now that your database and table are created, you can return to the open tab to continue configuring your AWS rule in AWS IoT Core.

Now add in DynaomoDBv2 as an 'rule action' to your rule.

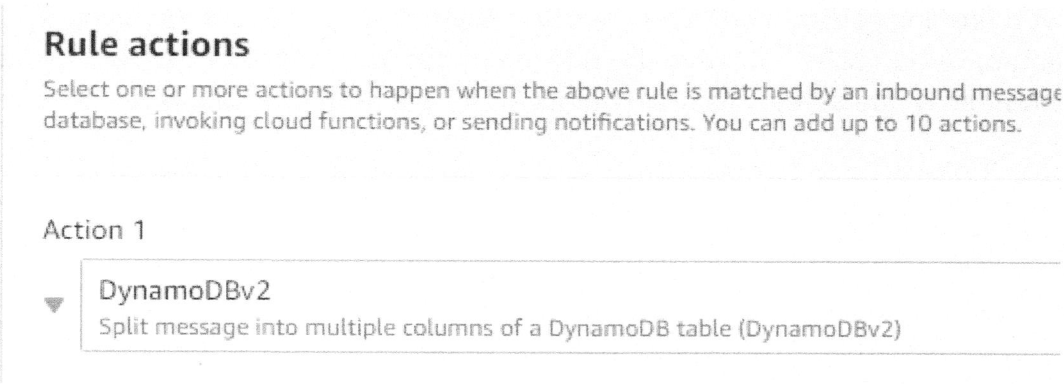
Rule actions
Select one or more actions to happen when the above rule is matched by an inbound message
database, invoking cloud functions, or sending notifications. You can add up to 10 actions.
Action 1
DynamoDBv2
Split message into multiple columns of a DynamoDB table (DynamoDBv2)

At this point you can select the database table you just created and “Create new role” to give the rule the needed permissions in which to move IoT data from AWS IoT Core into DynamoDB.

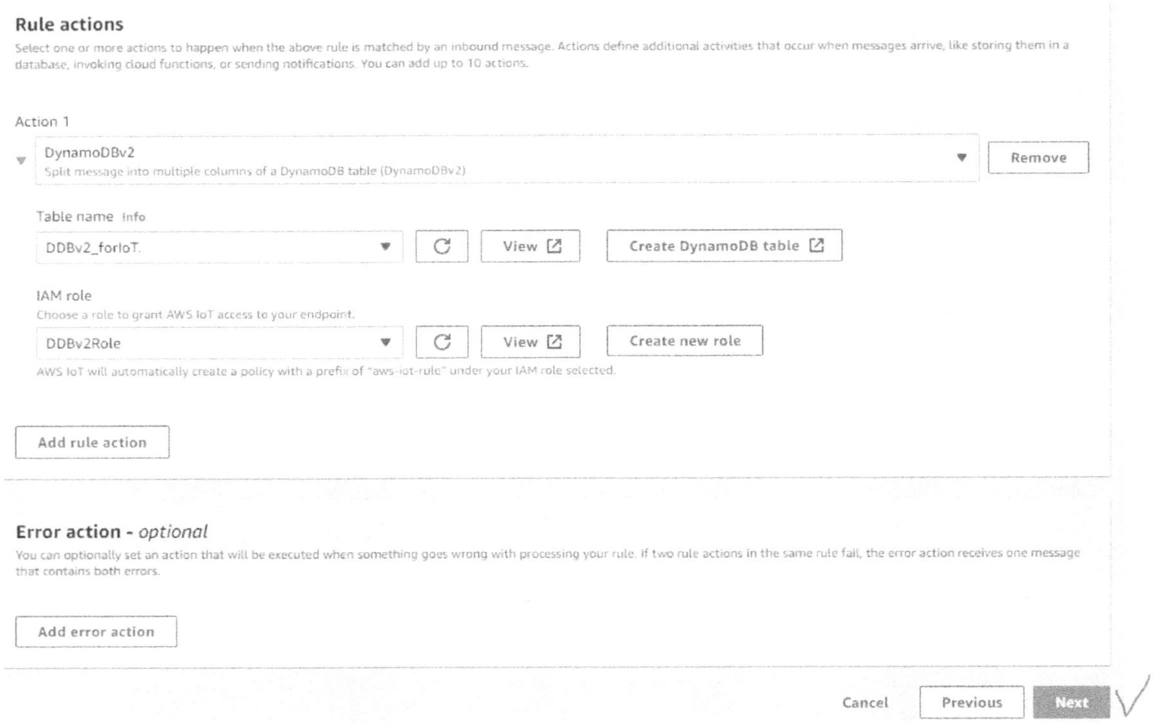
Rule actions
Select one or more actions to happen when the above rule is matched by an inbound message. Actions define additional activities that occur when messages arrive, like storing them in a database, invoking cloud functions, or sending notifications. You can add up to 10 actions.
Action 1
DynamoDBv2
Split message into multiple columns of a DynamoDB table (DynamoDBv2)
Remove
Table name Info
DDBv2_forIoT
View
Create DynamoDB table
IAM role
Choose a role to grant AWS IoT access to your endpoint.
DDBv2Role
View
Create new role
AWS IoT will automatically create a policy with a prefix of "aws-iot-rule" under your IAM role selected.
Add rule action
Error action - optional
You can optionally set an action that will be executed when something goes wrong with processing your rule. If two rule actions in the same rule fail, the error action receives one message that contains both errors.
Add error action
Cancel
Previous
Next

Now Click the “Next” button after you are done configuring the ‘rule action’.

Next

Now you are finished with creating your IoT Rule which adds your incoming JSON IoT data to DynamoDB. To save the rule you must now select the “Create” button at the bottom of the screen as seen below after reviewing everything.

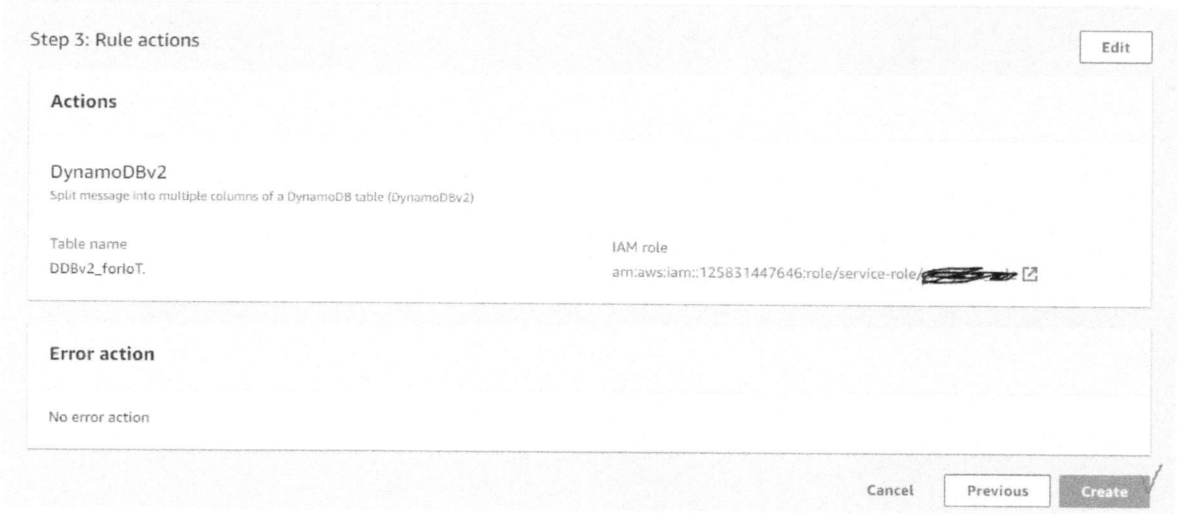
Step 3: Rule actions
Edit
Actions
DynamoDBv2
Split message into multiple columns of a DynamoDB table (DynamoDBv2)
Table name
DDBv2_forIoT.
IAM role
arn:aws:iam::125831447646:role/service-role/[redacted]
Error action
No error action
Cancel
Previous
Create

Step 4 – Produce and Ingest IoT Data Payloads into DynamoDB

After completing making this Rule and adding your DynamoDB action you are now ready to fill your database with IoT data. You will use a familiar JSON IoT payload consisting of temperature and humidity.

```
{
  "temperature": 55,
  "humidity": 66
}
```

Remember that your timestamp will be added to the Dynamo table by IoT Core as well as a feature facilitating a "Time-To-Live" for IoT data of a little over one day.

After programming your physical or virtual MQTT capable IoT device to transmit the sensor payload to AWS you can publish your IoT data under the topic of "iot/test" and display the results in AWS by subscribing to that topic in the MQTT test client on IoT Core. To see the IoT data come in to the test console navigate to IoT Core→MQTT test client, and subscribe to "iot/#".

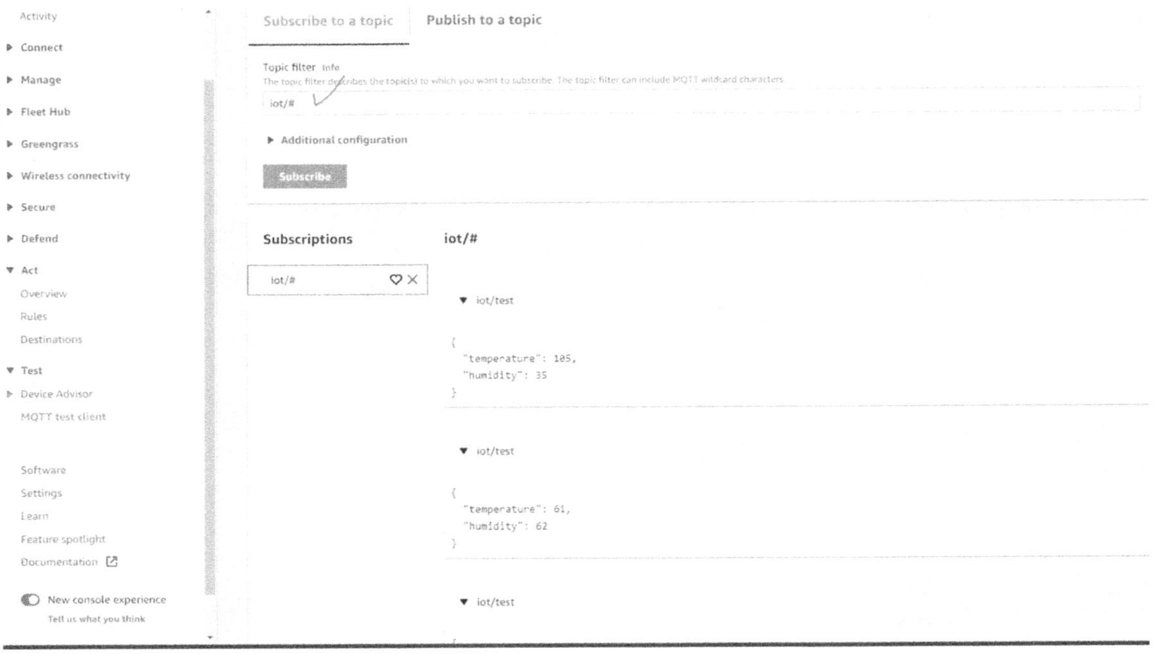
Activity
Connect
Manage
Fleet Hub
Greengrass
Wireless connectivity
Secure
Defend
Act
Overview
Rules
Destinations
Test
Device Advisor
MQTT test client
Software
Settings
Learn
Feature spotlight
Documentation
New console experience
Tell us what you think
Subscribe to a topic
Publish to a topic
Topic filter Info
iot/#
Additional configuration
Subscribe
Subscriptions
iot/#
iot/#
iot/test
{
"temperature": 105,
"humidity": 35
}
iot/test
{
"temperature": 61,
"humidity": 62
}
iot/test

Step 5 – Scan DynamoDB for the IoT Items

After publishing a reasonable number of IoT sensor readings return to your database table to make sure all the IoT items got inserted correctly into the table. If the DynamoDB table is still empty, then it is time to review the previous steps and remedy any issue causing the omission of the IoT data. To navigate back to DDB item list in the console go to:

DynamoDBv2→Tables→Explore Items

Alternately, you can just click this link.

https://console.aws.amazon.com/dynamodbv2#item-explorer

From this point forward you will want to scan your entire database. This can be an inherently expensive operation depending on the size of each database item and the number of objects in the database. If you are still on the AWS free tier, you have a good amount of free scanning capacity available. In any case the costs for scanning 5-20 small IoT objects is nominal, not more than a couple of cents.

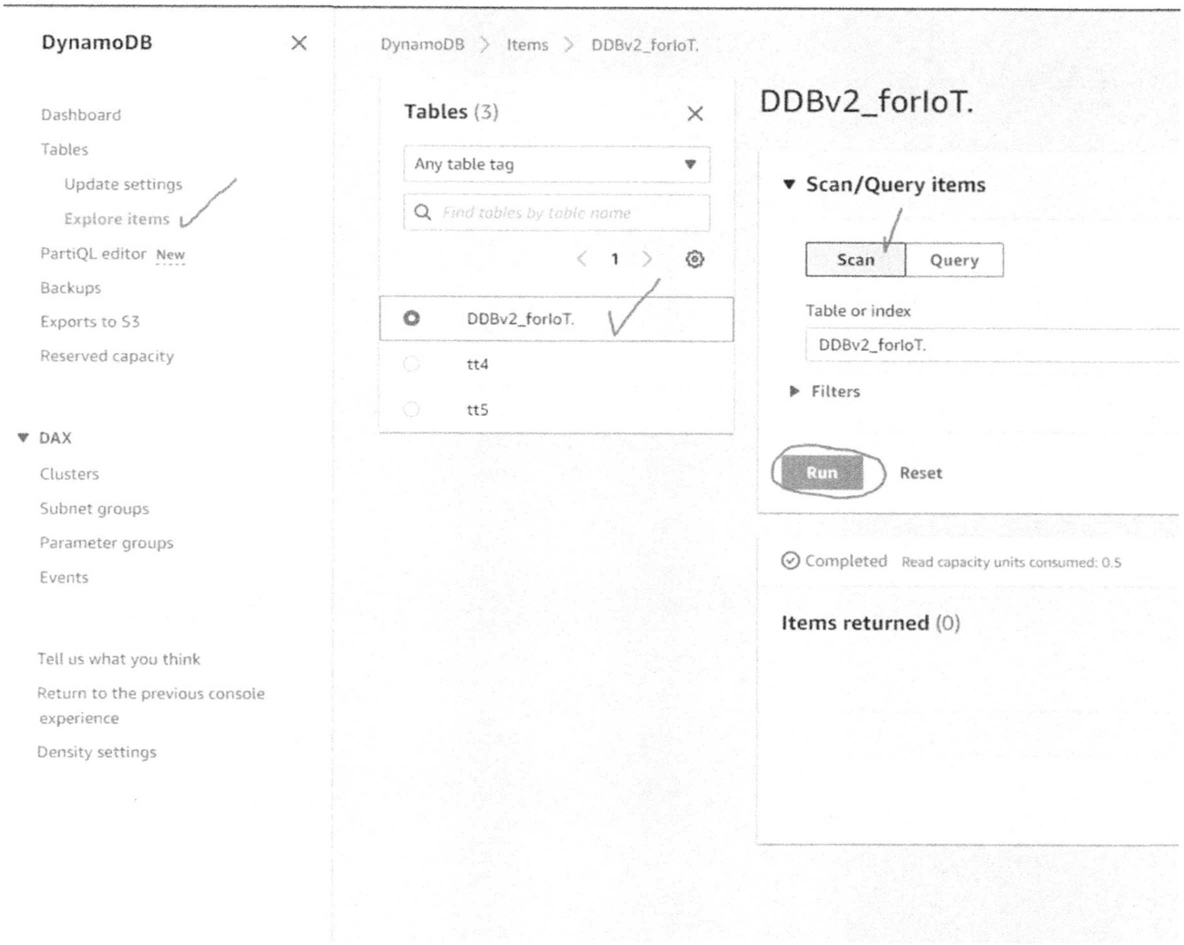
DynamoDB
Dashboard
Tables
Update settings
Explore items
PartiQL editor New
Backups
Exports to S3
Reserved capacity
DAX
Clusters
Subnet groups
Parameter groups
Events
Tell us what you think
Return to the previous console experience
Density settings
DynamoDB > Items > DDBv2_forIoT.
Tables (3)
Any table tag
Find tables by table name
DDBv2_forIoT.
tt4
tt5
DDBv2_forIoT.
Scan/Query items
Scan
Query
Table or index
DDBv2_forIoT.
Filters
Run
Reset
Completed Read capacity units consumed: 0.5
Items returned (0)

After running the scan of your data table, you should get all the data values as the result, as well as the Time-to-Live.

Run Reset

Completed Read capacity units consumed: 0.5

Items returned (10)

	timestamps	humidity	tempera...	ttlExpireOn (TTL)
	1649806918150	17	6	1649906918
	1649806920313	46	55	1649906920
	1649806912140	35	105	1649906912
	1649806904104	98	126	1649906904
	1649806910139	62	61	1649906910
	1649806914148	41	69	1649906914
	1649806916142	8	45	1649906916
	1649806908135	9	51	1649906908
	1649806906132	42	118	1649906906
	1649806922307	95	30	1649906922

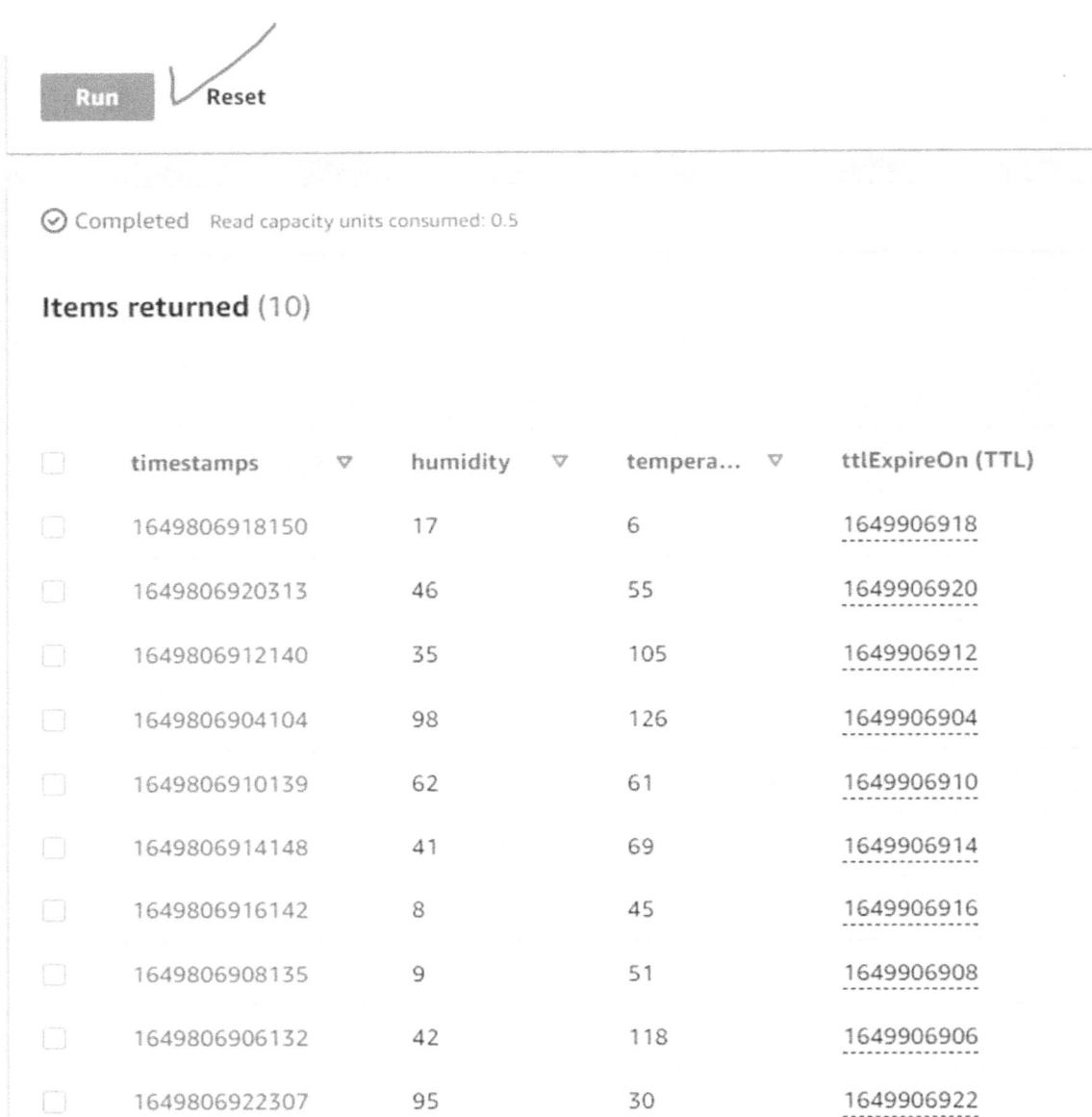

Awesome! Hopefully all your items in your table have a day or so to live so that you can still play with them before they disappear from your database table. The expiration period should be more than enough time to accomplish what you need to complete in this chapter.

Step 6 – Visualize the DDB Data with AWS QuickSight (Optional)

AWS QuickSight does not have a built-in connector yet for DynamoDB but there is a workaround for ad-hoc visualizations for DynamoDB data. To start using QuickSight you will need to download a .csv file of your DynamoDB data. To do this return to last screen you left off at in which you ran your DDB scan. From the "Items" screen go to the drop-down menu under "Actions" then select "download results to CSV."

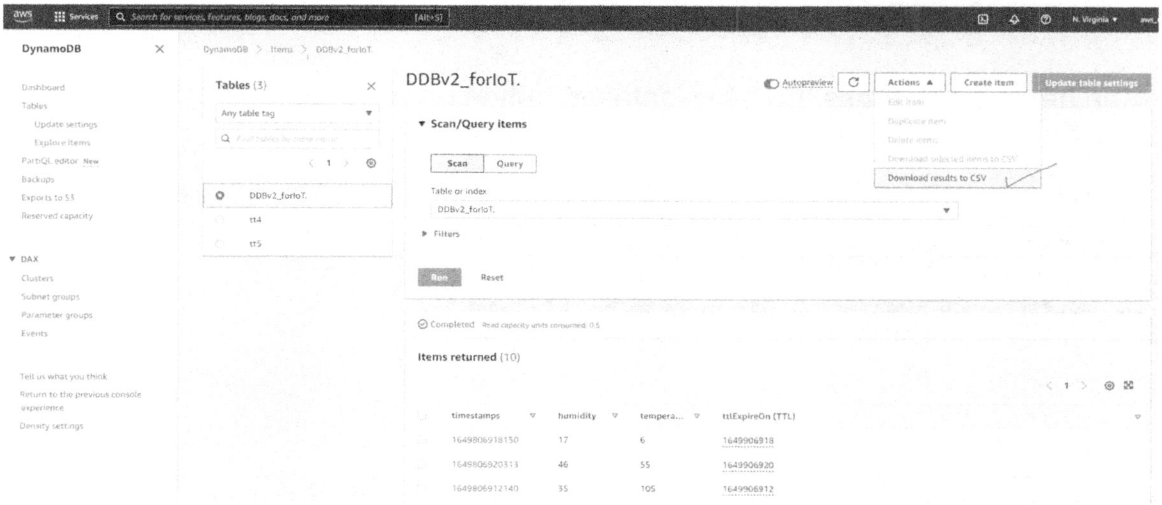

DynamoDB
Tables (3)
DDBv2_forIoT.
Scan/Query items
Scan
Query
Actions
Create item
Update table settings
Download results to CSV
Run
Reset
Items returned (10)
timestamps
humidity
ttlExpireOn (TTL)

Make a note of where you just downloaded your CSV file on your computer and then navigate to "QuickSight" in the AWS search box at the top of your screen or go to:

https://quicksight.aws.amazon.com

Once in QuickSight press the "New analysis" button on the upper right.

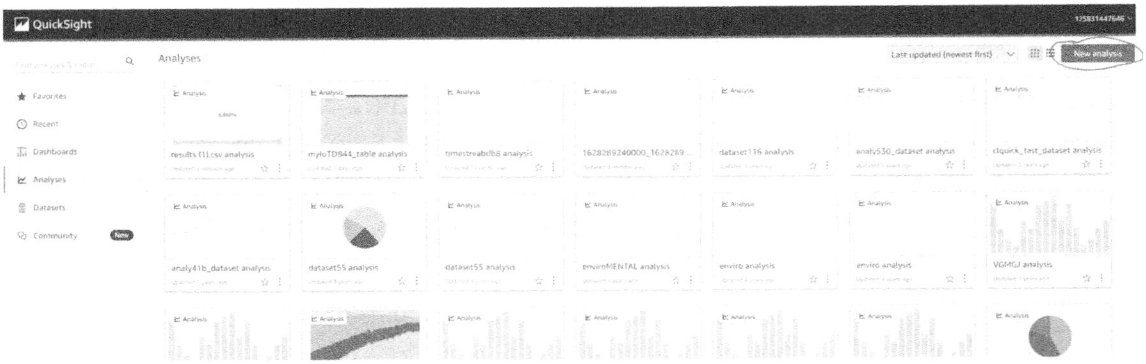
QuickSight
Analyses
Last updated (newest first)
New analysis
Favorites
Recent
Dashboards
Analyses
Datasets
Community
New

On the next screen press the “New dataset” button on the upper left of your screen.

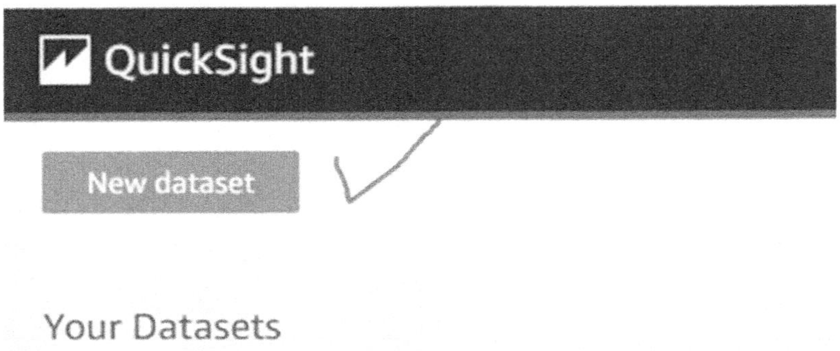
QuickSight
New dataset
Your Datasets

On the next screen the first selection box allows you to upload the data values CSV file you just downloaded.

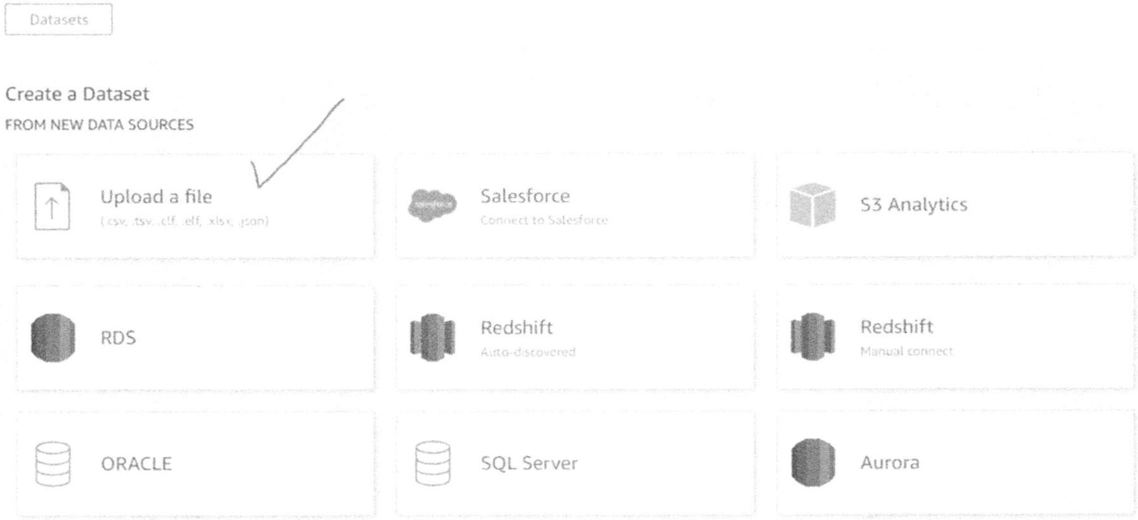
Datasets
Create a Dataset
FROM NEW DATA SOURCES
Upload a file
(.csv, .tsv, .clf, .elf, .xlsx, .json)
Salesforce
Connect to Salesforce
S3 Analytics
RDS
Redshift
Auto-discovered
Redshift
Manual connect
ORACLE
SQL Server
Aurora

Just navigate to your "results.csv" file and upload

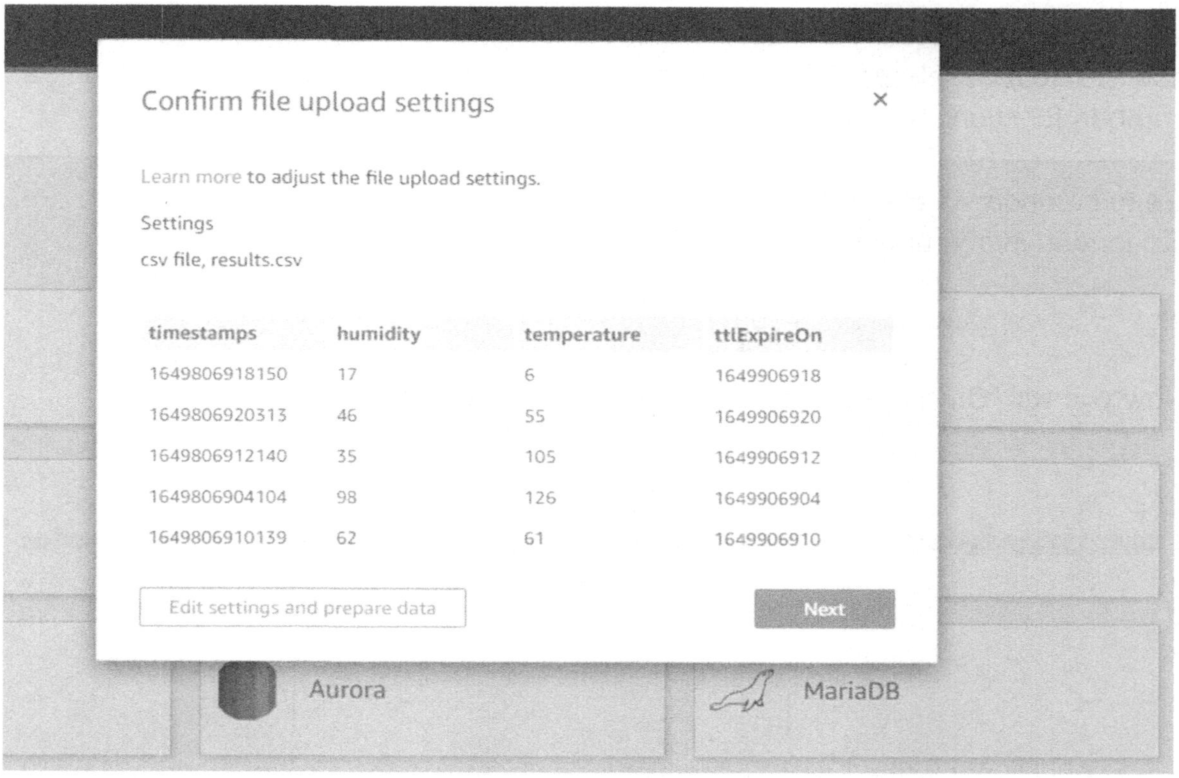
Confirm file upload settings
Learn more to adjust the file upload settings.
Settings
csv file, results.csv
timestamps humidity temperature ttlExpireOn
1649806918150 17 6 1649906918
1649806920313 46 55 1649906920
1649806912140 35 105 1649906912
1649806904104 98 126 1649906904
1649806910139 62 61 1649906910
Edit settings and prepare data
Next
Aurora
MariaDB

After uploading the CSV file, you will be presented with a range of business intelligence (BI) visualization options. I won't go any further, but it is worthwhile to note the range of charts and dashboards you have in which to visualize your IoT data from DynamoDB. After a lot of QuickSight use you may consume all your "SPICE" quota and need to purchase more capacity piecemeal or elevate your QuickSight subscription for further fun. Be careful of QuickSight costs for running the Spice engine excessively, it can get costly.

For now, let's return the main storyline of the project and move on to designing a Lambda function to consume your DynamoDB data for web visualization and dashboarding. Creating your own visualizations on a static web host in S3 will be extremely inexpensive compared to using QuickSight.

Step 7 – Design a Lambda Function to Consume the DynamoDB Data

If you want to do more than just store and query your DynamoDB IoT data, you can now create a dashboard for visualization using several different search criteria in a Lambda function.

Go to Lambda via the console or simply use this link to return to Lambda if you are still logged into your account:

https://console.aws.amazon.com/Lambda

Now you will “Create function” by pressing the button on the upper left:

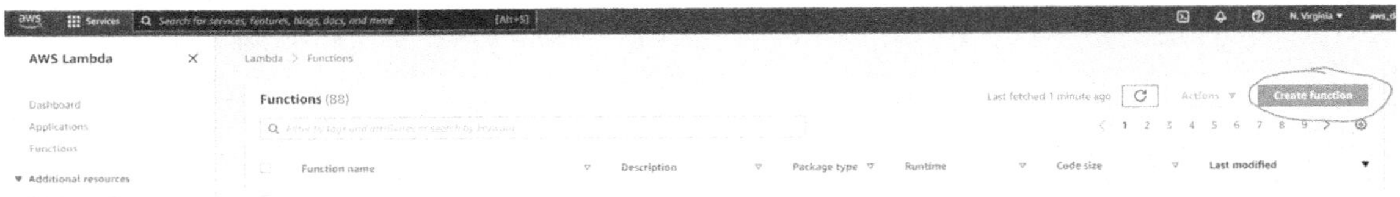

Services
AWS Lambda
Lambda > Functions
Functions (88)
Dashboard
Applications
Functions
Additional resources
Function name
Description
Package type
Runtime
Code size
Last modified
Create function

Here you will name the Lambda function and choose Python 3.8 or Node.js 14.x. I will provide the same functionality for a scan operation in both languages for whichever language option you prefer to use.

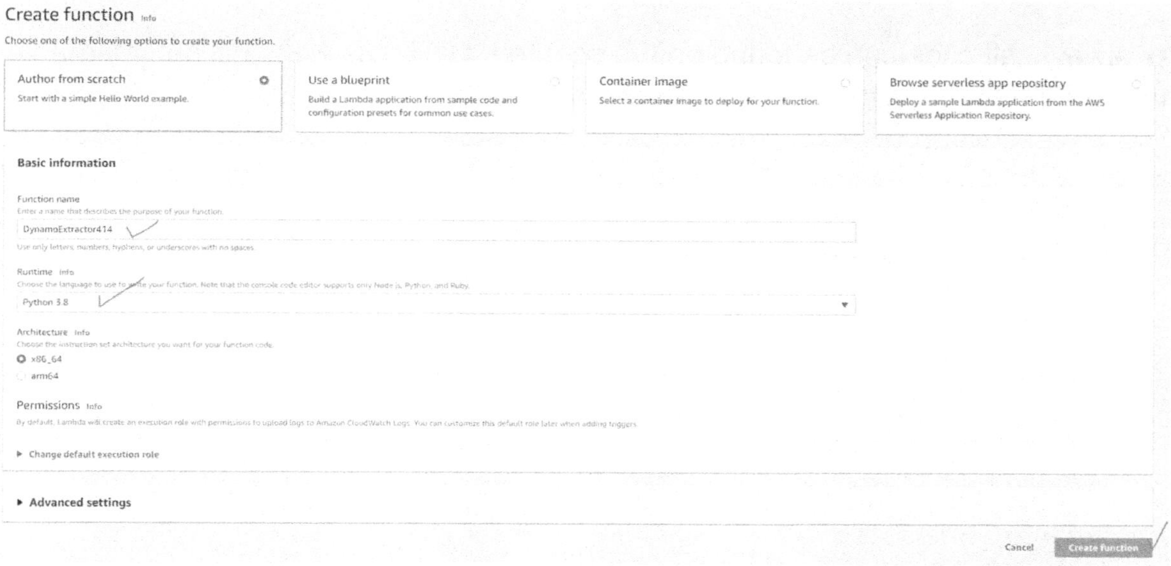

Create function
Choose one of the following options to create your function.
Author from scratch
Start with a simple Hello World example.
Use a blueprint
Build a Lambda application from sample code and configuration presets for common use cases.
Container image
Select a container image to deploy for your function.
Browse serverless app repository
Deploy a sample Lambda application from the AWS Serverless Application Repository.
Basic information
Function name
DynamoExtractor414
Runtime
Python 3.8
Architecture
x86_64
arm64
Permissions
Change default execution role
Advanced settings
Cancel
Create function

To write your function simply copy and paste the included code below into your new Lambda function. Don’t forget to fill out the line in the code with the name of your own DynamoDB table into the Lambda function. As always, all code can be found on the chapters GitHib as well.

As always, all code can be found on the chapters GitHib as well. Fill out your table name in the Lambda function for Python code here:

```
table = dynamodb.Table(‘<YOUR-DDB-TABLE-HERE>’)
```

The Python code below:

```
import boto3

def lambda_handler(event,context):
    dynamodb = boto3.resource(‘dynamodb’)

    table = dynamodb.Table(‘<YOUR-DDB-TABLE-HERE>’)

    response = table.scan()
    data = response[‘Items’]

    while ‘LastEvaluatedKey’ in response:
        response = table.scan(ExclusiveStartKey=response[‘LastEvaluatedKey’])
        data.extend(response[‘Items’])
    return(data)
```

As always, all code can be found on the chapters GitHib as well. Fill out your table name in the Lambda function for JavaScript code here:

```
const tableName = '<YOUR-DDB-TABLE-HERE>';
```

The Node.js Lambda code would be:

```
const AWS = require('aws-sdk');
const docClient = new AWS.DynamoDB.DocumentClient({
    apiVersion: '2012-08-10',
    sslEnabled: false,
    paramValidation: false,
    convertResponseTypes: false
});

const tableName = '<YOUR-DDB-TABLE-HERE>';

exports.handler = async (event, context, callback) => {
    let params = { TableName: tableName };

    let scanResults = [];
    let items;

    do {
        items = await docClient.scan(params).promise();
        items.Items.forEach((item) => scanResults.push(item));
        params.ExclusiveStartKey = items.LastEvaluatedKey;
    } while (typeof items.LastEvaluatedKey != "undefined");

    callback(null, scanResults);
};
```

As you can see, both functions scan the entire database using the DDB built-in keywords of “ExclusiveStartKey” and “LastEvaluatedKey.”

Here is what the code looks like in Lambda with Python. The important things to remember are to insert the name of your own DynamoDB table as well as to “Deploy” your function to save it.

Code
Test
Monitor
Configuration
Aliases
Versions
Code source Info
File Edit Find View Go Tools Window
Test
Deploy
Go to Anything (Ctrl-P)
lambda_function
Environment
DynamoExtractor41
lambda_function.py
import boto3

def lambda_handler(event,context):
    dynamodb = boto3.resource('dynamodb')

    table = dynamodb.Table('DDBv2_forIoT.')

    response = table.scan()
    data = response['Items']

    while 'LastEvaluatedKey' in response:
        response = table.scan(ExclusiveStartKey=response['LastEvaluatedKey'])
        data.extend(response['Items'])
    return(data)

After you have inserted your own table name and deployed your function, there is one last step to complete before you can test your Lambda function and observe the results. You need to give your function access to DynamoDB. Currently your function only has permission to execute itself, which won't get you very far. To give it DDB permission Go to the configuration tab in Lambda and then right click the role name:

Configuration
Aliases
Versions
Execution role
Role name
DynamoExtractor414-role-flz2bj58

Clicking on the role name will open a window in AWS IAM in which you can add an inline policy for including a DDB permission policy to your Lambda function. To do so, go to the right side of the screen and use the drop-down box to select "Create inline policy" for your role:

DynamoExtractor414-role-flz2bj58
Delete
Summary
Edit
Creation date
April 14, 2022, 12:06 (UTC-07:00)
ARN
Last activity
None
Maximum session duration
1 hour
Permissions
Trust relationships
Tags
Access Advisor
Revoke sessions
Permissions policies (1)
Simulate
Remove
Add permissions
Attach policies
Create inline policy
Policy name
Type
Description
AWSLambdaBasicExecutionRole-a1cdfde2-425c-42c2-9118-b88392148eef
Customer managed
Permissions boundary - (not set)
Set permissions boundary

After selecting to create your inline policy to add to the Lambda basic execution role, search and select DynamoDB and all actions and all resources. Again, this violates AWS's "least privilege" model, but for low volume prototyping in a non-shared AWS account it is the easiest method. Also just giving the Lambda function DDB read permission won't work.

Choose to "Review policy" when done:

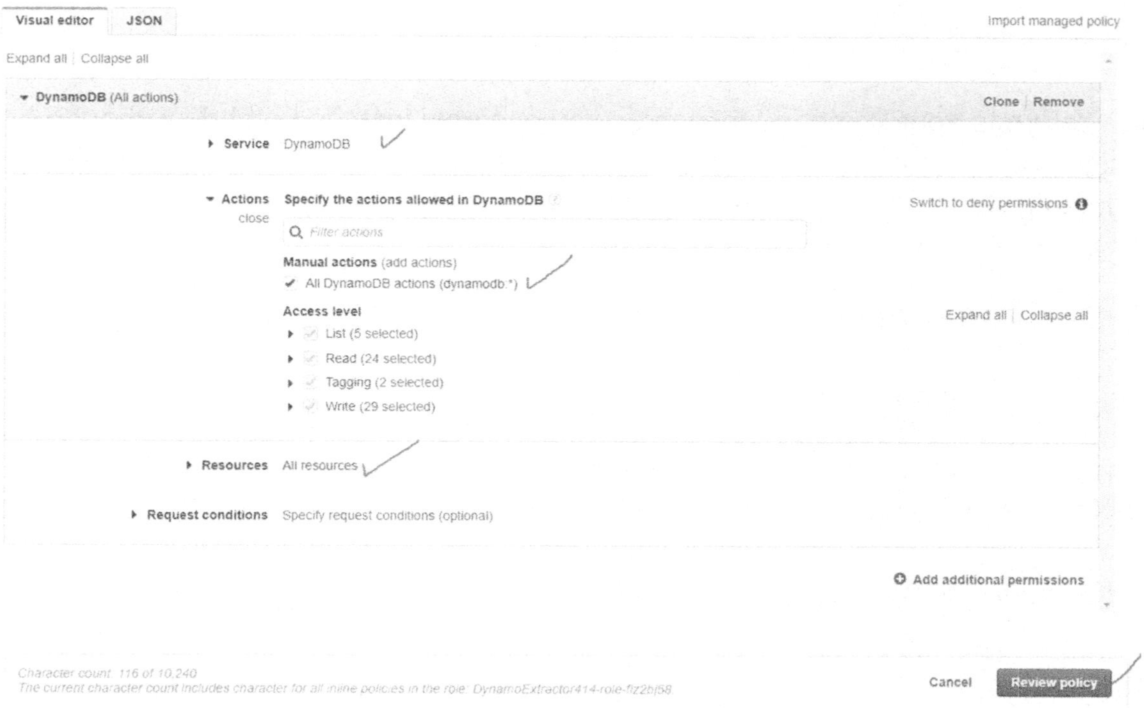
Visual editor
JSON
Import managed policy
Expand all | Collapse all
DynamoDB (All actions)
Clone | Remove
Service DynamoDB
Actions
close
Specify the actions allowed in DynamoDB
Switch to deny permissions
Filter actions
Manual actions (add actions)
All DynamoDB actions (dynamodb:*)
Access level
Expand all | Collapse all
List (5 selected)
Read (24 selected)
Tagging (2 selected)
Write (29 selected)
Resources All resources
Request conditions Specify request conditions (optional)
Add additional permissions
Character count: 116 of 10,240
Cancel
Review policy

Name and create your inline policy and you are now done with adding Lambda permissions. You can now close out the IAM window.

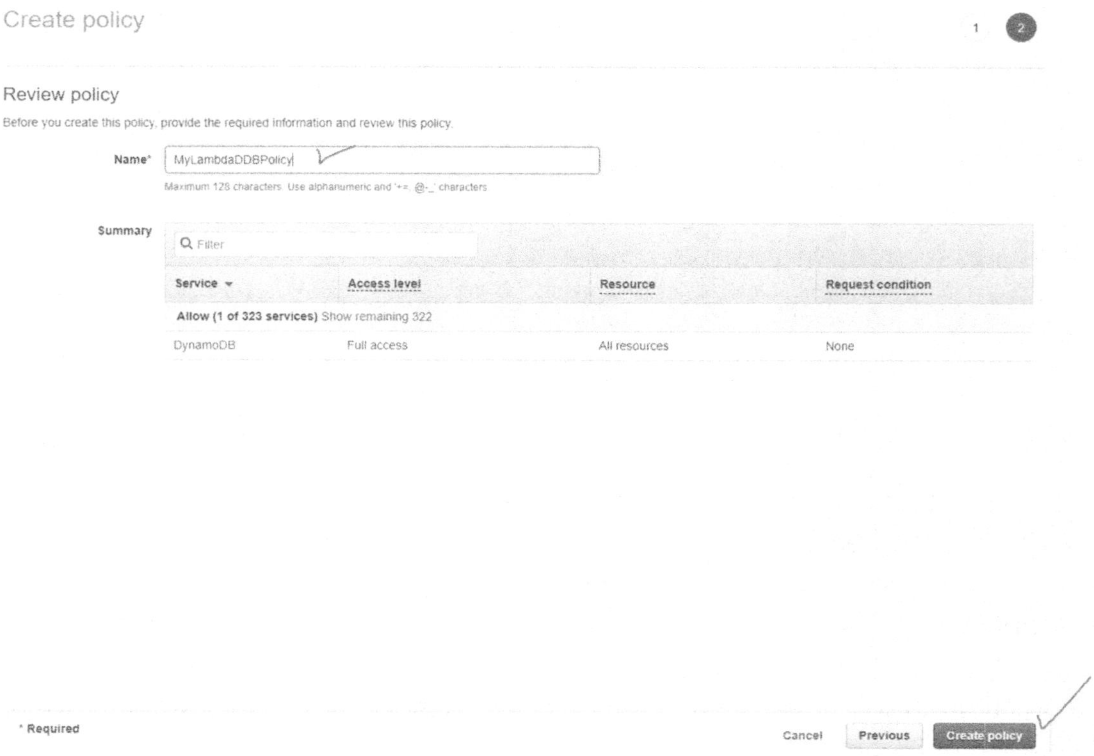
Create policy
1
2
Review policy
Before you create this policy, provide the required information and review this policy.
Name* MyLambdaDDBPolicy
Maximum 128 characters. Use alphanumeric and '+=,.@-_' characters
Summary
Filter
Service
Access level
Resource
Request condition
Allow (1 of 323 services) Show remaining 322
DynamoDB
Full access
All resources
None
* Required
Cancel
Previous
Create policy

Now return to your Lambda function as you can now test the Lambda without getting an "access denied/violation exception" type error that you would get if you forgot to give your Lambda the permissions needed to scan the Dynamo table.

Step 8 – Test the Lambda Function to Scan the Database

It is time to test the Lambda function before moving forwards, this is a best practice, so you don't waste time debugging a harder problem later when your Lambda function was the original culprit of the error.

To test your Lambda function, go to Test→ Configure test event.

Code
Test
Monitor
Configuration
Aliases
Versions
Code source Info
File Edit Find View Go Tools Window
Test
Deploy
Go to Anything (Ctrl-P)
lambda_functio
Configure test event Ctrl-Shift-C
Environment
DynamoExtractor41
lambda_function.py
import boto3
def lambda_handler(event,context):
dynamodb = boto3.resource('dynamodb')
table = dynamodb.Table('DDBv2_forIoT.')
response = table.scan()
data = response['Items']
while 'LastEvaluatedKey' in response:
response = table.scan(ExclusiveStartKey=response['LastEvaluatedKey'])
data.extend(response['Items'])
return(data)

From here you can leave the default JSON payload as it is. This is because your Lambda function has no "event" object", this means there is no incoming data object that you are going to operate on or perform ETL with. In these circumstances you are simply using the test feature to execute the Lambda function. If you had a Lambda function that needed access to the values of a real IoT JSON payload, which you often will, then the actual content of the JSON test event object would be relevant.

In this case simply give the test event a name and leave the default payload as it is.

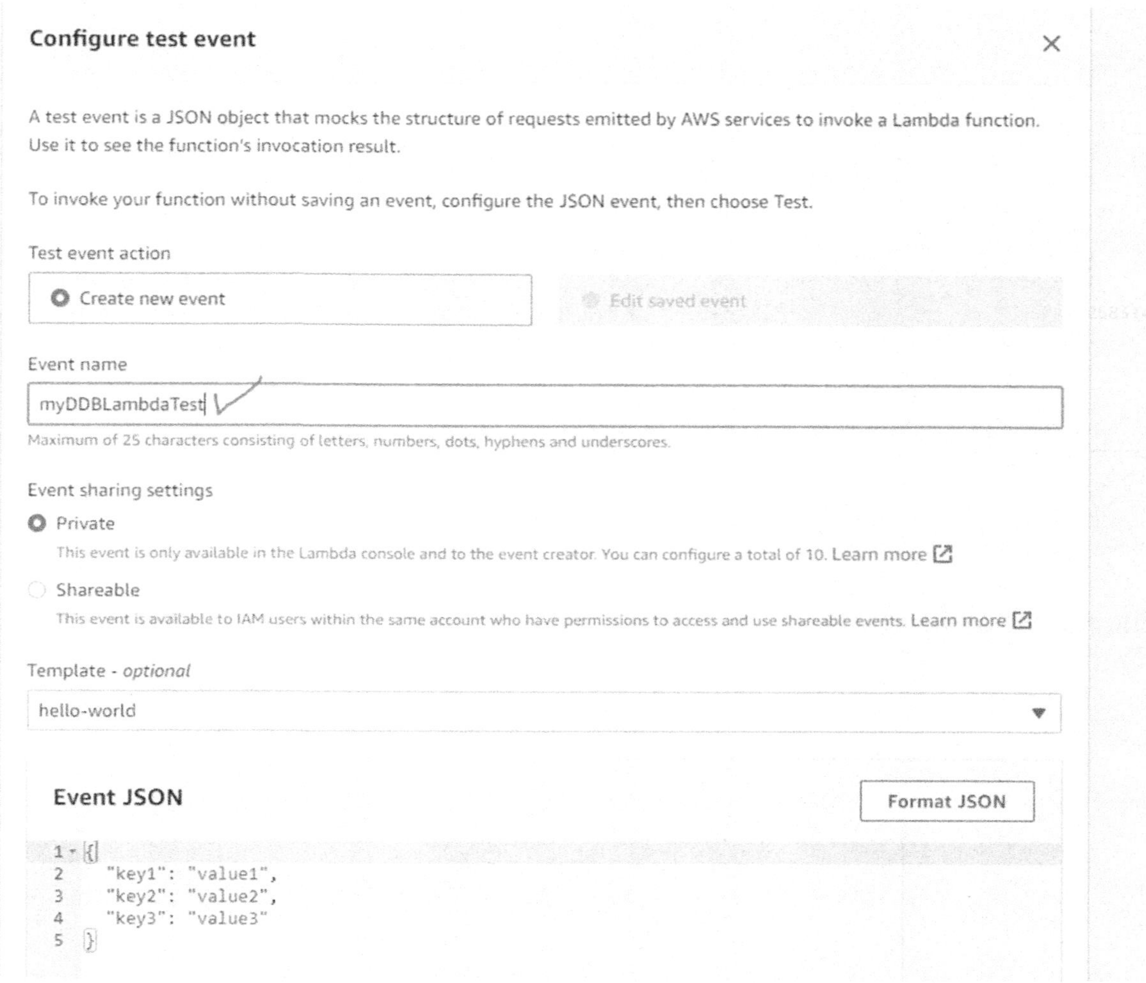

Configure test event
A test event is a JSON object that mocks the structure of requests emitted by AWS services to invoke a Lambda function. Use it to see the function's invocation result.
To invoke your function without saving an event, configure the JSON event, then choose Test.
Test event action
Create new event
Edit saved event
Event name
myDDBLambdaTest
Maximum of 25 characters consisting of letters, numbers, dots, hyphens and underscores.
Event sharing settings
Private
This event is only available in the Lambda console and to the event creator. You can configure a total of 10. Learn more
Shareable
This event is available to IAM users within the same account who have permissions to access and use shareable events. Learn more
Template - optional
hello-world
Event JSON
Format JSON
{
"key1": "value1",
"key2": "value2",
"key3": "value3"
}

Now save it:

Save

You can now test your Lambda by hitting the test button.

Tools Window Test Deploy

lambda_function ×

```
import boto3

def lambda_handler(event,context):
    dynamodb = boto3.resource('dynamodb')

    table = dynamodb.Table('DDBv2_forIoT.')

    response = table.scan()
    data = response['Items']

    while 'LastEvaluatedKey' in response:
        response = table.scan(ExclusiveStartKey=response['LastEvaluatedKey'])
        data.extend(response['Items'])
    return(data)
```

The results should be nicely formatted as JSON objects of all your database items.

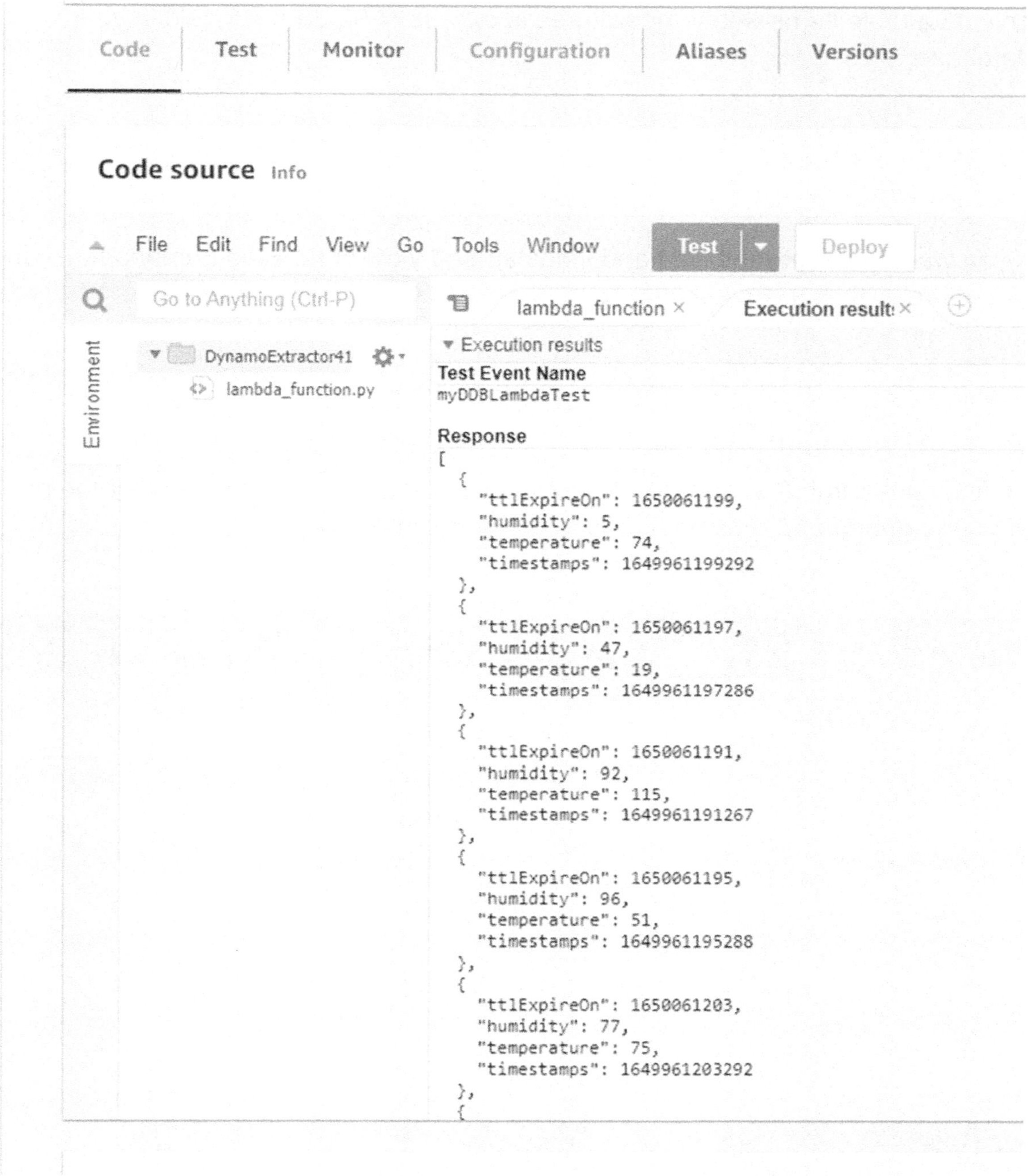
Code
Test
Monitor
Configuration
Aliases
Versions
Code source Info
File Edit Find View Go Tools Window
Test
Deploy
Go to Anything (Ctrl-P)
lambda_function
Execution result:
Environment
DynamoExtractor41
lambda_function.py
Execution results
Test Event Name
myDDBLambdaTest
Response
[
{
"ttlExpireOn": 1650061199,
"humidity": 5,
"temperature": 74,
"timestamps": 1649961199292
},
{
"ttlExpireOn": 1650061197,
"humidity": 47,
"temperature": 19,
"timestamps": 1649961197286
},
{
"ttlExpireOn": 1650061191,
"humidity": 92,
"temperature": 115,
"timestamps": 1649961191267
},
{
"ttlExpireOn": 1650061195,
"humidity": 96,
"temperature": 51,
"timestamps": 1649961195288
},
{
"ttlExpireOn": 1650061203,
"humidity": 77,
"temperature": 75,
"timestamps": 1649961203292
},
{

- If your Lambda function test return results just show an empty "[ ]" it is likely the time-to-live function has expired your data items and you will need to refill your data table.

If you wanted to do a database 'query' for specific items rather than just a 'scan' of every item in your table, you would need to adjust your Lambda function to retrieve those desired results instead. An example of a relevant query could be querying for only data table items with temperatures in excess of 90 degrees held in your database.

Step 9 – Observe the Return Values in AWS CloudWatch

If you wanted a more detailed and timestamped view of how the Lambda function executed, then you can view those logs in AWS CloudWatch found here:

https://console.aws.amazon.com/cloudwatch

To find your Lambda results in CloudWatch just search the log groups for the name of your Lambda and click on the name of your Lambda function.

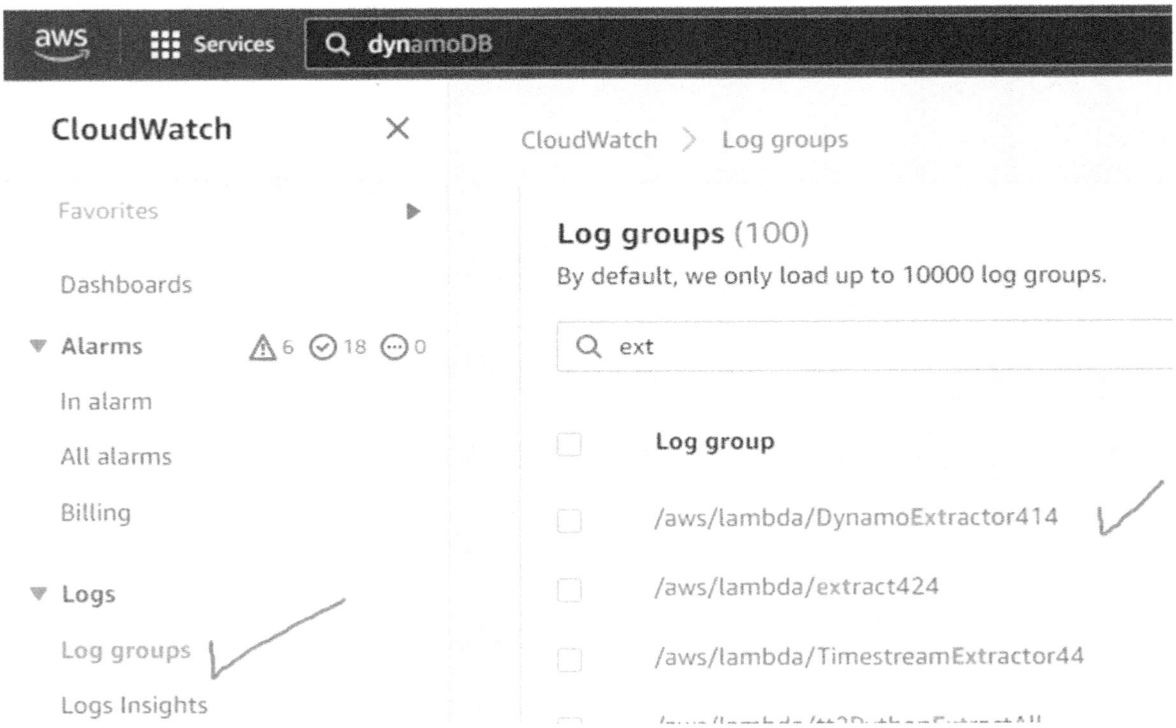
aws
Services
dynamoDB
CloudWatch
CloudWatch > Log groups
Favorites
Dashboards
Alarms 6 18 0
In alarm
All alarms
Billing
Logs
Log groups
Logs Insights
Log groups (100)
By default, we only load up to 10000 log groups.
ext
Log group
/aws/lambda/DynamoExtractor414
/aws/lambda/extract424
/aws/lambda/TimestreamExtractor44

You won't go further with CloudWatch here other than to note that it is a great debugging tool and automatically available through default permissions in the basic

Lambda execution role, so every time you run your Lambda functions a CloudWatch log is produced for every Lambda evocation. However, note that CloudWatch is not free.

Now that you know your Lambda function works and returns the expected results, you will need to generate a URL endpoint so that the results of your Lambda function can be retrieved by your static website for visualization.

Step 10 – Create a Rest API for your Lambda Function with API Gateway

AWS provides a dedicated service called API Gateway in which to create URL endpoints, not just to Lambda, but to a variety of AWS services you may need to access via a HTTP endpoint. Testing, security, and package transforms are all possible using API Gateway. For the needs of this project, you are simply going to create a "GET" request and link it to your DynamoDB extraction Lambda function. The results of invoking the API endpoint will produce the same JSON payload you observed when you tested the Lambda function in the previous section.

Note: A new and easier method is a Lambda "Function URL" which is a URL endpoint created directly from your Lambda function:

https://aws.amazon.com/blogs/aws/announcing-aws-Lambda-function-urls-built-in-https-endpoints-for-single-function-microservices/

This Lambda generated endpoint is easier to develop and can often be cheaper than an API Gateway created endpoint, however it is also less powerful and lacks many of the "bells and whistles" of the API Gateway features. For this example, I will stick with API Gateway for this chapter, but you may want to try to also compose a Function URL Lambda endpoint on your own as it should work just as well for this specific, basic use case. Even "Function URL's" from Lambda are just API Gateway created endpoints, as an abstracted underlying service, with HTTPS defaults chosen for you.

To go to API Gateway search in services box for "API Gateway" or go to:

https://console.aws.amazon.com/apigateway

- Make sure you are in the same region as your Lambda function.

Once in API Gateway, go to the upper right of the screen and select the: "Create API" button.

N. Virginia
aws
Actions
Create API

For this project you will create a REST API as it gives you the most flexibility. Select build.

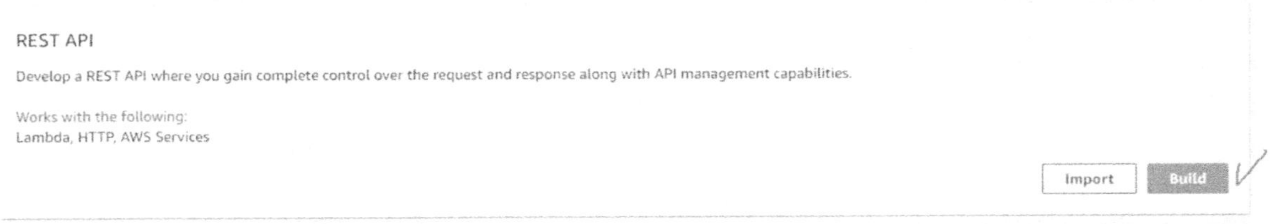
REST API
Develop a REST API where you gain complete control over the request and response along with API management capabilities.
Works with the following:
Lambda, HTTP, AWS Services
Import
Build

On the next screen you only need to provide a name for your API, the rest of the fields you can leave at the default settings. Once you provide a name for your API select the "Create API" button again.

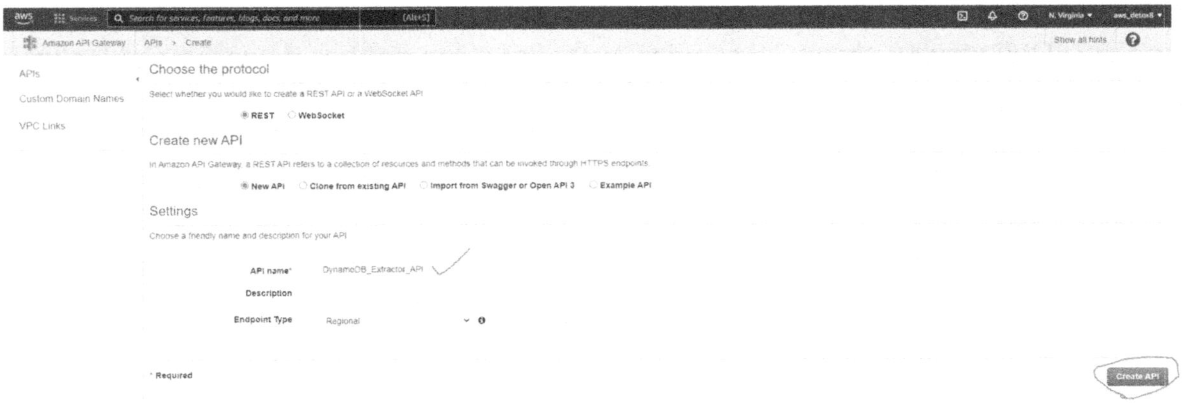
APIs
Custom Domain Names
VPC Links
Choose the protocol
REST
WebSocket
Create new API
New API
Clone from existing API
Import from Swagger or Open API 3
Example API
Settings
API name*
DynamoDB_Extractor_API
Description
Endpoint Type
Regional
* Required
Create API

Now, on the next screen navigate to the resources tab. On this screen you are going to perform several actions from the drop down "Actions" bar.

Steps to accomplish in this section

A) First "Create Method", you will be creating a GET request method.
B) Then "Enable CORS", this allows some cross-origin security.
C) Finally, "Deploy API", this creates the endpoint for use anywhere in the world.

Now to go over each action separately, as they involve some contingent sub-steps to accomplish.

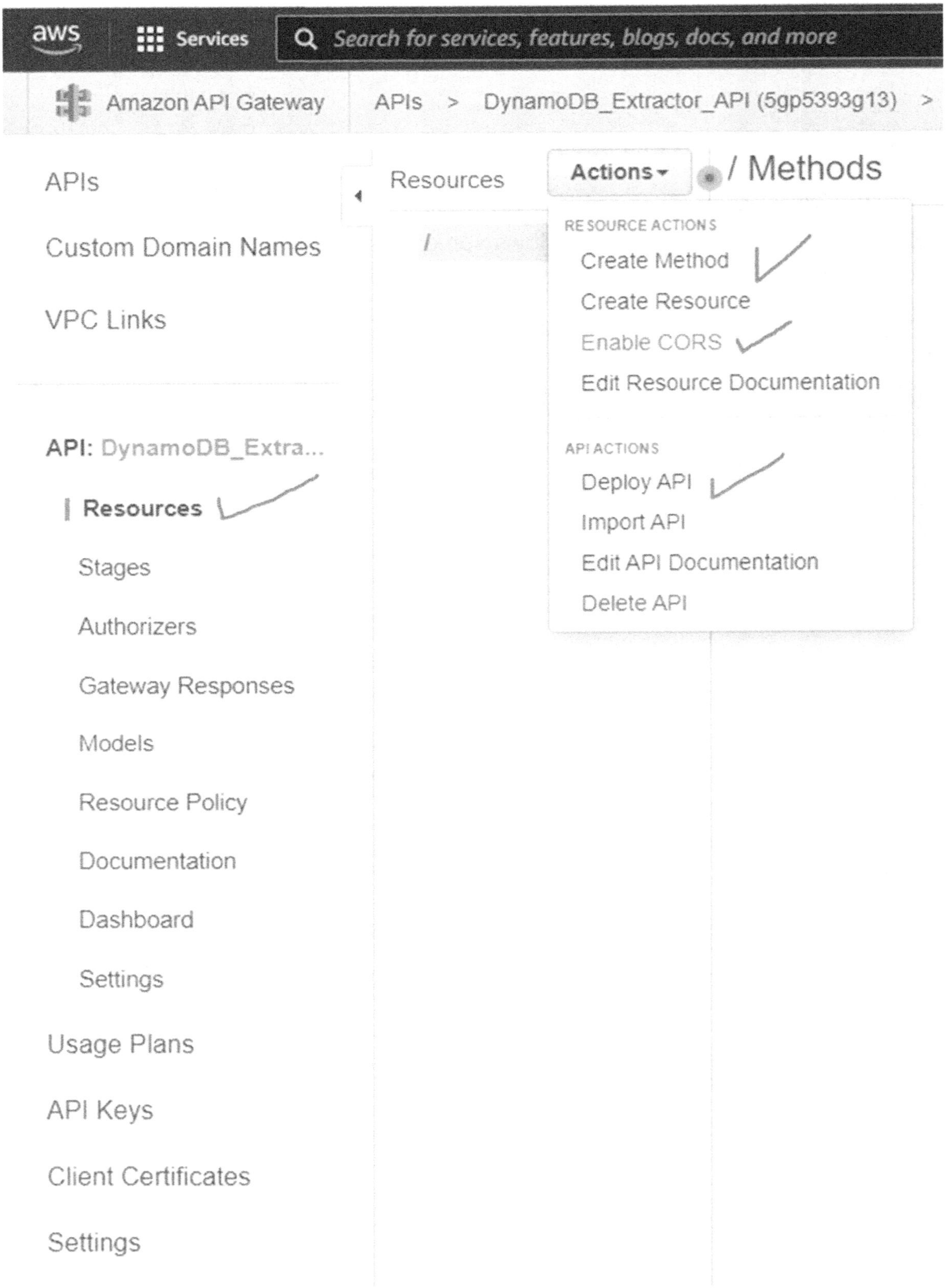
aws
Services
Search for services, features, blogs, docs, and more
Amazon API Gateway
APIs > DynamoDB_Extractor_API (5gp5393g13) >
APIs
Custom Domain Names
VPC Links
API: DynamoDB_Extra...
Resources
Stages
Authorizers
Gateway Responses
Models
Resource Policy
Documentation
Dashboard
Settings
Usage Plans
API Keys
Client Certificates
Settings
Resources
Actions
/ Methods
RESOURCE ACTIONS
Create Method
Create Resource
Enable CORS
Edit Resource Documentation
API ACTIONS
Deploy API
Import API
Edit API Documentation
Delete API

First, “Create Method” and select the “GET” method and then press the checkmark button. Then you will need to link the GET request to your Lambda. To accomplish this, use the drop-down menu and search for the Lambda function you recently created to extract your DynamoDB IoT data in either Python or Node.js.

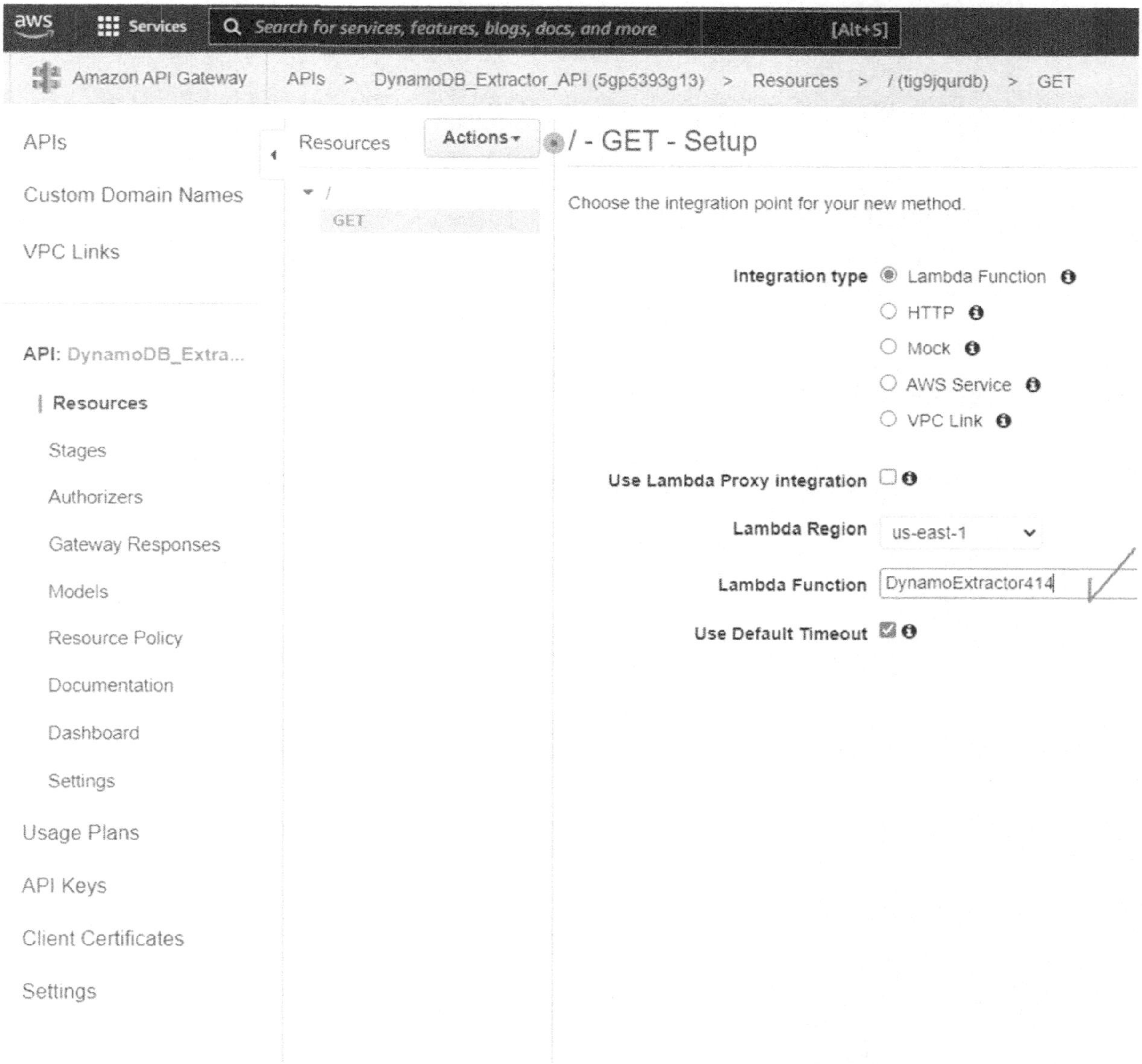
aws
Services
Search for services, features, blogs, docs, and more
[Alt+S]
Amazon API Gateway
APIs > DynamoDB_Extractor_API (5gp5393g13) > Resources > / (tig9jqurdb) > GET
APIs
Custom Domain Names
VPC Links
API: DynamoDB_Extra...
Resources
Stages
Authorizers
Gateway Responses
Models
Resource Policy
Documentation
Dashboard
Settings
Usage Plans
API Keys
Client Certificates
Settings
Resources
Actions
/
GET
/ - GET - Setup
Choose the integration point for your new method.
Integration type
Lambda Function
HTTP
Mock
AWS Service
VPC Link
Use Lambda Proxy integration
Lambda Region
us-east-1
Lambda Function
DynamoExtractor414
Use Default Timeout

On the lower right of your screen confirm the permission for API gateway to invoke your Lambda function by selecting “OK” in the permissions box.

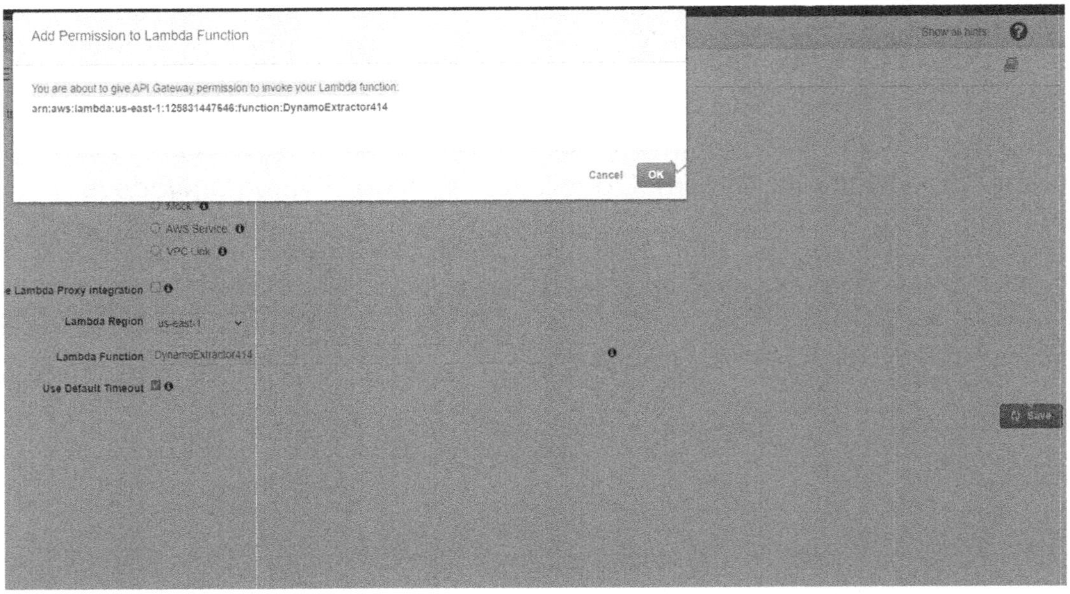
Add Permission to Lambda Function
You are about to give API Gateway permission to invoke your Lambda function:
arn:aws:lambda:us-east-1:125831447646:function:DynamoExtractor414
Cancel
OK
AWS Service
VPC Link
Lambda Proxy integration
Lambda Region
us-east-1
Lambda Function
DynamoExtractor414
Use Default Timeout
Save

Next, “Enable CORS” from the “Actions” drop down box.

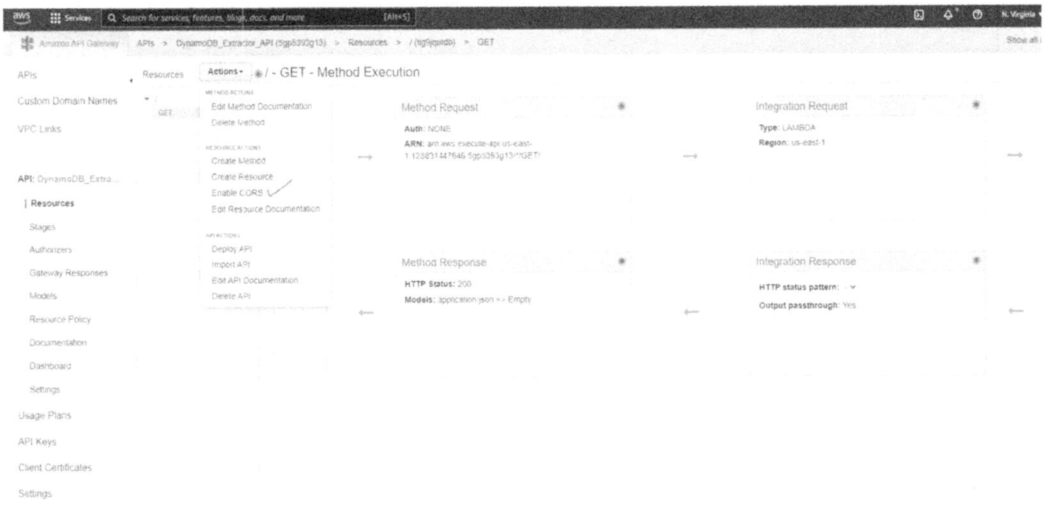
Actions
/ - GET - Method Execution
APIs
Custom Domain Names
VPC Links
Resources
Stages
Authorizers
Gateway Responses
Models
Resource Policy
Documentation
Dashboard
Settings
Usage Plans
API Keys
Client Certificates
Settings
Edit Method Documentation
Delete Method
Create Method
Create Resource
Enable CORS
Edit Resource Documentation
Deploy API
Import API
Edit API Documentation
Delete API
Method Request
Integration Request
Method Response
Integration Response

In the next step you are going enable CORS. Cross-origin resource sharing (CORS) is a browser security feature that restricts cross-origin HTTP requests that are initiated from scripts running in the browser. You could also add some header controls to your Lambda function instead, but you won’t do this either. To clear out CORS out simply select all the headers and then enter space or backspace to remove them.

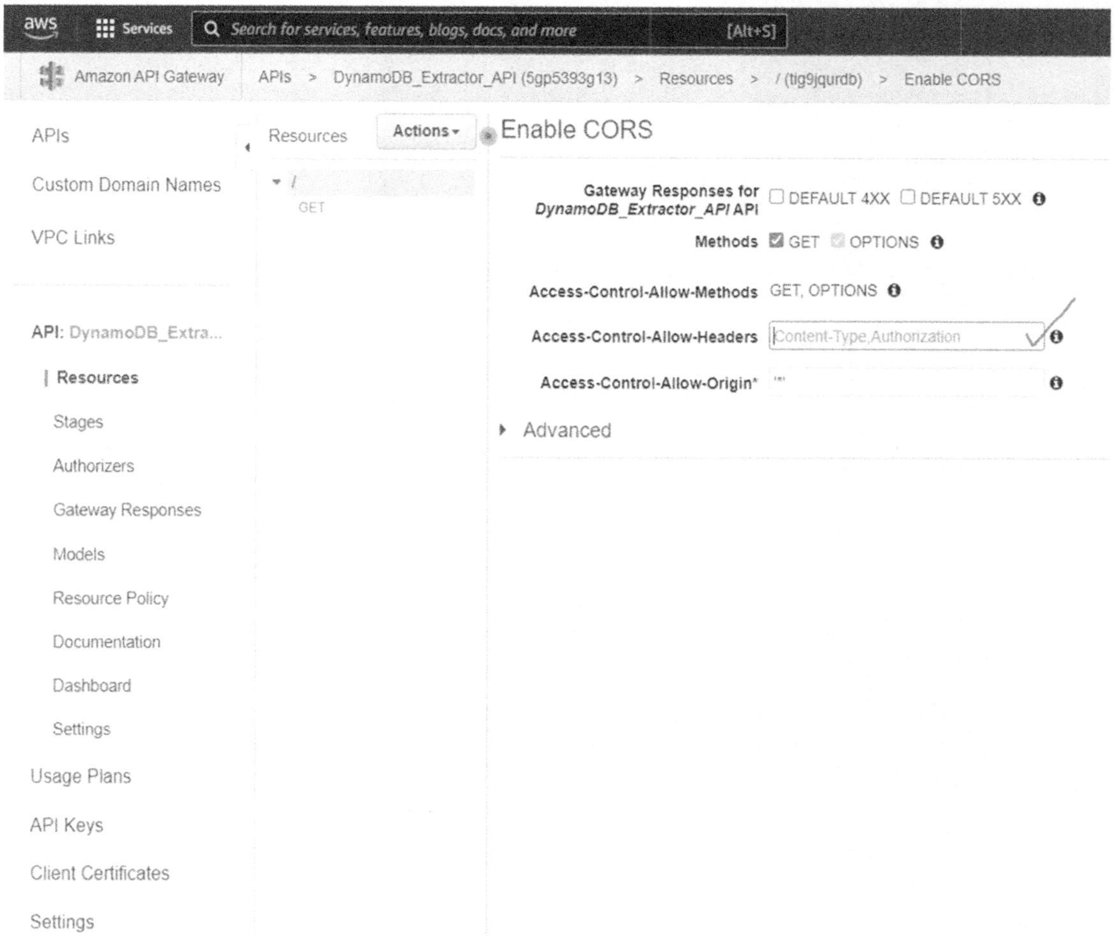
aws
Services
Search for services, features, blogs, docs, and more
[Alt+S]
Amazon API Gateway
APIs > DynamoDB_Extractor_API (5gp5393g13) > Resources > / (tig9jqurdb) > Enable CORS
APIs
Custom Domain Names
VPC Links
API: DynamoDB_Extra...
Resources
Stages
Authorizers
Gateway Responses
Models
Resource Policy
Documentation
Dashboard
Settings
Usage Plans
API Keys
Client Certificates
Settings
Resources
Actions
/
GET
Enable CORS
Gateway Responses for DynamoDB_Extractor_API API
DEFAULT 4XX
DEFAULT 5XX
Methods
GET
OPTIONS
Access-Control-Allow-Methods
GET, OPTIONS
Access-Control-Allow-Headers
Content-Type,Authorization
Access-Control-Allow-Origin*
'*'
Advanced

Then, select to enable CORS header by the long blue button on the right:

Enable CORS and replace existing CORS headers

Now conform your CORS changes to your HTTP headers.

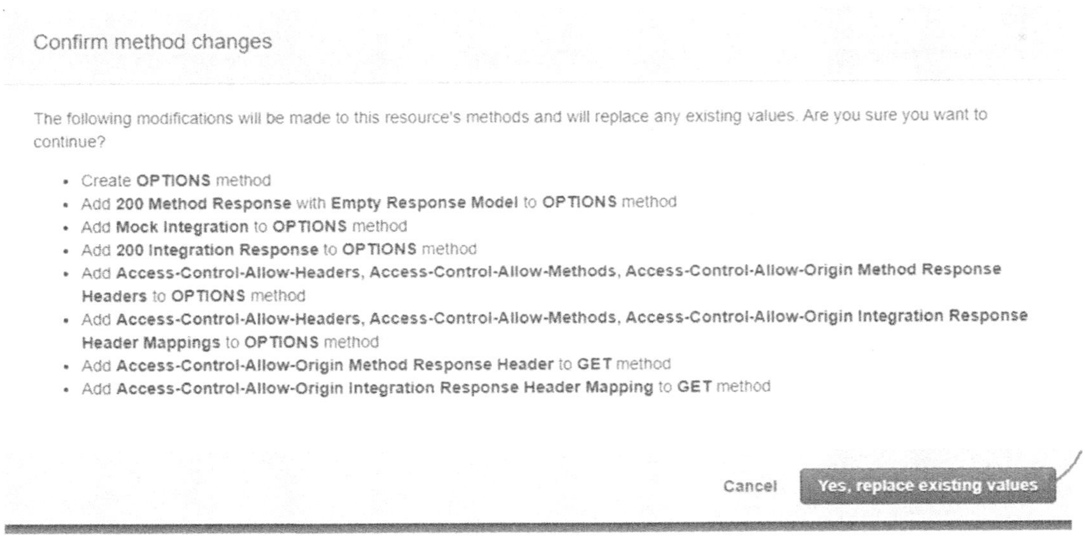
Confirm method changes
The following modifications will be made to this resource's methods and will replace any existing values. Are you sure you want to continue?
Create OPTIONS method
Add 200 Method Response with Empty Response Model to OPTIONS method
Add Mock Integration to OPTIONS method
Add 200 Integration Response to OPTIONS method
Add Access-Control-Allow-Headers, Access-Control-Allow-Methods, Access-Control-Allow-Origin Method Response Headers to OPTIONS method
Add Access-Control-Allow-Headers, Access-Control-Allow-Methods, Access-Control-Allow-Origin Integration Response Header Mappings to OPTIONS method
Add Access-Control-Allow-Origin Method Response Header to GET method
Add Access-Control-Allow-Origin Integration Response Header Mapping to GET method
Cancel
Yes, replace existing values

Now that you have changed your CORS headers, you are now able to deploy your API and receive the API Gateway endpoint. To do so return to the drop down "Action" menu and choose "Deploy API."

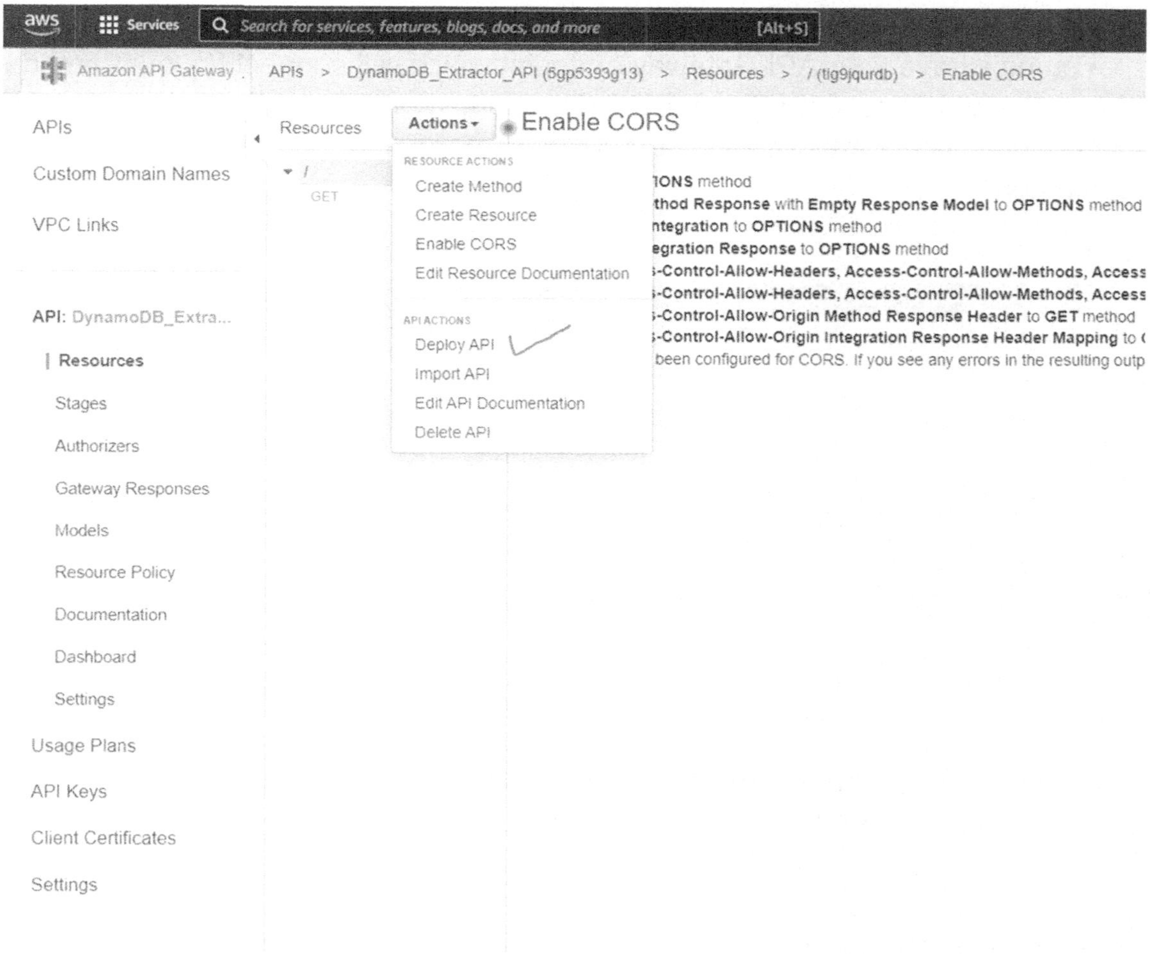
aws
Services
Search for services, features, blogs, docs, and more
[Alt+S]
Amazon API Gateway
APIs > DynamoDB_Extractor_API (5gp5393g13) > Resources > / (tig9jqurdb) > Enable CORS
APIs
Custom Domain Names
VPC Links
API: DynamoDB_Extra...
Resources
Stages
Authorizers
Gateway Responses
Models
Resource Policy
Documentation
Dashboard
Settings
Usage Plans
API Keys
Client Certificates
Settings
Resources
Actions
Enable CORS
RESOURCE ACTIONS
Create Method
Create Resource
Enable CORS
Edit Resource Documentation
API ACTIONS
Deploy API
Import API
Edit API Documentation
Delete API

You will deploy to a ‘New stage’ and call it “prod”, now select the “Deploy” button:

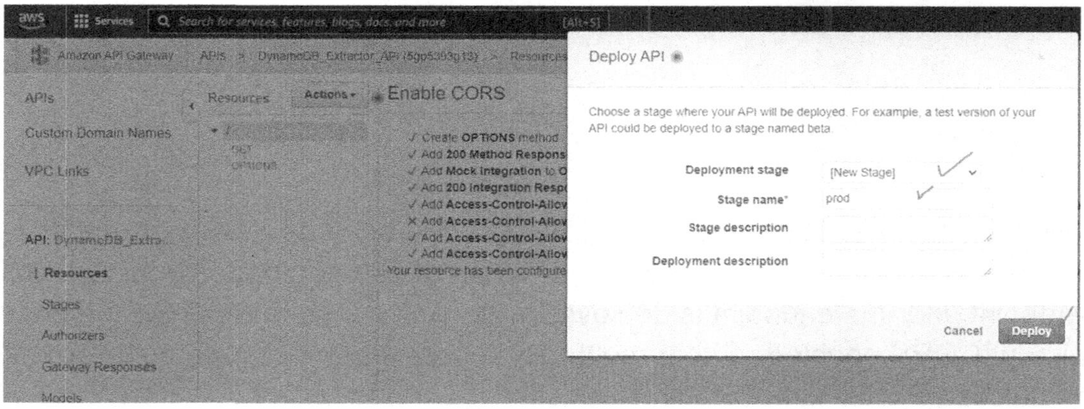
Deploy API
Choose a stage where your API will be deployed. For example, a test version of your API could be deployed to a stage named beta.
Deployment stage
[New Stage]
Stage name*
prod
Stage description
Deployment description
Cancel
Deploy

You now have your API Gateway endpoint which will connect to your Lambda function to extract your DynamoDB data from your data table. To see your HTTPS endpoint, select the "Stages" tab on the left pane and then select your "Get" method.

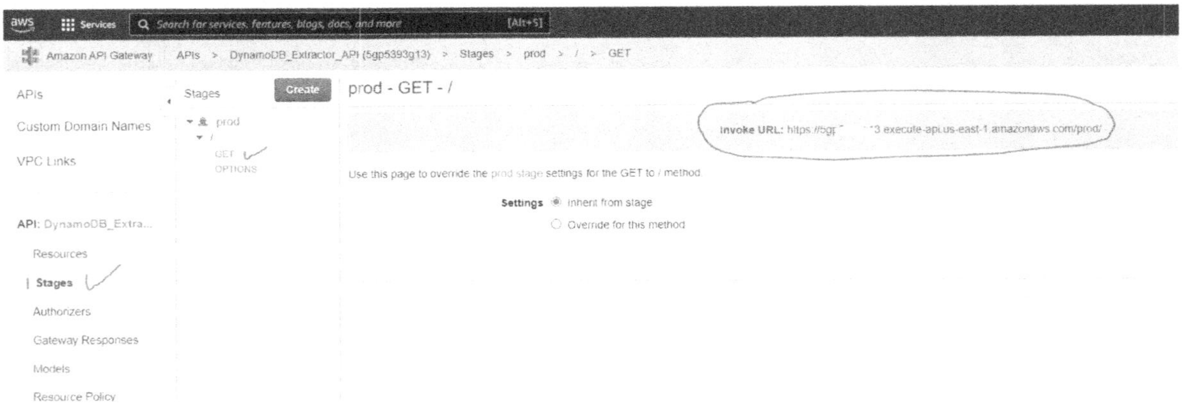
aws
Services
Search for services, features, blogs, docs, and more
[Alt+S]
Amazon API Gateway
APIs > DynamoDB_Extractor_API (5gp5393g13) > Stages > prod > / > GET
APIs
Custom Domain Names
VPC Links
Stages
Create
prod
GET
OPTIONS
prod - GET - /
Use this page to override the prod stage settings for the GET to / method
Settings
Inherit from stage
Override for this method
API: DynamoDB_Extra...
Resources
Stages
Authorizers
Gateway Responses
Models
Resource Policy

- Make sure to keep your new endpoint a secret or someone could continually access your DynamoDB scanning Lambda function and run up your bill.

As a last step you will want to test your endpoint within the API Gateway service before you use it in your static website dashboard visualization. To test it, simply either select the endpoint or right click the endpoint to open it in a new tab on your browser.

Here are the results for my ten readings from the database.

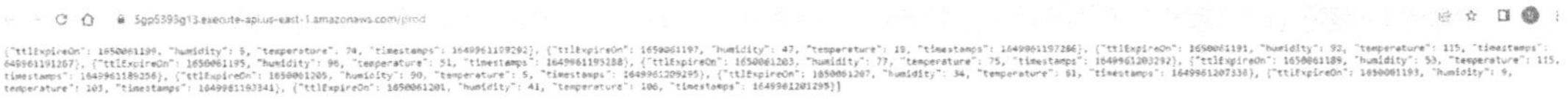

If your readings do not appear and you get a "Forbidden Exception" error on your browser and are unable to access you DynamoDB data through your API Gateway endpoint after the endpoint is deployed, you can choose to redeploy the endpoint without CORS enabled. Either method is OK for non-production use. Do not move on unless your DynamoDB items appear in your bowser window from the provided endpoint URL.

There is also a test function in the “Resources” tab of API Gateway (which looks like a lightning bolt). The built-in test function is useful if you have not deployed your API yet.

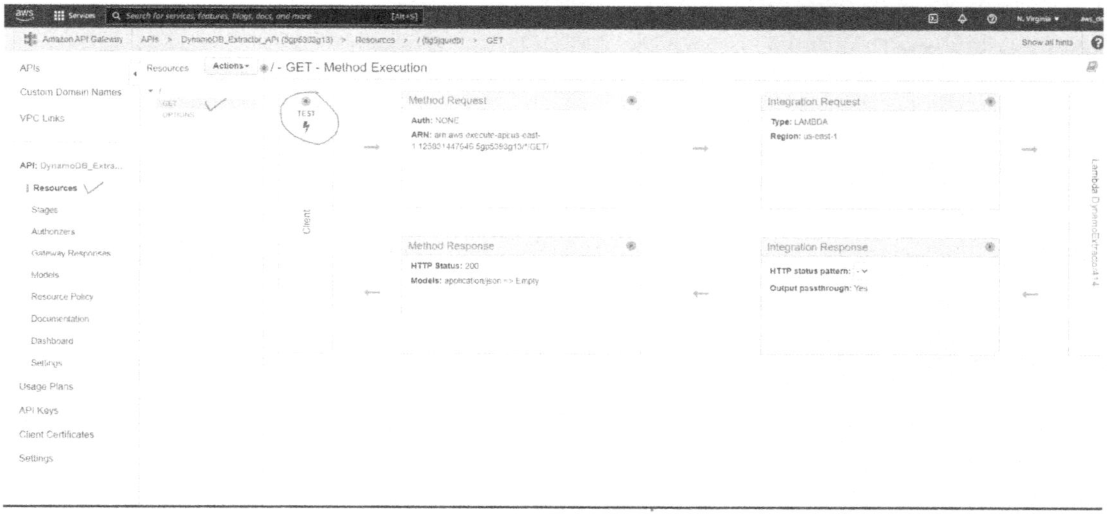
Amazon API Gateway
APIs
Custom Domain Names
VPC Links
Resources
Stages
Authorizers
Models
Resource Policy
Documentation
Dashboard
Settings
Usage Plans
API Keys
Client Certificates
Settings
Actions
/ - GET - Method Execution
TEST
Method Request
Auth: NONE
Integration Request
Type: LAMBDA
Region: us-east-1
Client
Method Response
HTTP Status: 200
Integration Response
Output passthrough: Yes

This should return the same scan results as those seen above in your browser but without the endpoint having to be “deployed”.

Step 11 – Create a Static Website in S3 for Visualization of the DynamoDB IoT Sensor Readings

Following the directions in the prerequisite chapter on creating an S3 bucket and a static website you can now upload the “index.html” webpage below to your S3 bucket. This webpage will use the API Gateway generated endpoint to invoke the Lambda function which returns the results from scanning the entire DynamoDB table. The only thing you need to do is fill in the following field in the below index.html page with the API Gateway generated endpoint that you just created:

```
x.open(“GET”,”<YOUR-API-GATEWAY-ENDPOINT-HERE>”, true);
```

After configuring the code with your own API Gateway URL, upload the code below as ‘*index.html*’ into the S3 bucket with and enabled static webhost that you just created.

```
<!DOCTYPE html>
<html lang="en">
<head>
  <meta charset="UTF-8">
  <meta name="viewport" content="width=device-width, initial-scale=1.0">
  <meta http-equiv="X-UA-Compatible" content="ie=edge">
  <title>Enviro Charts from DDB</title>
</head>
<body>
  <!-Latest compiled and minified CSS ->
  <link rel="stylesheet"
href="https://maxcdn.bootstrapcdn.com/bootstrap/3.3.7/css/bootstrap.min.css"
integrity="sha384-
BVYiiSIFeK1dGmJRAkycuHAHRg32OmUcww7on3Rydg4Va+PmSTsz/K68vbdEjh4u"
    crossorigin="anonymous">

  <script src="https://code.highcharts.com/highcharts.js"></script>

  <div class="container">

    <div class="row">
        <div class="col-sm-6"><h1>Dashboard</h1></div>
        <div class="col-sm-6" style="margin-top: 25px">
            <button id="fetch" class="btn btn-primary">Fetch</button>
            <span id="indicator" style="display: none;">Fetching...</span>
        </div>
      </div>

    <div class="panel panel-info">
      <div class="panel-heading">
        <h3 class="panel-title">
          <strong>Line Chart</strong>
        </h3>
      </div>
      <div class="panel-body">
        <div id="container1"></div>
      </div>
    </div>


    <div class="panel panel-info">
      <div class="panel-heading">
        <h3 class="panel-title">
          <strong>Bar Chart</strong>
```

```
        </h3>
      </div>
      <div class="panel-body">
        <div id="container"></div>
      </div>
    </div>
  </div>
  <script>

    window.onload = function exampleFunction() {

      document.getElementById('fetch').addEventListener('click',
fetchDDBData)

      function fetchDDBData() {
        document.getElementById('indicator').style.display = 'inline';
        var x = new XMLHttpRequest();

        // API Gateway Example:
        x.open("GET","<YOUR-API-GATEWAY-ENDPOINT-HERE>", true);
        ///----------------------////
        x.onreadystatechange = function () {
          if (x.readyState == 4 && x.status == 200) {
            let abcData = JSON.parse(x.responseText)
            // sort data based on timestamps
            abcData = abcData.sort((a,b) => a.timestamps - b.timestamps);
            let barGraphXaxisName = ['Humidity', 'Temperature'];
            let humiditySum = 0, temperatureSum = 0, timestampsSum = 0;
            let lineXaxisData = [], humArr = [], tempArr = [], 329sar = [];
            for (let I = 0; I < abcData.length; i++) {
              (humiditySum += Number(abcData[i].humidity)/abcData.length);
              (temperatureSum +=
Number(abcData[i].temperature)/abcData.length);

              var timestamp = Number(abcData[i].timestamps)
              var date = new Date(timestamp);
              console.log(date.getTime())
              console.log(date)

             humArr.push(Number(abcData[i].humidity));  //humidity
             tempArr.push(Number(abcData[i].temperature));
             329sar.push(date);  //date on X-Axis

            }
```

```
// round number up to twp decimal number for bar chart
humiditySum = Math.round(humiditySum * 100) / 100;
temperatureSum = Math.round(temperatureSum* 100) / 100;

Highcharts.chart('container', {
  chart: {
    type: 'column'
  },
  title: {
    text: 'Bar Chart'
  },
  xAxis: {
    categories: barGraphXaxisName
  },
  yAxis: {
    title: {
      text: 'Value'
    }
  },
  tooltip: {
formatter: function() {
    return this.x + ' average ' + this.y;
}
},
  series: [{
    data: [humiditySum, temperatureSum],
    name: "Temperature and Humidity Averages"
  }],

  responsive: {
    rules: [{
      condition: {
        maxWidth: 500
      },
      chartOptions: {
        chart: {
          className: 'small-chart'
        }
      }
    }]
  }
});

Highcharts.chart('container1', {
```

```
title: {
  text: 'Line chart'
},

yAxis: {
  title: {
    text: 'Value'
  }
},

xAxis: {
  categories: 331sar
},

legend: {
  layout: 'vertical',
  align: 'right',
  verticalAlign: 'middle'
},

plotOptions: {
  series: {
    label: {
      connectorAllowed: false
    }
  }
},
series: [{
  name: 'Humdity',
  data: humArr
}, {
  name: 'Temperature',
  data: tempArr
}],

responsive: {
  rules: [{
    condition: {
      maxWidth: 500
    },
    chartOptions: {
      legend: {
        layout: 'horizontal',
        align: 'center',
        verticalAlign: 'bottom'
```

```
                    }
                  }
                }]
              }
            });

            document.getElementById('indicator').style.display = 'none';
          }
        }
        x.send(null);
      }
    }
  </script>
</body>
</html>
```

I uploaded the index.html to my new bucket called "ddb4indexonly" which I configured to host a static website. Now open your web page by selecting to the index.html page by using the 'Object URL' as show below:

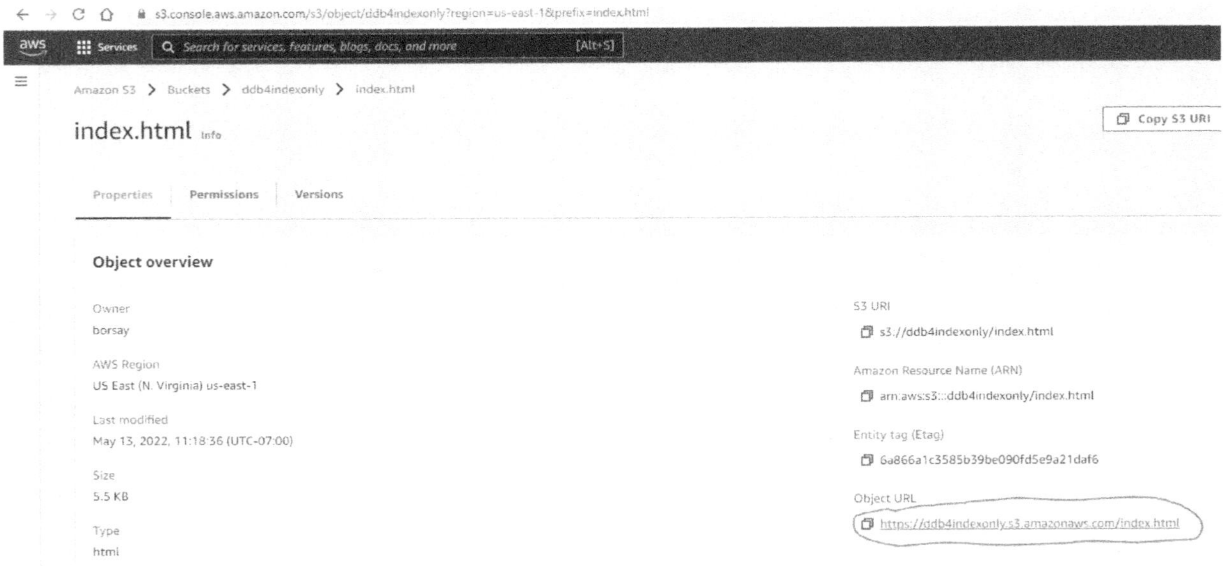

s3.console.aws.amazon.com/s3/object/ddb4indexonly?region=us-east-1&prefix=index.html
Services
Search for services, features, blogs, docs, and more
[Alt+S]
Amazon S3 > Buckets > ddb4indexonly > index.html
index.html Info
Copy S3 URI
Properties
Permissions
Versions
Object overview
Owner
borsay
AWS Region
US East (N. Virginia) us-east-1
Last modified
May 13, 2022, 11:18:36 (UTC-07:00)
Size
5.5 KB
Type
html
S3 URI
s3://ddb4indexonly/index.html
Amazon Resource Name (ARN)
arn:aws:s3:::ddb4indexonly/index.html
Entity tag (Etag)
6a866a1c3585b39be090fd5e9a21daf6
Object URL
https://ddb4indexonly.s3.amazonaws.com/index.html

Upon opening the index.html page the visualization should appear with your environmental readings.

One thing worth noting is that DynamoDB "*does not intend to support ordering in its scan operations*", thus the JavaScript code uses a sort() function:

```
abcData = abcData.sort((a,b) => a.timestamps - b.timestamps);
```

You could have also opted to sort the database items in the Lambda function instead, although that would have added to the runtime in Lambda instead of on the static webpage which could result in a slightly high expense.

The resulting visualization should appear like the image below:

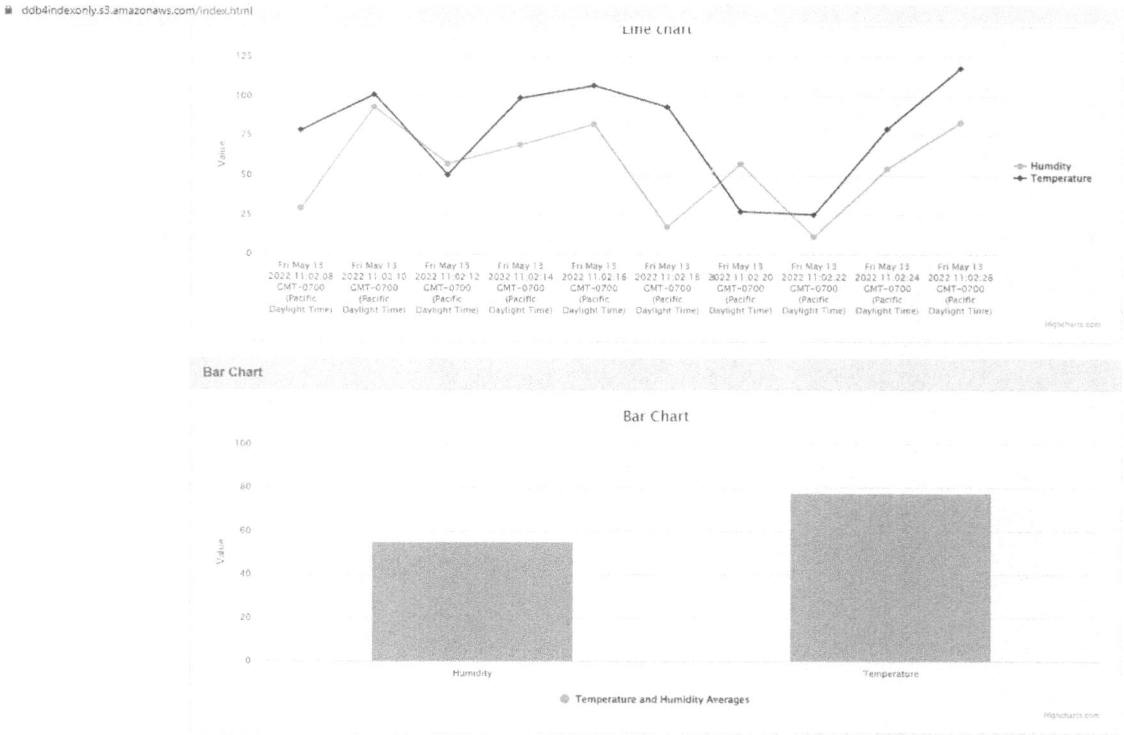

ddb4indexonly.s3.amazonaws.com/index.html
Line chart
Value
125
100
75
50
25
0
Fri May 13 2022 11:02:08 GMT-0700 (Pacific Daylight Time)
Fri May 13 2022 11:02:10 GMT-0700 (Pacific Daylight Time)
Fri May 13 2022 11:02:12 GMT-0700 (Pacific Daylight Time)
Fri May 13 2022 11:02:14 GMT-0700 (Pacific Daylight Time)
Fri May 13 2022 11:02:16 GMT-0700 (Pacific Daylight Time)
Fri May 13 2022 11:02:18 GMT-0700 (Pacific Daylight Time)
Fri May 13 2022 11:02:20 GMT-0700 (Pacific Daylight Time)
Fri May 13 2022 11:02:22 GMT-0700 (Pacific Daylight Time)
Fri May 13 2022 11:02:24 GMT-0700 (Pacific Daylight Time)
Fri May 13 2022 11:02:26 GMT-0700 (Pacific Daylight Time)
Humidity
Temperature
Bar Chart
Bar Chart
Value
100
80
60
40
20
0
Humidity
Temperature
Temperature and Humidity Averages

Remember to use (CNTL+SHIFT+I) in Chrome or (CNTL+Shift+J) in most other browsers to open the browsers developer console for debugging any JavaScript problems on your webpage.

Congratulations, you have filled the Dynamo database with IoT data, set the DDB table to expire old data to save costs, used a Lambda function to extract the Dynamo IoT data, created an API gateway Rest API to extract the DDB data, and designed a website visualization for the current items in the database.

A logical next step would be changing the Lambda function *scan* to a Lambda function *query* to bring up custom items, rather than all the IoT sensor readings from the data table to visualize on your webpage.

Chapter 16 -
AWS Timestream for IoT

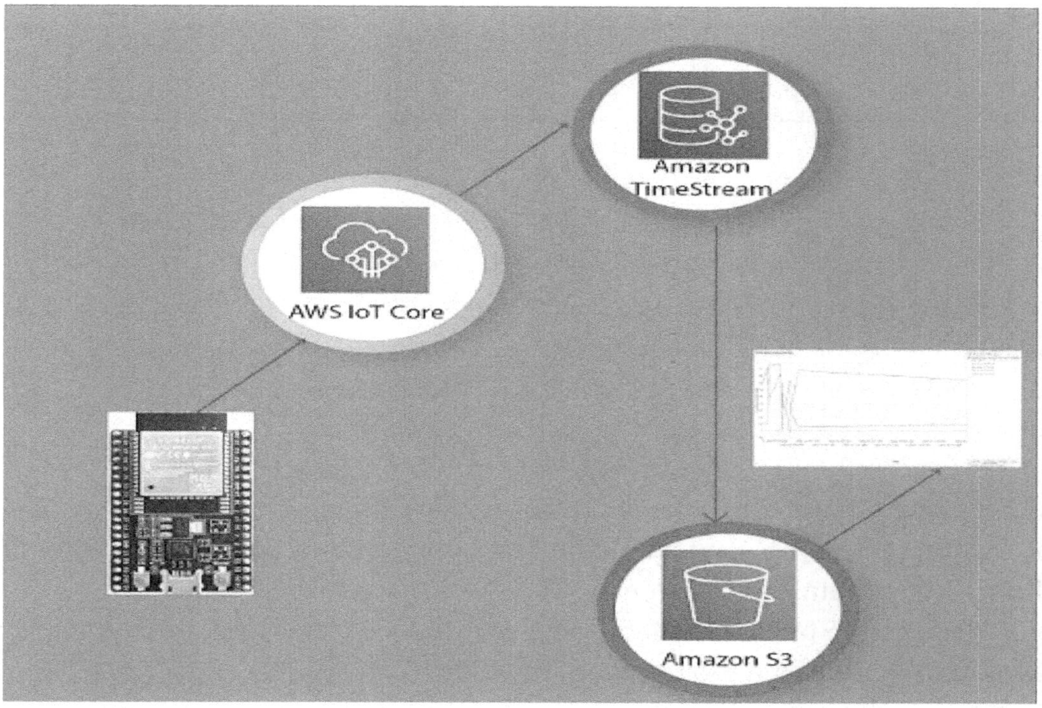

Amazon TimeStream
AWS IoT Core
Amazon S3

AWS Timestream is a fast, scalable, and serverless time series database service which provides functionality specifically applicable to IoT data. Timestream aims to overcome the limitations of relational DBs in analyzing time-series data, given that traditional RDB's lack the capacity to store and retrieve data by time intervals. Does this always make Timestream the best database choice for IoT? No, there are plenty of articles covering the pros and cons of Timestream vs. DynamoDB, as well as other database offerings on AWS. However, Timestream is a worthwhile option to explore for using IoT data with a time-series database integrated with IoT Core.

For this chapter we are mainly concerned with a typical, if simplified, IoT design flow for Timestream which will accomplish tasks similar to those we accomplished previously with DynamoDB, but with Timestream specific architecture. The following steps will be covered the in this chapter.

Amazon TimeStream

Step 1 – Create a Timestream Rule
Step 2 – Develop a Timestream Database and Data Table for IoT Data
Step 3 – Populate the Timestream Table with IoT Data
Step 4 – Test the Built-In Timestream Analytical Functions with AWS Athena Like SQL Queries
Step 5 – Configure a Timestream Connector to Grafana
Step 6 – Visualize the Timestream IoT Data in Grafana
Step 7 – Visualize the Timestream IoT Data in AWS QuickSight
Step 8 – Design a Lambda Function to Query the Timestream IoT Data
Step 9 – Develop a HTTP Endpoint as a Lambda Function URL to Access the IoT Data from Timestream on an External Website
Step 10 – Deploy a Static Website in S3 Using the Function URL to Query the Timestream IoT Data from the Lambda Function

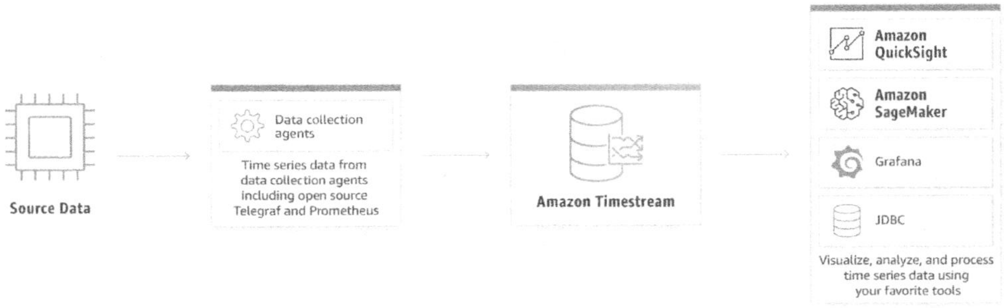
Source Data
Data collection agents
Time series data from data collection agents including open source Telegraf and Prometheus
Amazon Timestream
Amazon QuickSight
Amazon SageMaker
Grafana
JDBC
Visualize, analyze, and process time series data using your favorite tools

Step 1 – Create a Timestream Rule

Not all regions support AWS Timestream so make sure your preferred AWS region has the Timestream database available.

Go to AWS IoT Core:

https://console.aws.amazon.com/iot

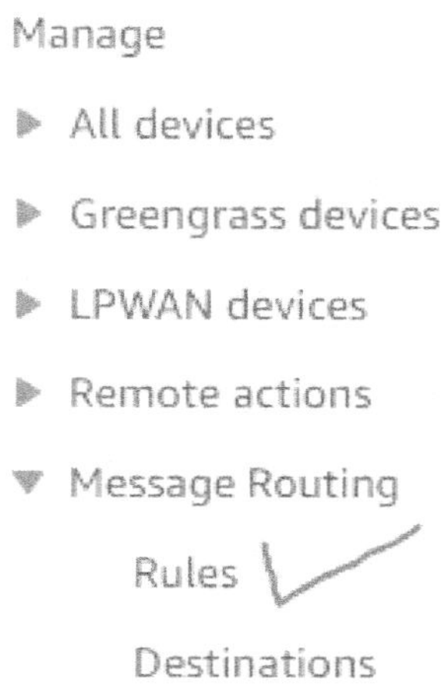
Manage
All devices
Greengrass devices
LPWAN devices
Remote actions
Message Routing
Rules
Destinations

Now create an "Rule" in IoT Core which you have done multiple times by now. Give the new Rule any name you like and set the Rules Query Statement for your rule to be:

```
SELECT temperature, humidity FROM 'iot/#'
```

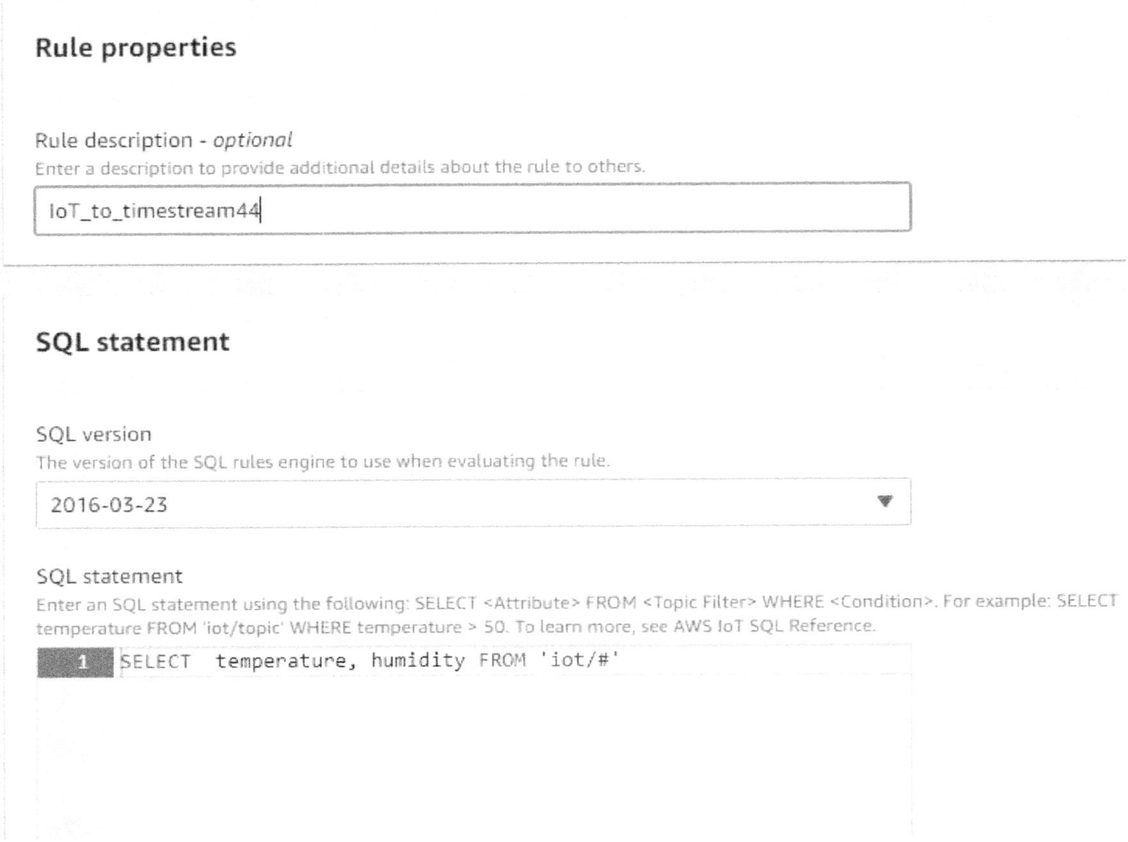
Rule properties
Rule description - optional
Enter a description to provide additional details about the rule to others.
IoT_to_timestream44
SQL statement
SQL version
The version of the SQL rules engine to use when evaluating the rule.
2016-03-23
SQL statement
Enter an SQL statement using the following: SELECT <Attribute> FROM <Topic Filter> WHERE <Condition>. For example: SELECT temperature FROM 'iot/topic' WHERE temperature > 50. To learn more, see AWS IoT SQL Reference.
1 SELECT temperature, humidity FROM 'iot/#'

The RQS may seem odd compared to what you have done before, but that is because Timestream has some unique features. One of these features you used previously is that the RQS automatically adds a timestamp to the IoT JSON payload with a built-in function. However, for the Timestream service a time is automatically added in the data table. For this reason, you do not need to send it a device side timestamp generated by the RQS unless you want a UNIX/Epoch timestamp specifically enumerated on the data table.

Now Select “Next”:

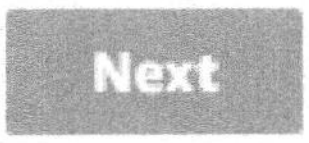
Next

Now you are ready for the net step.

Step 2 – Develop a Timestream Database and Data Table for IoT Data

Now you must create and configure your Timestream database and create a table within the Timestream database to hold your IoT data. To do this select "Create Timestream database" as a 'rule action'. This should open another tab in which you can create your database and then your data table. Leave the Timestream screen open and you will return to IoT core to finish your rule after you create the Timestream Database and table.

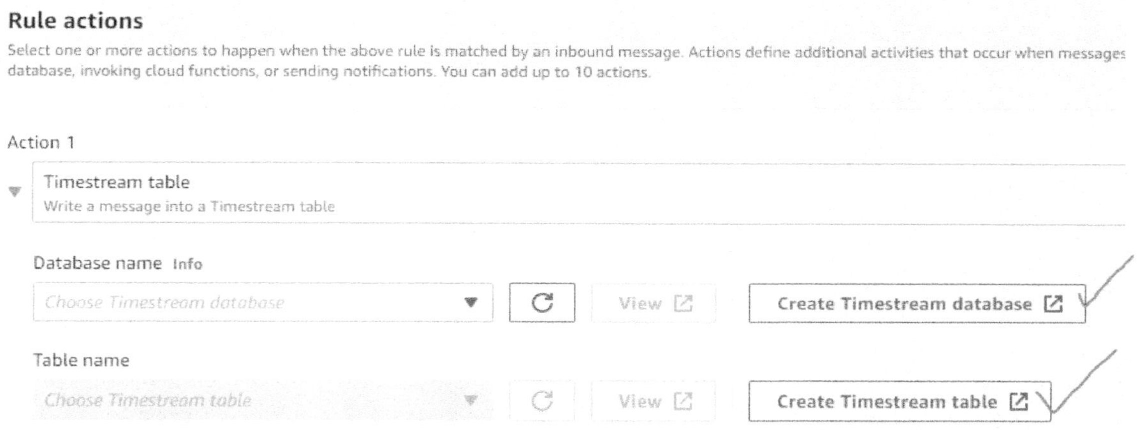
Rule actions
Select one or more actions to happen when the above rule is matched by an inbound message. Actions define additional activities that occur when messages
database, invoking cloud functions, or sending notifications. You can add up to 10 actions.
Action 1
Timestream table
Write a message into a Timestream table
Database name Info
Choose Timestream database
View
Create Timestream database
Table name
Choose Timestream table
View
Create Timestream table

For your database, give it any name you like, and choose "Standard database" for the configuration. Timestream allows for a couple of sample databases that can be filled with pre-structured sample data. These sample databases are useful for experimentation and learning how to structure queries on your data tables, but you will not use these here. For this chapter you can just use the "Standard database" configuration with no encryption. Leave the KMS encryption field blank or use the pre-populated 'aws/timestream' statement inserted by default.

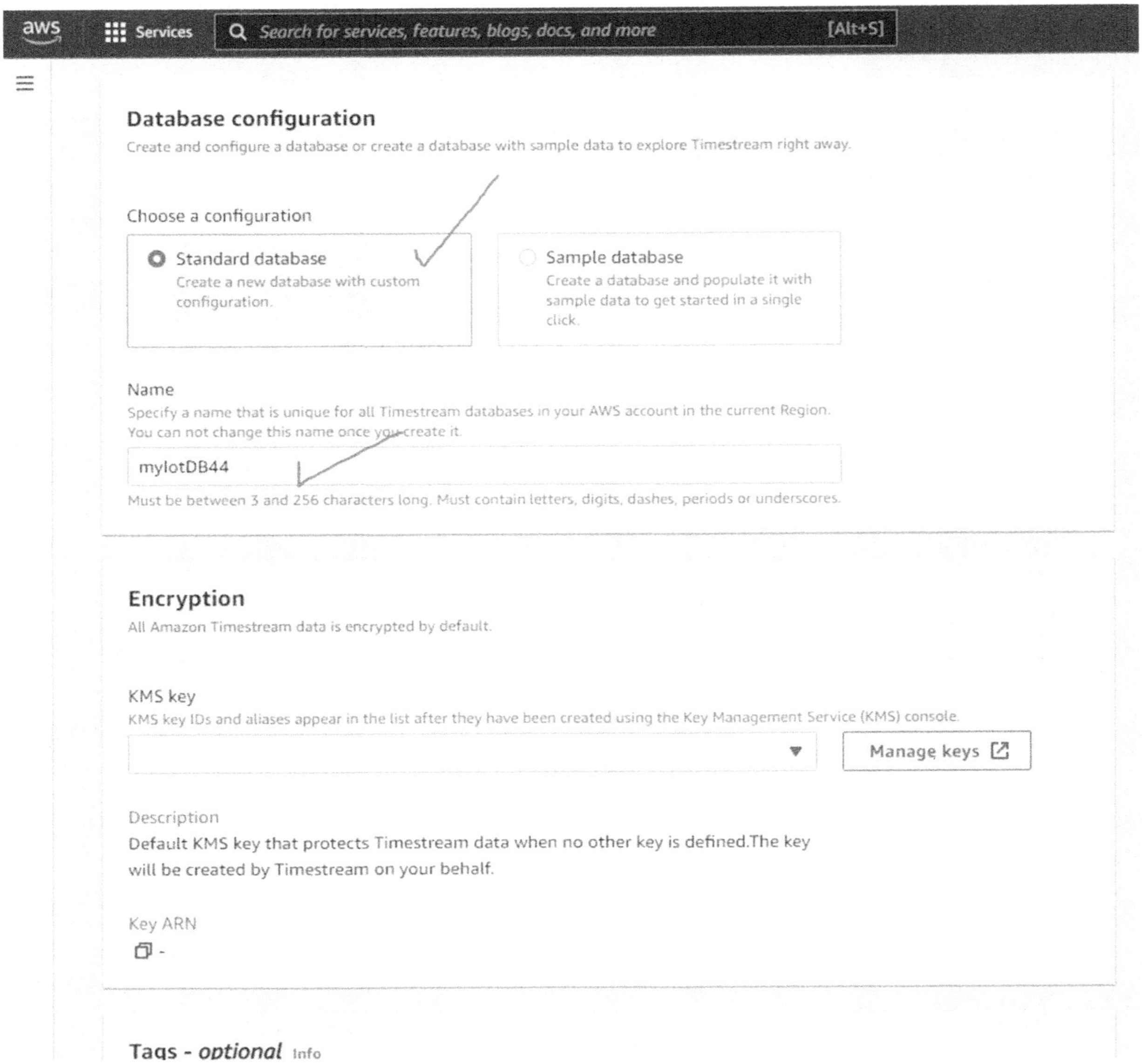
aws
Services
Search for services, features, blogs, docs, and more
[Alt+S]
Database configuration
Create and configure a database or create a database with sample data to explore Timestream right away.
Choose a configuration
Standard database
Create a new database with custom configuration.
Sample database
Create a database and populate it with sample data to get started in a single click.
Name
Specify a name that is unique for all Timestream databases in your AWS account in the current Region. You can not change this name once you create it.
myIotDB44
Must be between 3 and 256 characters long. Must contain letters, digits, dashes, periods or underscores.
Encryption
All Amazon Timestream data is encrypted by default.
KMS key
KMS key IDs and aliases appear in the list after they have been created using the Key Management Service (KMS) console.
Manage keys
Description
Default KMS key that protects Timestream data when no other key is defined.The key will be created by Timestream on your behalf.
Key ARN
Tags - optional Info

On the next field choose to “Create database”:

Cancel
Create database

Now that your Timestream database is created you must create a data table within your new database to hold your IoT data. To do this on the next screen select the

"Tables" tab on the left-hand side of the screen, or in IoT Core, select the "Create Timestream table" button.

Amazon Timestream
Databases
Tables
Scheduled queries New
Query editor
Monitoring
Tutorials
Timestream > Databases
Databases (1)
Filter
Name
Creation time (UTC)
myIotDB44
4/4/2022, 11:32:47 PM

On the next screen you can use the "Create table" to create a table within your new database.

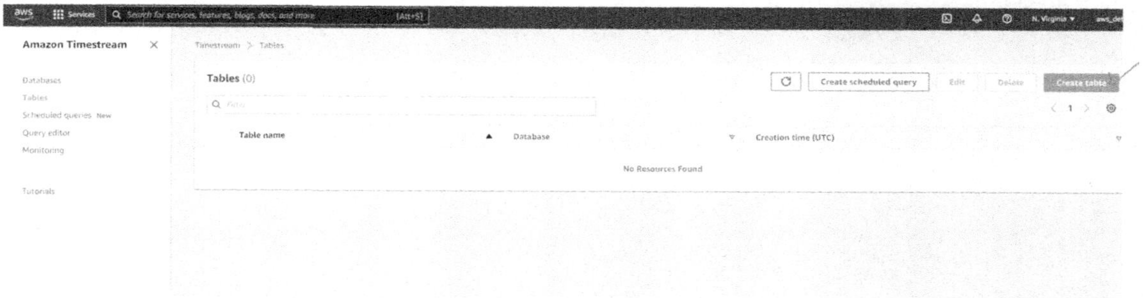
Amazon Timestream
Tables (0)
Create scheduled query
Create table
Table name
Database
Creation time (UTC)
No Resources Found

Going to the next screen you must choose which database you are creating your data table in. Of course, this will be the database you just created. Next, you need to choose a retention period for your data items. Remember the larger your database, and the longer you retain data in your data table, the more it will cost. However, you always have the option of deleting your database and data tables before the retention period expires. In the configuration below I choose three months for both fields, but you can choose a shorter time if you don't want to remember to manually destroy your database and data table when you are done.

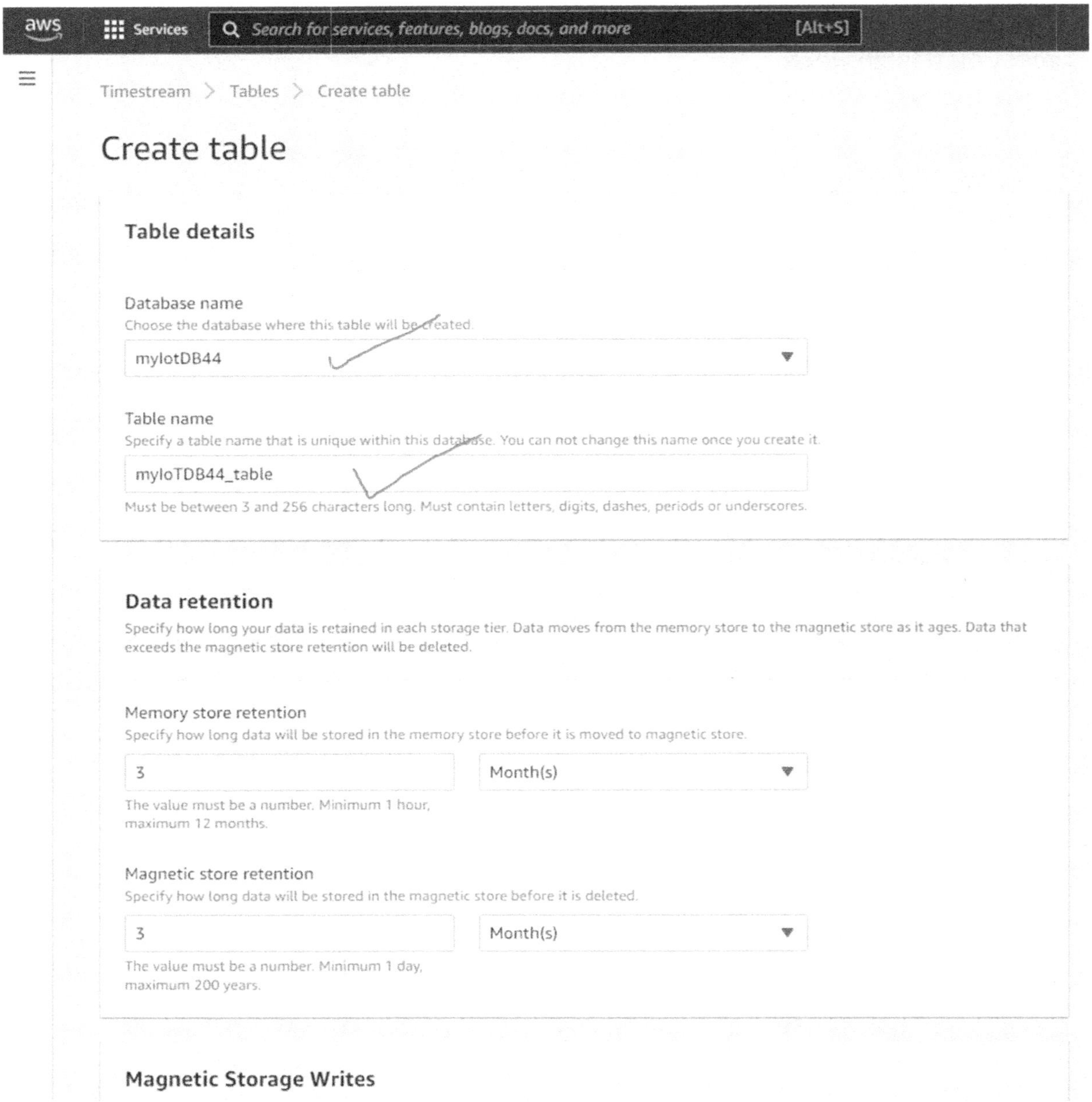
aws
Services
Search for services, features, blogs, docs, and more
[Alt+S]
Timestream > Tables > Create table
Create table
Table details
Database name
Choose the database where this table will be created.
myIotDB44
Table name
Specify a table name that is unique within this database. You can not change this name once you create it.
myIoTDB44_table
Must be between 3 and 256 characters long. Must contain letters, digits, dashes, periods or underscores.
Data retention
Specify how long your data is retained in each storage tier. Data moves from the memory store to the magnetic store as it ages. Data that exceeds the magnetic store retention will be deleted.
Memory store retention
Specify how long data will be stored in the memory store before it is moved to magnetic store.
3
Month(s)
The value must be a number. Minimum 1 hour, maximum 12 months.
Magnetic store retention
Specify how long data will be stored in the magnetic store before it is deleted.
3
Month(s)
The value must be a number. Minimum 1 day, maximum 200 years.
Magnetic Storage Writes

Leave 'Tags' and 'Magnetic storage writes' alone. Magnetic storage writes can be a good feature to save you money for IoT applications that don't require high frequency ingestion but for this small use case it shouldn't make a difference in nominal costs. Now select to "Create table." You can now return to AWS IoT Core tab and return to configuring your rule action.

The next screen requires you to fill out multiple fields to complete the process of implementing your database and data table successfully. First use the refresh wheel to populate your recently created database and data table within the relevant boxes.

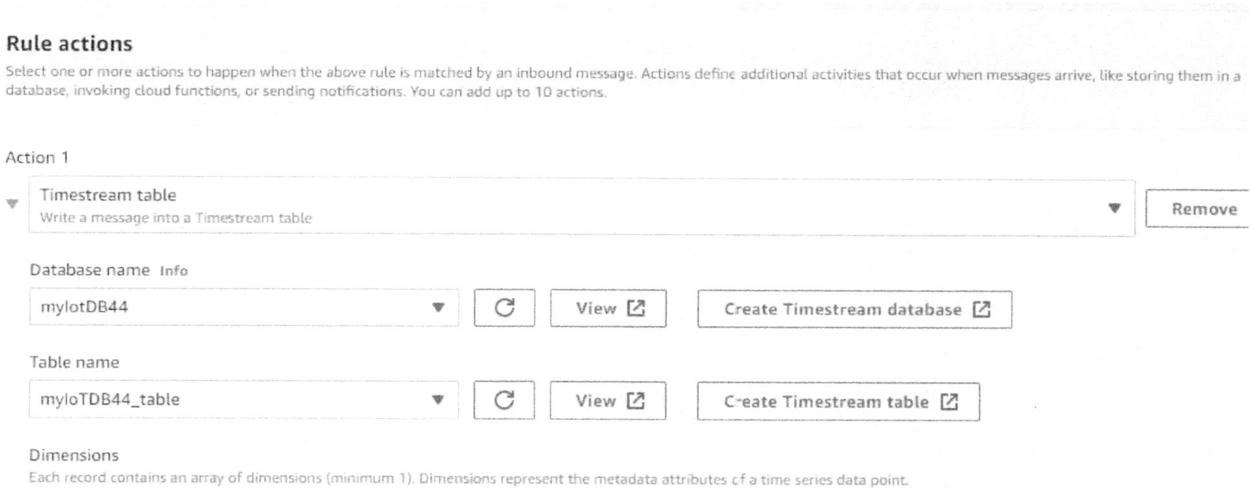
Rule actions
Select one or more actions to happen when the above rule is matched by an inbound message. Actions define additional activities that occur when messages arrive, like storing them in a database, invoking cloud functions, or sending notifications. You can add up to 10 actions.
Action 1
Timestream table
Write a message into a Timestream table
Remove
Database name Info
myIotDB44
View
Create Timestream database
Table name
myIoTDB44_table
View
Create Timestream table
Dimensions
Each record contains an array of dimensions (minimum 1). Dimensions represent the metadata attributes of a time series data point.

Next, you will designate a "Dimension Name" for your database which is the Timestream equivalent of a sort or partition key when using DynamoDB.

As a useful and common use case you may have multiple IoT devices that are sending IoT data simultaneously. Each device can identify itself in the payload with a unique ID. Publishing from your device you will use "device_ID " in the payload, however in the database it will appear linked to a literal string of "Device_ID". Using the ${*variable*} format tells AWS that this is a string literal and expect an exact matching name in your IoT payload. Thus, the name of the variable incoming from your IoT device to the AWS message broker is "device_ID" but it is written to your data table as "Device_ID."

It is also common to identify the specific IoT device in the MQTT publishing topic rather than in the IoT payload. For advanced production applications, it is also common to identify each specific device by the ClientID which is always unique for each device as a requirement of the MQTT protocol. AWS allows you to specify ClientID's as unique identifiers in the IoT policy you attached to your security certificates.

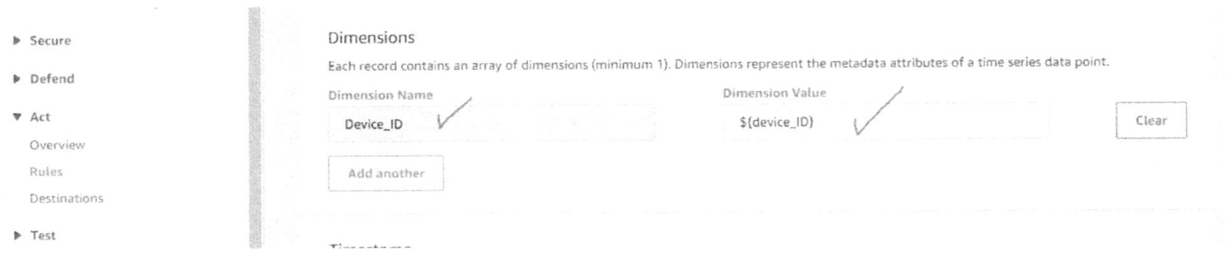

Secure
Defend
Act
Overview
Rules
Destinations
Test
Dimensions
Each record contains an array of dimensions (minimum 1). Dimensions represent the metadata attributes of a time series data point.
Dimension Name
Device_ID
Dimension Value
${device_ID}
Clear
Add another

The last part of the rule setup is to create a role for your IoT rule. At this point you should be quite familiar with making roles. Your role simply allows your IoT Core rule to access and write to Timestream. You may also notice the timestamp function is available in the Timestream configuration menu, however you do not need to utilize it. The reason for this is Timescale will automatically provide a date/time for you as discussed earlier.

The default Timestream date takes the format shown below as an example:

```
6466148147$66>4:>94285744444$
```

This feature automatically adds the timestamp, in milliseconds, to your IoT payload. To finish up the Timestream configuration process within the rule creation press the "the "Next" button:

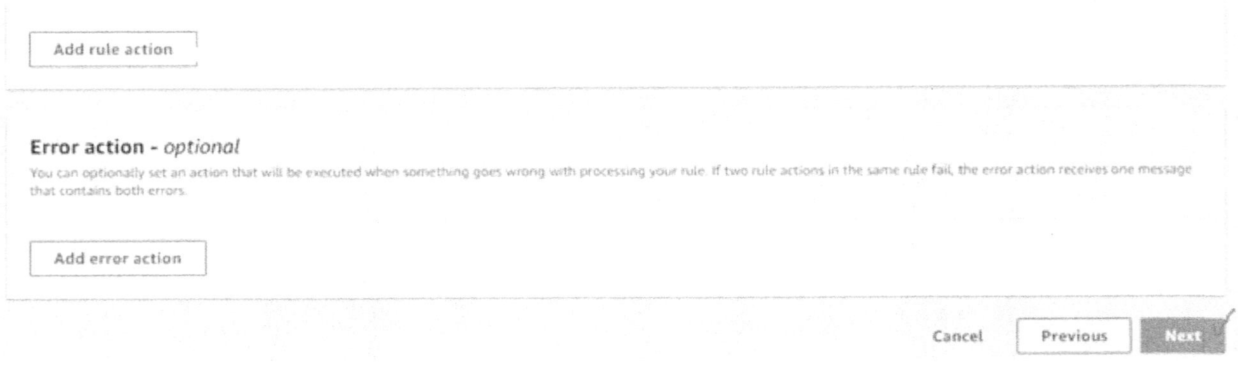

Add rule action
Error action - optional
You can optionally set an action that will be executed when something goes wrong with processing your rule. If two rule actions in the same rule fail, the error action receives one message that contains both errors.
Add error action
Cancel
Previous
Next

You can now complete your rule by selecting "Create" on the next screen.

Error action
No error action
Cancel
Previous
Create

You should now have the newly created Timestream rule in your menu of rules in IoT Core and it should be shown as active.

Step 3 – Populate the Timestream Table with IoT Data

After your Rule is created in IoT Core, you are now ready to fill the data table in your database with your IoT device generated readings. Below is a sample of a simple incoming JSON IoT payload to be published by the physical or virtual device:

```
{
    "device_ID": "ESP32_Alpha1",
    "temperature": 83,
    "humidity": 77
}
```

For this chapter I use sample environmental sensor input from three different devices named:

ESP32_Alpha1
ESP32_Bravo2
ESP32_Charlie3

These names are literal as they must match the variables names in the JavaScript code in the '*index.html*' web page you will use at the end of the chapter. So, if you are going to send IoT data to Timestream then it is a good idea to use all three device names with your data sensor readings or else change the JavaScript code in the index.html (to be discussed later) to suit your needs.

As always you are welcome to generate fake data from the MQTT test client in AWS IoT Core by simply publishing the JSON IoT sample payload a few times while changing the device name and the variable values. Otherwise, you can generate

IoT data organically with a physical IoT device or by using any of the virtual IoT data producers discussed previously. In the chapters GitHub I have made available a MQTTfx script you can use to generate the three enumerated device names randomly with an included sensor IoT payload sent to IoT Core by configurable iterations.

Below I just published some IoT JSON payloads from the MQTT test client in AWS IoT Core. I used the three different device names as noted above with some random sensor values.

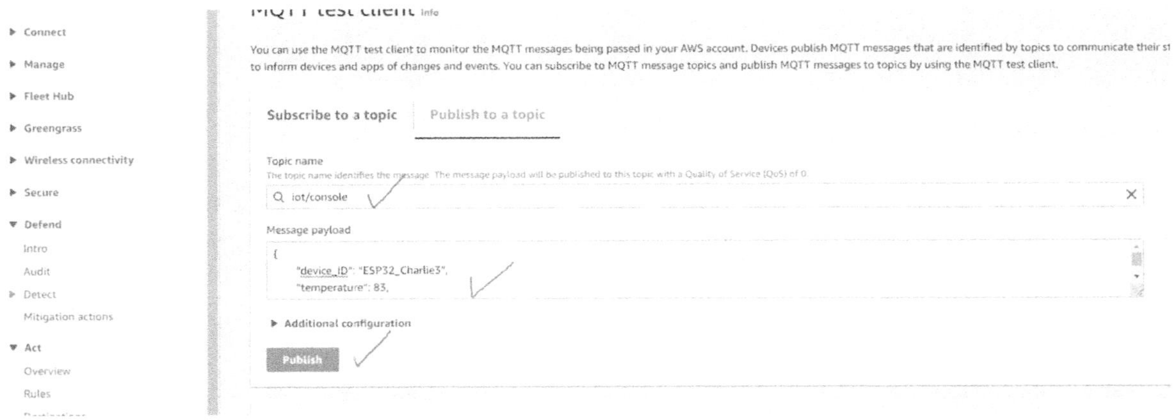

Connect
Manage
Fleet Hub
Greengrass
Wireless connectivity
Secure
Defend
Intro
Audit
Detect
Mitigation actions
Act
Overview
Rules
Subscribe to a topic
Publish to a topic
Topic name
iot/console
Message payload
{
"device_ID": "ESP32_Charlie3",
"temperature": 83,
Additional configuration
Publish

After you have published ten to twenty IoT JSON payloads under the topic of 'iot/Any-Name-You-Like'', it is time to check your Timestream database table to ensure the sensor readings have all been captured in your table to verify the design flow thus far.

Step 4 – Test the Built-In Timestream Analytical Functions with AWS Athena Like SQL Queries

To check the new items in your Timestream table after uploading the IoT sensor readings, return to:

https://console.aws.amazon.com/timestream

Now select tables:

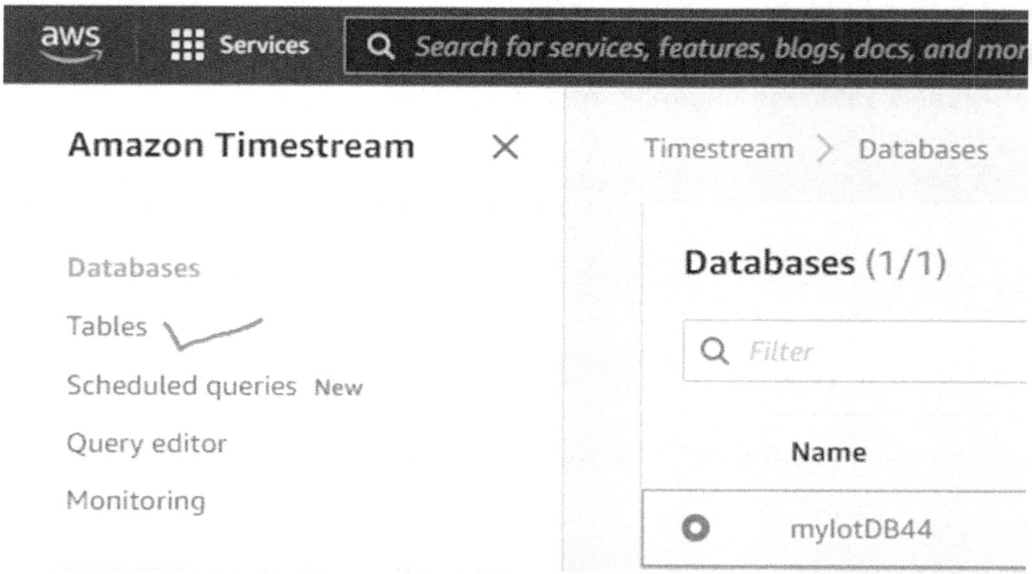
aws
Services
Search for services, features, blogs, docs, and mor
Amazon Timestream
Timestream > Databases
Databases
Tables
Scheduled queries New
Query editor
Monitoring
Databases (1/1)
Filter
Name
myIotDB44

Next select the “Query editor” so that you can run the AWS Athena like queries against your database table.

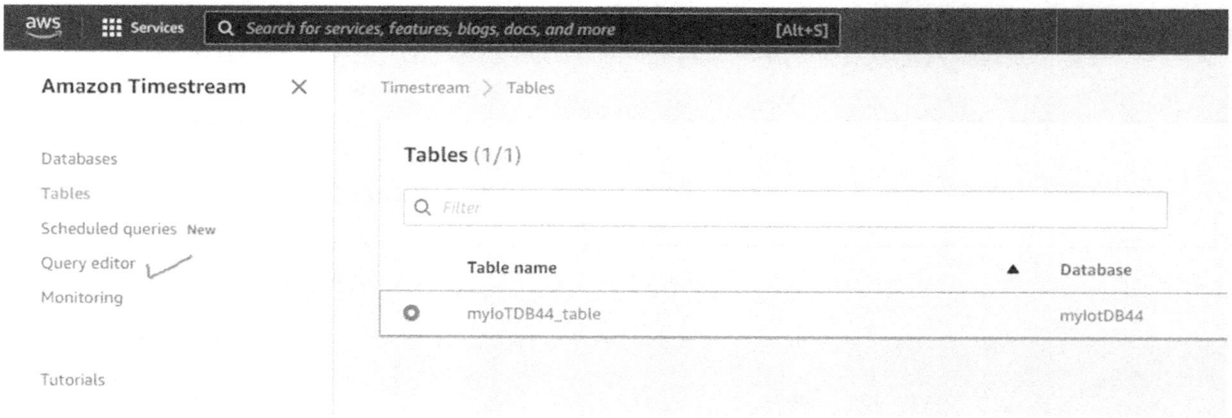
aws
Services
Search for services, features, blogs, docs, and more
[Alt+S]
Amazon Timestream
Timestream > Tables
Tables (1/1)
Filter
Databases
Tables
Scheduled queries New
Query editor
Monitoring
Tutorials
Table name
Database
myIoTDB44_table
myIotDB44

There are all types of Timestream SQL queries available. A default query may be populated on your screen. Be careful not to do repeated queries on huge data tables as it can be expensive. To see all the Timestream query operators available explore the documentation link below:

https://docs.aws.amazon.com/timestream/latest/developerguide/reference.html

Below is the default query and a modified, and simplified query in which to examine your data table items. Simply change my database and data table names into your own designated database and table names:

```
SELECT * FROM “myIotDB44”.”myIoTDB44_table” WHERE time between ago(999m) and now() ORDER BY time DESC LIMIT 10
```

Or a simplified query for small data tables:

```
SELECT * FROM “myIotDB44”.”myIoTDB44_table”
```

After running the query against my Timestream database here are the results:

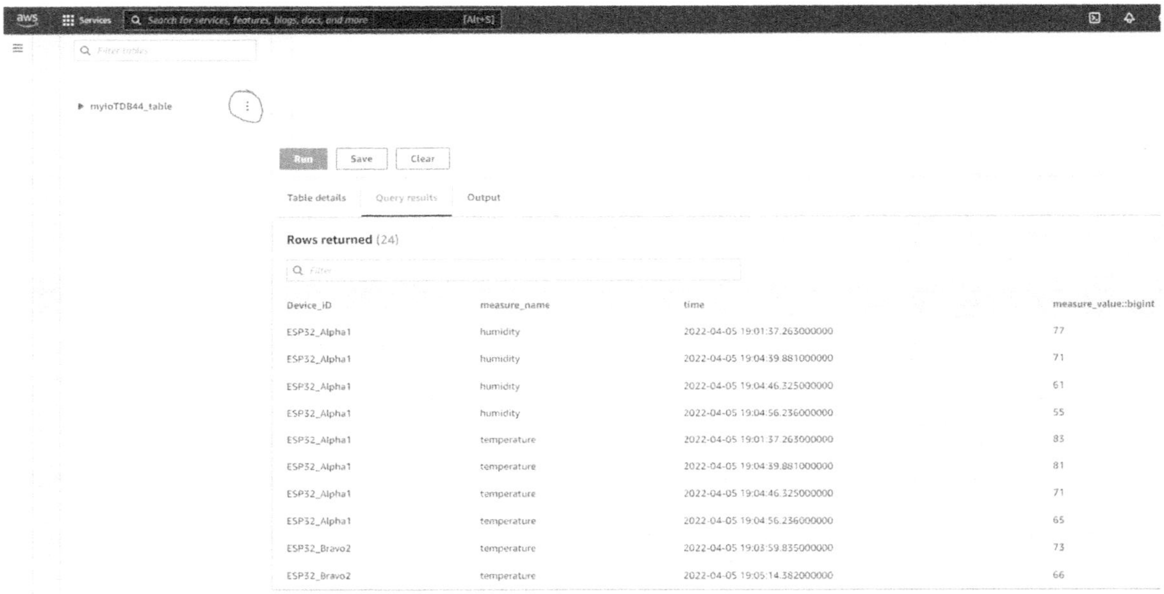

aws
Services
Search for services, features, blogs, docs, and more
[Alt+S]
myIoTDB44_table
Run
Save
Clear
Table details
Query results
Output
Rows returned (24)
Device_ID
measure_name
time
measure_value::bigint
ESP32_Alpha1 humidity 2022-04-05 19:01:37.263000000 77
ESP32_Alpha1 humidity 2022-04-05 19:04:39.881000000 71
ESP32_Alpha1 humidity 2022-04-05 19:04:46.325000000 61
ESP32_Alpha1 humidity 2022-04-05 19:04:56.236000000 55
ESP32_Alpha1 temperature 2022-04-05 19:01:37.263000000 83
ESP32_Alpha1 temperature 2022-04-05 19:04:39.881000000 81
ESP32_Alpha1 temperature 2022-04-05 19:04:46.325000000 71
ESP32_Alpha1 temperature 2022-04-05 19:04:56.236000000 65
ESP32_Bravo2 temperature 2022-04-05 19:03:59.835000000 73
ESP32_Bravo2 temperature 2022-04-05 19:05:14.382000000 66

Notice the order of the results. They are listed by ‘Device_ID’ first by default. If you run the query by time interval, they will be listed by time first with humidity and temperature interspersed. For a time series database this later query format would normally make more sense but you have many options in any case. Also notice the ellipsis to the right of the table name that is circled in red. Selecting this allows you to explore your database schema and setup. It has other useful functions like “Preview data” and “Show measurements”.

Step 5 – Configure a Timestream Connector to Grafana

IoT data in Timestream can be visualized with a few different AWS services like AWS QuickSight, which has a built-in connector for Timestream, or a Jupyter Notebook instance in AWS SageMaker. Both cost money and particularly SageMaker can get expensive for the large EC2 instances SageMaker utilizes. For this chapter you will use a free visualization tool called Grafana. While Grafana is external to AWS, they have worked with the engineers at AWS to create a middleware connector for Timestream to integrate SQL visualization services with AWS Timestream. Grafana is specially designed to handle time series data, so it is a good tool choice for IoT.

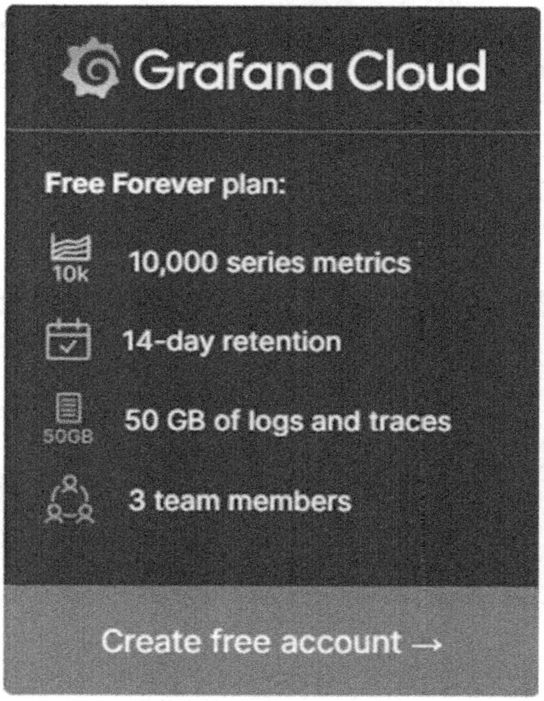

Grafana Cloud
Free Forever plan:
10k
10,000 series metrics
14-day retention
50GB
50 GB of logs and traces
3 team members
Create free account →

You can create your free Grafana account at:

https://grafana.com/

Once your free account is created you need to use the premade AWS Timestream connector to transmit your Timestream database and data table items to Grafana. To do this first go to the Grafana home page and then go to: Configuration icon →Data Sources

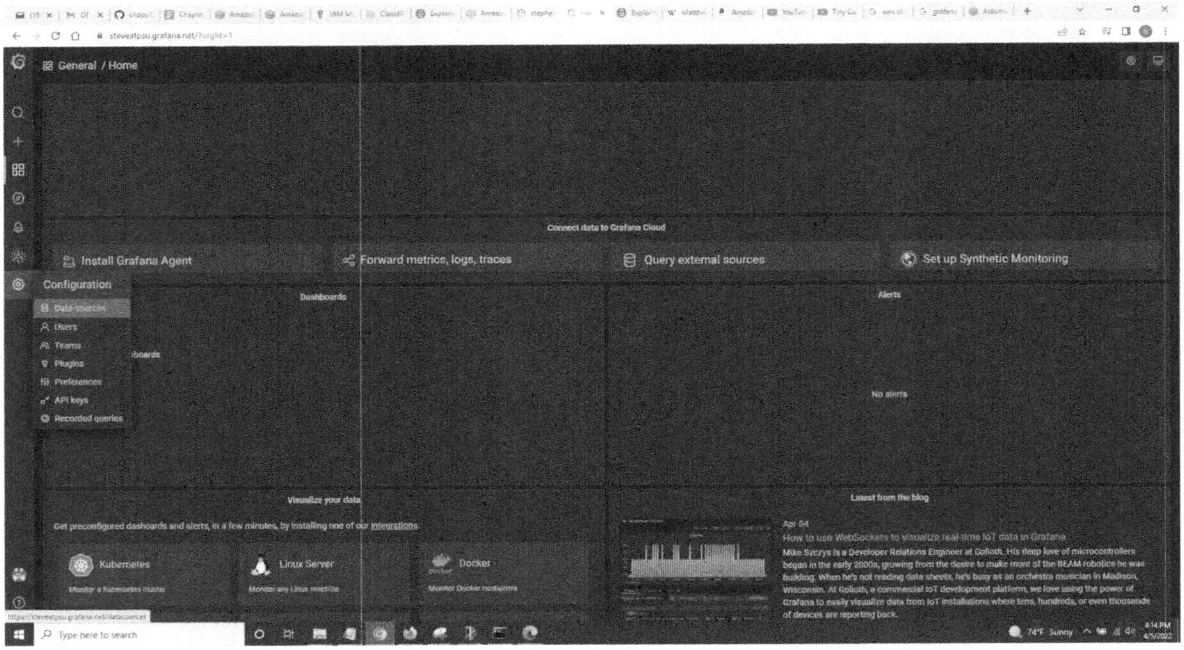
General / Home
Connect data to Grafana Cloud
Install Grafana Agent
Forward metrics, logs, traces
Query external sources
Set up Synthetic Monitoring
Configuration
Data sources
Users
Teams
Plugins
Preferences
API keys
Recorded queries
Dashboards
Alerts
No alerts
Visualize your data
Latest from the blog
Kubernetes
Linux Server
Docker

After you select 'Data Sources,' select to "Add data source"

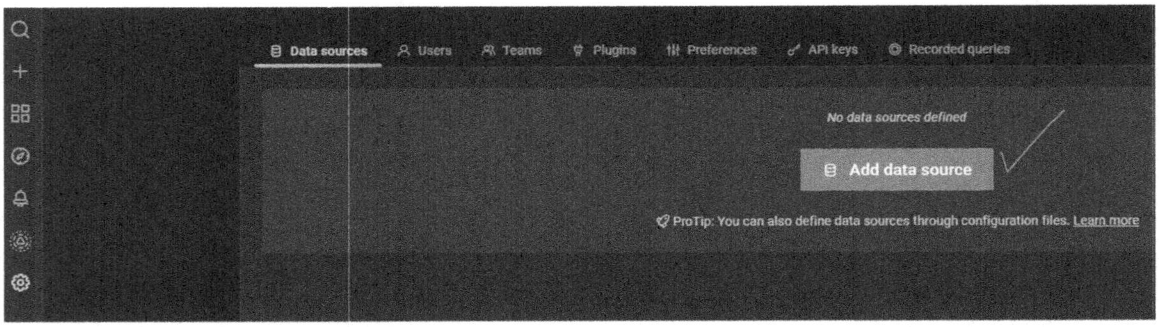
Data sources
Users
Teams
Plugins
Preferences
API keys
Recorded queries
No data sources defined
Add data source
ProTip: You can also define data sources through configuration files. Learn more

Next you should get a search screen for pre-built external connectors. Type "time" into the search box to bring up the Timestream connector.

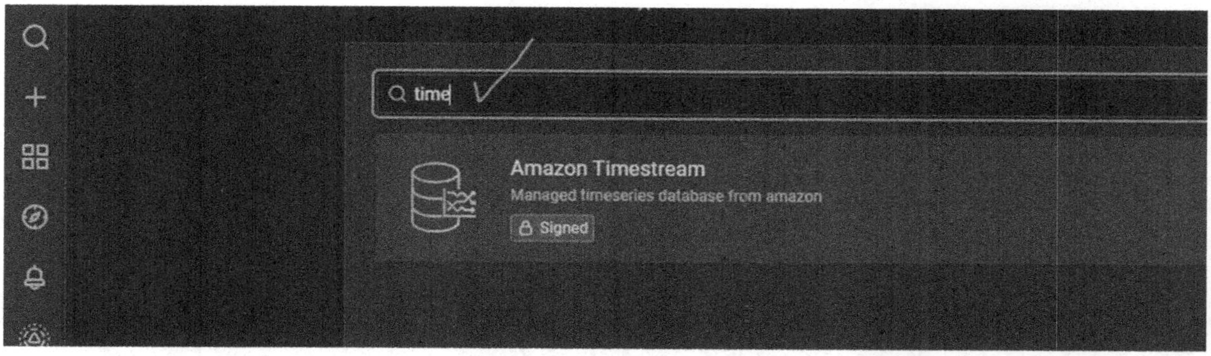

time
Amazon Timestream
Managed timeseries database from amazon
Signed

Select the timestream connector and then on the next screen you will configure your connection between Grafana and your AWS account.

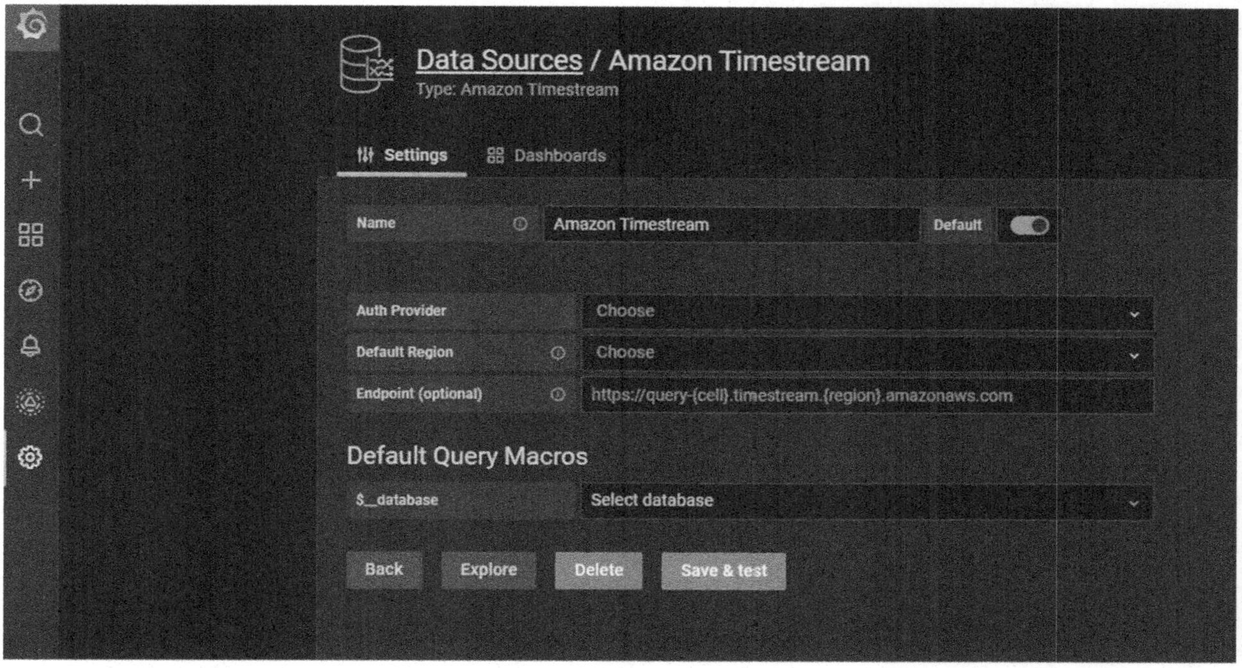

Data Sources / Amazon Timestream
Type: Amazon Timestream
Settings
Dashboards
Name
Amazon Timestream
Default
Auth Provider
Choose
Default Region
Choose
Endpoint (optional)
https://query-{cell}.timestream.{region}.amazonaws.com
Default Query Macros
$_database
Select database
Back
Explore
Delete
Save & test

For 'Auth Provider' you will use your "Access & secret key." Now this might seem like an odd choice, and if you use your root admin access and secret key (the SigV4 credentials you used to set up your AWS CLI with), then it would be a very poor choice. However, you are now going to create a new AWS user in IAM who has permission to only read Timestream databases and tables. For extra security don't forget to delete this user in AWS when you are done using Grafana.

You may have noticed throughout the book I am normally liberal with over-assigning privileges and permissions to AWS service roles, however when it comes to using the root admin credentials to your AWS account, I am far stricter, you should be very careful never to expose your root SigV4 credentials (Access key and secret access key).

Auth Provider
Access & secret key

At this point you must create your "Timestream User" and get the access key and secret access key for the new user. To do this return to IAM in AWS.

https://console.aws.amazon.com/iamv2

On the IAM screen choose "Users."

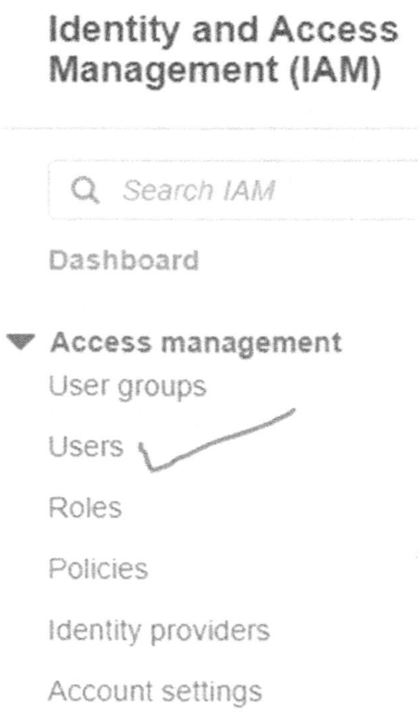
Identity and Access Management (IAM)
Search IAM
Dashboard
Access management
User groups
Users
Roles
Policies
Identity providers
Account settings

On the next screen choose the "Add users" button on the upper right

Add users

On the next screen you will create a new user. You can call your user something descriptive like "TimestreamReadOnlyUser." Also, you only need to grant your new user "Programmatic access" as there is no reason for the new user to have the ability to log into your account via the console.

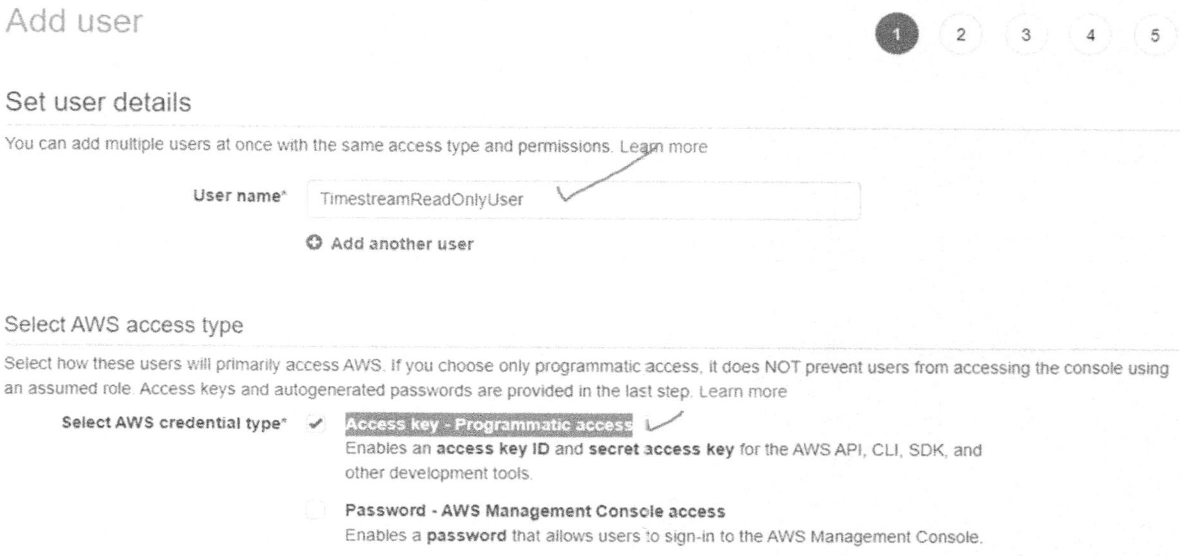
Add user
1
2
3
4
5
Set user details
You can add multiple users at once with the same access type and permissions. Learn more
User name*
TimestreamReadOnlyUser
Add another user
Select AWS access type
Select how these users will primarily access AWS. If you choose only programmatic access, it does NOT prevent users from accessing the console using an assumed role. Access keys and autogenerated passwords are provided in the last step. Learn more
Select AWS credential type*
Access key - Programmatic access
Enables an access key ID and secret access key for the AWS API, CLI, SDK, and other development tools.
Password - AWS Management Console access
Enables a password that allows users to sign-in to the AWS Management Console.

Select "Next: Permissions"

Next: Permissions

On this screen you are going to do three things. First, on the top bar select "Attach existing policies directly." This allows us to use a standard policy with a set of permissions already composed by AWS.

Secondly, type "timestream" into the search box to narrow down your policy choices to Timestream only related choices.

Finally, select the "*AmazonTimestreamReadOnlyAccess*" policy as there is no reason for Grafana to write to your database or perform other superfluous and possibly pernicious actions.

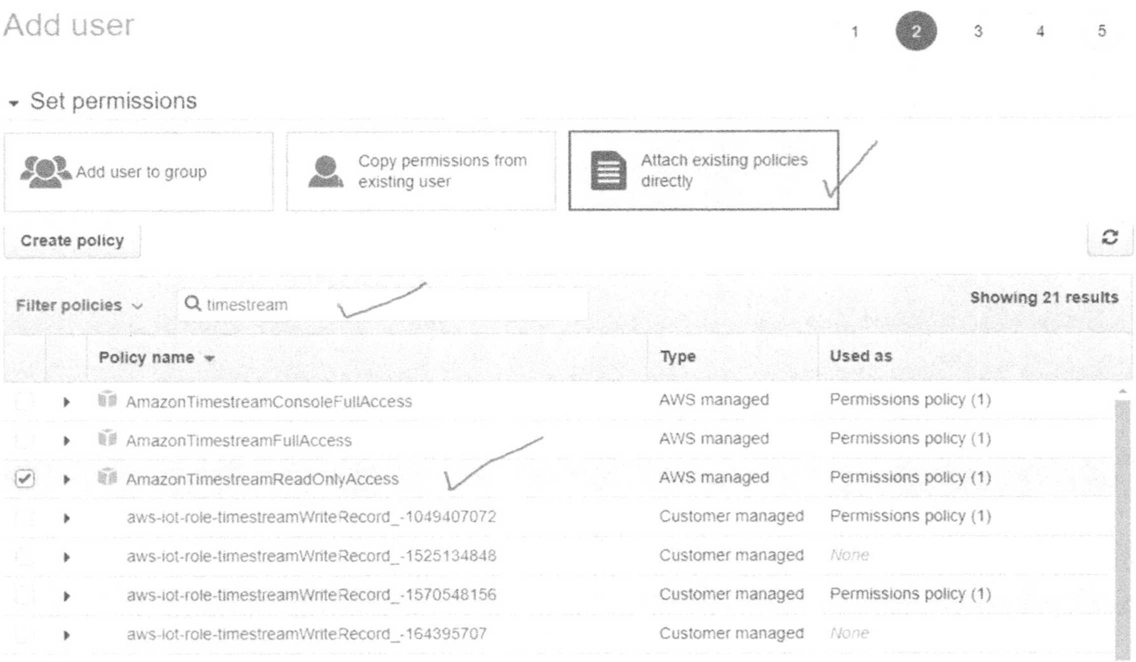

Add user
1 2 3 4 5
Set permissions
Add user to group
Copy permissions from existing user
Attach existing policies directly
Create policy
Filter policies
timestream
Showing 21 results
Policy name
Type
Used as
AmazonTimestreamConsoleFullAccess
AWS managed
Permissions policy (1)
AmazonTimestreamFullAccess
AWS managed
Permissions policy (1)
AmazonTimestreamReadOnlyAccess
AWS managed
Permissions policy (1)
aws-iot-role-timestreamWriteRecord_-1049407072
Customer managed
Permissions policy (1)
aws-iot-role-timestreamWriteRecord_-1525134848
Customer managed
None
aws-iot-role-timestreamWriteRecord_-1570548156
Customer managed
Permissions policy (1)
aws-iot-role-timestreamWriteRecord_-164395707
Customer managed
None

Choose:

Next: Tags

Leave these as blank and then choose:

Next: Review

Then review your choice if needed and select:

Create user

Now this is your final screen showing your new Timestream read-only user. To utilize your credentials, you must copy both your "Access key ID" and your "Secret access key." Again, these should look familiar to you from when you created your

AWS account and configured the AWS CLI, although they won't be the same keys obviously. Copy these keys to a secure location on your local computer.

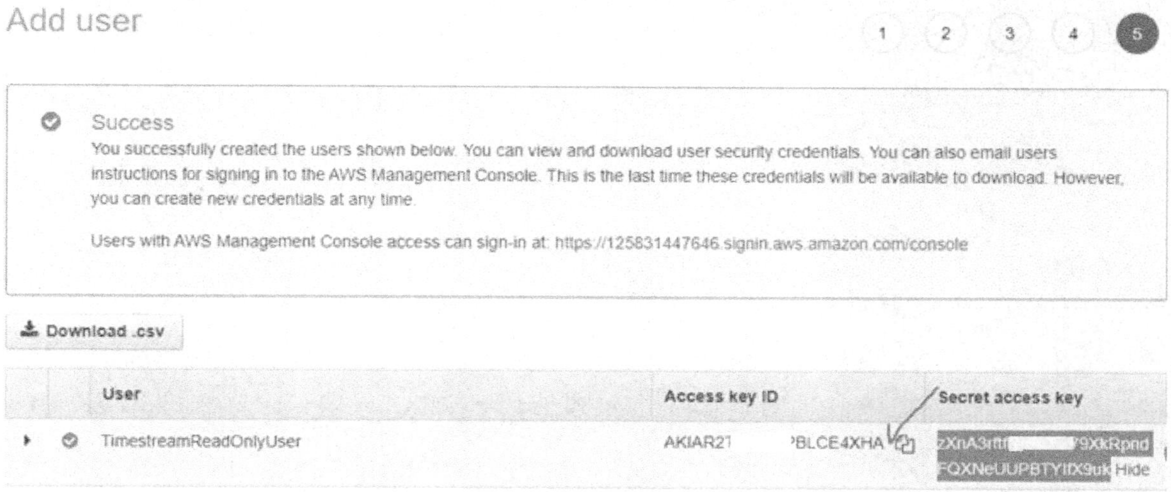

Add user
1
2
3
4
5
Success
You successfully created the users shown below. You can view and download user security credentials. You can also email users instructions for signing in to the AWS Management Console. This is the last time these credentials will be available to download. However, you can create new credentials at any time.
Users with AWS Management Console access can sign-in at: https://125831447646.signin.aws.amazon.com/console
Download .csv
User
Access key ID
Secret access key
TimestreamReadOnlyUser
AKIAR2 [redacted] BLCE4XHA
Hide

Remember if you fail to copy your 'Secret access key' you won't get the chance to copy it again later and you will be forced to create a new Timestream user in IAM.

Step 6 – Visualize the Timestream IoT Data in Grafana

Now that you are done creating your new AWS user credentials to link Timestream to Grafana feel free to close the IAM screen. Going back to the Grafana connector setup you can now enter your new access and secret keys directly into the Grafana connector configuration boxes. Also remember to select the region in which your Timestream database resides. Finally hit the "Save & Test" button.

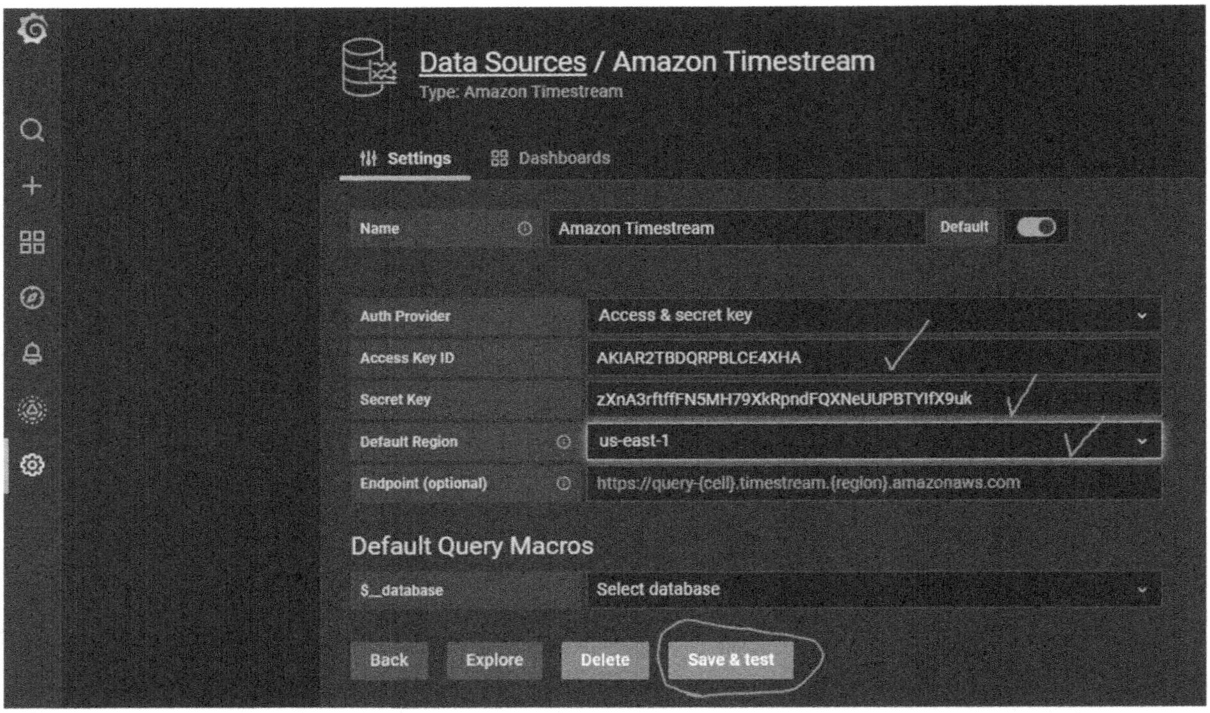
Data Sources / Amazon Timestream
Type: Amazon Timestream
Settings
Dashboards
Name
Amazon Timestream
Default
Auth Provider
Access & secret key
Access Key ID
AKIAR2TBDQRPBLCE4XHA
Secret Key
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
Default Region
us-east-1
Endpoint (optional)
https://query-{cell}.timestream.{region}.amazonaws.com
Default Query Macros
$_database
Select database
Back
Explore
Delete
Save & test

Now Grafana should be able to connect to your Timestream database on AWS. You can search for your data table by pressing “Save & test” button.

If the connector can’t find your database or table on the first attempt, sometimes there is a glitch in which you must manually refresh your browser to see the updated results.

Now that both your AWS Timestream database and your data table is connected to Grafana, you can create a visualization of your IoT data by using SQL like queries. To do this go to the left panel of the current screen and select:

+→Create→Dashboard

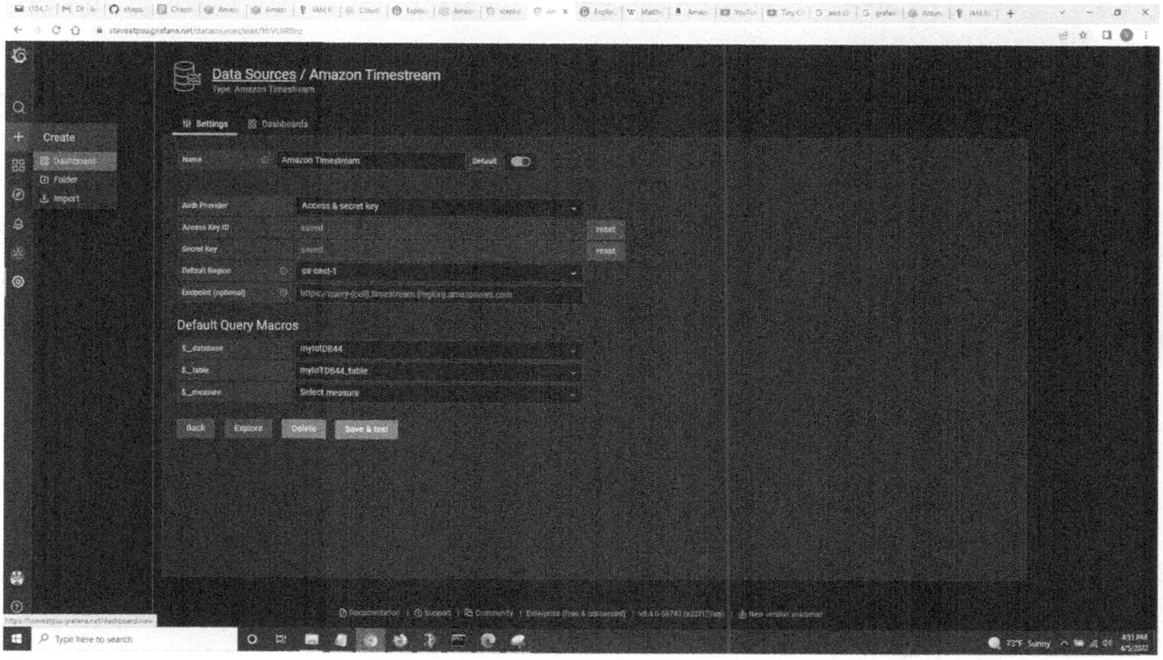
Data Sources / Amazon Timestream
Settings
Dashboards
Create
Dashboard
Folder
Import
Name
Amazon Timestream
Default
Auth Provider
Access & secret key
Access Key ID
reset
Secret Key
reset
Default Region
us-east-1
Endpoint (optional)
Default Query Macros
$_database
myIotDB44
$_table
myIoTDB44_table
$_measure
Select measure
Back
Explore
Delete
Save & test
Type here to search

On the next screen you can choose to "Add a new panel."

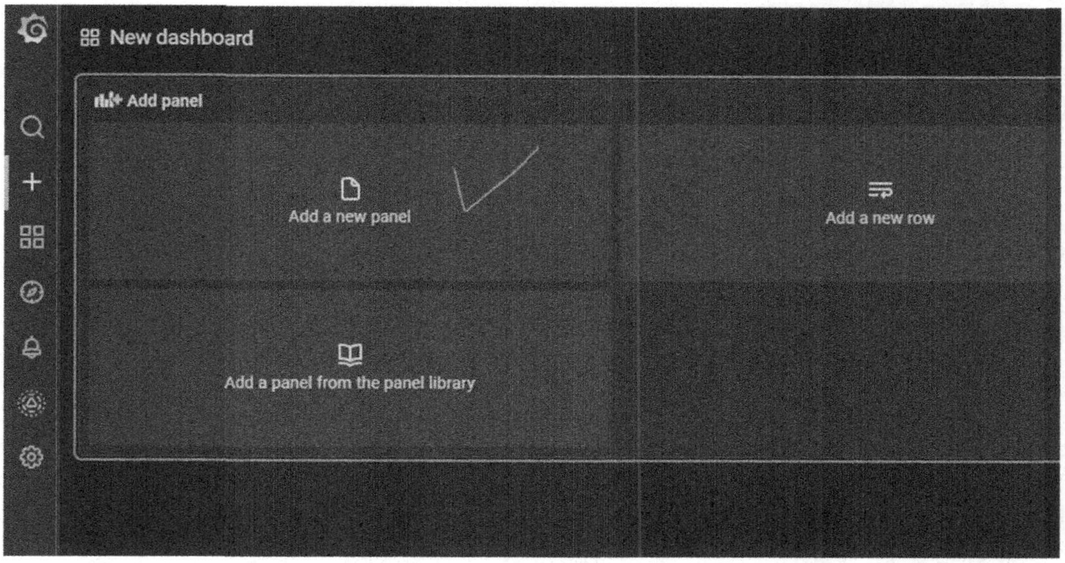
New dashboard
Add panel
Add a new panel
Add a new row
Add a panel from the panel library

On the next screen it is advisable to set your "Macros." These macros are the generic identifiers attached to your literal names for the database and data table. The macros work the same way environmental variables work in Lambda. Set your macros with the drop-down menu as shown below:

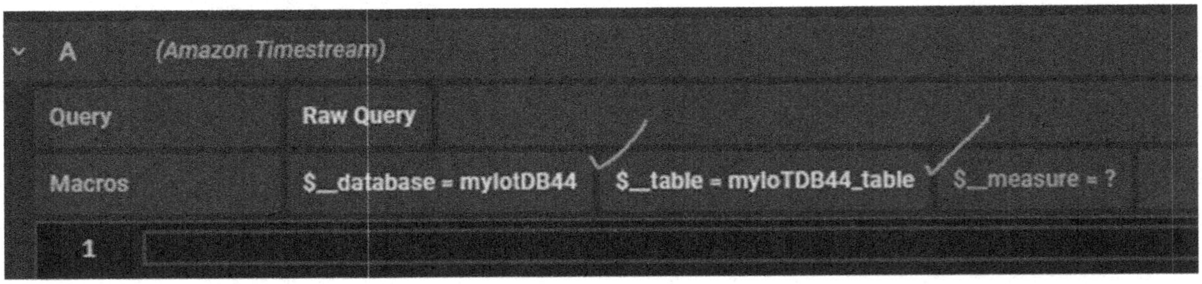
A
(Amazon Timestream)
Query
Raw Query
Macros
$__database = myIotDB44
$__table = myIoTDB44_table
$__measure = ?
1

Now you can use a “Raw Query or you can try a pre-built “samples” query. In any case there are near infinite ways to customize Grafana dashboards and use different query parameters to visualize your IoT data. Grafana is a very powerful tool although it is not always the easiest, or the most intuitive tool to use. To get started, below are two SQL queries you can try:

Query for combined graph (single entry)

```
FROM $__database.$__table WHERE ‘humidity’ = “measure_name” OR ‘temperature’
= “measure_name”
```

Use the query below to make two separate lines on your graph. You will need to make a Query “A” and a Query “B” as two different entries. Also make sure that the names and the data types match your data table (i.e., bigint or double).

Query A

```
SELECT CREATE_TIME_SERIES(time,measure_value::bigint) as temperature FROM
$__database.$__table where $__timeFilter and measure_name = ‘temperature’
```

Query B

```
SELECT CREATE_TIME_SERIES(time,measure_value::bigint) as humidity FROM
$__database.$__table where $__timeFilter and measure_name = ‘humidity’
```

The lines created may look rather small, no worries, simply drag your mouse over the region you want to zoom in on to get an expanded view.

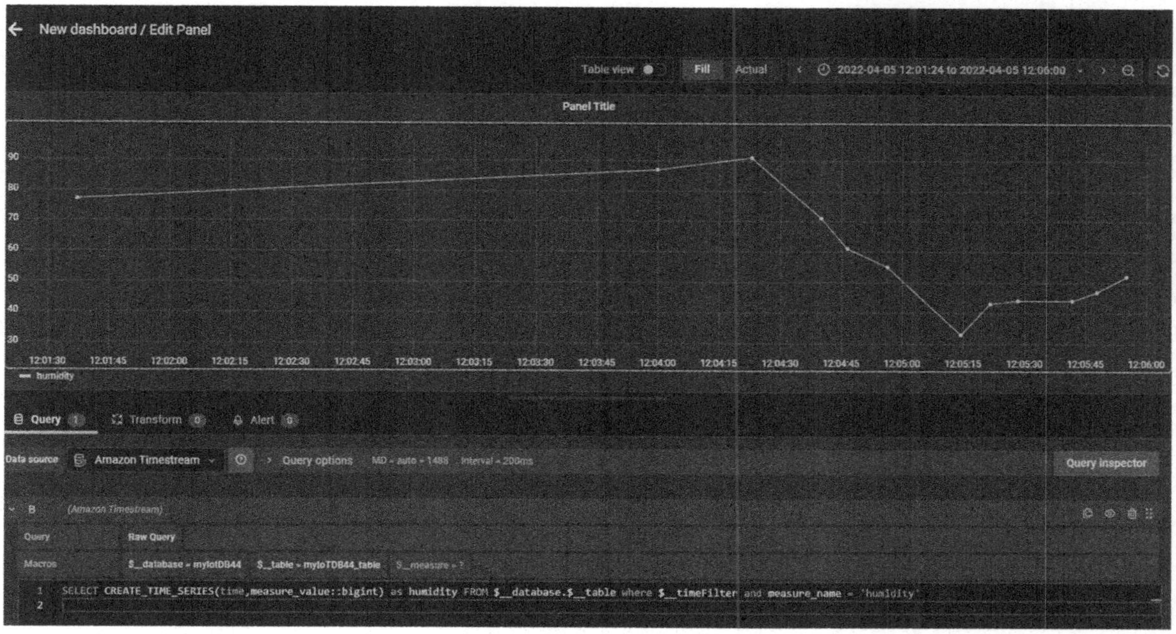
New dashboard / Edit Panel
Table view
Fill
Actual
2022-04-05 12:01:24 to 2022-04-05 12:06:00
Panel Title
90
80
70
60
50
40
30
12:01:30
12:01:45
12:02:00
12:02:15
12:02:30
12:02:45
12:03:00
12:03:15
12:03:30
12:03:45
12:04:00
12:04:15
12:04:30
12:04:45
12:05:00
12:05:15
12:05:30
12:05:45
12:06:00
humidity
Query 1
Transform 0
Alert 0
Data source
Amazon Timestream
Query options
Query inspector
B
(Amazon Timestream)
Query
Raw Query
Macros
$_database = myIotDB44
$_table = myIoTDB44_table
SELECT CREATE_TIME_SERIES(time,measure_value::bigint) as humidity FROM $__database.$__table where $__timeFilter and measure_name = 'humidity'

Congratulations, you now have the ability to use Grafana to visualize your Timestream data. You can also investigate embedding and sharing Grafana dashboards. Obviously, the visualizations you created here using simple SQL statements are not overly exciting, but with more complex time series data you can utilize more intricate SQL query's for more insightful results.

https://grafana.com/docs/grafana/latest/sharing/share-panel/

For the next sections you will first work on creating visualizations in AWS QuickSight, and then create your own visualizations for Timestream in a static website hosted on S3. Each visualization tool has its own advantages and disadvantages.

Step 7 – Visualize the Timestream IoT Data in AWS QuickSight

Unsurprisingly AWS QuickSight offers a built-in connector for Timestream to visualize data. Go to QuickSight and select a "New analysis" in the upper right:

New analysis

Then select “New dataset” in the upper left of your screen:

QuickSight
New dataset

Next, Select the Timestream connector:

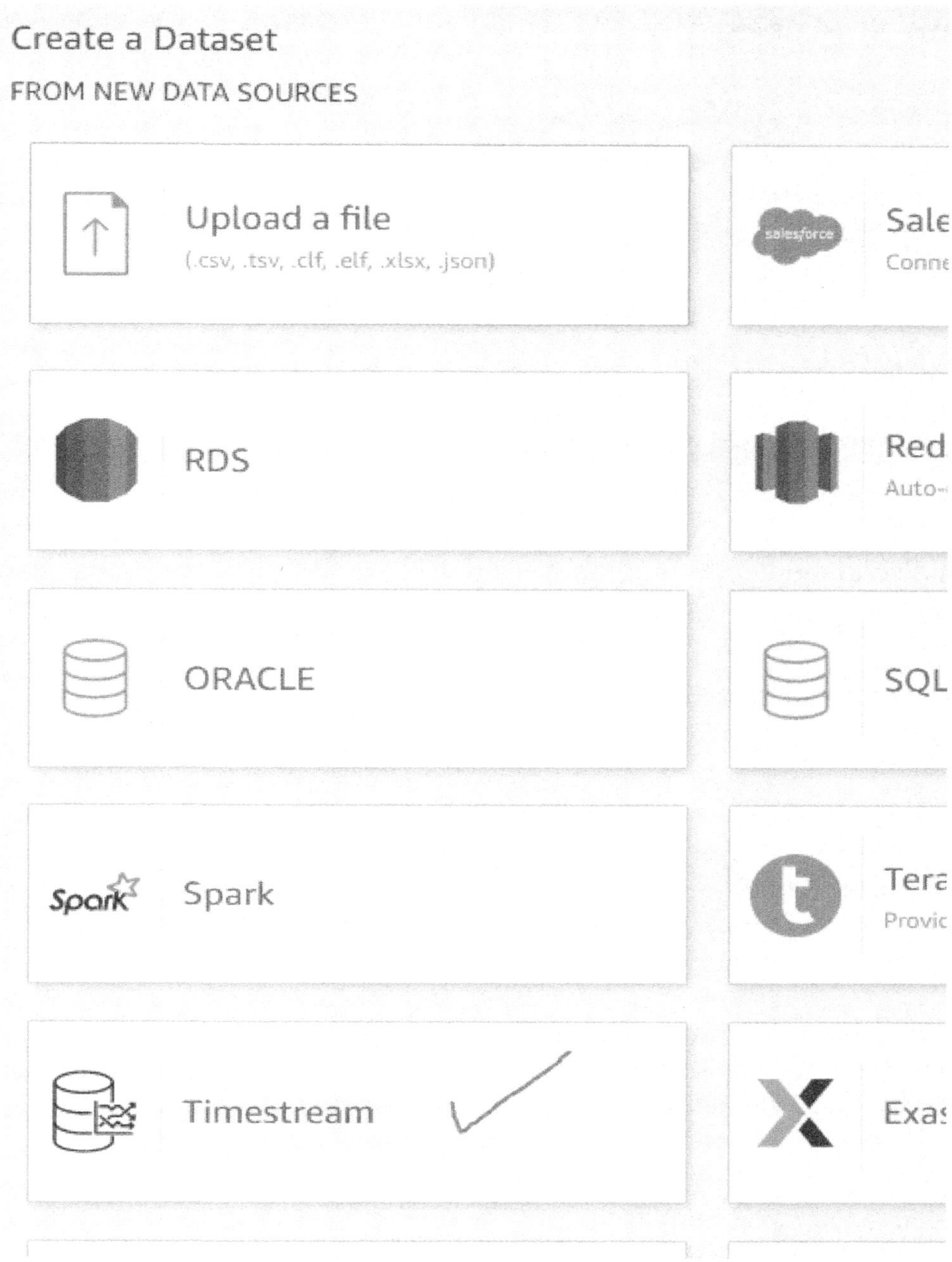
Create a Dataset
FROM NEW DATA SOURCES
Upload a file
(.csv, .tsv, .clf, .elf, .xlsx, .json)
salesforce
RDS
ORACLE
Spark
Spark
Timestream

On the next screen you will enter your Timestream database name and then data table name in the format as shown below:

"<Database Name>"."<Data Table Name>"

First "Validate" your data for the connection and then "Create data source"

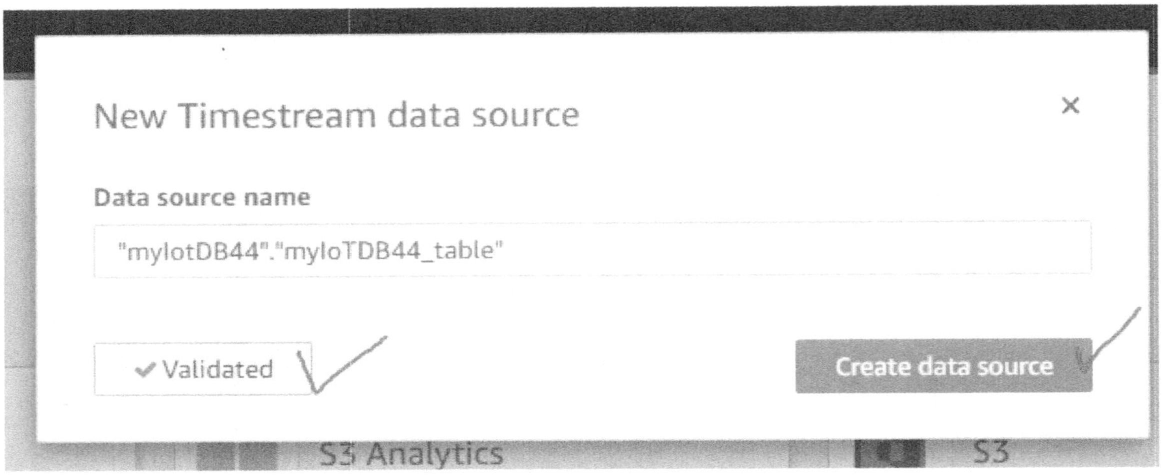
New Timestream data source
Data source name
"myIotDB44"."myIoTDB44_table"
Validated
Create data source
S3 Analytics
S3

You can also just enter your database alone in the 'Data source name' filed and then select a data table within that Timestream database.

From this point you are free to design whatever visualizations you like in QuickSight. Be mindful of your SPICE quota and costs on QucikSight as they can add up fast.

Step 8 – Design a Lambda Function to Query the Timestream IoT Data

In this section you will develop a Lambda function that can extract your time series data from Timestream. This will be useful as you can then link the extraction Lambda with an AWS API generated endpoint which you can then use in your own static website on S3 to visualize your Timestream data.

To proceed go to AWS Lambda at:

https://console.aws.amazon.com/lambda

On the upper right of your screen create a new Lambda function:

AWS Lambda
Functions (93)
Create function

Create a Python 3.8 Lambda function and call it anything you like, here I call mine "TimestreamExtractor44." When completed press the "Create function" button at the bottom of the screen.

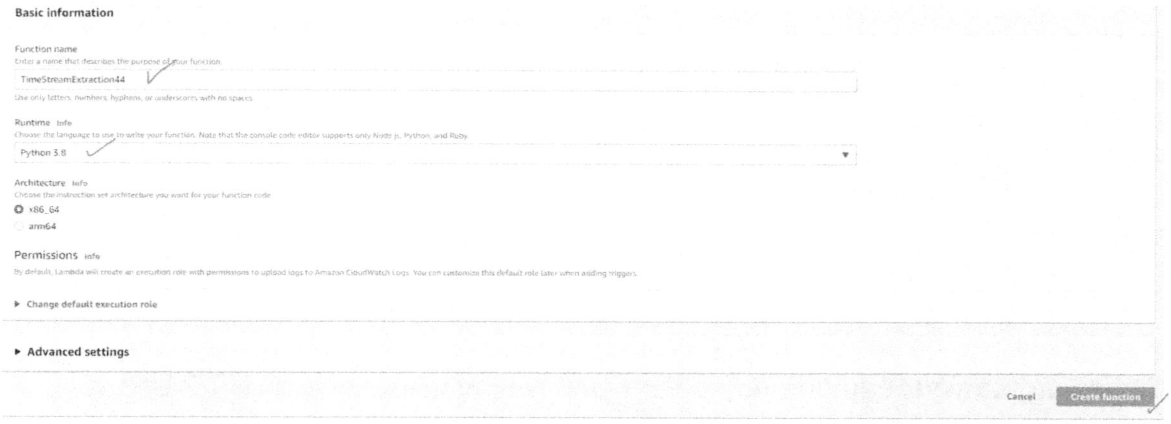
Basic information
Function name
TimeStreamExtraction44
Runtime
Python 3.8
Architecture
x86_64
arm64
Permissions
Change default execution role
Advanced settings
Cancel
Create function

Now you can copy and paste the following code into Lambda which is also available in the GitHub for this chapter. You must fill out two lines in the Lambda code to customize it for your own Timestream Database and table in your own region.

```
Config = Config(region_name = '<Your-Region>')
```

and

```
QueryString= 'SELECT * FROM "<YOUR-TIMESTREAM-DATABASE>"."<YOUR-TABLE-NAME>"'
```

Below is the code in Python:

```
import json
import boto3
from botocore.config import Config

config = Config(region_name = '<Your-Region>')
config.endpoint_discovery_enabled = True
timestream_query_client = boto3.client('timestream-query', config=config)

def lambda_handler(event, context):
```

```
    result = timestream_query_client.query(
        QueryString= ‘SELECT * FROM “<YOUR-TIMESTREAM-DATABASE>”.”<YOUR-
TABLE-NAME>”’
    )

    print(result[‘ColumnInfo’])
    print(result[‘Rows’])
    print(result)
    return(result)
```

The most important line of the Lambda function is:

```
QueryString= ‘SELECT * FROM “<YOUR-TIMESTREAM-DATABASE>”.”<YOUR-TABLE-NAME>”’
```

This unlocks the power of the AWS Athena like SQL Timestream query and puts that power into your Lambda function. Now by simply creating a HTTP URL (endpoint) connecting to this Lambda function you can return any query data from Timestream that you like.

It is important to note that to ingest that returned Timestream data from your Lambda query is contingent on the JavaScript code in the webhost. All query results won't be compatible with the same static web code.

Don't forget to give your Lambda function permission to access Timestream. To do this go to
Configuration→ Role name then click the Role name.

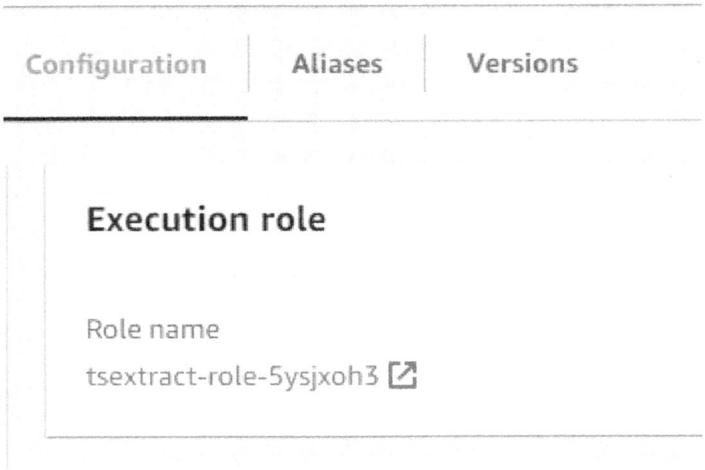
Configuration
Aliases
Versions
Execution role
Role name
tsextract-role-5ysjxoh3

Use the drop-down menu on the right to "Create inline policy":

Simulate
Remove
Add permissions
Attach policies
Create inline policy

Now search for "time" and give your inline policy "All Timestream actions" ,

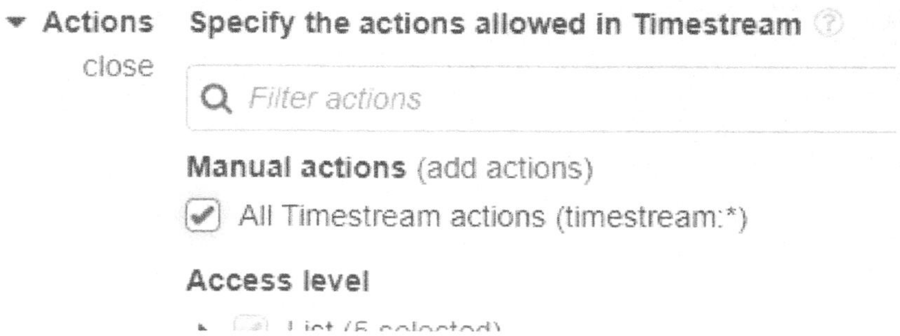

Actions
close
Specify the actions allowed in Timestream
Filter actions
Manual actions (add actions)
All Timestream actions (timestream:*)
Access level

and "All resources."

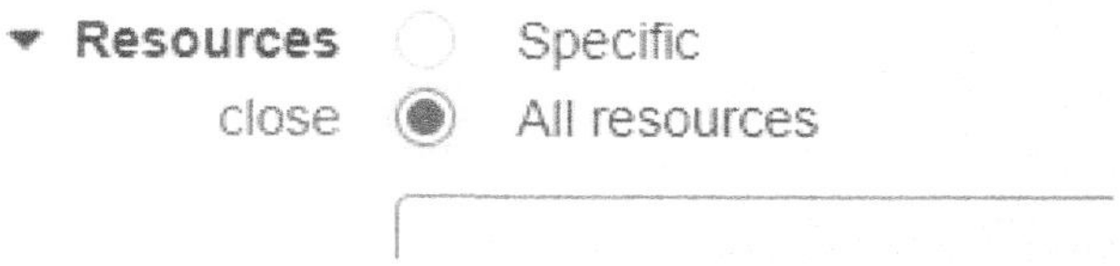

Resources
close
Specific
All resources

Then review and create a full access inline policy. Remember you can always restrict privileges later if you like.

Service	Access level	Resource	Request condition
Allow (1 of 325 services) Show remaining 324			
Timestream	Full access	All resources	None

Cancel Previous Create policy

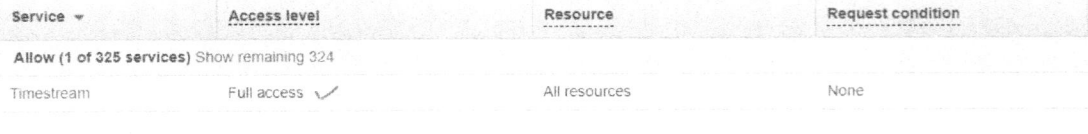

Once this is done it is time to test your Lambda function with Timestream. As the Lambda function just query's the Timestream database, and doesn't take any incoming event object or arguments, you can use the generic unedited test event just as you have done several times by now. Name the default test event anything you like ("t1" in this case) then "Save" the test event.

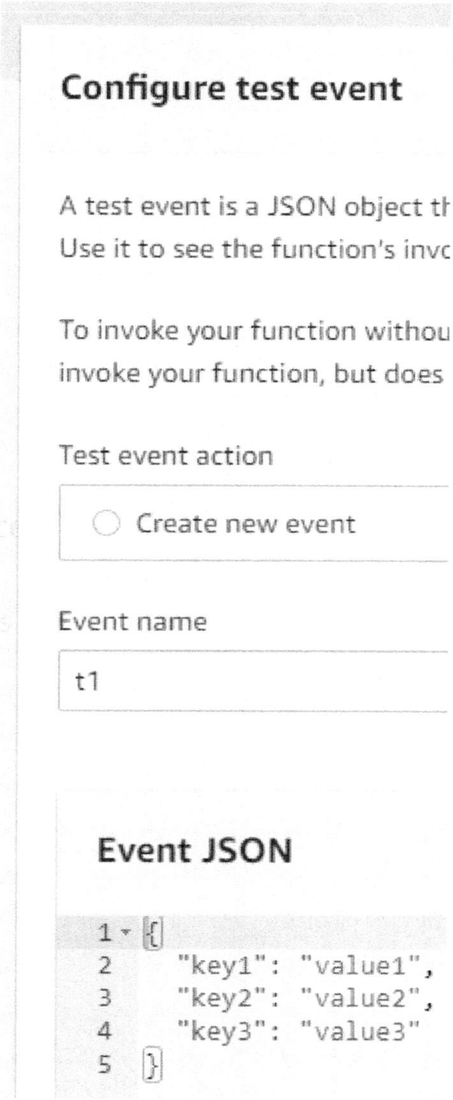
Configure test event
A test event is a JSON object tl
Use it to see the function's invc
To invoke your function withou
invoke your function, but does
Test event action
Create new event
Event name
t1
Event JSON
1 {
2 "key1": "value1",
3 "key2": "value2",
4 "key3": "value3"
5 }

Press the test button Then observe the test results. If everything works correctly the result should look like the image below:

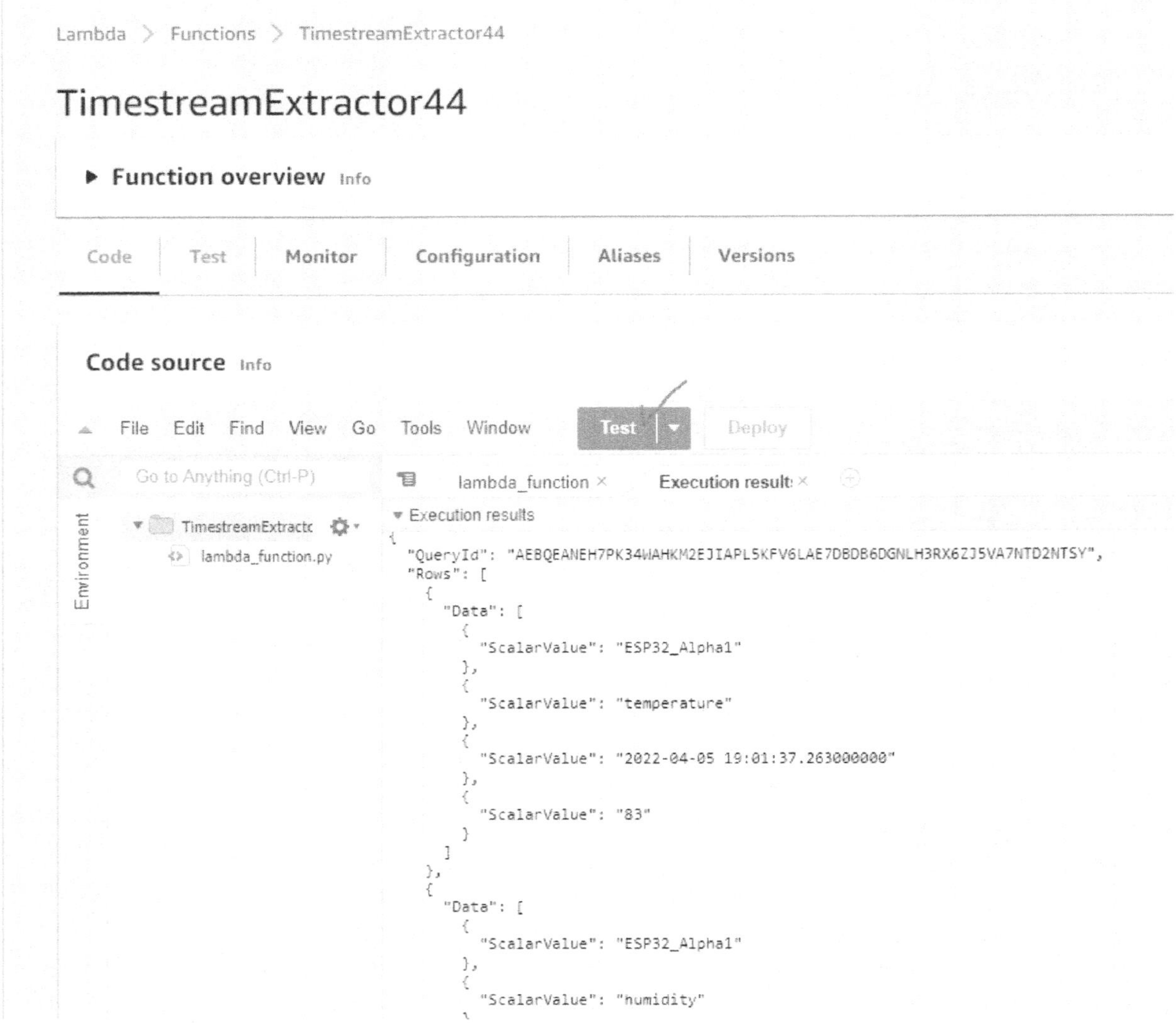
Lambda > Functions > TimestreamExtractor44
TimestreamExtractor44
Function overview Info
Code
Test
Monitor
Configuration
Aliases
Versions
Code source Info
File Edit Find View Go Tools Window
Test
Deploy
Go to Anything (Ctrl-P)
Environment
TimestreamExtractc
lambda_function.py
lambda_function
Execution result
Execution results
{
"QueryId": "AEBQEANEH7PK34WAHKM2EJIAPL5KFV6LAE7DBDB6DGNLH3RX6ZJ5VA7NTD2NTSY",
"Rows": [
{
"Data": [
{
"ScalarValue": "ESP32_Alpha1"
},
{
"ScalarValue": "temperature"
},
{
"ScalarValue": "2022-04-05 19:01:37.263000000"
},
{
"ScalarValue": "83"
}
]
},
{
"Data": [
{
"ScalarValue": "ESP32_Alpha1"
},
{
"ScalarValue": "humidity"

All database items should be displayed in scalar format. Don't forget you can change the query in your Lambda function to return different results from Timestream as desired.

Step 9 – Develop a HTTP Endpoint as a Lambda Function URL to Access the IoT Data from Timestream on an External Website

In the previous chapter you created a URL endpoint with the standard method using AWS API Gateway. I mentioned then that you could have used the new service called Lambda "Function URL," which is an endpoint creation tool directly accessible from Lambda itself. The endpoint is still created with API Gateway as the underlying service, but that creation process is abstracted away in configuring a Function URL.

You can now utilize the Lambda 'Function URL' to make the endpoint creation process easier. You can get away with this simplification because you are not passing the Lambda function any actual arguments, query string parameters, or an event object.

Within the Lambda function go to the configuration tab, choose the 'Function URL' tab and then press "Create function URL."

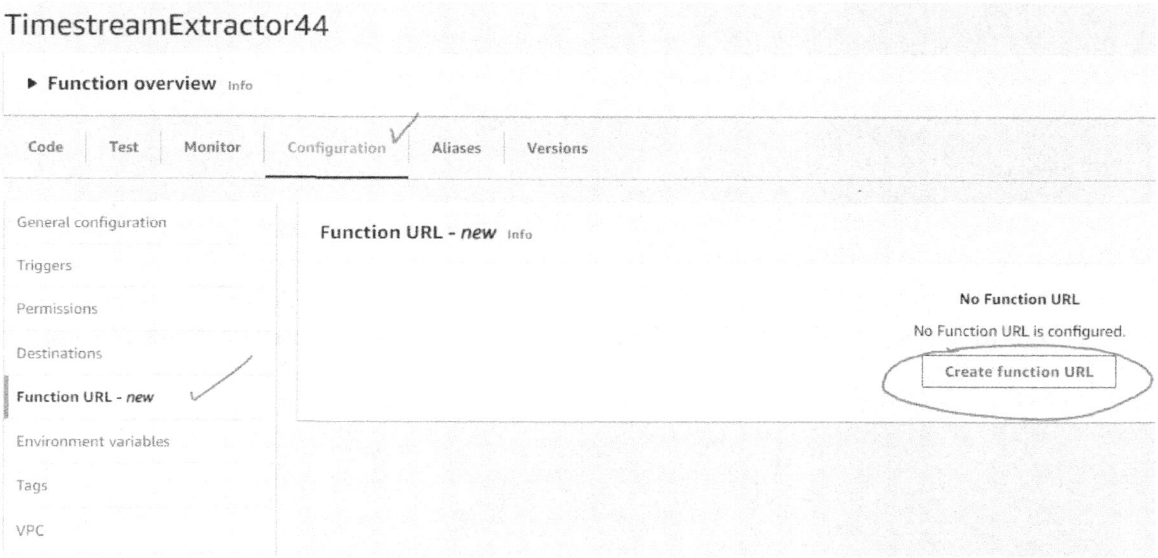

TimestreamExtractor44
Function overview Info
Code
Test
Monitor
Configuration
Aliases
Versions
General configuration
Triggers
Permissions
Destinations
Function URL - new
Environment variables
Tags
VPC
Function URL - new Info
No Function URL
No Function URL is configured.
Create function URL

You only have three fields to configure to get a working URL. First choose "None" for authentication type. You can always restrict this later as you like.

Then choose to 'Configure cross-region resource sharing (CORS).'

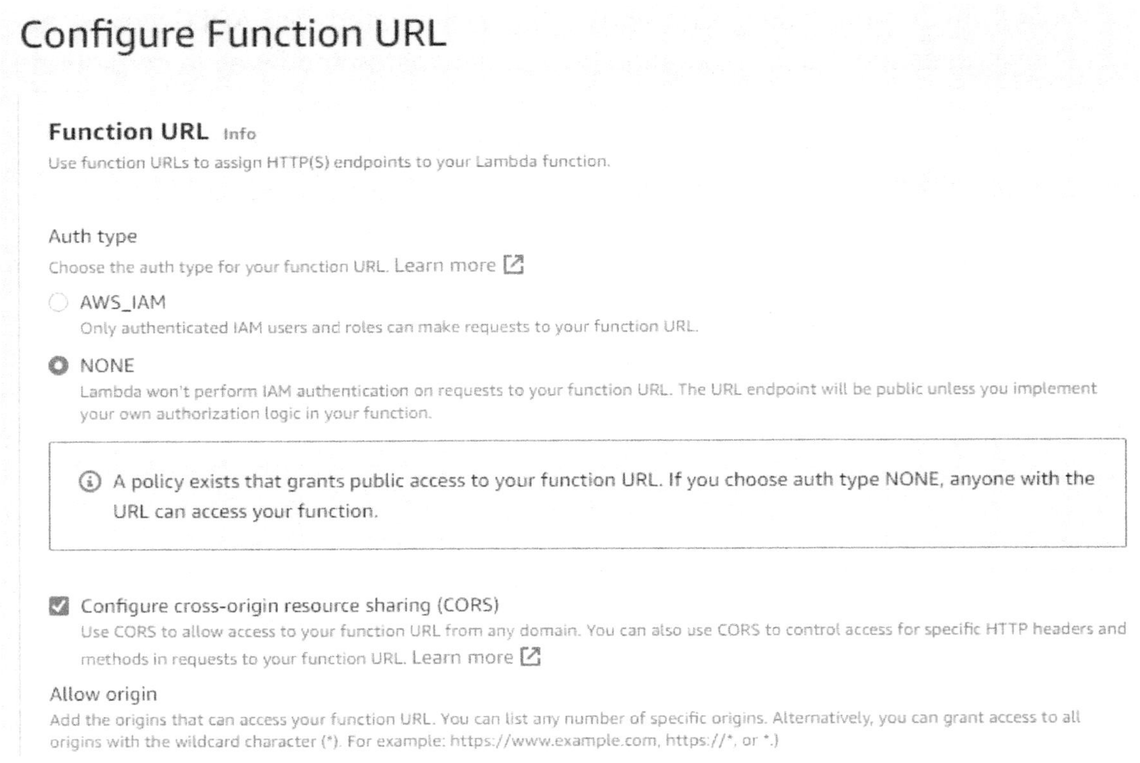
Configure Function URL
Function URL Info
Use function URLs to assign HTTP(S) endpoints to your Lambda function.
Auth type
Choose the auth type for your function URL. Learn more
AWS_IAM
Only authenticated IAM users and roles can make requests to your function URL.
NONE
Lambda won't perform IAM authentication on requests to your function URL. The URL endpoint will be public unless you implement your own authorization logic in your function.
A policy exists that grants public access to your function URL. If you choose auth type NONE, anyone with the URL can access your function.
Configure cross-origin resource sharing (CORS)
Use CORS to allow access to your function URL from any domain. You can also use CORS to control access for specific HTTP headers and methods in requests to your function URL. Learn more
Allow origin
Add the origins that can access your function URL. You can list any number of specific origins. Alternatively, you can grant access to all origins with the wildcard character (*). For example: https://www.example.com, https://*, or *.)

Scroll down to 'allow methods' and choose the "Get" method and then finally press "Save":

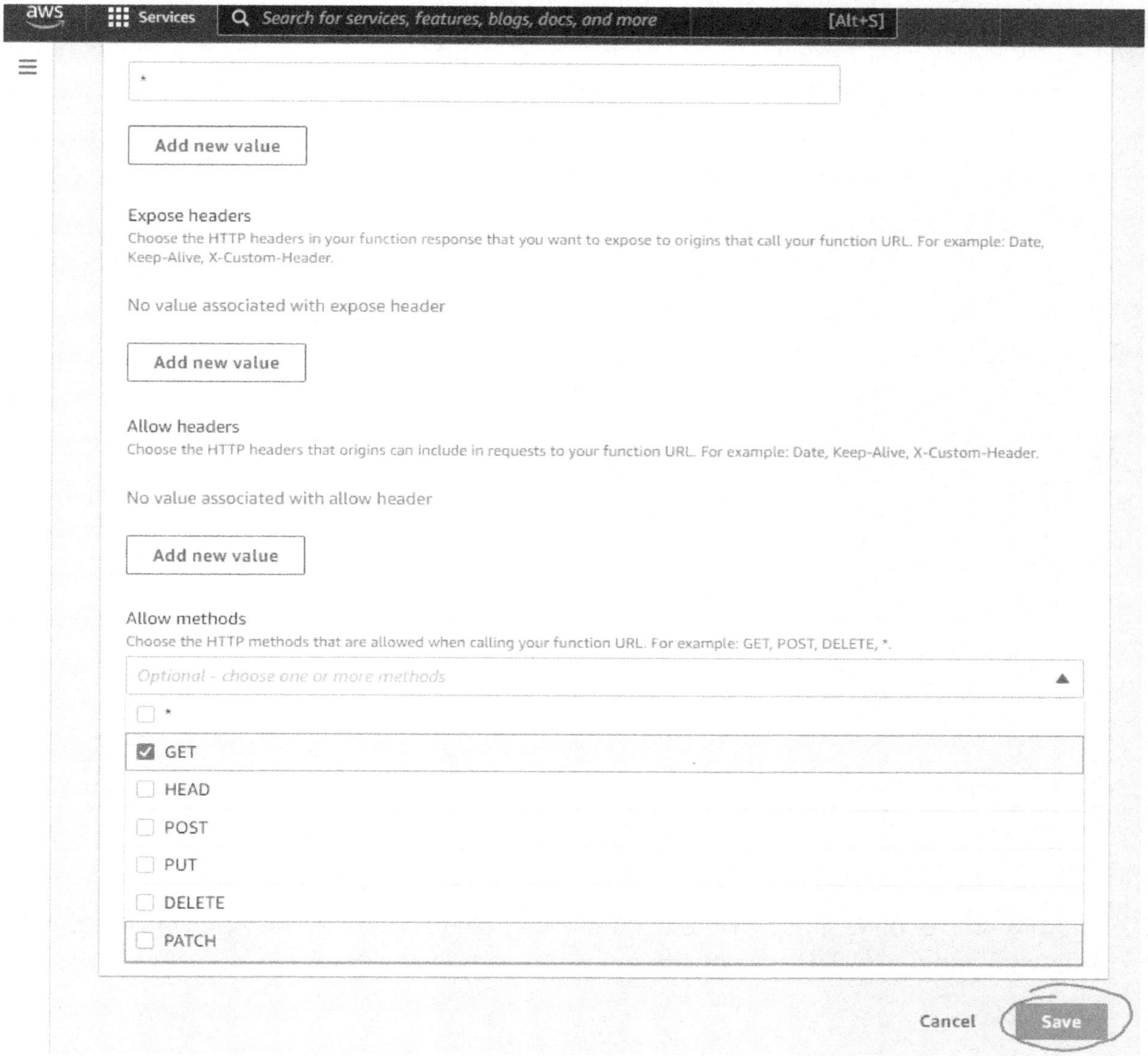
aws
Services
Search for services, features, blogs, docs, and more
[Alt+S]
*
Add new value
Expose headers
Choose the HTTP headers in your function response that you want to expose to origins that call your function URL. For example: Date, Keep-Alive, X-Custom-Header.
No value associated with expose header
Add new value
Allow headers
Choose the HTTP headers that origins can include in requests to your function URL. For example: Date, Keep-Alive, X-Custom-Header.
No value associated with allow header
Add new value
Allow methods
Choose the HTTP methods that are allowed when calling your function URL. For example: GET, POST, DELETE, *.
Optional - choose one or more methods
*
GET
HEAD
POST
PUT
DELETE
PATCH
Cancel
Save

After this you should receive your Lambda endpoint. Simply click it on to open the Function URL in a separate browser window.

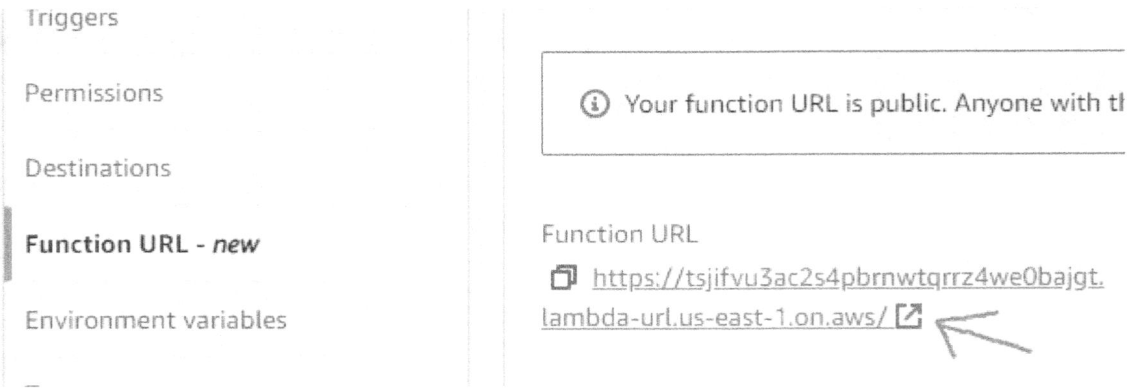
Triggers
Permissions
Destinations
Function URL - new
Environment variables
Your function URL is public. Anyone with tl
Function URL
https://tsjifvu3ac2s4pbrnwtqrrz4we0bajgt.
lambda-url.us-east-1.on.aws/

After clicking the link, you should get the query results from the Lambda function executing which returns all the items in your Timestream database. It should look like the scalar formatted JSON image below in the browser window:

If you did not receive similar Timestream query return results, then go back and check your function URL configuration.

Step 10 – Deploy a Static Website in S3 Using the Function URL to Query the Timestream IoT Data from the Lambda Function

Now create a public S3 bucket with static website hosting as shown in the prerequisite chapter on S3 public bucket creation. You will use this S3 bucket to host your website with the code included below.

You only need to fill out one field in the websites JavaScript code and that is your "Function URL" endpoint. In the last chapter you created this endpoint with AWS API Gateway, but in this chapter, you used the easier "Function URL" to create the endpoint directly from the Lambda function. Notice that the incoming trigger for the

Lambda function is still shown as API Gateway, this is because when you created your abbreviated Lambda 'Function URL' AWS created the endpoint with API Gateway behind the scenes and managed the abstractions for you.

Enter your own 'Function URL' endpoint on this line:

```
x.open("GET", "https://<YOUR-LAMBDA-FUNCTION-URL-HERE>", true);
```

After filling out the endpoint in the code below save the code as "*index.html*" in your public S3 bucket.

```
<!DOCTYPE html>
<html lang="en">
<head>
  <meta charset="UTF-8">
  <meta name="viewport" content="width=device-width, initial-scale=1.0">
  <meta http-equiv="X-UA-Compatible" content="ie=edge">
  <title>Dashboard</title>
  <link rel="stylesheet"
href="https://maxcdn.bootstrapcdn.com/bootstrap/3.3.7/css/bootstrap.min.css"
    integrity="sha384-
BVYiiSIFeK1dGmJRAkycuHAHRg32OmUcww7on3RYdg4Va+PmSTsz/K68vbdEjh4u"
crossorigin="anonymous">

</head>
<body>
  <div class="container">
    <h1>Dashboard</h1>
    <div class="panel panel-info">
      <div class="panel-heading">
        <h3 class="panel-title"><strong>ESP32_Charlie3 Chart</strong></h3>
      </div>
      <div class="panel-body">
        <div id="container"></div>
      </div>
    </div>

    <div class="panel panel-info">
      <div class="panel-heading">
        <h3 class="panel-title"><strong>Esp32_Alpha1 Chart</strong></h3>
      </div>
      <div class="panel-body">
```

```
        <div id="container1"></div>
      </div>
    </div>

    <div class="panel panel-info">
      <div class="panel-heading">
        <h3 class="panel-title"><strong>ESP32_Bravo2 Chart</strong></h3>
      </div>
      <div class="panel-body">
        <div id="container2"></div>
      </div>
    </div>
  </div>

  <script src="https://code.highcharts.com/highcharts.js"></script>
  <script>

    window.onload = function () {
      var x = new XMLHttpRequest();
      x.open("GET", "https://<YOUR-FUNCTION-URL-HERE>", true);
      x.onreadystatechange = function () {
        if (x.readyState == 4 && x.status == 200) {
          let resData = JSON.parse(x.responseText);
          let devicesArr = {
            'ESP32_Charlie3': { hum: [], temp: [], humtime: [], temptime: []
},
            'ESP32_Alpha1': { hum: [], temp: [], humtime: [], temptime: [] },
            'ESP32_Bravo2': { hum: [], temp: [], humtime: [], temptime: [] }
          };
          try {
            let { Rows } = resData;
            for (let key in devicesArr) {
              Rows.forEach(item => {
                let deviceKey = item.Data[0].ScalarValue;
                console.log('deviceKey', deviceKey);
                console.log('key', key);

                if (deviceKey.toLowerCase() == key.toLowerCase()) {
                  let dateTime = new
Date(item.Data[2].ScalarValue).toLocaleDateString() + new
Date(item.Data[2].ScalarValue).toLocaleTimeString();
                  if (item.Data[1].ScalarValue == 'humidity') {

devicesArr[key]['hum'].push(Number(item.Data[3].ScalarValue))
                    devicesArr[key]['humtime'].push(dateTime);
```

```
                }
                if (item.Data[1].ScalarValue == 'temperature') {

devicesArr[key]['temp'].push(Number(item.Data[3].ScalarValue))
                  devicesArr[key]['temptime'].push(dateTime);
                }
              }
            });
          }
          console.log('devicesArr', devicesArr);

          const ESP32_Charlie3ChartData = devicesArr['ESP32_Charlie3'];
          const xAxisData = ESP32_Charlie3ChartData['temptime'];
          const inhumidArr = ESP32_Charlie3ChartData['hum'];
          const intempArr = ESP32_Charlie3ChartData['temp'];
          Highcharts.chart('container', {
            title: {
              text: 'ESP32_Charlie3 Device'
            },
            tooltip: {
              useHTML: true,
              style: {
                padding: 0,
                pointerEvents: 'auto'
              },
              formatter: function () {
                return `
                  Time: ${this.x} <br>${this.series.name}: ${this.y}`
              }
            },
            yAxis: {
              title: {
                text: 'Value'
              }
            },
            xAxis: {
              categories: xAxisData
            },
            legend: {
              layout: 'vertical',
              align: 'right',
              verticalAlign: 'middle'
            },
            plotOptions: {
              series: {
```

```
          label: {
            connectorAllowed: false
          }
        }
      },
      series: [{
        name: 'Humdity',
        data: inhumidArr
      }, {
        name: 'Temperature',
        data: intempArr
      }]
    });

    const Esp32_Alpha1ChartData = devicesArr['ESP32_Alpha1'];
    const xAxisData1 = Esp32_Alpha1ChartData['temptime'];
    const inhumidArr1 = Esp32_Alpha1ChartData['hum'];
    const intempArr1 = Esp32_Alpha1ChartData['temp'];
    Highcharts.chart('container1', {
      title: {
        text: 'Esp32_Alpha1 Device'
      },
      tooltip: {
        useHTML: true,
        style: {
          padding: 0,
          pointerEvents: 'auto'
        },
        formatter: function () {
          return `
            Time: ${this.x} <br>${this.series.name}: ${this.y}`
        }
      },
      yAxis: {
        title: {
          text: 'Value'
        }
      },
      xAxis: {
        categories: xAxisData1
      },
      legend: {
        layout: 'vertical',
        align: 'right',
        verticalAlign: 'middle'
```

```
    },
    plotOptions: {
      series: {
        label: {
          connectorAllowed: false
        }
      }
    },
    series: [{
      name: 'Humdity',
      data: inhumidArr1
    }, {
      name: 'Temperature',
      data: intempArr1
    }]
  });

  const ESP_Bravo2ChartData = devicesArr['ESP32_Bravo2'];
  const xAxisData2 = ESP_Bravo2ChartData['temptime'];
  const inhumidArr2 = ESP_Bravo2ChartData['hum'];
  const intempArr2 = ESP_Bravo2ChartData['temp'];
  Highcharts.chart('container2', {
    title: {
      text: 'ESP_Bravo2 Device'
    },
    tooltip: {
      useHTML: true,
      style: {
        padding: 0,
        pointerEvents: 'auto'
      },
      formatter: function () {
        return `
          Time: ${this.x} <br>${this.series.name}: ${this.y}`
      }
    },
    yAxis: {
      title: {
        text: 'Value'
      }
    },
    xAxis: {
      categories: xAxisData2
    },
    legend: {
```

```
              layout: 'vertical',
              align: 'right',
              verticalAlign: 'middle'
            },
            plotOptions: {
              series: {
                label: {
                  connectorAllowed: false
                }
              }
            },
            series: [{
              name: 'Humdity',
              data: inhumidArr2
            }, {
              name: 'Temperature',
              data: intempArr2
            }]
          });

        } catch (error) {
          console.log(error)
        }
      }
    }
    x.onerror = function () {
    }
    x.send(null);
  }
  </script>
</body>
</html>
```

After uploading the code to your S3 bucket as index.html you can navigate to the 'Object URL' of the '*index.html'* file in your S3 bucket and select to open it.

index.html Info
Copy S3 U
Properties
Permissions
Versions
Object overview
Owner
borsay
AWS Region
US East (N. Virginia) us-east-1
Last modified
June 1, 2022, 14:28:23 (UTC-07:00)
Size
7.7 KB
Type
S3 URI
s3://timestreambuck/index.html
Amazon Resource Name (ARN)
arn:aws:s3:::timestreambuck/index.html
Entity tag (Etag)
bc8a7c7829e6ca37b5772023a6666c3a
Object URL
https://timestreambuck.s3.amazonaws.com/index.html

Right clicking the index.html Object URL as a new page should yield a visualization like that below with three graphs, one for each IoT device name assuming you implemented the same naming schema I recommended in Step 3.

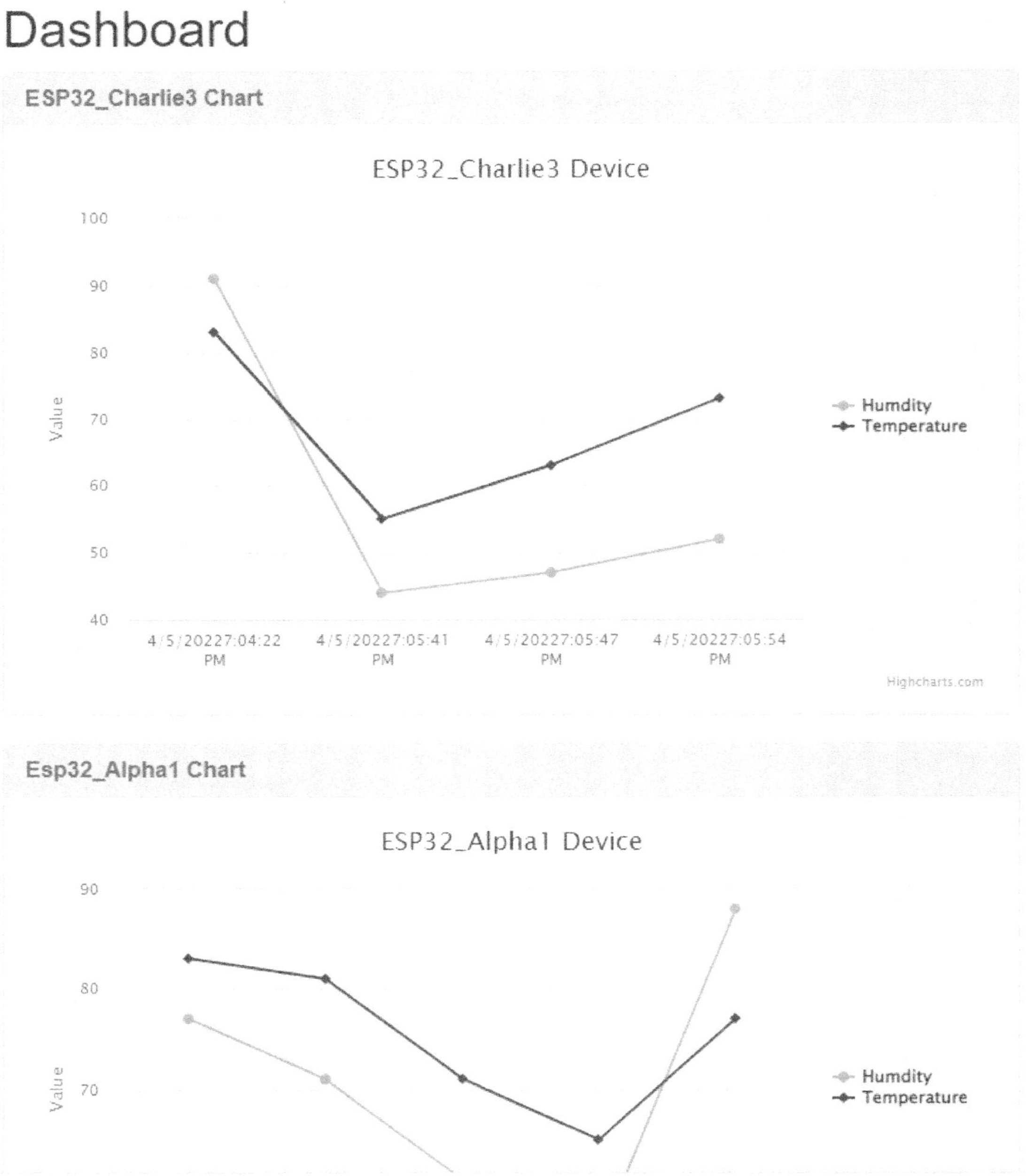
Dashboard
ESP32_Charlie3 Chart
ESP32_Charlie3 Device
100
90
80
70
60
50
40
Value
4/5/20227:04:22 PM
4/5/20227:05:41 PM
4/5/20227:05:47 PM
4/5/20227:05:54 PM
Humdity
Temperature
Highcharts.com
Esp32_Alpha1 Chart
ESP32_Alpha1 Device
90
80
70
Value
Humdity
Temperature

Congratulations, you were able to populate a Timestream table and visualize the IoT sensor readings in both Grafana and QuickSight. Then using a custom Lambda function you successfully queried your Timestream database. Finally, you were able to use a Function URL endpoint to develop a static website that produced graphs for all three IoT devices. As a next step try using different queries in the Lambda function to attain different results on you visualization website.

Chapter 17 - Putting it All Together with AWS IoT Analytics

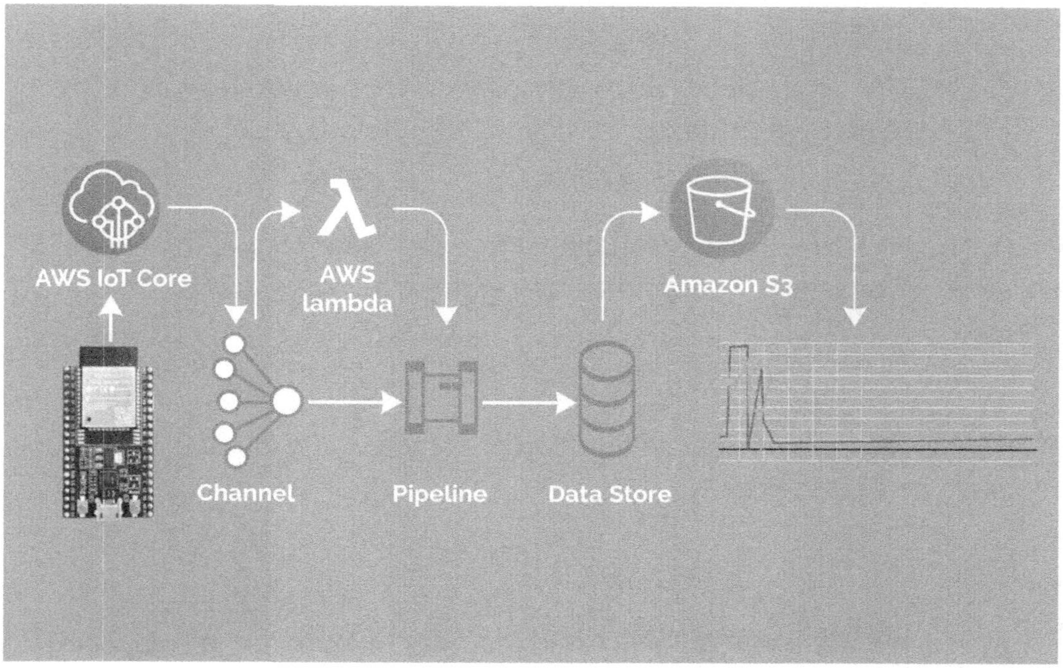
AWS IoT Core
AWS
lambda
Amazon S3
Channel
Pipeline
Data Store

IoT Analytics is AWS's first and only "All in one IoT solution" for some of the most common IoT services a typical IoT user would utilize on AWS. I believe the original intention of the service was to allow users to get up and running with a typical yet powerful AWS design flow that covered many of the major IoT-centric services offered on AWS. Whether you decide to use this consolidated service or decide to use your own chain of customized AWS services, IoT Analytics is still worth exploring as it is easy to get started with and accomplishes a lot without having to worry about all the implementation details of the underlying services.

IoT Analytics is a semi-managed process in which to ingest, filter, analysis and visualize your IoT data. By using IoT Analytics we can offset much of the overhead, inefficiencies, and hassle of chaining together the underlying AWS services ourselves. By providing a ready-made services template, AWS IoT Analytics reduces the complexity typically required to build an IoT analytics platform. We are already familiar with most of the key underlying services used in IoT Analytics from previous chapters.

Some of the advantages of AWS IoT Analytics are listed below:

A) IoT Analytics provides IoT batching for Data Lakes in efficient and readable CSV format. The batching will write to same csv file for every "Run."

B) IoT Analytics is integrated into many ancillary AWS services such as QuickSight, and SageMaker.

C) With the CSV storage option to S3, IoT Analytics integrates with services like AWS Glue and AWS Athena for advanced data analytics.

D) IoT Analytics modularizes its components, so you can use the Channel, Pipeline, Datastore, and Dataset as separate services in your own design flow.

E) IoT Analytics allows easy integration of Lambda functions for ETL on IoT data in its design flow.

For this project we will use AWS IoT Analytics, with Lambda for IoT payload enrichment, and built-in S3 data delivery to place the sensor readings into a S3 bucket. Using the object URL of your data in S3 you will then code a simple JavaScript static website, also hosted on S3, to parse the IoT data and then use Google Charts to visualize your environmental sensor readings. It should be noted that this method is totally flexible. Other free CDN based packages like Plotly, Highcharts.js, or Chart.js can also easily be implemented instead of Google Charts. Also, I will briefly show how to use the built in IoT Analytics connector in AWS QuickSight to visualize data if this "code-free" method is preferred for business analytics visualizations.

A key benefit of IoT Analytics is how well it integrates with Lambda for data enrichment. I will demonstrate a very simple Lambda function that we can implement in the IoT Analytics 'Pipeline' which demonstrates useful IoT data enrichment. I chose to demonstrate a simple Lambda function in both Python and Node.js because my function doesn't require rolling up and uploading any Node.js modules or Python packages to Lambda and can be developed directly from the Lambda editor, and then integrated in the IoT Analytics 'Pipeline.'

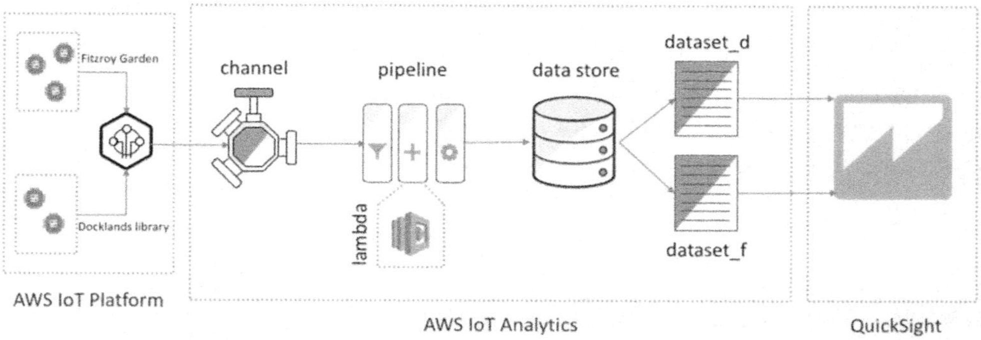

Fitzroy Garden
Docklands library
AWS IoT Platform
channel
pipeline
lambda
data store
dataset_d
dataset_f
AWS IoT Analytics
QuickSight

Step 1 – Create an IoT Analytics Channel, Pipeline, Datastore and Dataset
Step 2 – Connect IoT Analytics with an IoT Core Rule
Step 3 – Test the IoT Analytics Configuration by Running a Dataset
Step 4 – Create a S3 Public Bucket and Configure Retention Settings for the IoT Dataset
Step 5 – Design a Lambda Function for IoT Payload Transformation and Grant Integration Permissions with the AWS CLI
Step 6 – Integrate the Lambda Function into the Pipeline
Step 7 – Publish IoT Data and then Run the Dataset
Step 8 – Visualize the Timestream IoT Data in AWS QuickSight
Step 9 – Discover Insights into your IoT Data with AWS SageMaker
Step 10 – Configure, Upload, and Visualize the IoT Data in S3 with a Static Website

---

Step 1 – Create a IoT Analytics Channel, Pipeline, Datastore, and Dataset

To start the design process, go to IoT Analytics in a supported region:

https://console.aws.amazon.com/iotanalytics

To start, use the "Create resources" for IoT Analytics, simply type in a name for your Analytics chain and at this point do not offer a MQTT topic name, you will have more flexibility by doing that in IoT Core soon. If you do use a topic name here it will create a IoT Core Rule automatically for you, but I do not recommend this it reduces your flexibility in using the RQS.

Previously you had to individually create the Channel, Pipeline, and Data Store but now you can conveniently create all three with one click and then edit them separately later (which you will do for the two options when you enrich and store the IoT data). Add your own "Resources prefix" and, now press "Create resources". All your components will be automatically created.

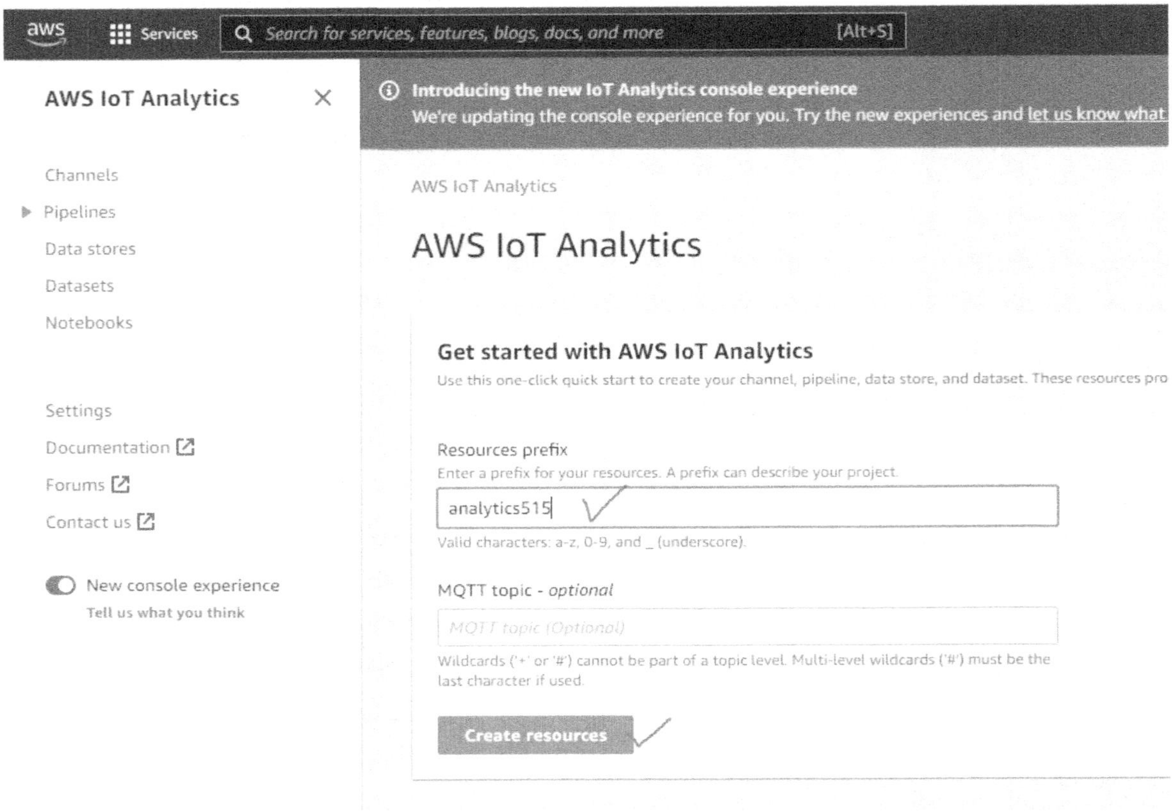

aws
Services
Search for services, features, blogs, docs, and more
[Alt+S]
AWS IoT Analytics
Introducing the new IoT Analytics console experience
We're updating the console experience for you. Try the new experiences and let us know what
Channels
Pipelines
Data stores
Datasets
Notebooks
Settings
Documentation
Forums
Contact us
New console experience
Tell us what you think
AWS IoT Analytics
AWS IoT Analytics
Get started with AWS IoT Analytics
Use this one-click quick start to create your channel, pipeline, data store, and dataset. These resources pro
Resources prefix
Enter a prefix for your resources. A prefix can describe your project.
analytics515
Valid characters: a-z, 0-9, and _ (underscore).
MQTT topic - optional
MQTT topic (Optional)
Wildcards ('+' or '#') cannot be part of a topic level. Multi-level wildcards ('#') must be the last character if used.
Create resources

After a short time, all the resources in the IoT Analytics process chain should be created for you.

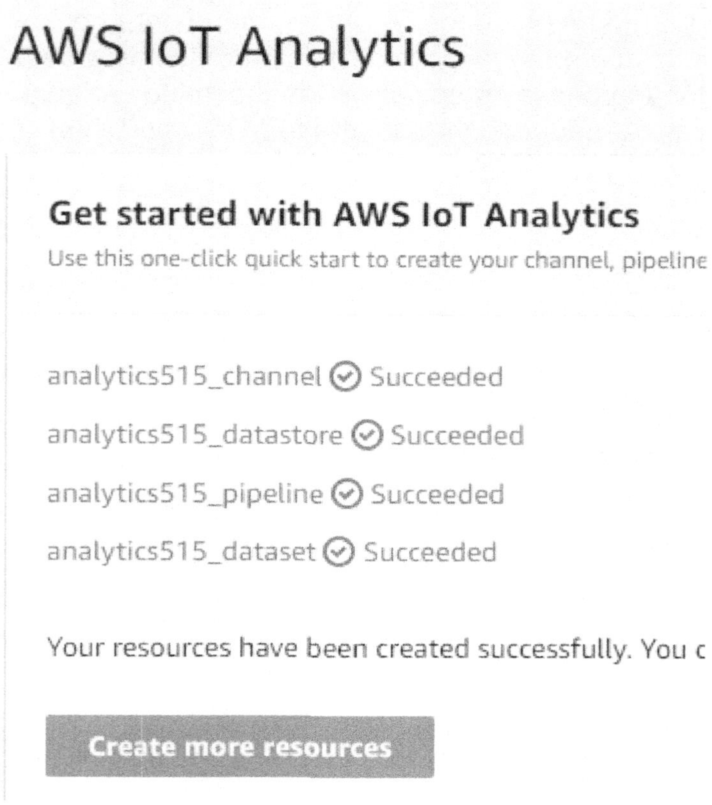
AWS IoT Analytics
Get started with AWS IoT Analytics
Use this one-click quick start to create your channel, pipeline
analytics515_channel Succeeded
analytics515_datastore Succeeded
analytics515_pipeline Succeeded
analytics515_dataset Succeeded
Your resources have been created successfully. You c
Create more resources

You just created all your resources with one click, easy so far. Notice that the resources have the same prefix from your "Resources prefix" selection. Now you can connect the MQTT broker in IoT Core so that you can send IoT messages to the IoT Analytics 'Channel". Once the IoT sensor readings are in the channel those messages will be propagated through the IoT Analytics Pipeline where you will enhance or transform them with a Lambda function.

Step 2 – Connect IoT Analytics with an IoT Core Rule

At this point you have done this many times. Navigate to AWS IoT Core and create a new Rule in IoT Core:

https://console.aws.amazon.com/iot/#/rulehub

Create a new Rule and give it a name of your choice. Here I called mine "analytics515."

Next, you will use the Rules Query Statement to ingest your incoming data package under a user provided topic name. Remember you can delimit your incoming data to any field you like or set up conditional processing based on the incoming variable values. However, for most purposes it's useful to grab all the IoT Data and then parse it later as needed, which is what you will do here.
For the Rules Query Statement, you will use a simple one for this project:

```
SELECT * FROM 'iot/#'
```

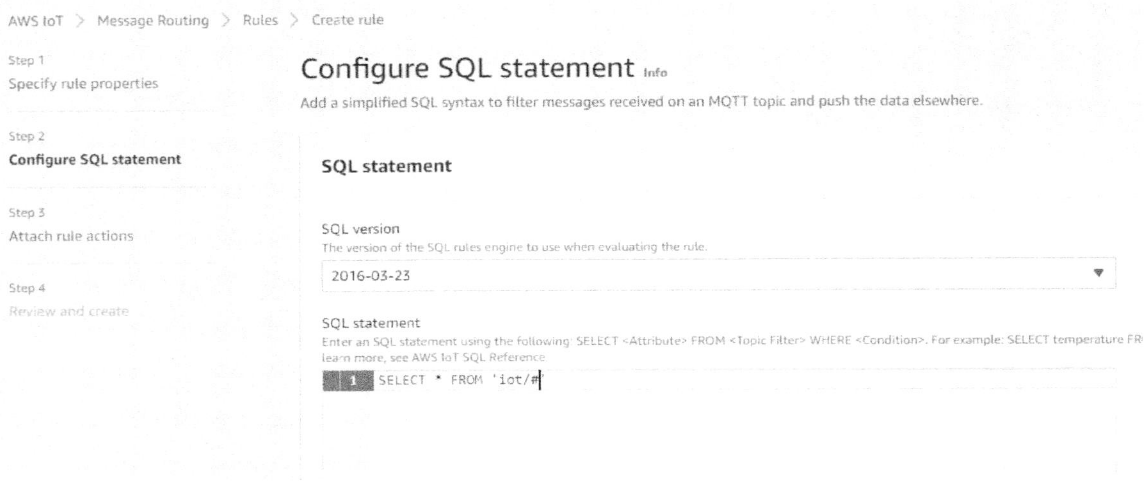

AWS IoT > Message Routing > Rules > Create rule
Step 1
Specify rule properties
Step 2
Configure SQL statement
Step 3
Attach rule actions
Step 4
Review and create
Configure SQL statement Info
Add a simplified SQL syntax to filter messages received on an MQTT topic and push the data elsewhere.
SQL statement
SQL version
The version of the SQL rules engine to use when evaluating the rule.
2016-03-23
SQL statement
1 SELECT * FROM 'iot/#'

Select the "Next" button where you can add in your IoT Analytics service to process your IoT data coming through IoT Core.

Next

Select "Send a message to IoT Analytics." To configure your action, choose to manually add in the resources you just created for IoT Analytics. Choose the channel you just created at the beginning of your processing chain; the messages will get propagated from the channel to the rest of the IoT Analytics resources. Leave "Batch Mode" unselected, you are not sending enough payloads at a frequency to warrant the batching of IoT data payloads. Finally, create a "Role" which will give the necessary permissions to link IoT Core with the IoT Analytics Channel.

If you are using the new console experience in IoT Core rather than the classic view your configuration page should look as below:

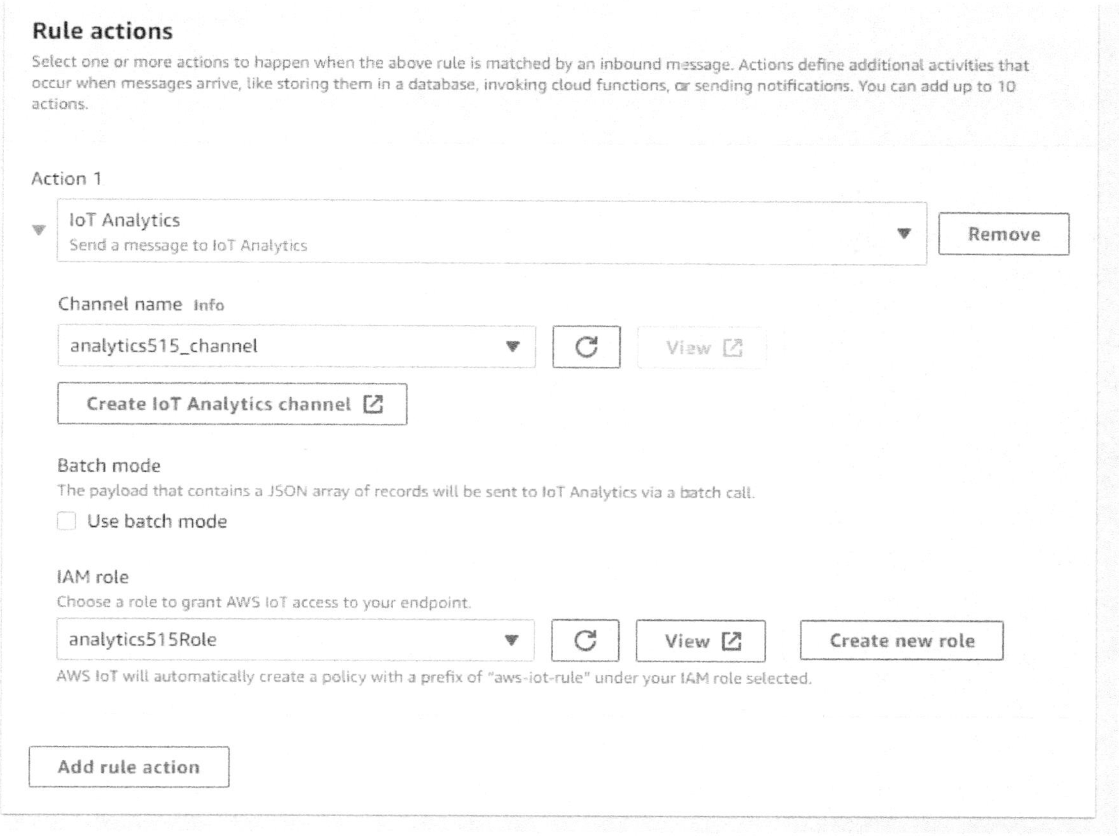
Rule actions
Select one or more actions to happen when the above rule is matched by an inbound message. Actions define additional activities that occur when messages arrive, like storing them in a database, invoking cloud functions, or sending notifications. You can add up to 10 actions.
Action 1
IoT Analytics
Send a message to IoT Analytics
Remove
Channel name Info
analytics515_channel
View
Create IoT Analytics channel
Batch mode
The payload that contains a JSON array of records will be sent to IoT Analytics via a batch call.
Use batch mode
IAM role
Choose a role to grant AWS IoT access to your endpoint.
analytics515Role
View
Create new role
AWS IoT will automatically create a policy with a prefix of "aws-iot-rule" under your IAM role selected.
Add rule action

Since you do not have any more ‘rule actions’ to add to your rule go ahead and press “Next”:

Next

Review your rule details and then select “Create” to finalize your rule:

Create

At this point you have successfully configured IoT Core to dispatch IoT payloads as messages to the “Channel” in IoT Analytics which will then propagate through the rest of the IoT Analytics services chain.

Step 3 – Test the IoT Analytics Configuration by Running a Dataset

Now you will test the rule you just created by connecting IoT Core to IoT Analytics to ensure that everything is configured correctly. To do this simply publish your typical JSON IoT payload consisting of temperature and humidity. Since you subscribed to the topic of 'iot/#' in your RQS you can send the payload from the virtual or physical IoT device with an applicable topic with 'iot/<Use-Anything-Here>'.

Below are the payloads being received by IoT Core from an IoT device and dispatched to IoT Analytics from the rule you just created:

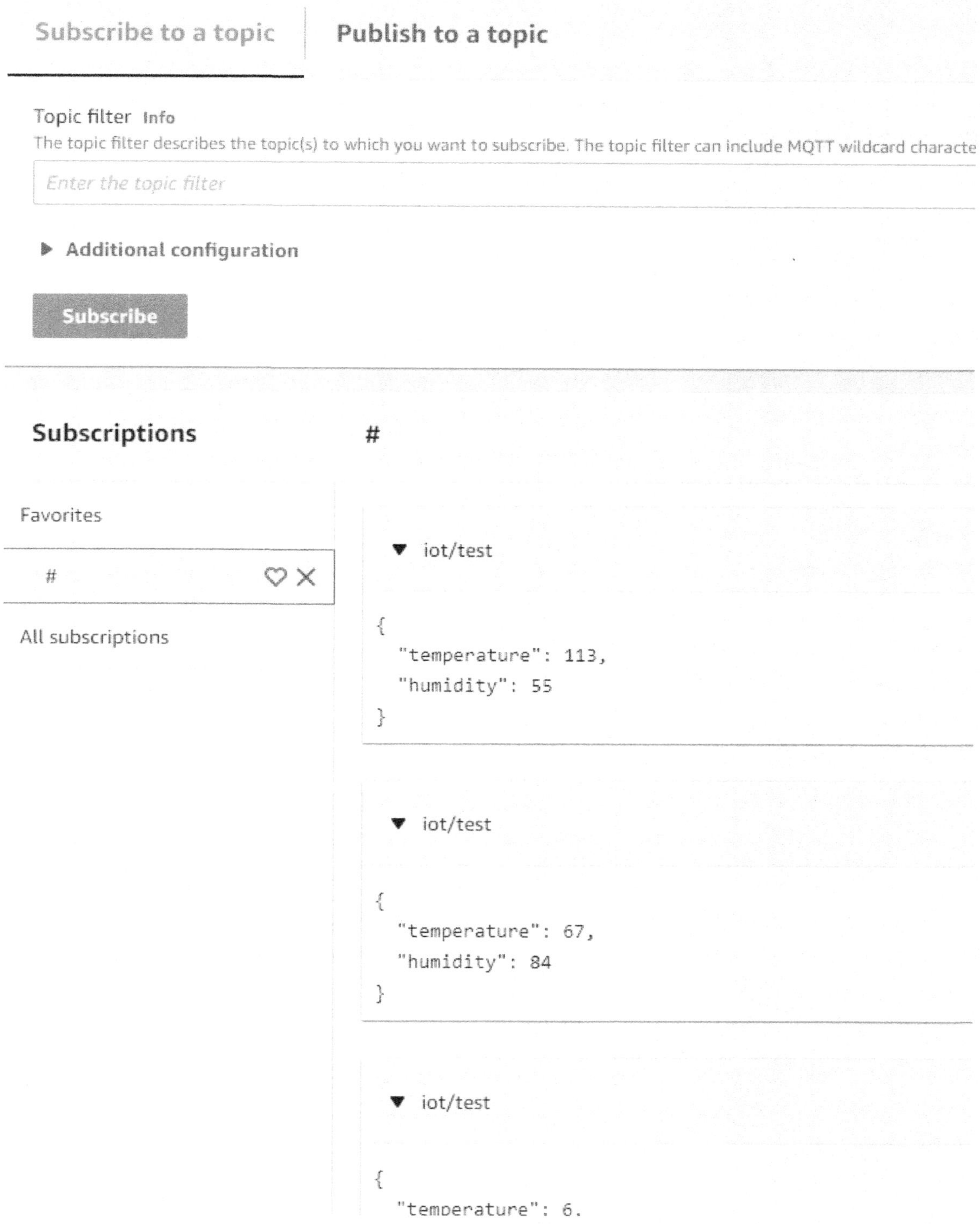
Subscribe to a topic
Publish to a topic
Topic filter Info
The topic filter describes the topic(s) to which you want to subscribe. The topic filter can include MQTT wildcard characte
Enter the topic filter
Additional configuration
Subscribe
Subscriptions
#
Favorites
#
All subscriptions
iot/test
{
"temperature": 113,
"humidity": 55
}
iot/test
{
"temperature": 67,
"humidity": 84
}
iot/test
{
"temperature": 6.

Now go to the IoT Analytics "Channel" page:

IoT Analytics→Channels

https://console.aws.amazon.com/iotanalytics/#/channels

Make sure your IoT payloads have propagated successfully through IoT Analytics. First check the IoT Analytics channel and look for the "Last message arrival time" to be the current time:

Channels (16)

Name	Storage type	Status	Last message arrival time
analy41a_channel	Service managed	Active	-
analy41b_channel	Service managed	Active	-
analy530_channel	Service managed	Active	-
analytics515_channel	Service managed	Active	May 16, 2022 10:34:02 AM -0700
chal55	Service managed	Active	-

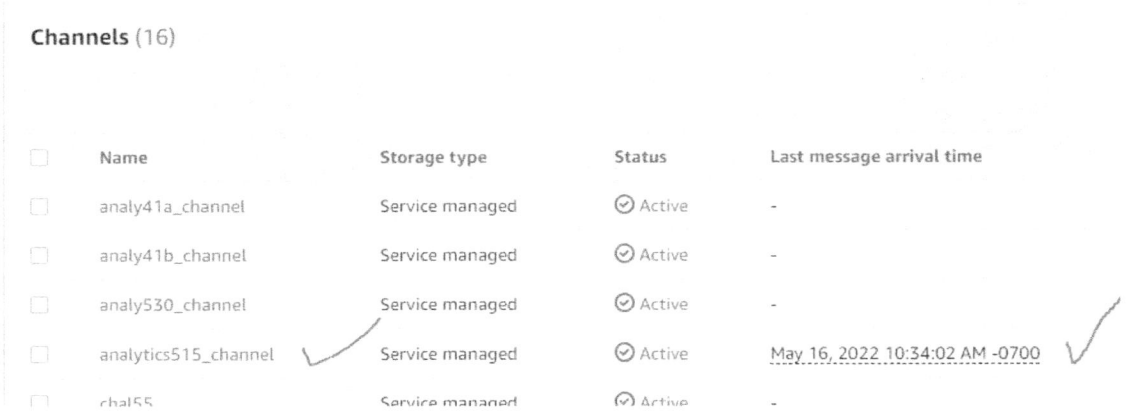

Above, the channel shows the IoT data being ingested at exactly the time expected. As a final check go to the end of the analytics chain and run your Dataset to ensure it has received all the IoT readings you published from your device.

IoT Analytics→Datasets

Or click:

https://console.aws.amazon.com/iotanalytics/#/datasets

Select your specific dataset. Now you have two options that have the same result. You can either press the "Run now" button and then check your contents, or check your contents and then use the "Run now" button to receive the results of your query on the next page under the "Content" tab.

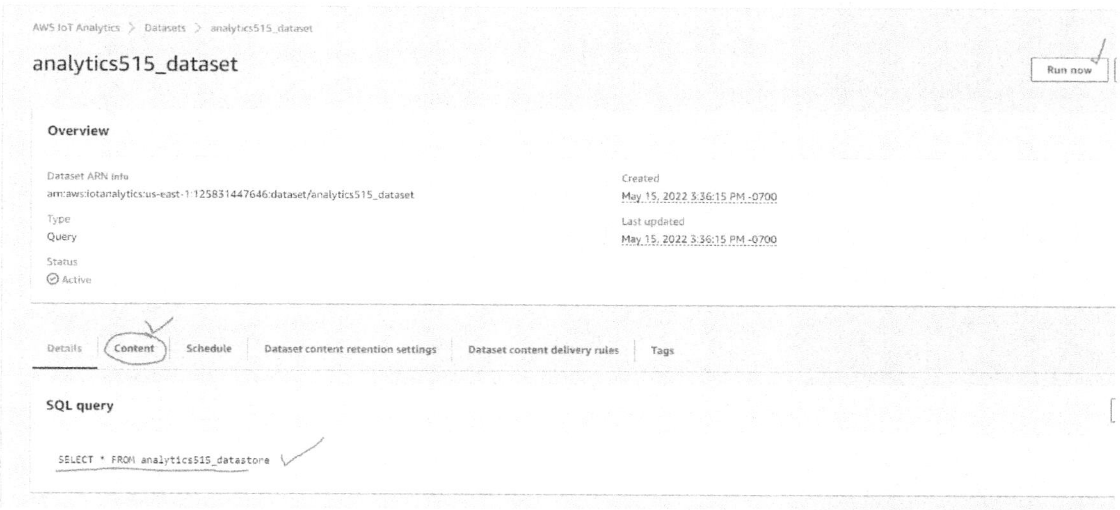
AWS IoT Analytics > Datasets > analytics515_dataset
analytics515_dataset
Run now
Overview
Dataset ARN Info
arn:aws:iotanalytics:us-east-1:125831447646:dataset/analytics515_dataset
Created
May 15, 2022 3:36:15 PM -0700
Type
Query
Last updated
May 15, 2022 3:36:15 PM -0700
Status
Active
Details
Content
Schedule
Dataset content retention settings
Dataset content delivery rules
Tags
SQL query
SELECT * FROM analytics515_datastore

Also notice the Athena like SQL query statement inserted by default. If you have a large data set of IoT sensor readings, you may want to confine your results to only readings in which the temperature exceeded some threshold value, or just a specified number of readings by ascending or descending order. For now, use the default SQL statement and query for every IoT payload delivered to IoT Analytics.

After some time, the IoT data is ready for you to view, you may have to press the refresh dial to see when your report is available.

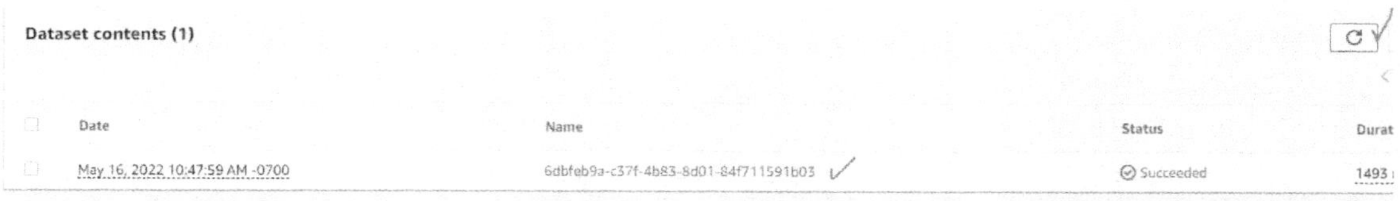
Dataset contents (1)
Date
Name
Status
Durat
May 16, 2022 10:47:59 AM -0700
6dbfeb9a-c37f-4b83-8d01-84f711591b03
Succeeded
1493

Now you can click the report to see your IoT data:

Result preview

44091084-e16c-4b02-bd10-aaa9484c6ce3.csv

temperature	humidity	__dt
126	99	2022-05-16 00:00:00.000
84	15	2022-05-16 00:00:00.000
59	9	2022-05-16 00:00:00.000
110	59	2022-05-16 00:00:00.000
75	28	2022-05-16 00:00:00.000
101	96	2022-05-16 00:00:00.000
62	96	2022-05-16 00:00:00.000
6	86	2022-05-16 00:00:00.000
67	84	2022-05-16 00:00:00.000

Great, hopefully everything is working, and your dataset appears, if not review the previous step.

You may have noticed the mysterious '_dt' field in the results table. This is the "delta time "which is automatically added to your dataset. The __dt field still appears even if you run an unsuccessful query which will appear as an empty data set. You can ignore the __dt field, as you are not using this option.

Now that you know that the IoT Analytics design works successfully thus far, you can move on. If you don't have any data, then review the previous steps before moving on. Remember it can take a few minutes for your data to appear after the sensor readings reach the AWS message broker and IoT Core. A good way to check the status of your IoT readings before you run the dataset report is to look at the "Last message arrival time" in the 'Channel' and then the 'Datastore' as mentioned earlier.

Step 4 – Create a S3 Public Bucket and Configure Retention Settings for the IoT Dataset

Follow the prerequisite directions to create a public S3 bucket with a static web host using a 'index.html' launch page. You will be using this bucket later for the visualization of the IoT Analytics 'Dataset'. Once you create your public bucket in S3, you now need to set the bucket as a data repository for IoT Analytics. This is required to allow your ephemeral dataset to become a permanent CSV data object held in a S3 partition as a data lake.

Name your S3 bucket something globally unique, below is my bucket:

analytics515-bucket
US East (N. Virginia) us-east-1

Close out your data run results and select the “Dataset content delivery rules” tab, then “Add dataset content delivery rules.”

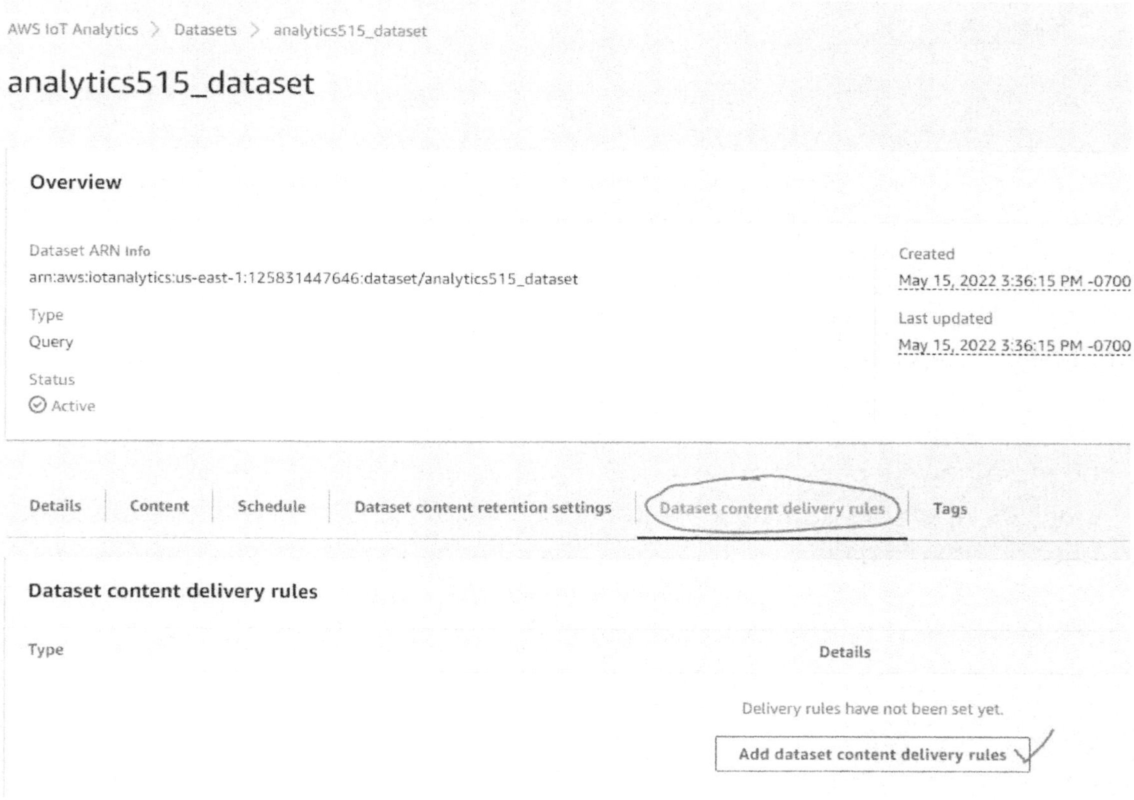

AWS IoT Analytics > Datasets > analytics515_dataset
analytics515_dataset
Overview
Dataset ARN Info
arn:aws:iotanalytics:us-east-1:125831447646:dataset/analytics515_dataset
Type
Query
Status
Active
Created
May 15, 2022 3:36:15 PM -0700
Last updated
May 15, 2022 3:36:15 PM -0700
Details
Content
Schedule
Dataset content retention settings
Dataset content delivery rules
Tags
Dataset content delivery rules
Type
Details
Delivery rules have not been set yet.
Add dataset content delivery rules

Now select “Delivery result to S3” in “Add rule” and then press “Add”

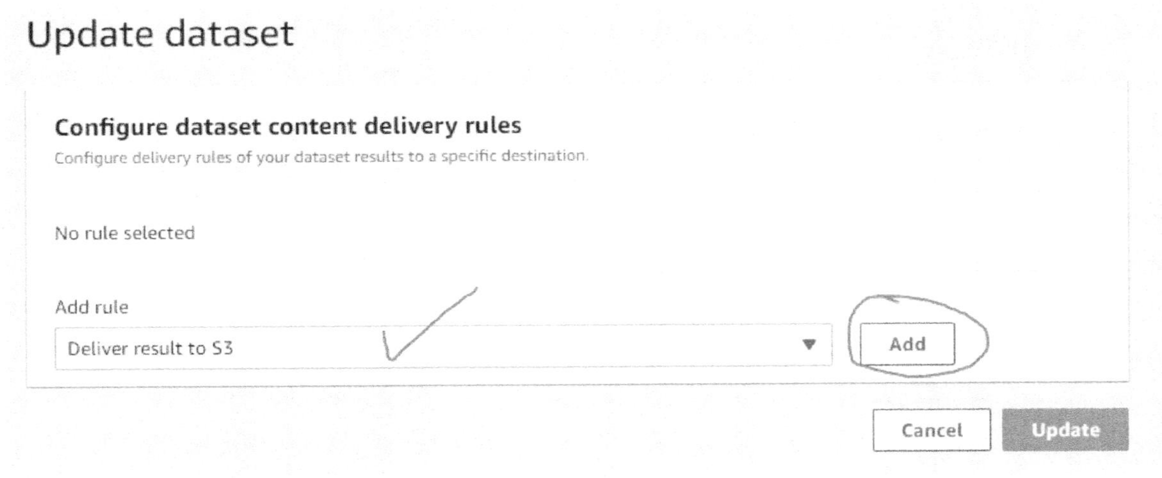
Update dataset
Configure dataset content delivery rules
Configure delivery rules of your dataset results to a specific destination.
No rule selected
Add rule
Deliver result to S3
Add
Cancel
Update

On the next screen there are three things to configure:

1. For "S3 bucket name" choose the public bucket you just created to host the dataset readings.

2. For "Bucket key expression" provide a file path to save your dataset. Here I choose a new key I called "enviro" that will be automatically created by IoT Analytics when the dataset is written to the S3 bucket. Then I chose to call my sensor readings data object "iot.csv." It is a good idea to use the .csv file extension as IoT Analytics will deliver the dataset with CSV formatting by default, but otherwise as a blob object without a file extension.

3. For "IAM Role" create a new role that will allow IoT Analytics to write (Put) the dataset to S3.

4. Press "Update"

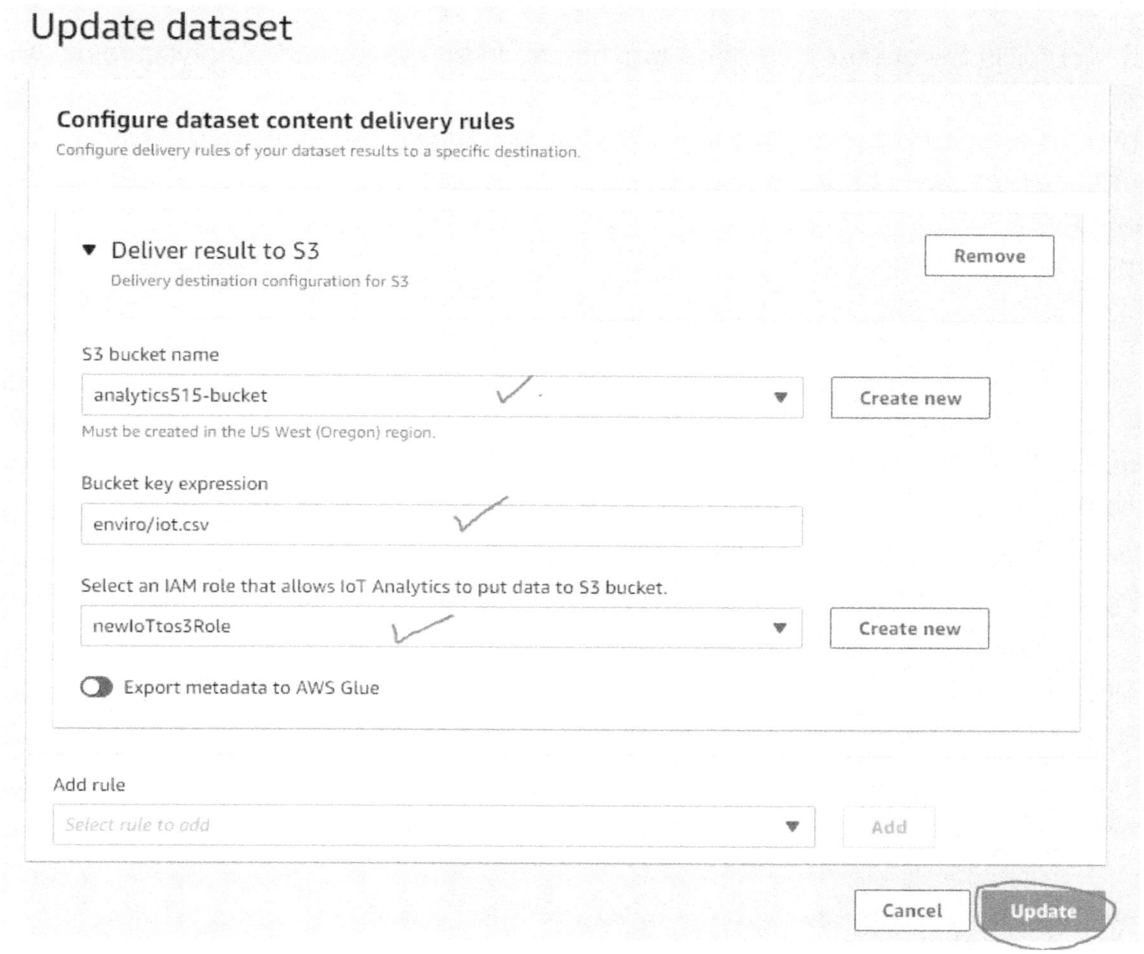
Update dataset
Configure dataset content delivery rules
Configure delivery rules of your dataset results to a specific destination.
Deliver result to S3
Delivery destination configuration for S3
Remove
S3 bucket name
analytics515-bucket
Create new
Must be created in the US West (Oregon) region.
Bucket key expression
enviro/iot.csv
Select an IAM role that allows IoT Analytics to put data to S3 bucket.
newIoTtos3Role
Create new
Export metadata to AWS Glue
Add rule
Select rule to add
Add
Cancel
Update

As an aside there are three opportunities to set up S3 storage for data in IoT Analytics. Once in the channel, once in the datastore, and finally here in the dataset as you just completed the configuration for. The problem with the first two S3 storage "offramps" is that they both save data in compressed format (.gz). Thus, if you wanted to work with this data, it would require extra processing logic (like decompressing the S3 object in Lambda).

You are welcome to *offload* your IoT data from any or all the three services in IoT Analytics. However, for this project you will only be using the CSV data delivered to S3 from the 'Dataset' at the end of the IoT Analytics services chain.

Step 5 – Design a Lambda Function for IoT Payload Transformation and Grant Integration Permissions with the AWS CLI

Now you will now create a Lambda function to insert into the IoT Analytics pipeline to transform and enrich your incoming IoT data. This transformed data then will be sent from the pipeline through the rest of the IoT Analytics processing chain. For your transform you will do something very trivial just to demonstrate the Lambda transformation. You will just be adding a "serverside" timestamp to your temperature and humidity IoT payload. The real use for inserting a Lambda function in the pipeline would usually be a much more extensive transformation or enrichment of your IoT payload. The sky is the limit.

First go to Lambda and then create a new Lambda function in your region in Python 3.8. Below is the code for the simple Lambda function for integration with pipeline activities:

```
import json
import time

def lambda_handler(event, context):
    event[0]['serversidetimestamp'] = round(time.time() * 1000)

    print(event)
    return event
```

Shown in the image below, you can also create a Lambda function in Node.js 16x called "SS-timestamp" for serverside timestamp

Basic information
Function name
SS-timestamp
Runtime
Node.js 16.x
Architecture
x86_64
arm64
Permissions
Change default execution role
Advanced settings
Cancel
Create function

Here is the ultra-simple code for the Lambda function in Node.js (16.x) which accomplishes the same thing as the Python Lambda function above:

```
exports.handler = function handler(event) {

    console.log("event whole: ", event);
    console.log("event element: ", event[0]);

//add timestamp to data and name it "Serversidetimestamp"
        event[0].serversidetimestamp = Date.now();
        console.log("event whole mod: ", event);

       return event;
};
```

After pasting the Python or Node.js code into your own Lambda function, deploy the Lambda function to save it.

Lambda > Functions > SS-timestamp
SS-timestamp
Function overview Info
Code
Test
Monitor
Configuration
Aliases
Versions
Code source Info
File Edit Find View Go Tools Window
Test
Deploy
Go to Anything (Ctrl-P)
index.js
Environment
SS-timestamp
index.js
exports.handler = function handler(event) {
console.log("event whole: ", event);
console.log("event element: ", event[0]);
//add timesteamp to incoming data and name it "ServersideTimestamp"
event[0].ServersideTimestamp = Date.now();
console.log("event whole mod: ", event);
return event;
};

I have added in extra console logging print statements to the code so that you can debug the Lambda function later in CloudWatch if you want to. However, there is something very important to note about this Lambda function related to how it will be processed in the IoT Analytics Pipeline. The format of the incoming event object from the IoT channel is not what you would normally expect. This is because it is a Kinesis like nested JSON array event even though you already choose not to select batch processing. The IoT payload to be processed has a batch of one object in this case. So, if you want to debug or use the "Test" feature in Lambda you cannot use a standard JSON payload to test it with. You will have to use the nested JSON array format as shown below as an example test payload:

```
[
  {
      "temperature": 55,
      "humidity": 66
  }
]
```

Notice the opening [and closing] brackets as nested array notation JSON.

Lambda Permission

Now you must give the Lambda function that you just created the permission to be integrated into IoT Analytics. Unlike in any other section of this book, you cannot configure these permissions in AWS IAM by attaching a inline policy to your Lambda function. I do not know why this is. Rather, you must add the permissions from the AWS CLI as currently listed on page 41 of the IoT Analytics User Guide.

https://docs.aws.amazon.com/iotanalytics/latest/userguide/iotanalytics-ug.pdf

Below is the command to create the needed permissions for Lambda integration into IoT Analytics using the AWS CLI. As always, use the region flag if you are using another region for IoT Analytics than your AWS CLI configured 'home' region. Remember to also customize the command below for the name of your Lambda function and a unique statement ID.

```
Aws lambda add-permission –function-name <Your-Lambda-Name> --region <Your-AWS-Region> --statement-id <Some-ID> --principal iotanalytics.amazonaws.com –action lambda:InvokeFunction
```

Here is what the command from the AWS CLI looks like

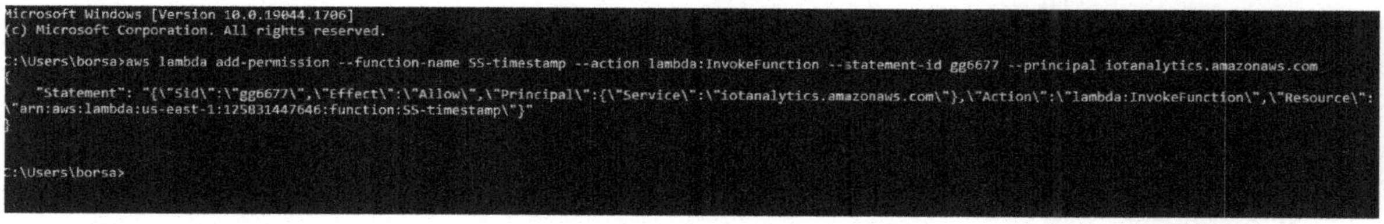
Microsoft Windows [Version 10.0.19044.1706]
(c) Microsoft Corporation. All rights reserved.
C:\Users\borsa>aws lambda add-permission --function-name SS-timestamp --action lambda:InvokeFunction --statement-id gg6677 --principal iotanalytics.amazonaws.com
{
"Statement": "{\"Sid\":\"gg6677\",\"Effect\":\"Allow\",\"Principal\":{\"Service\":\"iotanalytics.amazonaws.com\"},\"Action\":\"lambda:InvokeFunction\",\"Resource\":\"arn:aws:lambda:us-east-1:125831447646:function:SS-timestamp\"}"
}
C:\Users\borsa>

Notice the CLI statement return acknowledging that the command went through successfully. Also note that if you try to give these permissions after you insert the Lambda function into the pipeline it sometimes will not work. Your "statement id" can be any random alphanumeric string that you like so long as it is unique.

Step 6 – Integrate the Lambda Function into the Pipeline

Now return to the IoT Analytics Pipeline:

https://console.aws.amazon.com/iotanalytics/#/pipelines

Go to your pipeline, then click to open it, then go to the "Activities" tab and then press the "Add activities" button.

Monitoring
Activities
Tags
Channel inputs
Name
Type
analytics515_channel
Channel
Activities
Name
Type
No activities
You don't have any activities for this pipeline.
Add activities

The message attributes from your JSON payload may appear from when you tested the processing chain. You can ignore this screen and hit "Next."

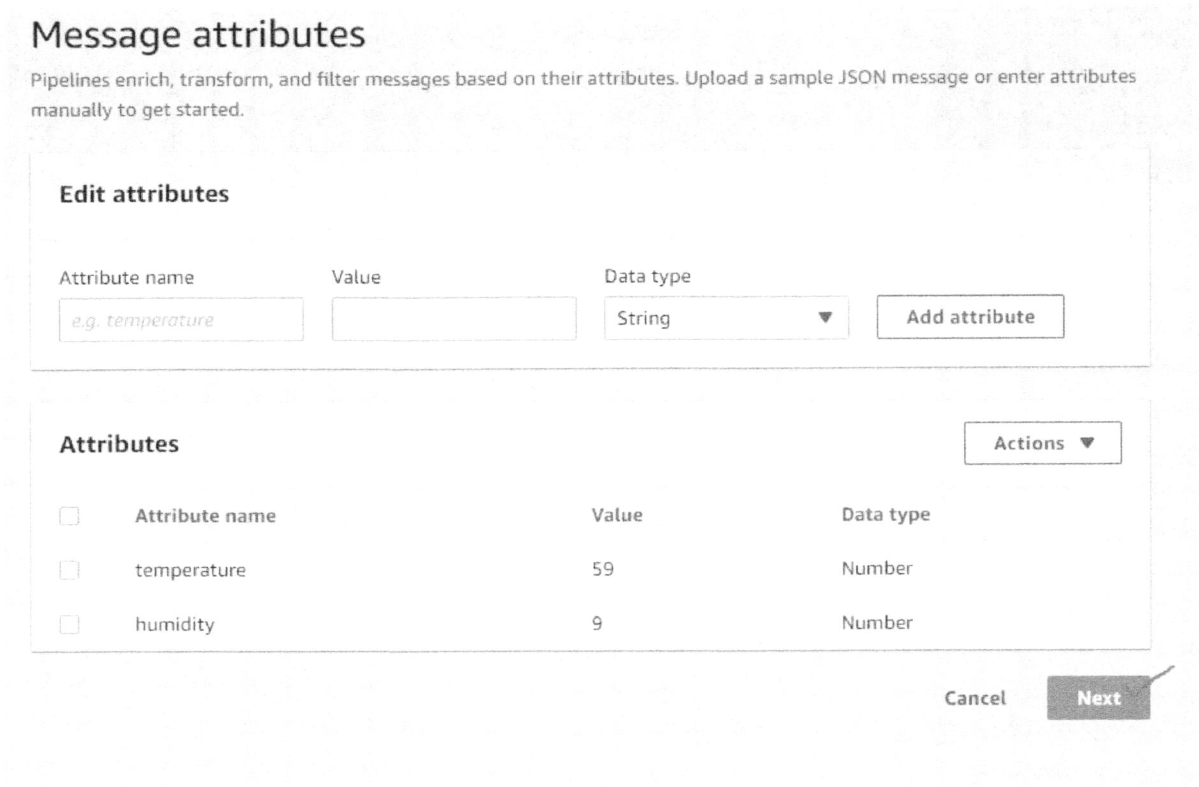
Message attributes
Pipelines enrich, transform, and filter messages based on their attributes. Upload a sample JSON message or enter attributes manually to get started.
Edit attributes
Attribute name
Value
Data type
e.g. temperature
String
Add attribute
Attributes
Actions
Attribute name
Value
Data type
temperature
59
Number
humidity
9
Number
Cancel
Next

Choose to "Transform message with a Lambda function" from the drop-down menu of options and then press "Add"

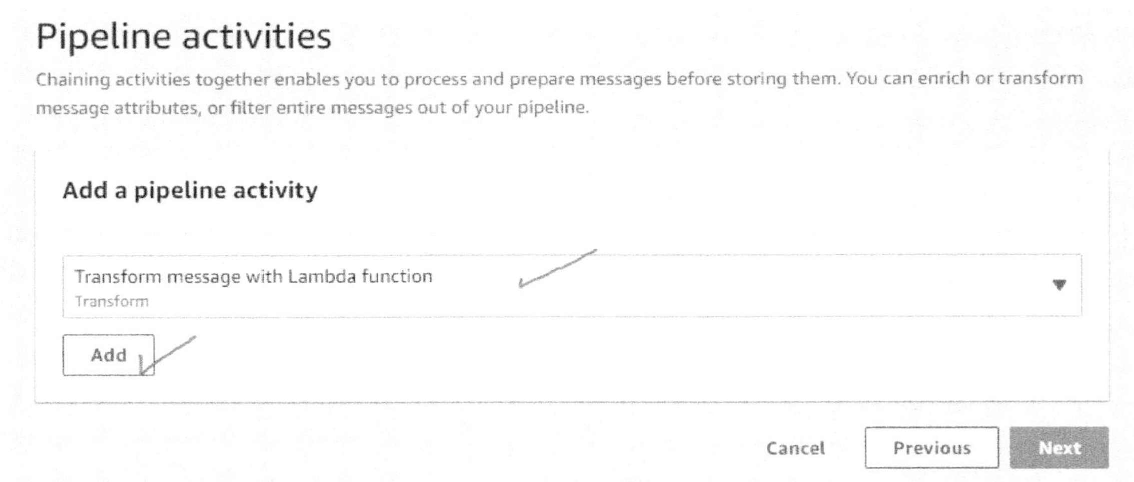
Pipeline activities
Chaining activities together enables you to process and prepare messages before storing them. You can enrich or transform message attributes, or filter entire messages out of your pipeline.
Add a pipeline activity
Transform message with Lambda function
Transform
Add
Cancel
Previous
Next

Now you will add the Lambda function that you just created by selecting it from the drop-down menu. Keep the batch size as one and press "Next."

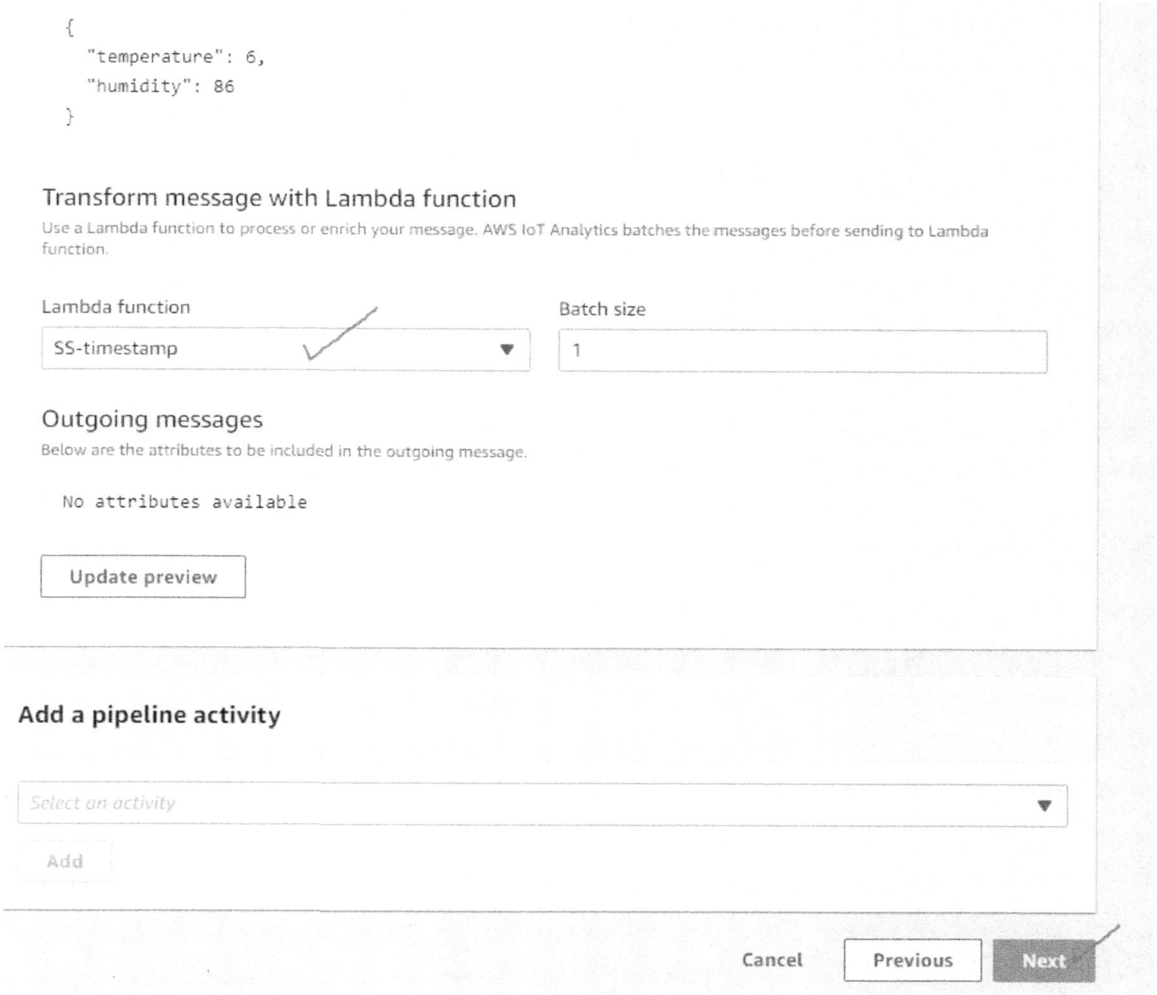
{
"temperature": 6,
"humidity": 86
}
Transform message with Lambda function
Use a Lambda function to process or enrich your message. AWS IoT Analytics batches the messages before sending to Lambda function.
Lambda function
SS-timestamp
Batch size
1
Outgoing messages
Below are the attributes to be included in the outgoing message.
No attributes available
Update preview
Add a pipeline activity
Select an activity
Add
Cancel
Previous
Next

Finally review and "Update".

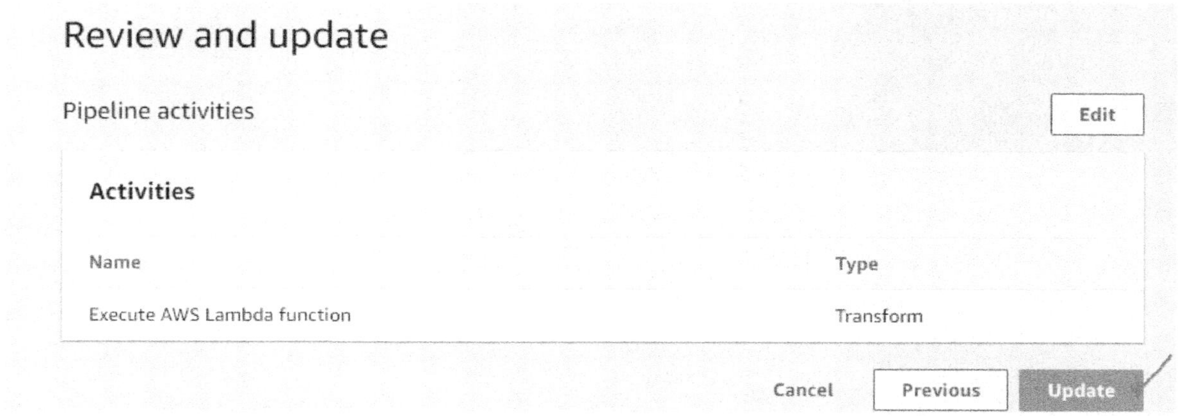
Review and update
Pipeline activities
Edit
Activities
Name
Type
Execute AWS Lambda function
Transform
Cancel
Previous
Update

Now you are done adding the Lambda function timestamp transformation as a "pipeline activity" into the IoT Analytics processing chain.

Step 7 – Publish IoT Data and then Run the Dataset

Now it is time to send your IoT sensor readings through the entire IoT Analytics processing chain to be transformed and enhanced by your Lambda function and then delivered to your S3 bucket for storage and future analysis and visualization.

Use a physical or virtual IoT device to send environmental data to IoT Core with the "iot/<something>" topic. To do this return to the MQTT test client here:

https://aws.amazon.com/iot

Shown below I am receiving IoT data in the IoT Core MQTT test client:

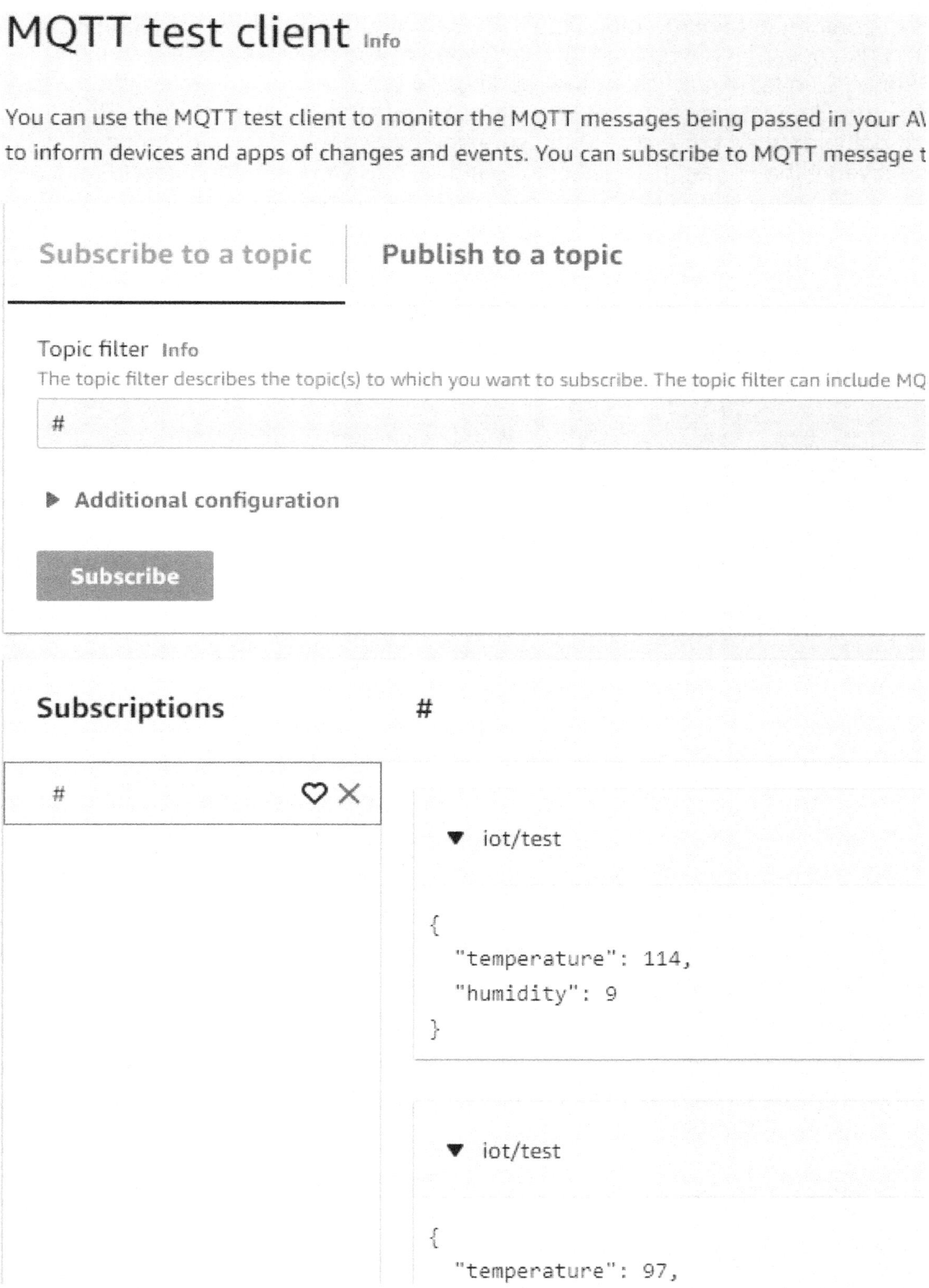
MQTT test client Info
You can use the MQTT test client to monitor the MQTT messages being passed in your A\
to inform devices and apps of changes and events. You can subscribe to MQTT message t
Subscribe to a topic
Publish to a topic
Topic filter Info
The topic filter describes the topic(s) to which you want to subscribe. The topic filter can include MQ
#
Additional configuration
Subscribe
Subscriptions
#
#
iot/test
{
"temperature": 114,
"humidity": 9
}
iot/test
{
"temperature": 97,

Next, confirm that your Lambda function was integrated properly, to do this check the "Last message arrival time" in the 'Channel' and then the same field in the 'Datastore' in IoT Analytics. If the readings hit the channel but never made it to the datastore it usually means that your timestamp Lambda function in the 'Pipeline' was not integrated correctly. Make sure you have deployed your Lambda function and given it the correct permissions from the AWS CLI as demonstrated earlier.

Now to place the contents of the Dataset as a CSV file (enviro/iot.csv) into your S3 bucket you must run a new query with your dataset. This SQL statement will put the contents of the CSV file in timestamp order:

IoT Analytics→Datasets-→ Edit SQL Query

```
SELECT * FROM <Your-IoT-Analytics-Prefix>_datastore order by
serversidetimestamp
```

Use your own IoT Analytics prefix name with your SQL query.

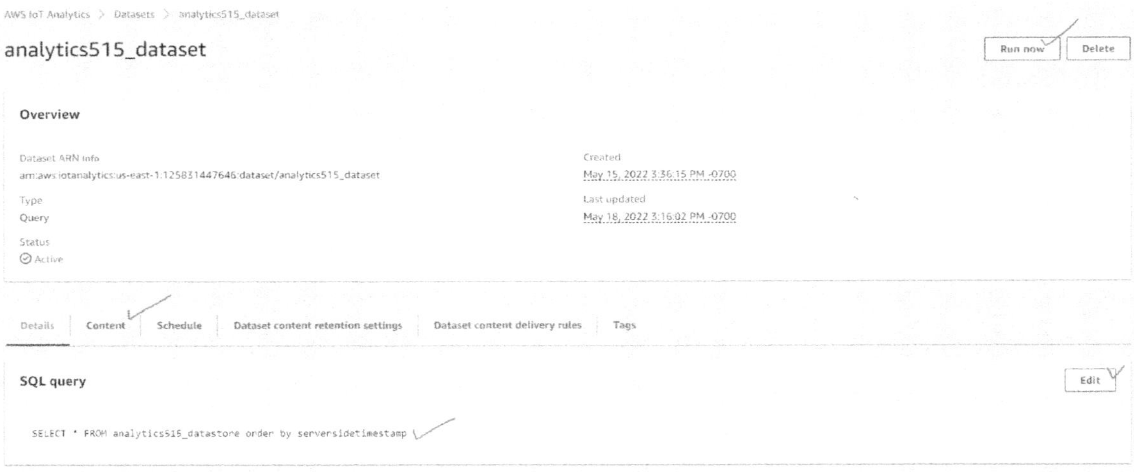
AWS IoT Analytics > Datasets > analytics515_dataset
analytics515_dataset
Run now
Delete
Overview
Dataset ARN info
arn:aws:iotanalytics:us-east-1:125831447646:dataset/analytics515_dataset
Created
May 15, 2022 3:36:15 PM -0700
Type
Query
Last updated
May 18, 2022 3:16:02 PM -0700
Status
Active
Details
Content
Schedule
Dataset content retention settings
Dataset content delivery rules
Tags
SQL query
Edit
SELECT * FROM analytics515_datastore order by serversidetimestamp

You can customize your own Athena style SQL queries on your dataset by reading the reference documentation:

https://docs.aws.amazon.com/iotanalytics/latest/userguide/sql-support.html

Press the "Run now" button and then view the "Content" tab. Once in the content pane open your latest query. The query results were automatically sent to your S3 bucket as 'enviro/iot.csv' from when you configured the S3 retention settings earlier in Step 4.

Result preview

420de66a-fafa-41c3-af12-8d627acb8a1b.csv

temperature	humidity	serversidetimestamp	__dt
31	12	1652911388001	2022-05-18 00:00:00.000
119	40	1652911388006	2022-05-18 00:00:00.000
122	67	1652911388014	2022-05-18 00:00:00.000
57	86	1652911388018	2022-05-18 00:00:00.000
57	12	1652911388034	2022-05-18 00:00:00.000
64	70	1652911388041	2022-05-18 00:00:00.000
85	78	1652911388054	2022-05-18 00:00:00.000
8	70	1652911388059	2022-05-18 00:00:00.000
57	12	1652911388074	2022-05-18 00:00:00.000

Important S3 dataset retention facts to remember

1. The dataset that is written (PUT) to S3 as 'iot.csv' is contingent upon your SQL query, thus the 'iot.csv object will be the results of your specific query and not all the historical IoT readings that are held in the datastore.

2. S3 is incapable of appending or concatenating data objects, thus all new queries of the datastore will produce a dataset that overwrites previous "iot.csv" objects in S3 unless you specify bucket key retention settings for storage to another folder location in S3.

3. If you edit the CSV object ('iot.csv') from S3 do so only in a UTF-8 editor. If you use Excel or a similar spreadsheet application, the application will add special characters to the CSV object that you can't see, and then you won't be able to parse your modified CSV object, and it will no longer work with the website visualizations.

Now return to S3 and check you IoT Analytics dataset destination bucket and search for the S3 object to make sure it was successfully created. Then "Download" the 'iot.csv' object and examine the IoT sensor readings.

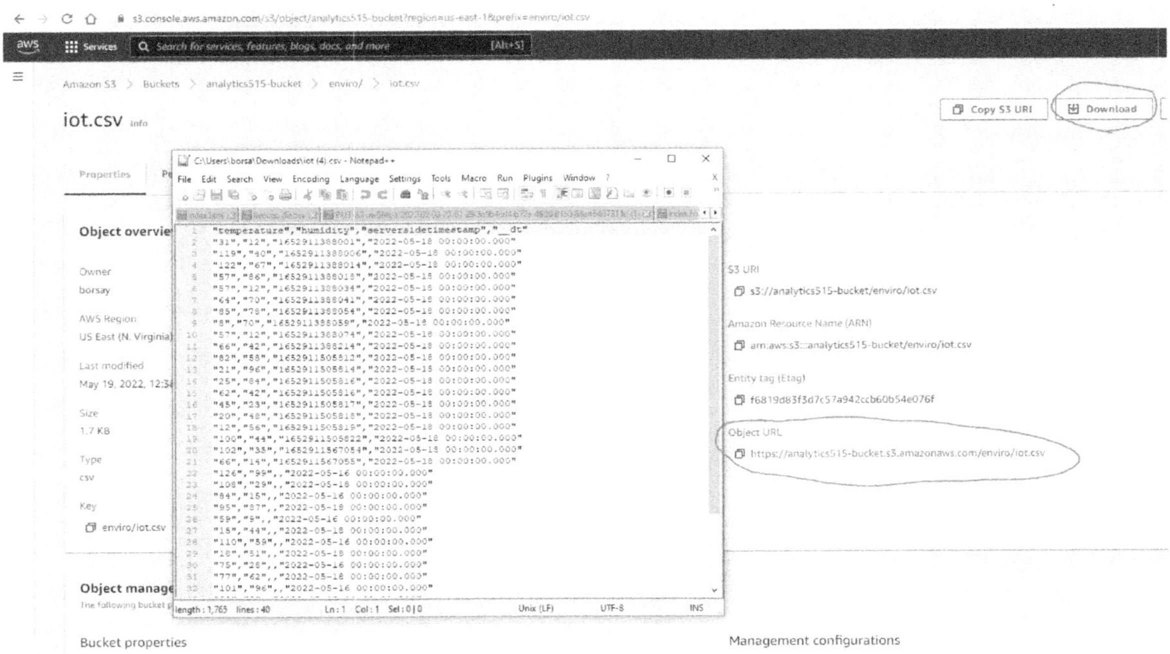
iot.csv
Copy S3 URI
Download
Object overview
Owner
borsay
AWS Region
US East (N. Virginia)
Type
csv
Key
enviro/iot.csv
S3 URI
s3://analytics515-bucket/enviro/iot.csv
Object URL
Bucket properties
Management configurations

If everything looks correct, then you are ready to upload the "index.html" file for visualization of your IoT data in S3.

Step 8 – Visualize the Timestream IoT Data in AWS QuickSight

Unsurprisingly AWS QuickSight offers a built-in connector for IoT Analytics to visualize your IoT dataset. Go to QuickSight and select a "New analysis" in the upper right:

New analysis

Then select "New dataset" in the upper left of your screen:

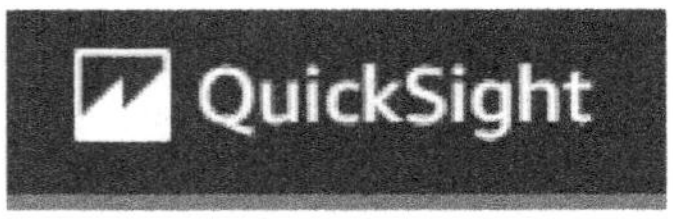
QuickSight

New dataset

Next, Select the “AWS IoT Analytics” connector:

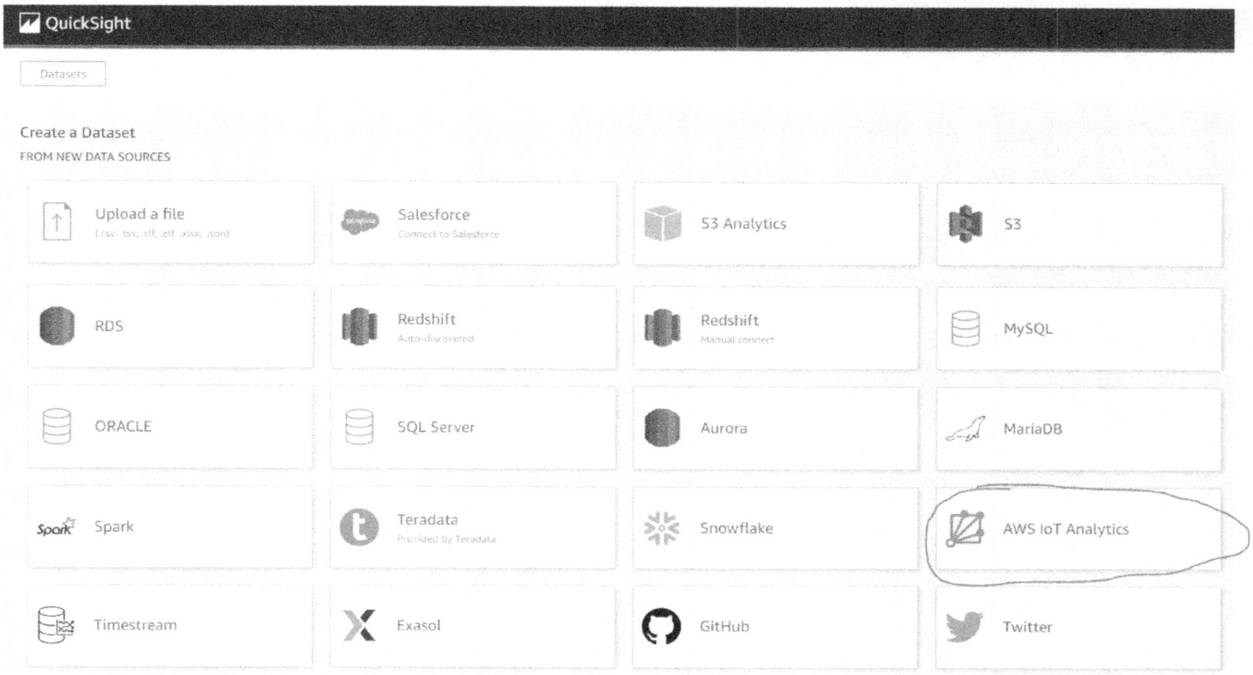
QuickSight
Datasets
Create a Dataset
FROM NEW DATA SOURCES
Upload a file
Salesforce
Connect to Salesforce
S3 Analytics
S3
RDS
Redshift
Auto-discovered
Redshift
Manual connect
MySQL
ORACLE
SQL Server
Aurora
MariaDB
Spark
Teradata
Provided by Teradata
Snowflake
AWS IoT Analytics
Timestream
Exasol
GitHub
Twitter

On the next screen you will select the name of your desired dataset to visualize in QuickSight and then press the “Create data source” button.

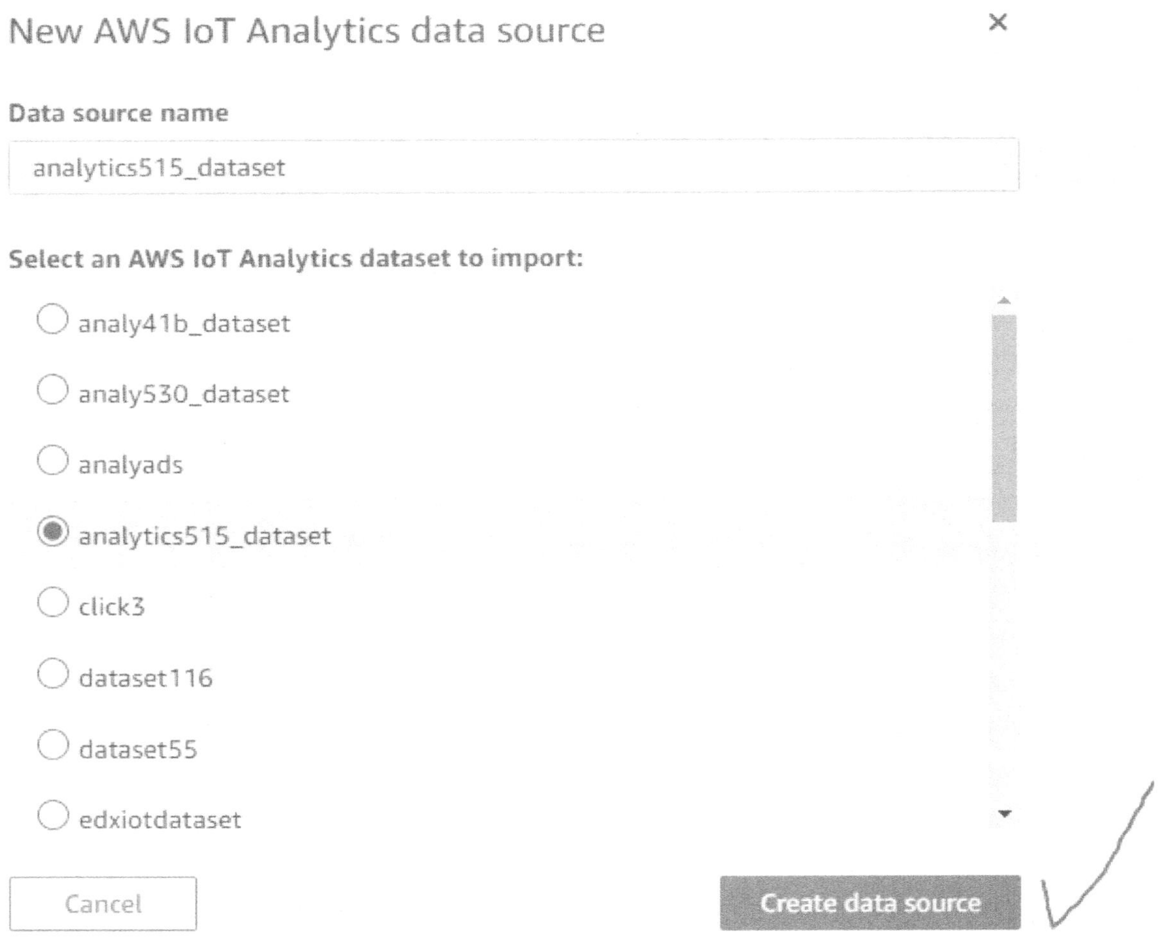
New AWS IoT Analytics data source
Data source name
analytics515_dataset
Select an AWS IoT Analytics dataset to import:
analy41b_dataset
analy530_dataset
analyads
analytics515_dataset
click3
dataset116
dataset55
edxiotdataset
Cancel
Create data source

After you select "Create data source" you can now visualize your IoT Analytics dataset by selecting "Visualize."

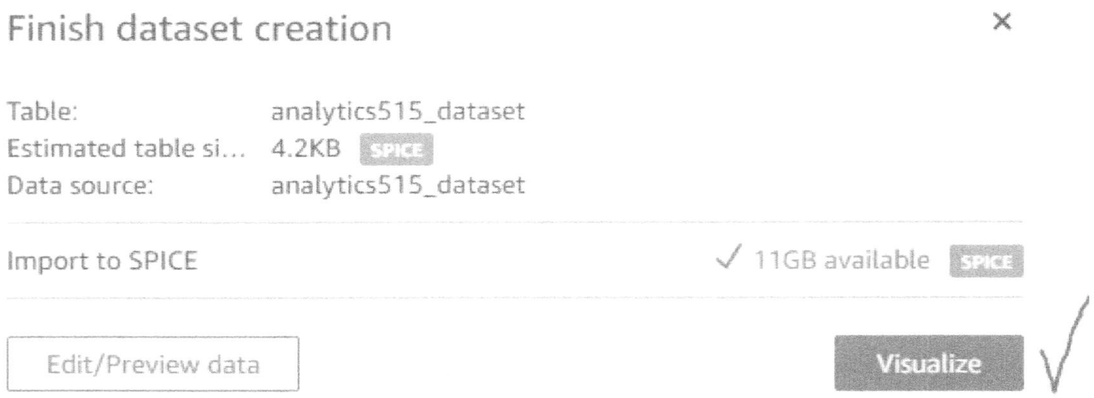
Finish dataset creation
Table: analytics515_dataset
Estimated table si... 4.2KB SPICE
Data source: analytics515_dataset
Import to SPICE
11GB available SPICE
Edit/Preview data
Visualize

Now you can drag your dataset variables to any prebuilt visualization in QuickSight that you like.

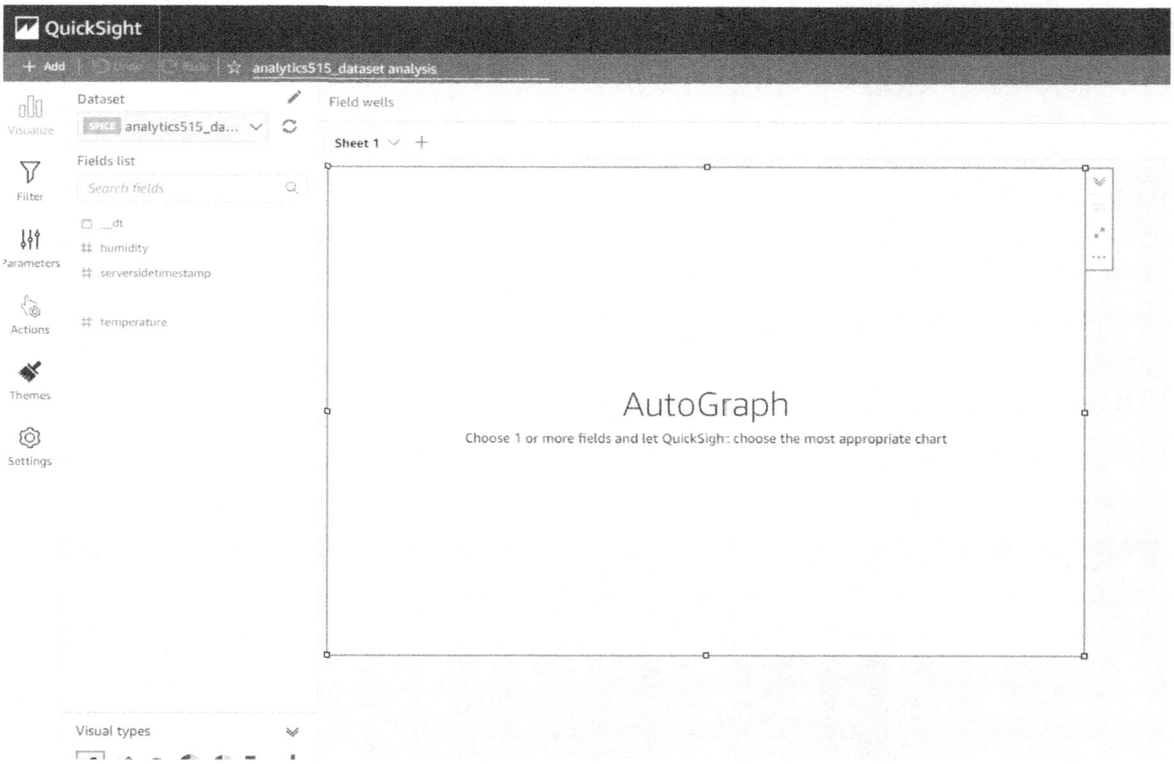
QuickSight
Add
analytics515_dataset analysis
Visualize
Filter
Parameters
Actions
Themes
Settings
Dataset
analytics515_da...
Fields list
Search fields
__dt
humidity
serversidetimestamp
temperature
Visual types
Field wells
Sheet 1
AutoGraph
Choose 1 or more fields and let QuickSight choose the most appropriate chart

From this point you are free to design whatever visualizations you desire in QuickSight. Be mindful of your SPICE quota and other costs on QucikSight.

Step 9 - Discover Insights into your IoT Data with AWS SageMaker

Warning: SageMaker can be very expensive as an instanced AWS service. Remember to "Stop" and then "Delete" any SageMaker instance after use.

AWS SageMaker enables developers to work with training and deploying machine learning models. For IoT data Sagemaker can provide many insights useful for discovering patterns and leading to innovative solutions.

I don't discuss SageMaker in this book much for two main reasons

A) SageMaker is not a "serverless" service and uses a server instance space to run.

B) SageMaker is relatively expensive.

I will mitigate the costs by emphasizing shutting down and destroying SageMaker instances after use.
Launch a Sagemaker instance by going to AWS→SageMaker or go to:

https://console.aws.amazon.com/sagemaker

On the left-side pane in "Notebook" open a "Notebook instance" to work with a Jupyter notebook.

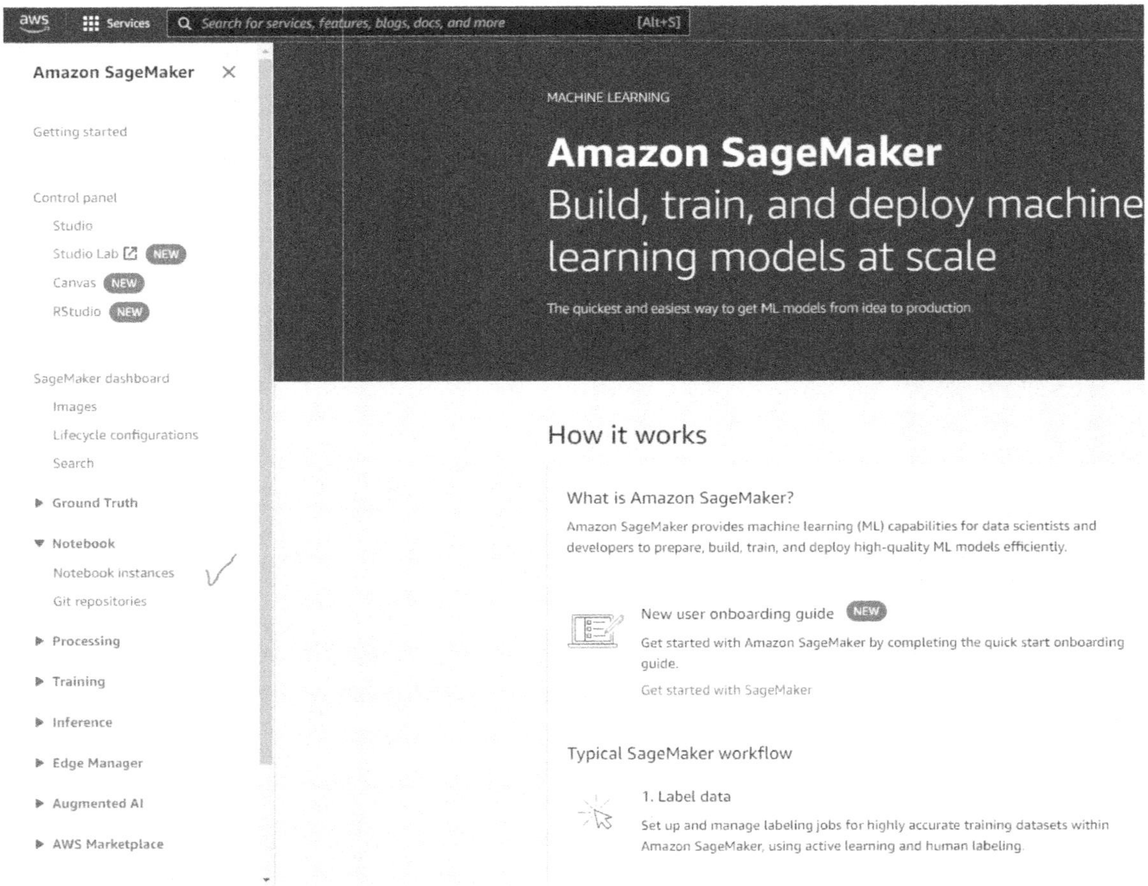

aws
Services
Search for services, features, blogs, docs, and more
[Alt+S]
Amazon SageMaker
Getting started
Control panel
Studio
Studio Lab
NEW
Canvas
NEW
RStudio
NEW
SageMaker dashboard
Images
Lifecycle configurations
Search
Ground Truth
Notebook
Notebook instances
Git repositories
Processing
Training
Inference
Edge Manager
Augmented AI
AWS Marketplace
MACHINE LEARNING
Amazon SageMaker
Build, train, and deploy machine learning models at scale
The quickest and easiest way to get ML models from idea to production
How it works
What is Amazon SageMaker?
Amazon SageMaker provides machine learning (ML) capabilities for data scientists and developers to prepare, build, train, and deploy high-quality ML models efficiently.
New user onboarding guide
NEW
Get started with Amazon SageMaker by completing the quick start onboarding guide.
Get started with SageMaker
Typical SageMaker workflow
1. Label data
Set up and manage labeling jobs for highly accurate training datasets within Amazon SageMaker, using active learning and human labeling.

More information on Jupyter notebooks can be found at the URL below if you wish to explore the tool further:

https://jupyter.org/

Now select to "Create notebook instance" on the upper right corner of the screen:

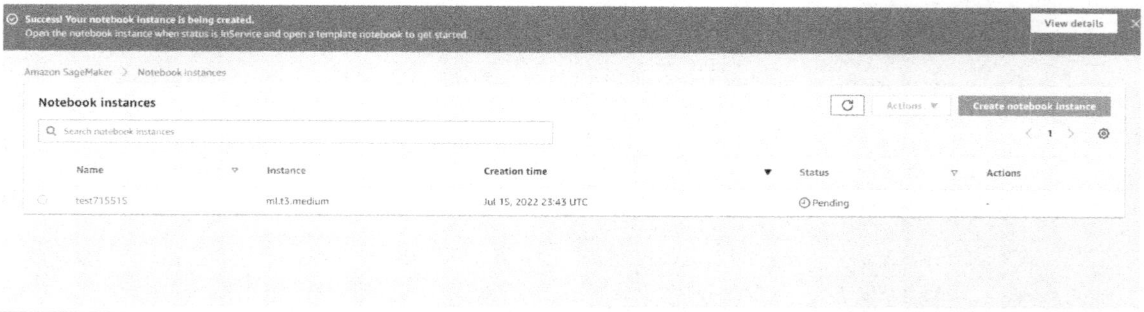
Success! Your notebook instance is being created.
Open the notebook instance when status is InService and open a template notebook to get started.
View details
Amazon SageMaker > Notebook instances
Notebook instances
Actions
Create notebook instance
Search notebook instances
Name
Instance
Creation time
Status
Actions
ml.t3.medium
Jul 15, 2022 23:43 UTC
Pending

On the next screen you will configure your notebook. As you can see it takes a medium size or larger EC2 instance to work with a SageMaker. Notebook instances can be rather expensive over time. Leave all the default settings as they are.

Warning: SageMaker can be a very expensive AWS service. Remember to "Stop" and then "Delete" any SageMaker instance after use.

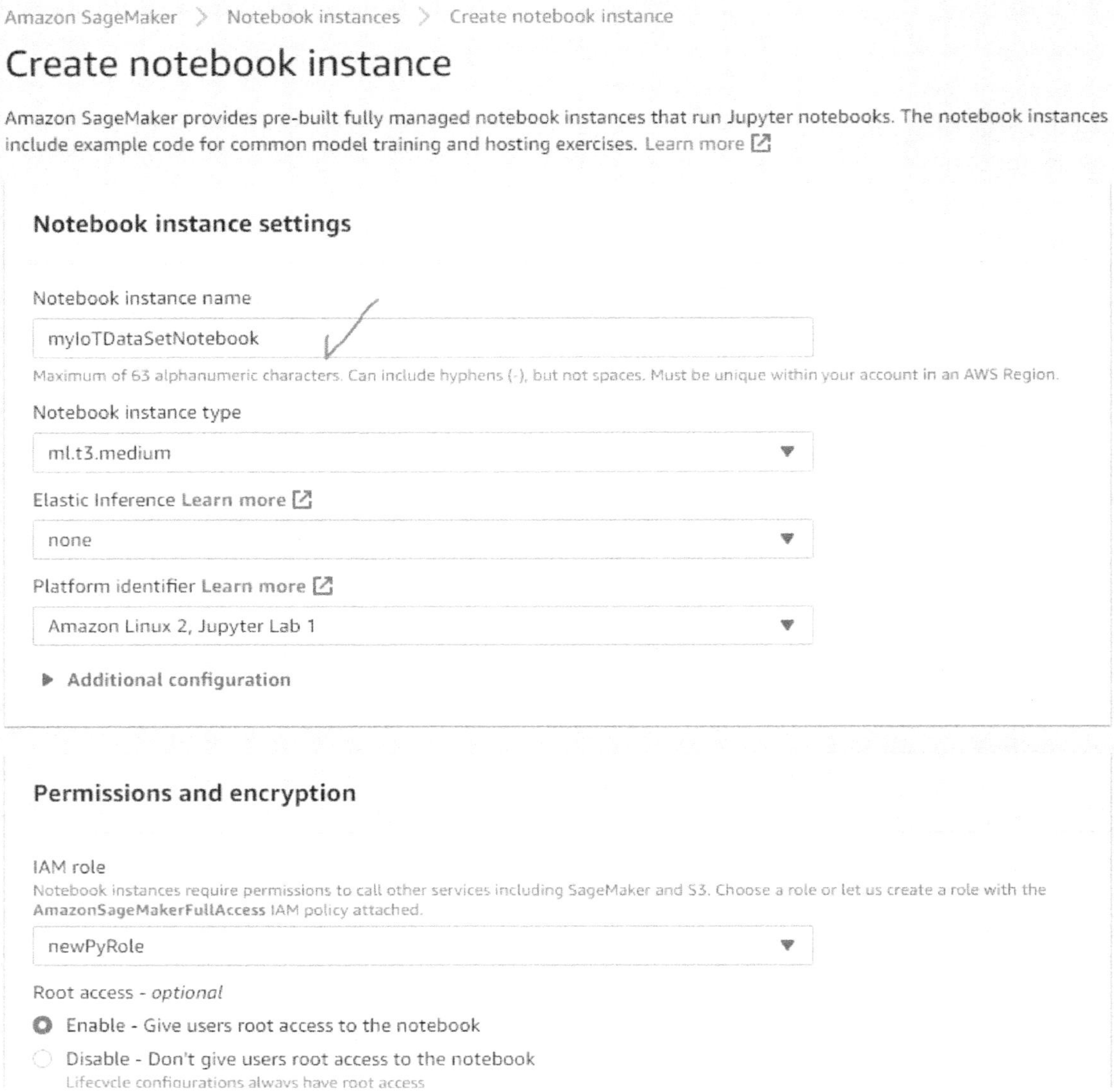

Amazon SageMaker > Notebook instances > Create notebook instance
Create notebook instance
Amazon SageMaker provides pre-built fully managed notebook instances that run Jupyter notebooks. The notebook instances include example code for common model training and hosting exercises. Learn more
Notebook instance settings
Notebook instance name
myIoTDataSetNotebook
Maximum of 63 alphanumeric characters. Can include hyphens (-), but not spaces. Must be unique within your account in an AWS Region.
Notebook instance type
ml.t3.medium
Elastic Inference Learn more
none
Platform identifier Learn more
Amazon Linux 2, Jupyter Lab 1
Additional configuration
Permissions and encryption
IAM role
Notebook instances require permissions to call other services including SageMaker and S3. Choose a role or let us create a role with the AmazonSageMakerFullAccess IAM policy attached.
newPyRole
Root access - optional
Enable - Give users root access to the notebook
Disable - Don't give users root access to the notebook
Lifecycle configurations always have root access

After giving your notebook a name, select “Create notebook instance”:

Create notebook instance

The notebook instance can take a good amount of time to create. For my test case it took about eight minutes. Your creation may be slower or faster depending on time of day, external server load, and AWS region.

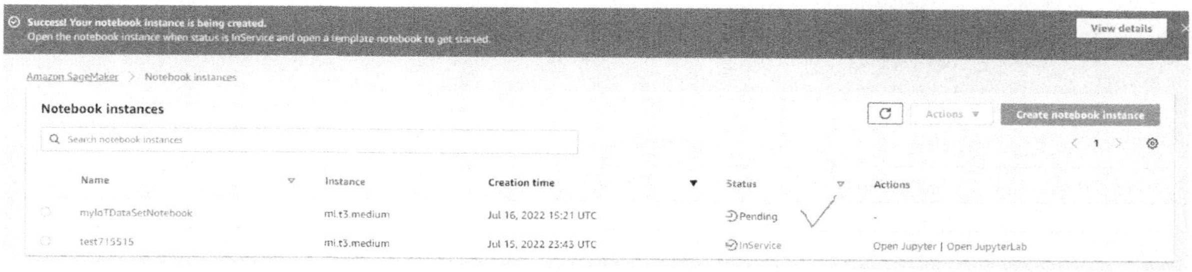
Success! Your notebook instance is being created.
Open the notebook instance when status is InService and open a template notebook to get started.
View details
Amazon SageMaker > Notebook instances
Notebook instances
Actions
Create notebook instance
Name
Instance
Creation time
Status
Actions
myIoTDataSetNotebook
ml.t3.medium
Jul 16, 2022 15:21 UTC
Pending
test715515
ml.t3.medium
Jul 15, 2022 23:43 UTC
InService
Open Jupyter | Open JupyterLab

Once the “State” has changed from “Pending” to “InService” you are ready to “Open Jupyter” from the “Actions” column on the right.

Status
Actions
InService
Open Jupyter | Open JupyterLab

In your notebook menu choose “New” and then “conda_pytorch_38”. This abstruse moniker stands for “Anaconda Pytorch package using Python version 3.8”
More information about the popular and free Anaconda Python package of packages and Pytorch can be found at the URLs below

https://www.anaconda.com/products/distribution
https://pytorch.org/

Now you should be in your Jupyter notebook instance and selected the correct Python package to manipulate your dataset from IoT Analytics.

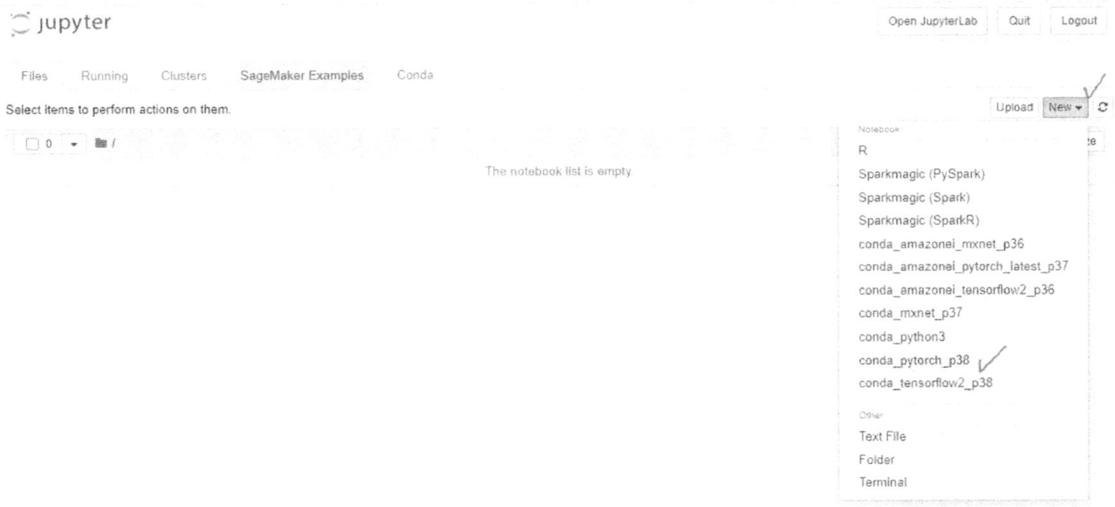
jupyter
Open JupyterLab
Quit
Logout
Files
Running
Clusters
SageMaker Examples
Conda
Select items to perform actions on them.
Upload
New
The notebook list is empty.
R
Sparkmagic (PySpark)
Sparkmagic (Spark)
Sparkmagic (SparkR)
conda_amazonei_mxnet_p36
conda_amazonei_pytorch_latest_p37
conda_amazonei_tensorflow2_p36
conda_mxnet_p37
conda_python3
conda_pytorch_p38
conda_tensorflow2_p38
Text File
Folder
Terminal

Below is the Python code for you to use on your Jupyter notebook instance. You must customize just one line of the code as listed below for it to point it to your specific dataset in IoT Analytics. Fill out the following line in the code:

```
dataset = "YOUR_DATASET_HERE"  #Ex: "analytics515_dataset"
```

Now enter the following Python code by copy and pasting it into the Jupyter notebook instance:

```
#Using 'conda_chainer_p36'  or 'conda_pytorch_p38'
import boto3
import pandas as pd
from matplotlib import pyplot as plt
# Create IoT Analytics client
client = boto3.client('iotanalytics')
#run the code below with your own dataset
dataset = "YOUR_DATASET_HERE" #Ex: "analytics615_dataset"
dataset_url = client.get_dataset_content(datasetName =
dataset)['entries'][0]['dataURI']
# Start working with the data
df = pd.read_csv(dataset_url)
df.serversidetimestamp =
pd.to_datetime(pd.to_numeric(df.serversidetimestamp), unit='ms')
df.set_index(df.serversidetimestamp, inplace=True)
#df.sort_values('serversidetimestamp', inplace=True)

fig, ax = plt.subplots()
df.temperature.plot(legend=True)
```

```
df.humidity.plot(legend=True)
plt.show()

print('Average Humidity: ', df.humidity.mean())
print('Number of samples: ', len(df))
print('Average temperature: ', df.temperature.mean())
print('Number of samples: ', len(df))
```

As you can see the code imports the AWS-SDK for Python called 'Boto3' which you are already familiar with from using it in Lambda functions. Also, the Python program uses Pandas and Matplotlib as popular, robust, and free Python statistical packages which are great for the manipulation IoT data. More information on Pandas and Matplotlib can be found at the URLs below:

https://pandas.pydata.org/

https://matplotlib.org/

Now enter the Python code above into the editor on your Jupyter notebook instance:

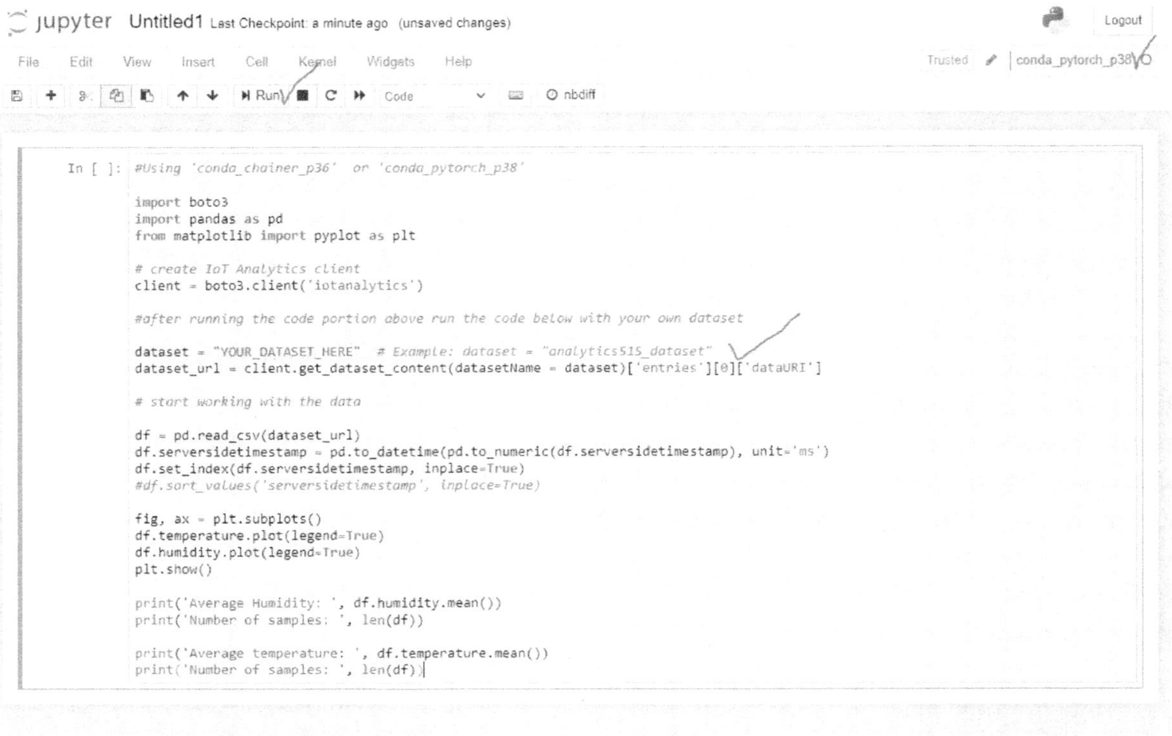
jupyter
Untitled1 Last Checkpoint: a minute ago (unsaved changes)
Logout
File
Edit
View
Insert
Cell
Kernel
Widgets
Help
Trusted
conda_pytorch_p38
Run
Code
nbdiff
In [ ]:

```
#Using 'conda_chainer_p36'  or 'conda_pytorch_p38'

import boto3
import pandas as pd
from matplotlib import pyplot as plt

# create IoT Analytics client
client = boto3.client('iotanalytics')

#after running the code portion above run the code below with your own dataset

dataset = "YOUR_DATASET_HERE"  # Example: dataset = "analytics515_dataset"
dataset_url = client.get_dataset_content(datasetName = dataset)['entries'][0]['dataURI']

# start working with the data

df = pd.read_csv(dataset_url)
df.serversidetimestamp = pd.to_datetime(pd.to_numeric(df.serversidetimestamp), unit='ms')
df.set_index(df.serversidetimestamp, inplace=True)
#df.sort_values('serversidetimestamp', inplace=True)

fig, ax = plt.subplots()
df.temperature.plot(legend=True)
df.humidity.plot(legend=True)
plt.show()

print('Average Humidity: ', df.humidity.mean())
print('Number of samples: ', len(df))

print('Average temperature: ', df.temperature.mean())
print('Number of samples: ', len(df))
```

Now press ‘Run’ button (you may have to press ‘Run’ twice if it does not complete the first time). The resultant graph and variable averages should look like the image below. Also note that the Python code does not handle empty or bad readings well, so you may need to delete the old dataset and re-run a good dataset by publishing all new IoT readings to IoT Analytics.

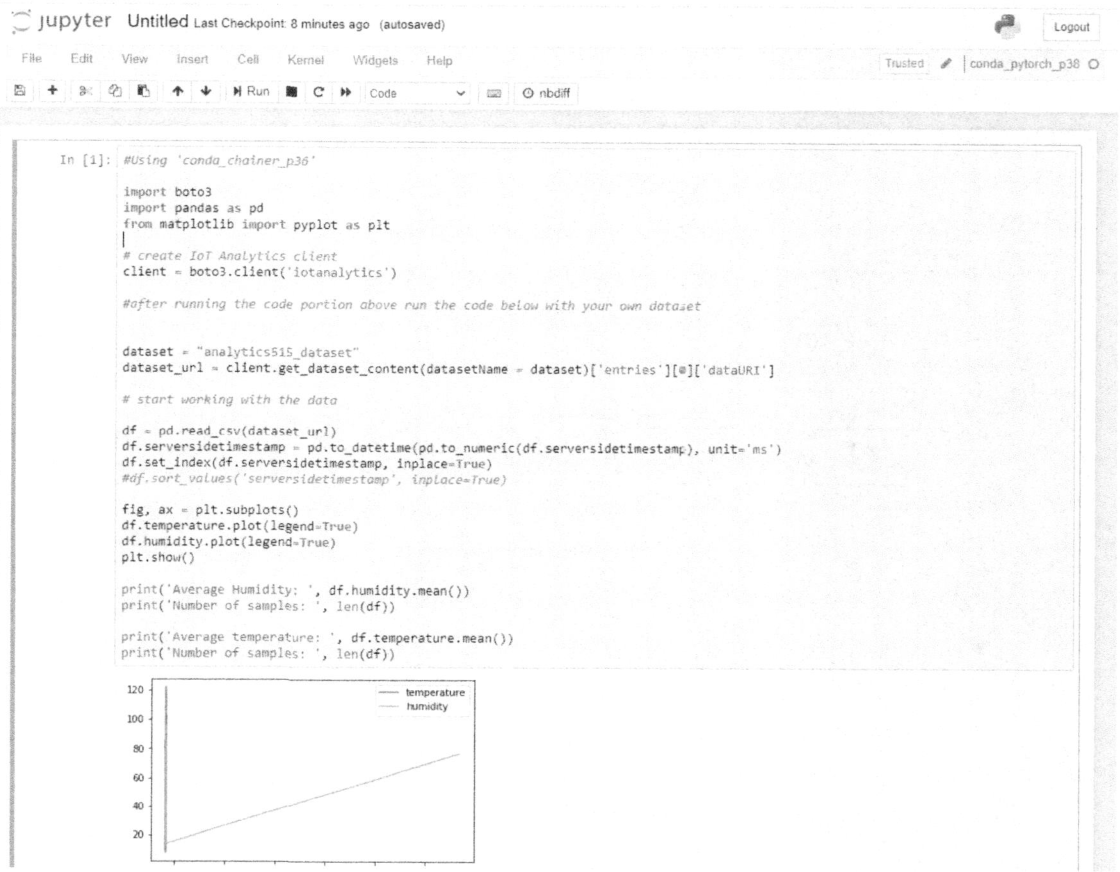

jupyter Untitled Last Checkpoint: 8 minutes ago (autosaved)
Logout
File Edit View Insert Cell Kernel Widgets Help
Trusted
conda_pytorch_p38
Run
Code
nbdiff
In [1]:
#Using 'conda_chainer_p36'
import boto3
import pandas as pd
from matplotlib import pyplot as plt
# create IoT Analytics client
client = boto3.client('iotanalytics')
#after running the code portion above run the code below with your own dataset
dataset = "analytics515_dataset"
dataset_url = client.get_dataset_content(datasetName = dataset)['entries'][0]['dataURI']
# start working with the data
df = pd.read_csv(dataset_url)
df.serversidetimestamp = pd.to_datetime(pd.to_numeric(df.serversidetimestamp), unit='ms')
df.set_index(df.serversidetimestamp, inplace=True)
#df.sort_values('serversidetimestamp', inplace=True)
fig, ax = plt.subplots()
df.temperature.plot(legend=True)
df.humidity.plot(legend=True)
plt.show()
print('Average Humidity: ', df.humidity.mean())
print('Number of samples: ', len(df))
print('Average temperature: ', df.temperature.mean())
print('Number of samples: ', len(df))
temperature
humidity
120
100
80
60
40
20

Cleaning Up:

To prevent high costs, stop and then delete your instance. Stop your instance buy selecting the “Stop” button on your Notebook instance console:

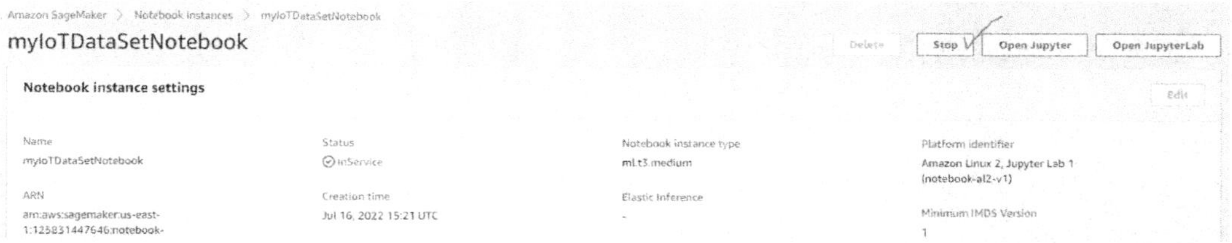

Amazon SageMaker > Notebook instances > myIoTDataSetNotebook
myIoTDataSetNotebook
Delete
Stop
Open Jupyter
Open JupyterLab
Notebook instance settings
Edit
Name
myIoTDataSetNotebook
Status
InService
Notebook instance type
ml.t3.medium
Platform identifier
Amazon Linux 2, Jupyter Lab 1 (notebook-al2-v1)
ARN
arn:aws:sagemaker:us-east-1:125831447646:notebook-
Creation time
Jul 16, 2022 15:21 UTC
Elastic Inference
-
Minimum IMDS Version
1

After a short amount of time the instance will stop:

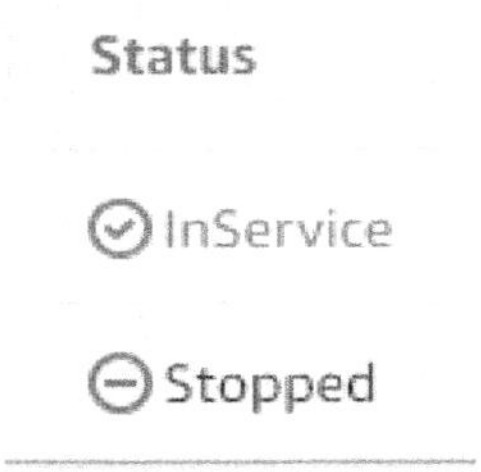
Status
InService
Stopped

Now 'Delete' the instance:

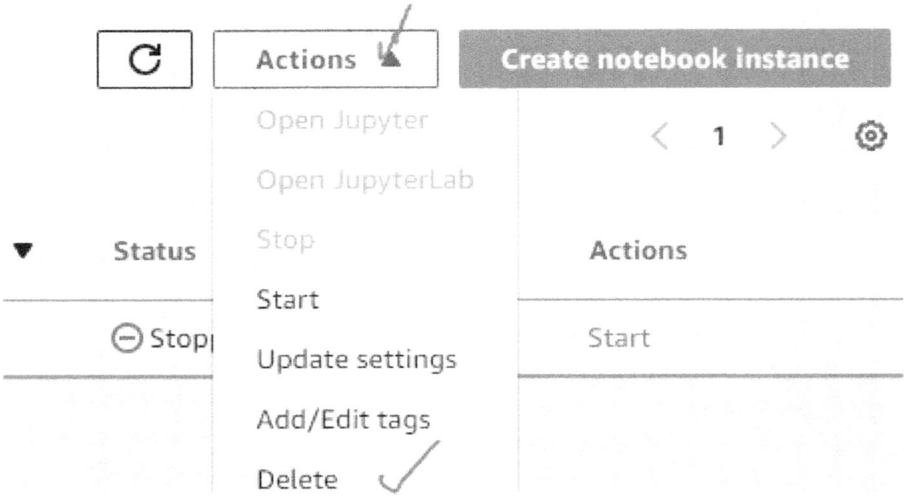
Actions
Create notebook instance
Open Jupyter
Open JupyterLab
Stop
Start
Update settings
Add/Edit tags
Delete
1
Status
Actions
Start

Warning: SageMaker can be very expensive as an instanced AWS service. Remember to "Stop" and then "Delete" any SageMaker instance after use.

Step 10 - Configure, Upload, and Visualize the IoT Data in S3 on a Static Website

Ensure your S3 bucket holding your 'iot.csv' file has static web hosting enabled when you upload the index.html file below. Make sure to replace the line below with the 'Object URL' of the 'iot.csv' file in your S3 bucket. In this example the key was 'enviro' and the object was 'iot.csv' in case you forgot (enviro/iot.csv).

```
"https://<YOUR-BUCKET-NAME>.s3.amazonaws.com/<YOUR-PATH>/<YOUR-DATA-
FILE>.csv"
```

The 'Object URL' is listed in your CSV file location in S3 (see image below).

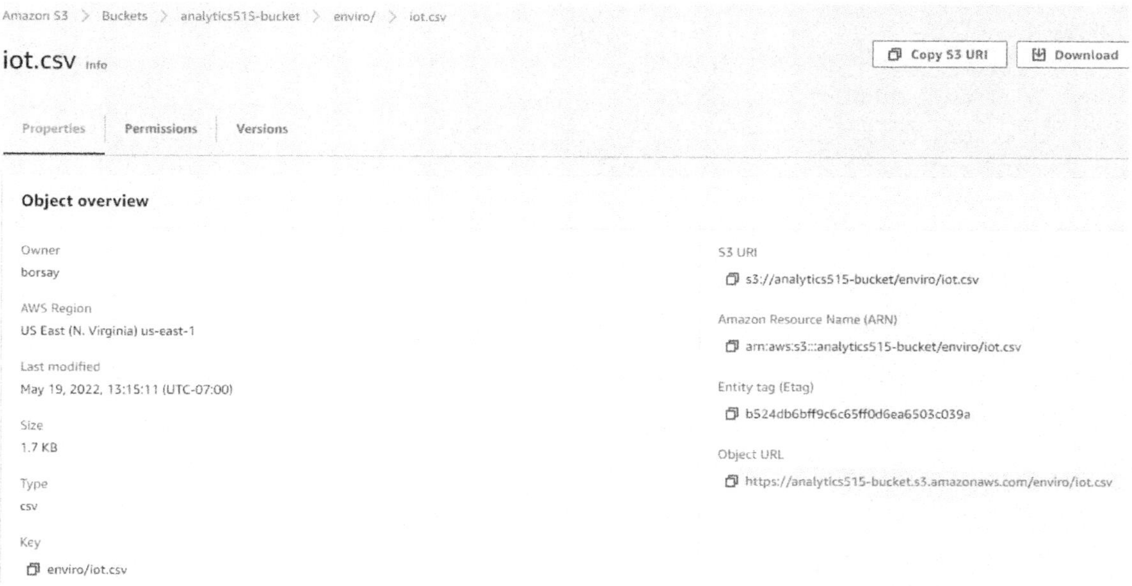
Amazon S3 > Buckets > analytics515-bucket > enviro/ > iot.csv
iot.csv Info
Copy S3 URI
Download
Properties
Permissions
Versions
Object overview
Owner
borsay
AWS Region
US East (N. Virginia) us-east-1
Last modified
May 19, 2022, 13:15:11 (UTC-07:00)
Size
1.7 KB
Type
csv
Key
enviro/iot.csv
S3 URI
s3://analytics515-bucket/enviro/iot.csv
Amazon Resource Name (ARN)
arn:aws:s3:::analytics515-bucket/enviro/iot.csv
Entity tag (Etag)
b524db6bff9c6c65ff0d6ea6503c039a
Object URL
https://analytics515-bucket.s3.amazonaws.com/enviro/iot.csv

The complete JavaScript code for the "*index.html*" is listed below:

```
<!DOCTYPE html>
<html>
<head>
  <script type="text/javascript"
src="https://www.gstatic.com/charts/loader.js"></script>
  <script src="https://code.jquery.com/jquery-3.2.1.min.js"></script>
  <script>

    $(document).ready(function () {
      $("button").click(function () {
        $.get("https://<YOUR-BUCKET-NAME>.s3.amazonaws.com/<YOUR-PATH>/<YOUR-
DATA-FILE>.csv", function (data) {

          data = data.replace(/"/g, '').split('\n');
          let allRecArr = data.map(x => {
            x = x.split(',').map(x => +x);
            return x;
          });

          google.charts.load('current', { packages: ['corechart', 'line'] });
          google.charts.setOnLoadCallback(drawBasic);

          function drawBasic() {
```

```
          var data = new google.visualization.DataTable();
          data.addColumn('number', 'time');
          data.addColumn('number', 'temperature');
          data.addColumn('number', 'humidity');

          for (i = 1; i < allRecArr.length; i++) {
            let item = allRecArr[i];
            if (item[2]) {
              data.addRows([
                [item[2], item[0], item[1]]
              ]);
            } else {
              console.log('skip record', item)
            }
          }

          var options = {
            chartArea:{left:50,top:50,width:"85%"},
            height: 780,
            hAxis: {
              title: 'Time'
            },
            vAxis: {
              title: 'Environmental Data'
            }
          };


          var chart = new
google.visualization.LineChart(document.getElementById('chart_div'));

          chart.draw(data, options);
        }

      });
    });
  });

  </script>
</head>
<body>
  <br>
  <button>Press to display your most recent data</button>
  <div id="chart_div"></div>
```

```
</body>
</html>
```

This is a simple Google chart. It is not as configurable as Highcharts.js or Chart.js and is especially deficient for streaming data. However, it is very easy to use. Also, there are many JavaScript packages for handling CSV files, even for static websites, so you can likely come up with a better visualization on your own.

Additional JavaScript code has been added so that when parsing the environmental readings, the code will skip over those sensor readings that do not have a 'serversidetimestamp'. This feature is useful for heterogenous data that may have contaminated IoT data that was not transformed with Lambda in the pipeline.

Now go to the index.html page in S3 where your new visualization file is located.

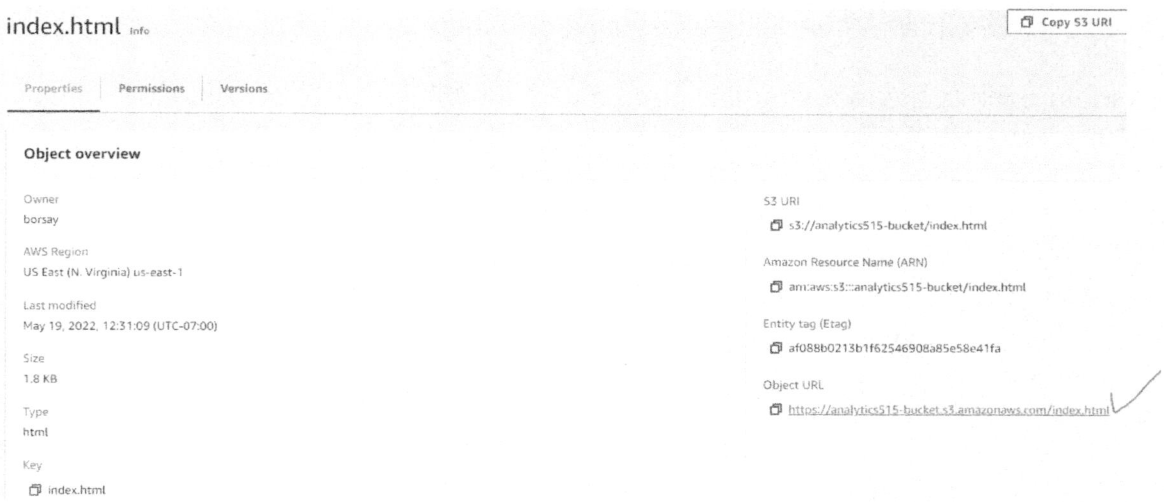

index.html Info
Copy S3 URI
Properties
Permissions
Versions
Object overview
Owner
borsay
AWS Region
US East (N. Virginia) us-east-1
Last modified
May 19, 2022, 12:31:09 (UTC-07:00)
Size
1.8 KB
Type
html
Key
index.html
S3 URI
s3://analytics515-bucket/index.html
Amazon Resource Name (ARN)
arn:aws:s3:::analytics515-bucket/index.html
Entity tag (Etag)
af088b0213b1f62546908a85e58e41fa
Object URL
https://analytics515-bucket.s3.amazonaws.com/index.html

If you try to open the index.html page and click the button no visualization will appear to graph your data. Why is this? This is because AWS helpfully, or unhelpfully, automatically enables KMS encryption on your iot.csv object by default. I've asked AWS to make this automatic encryption an optional feature for a few years now but no luck thus far. But this is OK as all you need to do is to manually turn off the automatic KMS encryption in your S3 bucket. To do this go to go back to your CSV file in S3 and under the properties" tab scroll down to "Server-side encryption." Now press the "Edit" button.

Storage class
Edit
Storage class
Standard
Server-side encryption settings
Edit
Default encryption
Enabled
Server-side encryption
AWS Key Management Service key (SSE-KMS)
AWS KMS key ARN
Bucket Key
Disabled
Additional checksums
Additional checksums

Choose to "Disable" Server-side encryption and then "Save Changes."

Navigate back to the index.html file and select the Object URL of your index.html object.

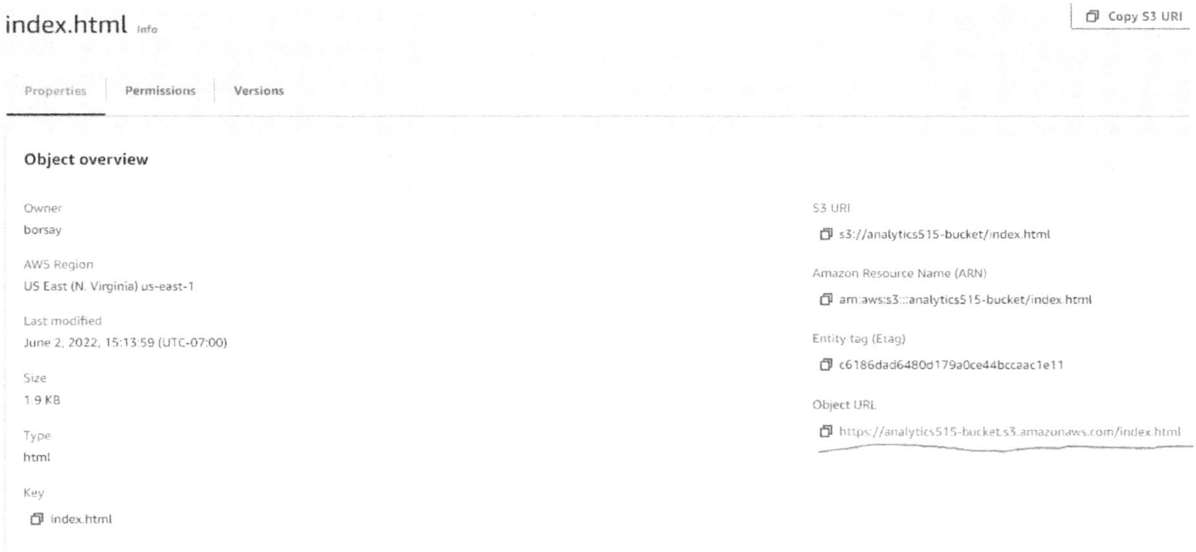
index.html Info
Copy S3 URI
Properties
Permissions
Versions
Object overview
Owner
borsay
AWS Region
US East (N. Virginia) us-east-1
Last modified
June 2, 2022, 15:13:59 (UTC-07:00)
Size
1.9 KB
Type
html
Key
index.html
S3 URI
s3://analytics515-bucket/index.html
Amazon Resource Name (ARN)
arn:aws:s3:::analytics515-bucket/index.html
Entity tag (Etag)
c6186dad6480d179a0ce44bccaac1e11
Object URL
https://analytics515-bucket.s3.amazonaws.com/index.html

Open the Object URL and initiate the webpage by pressing the "Display IoT Data" button.

Now the graph should work and display as below just with different data:

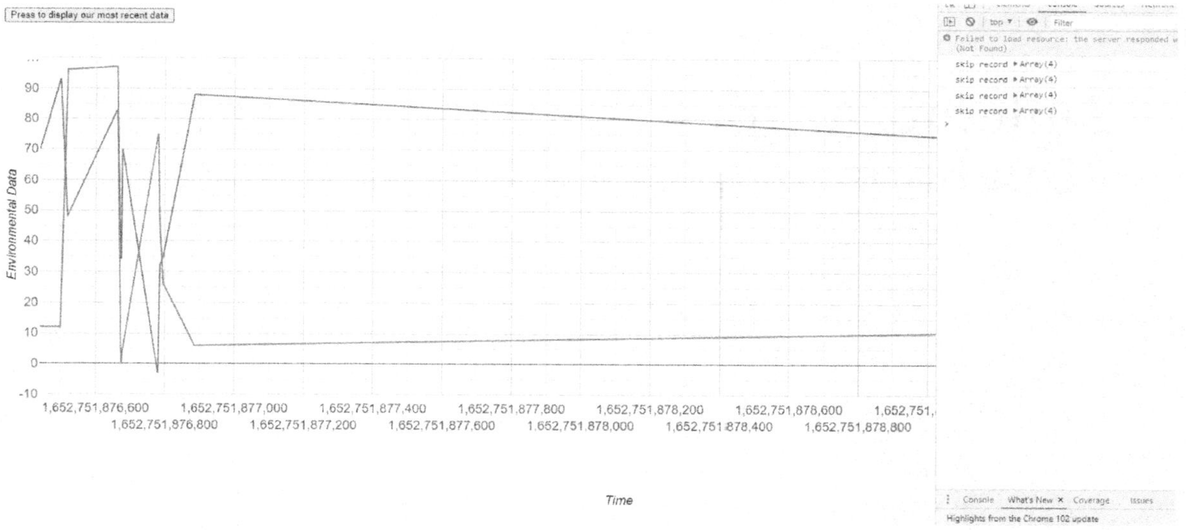

Press to display our most recent data
Environmental Data
Time
skip record ▸Array(4)

Also notice how readings without timestamps are skipped as indicated in the developer's console pane of the browser.

Congratulations, you have completed all the steps necessary to set up IoT Analytics and then added in the bonus features of Lambda enhancement as well as S3 repository storage with a Google charts visualization of queried IoT data. Also, just as with Timestream, IoT Analytics has a built-in connector for AWS QuickSight for business intelligence (BI) visualizations as well as the facility for easy inclusion with AWS SageMaker.

Chapter 18 -
Building A Real-Time Serverless IoT Dashboard with AWS WebSockets

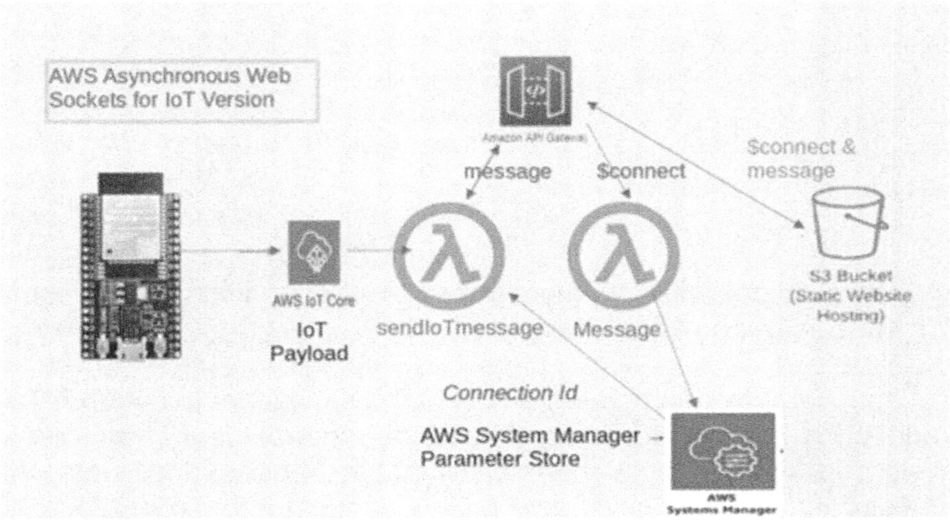

AWS Asynchronous Web Sockets for IoT Version
message
$connect
$connect & message
AWS IoT Core
IoT Payload
sendIoTmessage
Message
S3 Bucket (Static Website Hosting)
Connection Id
AWS System Manager → Parameter Store

In the previous chapter I discussed IoT specific websites such as ThingSpeak, Loasant, and Ubidots, which specialize in IoT applications on the cloud. Although these website services are not competitive with AWS for production level IoT design, they do have one clear advantage over AWS: easy to use, real-time IoT dashboarding. In this chapter I offer what I believe to be the world's first complete serverless real-time dashboarding solution for AWS. It is especially enticing as it only costs pennies a day with the included inexpensive services.

In a previous chapter I showed you how to develop the "Worlds Simplest Synchronous Serverless IoT Dashboard on AWS," The design was relatively simple as listed below:

1. *Ingest IoT device data into AWS IoT Core.*

2. The JSON IoT payload is then put into a S3 bucket using an IoT Core rule.

3. A static website in a public S3 bucket, along with the IoT data, consumes the IoT data on an adjustable polling time interval.

4. The static website then graphs the IoT data in a line chart using Highcharts or Plotly.

While this IoT implementation was both simple and effective, in fact the "World's Simplest" as determined by extensive expert review, it did have some problems.

The main problem with the previous synchronous IoT design was that IoT data was only extracted on interval, which led to over-fetching of stale data as well as under-fetching of new IoT data that could easily have been missed if synchronous polling did not align with data replacement in the S3 bucket. It should be remembered that this back-end bifurcation between Lambda and the website is an inherent challenging issue in AWS serverless design. When we develop with "serverful" design, as with a Linux partition using AWS EC2, we have a live server instance that can "serve up" data on demand in a completely integrated manner. With a "serverless" model we rely on requests to AWS Lambda to execute server (back-end) code on demand, thus the web host and the server can't implicitly execute coordinated operations without special provisions.

So, the question becomes, how can we fix these communication issues? Well, the obvious answer is to move the IoT design flow from a synchronous polling model to an asynchronous pushing model. This can be also re-framed as moving from a "client pull" of IoT data from the website host to Lambda, to a "server push" of data from AWS Lambda to the website. There are several ways to do this in a serverless model, here are three:

1. AWS WebSockets in the web browser
2. MQTT over WebSockets using the AWS IoT device SDK for JavaScript in the web browser
3. GraphQL with AWS AppSync/Amplify in the web browser

AWS WebSockets to the rescue

In this chapter we will focus on the AWS WebSockets solution for asynchronous real-time serverless design.

Just like the MQTT protocol, which most of you are familiar with, the WebSockets API has a special protocol which allows a bi-directional communication "socket" so that the Lambda function can send and receive data directly from the website host in real time. This allows us to move from the synchronous client polling model to an asynchronous server pushing model. The AWS WebSockets API requires API Gateway to provide external and internal WebSockets endpoint URLs to accomplish this task.

Synchronous – The static Website pulling IoT data via polling from a data repository in S3 on interval (Client pull)

Asynchronous – The Lambda function pushing IoT Data via WebSockets to the static Website host as soon as the data is available (Server push)

Now that we have a basic understanding of the advantages of WebSockets for asynchronous IoT we can proceed to build the design flow on AWS to achieve these advantages. One word of warning, this chapter can be extremely confusing because we are working backwards to achieve the result. By the end of the project, you will understand the process much better than when you started.

Sockets

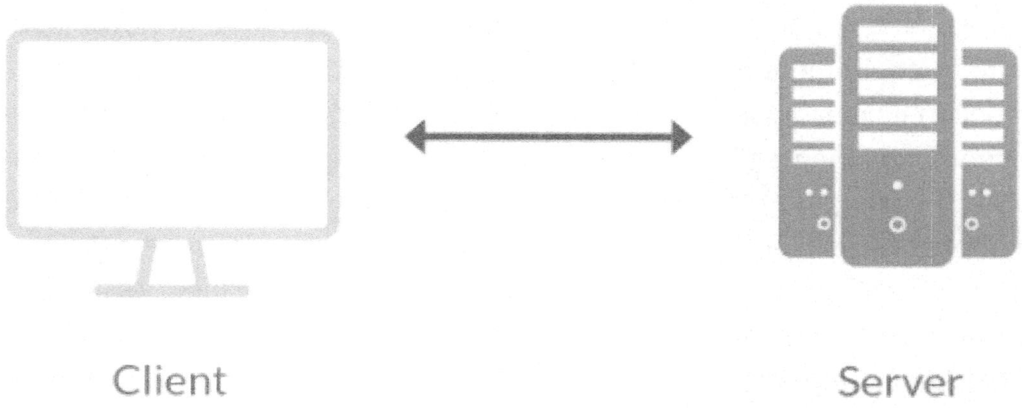
Client
Server

Step 1 - Create a Public Bucket in S3 and Enable Static Web Hosting
Step 2 - Set up a Variable String in the Systems Manager Parameter Store
Step 3 - Develop the Connection and Messaging Lambda Functions
Step 4 - Design WebSocket Endpoints in AWS API Gateway
Step 5 - Create an AWS IoT Core Rule to Send IoT Data to Lambda
Step 6 - Upload the Static Website Code to Create an Asynchronous Visualization of the IoT Data
Step 7 - Populate and Visualize the IoT Data in Real-Time on a Static Webhost

---

Step 1 - Create a Public Bucket in S3 and Enable Static Web Hosting

Refer to the prerequisite chapter on creating a public bucket in S3 with a static index.html page as a web host. You can name you bucket something related to a WebSockets real-time IoT dashboard.

Step 2 - Set up a Variable String in the Systems Manager Parameter Store

You need to retain the unique session *connection ID* of the index.html webpage as a requirement of the WebSockets API protocol. This is similar to how unique Client IDs are a requirement of the MQTT protocol to keep track of device client. The connection ID is an identifier that API Gateway assigns as an auto-generated alphanumeric string and then it uses the string to keep a handle on the connection. You will be using the AWS Systems Manager Parameter Store, rather than DynamoDB (as is typical), to store the connection ID. You can get away with this massive simplification and cost saving mechanism of using the AWS Parameter Store over using a database because unlike a generic and overused “chatroom” WebSocket examples, which requires us to keep track of an unknown number of connection ID’s (chatroom participants), for this use case you can be assured that you only need one connection ID as you only have one client to serve - the webpage as the client in a one-to-one mapping. Even if you use a fan-in architecture with many IoT devices they do not count as clients as they are feeding into the same connection nexus. The connection clients consist only of web-based entities that each need their own webpage connected via WebSockets.

To get started, navigate in the AWS console to the “Systems Manager” service and select the “Parameter Store” on the panel on the left-hand side of the screen:

https://console.aws.amazon.com/systems-manager/parameters

On the upper right of the screen select the “Create parameter” button:

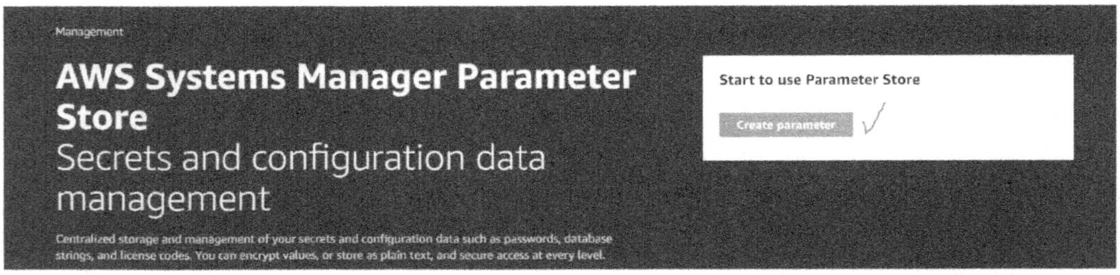
Management
AWS Systems Manager Parameter Store
Secrets and configuration data management
Centralized storage and management of your secrets and configuration data such as passwords, database strings, and license codes. You can encrypt values, or store as plain text, and secure access at every level.
Start to use Parameter Store
Create parameter

Choose a parameter name like “connection_id”, choose Type: “*String*”, and then put some dummy string value into the box below (The exact string value here is irrelevant because it will be overwritten by your connection Lambda). That's it, super easy, and for all effective purposes the Parameter Store is free for up to 10,000 strings. Compare this cost to DynamoDB once you are no longer on the free tier!

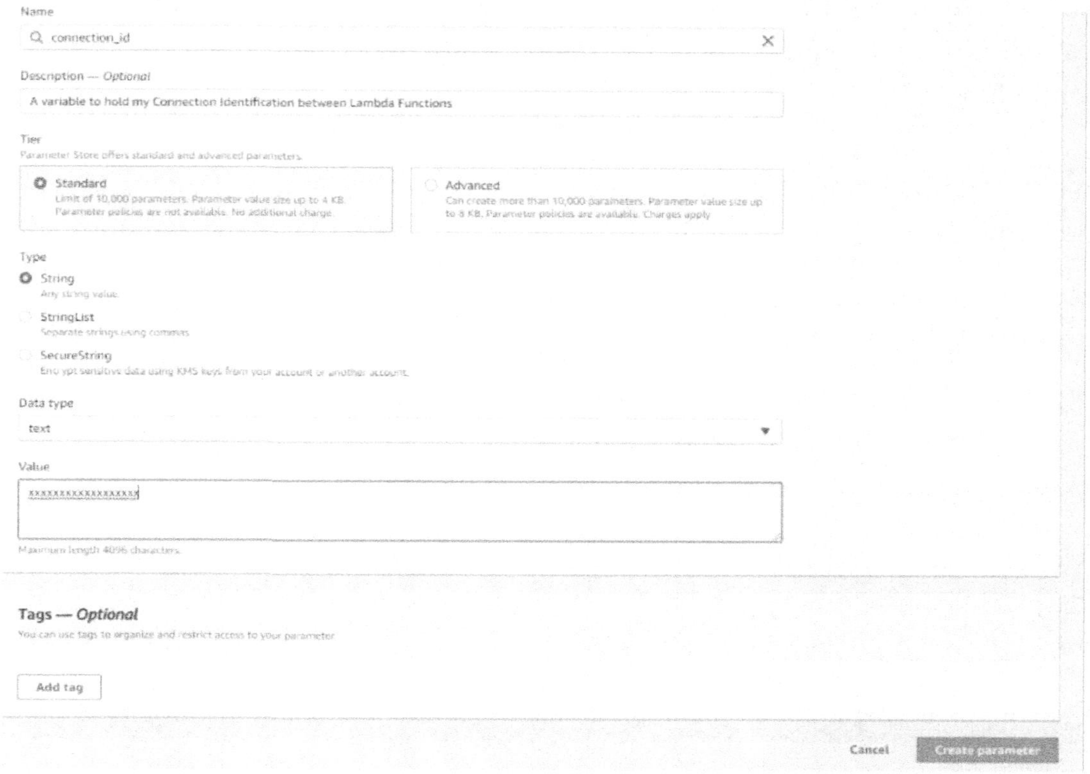

Name
connection_id
Description — Optional
A variable to hold my Connection Identification between Lambda Functions
Tier
Standard
Advanced
Type
String
StringList
SecureString
Data type
text
Value
xxxxxxxxxxxxxxxxx
Tags — Optional
Add tag
Cancel
Create parameter

Finally select the "Create parameter" button and you are done.

Step 3 - Develop the Connection and Messaging Lambda Functions

You will need two Lambda functions for this project:

A) *Lambda function one* – 'connection' Lambda: This Lambda function receives the connection ID from the website host via the $connect route and then stores the connection ID into the AWS Parameter Store as a string variable. The $connect route on API Gateway is mapped to this Lambda.

B) *Lambda function two* – 'sendIoTdata': This Lambda function will forward your

IoT data to your static website host through the 'message' route in API Gateway. You will need both the Lambda functions mapped 'message' route and the ability to execute an API Gateway 'post_to_connection()' function to achieve bi-directional IoT data transfer capabilities. API Gateway will be brokering the data pipe between your Lambda function and your website. You will also use an API invoking the AWS Parameter Store to retrieve the connection ID that was written from the 'connection' Lambda function.

If this all sounds confusing it is because it is. But by the end of the chapter you will understand the big picture and be able to use the project for your own purposes.

A) The Connection Lambda

Go to:

https://aws.amazon.com/Lambda

Navigate to Lambda in your desired region and create a new Lambda function in Node.js. Call it something like "myConnection", you can also choose your own name. You will be using the Node.js V. 14 runtime.

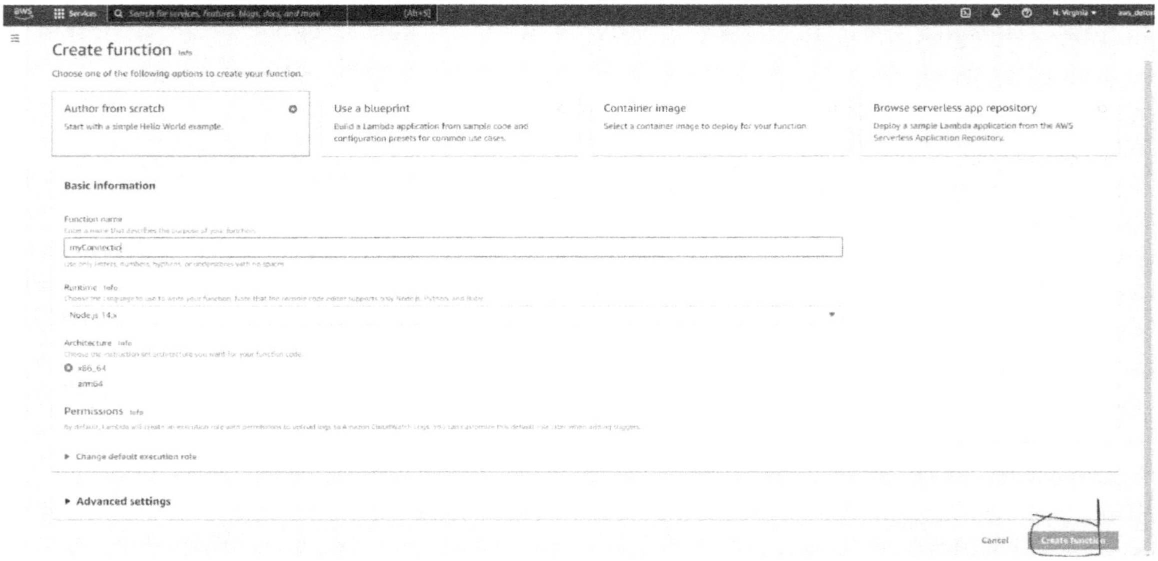

Create function
Choose one of the following options to create your function.
Author from scratch
Start with a simple Hello World example.
Use a blueprint
Container image
Browse serverless app repository
Basic information
Function name
myConnectio
Runtime
Node.js 14.x
Architecture
x86_64
arm64
Permissions
Change default execution role
Advanced settings
Cancel
Create function

At this point you should paste the name of your parameter variable string you created in the Parameter Store earlier into the 'connection' Lambda function:

```
Name: '<Insert-Your-SSM-Parameter-Name-Here>',
```

After you create your Lambda function, paste the following code into the function with your own SSM parameter name ('connection_id') inserted into the code as listed below:

```
//Extra Permission required: SSM

const AWS = require('aws-sdk')
var mySSM_Client = new AWS.SSM();   //new client object

exports.handler = async (event, context) => {

 console.log(event);
 let connectionId = event.requestContext.connectionId;
 console.log("myConnectionID is: ", connectionId)

//-----------------Begin SSM Code
// putParameter-property
var params = {
  Name: '<Insert-Your-SSM-Parameter-Name-Here>',
  Value: connectionId,
  Overwrite: true  //not required but default is False
};

//await and promise() stub are not documented but necessary
var mySSM_request = await mySSM_Client.putParameter(params, function(err,
data) {
  if (err) console.log(err, err.stack);     // an error occurred
  else     console.log("success: ", data);  // successful response
}).promise()
//var mySSM_request = await mySSM_Client.putParameter

console.log("My request: ", mySSM_request)

//------------------End SSM Code

    const response = {
       statusCode: 200,
       body: JSON.stringify('Hello from Lambda!'),
   };
   return response;
};
```

The image below shows the Lambda function with the SSM parameter name ('connection_id') inserted.

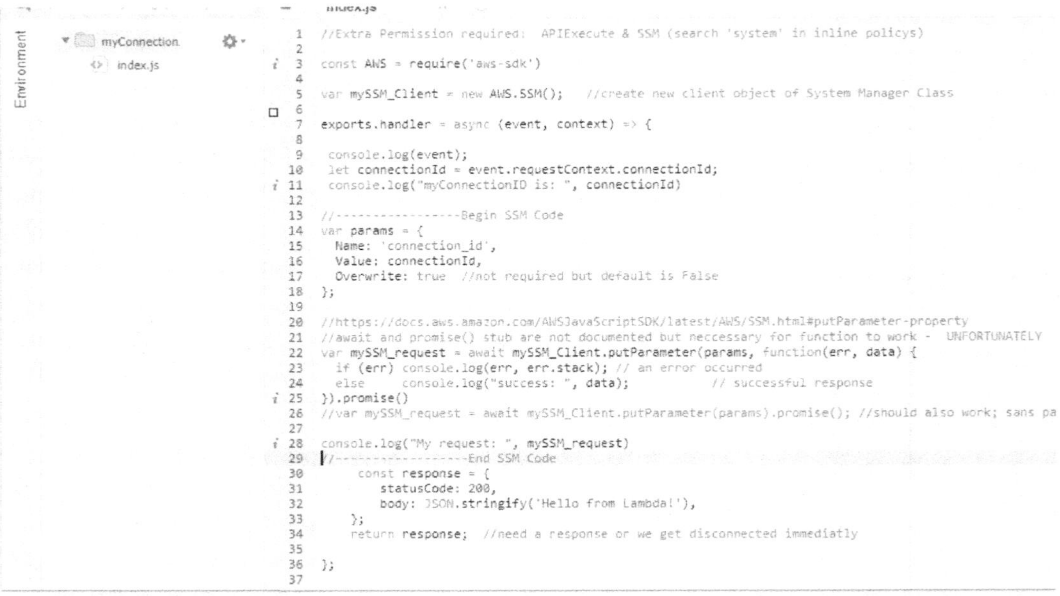
Environment
myConnection
index.js
index.js
//Extra Permission required: APIExecute & SSM (search 'system' in inline policys)
const AWS = require('aws-sdk')
var mySSM_Client = new AWS.SSM(); //create new client object of System Manager Class
exports.handler = async (event, context) => {
console.log(event);
let connectionId = event.requestContext.connectionId;
console.log("myConnectionID is: ", connectionId)
//-----------------Begin SSM Code
var params = {
Name: 'connection_id',
Value: connectionId,
Overwrite: true //not required but default is False
};
//https://docs.aws.amazon.com/AWSJavaScriptSDK/latest/AWS/SSM.html#putParameter-property
//await and promise() stub are not documented but neccessary for function to work - UNFORTUNATELY
var mySSM_request = await mySSM_Client.putParameter(params, function(err, data) {
if (err) console.log(err, err.stack); // an error occurred
else console.log("success: ", data); // successful response
}).promise()
//var mySSM_request = await mySSM_Client.putParameter(params).promise(); //should also work; sans pa
console.log("My request: ", mySSM_request)
//-----------------End SSM Code
const response = {
statusCode: 200,
body: JSON.stringify('Hello from Lambda!'),
};
return response; //need a response or we get disconnected immediatly
};

As you can see the function has two main routines.

1. The Lambda function receives the connection ID by extracting the necessary parameter by drilling down into the event blob of browser data that is returned from your static website as soon as you open index.html page. This will be done by integrating this connection Lambda with the *$connect* route key that you will set up in API Gateway soon.

The code below extracts the connection ID from the event object returned from the website (object blob of website data).:

```
let connectionId = event.requestContext.connectionId;
```

In AWS CloudWatch you can view details on this big blob of data your browser sent to the connection Lambda. Deep within this data blob is the connection ID that will be saved in the AWS System Manager Parameter Store.

2. After the connection ID is successfully extracted, the Lambda function uses

the “put” API from the Systems Manager Parameter Store to save the connection ID to a string variable. The connection ID is held in the ‘*params*’ object at this point.

```
mySSM_Client.putParameter(params, function(err, data)
```

The previous string variable in the Parameter Store (initiated as “xxxxxxx”) is now overwritten with the real connection ID and is made available for use when called by the "sendIoTdata" Lambda function that you will create next. Whenever a new connection to a website is made then a new and unique connection ID is returned from the new website, via the $connect route key that you will create soon.

A few notes about this function are in order:

You may notice that I have put a link to the ‘put’ Parameter API code documentation within the Lambda function as a comment. Notice that I had to modify the original API code, or it would not work as documented by AWS. I received no errors as to the problem with the 'put' API, but the parameter string value would not be stored. However, I have dealt with this issue before when using Node.js in Lambda and it seems to be an ongoing challenge with the AWS-SDK for Node.js. To fix this problem I had to add the additional await and promise() stub to the Lambda function.

Adding permissions to the connection Lambda function

No, you are not done with the connection Lambda yet, you still need to add the necessary permissions so that your Lambda function can write the connection ID string to the Parameter Store in the AWS Systems Manager. To accomplish this, navigate to IAM by going to:

Configuration tab → Permissions tab→ Role name → then open your role link to get to AWS IAM.

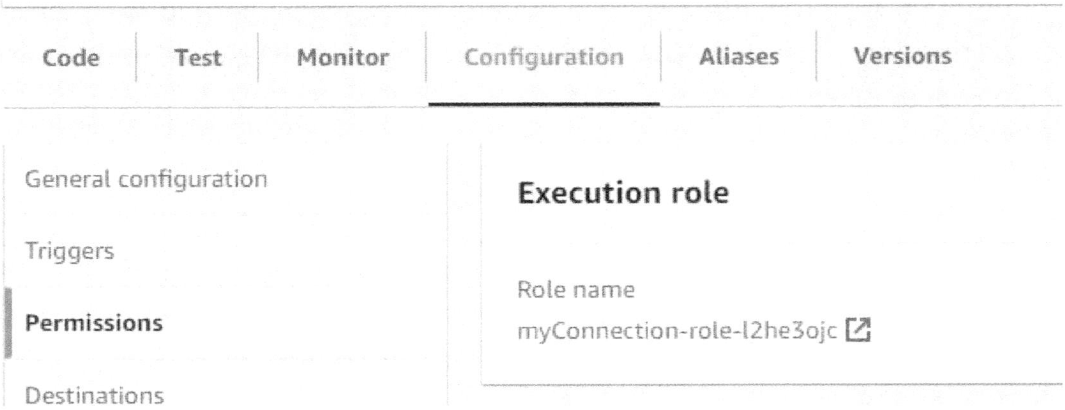
Code
Test
Monitor
Configuration
Aliases
Versions
General configuration
Triggers
Permissions
Destinations
Execution role
Role name
myConnection-role-l2he3ojc

Within IAM you need to add an inline permissions policy. Click the "Add inline policy" on the right-hand side of the screen.

Permissions
Trust relationships
Tags
Access Advisor
Revoke sessions
Permissions policies (1 policy applied)
Attach policies
Add inline policy
Policy name
Policy type
Managed policy
Permissions boundary (not set)

You will add Parameter Store permission, which is in the "Systems Manager" service. To add this permission search for it by typing in "sys" in the policy search box until "System Manager" comes up and then grant the inline policy 'All actions' and 'All resources'.

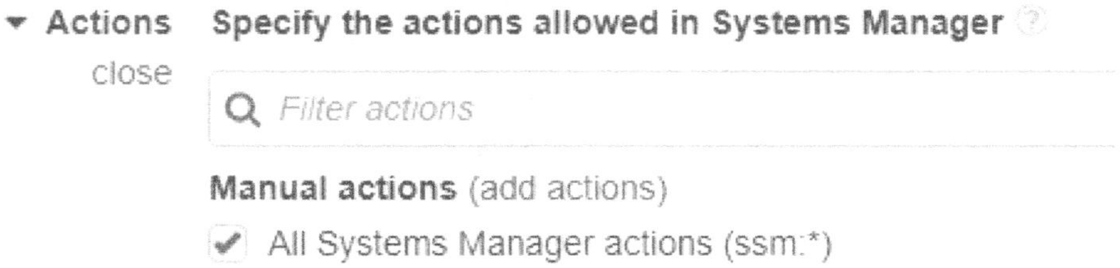
Actions
close
Specify the actions allowed in Systems Manager
Filter actions
Manual actions (add actions)
All Systems Manager actions (ssm:*)

And 'All Resources' permissions.

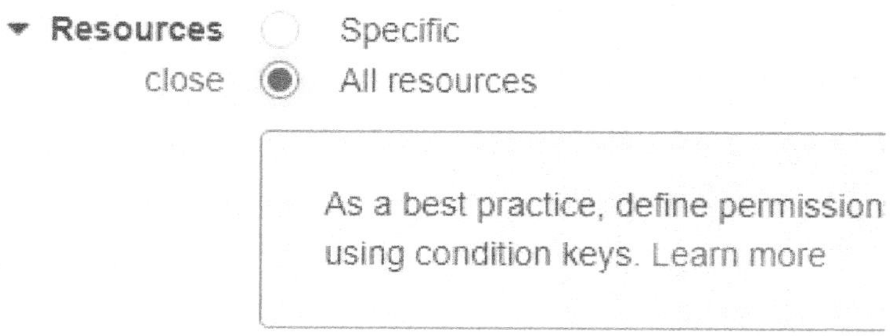
Resources
close
Specific
All resources
As a best practice, define permission
using condition keys. Learn more

Now click “Review Policy” and give your policy a name like “SysManager4connection” and then create the policy.

Your screen should look like this:

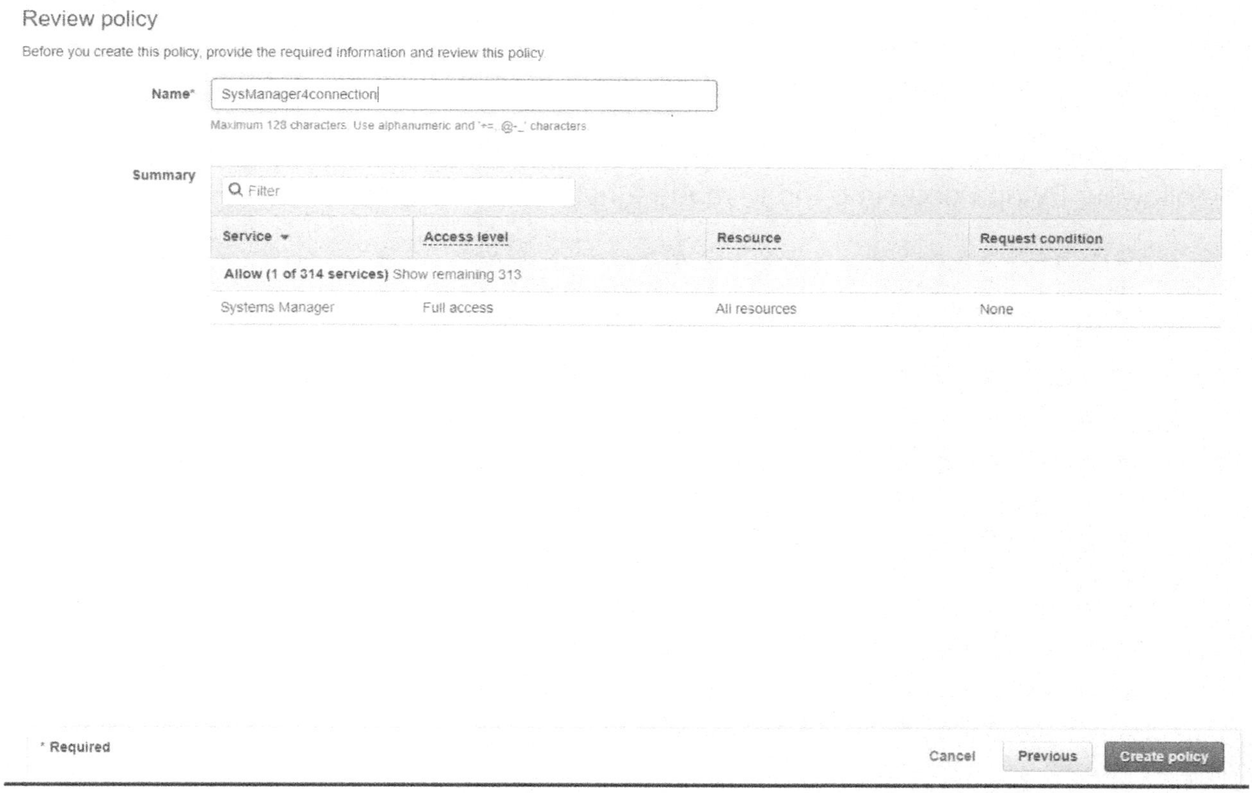
Review policy
Before you create this policy, provide the required information and review this policy
Name*
SysManager4connection
Summary
Filter
Service
Access level
Resource
Request condition
Allow (1 of 314 services) Show remaining 313
Systems Manager
Full access
All resources
None
* Required
Cancel
Previous
Create policy

Press “Create policy” and now you are done with the inline policy for SSM access. Now that you are done assigning the needed Systems Manager permission for your policy, you can create your second Lambda function.

B) sendIoTData Lambda:

Navigate back to Lambda and create a new Lambda function in Python 3.8. Call it something like "sendIoTData", you can also choose your own Lambda function name.

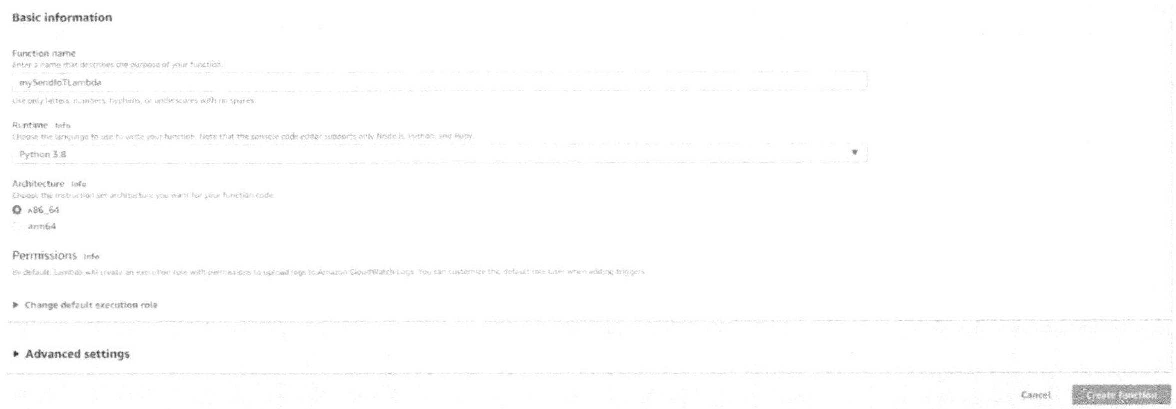
Basic information
Function name
Runtime
Python 3.8
Architecture
x86_64
arm64
Permissions
Change default execution role
Advanced settings
Cancel

Now select "Create function," and after the Lambda function is created paste the following Python code into the Lambda function code pane:

```
#Add both 'ExecuteAPI' and 'System' permissions

import json
import boto3
WebSocket_HTTPS_URL = "https://<Insert-WebSocket-HTTPS-Endpoint_Here>"
client = boto3.client("apigatewaymanagementapi", endpoint_url =
WebSocket_HTTPS_URL)
ssm_Client = boto3.client('ssm')

def lambda_handler(event, context):
    print(event)
    response_ssm = ssm_Client.get_parameter(Name='<Insert-Your-SSM-Parameter-
Name-Here>')
    print("my stored connection id: ", response_ssm['Parameter']['Value'] )
    connectionId =  response_ssm['Parameter']['Value']
    Test_Message = json.dumps({ "message": "Hello from Lambda, hardcoded test
message"})
    IoT_Message = json.dumps(event)
    #AWS API Gateway API's require 'key=value' arguments
```

```
    response = client.post_to_connection(ConnectionId = connectionId, Data =
IoT_Message)
```

This Lambda function accomplishes two main tasks

A) The Lambda function retrieves the stored connection ID written from the previous Lambda function and then adds it as a key-value parameter to the “post to connection” API. To accomplish this the Lambda function uses the "get_parameter()" API to retrieve the connection ID you saved in the Systems Manager Parameter Store using the connection Lambda you previously created.

B) The Lambda function receives the incoming IoT data payload from AWS IoT Core as an event object, and then dispatches the IoT JSON payload linked to the connection ID by invoking the "post_to_connection()" API (an API Gateway function). Then finally the IoT payload gets dispatched to your website via the WebSocket endpoint.

At this point you should insert the name of your parameter variable from the Parameter Store into the Lambda function:

```
response_ssm = ssm_Client.get_parameter(Name='<Insert-Your-SSM-Parameter-
Name-Here>')
```

Now deploy the ‘*sendIoTdata*’ Lambda function.

At this point you still need the internal WebSocket HTTPS endpoint in your Lambda function which you won’t receive until you create the WebSocket API in AWS API Gateway. You will accomplish this in the next section.

A few interesting notes to help explain the operation of this ‘sendIoTdata’ Lambda function. To retrieve your connection ID you have to drill down into the blob of data returned as a response when invoking the client object of type ‘SSM’. This is a different blob of information than what you received from your website host connection. If you want to see this information, or any other information in Lambda, simply 'print' out the response and then go to AWS CloudWatch to examine the blobs info. CloudWatch is a necessary tool for any Lambda debugging. For convenience, CloudWatch permissions are always included in the basic Lambda execution roles which are created automatically for you when you created your Lambda function.

A second thing to note is that the API:

```
post_to_connection(ConnectionId = connectionId, Data = IoT_Message)
```

requires a key-value pair as function parameters. The IoT message has the option of being any hardcoded message you add to the Lambda function, or just a JSON payload from a test event. Of course, you will be using a real IoT JSON payload when you add in the AWS IoT Core service in a coming step. This function is part of the API Gateway client ("*apigatewaymanagementapi*") and thus needs the related permission to execute the API.

Finally, you do not have your 'wss' WebSocket endpoint yet

```
WebSocket_HTTPS_URL = "https://<Insert-WebSocket-Endpoint_Here>"
```

You will get the endpoint by completing the next step in API Gateway. After you create this endpoint, you can then insert it into the Lambda function.

Adding permissions to your sendIoTdata Lambda function

Bad news, you must add two extra permissions for this Lambda function to integrate it properly with the complete design flow. Good news, you already know how to do this from the previous step. The two permissions you will add are "Systems Manager" and "ExecuteAPI."

While still in the Lambda function go to:

Permissions→Configuration and click on the "Role name," this will open up IAM, now "Create an inline policy" on the right side of the screen from the drop-down box.

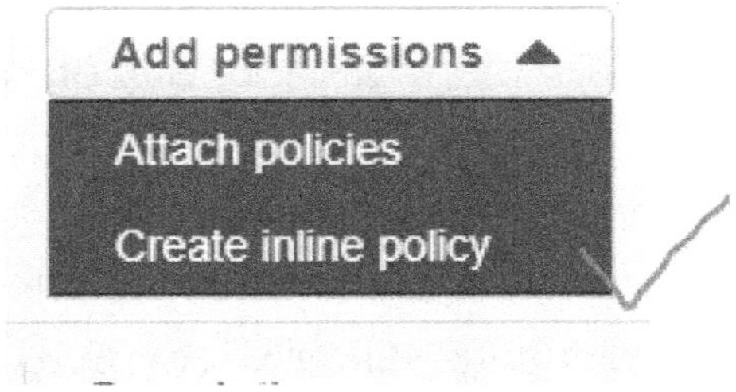
Add permissions
Attach policies
Create inline policy

To add the "Systems Manager" permission policy to give access to the Parameter Store, simply follow the same instructions from the previous ‘connection’ Lambda permissions. To find the "ExecuteAPI" permissions policy just search for "execute" in the policies search box. Duplicating the same process as before, you can give the ‘sendIoTdata’ Lambda function access to “All actions” and “All resources” to make things easy, or narrow the permissions down to your Lambda functions ARN if you want to be pedantic or are on a shared AWS corporate account.

Now you are ready to move to the next step. More good news, you have just completed the most difficult part of this chapter. You should now have three policies for this Lambda: default execution role, “Systems Manager” permissions policy, and “ExecuteAPI” permissions policy.

Permissions policies (3 policies applied)
Attach policies
Add inline policy
Policy name
Policy type
Managed policy
ExecuteAPI4connection
Inline policy
SysManager4connection
Inline policy

Finally, note that you need "ExecuteAPI" in the 'sendIoTdata' Lambda function because the *post_to_connection()* API needs to pass your IoT payloads through API Gateway before it can be sent to your webpage. The ExecuteAPI permission policy allows the Lambda function to 'execute' the internal HTTPS endpoint via the API Gateway 'client' using the *post_to_connection()* function. You will be creating those internal and external WebSocket endpoints in the next section discussing AWS API Gateway.

Step 4 - Design WebSocket Endpoints in AWS API Gateway

WebSockets form a direct connection with your website host using a URL endpoint which directs both the website and the Lambda function to direct the data exchange. API Gateway provides these endpoints for this exchange just as it would for a normal REST API.

You will be obtaining two WebSocket endpoints from the creation process in API Gateway. One internal endpoint (HTTPS) for use in the 'sendIoTdata' Lambda function, and one external WebSocket endpoint (*wss*) for use on your webpage.

1. External WebSocket endpoint: this is the URL with a 'wss' prefix. This is the AWS WebSockets endpoint to be embedded on your website to communicate with API Gateway.

2. Internal WebSocket Endpoint: this is the URL with a 'https' prefix. This is the AWS WebSocket endpoint needed for your 'sendIoTdata' Lambda function to communicate with API Gateway through the *post_to_connection()* API, and in turn, communicate with your static website in S3.

Create the API Gateway WebSocket endpoints and routes by navigating to:

API Gateway –> Create API and choosing to build a WebSocket API

https://console.aws.amazon.com/apigateway/main/precreate

- Make sure you are still in the same region as your other AWS services.

Select a name for your WebSocket API and then type *request.body.action* in the box for the 'Route selection expression'. This is the standard path to designate a WebSocket action like "message", "join", or "send".

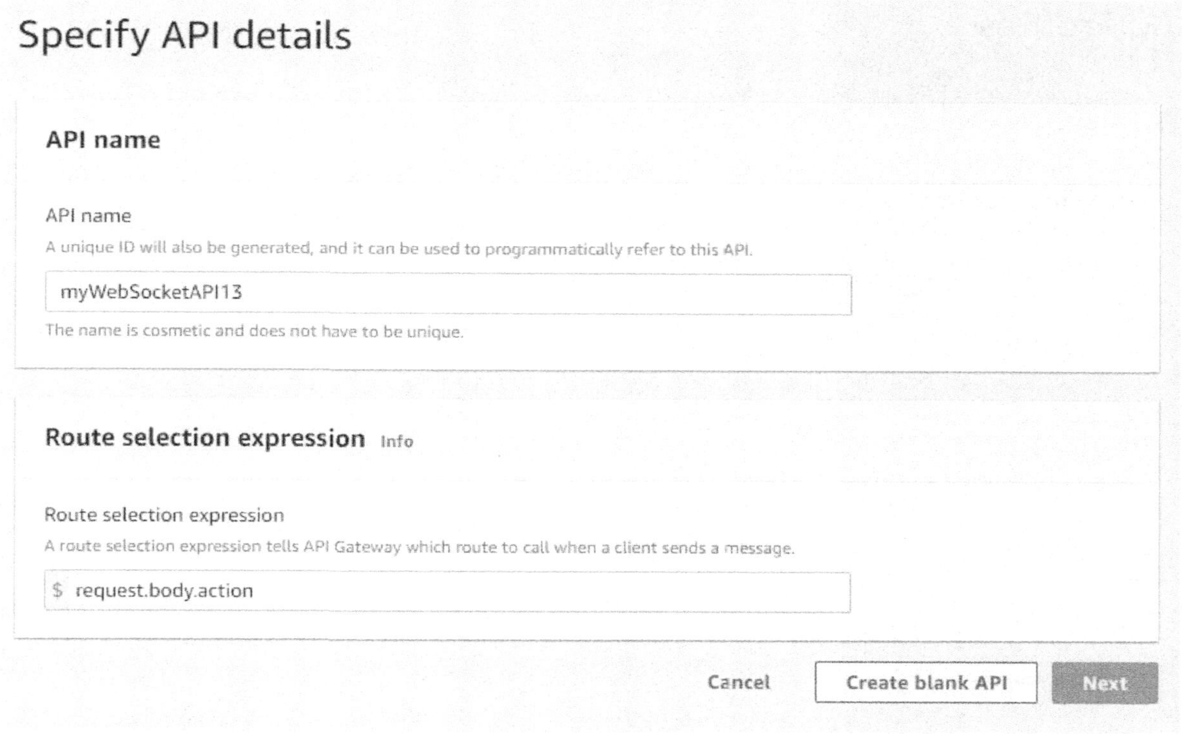
Specify API details
API name
API name
A unique ID will also be generated, and it can be used to programmatically refer to this API.
myWebSocketAPI13
The name is cosmetic and does not have to be unique.
Route selection expression Info
Route selection expression
A route selection expression tells API Gateway which route to call when a client sends a message.
$ request.body.action
Cancel
Create blank API
Next

Choose the “Next” button and then on the next screen you will select one pre-made macro route and one custom route. The one predefined route that you need here is the connection route. Elect to add a connection route with the macro called ‘*$connect*’ to route to your ‘connection’ Lambda function.

The second route you will designate is a “Custom” route called “message”. This is the custom route which forms a bi-directional pipe or "socket" between your website and AWS providing a conduit for incoming and outgoing data.

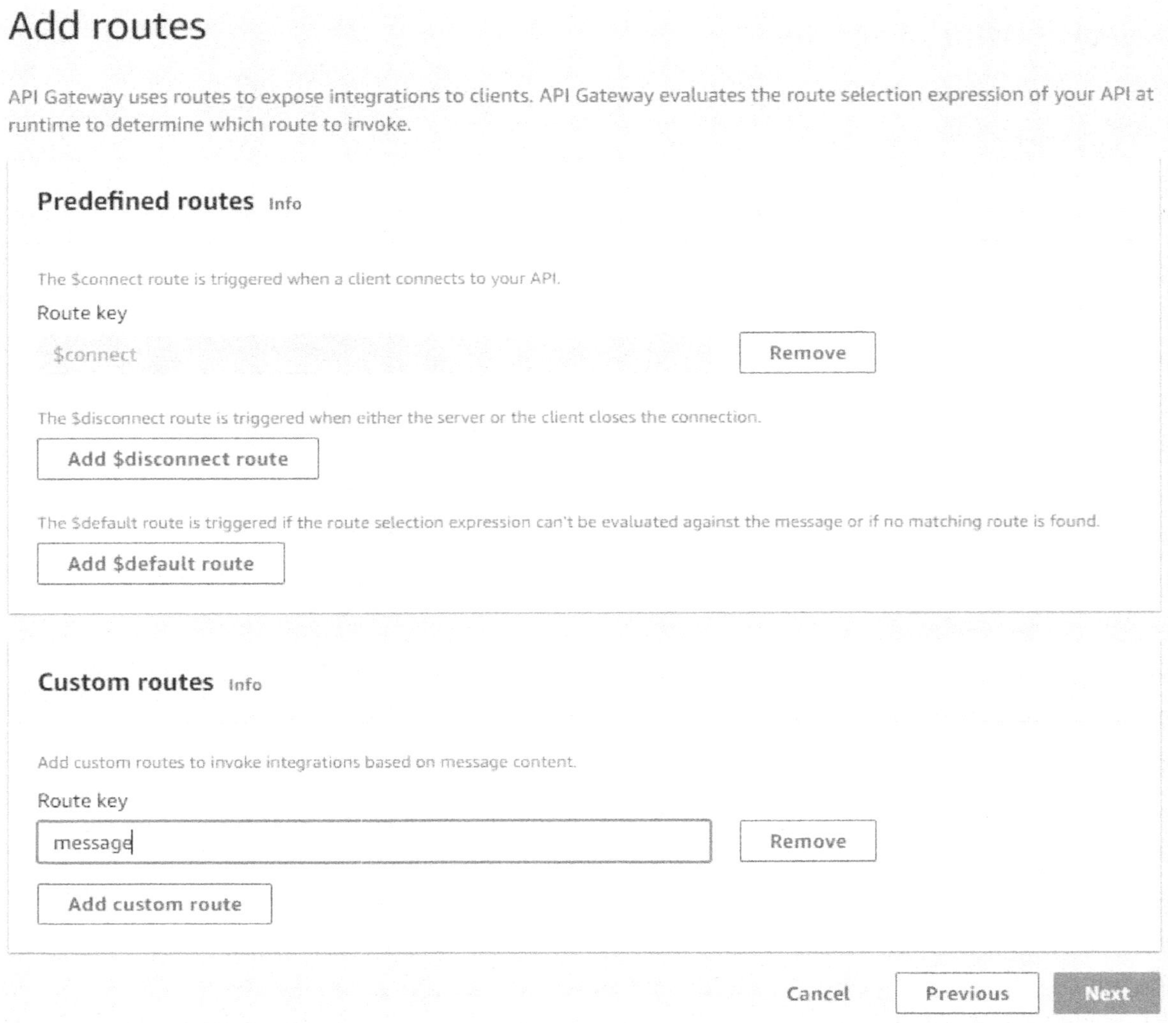
Add routes
API Gateway uses routes to expose integrations to clients. API Gateway evaluates the route selection expression of your API at runtime to determine which route to invoke.
Predefined routes Info
The $connect route is triggered when a client connects to your API.
Route key
$connect
Remove
The $disconnect route is triggered when either the server or the client closes the connection.
Add $disconnect route
The $default route is triggered if the route selection expression can't be evaluated against the message or if no matching route is found.
Add $default route
Custom routes Info
Add custom routes to invoke integrations based on message content.
Route key
message
Remove
Add custom route
Cancel
Previous
Next

Select "Next" to go to the next screen to configure your WebSocket API.

Now you must link your WebSockets API routes with your two previously created Lambda functions. You may now see why I had you created the Lambdas first even though it seems counter intuitive. This awkwardness in IoT architecture is typical for IoT design flows as you often must work backwards in AWS.

To link the two Lambdas to the two WebSocket route keys select the Lambda functions you just created and link them to the appropriate route keys shown in the image below. The Lambda names may appear slightly different as I revised them cosmetically and renamed them, do not let that confuse you.

'$connect' route key to 'connection' Lambda function

'message' route key to 'sendIoTdata' Lambda function

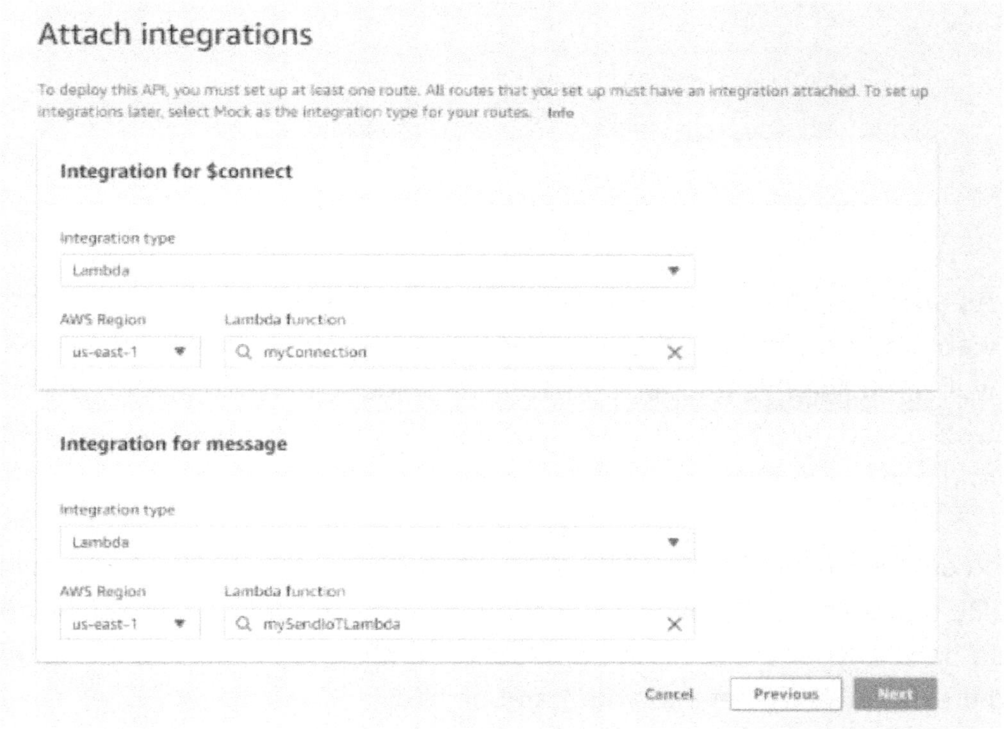
Attach integrations
To deploy this API, you must set up at least one route. All routes that you set up must have an integration attached. To set up integrations later, select Mock as the integration type for your routes. Info
Integration for $connect
Integration type
Lambda
AWS Region
Lambda function
us-east-1
myConnection
Integration for message
Integration type
Lambda
AWS Region
Lambda function
us-east-1
mySendIoTLambda
Cancel
Previous
Next

Select "Next" then leave the stage name as "production" and select "Next" again, and then finally "Create and deploy."

Now to view the WebSocket endpoints go to the tab called "stages" on the left of your screen. Click your only stage which should be in blue and called "production." After selecting the production stage, you should now see your two WebSocket endpoints on the top of your screen. Leave this screen open as you will need to copy both endpoints.

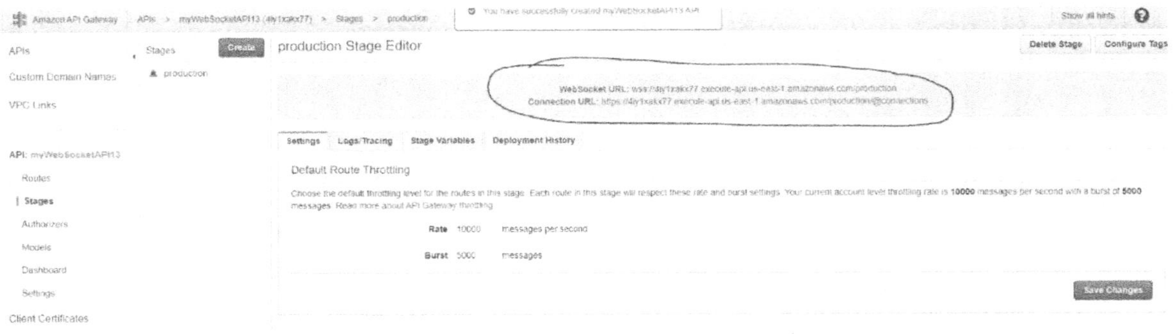
production Stage Editor
WebSocket URL: wss://4iy1xakx77.execute-api.us-east-1.amazonaws.com/production
Connection URL: https://4iy1xakx77.execute-api.us-east-1.amazonaws.com/production/@connections
Settings
Logs/Tracing
Stage Variables
Deployment History
Default Route Throttling
Rate 10000 messages per second
Burst 5000 messages
Save Changes

- As an aside, this single external "wss" socket URL can work with any static webhost external to AWS to connect to AWS. Thus, you can also host a website using this endpoint on JSbin, JSFiddle, Playcode.io, or any other web-based JavaScript IDE you like if all you want to do is test the IoT design and don't care about retaining your website after testing.

Now you can complete the "SendIoTdata" Lambda function with the new internal https URL and then re-deploy the Lambda function. To do this open a new tab and navigate back to your Lambda "sendIoTdata" Lambda function. The format for pasting the 'https' endpoint into your Lambda:

```
WebSocket_HTTPS_URL = 'https://<Insert-WebSocket-HTTPS-Endpoint-Here>'
```

The endpoint is now inserted into the Lambda function below:

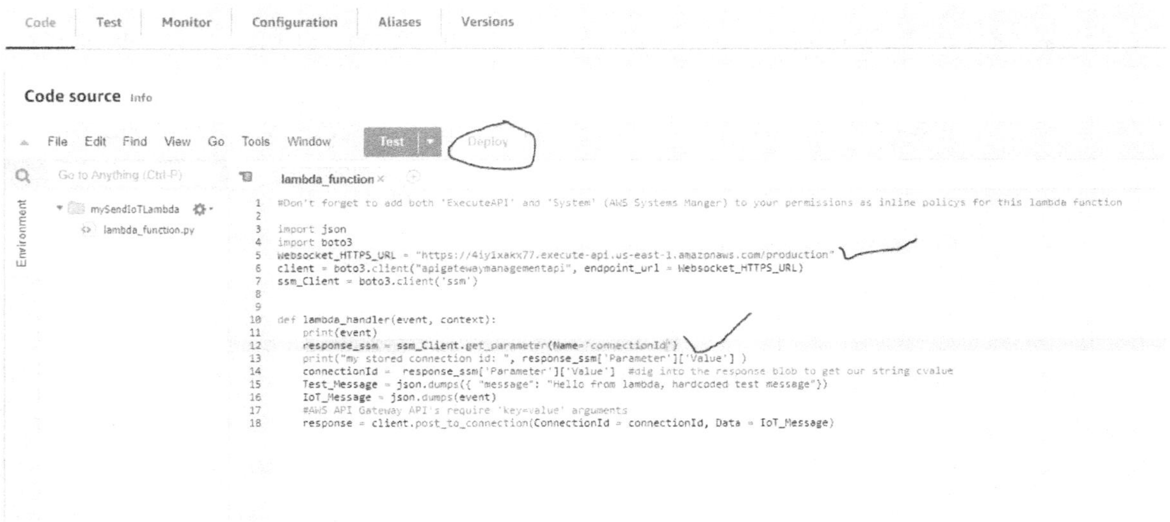
Code
Test
Monitor
Configuration
Aliases
Versions
Code source Info
File Edit Find View Go Tools Window Test Deploy
lambda_function
#Don't forget to add both 'ExecuteAPI' and 'System' (AWS Systems Manger) to your permissions as inline policys for this lambda function
import json
import boto3
Websocket_HTTPS_URL = "https://4iy1xakx77.execute-api.us-east-1.amazonaws.com/production"
client = boto3.client("apigatewaymanagementapi", endpoint_url = Websocket_HTTPS_URL)
ssm_Client = boto3.client('ssm')
def lambda_handler(event, context):
print(event)
response_ssm = ssm_Client.get_parameter(Name='connectionId')
print("my stored connection id: ", response_ssm['Parameter']['Value'])
connectionId = response_ssm['Parameter']['Value'] #dig into the response blob to get our string cvalue
Test_Message = json.dumps({ "message": "Hello from lambda, hardcoded test message"})
IoT_Message = json.dumps(event)
#AWS API Gateway API's require 'key=value' arguments
response = client.post_to_connection(ConnectionId = connectionId, Data = IoT_Message)

Don’t forget to 'Deploy' your Lambda function or your changes won’t be saved.

Step 5 - Create an AWS IoT Core Rule to Send IoT Data to Lambda

In this step you will create an AWS IoT Core Rule that will send the IoT data from the MQTT broker in IoT Core to your 'sendIoTData' Lambda function. Once the IoT payload is dispatched as an event object to the Lambda function then the IoT payload can be forwarded to your static website via the internal HTTPS WebSocket endpoint in your Lambda function.

In AWS IoT Core select: Rules→ Create or go to

https://console.aws.amazon.com/iot

Select a name for your Rule and then change the Rules Query Statement to the following:

```
SELECT *, timestamp() as timestamps FROM 'iot/#'
```

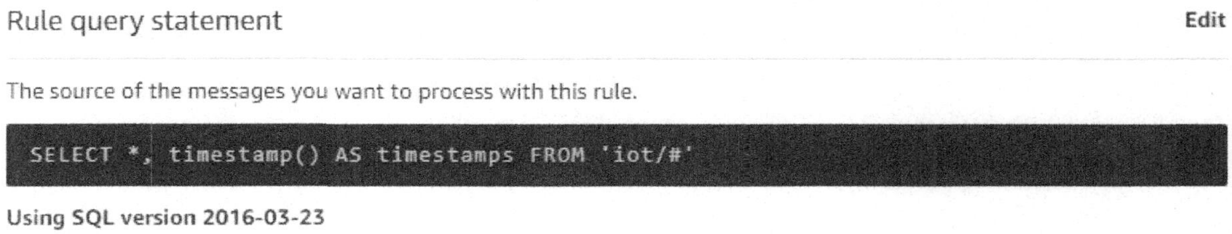

Rule query statement
Edit
The source of the messages you want to process with this rule.
SELECT *, timestamp() AS timestamps FROM 'iot/#'
Using SQL version 2016-03-23

This query does two important things that differ from a generic RQS. First, it adds a field to your incoming IoT payload called “timestamps." This “timestamps” field is a literal match for a variable extant in the JavaScript web code for the static website. Using the premade AWS timestamp() function also adds a UNIX/Epoch timestamp to your payload. You will need this timestamp for indexing the X-axis on the line chart visualization on the static website in S3. Of course, adding the timestamp can also be done in Lambda depending on your needs or your preferences. Often, on non-application level MCU’s in embedded devices like the ESP32 and ESP8266, UNIX timestamps cannot be programmed without additional RTC hardware or extra libraries, in these cases you can use “uptime” as a relative time index rather than an absolute time format like the timestamp() function provides.

The second important thing the RQS does is something you already are familiar with from earlier in this book. The RQS uses a wildcard topic from which the hash/pound allows a fungible extension to the incoming base topic. For instance, if you were using MQTT messaging to communicate between Lambda functions, you could have one topic published as 'iot/LambdaTopic' and another as 'iot/deviceTopic'. Using the 'iot/#' means that both formats will be picked up by the RQS and then you could discriminate how to handle multiple topics coming into the same or different Lambda function by topic extension. However, remember you may need some conditional topic testing in your Lambda function to prevent an infinite publish/subscribe loop as described in the second prerequisite chapter of the book.

Your Rule should now look something like this:

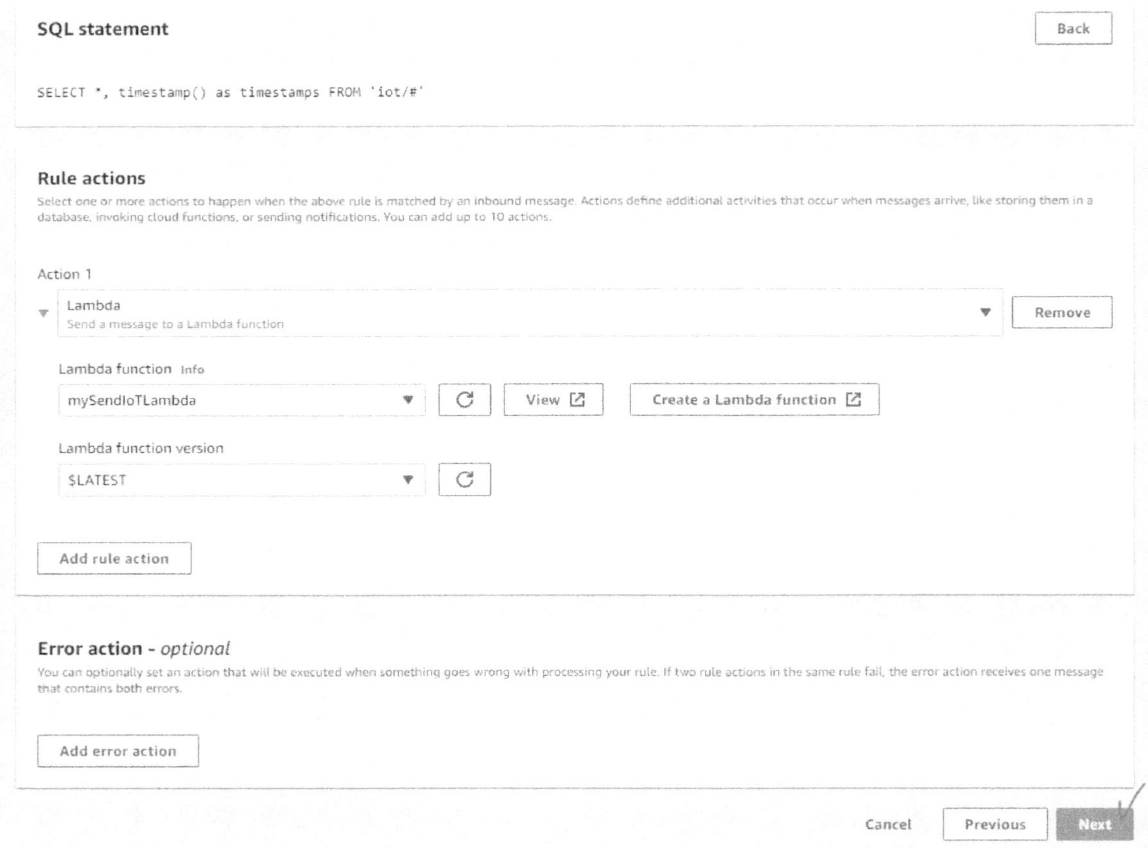

SQL statement
Back
SELECT *, timestamp() as timestamps FROM 'iot/#'
Rule actions
Select one or more actions to happen when the above rule is matched by an inbound message. Actions define additional activities that occur when messages arrive, like storing them in a database, invoking cloud functions, or sending notifications. You can add up to 10 actions.
Action 1
Lambda
Send a message to a Lambda function
Remove
Lambda function Info
mySendIoTLambda
View
Create a Lambda function
Lambda function version
$LATEST
Add rule action
Error action - optional
You can optionally set an action that will be executed when something goes wrong with processing your rule. If two rule actions in the same rule fail, the error action receives one message that contains both errors.
Add error action
Cancel
Previous
Next

Now select “Next”:

Next

Now review and finish by “Create” the rule:

Create

The final thing you must do is make sure the new rule is 'enabled' on the rules menu.

Now that your IoT rule is created and will dispath IoT payloads to your ‘sendIoTdata’ Lambda function, you should upload the web code to your website in S3.

Step 6 - Upload the Static Website Code to Create an Asynchronous Visualization of the IoT Data

There are two files to upload to your public bucket and your newly created static webhost. The files are called *'index.html'* and *'main.js'*.

Below is the index.html launch page. Copy the following code and save it to the S3 bucket, serving as a static webhost, as "*index.html*":

```
<!DOCTYPE html>
<html lang="en">
<head>
    <meta charset="UTF-8">
    <meta name="viewport" content="width=device-width, initial-scale=1.0">
    <meta http-equiv="X-UA-Compatible" content="ie=edge">
    <title>Dashboard</title>
</head>

<body>
    <div class="container">
        <h1>Asynchronous IoT Weather Data with AWS WebSockets</h1>

        <div class="panel panel-info">
            <div class="panel-heading">
                <h3 class="panel-title"><strong>Line Chart</strong></h3>
            </div>
            <div class="panel-body">
```

```
            <div class="col-sm-6 col-md-6">
            <div id="container1"></div>
            </div>
        </div>
    </div>

    <style>
        .row {
          box-sizing: border-box;
        }

        .row {
          display: flex;
          justify-content: space-between;
        }

        .row {
          width: 100%;
          padding: 10px;
        }

    </style>

<div class="row">

    <div class="col-sm-4">
        <figure class="highcharts-figure">

            <div id="container2"></div>
                <p class="highcharts-description">
                Temperature Gauge with Degrees in Fehr/Cel
            </p>
        </figure>
    </div>



    <div class="col-sm-4">
        <figure class="highcharts-figure">
            <div id="container3"></div>
                <p class="highcharts-description">
               Humidity Guage showing %of water saturation
            </p>
        </figure>
    </div>
```

```
        <figure class="col-sm-4">
            <figure class="highcharts-figure"></figure>
                <div id="container4"></div>
                    <p class="highcharts-description">
                    Epoch/UNIX time, expect many ticks per Second
                </p>
            </figure>
        </div>

    </div>

</div>
    </body>
    </html>

<script src="https://code.highcharts.com/highcharts.js"></script>
<script src="https://code.highcharts.com/highcharts-more.js"></script>
<script src="https://code.highcharts.com/modules/exporting.js"></script>
<script src="https://code.highcharts.com/modules/export-data.js"></script>
<script src="https://code.highcharts.com/modules/accessibility.js"></script>

    <script src="https://code.jquery.com/jquery-3.1.1.min.js"></script>
    <script src="./main.js"></script>
```

The *'main.js'* file below has WebSockets compatible asynchronous code as shown in the snippit below:

```
const socket = new WebSocket('<Insert-Your-WSS-Endpoint-With-Prefix-Here>')
socket.addEventListener('open', event => {
console.log('WebSocket is connected, now check for your new Connection ID in
Cloudwatch })
socket.addEventListener('message', event => {
console.log('Your iot payload is:', event.data);
drawChart(event.data);
})
```

With these few lines of code you can now take advantage of WebSockets to enable the “sendIoTdata” Lambda function to perform a “server push” and transmit event objects, as incoming IoT payloads, directly into your static web host. This is possible through the socket event listener as the ‘message’ which forms a bidirectional link with API Gateway given the external WebSockets endpoint and the route key of 'message'.

The only change you need to make to the code below is on line three of the main.js file. You will need to insert the external AWS WebSocket endpoint you got from API Gateway into the JavaScript code. This WebSocket endpoint is the external address that starts with '*wss://*" prefix. Make sure to include the 'wss://' prefix when pasting your WebSocket endpoint into the main.js code.

```
Const socket = new WebSocket('<Insert-Your-WebSocket-Endpoint-Here-With-WSS-
Prefix>')
```

Once the line above is customized and inserted into the code below, save the following code as 'main.js':

```
let humArr = [], tempArr = [], upArr = [];

const socket = new WebSocket('<Insert-Your-WebSocket-Endpoint-Here-With-WSS-
Prefix>')

socket.addEventListener('open', event => {
  console.log('WebSocket is connected, now check for your new Connection ID
in Cloudwatch and the Parameter Store on AWS')
})
socket.addEventListener('message', event => {

    console.log('Your iot payload is:', event.data);
    drawChart(event.data);  //Bar Graph
    drawChart2(event.data); //Temperature F
    drawChart3(event.data); //Humidity index %
    drawChart4(event.data); //Timestamps
    })

let myChart = Highcharts.chart('container1', {

    title: {
        text: 'Line chart'
    },

    subtitle: {
        text: 'subtitle'
    },
```

```
yAxis: {
    title: {
        text: 'Value'
    }
},

xAxis: {
    categories: upArr
},

legend: {
    layout: 'vertical',
    align: 'right',
    verticalAlign: 'middle'
},

plotOptions: {
    series: {
        label: {
            connectorAllowed: false
        }
    }
},
series: [{
    name: 'Humdity',
    data: []
}, {
    name: 'Temperature',
    data: []
}],

responsive: {
    rules: [{
        condition: {
            maxWidth: 500
        },
        chartOptions: {
            legend: {
                layout: 'horizontal',
                align: 'center',
                verticalAlign: 'bottom'
            }
        }
    }]
}
```

```
});

    let myChart2 = Highcharts.chart('container2', {

    chart: {
        type: 'gauge',
        plotBackgroundColor: null,
        plotBackgroundImage: null,
        plotBorderWidth: 0,
        plotShadow: false
    },

    title: {
        text: 'Temperature'
    },

    pane: {
        startAngle: -150,
        endAngle: 150,
        background: [{
            backgroundColor: {
                linearGradient: { x1: 0, y1: 0, x2: 0, y2: 1 },
                stops: [
                    [0, '#FFF'],
                    [1, '#333']
                ]
            },
            borderWidth: 0,
            outerRadius: '109%'
        }, {
            backgroundColor: {
                linearGradient: { x1: 0, y1: 0, x2: 0, y2: 1 },
                stops: [
                    [0, '#333'],
                    [1, '#FFF']
                ]
            },
            borderWidth: 1,
            outerRadius: '107%'
        }, {
            // default background
        }, {
            backgroundColor: '#DDD',
            borderWidth: 0,
```

```
            outerRadius: '105%',
            innerRadius: '103%'
        }]
    },

    // the value axis
    yAxis: {
        min: 0,
        max: 150,

        minorTickInterval: 'auto',
        minorTickWidth: 1,
        minorTickLength: 10,
        minorTickPosition: 'inside',
        minorTickColor: '#666',

        tickPixelInterval: 30,
        tickWidth: 2,
        tickPosition: 'inside',
        tickLength: 10,
        tickColor: '#666',
        labels: {
            step: 2,
            rotation: 'auto'
        },
        title: {
            text: 'Degrees °F'
        },
        plotBands: [{
            from: 0,
            to: 90,
            color: '#55BF3B' // green
        }, {
            from: 90,
            to: 105,
            color: '#DDDF0D' // yellow
        }, {
            from: 105,
            to: 150,
            color: '#DF5353' // red
        }]
    },

    series: [{
        name: 'Temp',
```

```
        data: [0],
        tooltip: {
            valueSuffix: ' degrees'
        }
    }]

},
// Add some life

);

let myChart3 = Highcharts.chart('container3', {

    chart: {
        type: 'gauge',
        plotBackgroundColor: null,
        plotBackgroundImage: null,
        plotBorderWidth: 0,
        plotShadow: false
    },

    title: {
        text: 'Humidity'
    },

    pane: {
        startAngle: -150,
        endAngle: 150,
        background: [{
            backgroundColor: {
                linearGradient: { x1: 0, y1: 0, x2: 0, y2: 1 },
                stops: [
                    [0, '#FFF'],
                    [1, '#333']
                ]
            },
            borderWidth: 0,
            outerRadius: '109%'
        }, {
            backgroundColor: {
                linearGradient: { x1: 0, y1: 0, x2: 0, y2: 1 },
                stops: [
                    [0, '#333'],
                    [1, '#FFF']
                ]
```

```
        },
        borderWidth: 1,
        outerRadius: '107%'
    }, {
        // default background
    }, {
        backgroundColor: '#DDD',
        borderWidth: 0,
        outerRadius: '105%',
        innerRadius: '103%'
    }]
},

// the value axis
yAxis: {
    min: 0,
    max: 100,

    minorTickInterval: 'auto',
    minorTickWidth: 1,
    minorTickLength: 10,
    minorTickPosition: 'inside',
    minorTickColor: '#666',

    tickPixelInterval: 30,
    tickWidth: 2,
    tickPosition: 'inside',
    tickLength: 10,
    tickColor: '#666',
    labels: {
        step: 2,
        rotation: 'auto'
    },
    title: {
        text: '%'
    },
    plotBands: [{
        from: 0,
        to: 40,
        color: '#55BF3B' // green
    }, {
        from: 40,
        to: 70,
        color: '#DDDF0D' // yellow
    }, {
```

```
            from: 70,
            to: 100,
            color: '#DF5353' // red
        }]
    },

    series: [{
        name: 'humid',
        data: [0],
        tooltip: {
            valueSuffix: ' degrees'
        }
    }]

},
// Add some life

);


let myChart4 = Highcharts.chart('container4', {

    chart: {
        type: 'gauge',
        plotBackgroundColor: null,
        plotBackgroundImage: null,
        plotBorderWidth: 0,
        plotShadow: false
    },

    title: {
        text: 'Time'
    },

    pane: {
        startAngle: -150,
        endAngle: 150,
        background: [{
            backgroundColor: {
                linearGradient: { x1: 0, y1: 0, x2: 0, y2: 1 },
                stops: [
                    [0, '#FFF'],
                    [1, '#333']
                ]
            },
```

```
            borderWidth: 0,
            outerRadius: '109%'
        }, {
            backgroundColor: {
                linearGradient: { x1: 0, y1: 0, x2: 0, y2: 1 },
                stops: [
                    [0, '#333'],
                    [1, '#FFF']
                ]
            },
            borderWidth: 1,
            outerRadius: '107%'
        }, {
            // default background
        }, {
            backgroundColor: '#DDD',
            borderWidth: 0,
            outerRadius: '105%',
            innerRadius: '103%'
        }]
    },

    // the value axis
    yAxis: {
        min: 0,
        max: 1000,

        minorTickInterval: 'auto',
        minorTickWidth: 1,
        minorTickLength: 10,
        minorTickPosition: 'inside',
        minorTickColor: '#666',

        tickPixelInterval: 30,
        tickWidth: 2,
        tickPosition: 'inside',
        tickLength: 10,
        tickColor: '#666',
        labels: {
            step: 2,
            rotation: 'auto'
        },
        title: {
            text: 'Ticks'
        },
```

```
        plotBands: [{
            from: 0,
            to: 1000,
            color: '#55BF3B' // green
        }, {
            from: 0,
            to: 0,
            color: '#DDDF0D' // yellow
        }, {
            from: 0,
            to: 0,
            color: '#DF5353' // red
        }]
    },

    series: [{
        name: 'Temp',
        data: [0],
        tooltip: {
            valueSuffix: 'ticks'
        }
    }]

},
// Add some life


);

let drawChart = function (data) {

    var IoT_Payload = JSON.parse(data);
    console.log("458au json object", IoT_Payload);
    //console.log(IoT_Payload.temperature);

        let { humidity, temperature, timestamps } = IoT_Payload;

        humArr.push(Number(IoT_Payload.humidity));
        tempArr.push(Number(IoT_Payload.temperature));
        upArr.push(Number(IoT_Payload.timestamps));


        myChart.series[0].setData(humArr , true)
        myChart.series[1].setData(tempArr , true)
    }
```

```
//------------------ 459auges

let drawChart2 = function (data) {

    var IoT_Payload = JSON.parse(data);
    console.log("our json object2", IoT_Payload);

    var newVal = (IoT_Payload.temperature);
    var point = myChart2.series[0].points[0];
    console.log('Your point:', point);
    console.log('Your newVal:', newVal);
    point.update(newVal);
}

let drawChart3 = function (data) {

    var IoT_Payload = JSON.parse(data);
    console.log("our json object3", IoT_Payload);

    var newVal = (IoT_Payload.humidity);
    var point = myChart3.series[0].points[0];
    console.log('Your point:', point);
    console.log('Your newVal:', newVal);
    point.update(newVal);
}

let drawChart4 = function (data) {

    var IoT_Payload = JSON.parse(data);
    console.log("our json object4", IoT_Payload);

    var newVal = (IoT_Payload.timestamps);
    var point = myChart4.series[0].points[0];
    console.log('Your point:', point);
    console.log('Your newVal:', newVal);
    point.update(newVal);

}
```

After adding your WebSocket endpoint into *'main.js'*, you are now ready to save it locally and then upload the files you just saved into your S3 bucket. To do this simply select the 'Objects' tab in your S3 bucket and drag both the '*main.js*' and '*index.html*' files to the base level of your bucket. Both files should be on the same level of the partition hierarchy in S3.

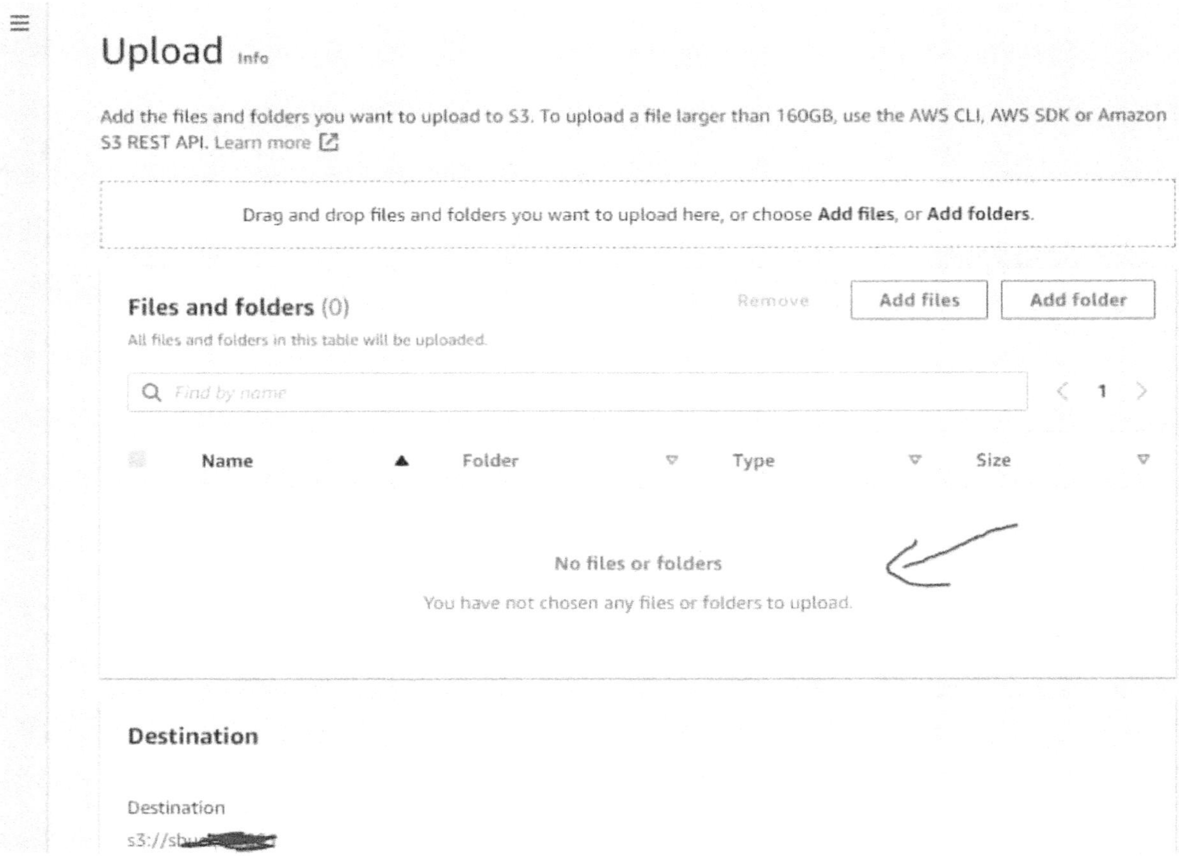
Upload Info
Add the files and folders you want to upload to S3. To upload a file larger than 160GB, use the AWS CLI, AWS SDK or Amazon S3 REST API. Learn more
Drag and drop files and folders you want to upload here, or choose Add files, or Add folders.
Files and folders (0)
All files and folders in this table will be uploaded.
Remove
Add files
Add folder
Find by name
1
Name
Folder
Type
Size
No files or folders
You have not chosen any files or folders to upload.
Destination
Destination
s3://s[redacted]

Press the 'upload' button on the bottom right of your screen, and then after both files have been uploaded select the 'close' button. You should now have two objects in your bucket; both web code files ('index.html' and 'main.js').

Now is a good time to initiate your static webhost by opening a new web browser tab with your static website URL. The address of your website can be found by going to the "*index.html*" object in your bucket and opening the 'Object URL.' Clicking this URL will bring up your website.

index.html Info
Copy S3 UR
Properties
Permissions
Versions
Object overview
Owner
borsay
AWS Region
US East (N. Virginia) us-east-1
Last modified
December 21, 2021, 12:00:10 (UTC-08:00)
Size
851.0 B
Type
html
Key
index.html
S3 URI
s3://[redacted]/index.html
Amazon Resource Name (ARN)
arn:aws:s3:::[redacted]/index.html
Entity tag (Etag)
a721bc8cb507d85c1fc6751a6cc693be
Object URL
https://[redacted].s3.amazonaws.com/index.html

The Highcharts code works by using AWS WebSockets with AWS Lambda for asynchronous invocations. You can see this message in the browser by pressing 'Ctrl + Shift + I' in most browsers, in Chrome the shortcut is 'Ctrl + Shift +J' . When your website connects the connect function in the 'main.js' first displays the message in your browsers dev tools console:

- *"WebSocket is connected, now check for your new Connection ID in Cloudwatch and the Parameter store on AWS"*

Now that the website is initiated, you can send your website some IoT data payloads and produce the visualization.

Step 7 - Populate and Visualize the IoT Data in Real-Time on a Static Webhost

For this last step you have three different ways to populate the visualization from IoT Core to your webhost. You have used all three methods throughout this book so you are free to choose any method of IoT data delivery you prefer.

1. Use a physical ESP device to publish IoT JSON payloads under an applicable topic name.

2. Manually publish JSON data payloads from the MQTT test client in IoT Core as demonstrated earlier in the book.

3. Use a virtual device to publish IoT data to your topic automatically at a configurable interval.

For Option A you can simply program your ESP8266, ESP32, or RPi physical device to publish data to IoT core as I instruct in my course.

For Option B you would have to spend some time manually altering and then publishing JSON payloads in the MQTT test client in IoT Core to generate the line chart in the visualization. I don't recommend this option because of the Real-Time nature of the visualization. It is going to be much more interesting to let the physical or virtual IoT device do the work for you and then you can just sit back and watch the visualization.

For this section I will explain how to use 'Option C.' So, you can use MQTT.fx or the IoT Bash script which utilizes the AWS CLI that you used earlier. If you have not realized, one advantage of the Bash script with the AWS CLI is that it is much easier to switch AWS regions. With MQTT.fx you would need to configure new, region-specific certificates to change your AWS region. The downside of the Bash script is that it cannot receive (subscribe) to MQTT topics. This is due to the fact that the AWS CLI communicates through HTTPS, not MQTT(S). For this chapter you are not using the MQTT subscribe function, so the Bash script is fine to use.

Your test IoT JSON payload should look something like this:

```
{
    "temperature": 83,
    "humidity": 77
}
```

I have already altered the Bash test script below to send just temperature and humidity data. Simply insert your AWS region and MQTT topic name ('iot/whatever') into the test script where indicated. The Bash script uses your AWS CLI to deliver the payload to IoT Core (using your SigV4 credentials over HTTPS from the AWS CLI). You can also change the number of payloads published (iterations) and wait time between each payload publish (interval) to produce as much fake IoT data as you like.

Edit these fields for your own info:

```
mqtttopic='<Insert-Your-IoT-Topic-Here>'
iterations=10
wait=3
region='<Insert-Your-AWS-Test-Region-Here>'
profile='default'
```

You must change fields at the top of the page in the bash script to customize it for your MQTT topic name (‘iot/whatever’) and AWS region ('us-east-1’ or other) in which you developed your AWS services for this tutorial. The other two fields, 'iterations' and 'wait time', are optional to edit.

```
#!/bin/bash
mqtttopic='<Insert-Your-IoT-Topic-Here>'
iterations=10
wait=3
region='<Insert-Your-AWS-Test-Region-Here>'
profile='default'

for (( i = 1; i <=$iterations; i++)) {

    #Added these randomizers because old ones didn't generate good numbers

    #Temperature in Fehr
    minT=-20
    maxT=120
    numberT=$(expr $minT + $RANDOM % $maxT)

    #humidity % cannot exceed 100
    minH=0
    maxH=100
    numberH=$(expr $minH + $RANDOM % $maxH)

  temperature=$(($numberT ))
  humidity=$(($numberH ))

  echo "Publishing message $i/$ITERATIONS to IoT topic $mqtttopic:"
```

```
  echo "temperature: $temperature"
  echo "humidity: $humidity"

 #use below for AWS CLI V2
 aws iot-data publish --topic "$mqtttopic" --cli-binary-format raw-in-base64-
out --payload "{\"temperature\":$temperature,\"humidity\":$humidity}" --
profile "$profile" --region "$region"

  sleep $wait
}
```

Now save the above code, giving it a name like "IoT_tester.sh". You can run the script by simply installing the Bash script (listed above) locally and then from the command prompt typing the name of the Bash script. Bash scripts are neat because they should work on any operating system. If Bash does not work on your Windows system, simply install the free "Git for Windows" as demonstrated in chapters 1 and 2. Also check the chapters GitHub as I added a second web visualization using Plotly.

Activating the Bash script in Windows looks like the image below but with your own environmental sensor values:

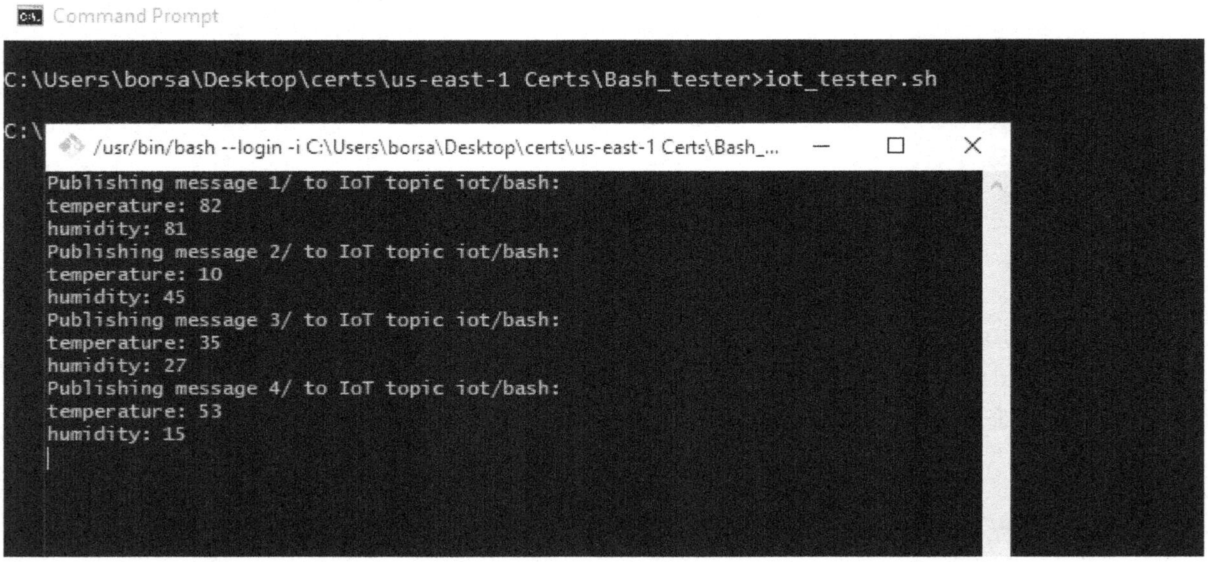
Command Prompt
C:\Users\borsa\Desktop\certs\us-east-1 Certs\Bash_tester>iot_tester.sh
/usr/bin/bash --login -i C:\Users\borsa\Desktop\certs\us-east-1 Certs\Bash_...
Publishing message 1/ to IoT topic iot/bash:
temperature: 82
humidity: 81
Publishing message 2/ to IoT topic iot/bash:
temperature: 10
humidity: 45
Publishing message 3/ to IoT topic iot/bash:
temperature: 35
humidity: 27
Publishing message 4/ to IoT topic iot/bash:
temperature: 53
humidity: 15

If you also open the developer tools console pane (Ctrl + Shift + J in Chrome, and Ctrl + Shift + I in most other browsers) you could observe incoming IoT payloads in real-time.

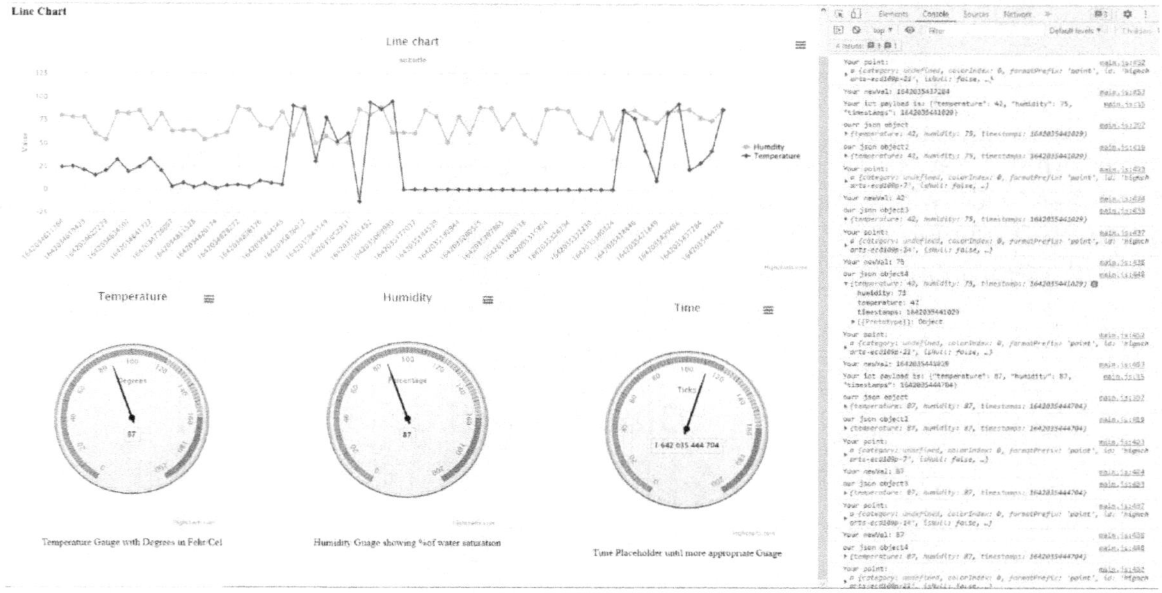

Line Chart
Line chart
Humidity
Temperature
Temperature
Humidity
Time
Temperature Gauge with Degrees in Fehr/Cel
Humidity Guage showing %of water saturation
Time Placeholder until more appropriate Guage

Congratulations! You finished this chapter and created an asynchronous serverless AWS IoT Dashboard using AWS WebSockets. The possibilities of designing Real-Time IoT dashboards for very little cost are endless. Perhaps you can come up with your own visualizations or improvements for this unique project.

Introducing the Cloudboard

Check out my new Cloudboard, an IoT device to cloud training tool. No need to buy and mess with wiring up sensors. Cloud tutorials designed specifically for the Cloudboard coming soon. All the sensors that you need to get started with device to cloud integration.

Cloudboard.cc

HEROES
C5
POW
R17
C7
R13
R12
C6
Q1
R1
U2
BOOTRESET
C4
B1
B2
R4
B
G
Y
USBC
R10
R8
IO14
IO27
IO26
IO23
IO13
GND
3V3
5V
H1
C2
C8

Made in United States
Orlando, FL
29 December 2022

27877501R00265